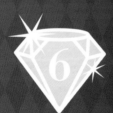

HIROHIKO ARAKI

JoJo's BIZARRE ADVENTURE

PART 4 ★ DIAMOND IS UNBREAKABLE

6

JoJo's

BIZARRE ADVENTURE

PART 4 ★ DIAMOND IS UNBREAKABLE

CONTENTS

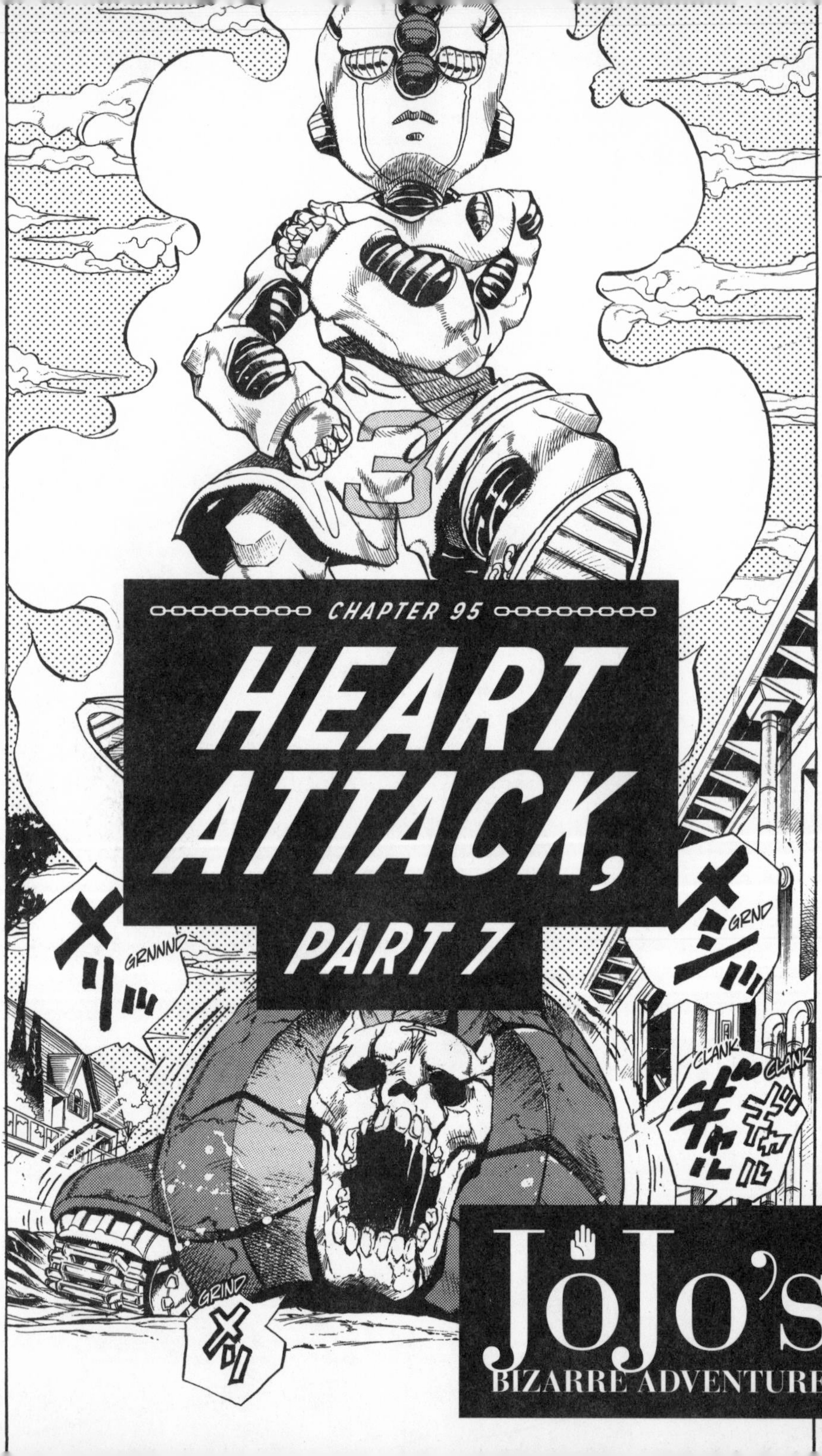
CHAPTER 95
HEART ATTACK,
PART 7
GRND
GRNNND
CLANK
CLANK
GRIND
JoJo's
BIZARRE ADVENTURE

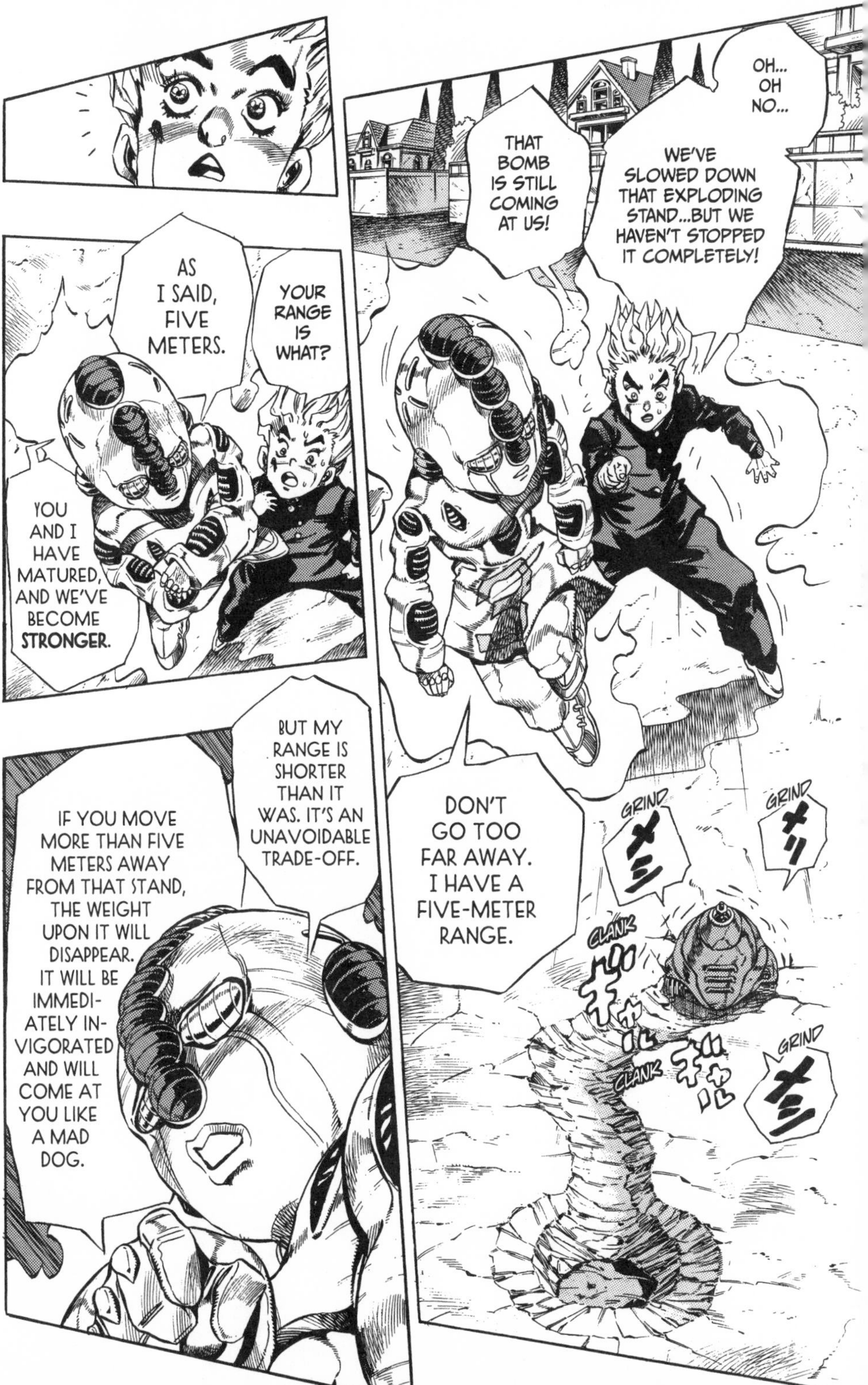

OH... OH NO...
WE'VE SLOWED DOWN THAT EXPLODING STAND...BUT WE HAVEN'T STOPPED IT COMPLETELY!
THAT BOMB IS STILL COMING AT US!
DON'T GO TOO FAR AWAY. I HAVE A FIVE-METER RANGE.
GRIND
GRIND
CLANK
CLANK
GRIND
YOUR RANGE IS WHAT?
AS I SAID, FIVE METERS.
YOU AND I HAVE MATURED, AND WE'VE BECOME **STRONGER**.
BUT MY RANGE IS SHORTER THAN IT WAS. IT'S AN UNAVOIDABLE TRADE-OFF.
IF YOU MOVE MORE THAN FIVE METERS AWAY FROM THAT STAND, THE WEIGHT UPON IT WILL DISAPPEAR. IT WILL BE IMMEDI-ATELY IN-VIGORATED AND WILL COME AT YOU LIKE A MAD DOG.

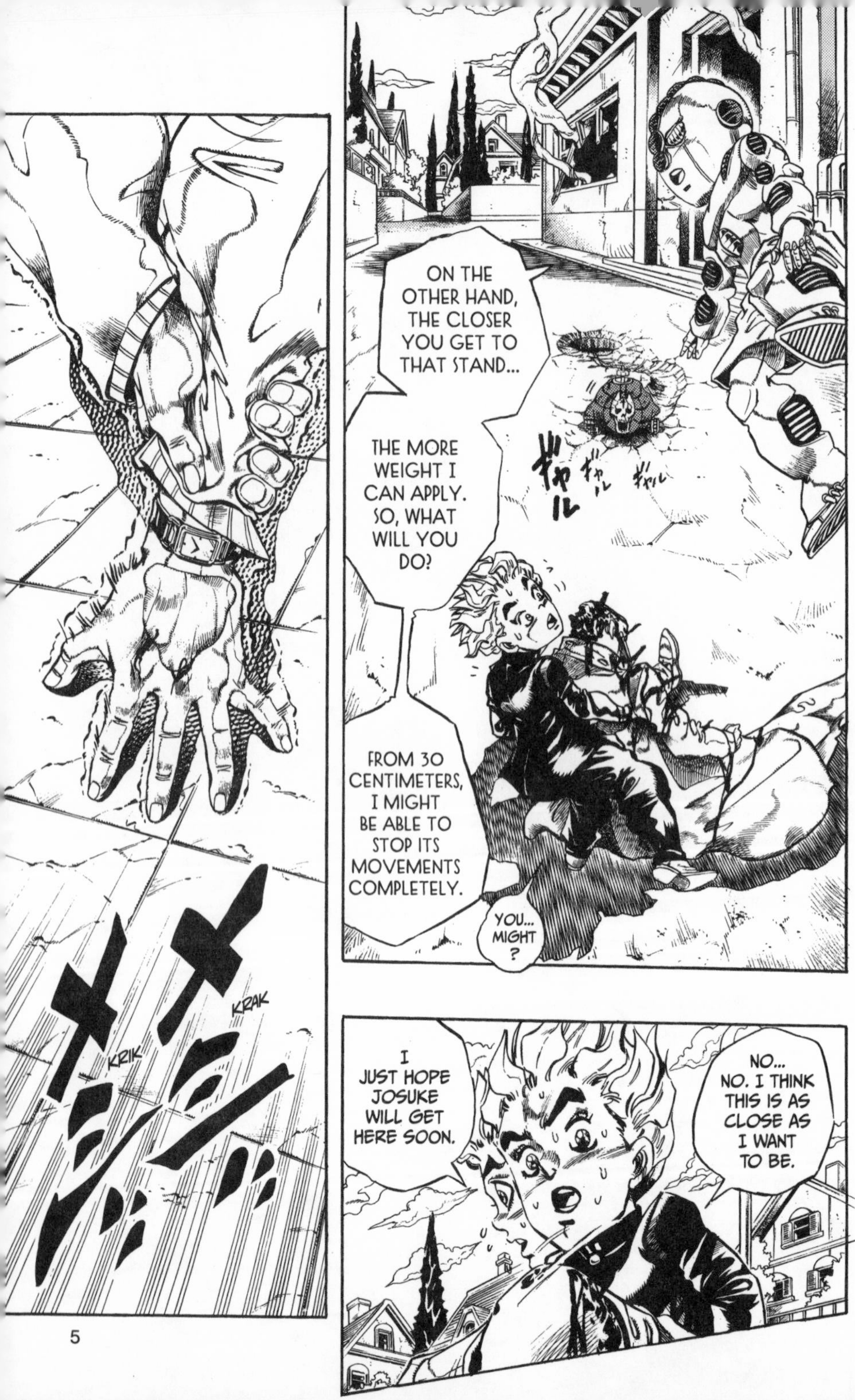
ON THE OTHER HAND, THE CLOSER YOU GET TO THAT STAND...
THE MORE WEIGHT I CAN APPLY. SO, WHAT WILL YOU DO?
FROM 30 CENTIMETERS, I MIGHT BE ABLE TO STOP ITS MOVEMENTS COMPLETELY.
YOU... MIGHT?
NO... NO. I THINK THIS IS AS CLOSE AS I WANT TO BE.
I JUST HOPE JOSUKE WILL GET HERE SOON.
KRIK
KRAK

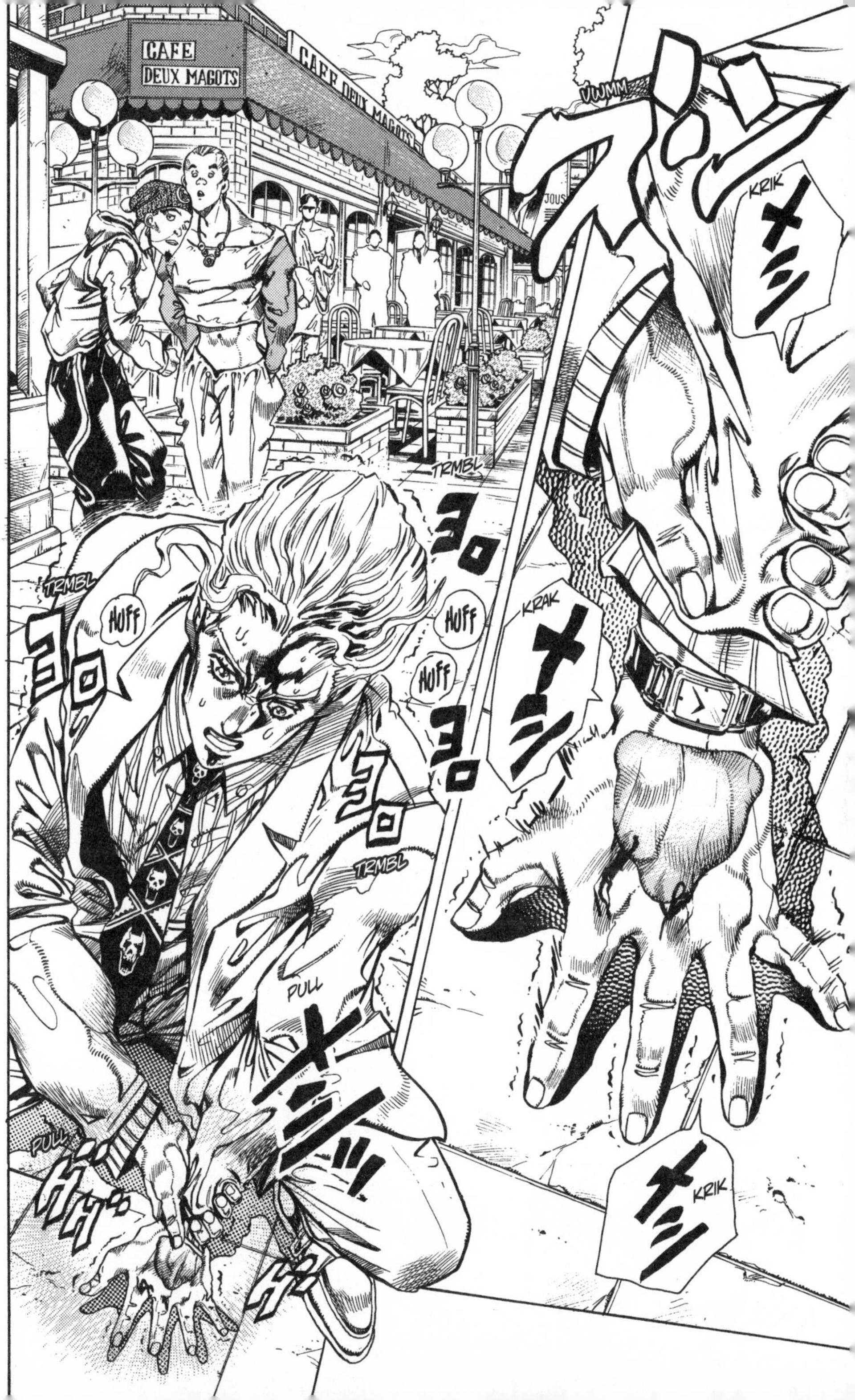
VWMM
KRIK
KRAK
KRIK
CAFE
DEUX MAGOTS
CAFE DEUX MAGOTS
TRMBL
HUFF
HUFF
HUFF
TRMBL
TRMBL
PULL
PULL

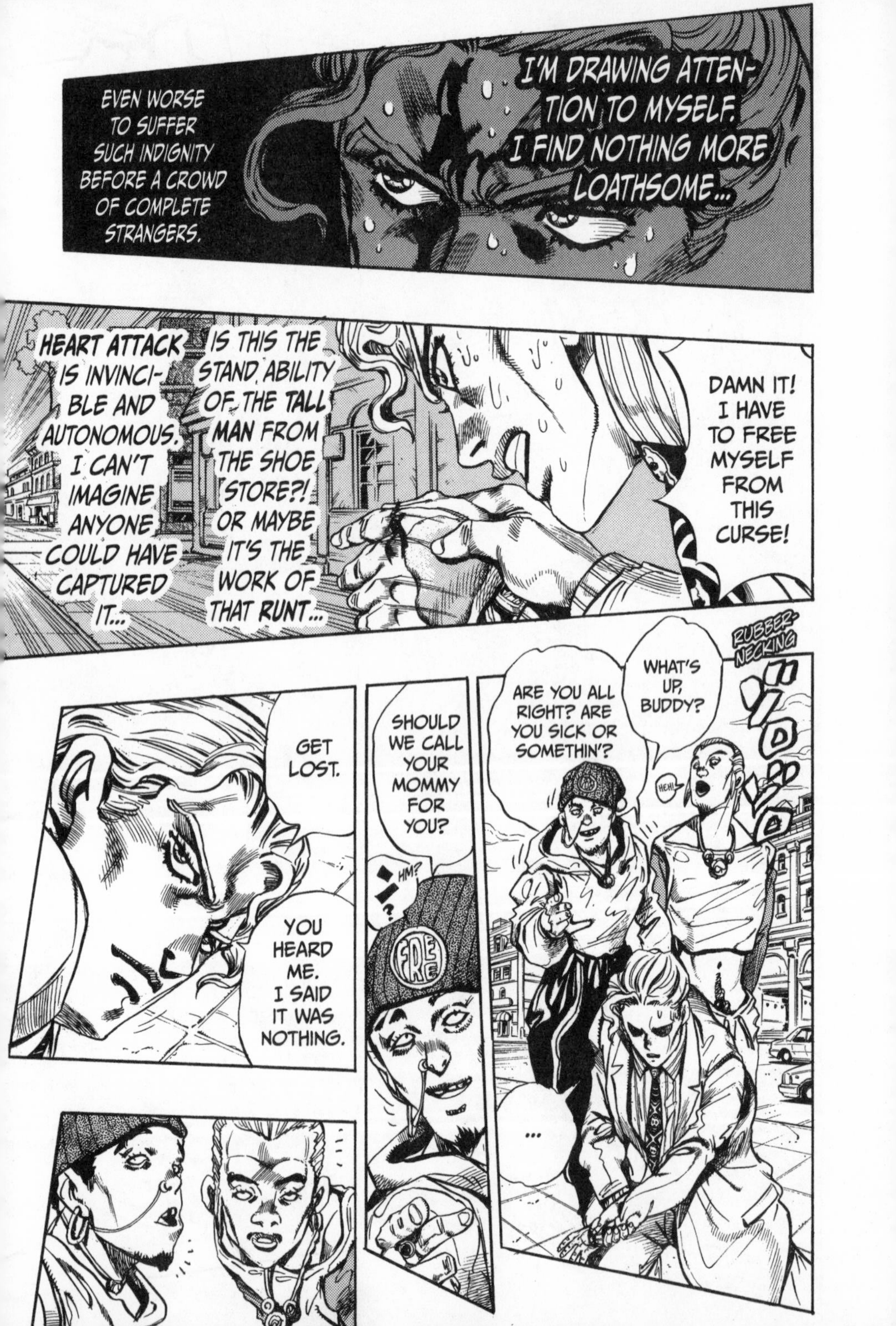
I'M DRAWING ATTENTION TO MYSELF. I FIND NOTHING MORE LOATHSOME...
EVEN WORSE TO SUFFER SUCH INDIGNITY BEFORE A CROWD OF COMPLETE STRANGERS.
DAMN IT! I HAVE TO FREE MYSELF FROM THIS CURSE!
IS THIS THE STAND ABILITY OF THE TALL MAN FROM THE SHOE STORE?! OR MAYBE IT'S THE WORK OF THAT RUNT...
HEART ATTACK IS INVINCIBLE AND AUTONOMOUS. I CAN'T IMAGINE ANYONE COULD HAVE CAPTURED IT...
RUBBERNECKING
WHAT'S UP, BUDDY?
HEH!
ARE YOU ALL RIGHT? ARE YOU SICK OR SOMETHIN'?
...
SHOULD WE CALL YOUR MOMMY FOR YOU?
HM?
GET LOST.
YOU HEARD ME. I SAID IT WAS NOTHING.

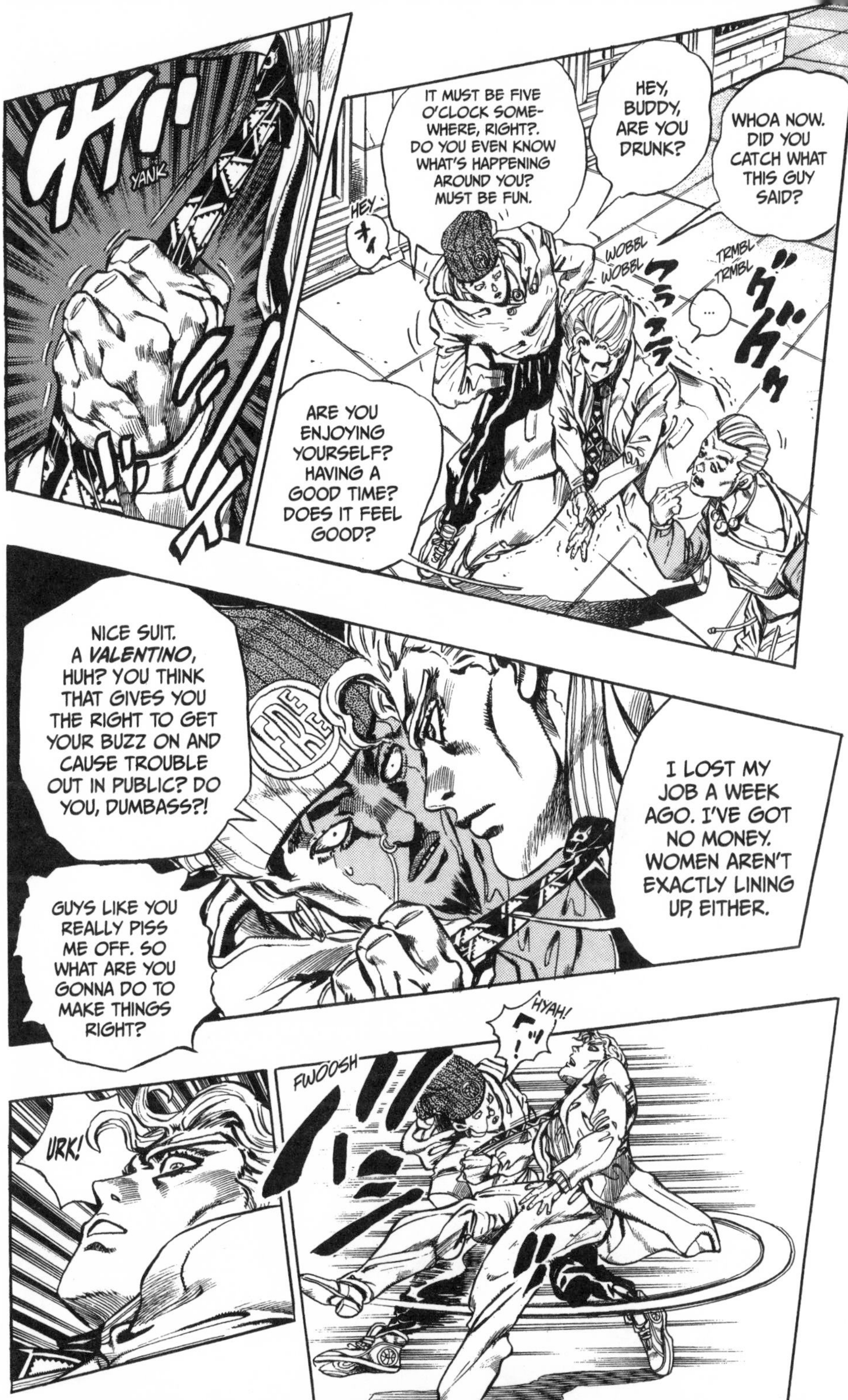
WHOA NOW. DID YOU CATCH WHAT THIS GUY SAID?
HEY, BUDDY, ARE YOU DRUNK?
IT MUST BE FIVE O'CLOCK SOMEWHERE, RIGHT?. DO YOU EVEN KNOW WHAT'S HAPPENING AROUND YOU? MUST BE FUN.
HEY.
TRMBL TRMBL
WOBBL WOBBL
...
ARE YOU ENJOYING YOURSELF? HAVING A GOOD TIME? DOES IT FEEL GOOD?
YANK
NICE SUIT. A *VALENTINO*, HUH? YOU THINK THAT GIVES YOU THE RIGHT TO GET YOUR BUZZ ON AND CAUSE TROUBLE OUT IN PUBLIC? DO YOU, DUMBASS?!
I LOST MY JOB A WEEK AGO. I'VE GOT NO MONEY. WOMEN AREN'T EXACTLY LINING UP, EITHER.
GUYS LIKE YOU REALLY PISS ME OFF. SO WHAT ARE YOU GONNA DO TO MAKE THINGS RIGHT?
HYAH!
FWOOSH
URK!

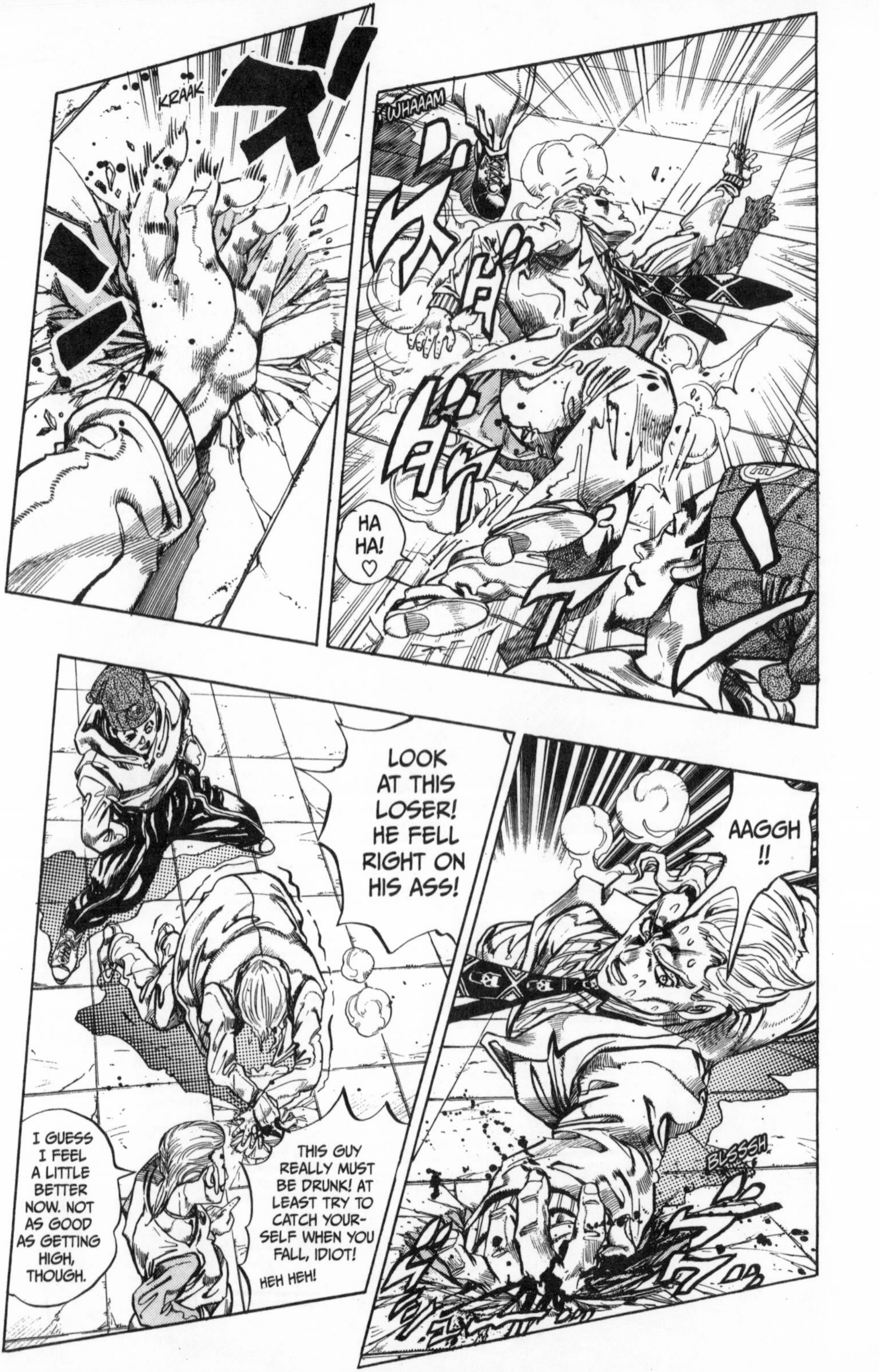
WHAAAM
HA HA! ♡
KRAAK
AAGGH !!
BLSSSH
LOOK AT THIS LOSER! HE FELL RIGHT ON HIS ASS!
THIS GUY REALLY MUST BE DRUNK! AT LEAST TRY TO CATCH YOURSELF WHEN YOU FALL, IDIOT!
HEH HEH!
I GUESS I FEEL A LITTLE BETTER NOW. NOT AS GOOD AS GETTING HIGH, THOUGH.

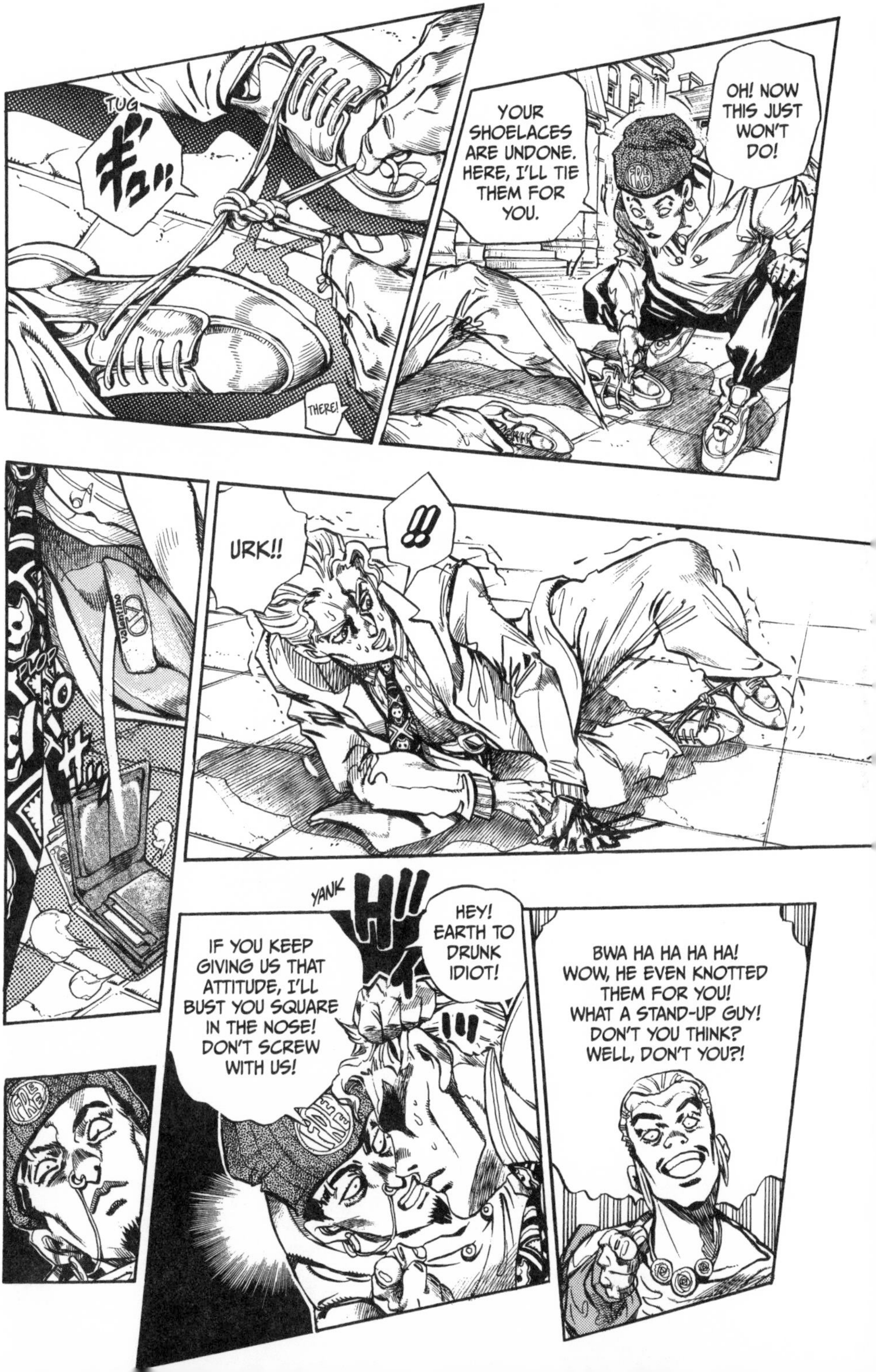
OH! NOW THIS JUST WON'T DO!
YOUR SHOELACES ARE UNDONE. HERE, I'LL TIE THEM FOR YOU.
TUG
ギュッ
THERE!
!!
URK!!
PLOP
BWA HA HA HA HA! WOW, HE EVEN KNOTTED THEM FOR YOU! WHAT A STAND-UP GUY! DON'T YOU THINK? WELL, DON'T YOU?!
HEY! EARTH TO DRUNK IDIOT!
YANK
IF YOU KEEP GIVING US THAT ATTITUDE, I'LL BUST YOU SQUARE IN THE NOSE! DON'T SCREW WITH US!

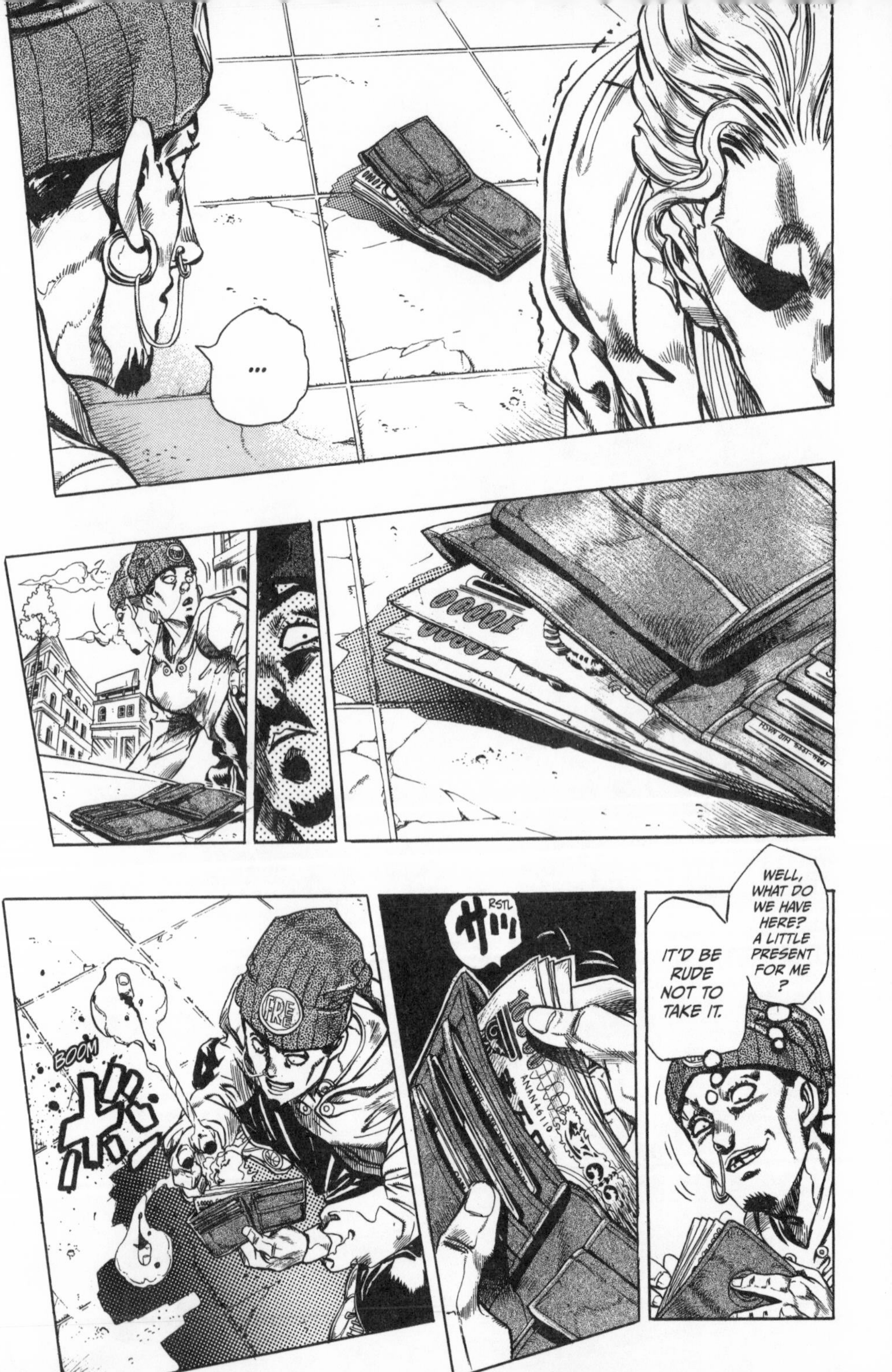
...
WELL, WHAT DO WE HAVE HERE? A LITTLE PRESENT FOR ME?
IT'D BE RUDE NOT TO TAKE IT.
RSTL
BOOM

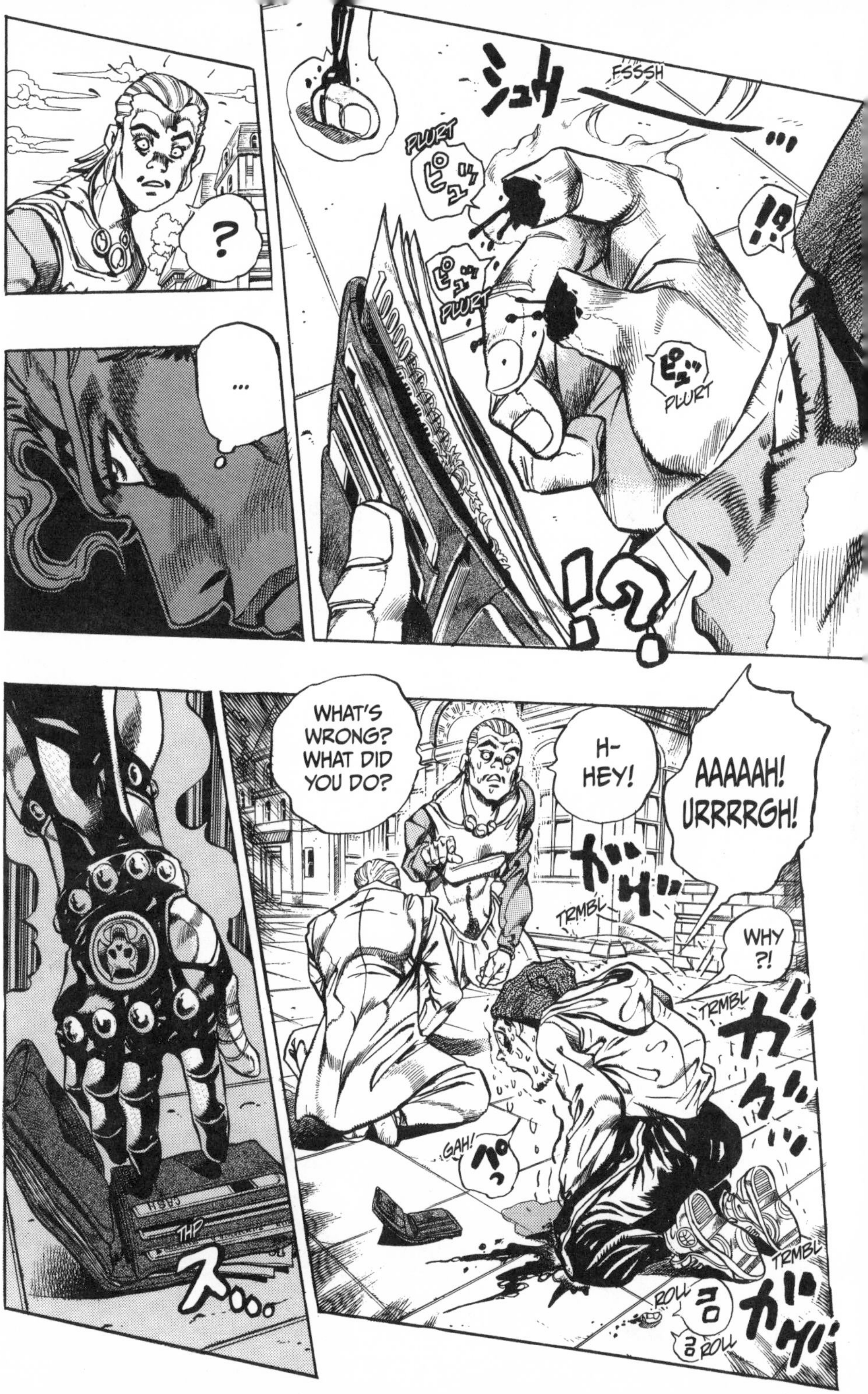

FSSSH
PLURT
PLURT
PLURT
!?
!?
?
...
AAAAAH! URRRRGH!
TRMBL
H- HEY!
WHAT'S WRONG? WHAT DID YOU DO?
WHY ?!
TRMBL
TRMBL
GAH!
ROLL
ROLL
THP

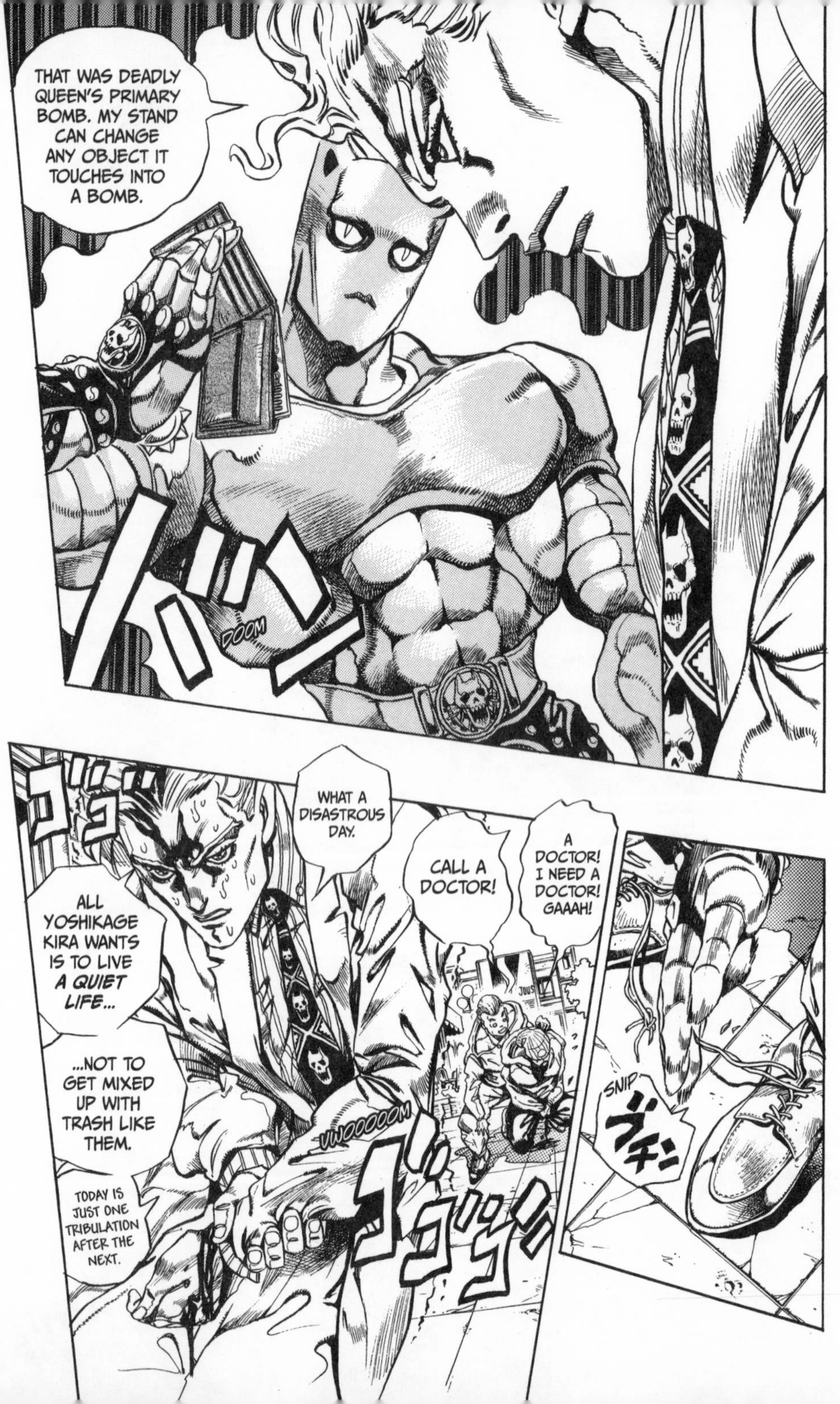
THAT WAS DEADLY QUEEN'S PRIMARY BOMB. MY STAND CAN CHANGE ANY OBJECT IT TOUCHES INTO A BOMB.
DOOM
SNIP
A DOCTOR! I NEED A DOCTOR! GAAAH!
CALL A DOCTOR!
WHAT A DISASTROUS DAY.
ALL YOSHIKAGE KIRA WANTS IS TO LIVE *A QUIET LIFE*...
...NOT TO GET MIXED UP WITH TRASH LIKE THEM.
VWOOOOOM
TODAY IS JUST ONE TRIBULATION AFTER THE NEXT.

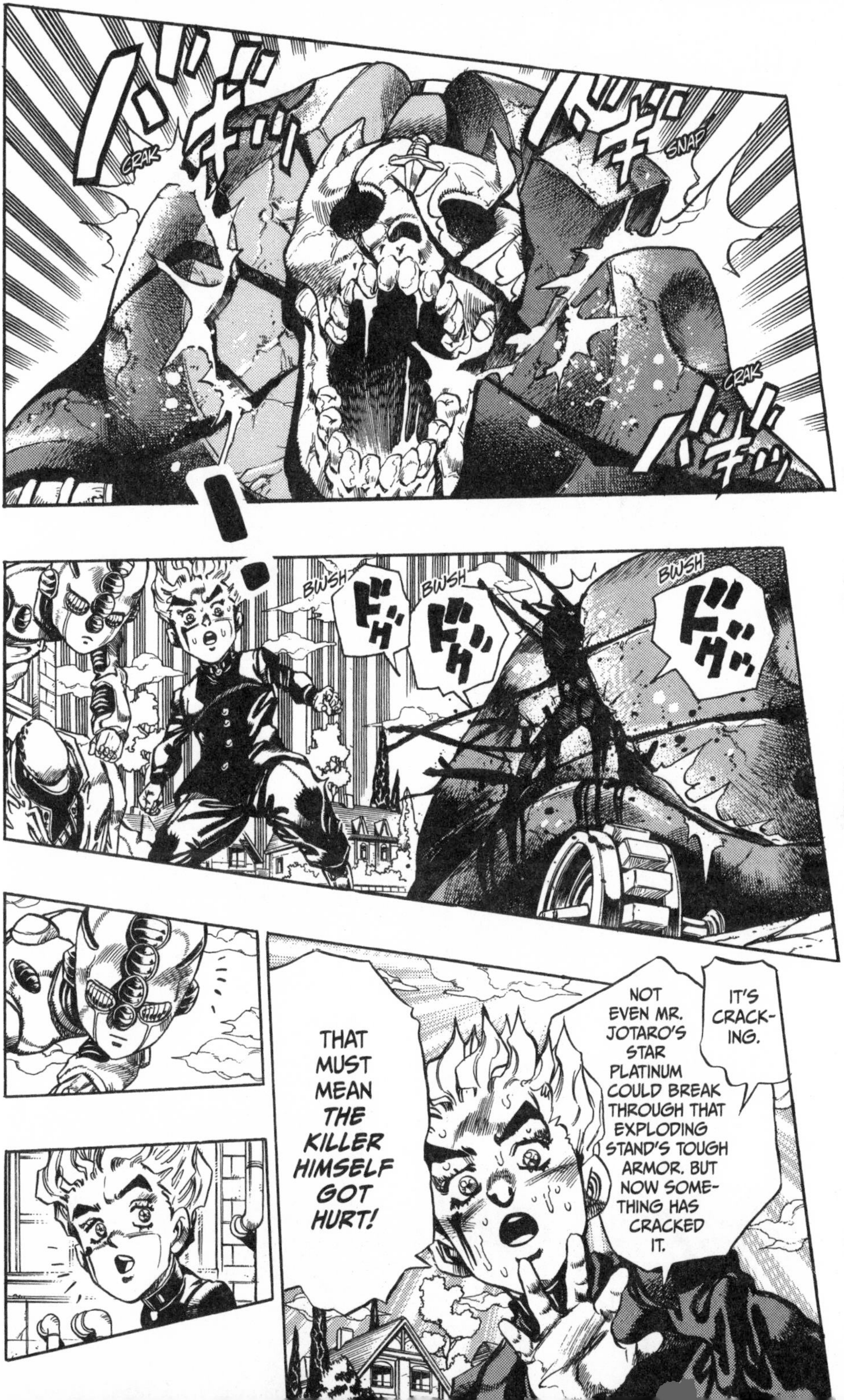
SNAP
CRAK
CRAK
BWSH
BWSH
BWSH
IT'S CRACKING.
NOT EVEN MR. JOTARO'S STAR PLATINUM COULD BREAK THROUGH THAT EXPLODING STAND'S TOUGH ARMOR. BUT NOW SOMETHING HAS CRACKED IT.
THAT MUST MEAN *THE KILLER HIMSELF* GOT HURT!

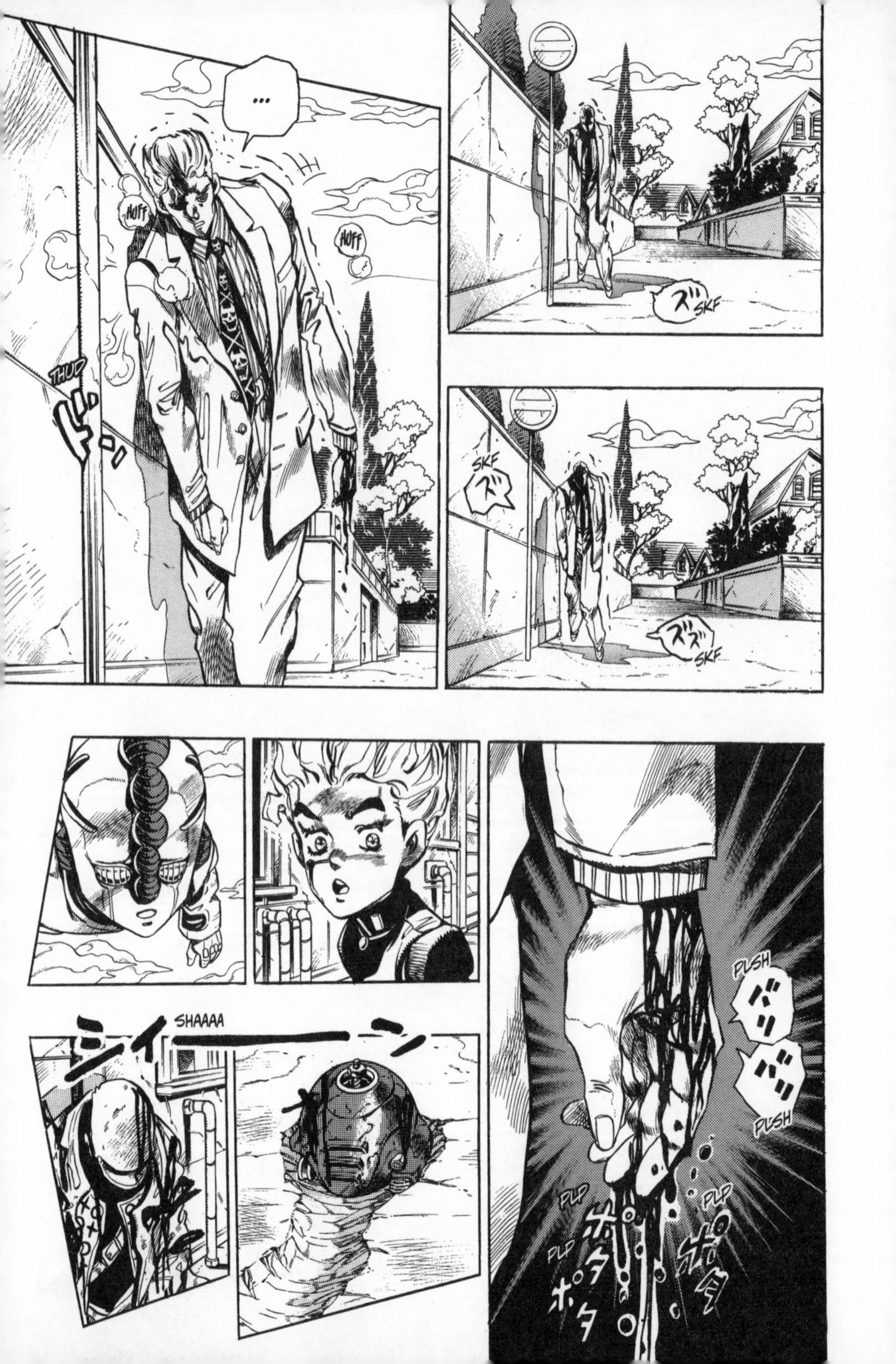

ズ SKF
SKF ズ
ズズ SKF
...
HUFF
HUFF
THUD
PLSH バリ
バリ PLSH
PLP
PLP
PLP
SHAAAA

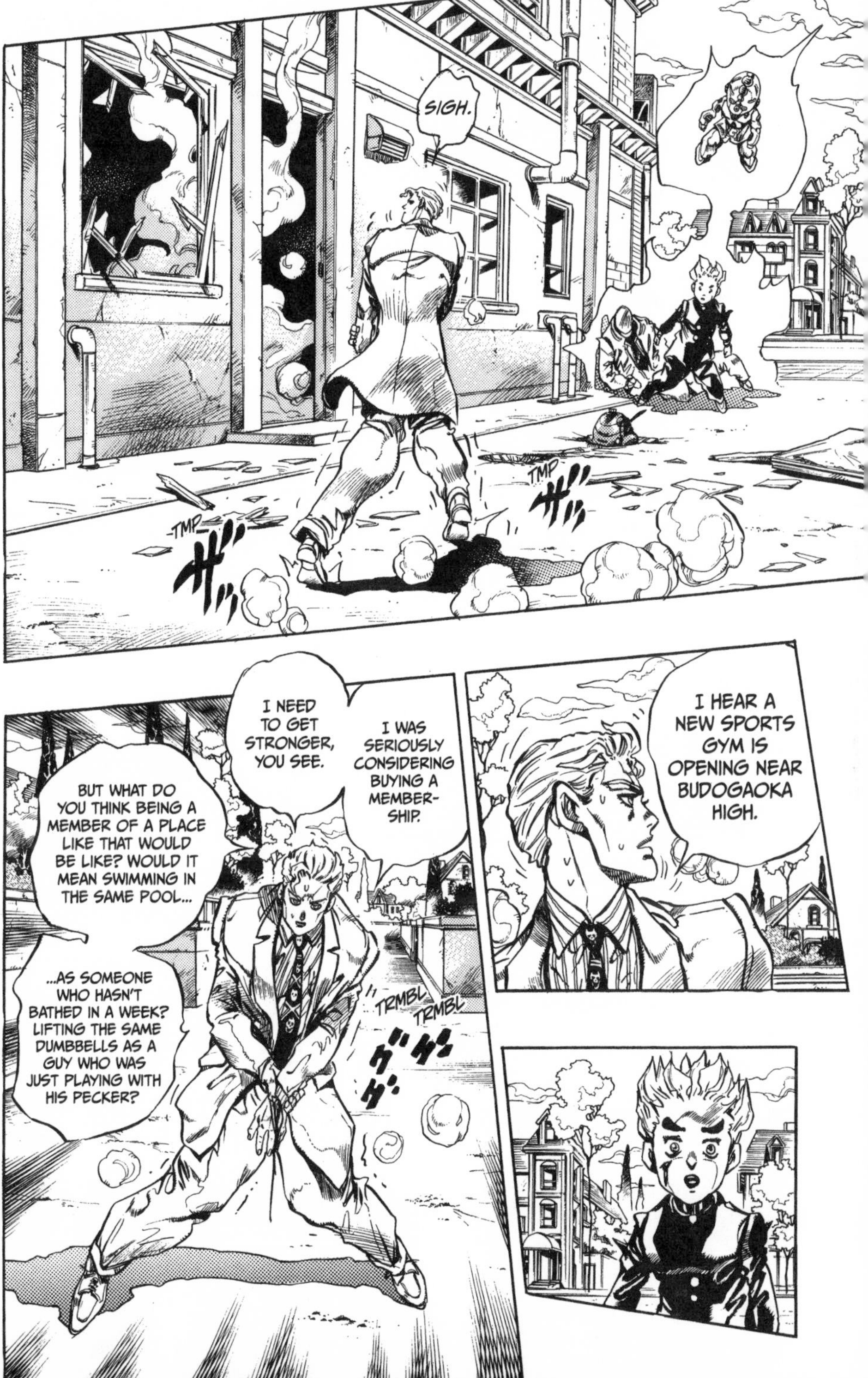
SIGH.
TMP
TMP
I HEAR A NEW SPORTS GYM IS OPENING NEAR BUDOGAOKA HIGH.
I WAS SERIOUSLY CONSIDERING BUYING A MEMBER-SHIP.
I NEED TO GET STRONGER, YOU SEE.
BUT WHAT DO YOU THINK BEING A MEMBER OF A PLACE LIKE THAT WOULD BE LIKE? WOULD IT MEAN SWIMMING IN THE SAME POOL...
TRMBL TRMBL
...AS SOMEONE WHO HASN'T BATHED IN A WEEK? LIFTING THE SAME DUMBBELLS AS A GUY WHO WAS JUST PLAYING WITH HIS PECKER?

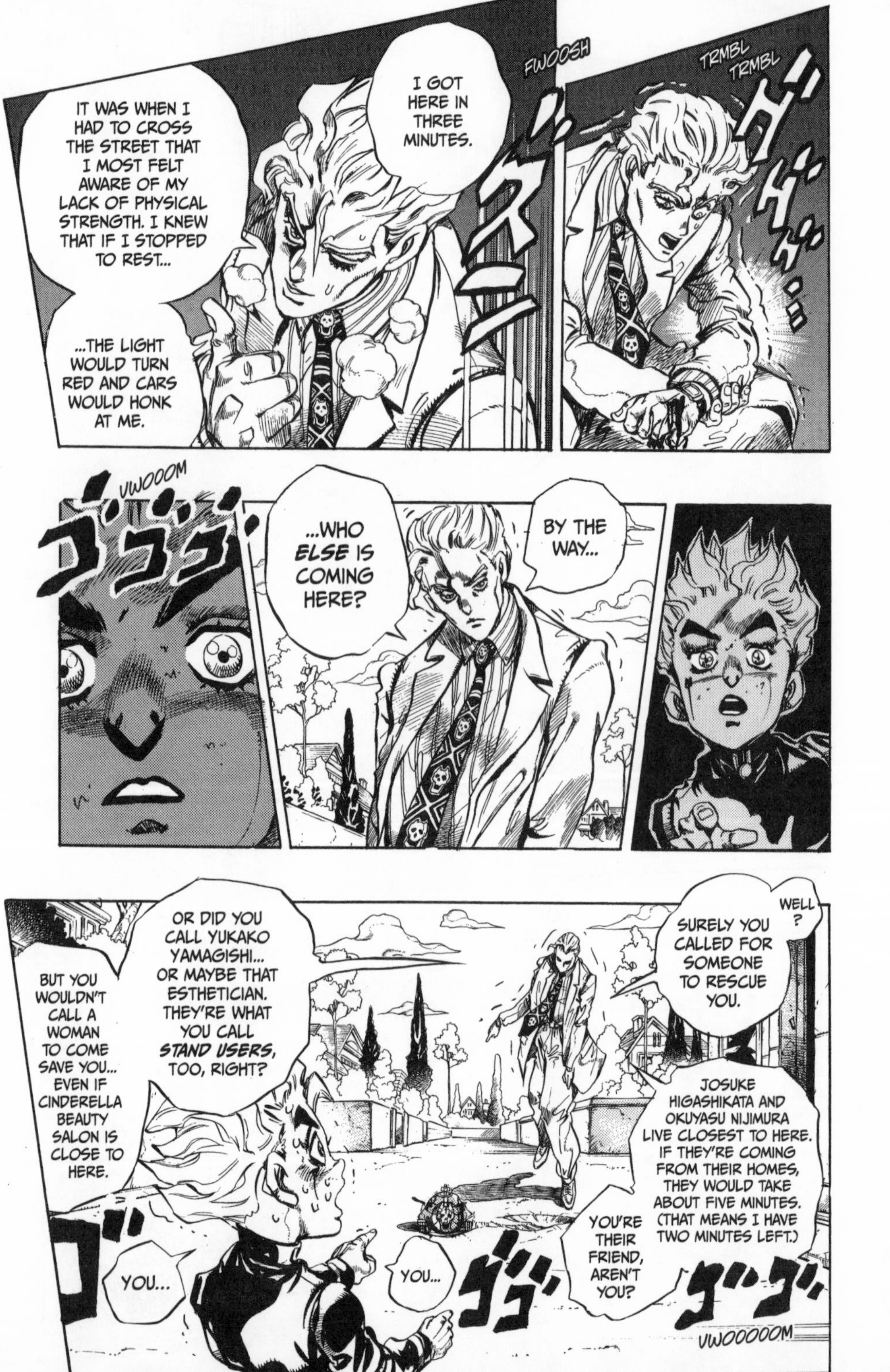
TRMBL TRMBL
FWOOSH
I GOT HERE IN THREE MINUTES.
IT WAS WHEN I HAD TO CROSS THE STREET THAT I MOST FELT AWARE OF MY LACK OF PHYSICAL STRENGTH. I KNEW THAT IF I STOPPED TO REST...
...THE LIGHT WOULD TURN RED AND CARS WOULD HONK AT ME.
BY THE WAY...
...WHO *ELSE* IS COMING HERE?
UWOOOM
WELL?
SURELY YOU CALLED FOR SOMEONE TO RESCUE YOU.
JOSUKE HIGASHIKATA AND OKUYASU NIJIMURA LIVE CLOSEST TO HERE. IF THEY'RE COMING FROM THEIR HOMES, THEY WOULD TAKE ABOUT FIVE MINUTES. (THAT MEANS I HAVE TWO MINUTES LEFT.)
UWOOOOOM
YOU'RE THEIR FRIEND, AREN'T YOU?
YOU...
OR DID YOU CALL YUKAKO YAMAGISHI... OR MAYBE THAT ESTHETICIAN. THEY'RE WHAT YOU CALL *STAND USERS*, TOO, RIGHT?
BUT YOU WOULDN'T CALL A WOMAN TO COME SAVE YOU... EVEN IF CINDERELLA BEAUTY SALON IS CLOSE TO HERE.
YOU...

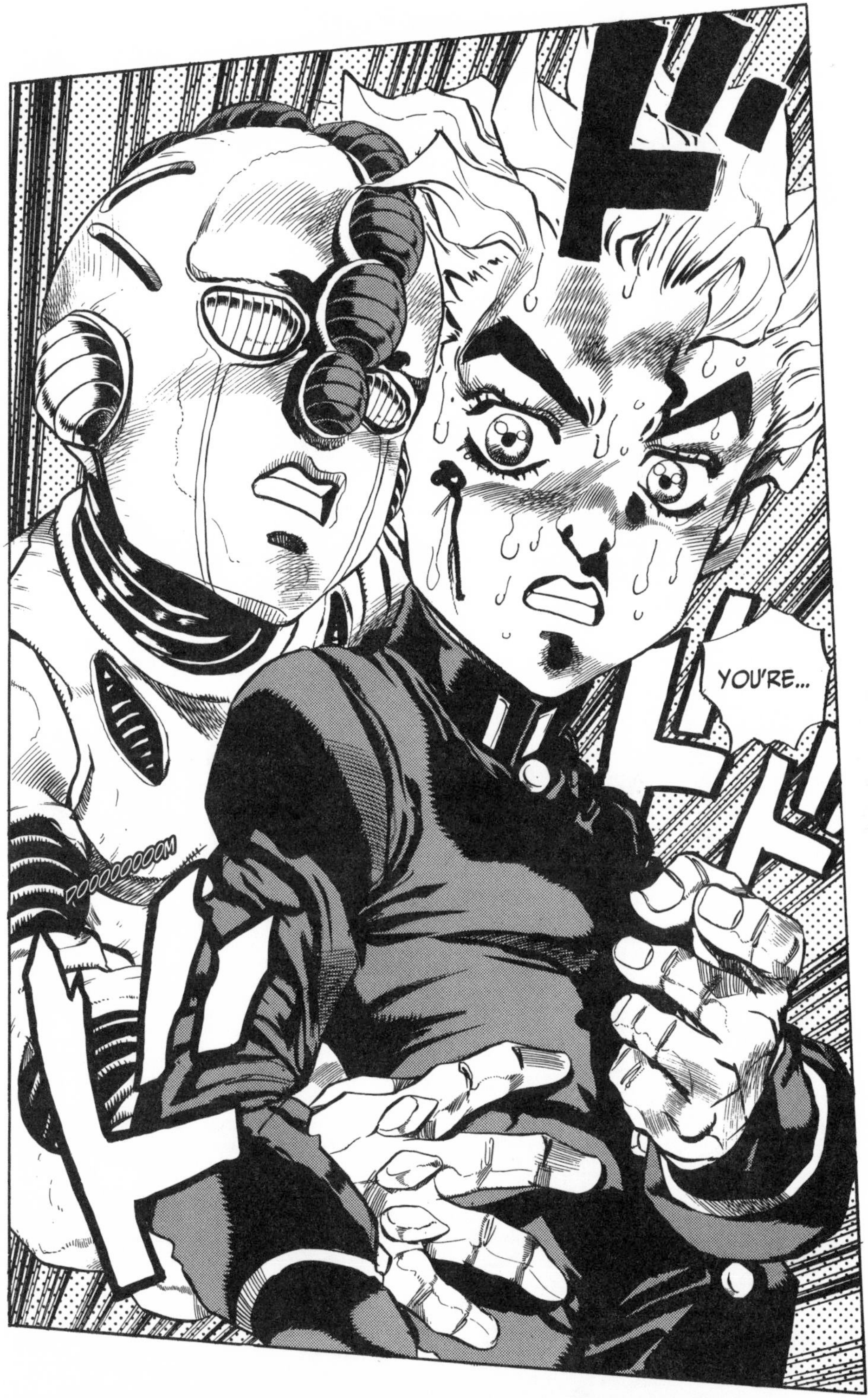
YOU'RE...
DOOOOOOOOOM

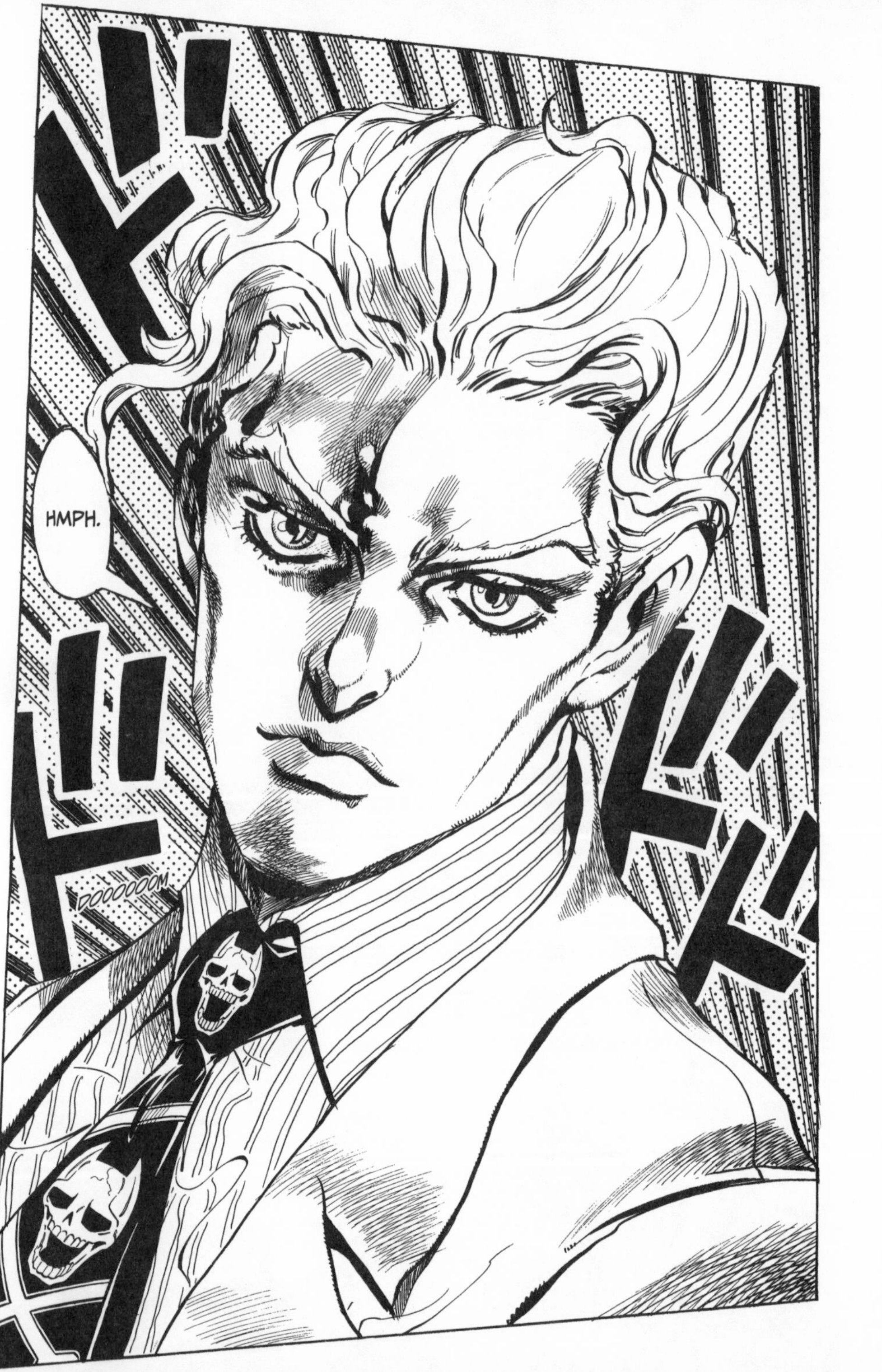
HMPH.
DOOOOOOM

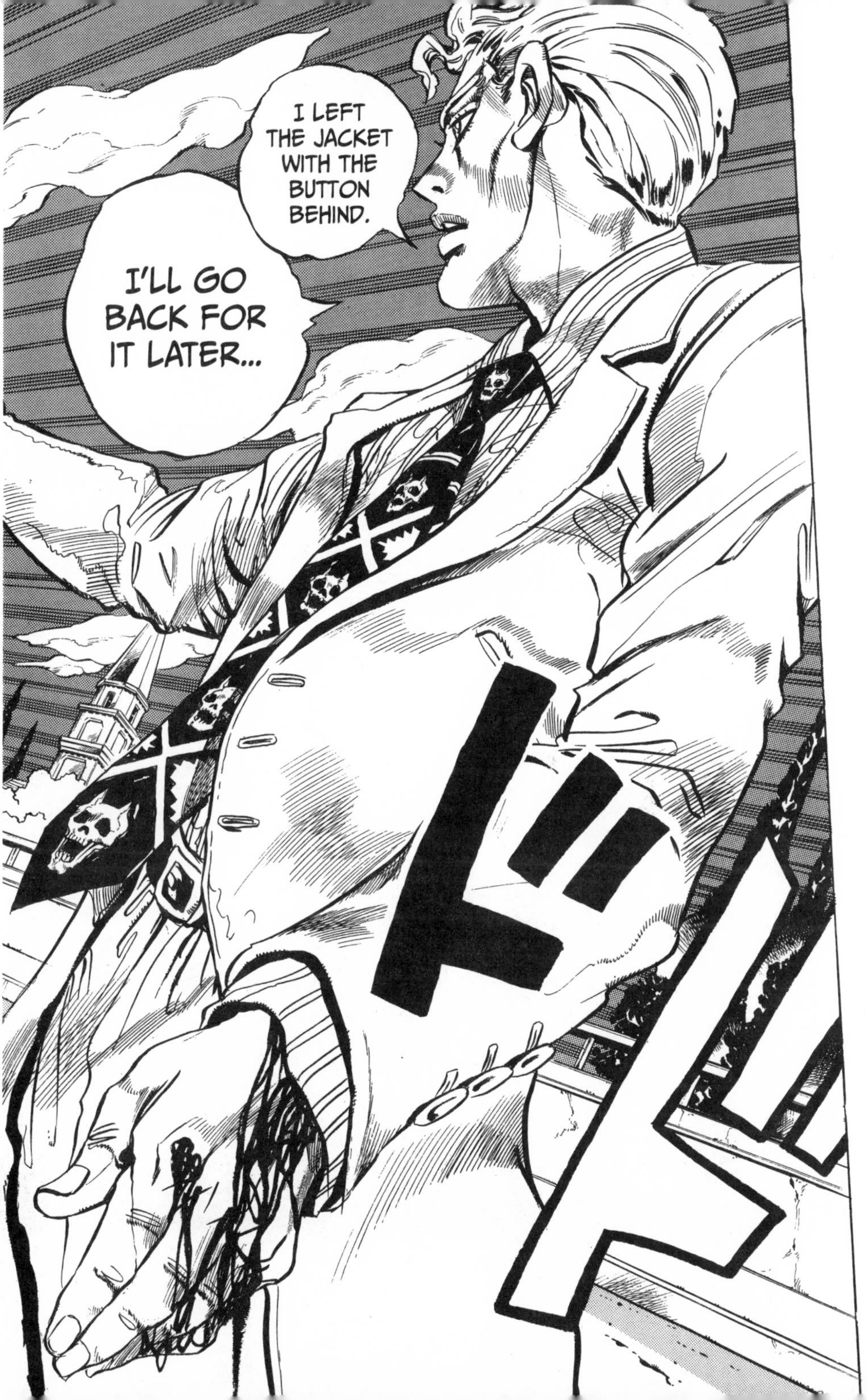
I LEFT THE JACKET WITH THE BUTTON BEHIND.
I'LL GO BACK FOR IT LATER...

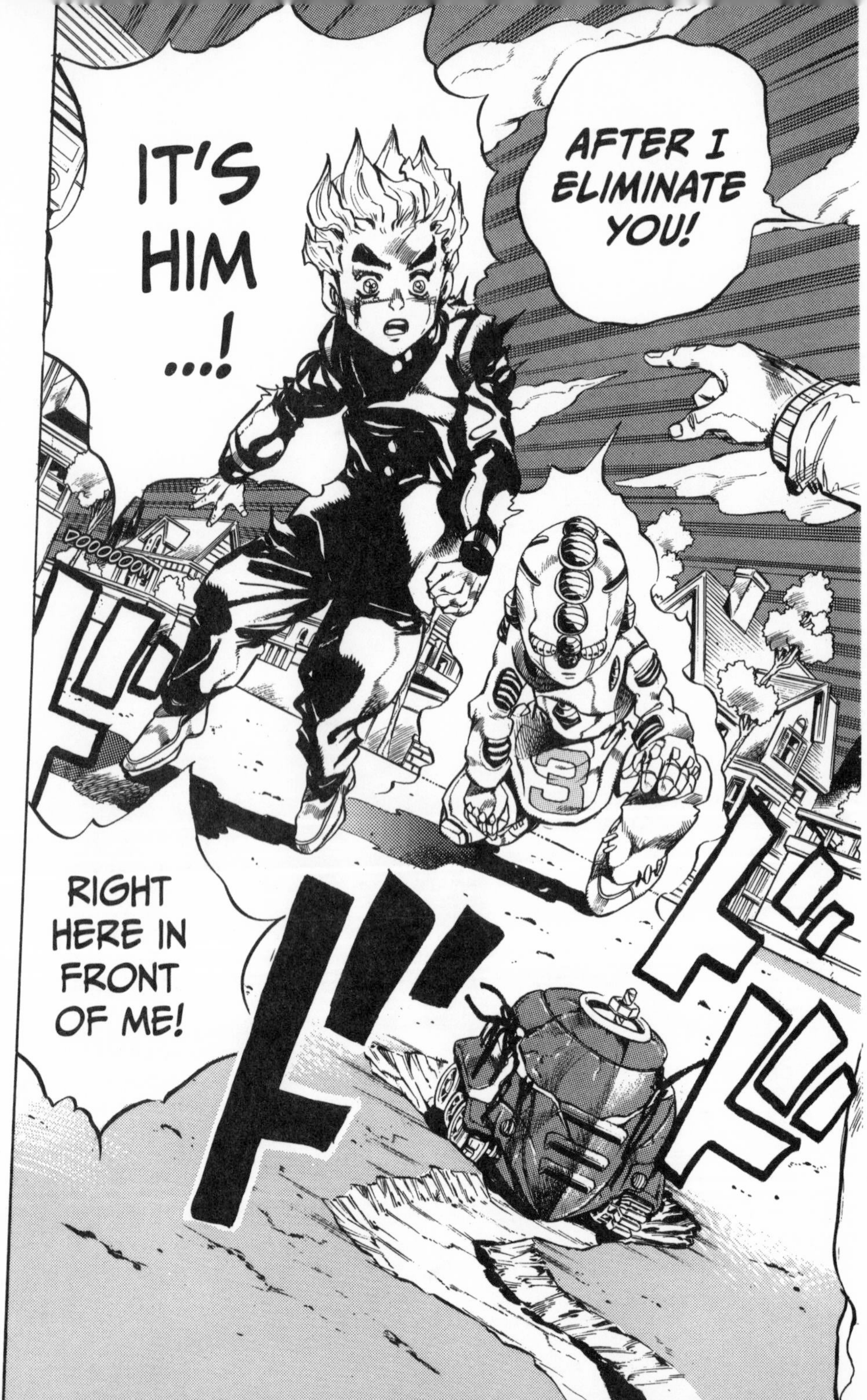
AFTER I ELIMINATE YOU!
IT'S HIM ...!
DOOOOOOOM
RIGHT HERE IN FRONT OF ME!

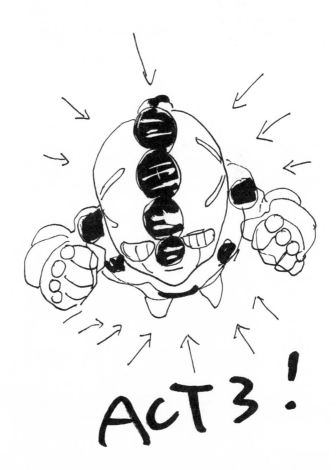

ACT 3!

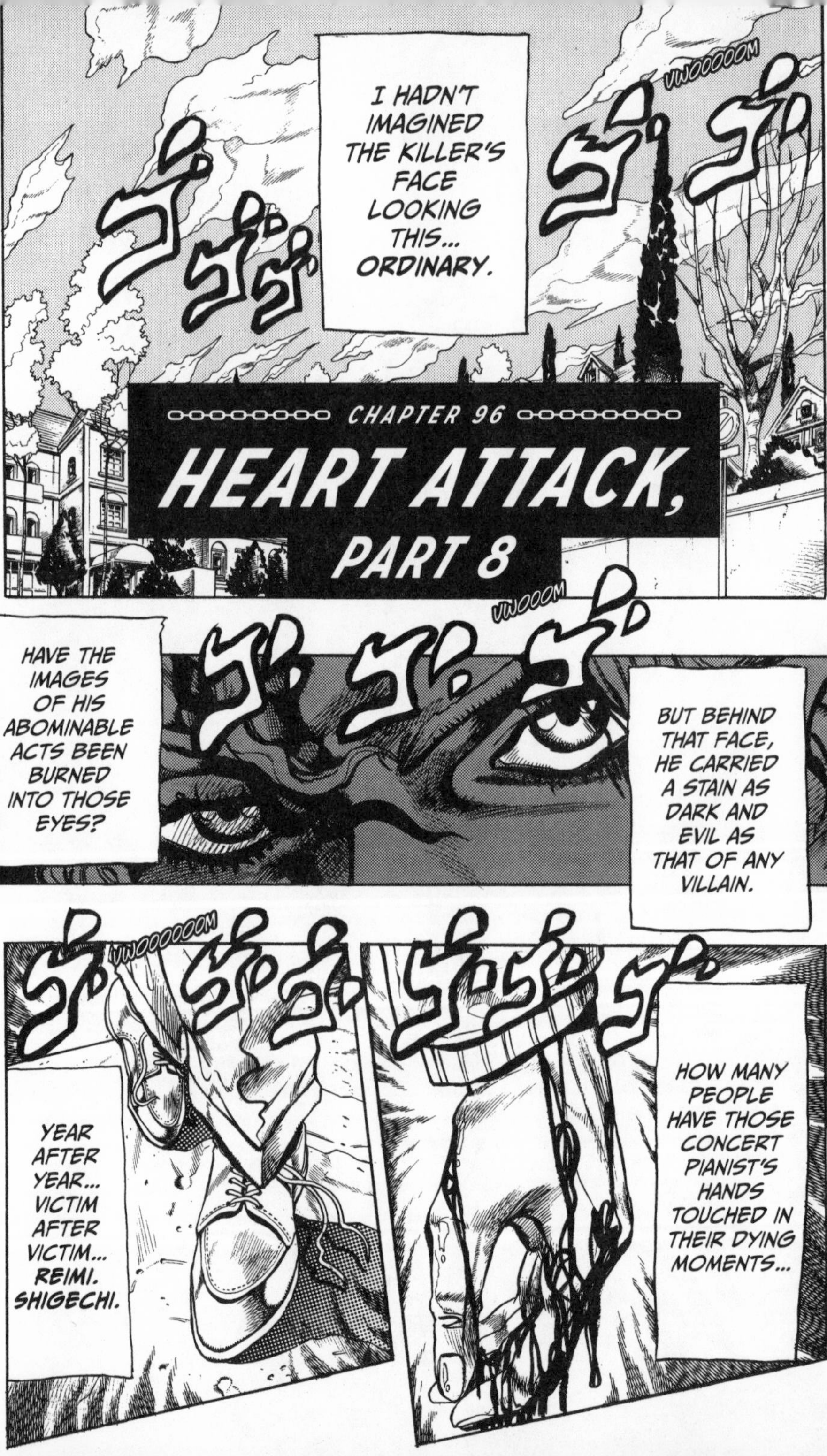
VWOOOOOM
I HADN'T IMAGINED THE KILLER'S FACE LOOKING THIS... ORDINARY.
CHAPTER 96
HEART ATTACK, PART 8
BUT BEHIND THAT FACE, HE CARRIED A STAIN AS DARK AND EVIL AS THAT OF ANY VILLAIN.
VWOOOM
HAVE THE IMAGES OF HIS ABOMINABLE ACTS BEEN BURNED INTO THOSE EYES?
HOW MANY PEOPLE HAVE THOSE CONCERT PIANIST'S HANDS TOUCHED IN THEIR DYING MOMENTS...
VWOOOOOOM
YEAR AFTER YEAR... VICTIM AFTER VICTIM... REIMI. SHIGECHI.

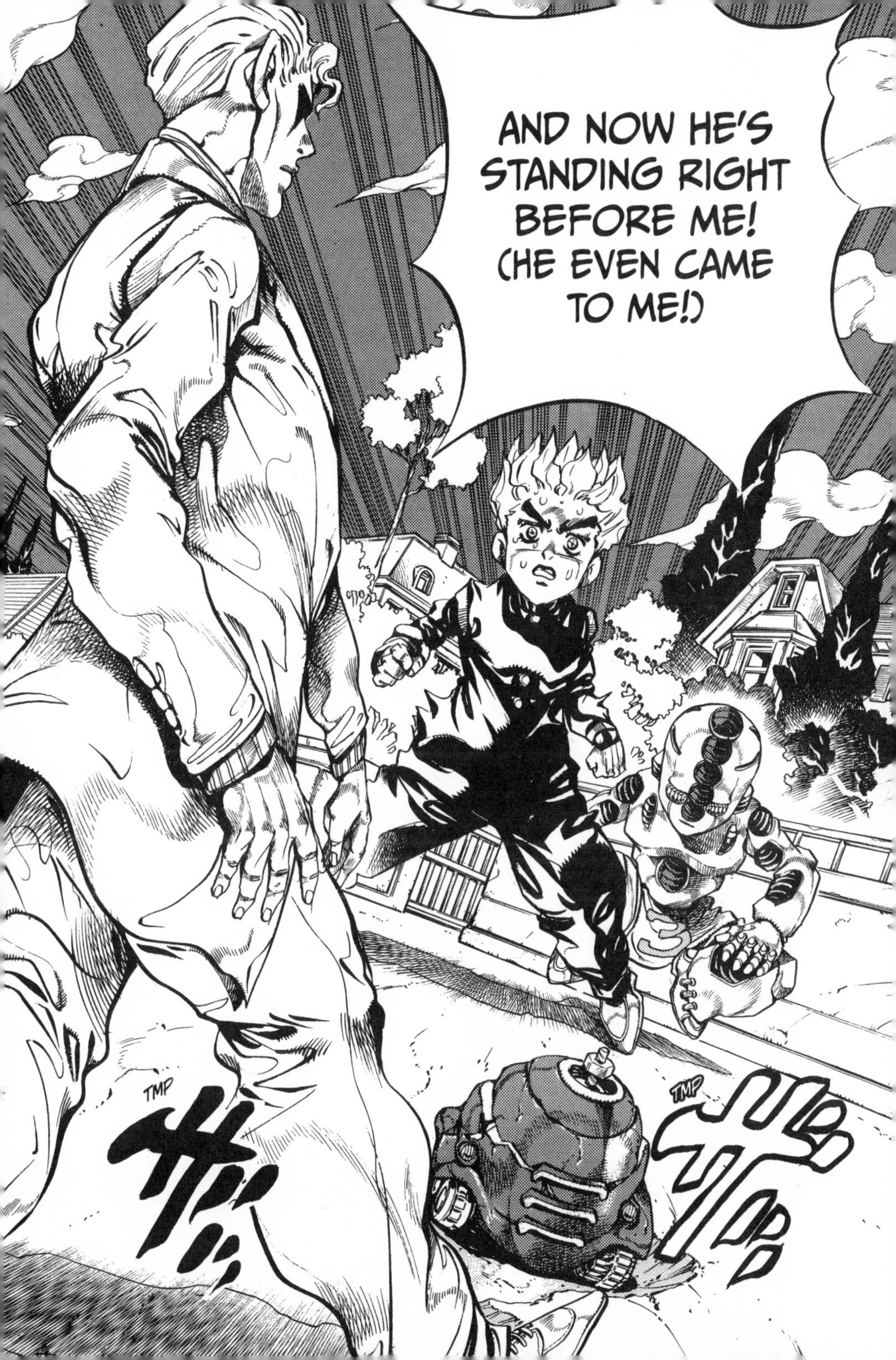
AND NOW HE'S STANDING RIGHT BEFORE ME! (HE EVEN CAME TO ME!)
TMP
TMP

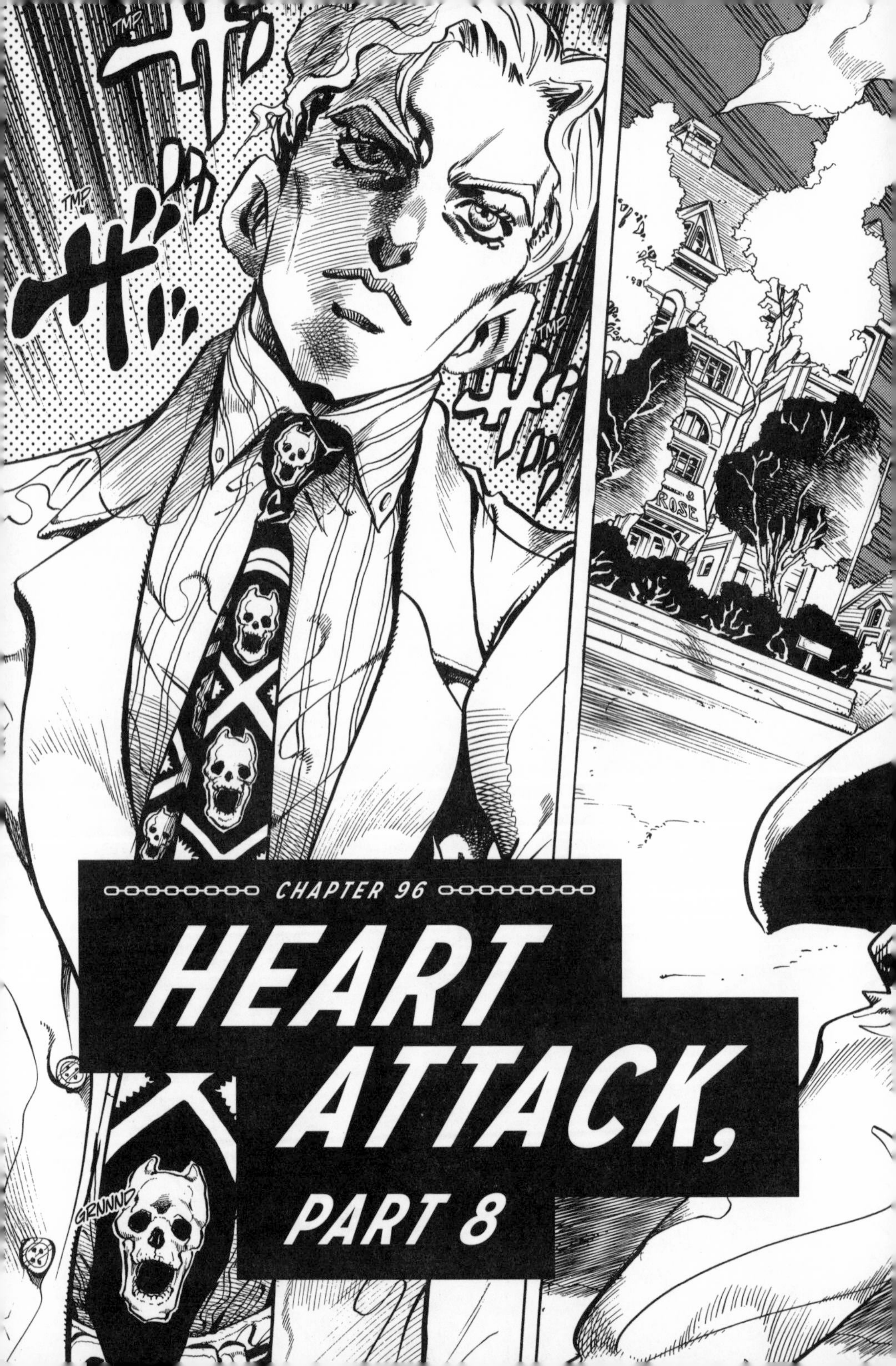
TMP
TMP
TMP
ROSE
CHAPTER 96
HEART ATTACK, PART 8
GRNNND

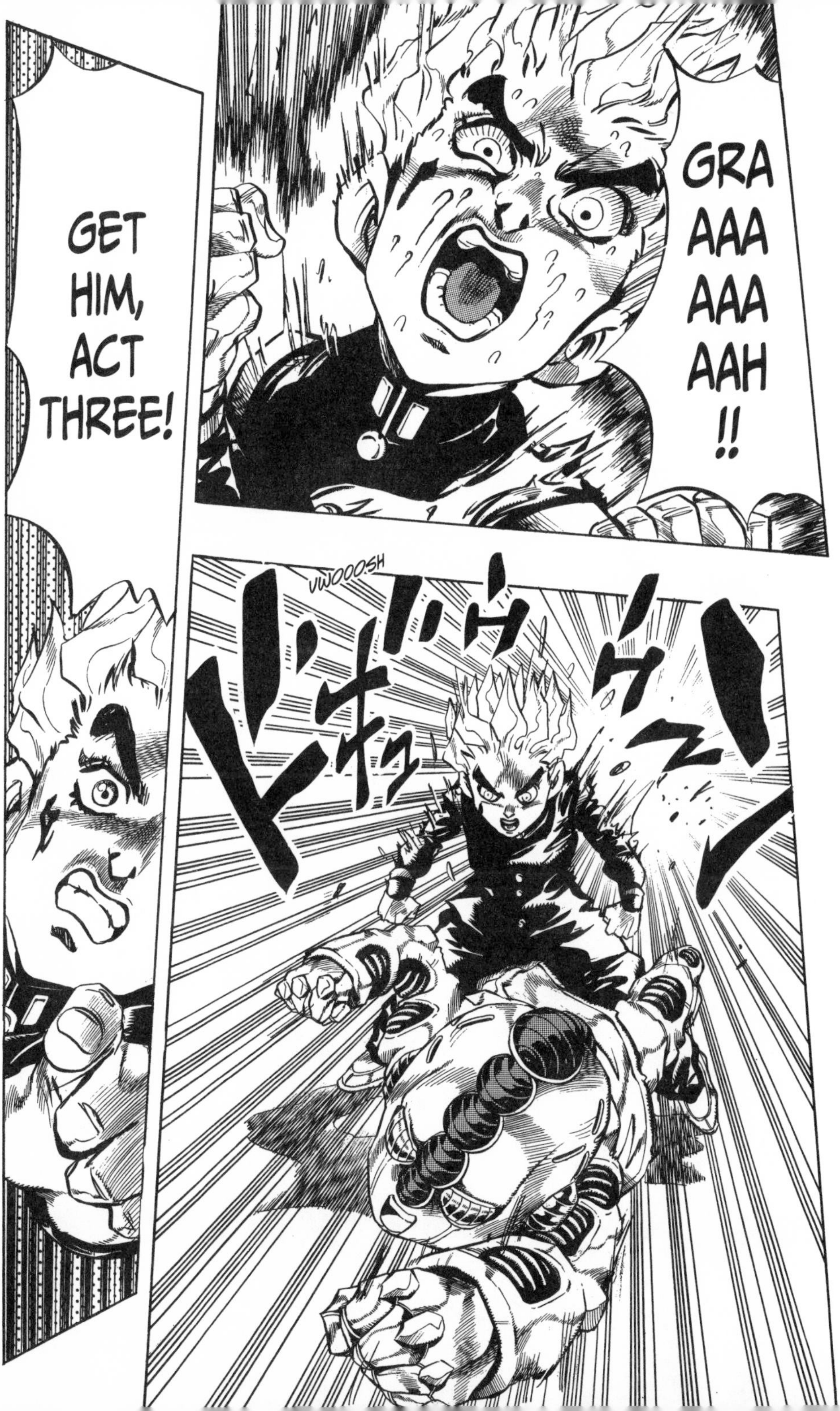
GRAAAAAAAAAAAH!!
GET HIM, ACT THREE!
VWOOOSH

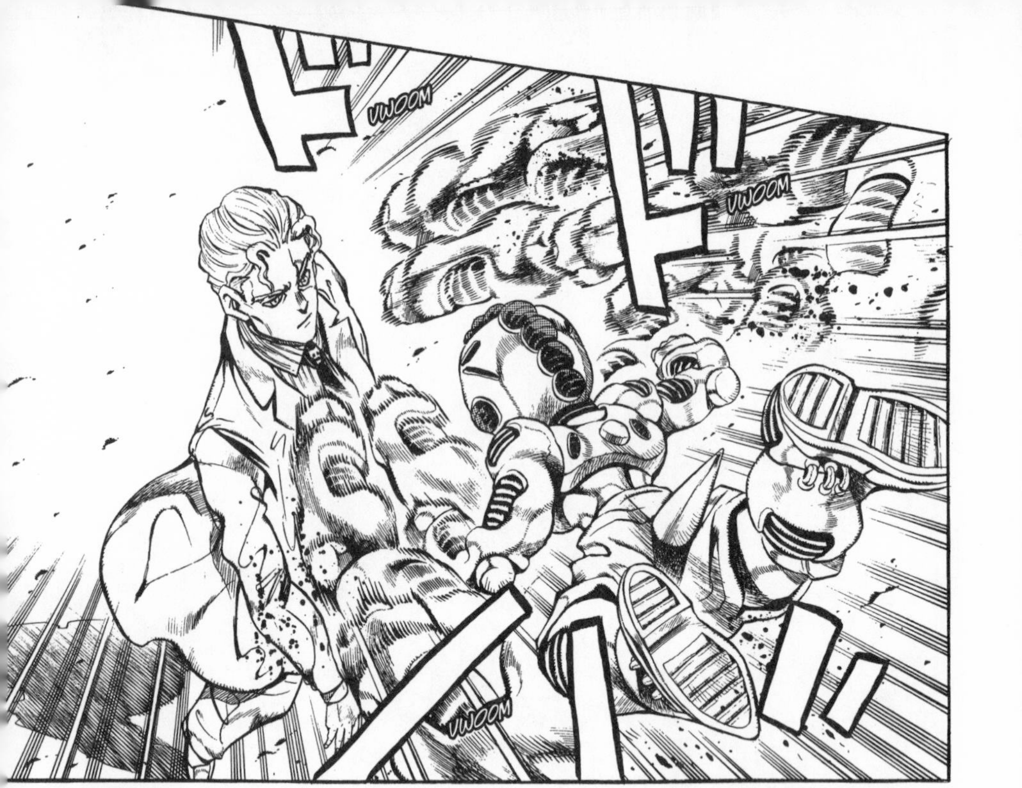
UWOOM
UWOOM
UWOOM
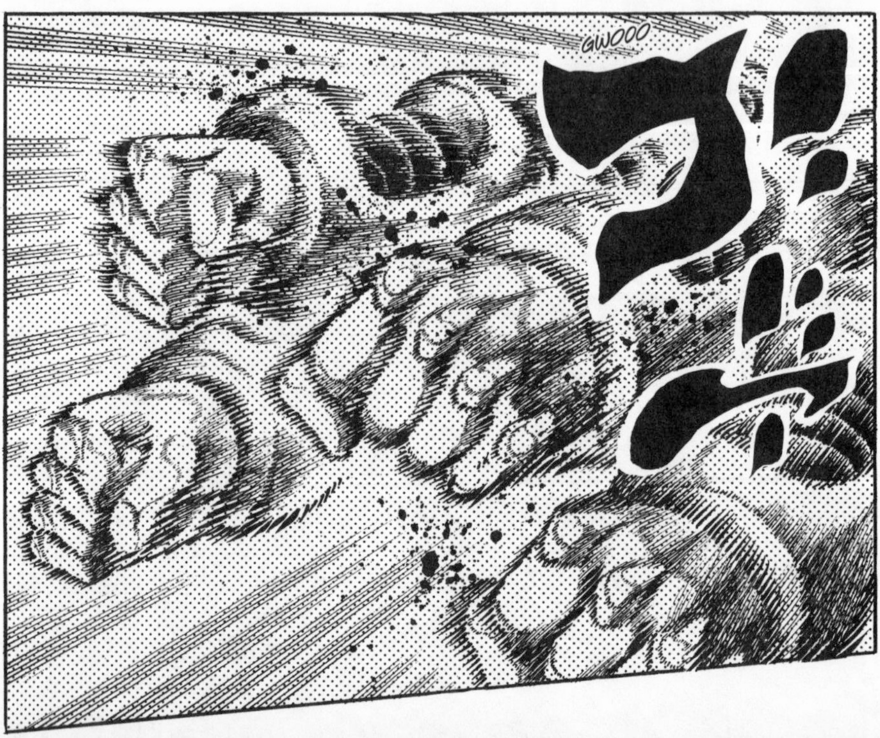
GWOOO

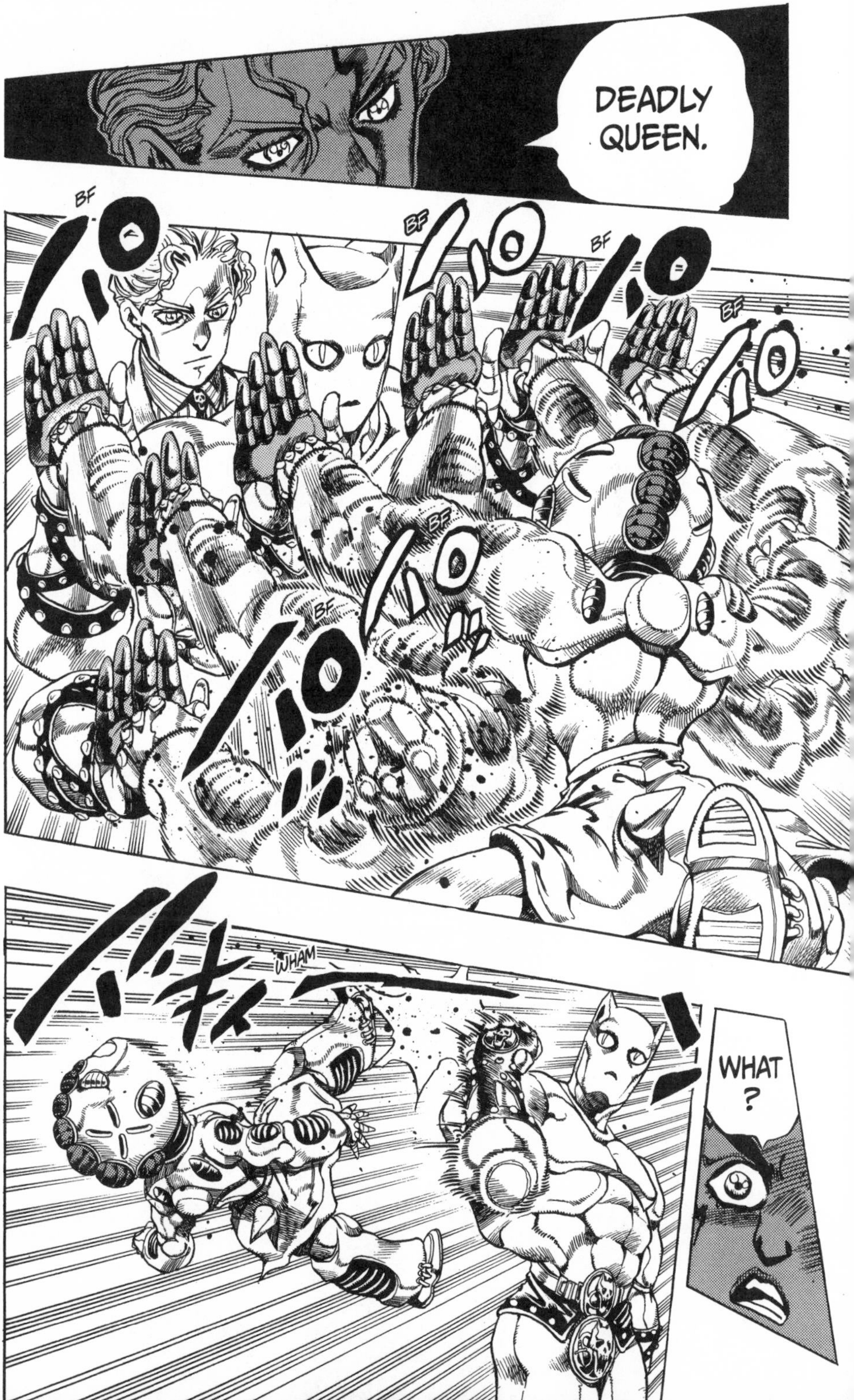
DEADLY QUEEN.
BF
BF
BF
BF
BF
BF
WHAM
WHAT?

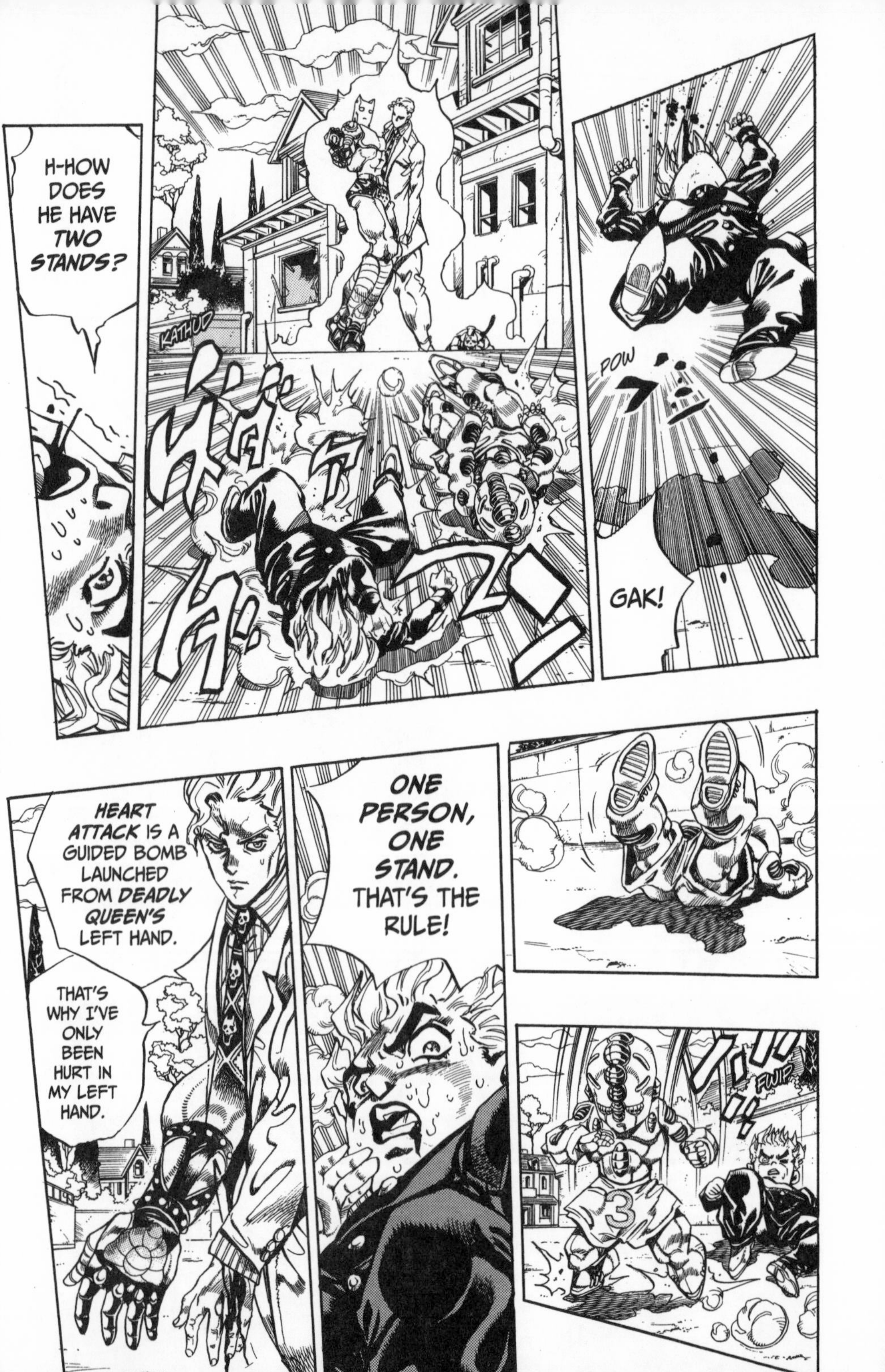
POW
GAK!
KATHUD
H-HOW DOES HE HAVE *TWO STANDS?*
FWIP
ONE PERSON, ONE STAND. THAT'S THE RULE!
HEART ATTACK IS A GUIDED BOMB LAUNCHED FROM *DEADLY QUEEN'S* LEFT HAND.
THAT'S WHY I'VE ONLY BEEN HURT IN MY LEFT HAND.

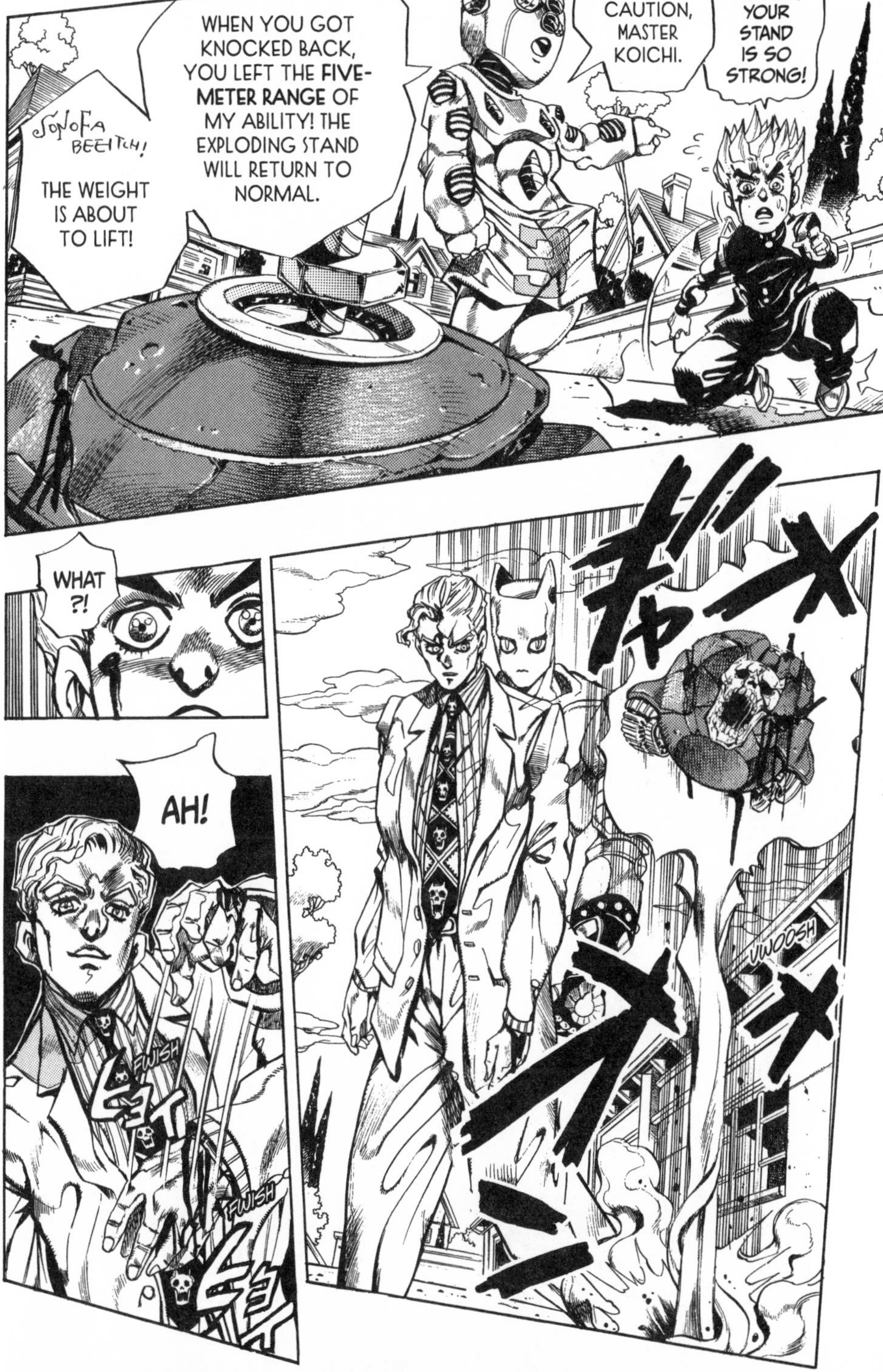
EVEN WORSE, YOUR STAND IS SO STRONG!
A WORD OF CAUTION, MASTER KOICHI.
WHEN YOU GOT KNOCKED BACK, YOU LEFT THE FIVE-METER RANGE OF MY ABILITY! THE EXPLODING STAND WILL RETURN TO NORMAL.
SONOFA BEEITCH!
THE WEIGHT IS ABOUT TO LIFT!
VWOOSH
WHAT ?!
AH!
FWISH
FWISH

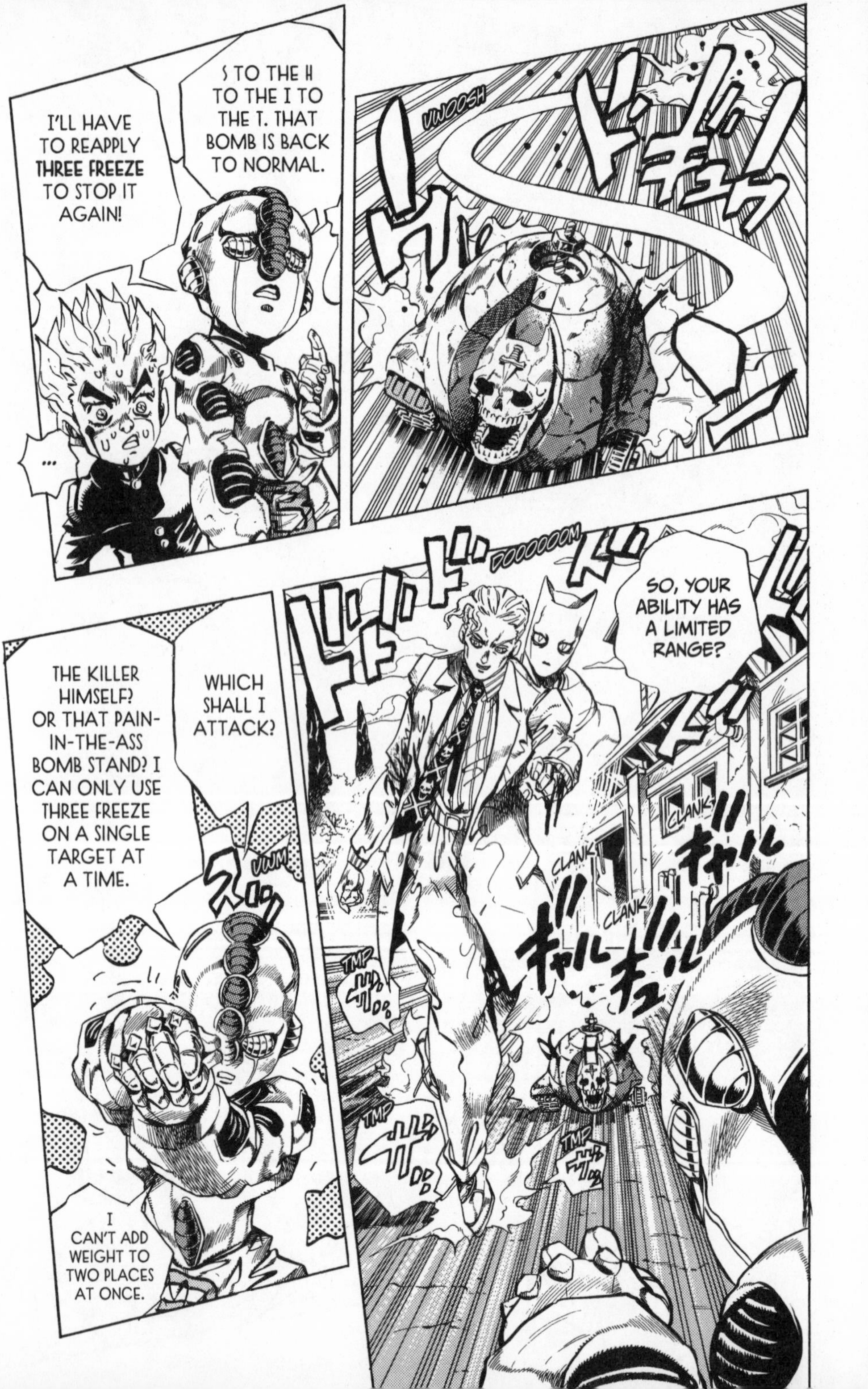
VWOOSH
S TO THE H TO THE I TO THE T. THAT BOMB IS BACK TO NORMAL.
I'LL HAVE TO REAPPLY **THREE FREEZE** TO STOP IT AGAIN!
...
DOOOOOOOM
SO, YOUR ABILITY HAS A LIMITED RANGE?
CLANK
CLANK
CLANK
TMP
TMP
TMP
WHICH SHALL I ATTACK?
THE KILLER HIMSELF? OR THAT PAIN-IN-THE-ASS BOMB STAND? I CAN ONLY USE THREE FREEZE ON A SINGLE TARGET AT A TIME.
VWM
I CAN'T ADD WEIGHT TO TWO PLACES AT ONCE.

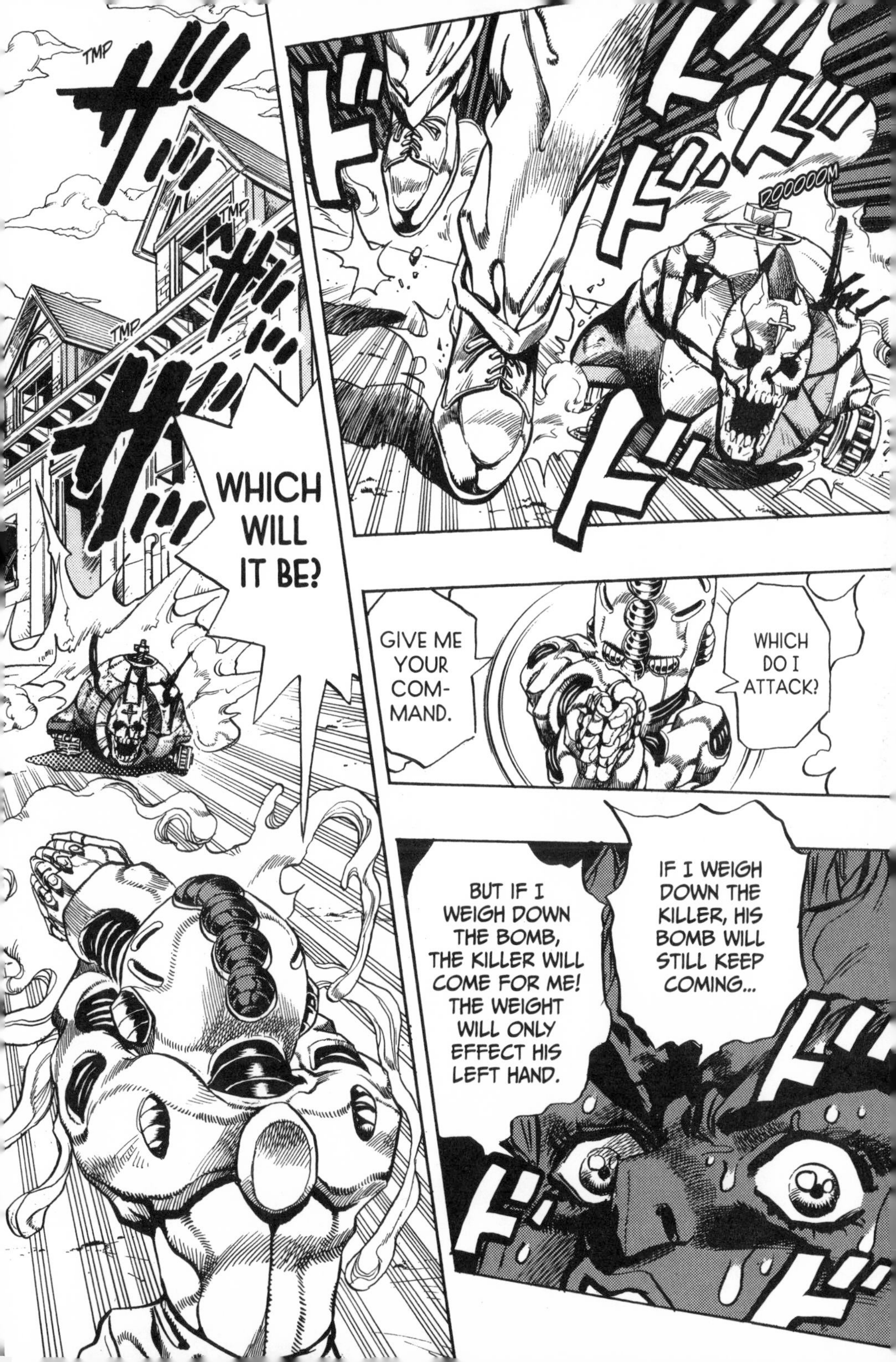
DOOOOOM
WHICH DO I ATTACK?
GIVE ME YOUR COMMAND.
IF I WEIGH DOWN THE KILLER, HIS BOMB WILL STILL KEEP COMING...
BUT IF I WEIGH DOWN THE BOMB, THE KILLER WILL COME FOR ME! THE WEIGHT WILL ONLY EFFECT HIS LEFT HAND.
TMP
TMP
TMP
WHICH WILL IT BE?

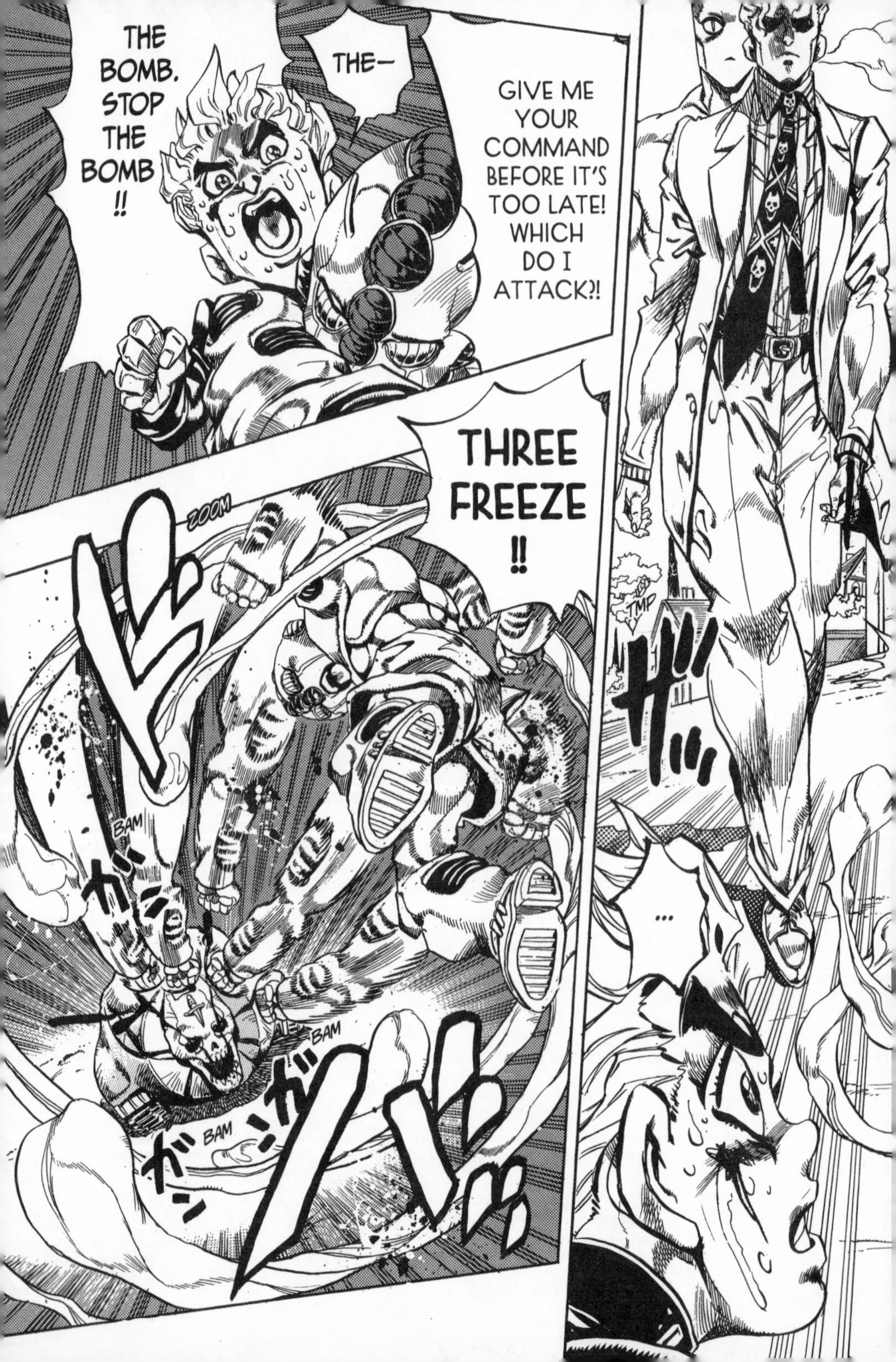
TMP
...
GIVE ME YOUR COMMAND BEFORE IT'S TOO LATE! WHICH DO I ATTACK?!
THE—
THE BOMB. STOP THE BOMB!!
THREE FREEZE!!
ZOOM
BAM
BAM
BAM

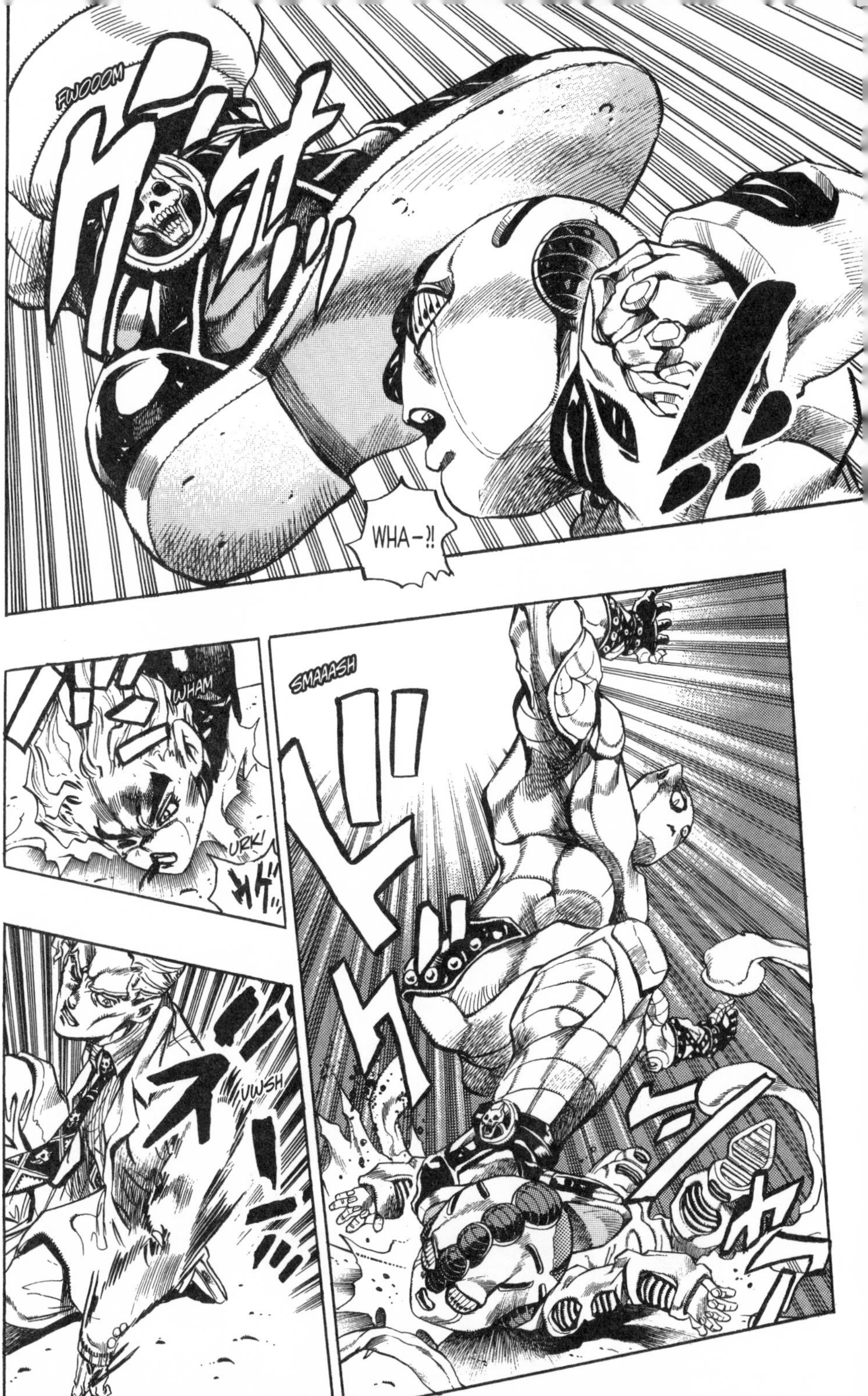
FWOOOM
WHA–?!
SMAAASH
WHAM
URK!
VWSH

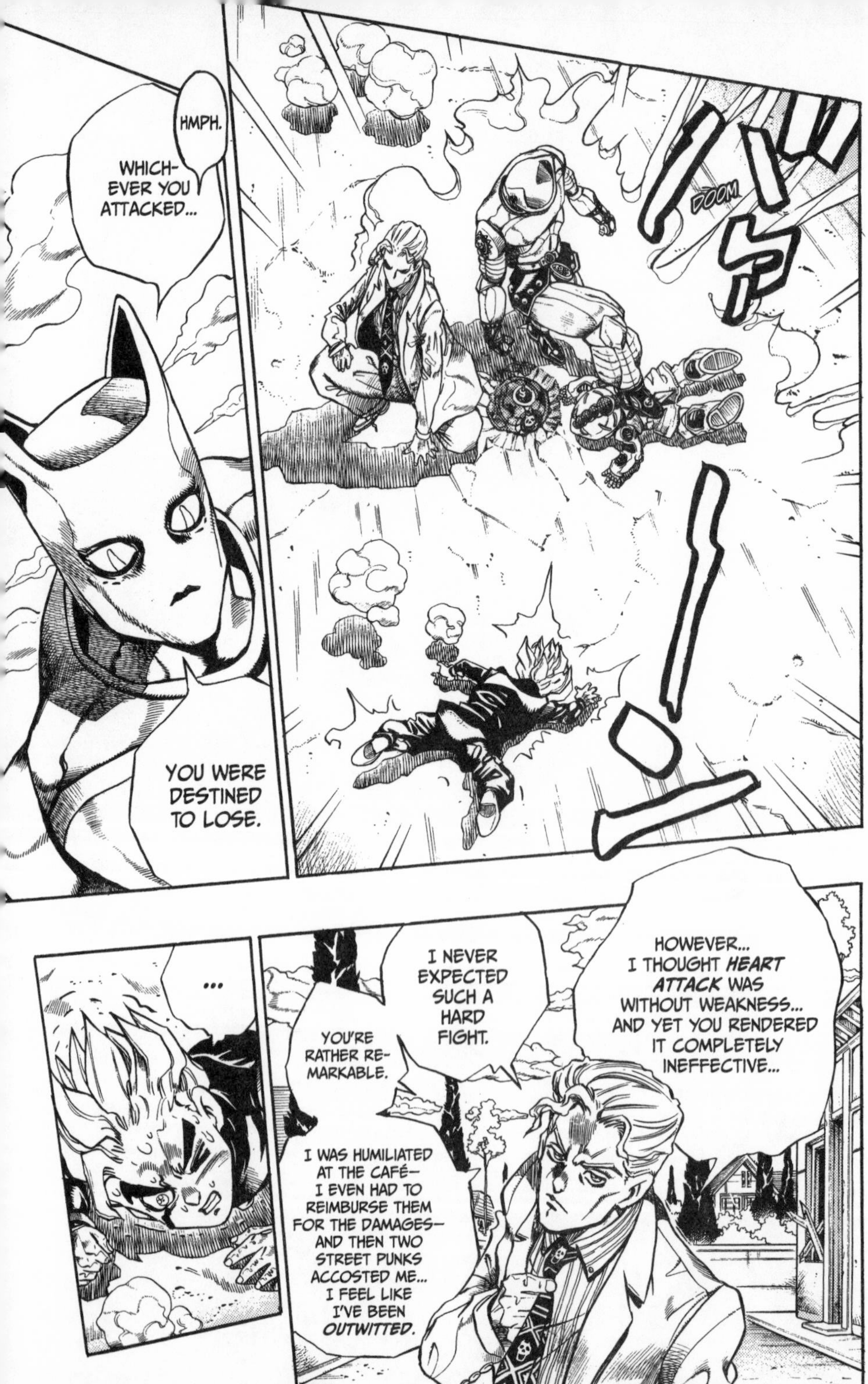
DOOM
HMPH.
WHICH-EVER YOU ATTACKED...
YOU WERE DESTINED TO LOSE.
HOWEVER... I THOUGHT *HEART ATTACK* WAS WITHOUT WEAKNESS... AND YET YOU RENDERED IT COMPLETELY INEFFECTIVE...
I NEVER EXPECTED SUCH A HARD FIGHT.
YOU'RE RATHER RE-MARKABLE.
I WAS HUMILIATED AT THE CAFÉ— I EVEN HAD TO REIMBURSE THEM FOR THE DAMAGES— AND THEN TWO STREET PUNKS ACCOSTED ME... I FEEL LIKE I'VE BEEN *OUTWITTED*.
...

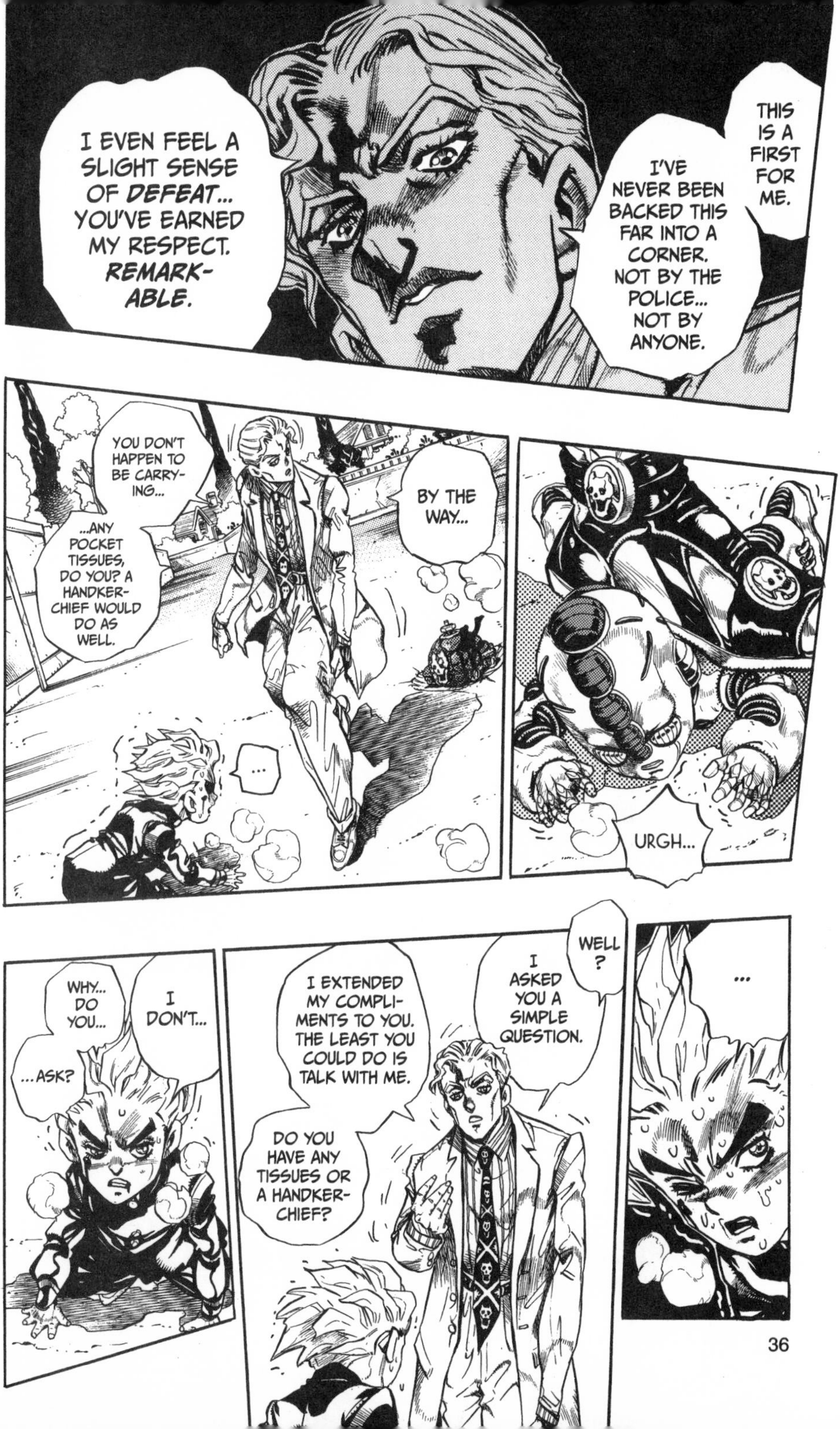
THIS IS A FIRST FOR ME.
I'VE NEVER BEEN BACKED THIS FAR INTO A CORNER. NOT BY THE POLICE... NOT BY ANYONE.
I EVEN FEEL A SLIGHT SENSE OF DEFEAT... YOU'VE EARNED MY RESPECT. REMARKABLE.
URGH...
BY THE WAY...
YOU DON'T HAPPEN TO BE CARRYING...
...ANY POCKET TISSUES, DO YOU? A HANDKERCHIEF WOULD DO AS WELL.
...
...
WELL?
I ASKED YOU A SIMPLE QUESTION.
I EXTENDED MY COMPLIMENTS TO YOU. THE LEAST YOU COULD DO IS TALK WITH ME.
DO YOU HAVE ANY TISSUES OR A HANDKERCHIEF?
I DON'T...
WHY... DO YOU...
...ASK?

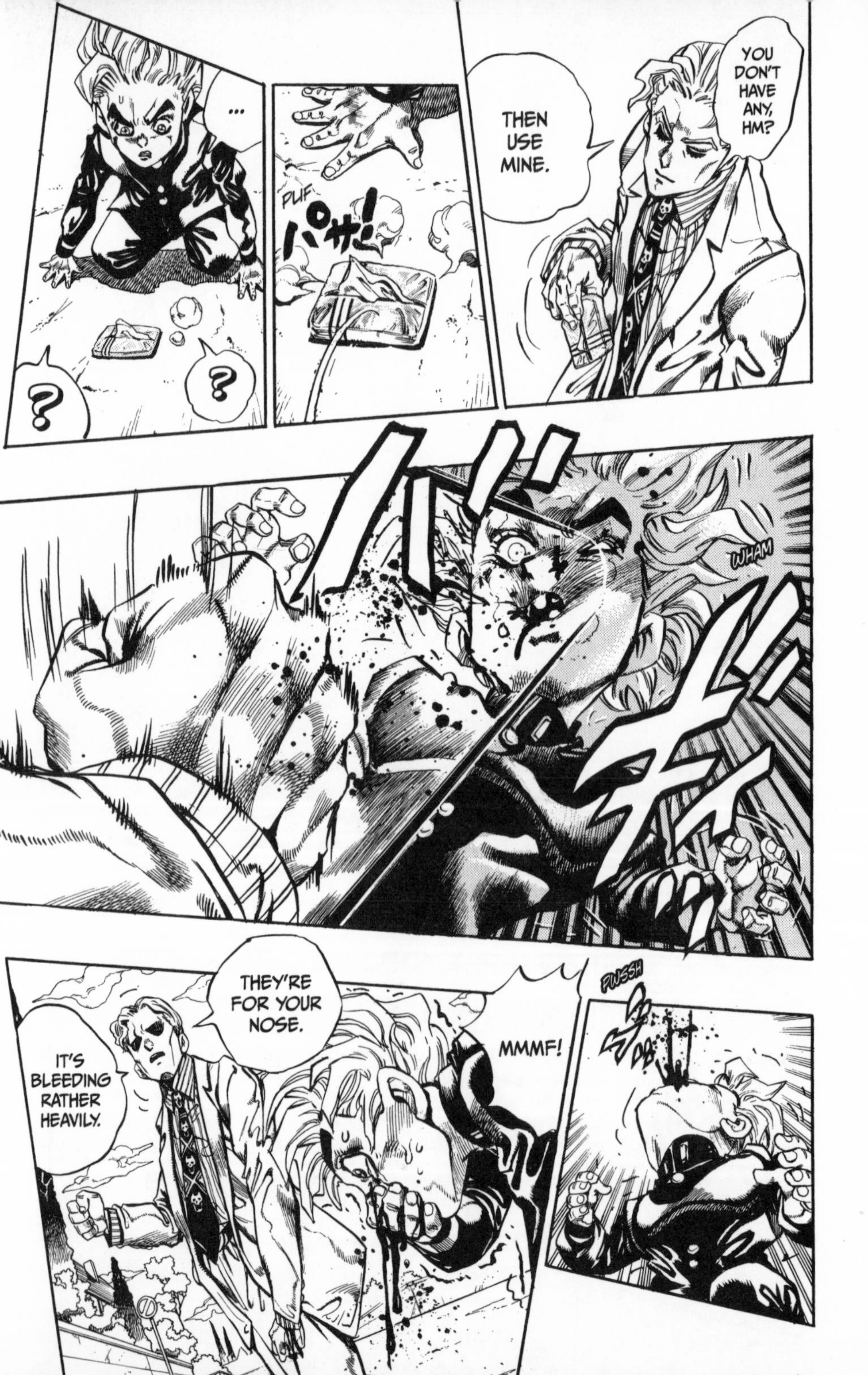
YOU DON'T HAVE ANY, HM?
THEN USE MINE.
PUF
パサッ！
...
?
?
WHAM
PWSSH
MMMF!
THEY'RE FOR YOUR NOSE.
IT'S BLEEDING RATHER HEAVILY.

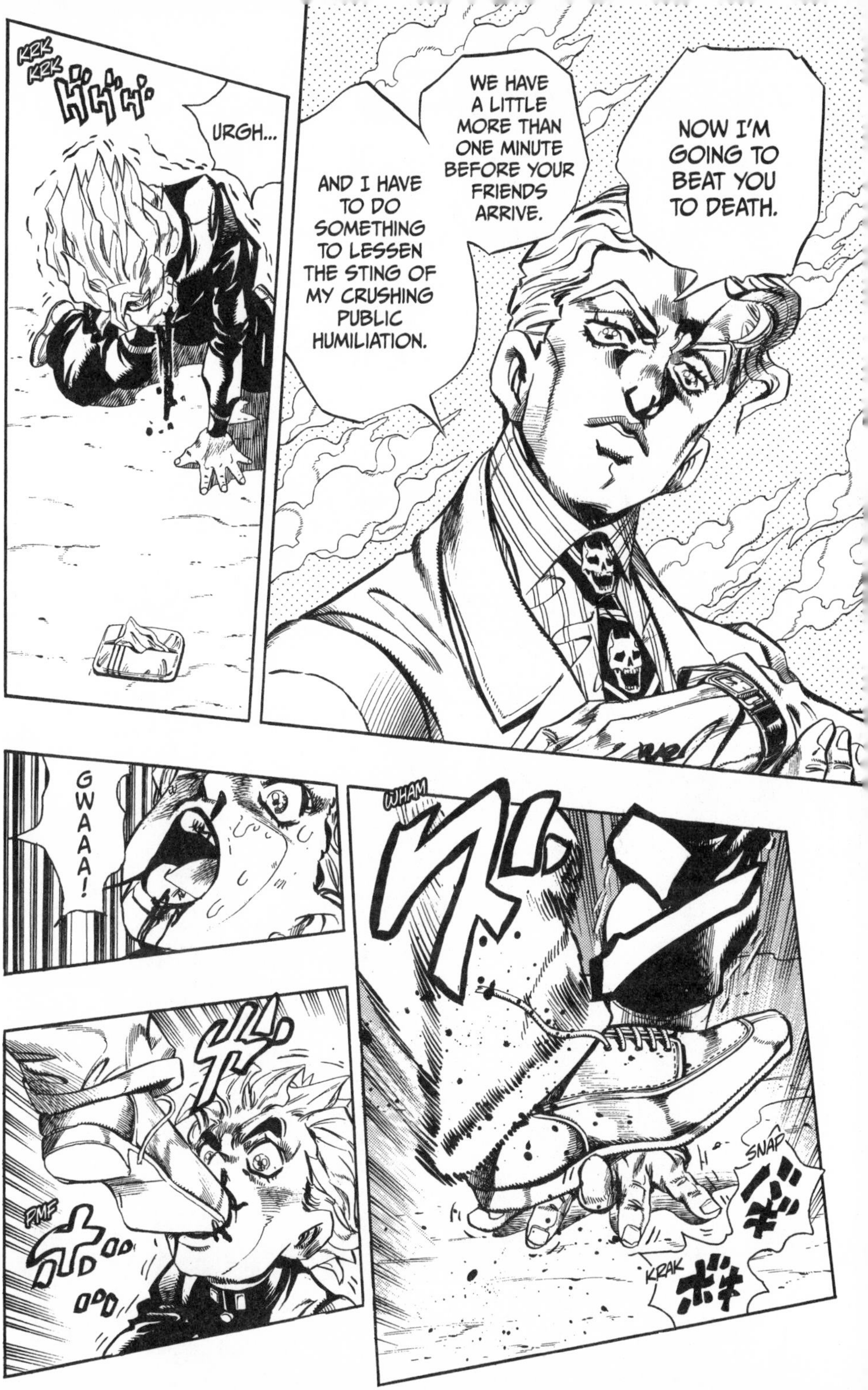
NOW I'M GOING TO BEAT YOU TO DEATH.
WE HAVE A LITTLE MORE THAN ONE MINUTE BEFORE YOUR FRIENDS ARRIVE.
AND I HAVE TO DO SOMETHING TO LESSEN THE STING OF MY CRUSHING PUBLIC HUMILIATION.
KRK KRK
URGH...
WHAM
SNAP
KRAK
GWAAAA!
PMF

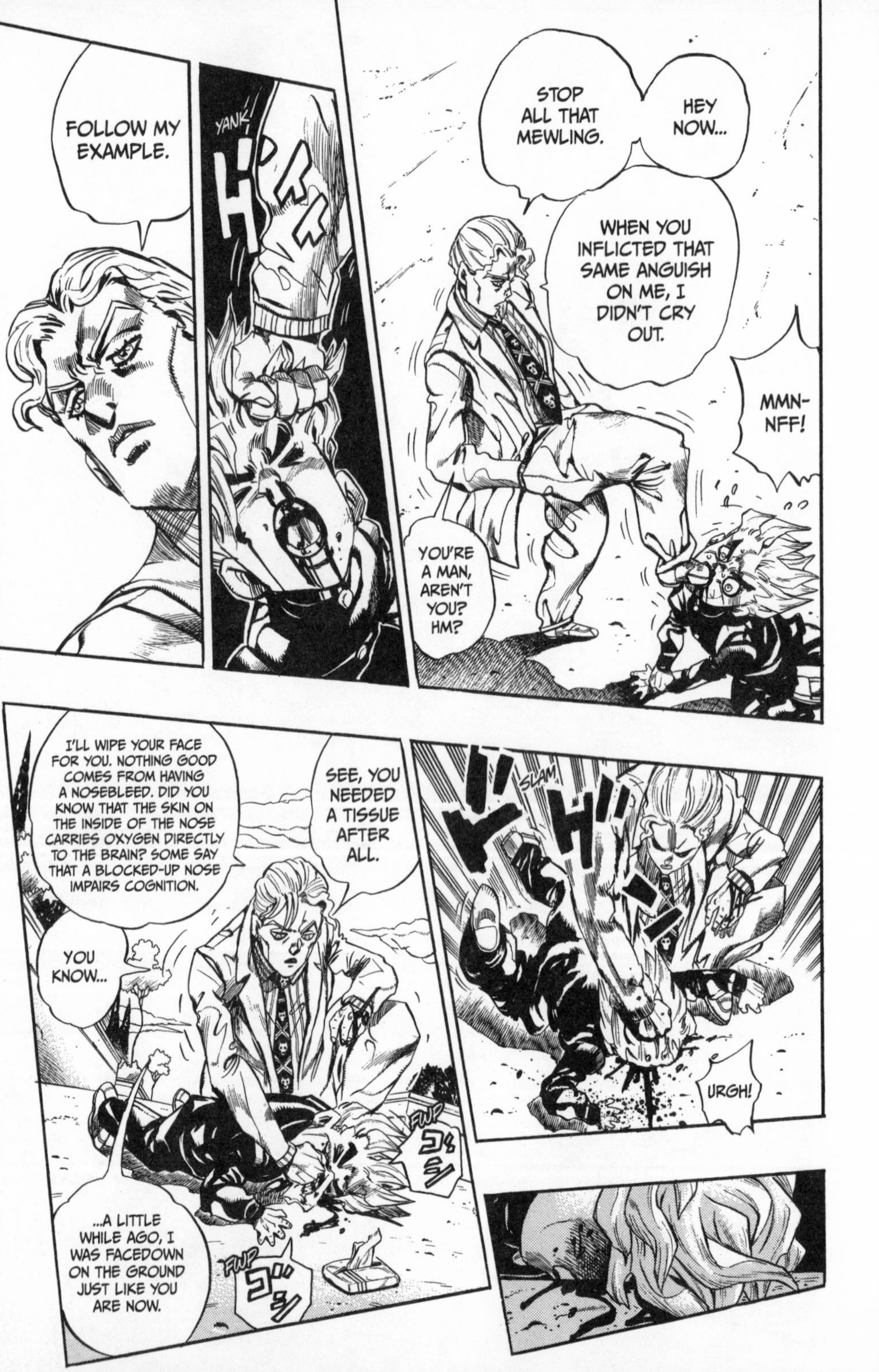
HEY NOW...
STOP ALL THAT MEWLING.
WHEN YOU INFLICTED THAT SAME ANGUISH ON ME, I DIDN'T CRY OUT.
MMN-NFF!
YOU'RE A MAN, AREN'T YOU? HM?
YANK!
FOLLOW MY EXAMPLE.
SLAM
URGH!
SEE, YOU NEEDED A TISSUE AFTER ALL.
I'LL WIPE YOUR FACE FOR YOU. NOTHING GOOD COMES FROM HAVING A NOSEBLEED. DID YOU KNOW THAT THE SKIN ON THE INSIDE OF THE NOSE CARRIES OXYGEN DIRECTLY TO THE BRAIN? SOME SAY THAT A BLOCKED-UP NOSE IMPAIRS COGNITION.
YOU KNOW...
FWP
FWP
...A LITTLE WHILE AGO, I WAS FACEDOWN ON THE GROUND JUST LIKE YOU ARE NOW.

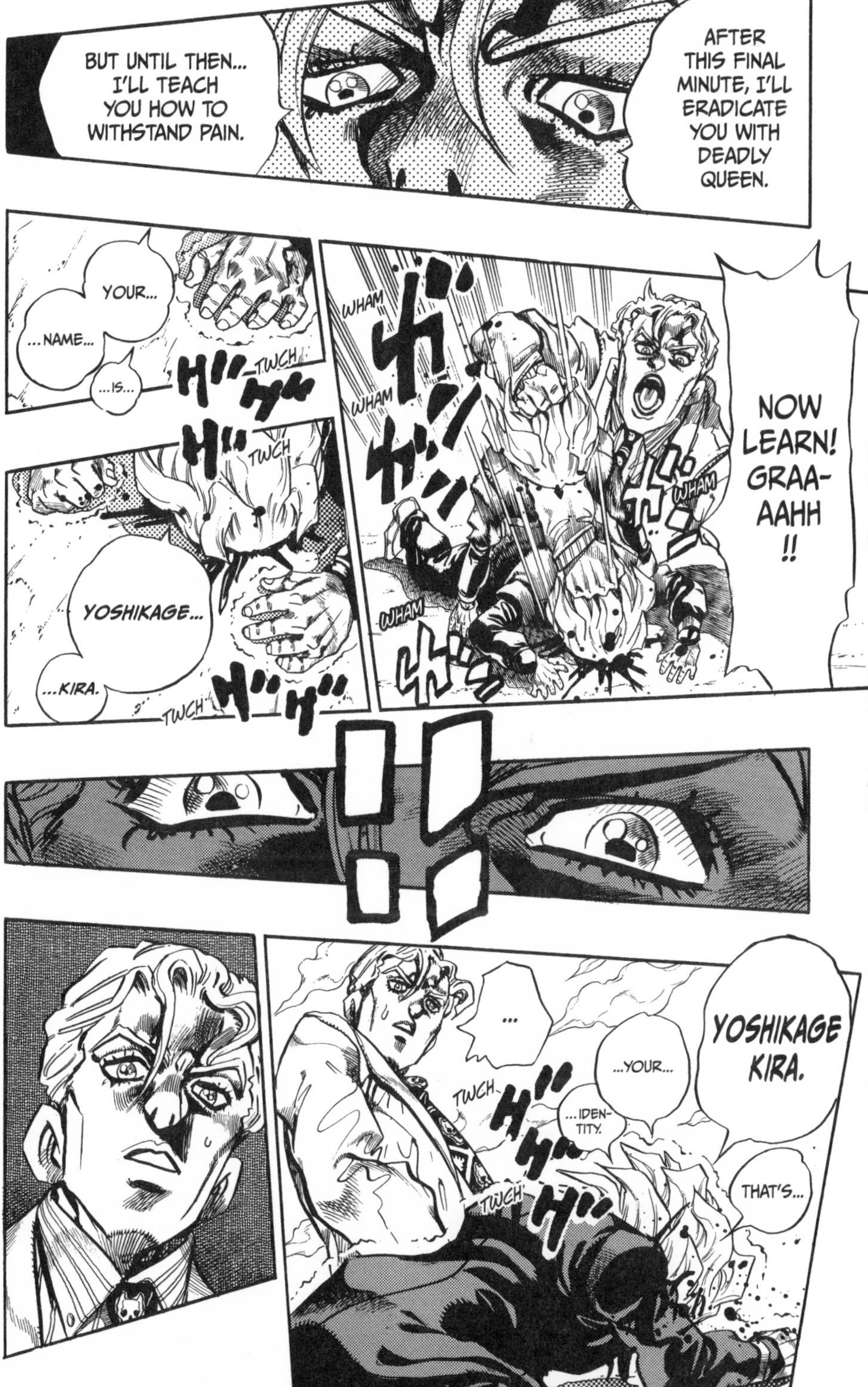
AFTER THIS FINAL MINUTE, I'LL ERADICATE YOU WITH DEADLY QUEEN.
BUT UNTIL THEN... I'LL TEACH YOU HOW TO WITHSTAND PAIN.
NOW LEARN! GRAA-AAHH!!
WHAM
WHAM
WHAM
WHAM
YOUR...
...NAME...
...IS...
TWCH
TWCH
YOSHIKAGE...
...KIRA.
TWCH
YOSHIKAGE KIRA.
THAT'S...
...YOUR...
...IDEN-TITY.
...
TWCH
TWCH

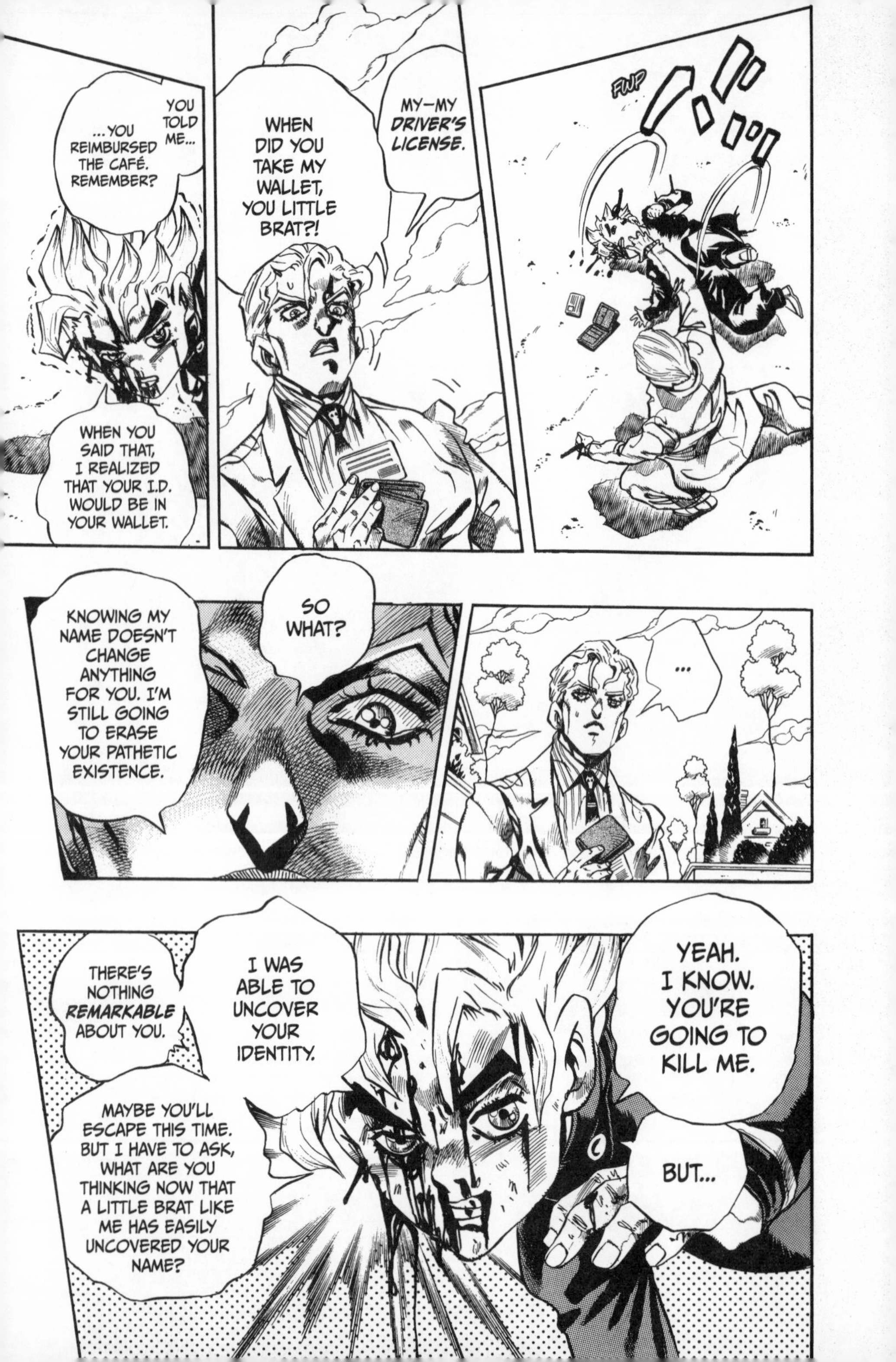
FWUP
MY—MY DRIVER'S LICENSE.
WHEN DID YOU TAKE MY WALLET, YOU LITTLE BRAT?!
YOU TOLD ME...
...YOU REIMBURSED THE CAFÉ. REMEMBER?
WHEN YOU SAID THAT, I REALIZED THAT YOUR I.D. WOULD BE IN YOUR WALLET.
...
SO WHAT?
KNOWING MY NAME DOESN'T CHANGE ANYTHING FOR YOU. I'M STILL GOING TO ERASE YOUR PATHETIC EXISTENCE.
YEAH. I KNOW. YOU'RE GOING TO KILL ME.
BUT...
I WAS ABLE TO UNCOVER YOUR IDENTITY.
THERE'S NOTHING REMARKABLE ABOUT YOU.
MAYBE YOU'LL ESCAPE THIS TIME. BUT I HAVE TO ASK, WHAT ARE YOU THINKING NOW THAT A LITTLE BRAT LIKE ME HAS EASILY UNCOVERED YOUR NAME?

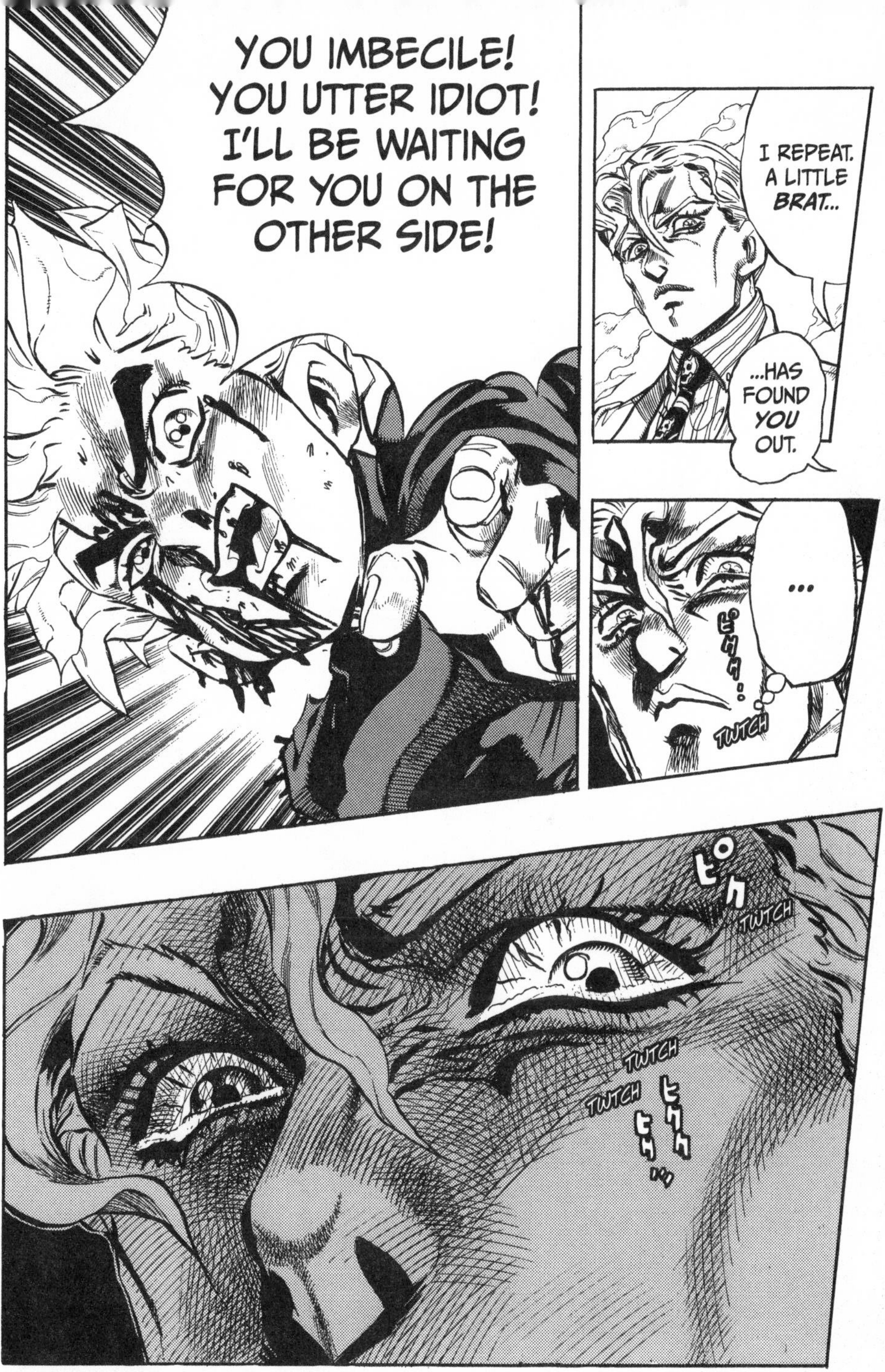
I REPEAT. A LITTLE BRAT...
...HAS FOUND YOU OUT.
...
TWTCH
YOU IMBECILE! YOU UTTER IDIOT! I'LL BE WAITING FOR YOU ON THE OTHER SIDE!
TWTCH
TWTCH
TWTCH

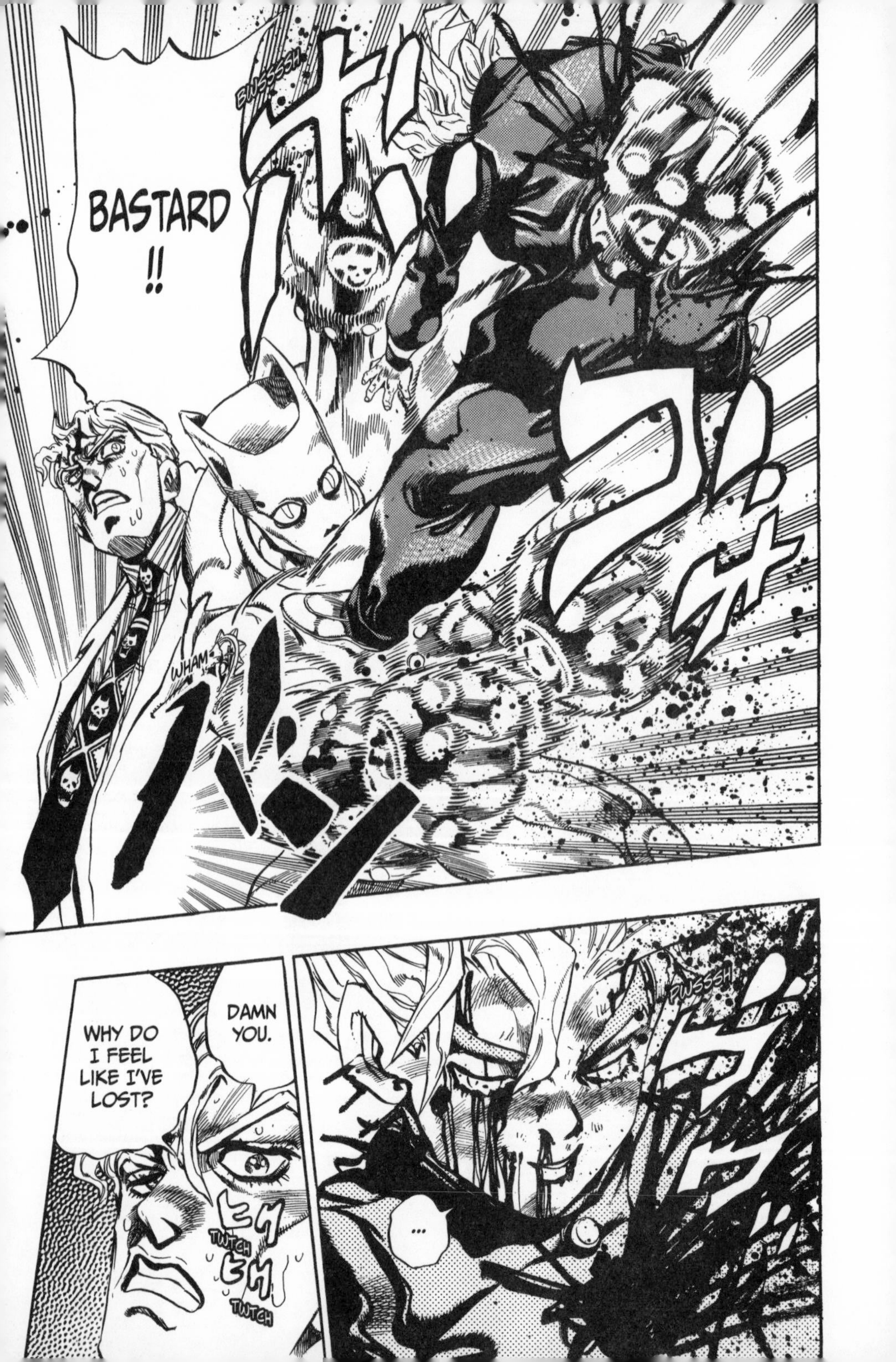
BWSSSSH
BASTARD!!
WHAM
PWSSSH
...
DAMN YOU.
WHY DO I FEEL LIKE I'VE LOST?
TWITCH
TWITCH

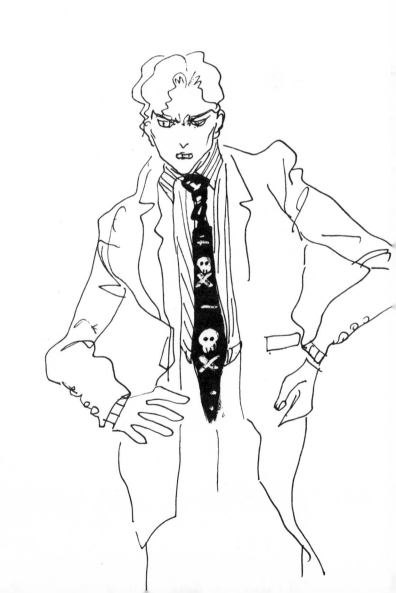

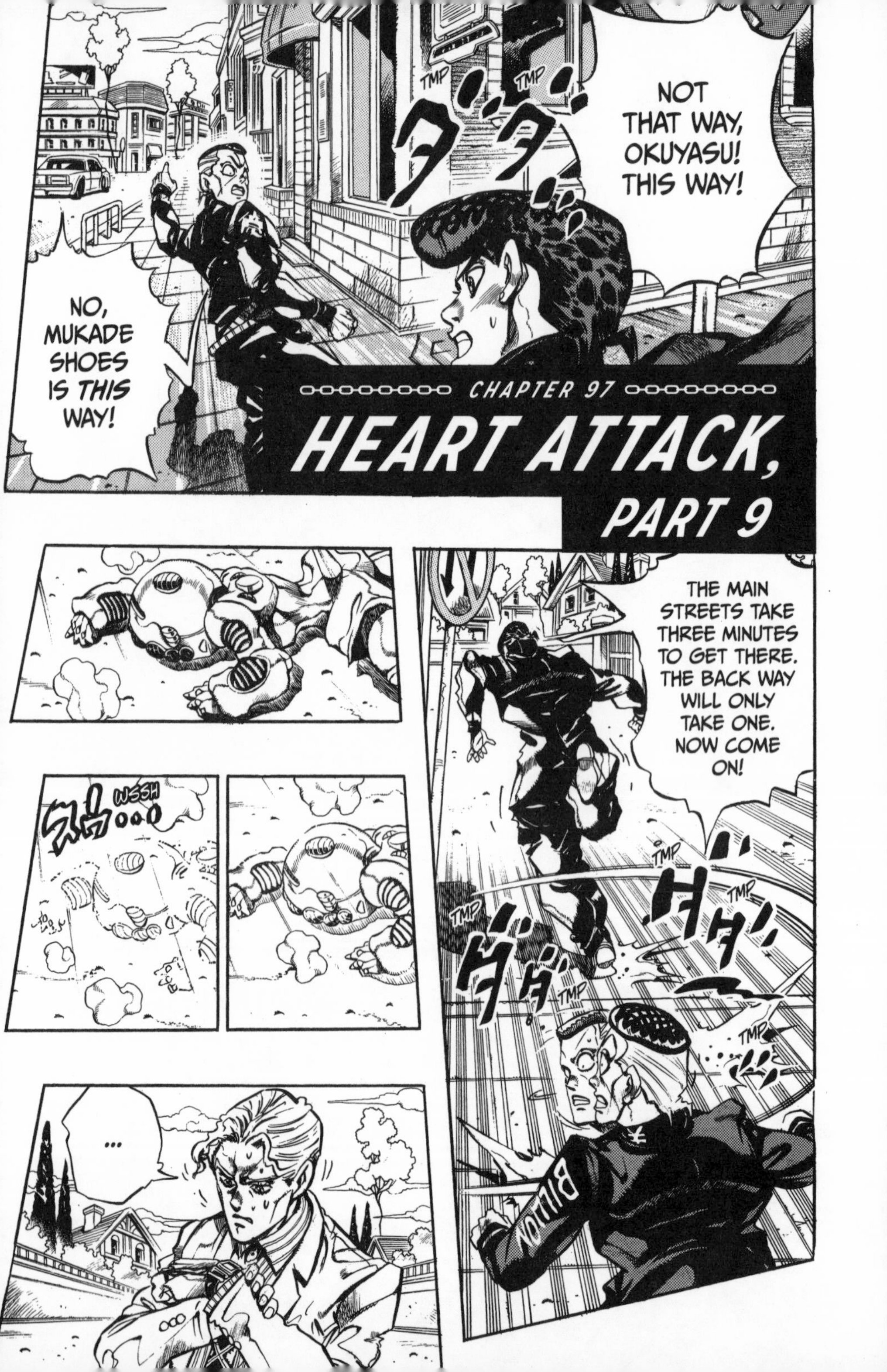
TMP
TMP
NOT THAT WAY, OKUYASU! THIS WAY!
NO, MUKADE SHOES IS THIS WAY!
CHAPTER 97
HEART ATTACK, PART 9
THE MAIN STREETS TAKE THREE MINUTES TO GET THERE. THE BACK WAY WILL ONLY TAKE ONE. NOW COME ON!
TMP
TMP
TMP
TMP
TMP
BILLION
WSSH
...

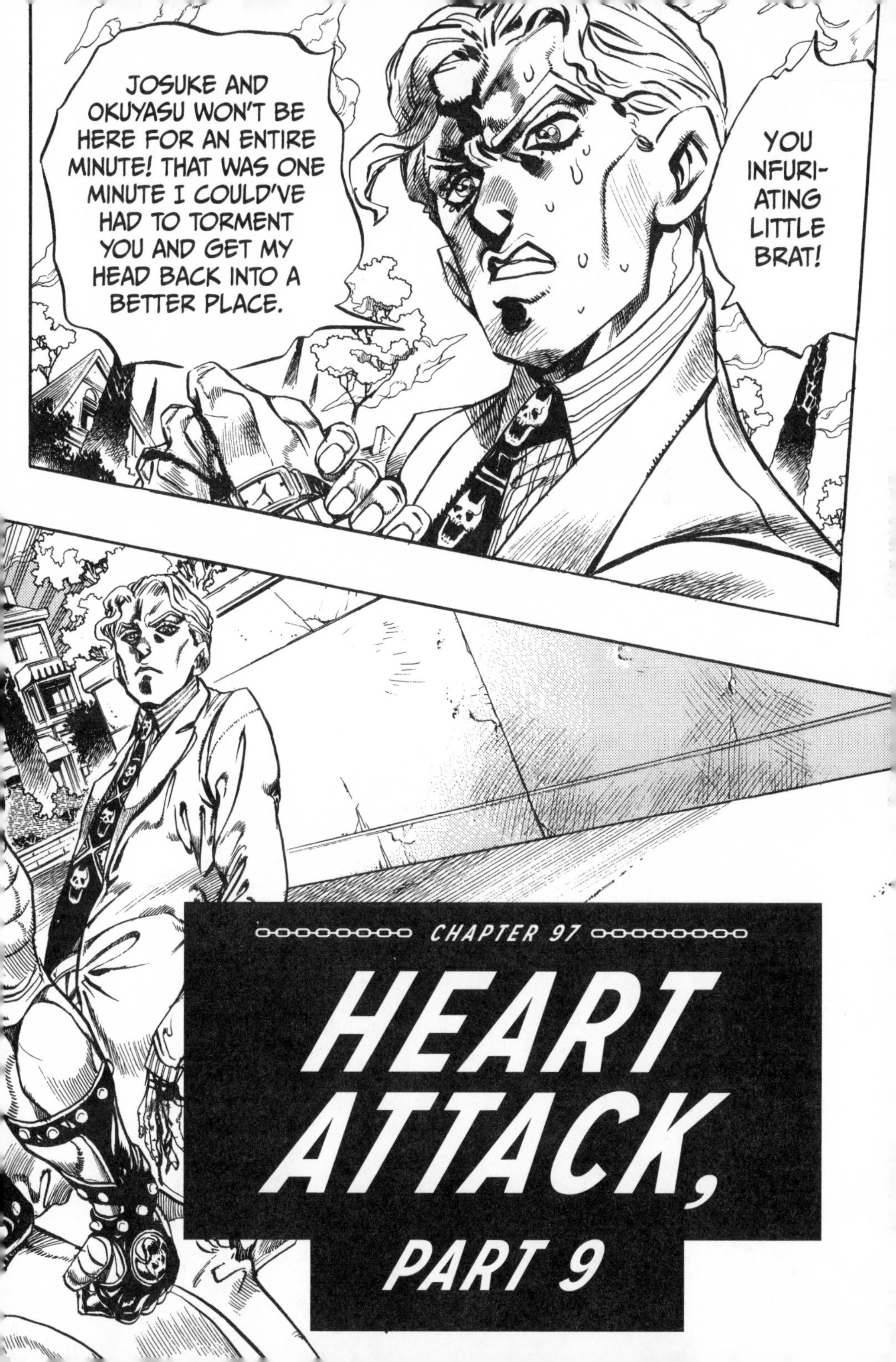
YOU INFURIATING LITTLE BRAT!
JOSUKE AND OKUYASU WON'T BE HERE FOR AN ENTIRE MINUTE! THAT WAS ONE MINUTE I COULD'VE HAD TO TORMENT YOU AND GET MY HEAD BACK INTO A BETTER PLACE.
CHAPTER 97
HEART ATTACK, PART 9

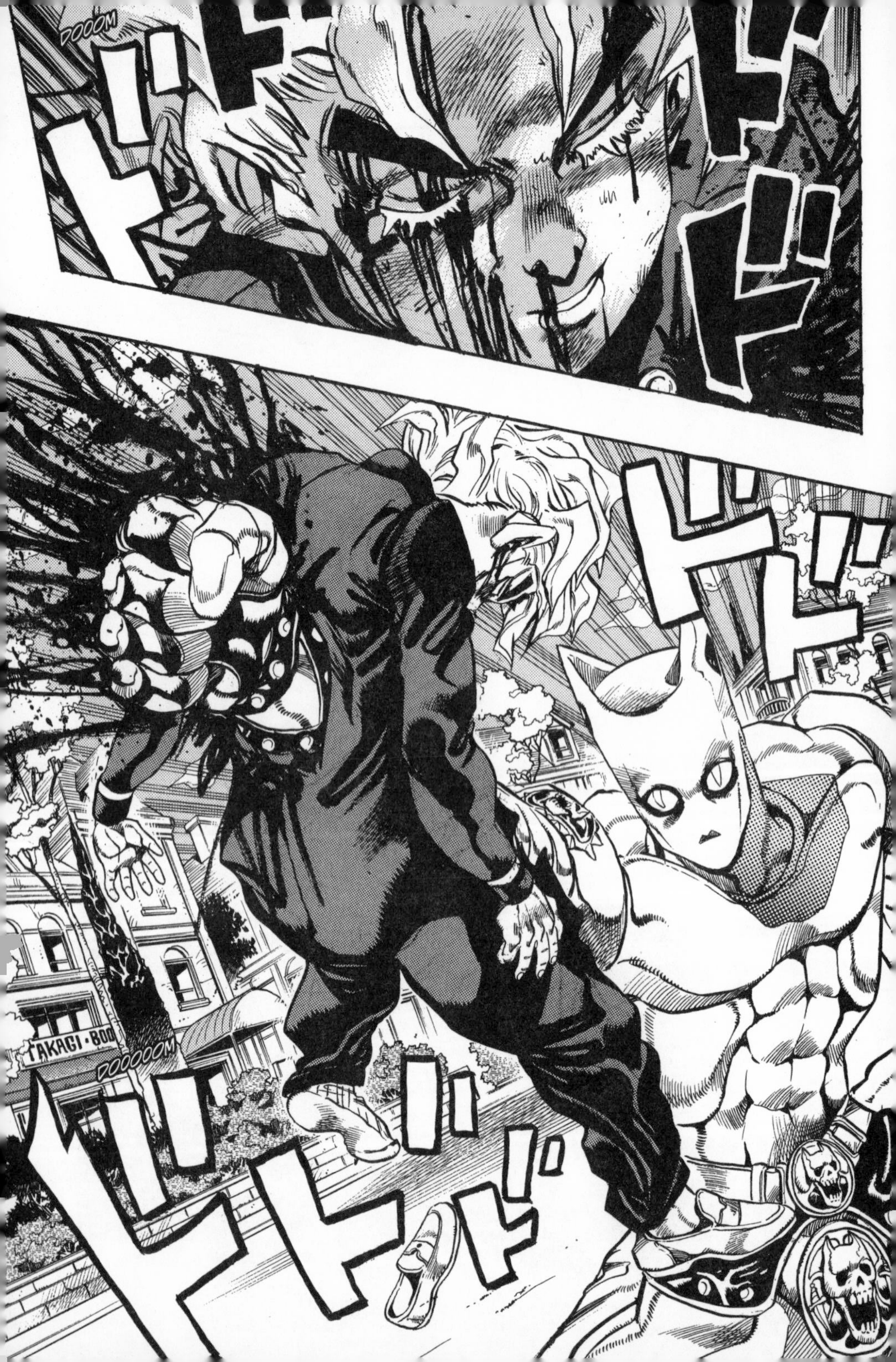
DOOOM
TAKAGI·BOO
DOOOOOM

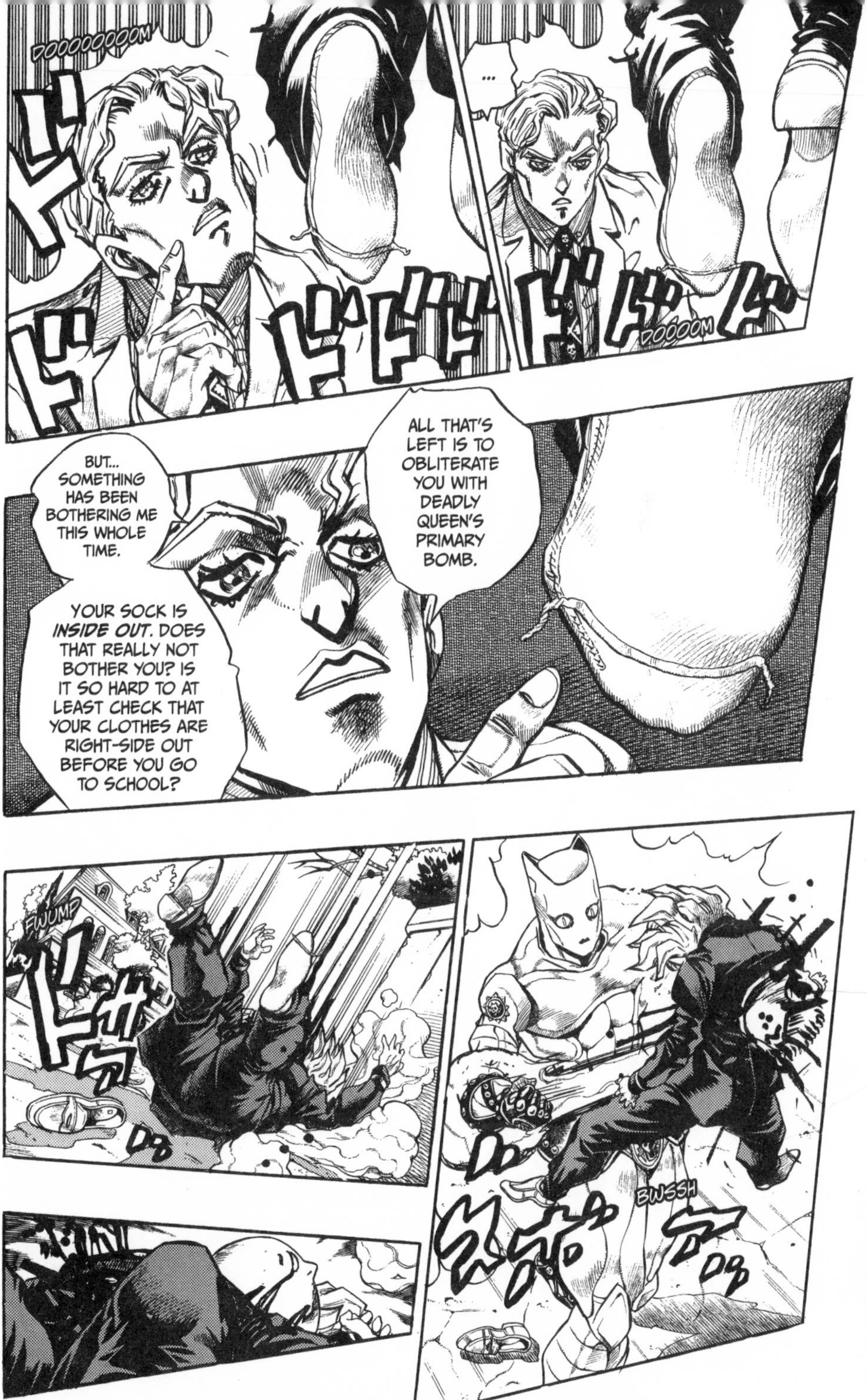

...
DOOOOM
DOOOOOOOOM
ALL THAT'S LEFT IS TO OBLITERATE YOU WITH DEADLY QUEEN'S PRIMARY BOMB.
BUT... SOMETHING HAS BEEN BOTHERING ME THIS WHOLE TIME.
YOUR SOCK IS *INSIDE OUT*. DOES THAT REALLY NOT BOTHER YOU? IS IT SO HARD TO AT LEAST CHECK THAT YOUR CLOTHES ARE RIGHT-SIDE OUT BEFORE YOU GO TO SCHOOL?
DB
BWSSH
DB
FWUMP
DB

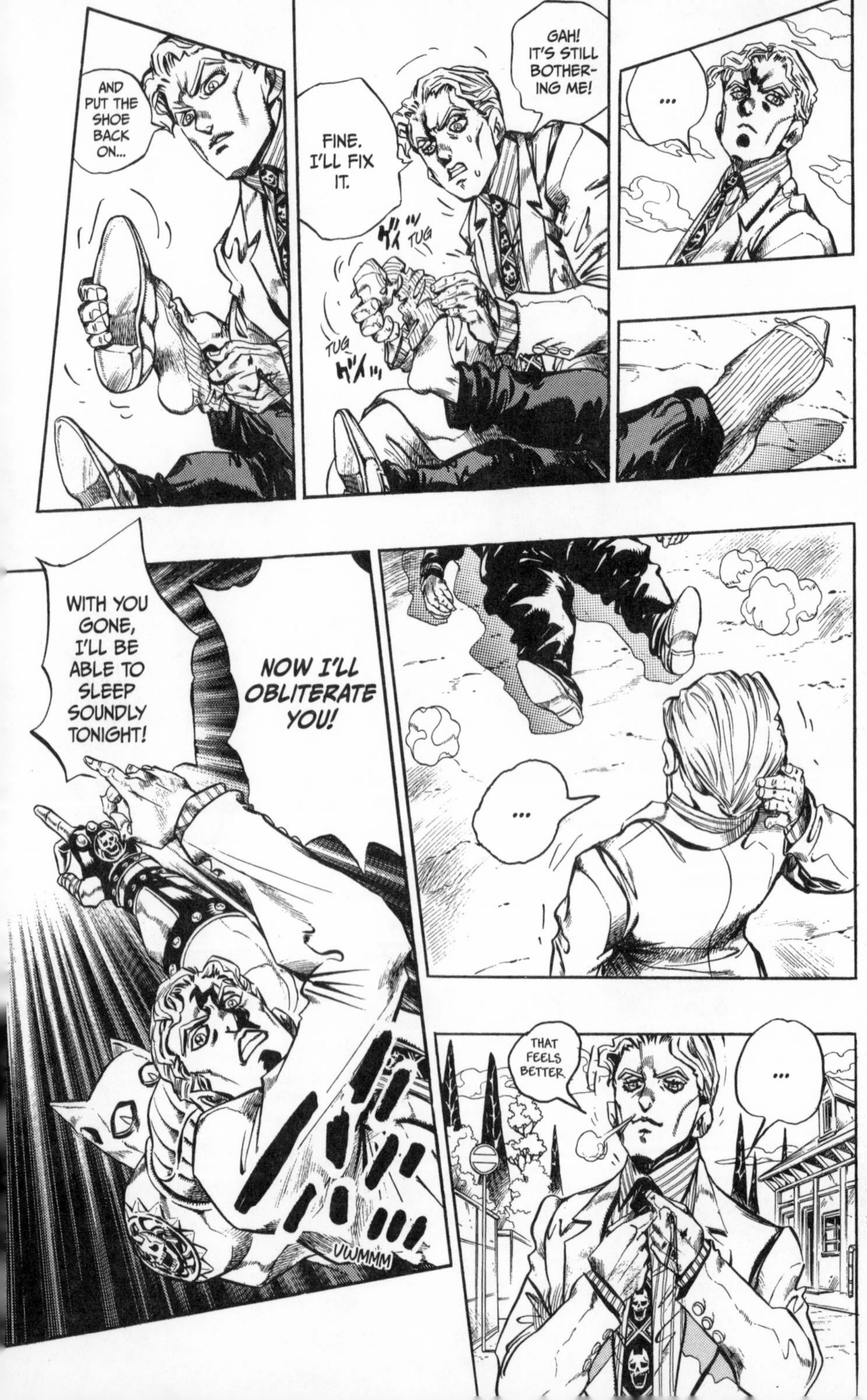
...
GAH! IT'S STILL BOTHERING ME!
FINE. I'LL FIX IT.
TUG
TUG
AND PUT THE SHOE BACK ON...
...
...
THAT FEELS BETTER
NOW I'LL OBLITERATE YOU!
WITH YOU GONE, I'LL BE ABLE TO SLEEP SOUNDLY TONIGHT!
VWMMM

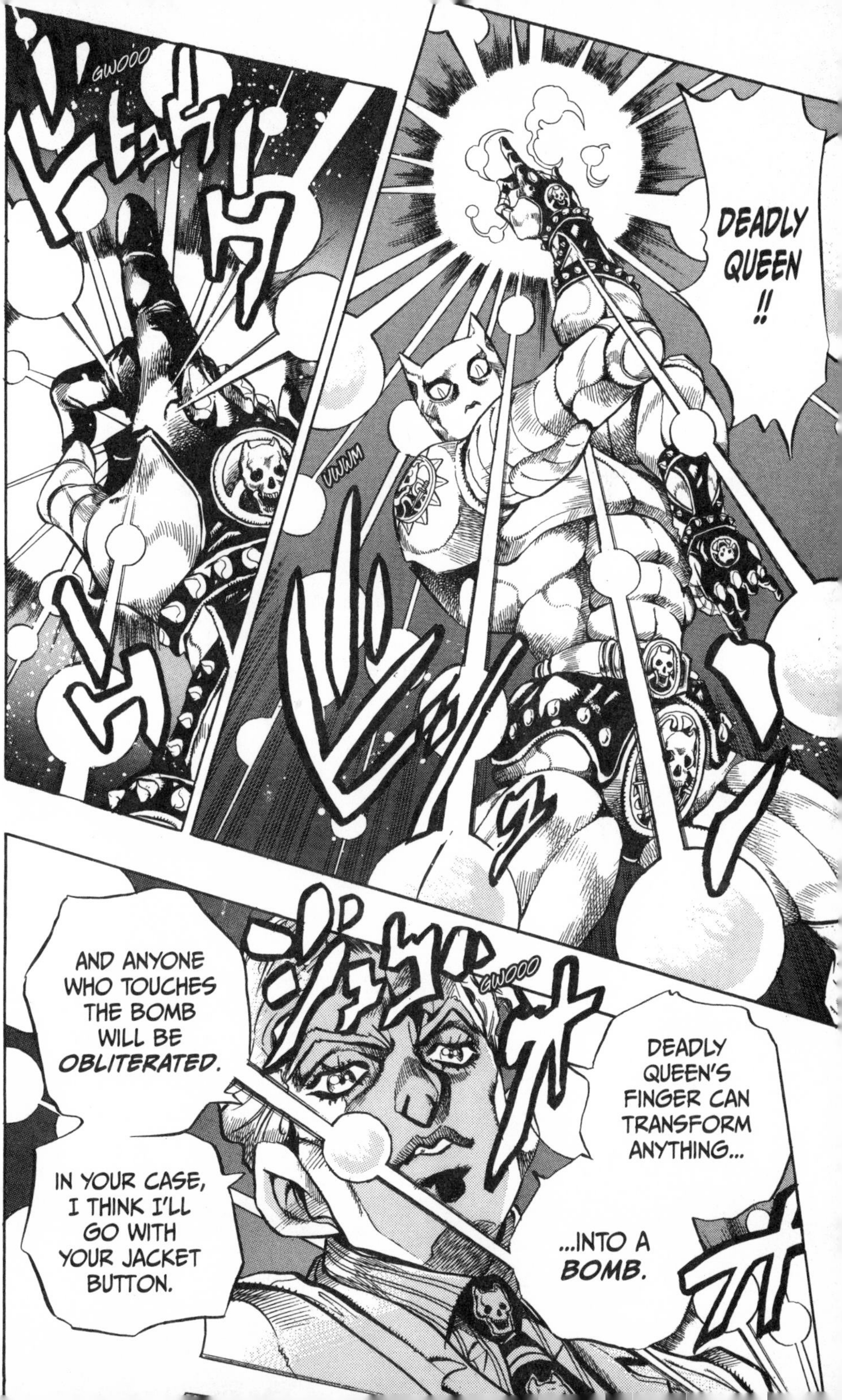
DEADLY QUEEN !!
VWWM
GWOOO
DEADLY QUEEN'S FINGER CAN TRANSFORM ANYTHING...
...INTO A BOMB.
GWOOO
AND ANYONE WHO TOUCHES THE BOMB WILL BE OBLITERATED.
IN YOUR CASE, I THINK I'LL GO WITH YOUR JACKET BUTTON.

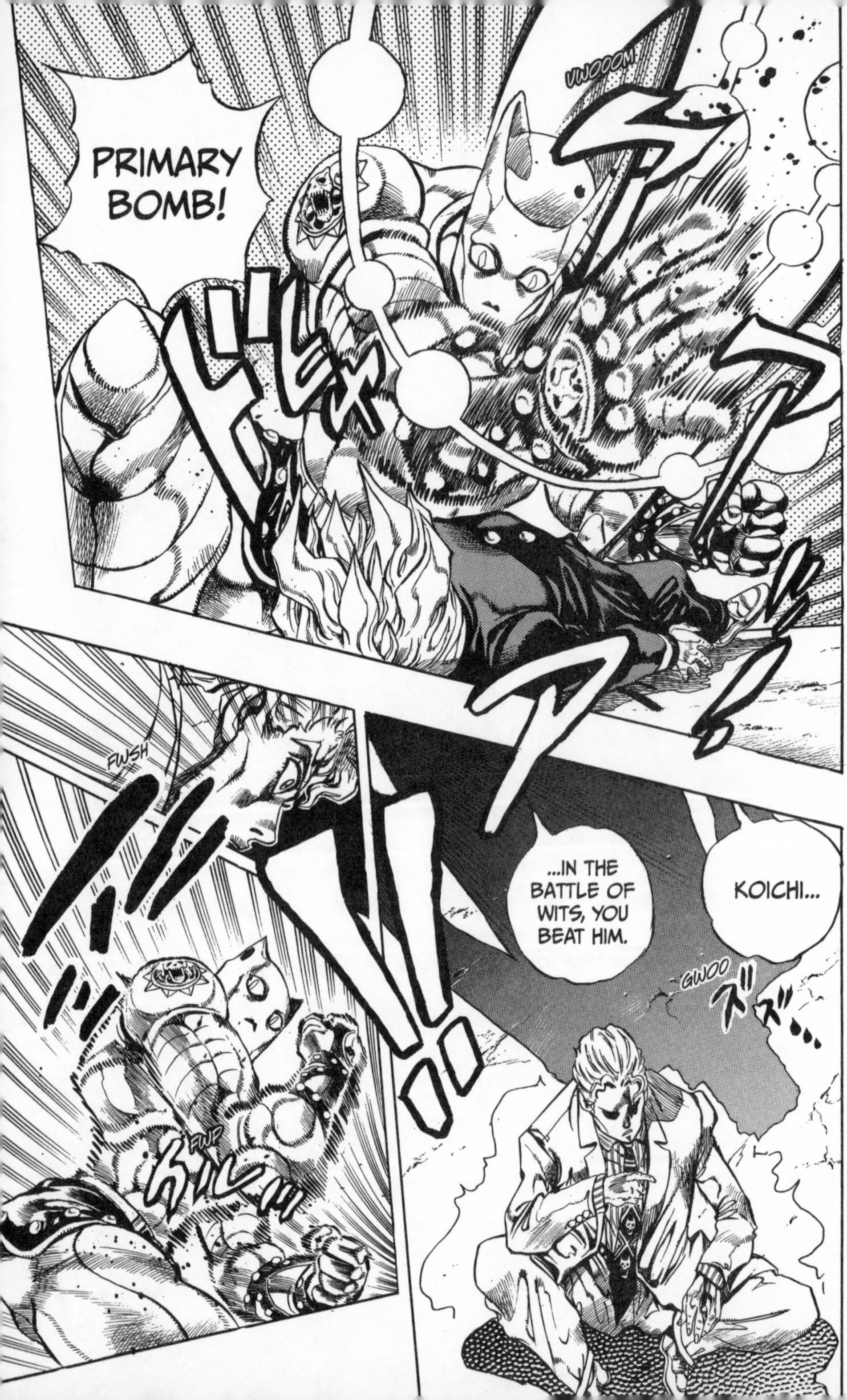
UWOOOM
PRIMARY BOMB!
KOICHI...
...IN THE BATTLE OF WITS, YOU BEAT HIM.
GWOO
ズズ...
FWSH
FWP

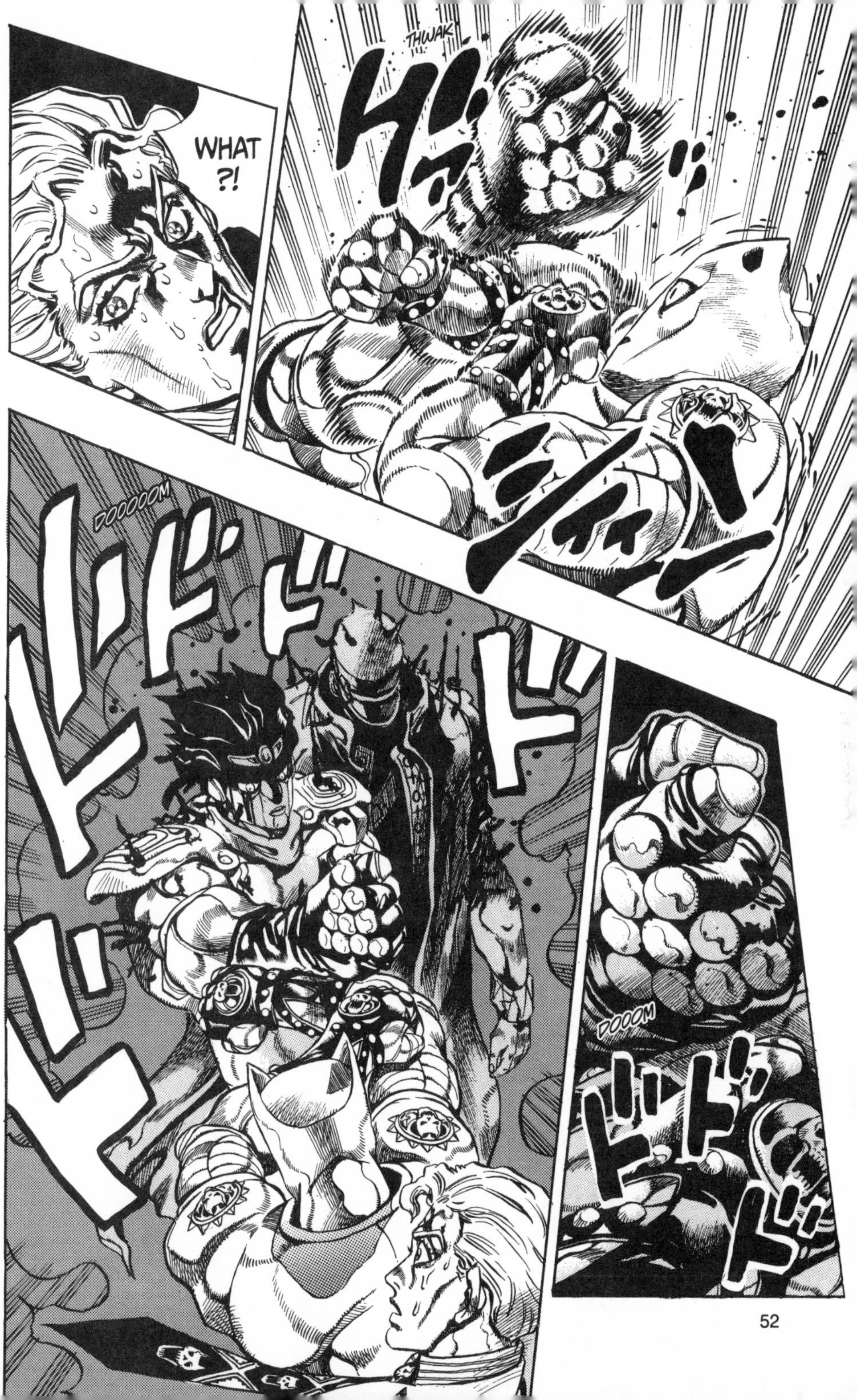
THWAK
WHAT ?!
DOOOM
DOOOOOM

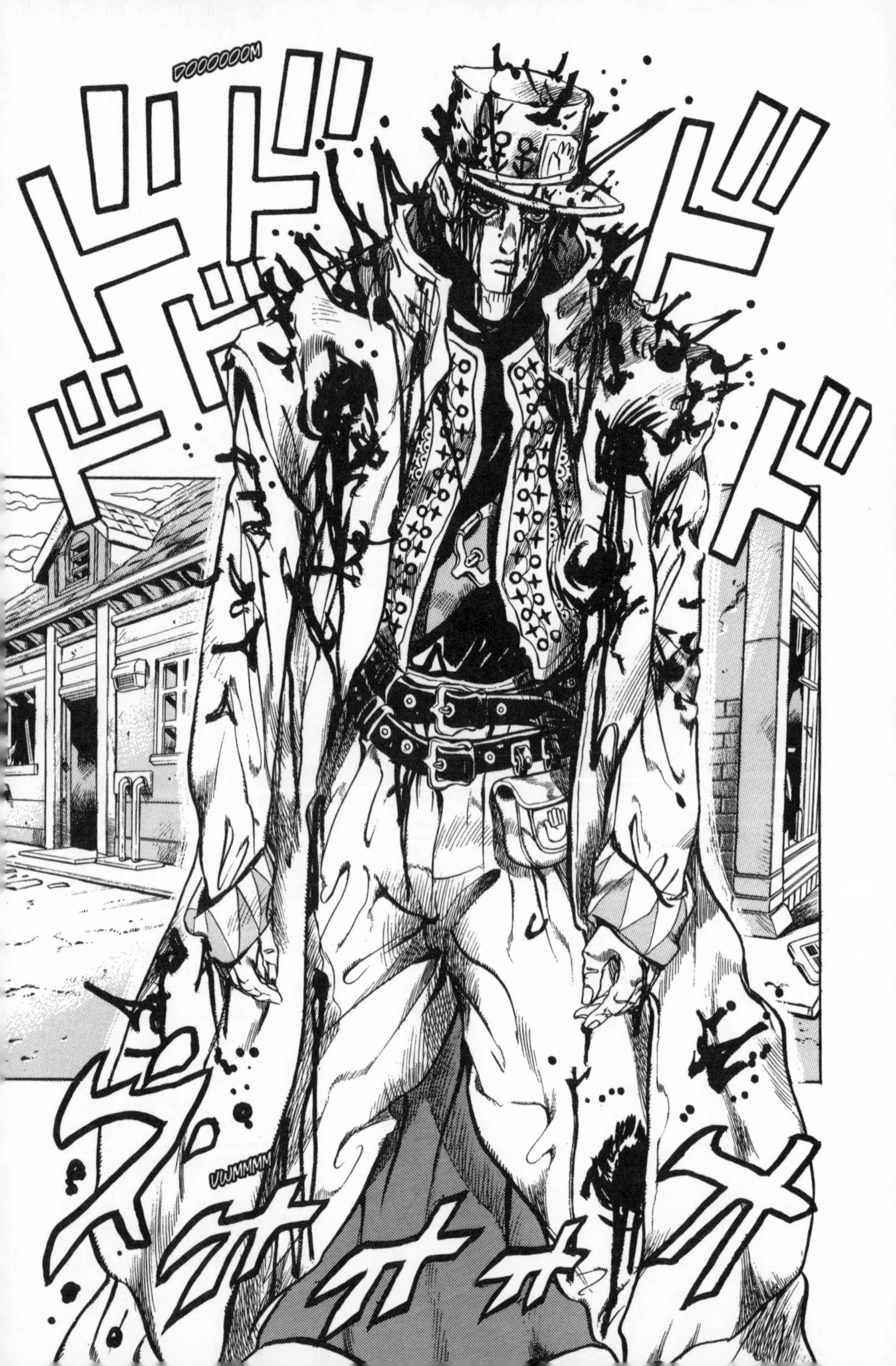
ドドドドドドド
DOOOOOOM
ズオオオ
VWMMMM

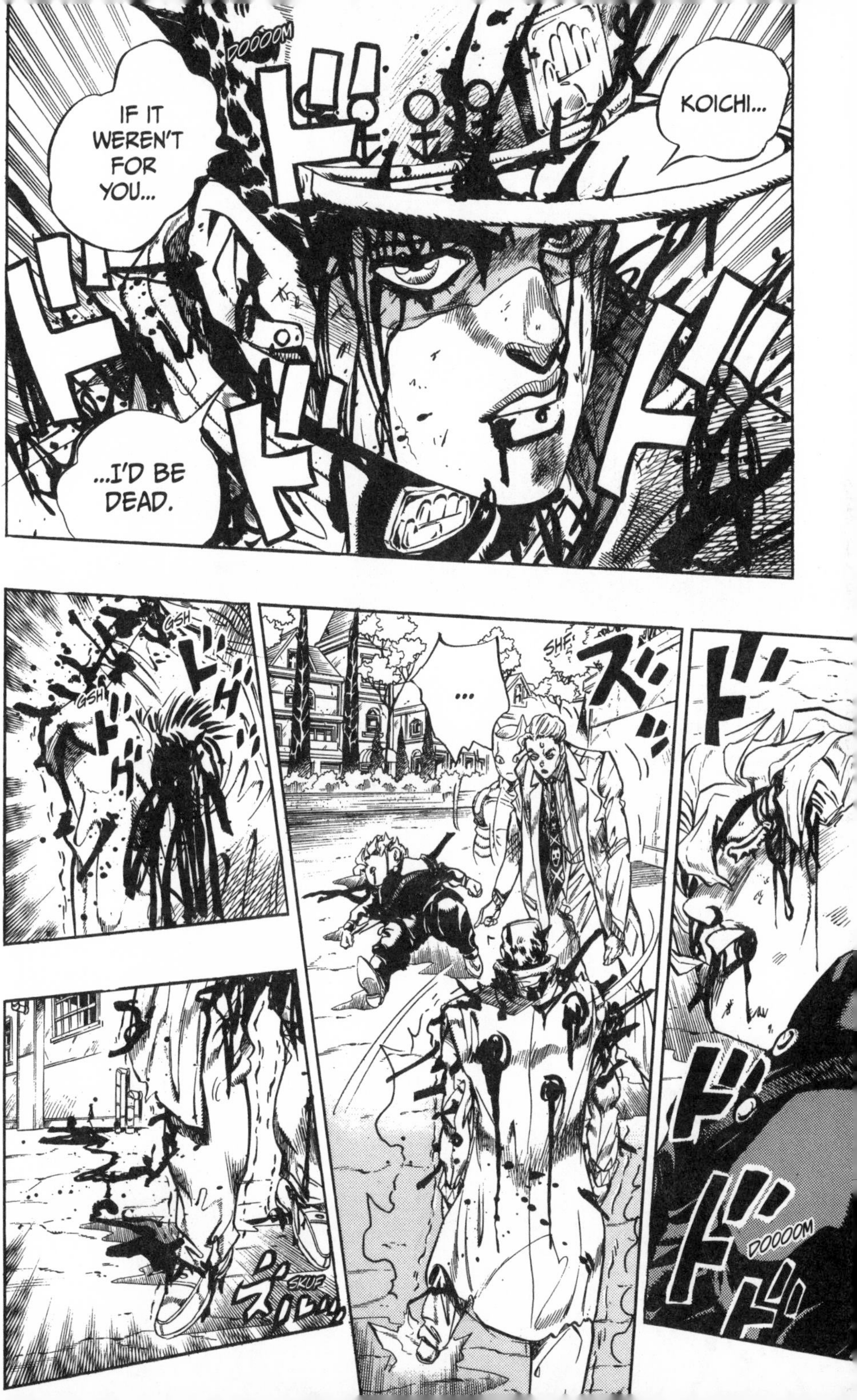
DOOOOM
KOICHI...
IF IT WEREN'T FOR YOU...
...I'D BE DEAD.
DOOOOM
SHF
...
GSH
GSH
SKUF

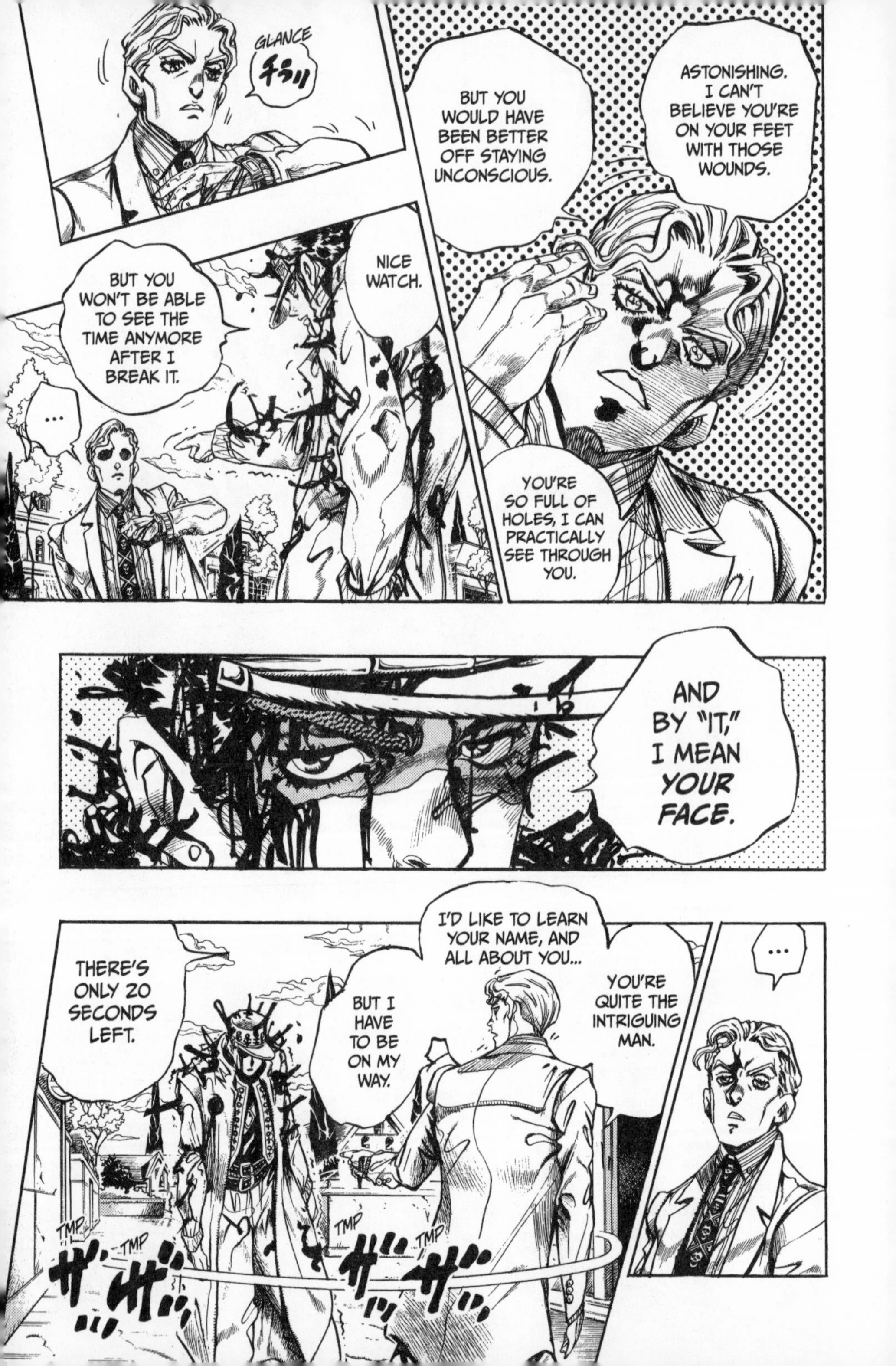
ASTONISHING. I CAN'T BELIEVE YOU'RE ON YOUR FEET WITH THOSE WOUNDS.
BUT YOU WOULD HAVE BEEN BETTER OFF STAYING UNCONSCIOUS.
YOU'RE SO FULL OF HOLES, I CAN PRACTICALLY SEE THROUGH YOU.
GLANCE
チラッ
NICE WATCH.
BUT YOU WON'T BE ABLE TO SEE THE TIME ANYMORE AFTER I BREAK IT.
...
AND BY "IT," I MEAN *YOUR FACE*.
...
I'D LIKE TO LEARN YOUR NAME, AND ALL ABOUT YOU...
YOU'RE QUITE THE INTRIGUING MAN.
BUT I HAVE TO BE ON MY WAY.
THERE'S ONLY 20 SECONDS LEFT.
TMP
TMP
TMP
TMP

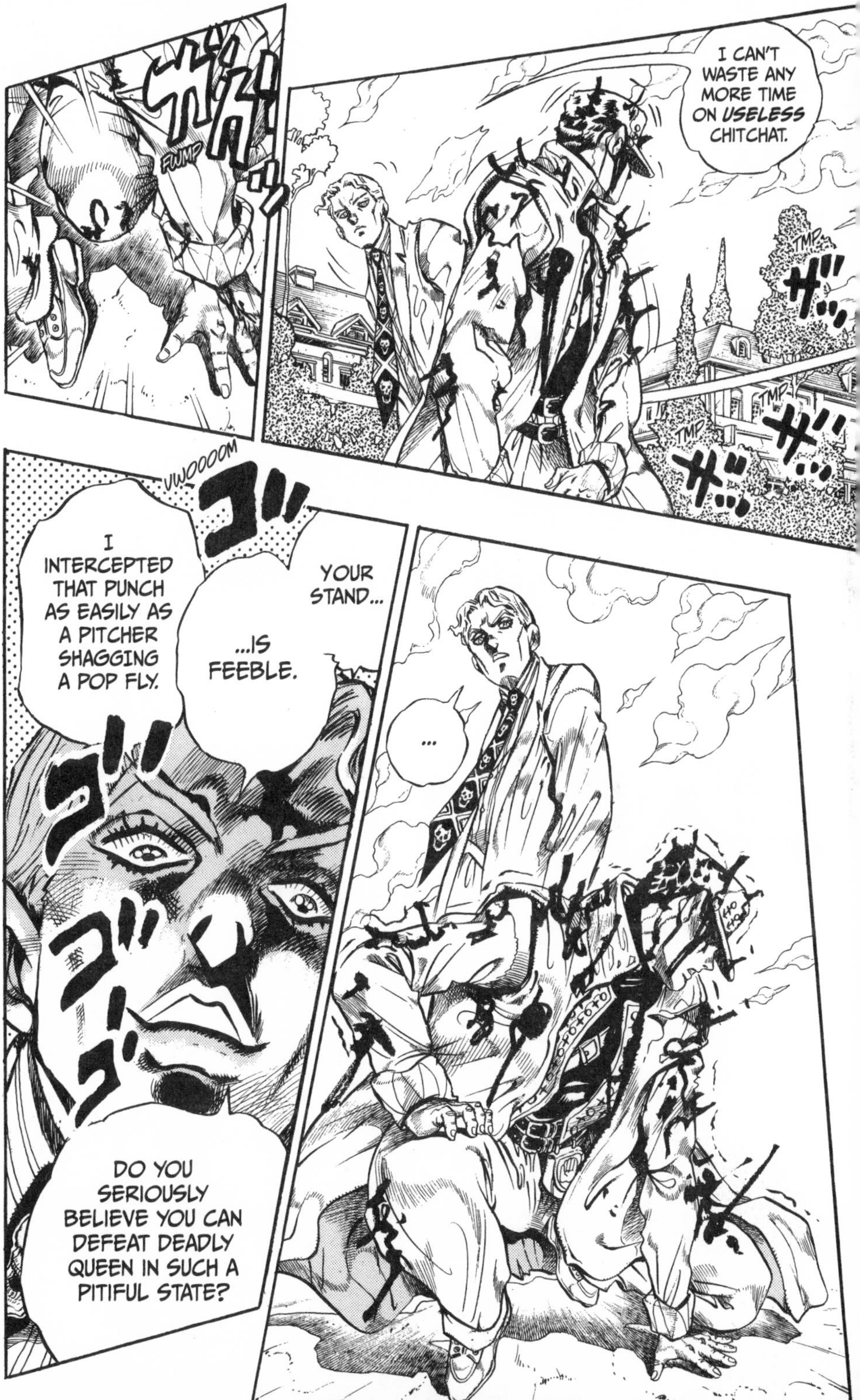
I CAN'T WASTE ANY MORE TIME ON *USELESS* CHITCHAT.
TMP
TMP
TMP
FWUMP
...
UWOOOOM
YOUR STAND...
...IS FEEBLE.
I INTERCEPTED THAT PUNCH AS EASILY AS A PITCHER SHAGGING A POP FLY.
DO YOU SERIOUSLY BELIEVE YOU CAN DEFEAT DEADLY QUEEN IN SUCH A PITIFUL STATE?

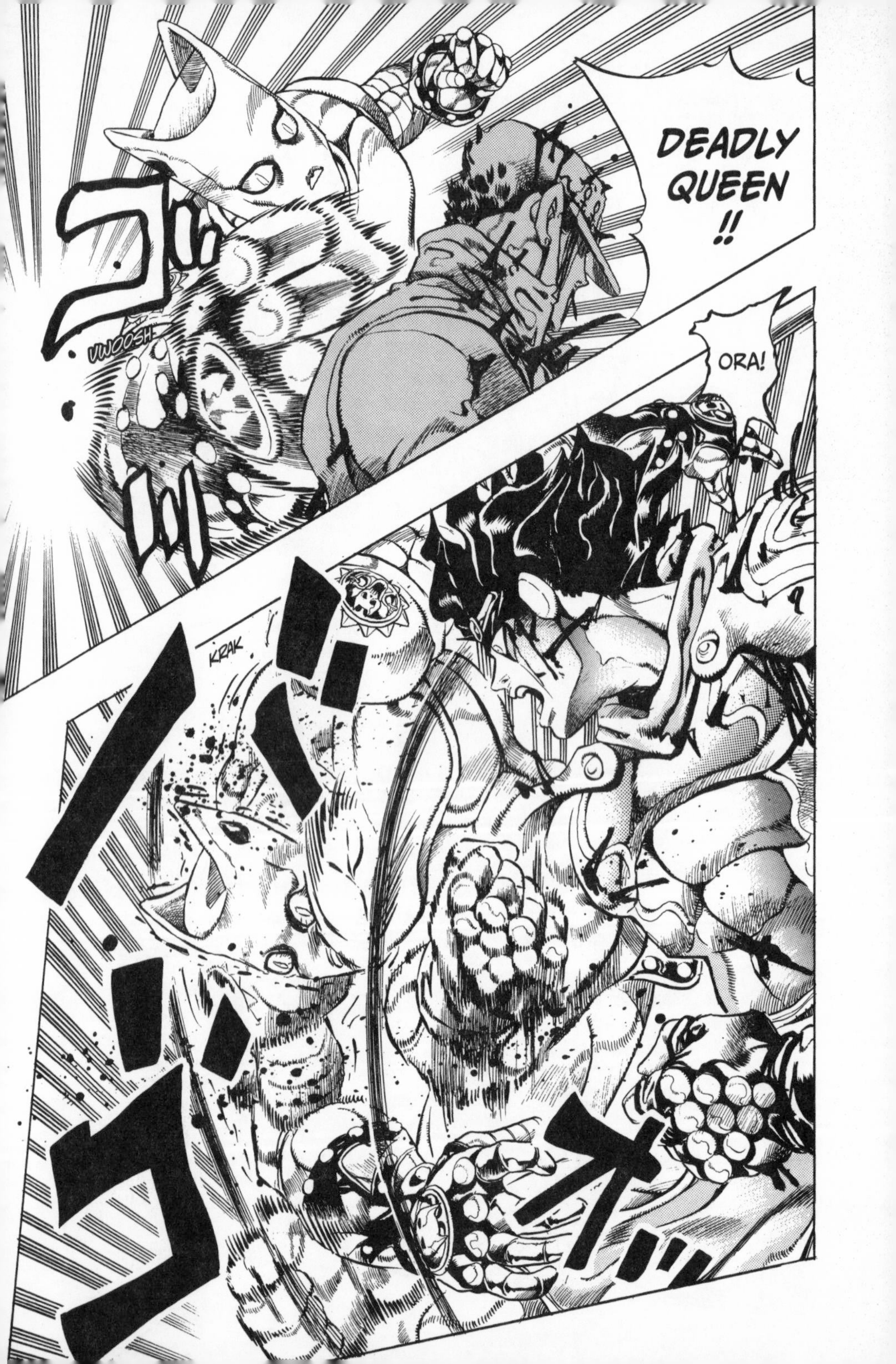
DEADLY QUEEN !!
UWOOSH
ORA!
KRAK

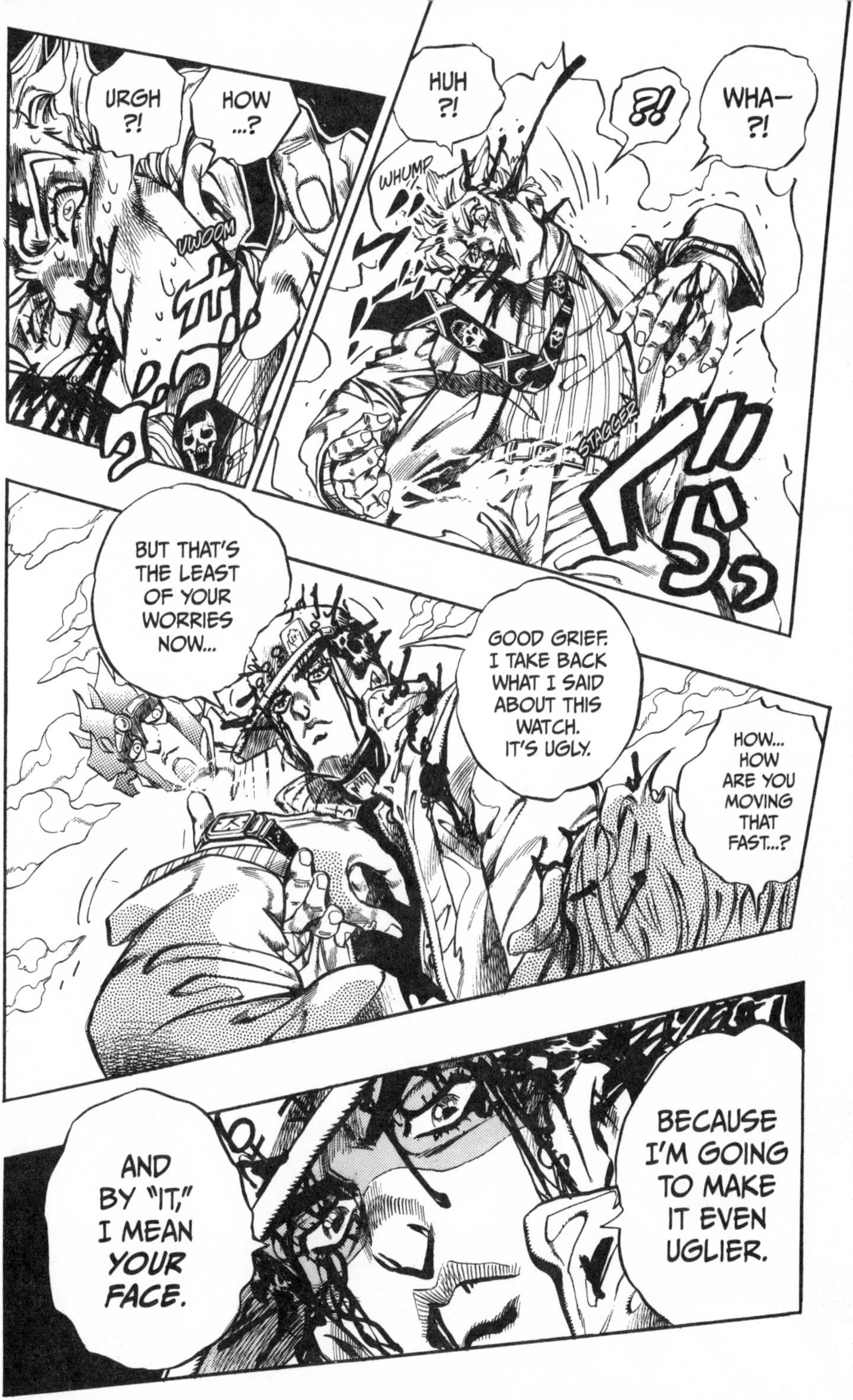
WHA– ?!
?!
HUH ?!
WHUMP
STAGGER
HOW ...?
URGH ?!
VWOOM
HOW... HOW ARE YOU MOVING THAT FAST...?
GOOD GRIEF. I TAKE BACK WHAT I SAID ABOUT THIS WATCH. IT'S UGLY.
BUT THAT'S THE LEAST OF YOUR WORRIES NOW...
BECAUSE I'M GOING TO MAKE IT EVEN UGLIER.
AND BY "IT," I MEAN *YOUR FACE.*

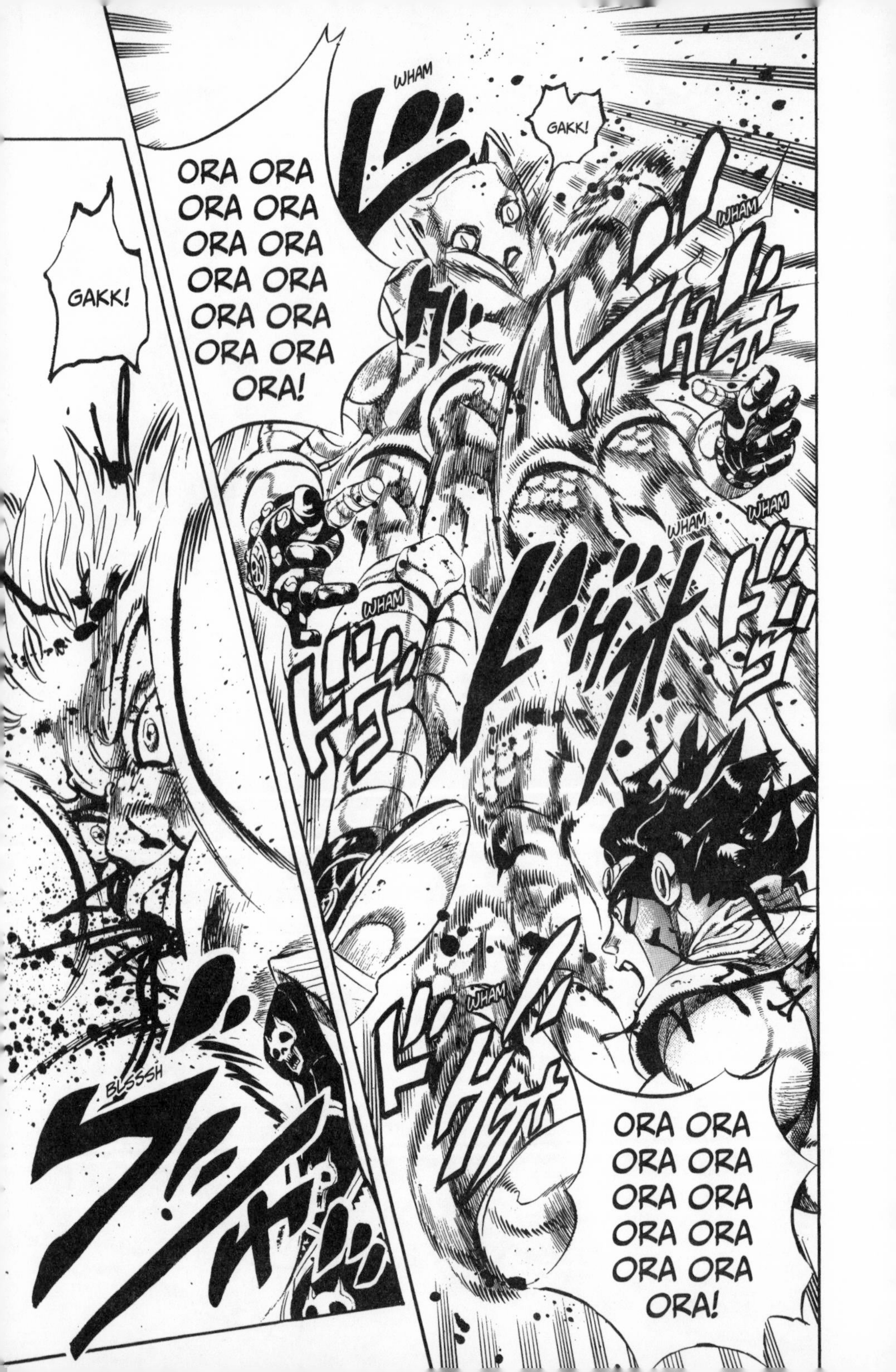
WHAM
GAKK!
ORA ORA ORA ORA ORA ORA ORA ORA ORA ORA ORA ORA ORA!
WHAM
WHAM
WHAM
WHAM
WHAM
ORA ORA ORA ORA ORA ORA ORA ORA ORA ORA ORA!
GAKK!
BLSSSH

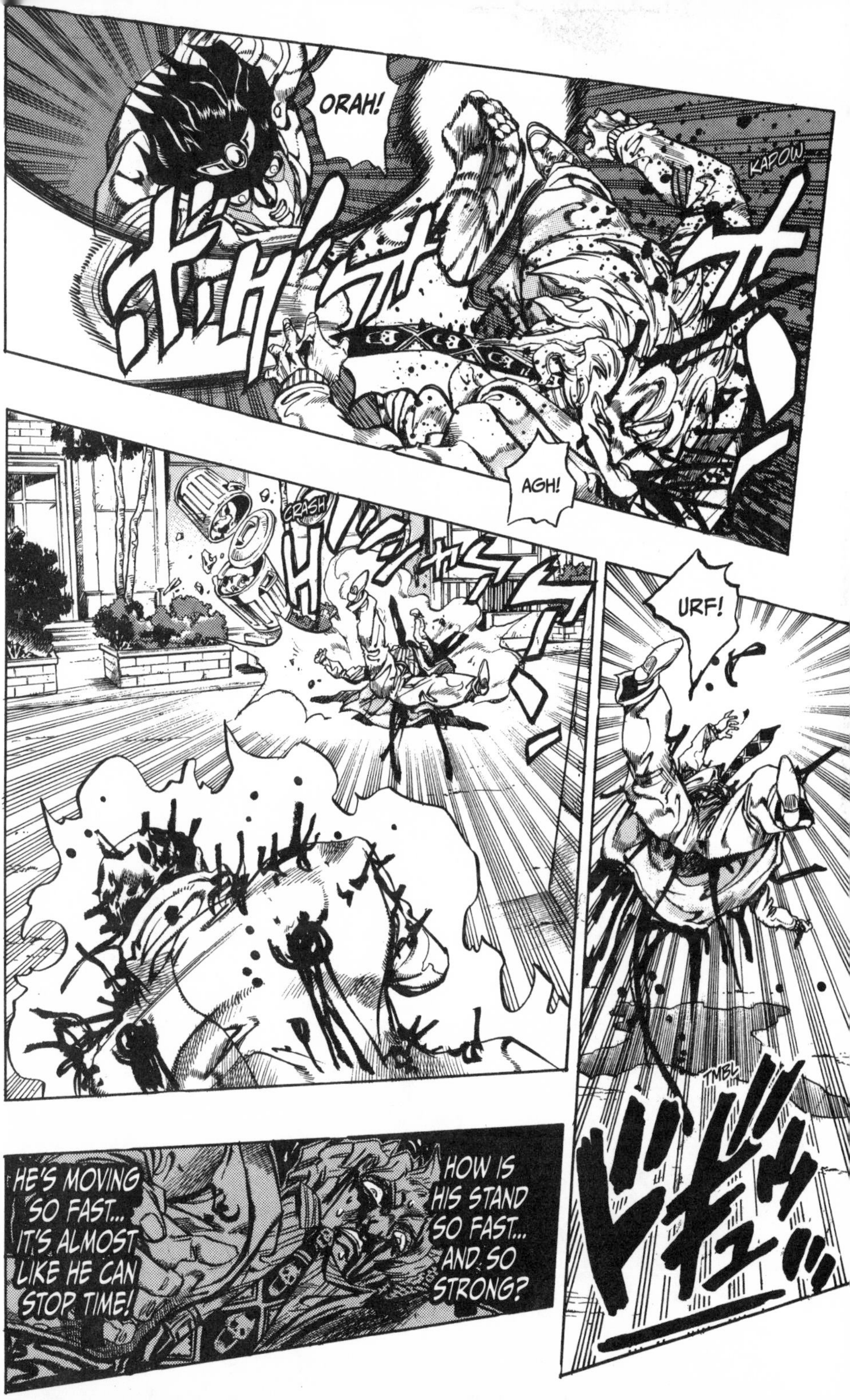
KAPOW
ORAH!
AGH!
URF!
TMBL
CRASH
HOW IS HIS STAND SO FAST... AND SO STRONG?
HE'S MOVING SO FAST... IT'S ALMOST LIKE HE CAN STOP TIME!

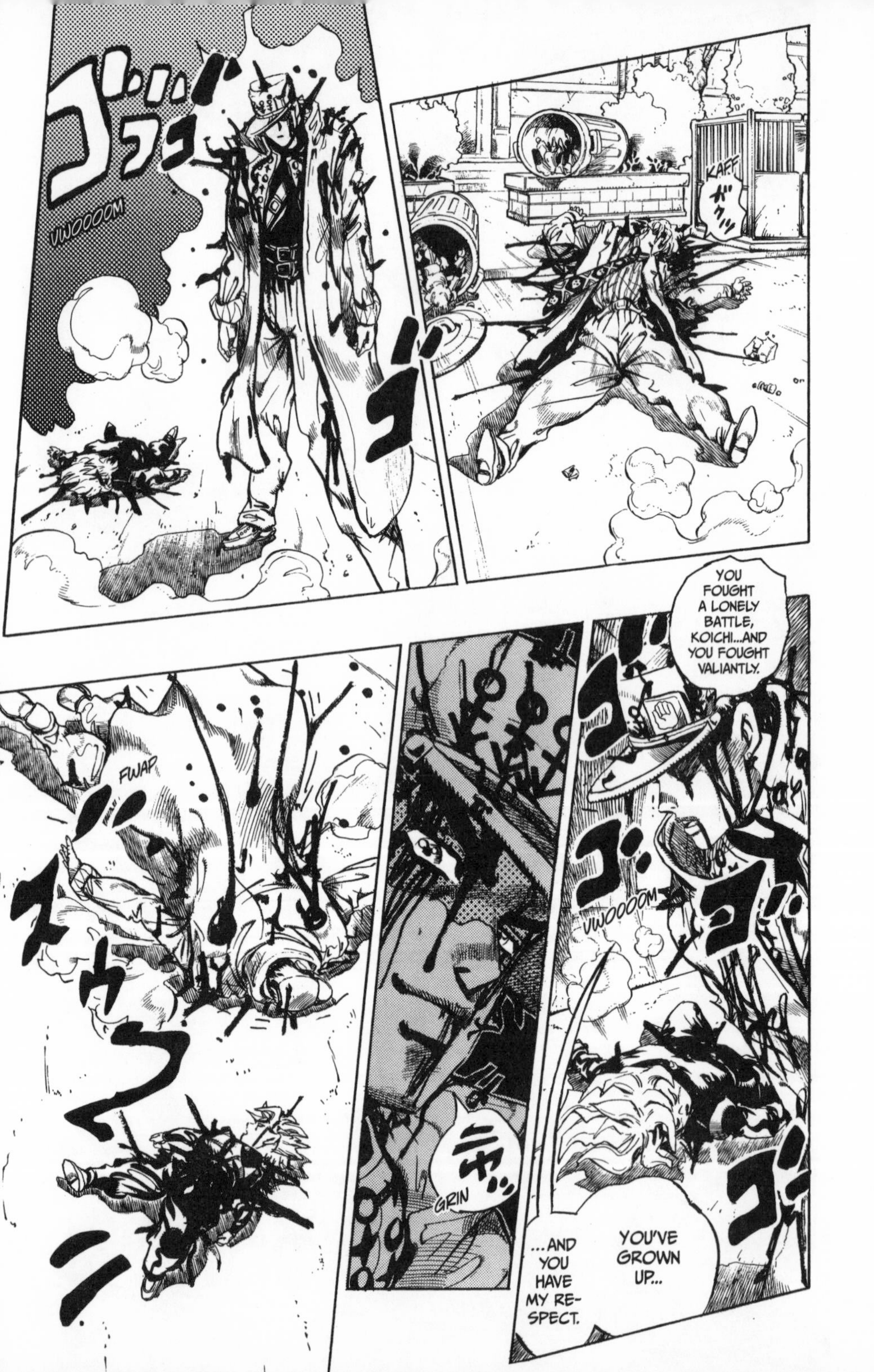
KAFF
ガクッ
VWOOOOM
YOU FOUGHT A LONELY BATTLE, KOICHI...AND YOU FOUGHT VALIANTLY.
VWOOOOM
YOU'VE GROWN UP...
...AND YOU HAVE MY RESPECT.
ニヤッ
GRIN
FWAP

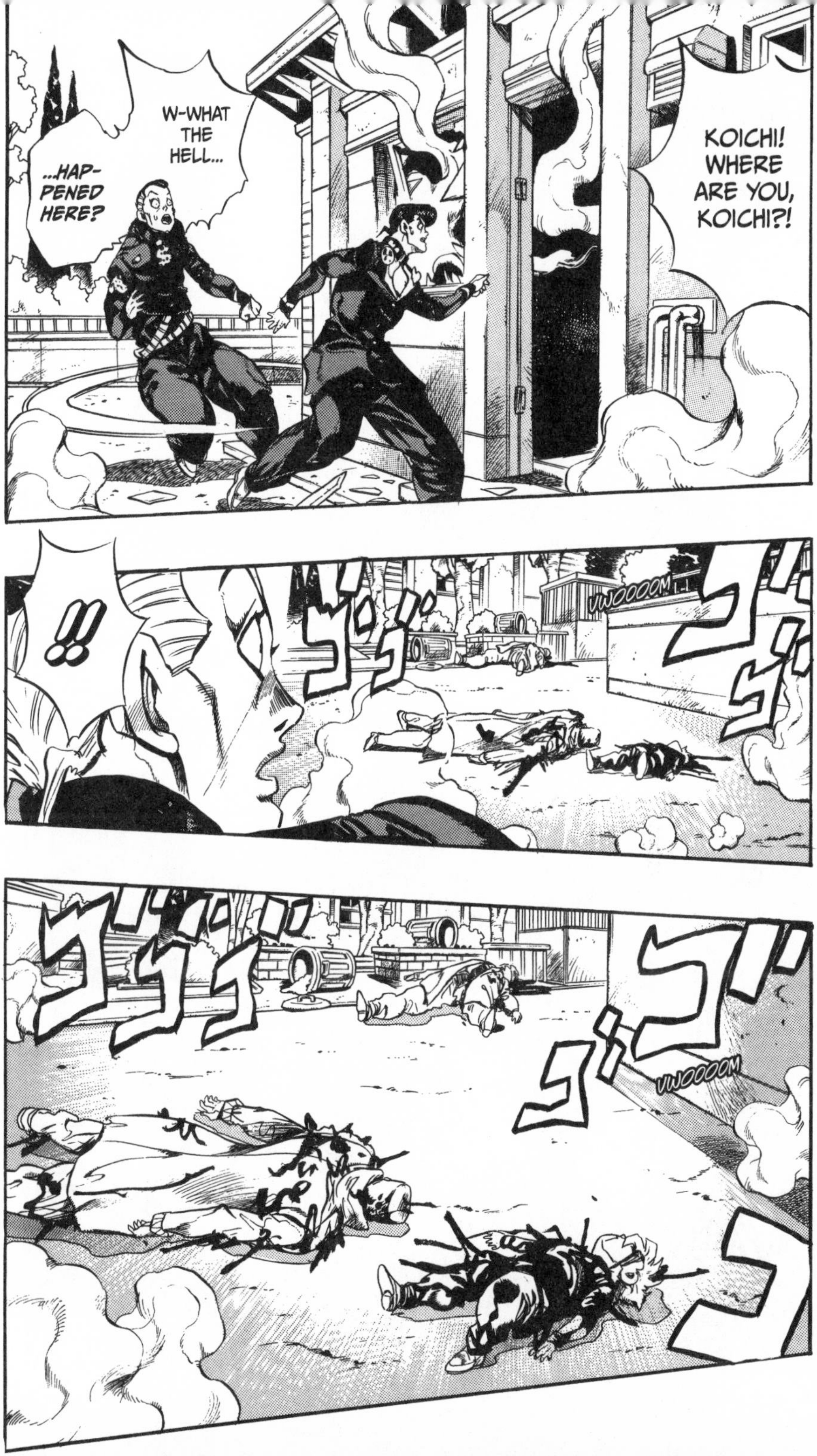
KOICHI! WHERE ARE YOU, KOICHI?!
W-WHAT THE HELL...
...HAP-PENED HERE?
!!
VWOOOOM
VWOOOOM

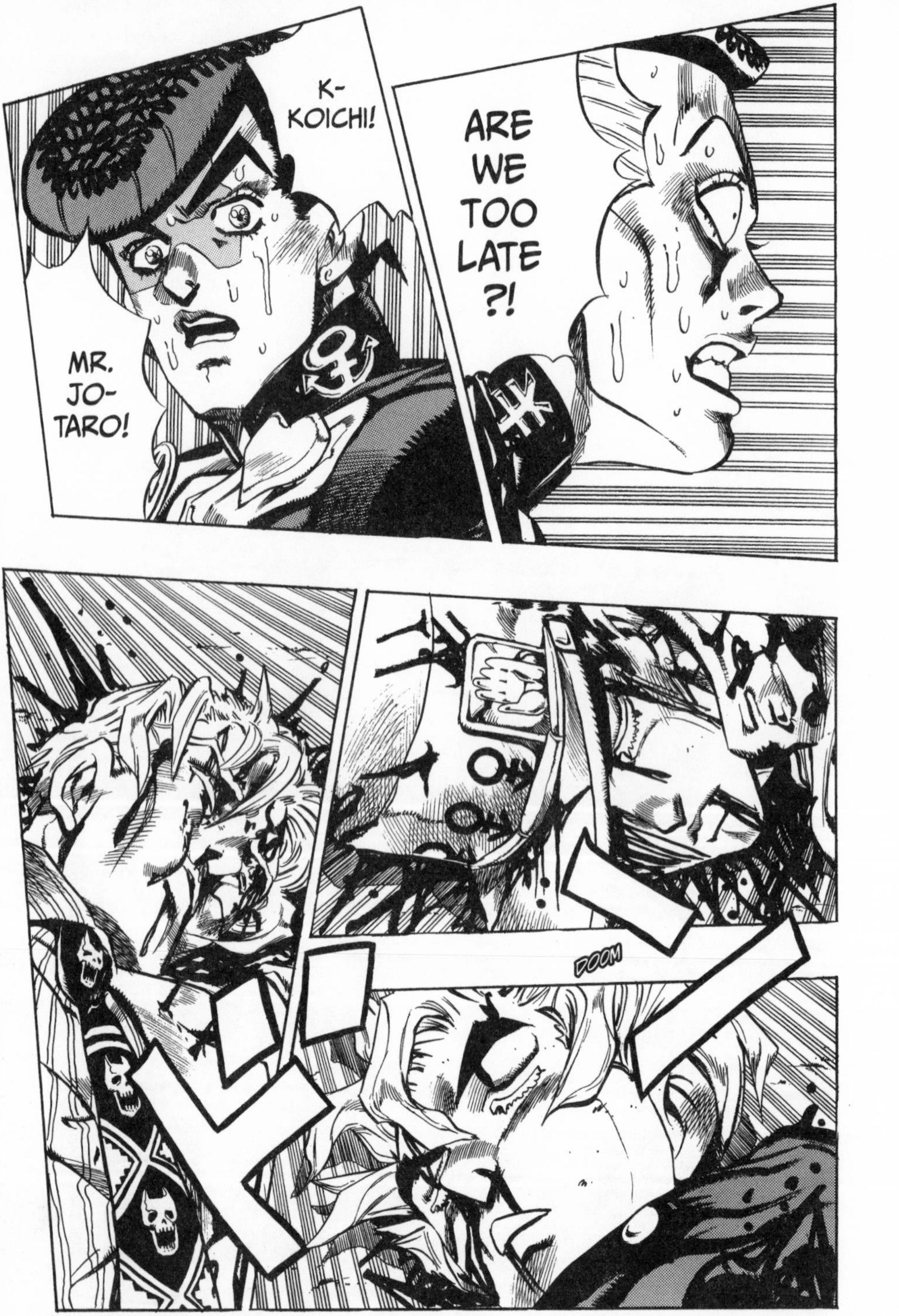
ARE WE TOO LATE?!
K-KOICHI!
MR. JO-TARO!
DOOM

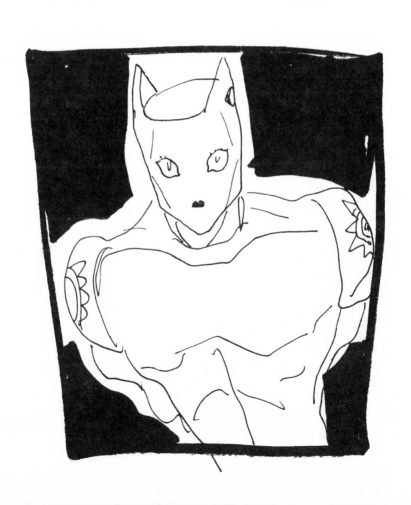

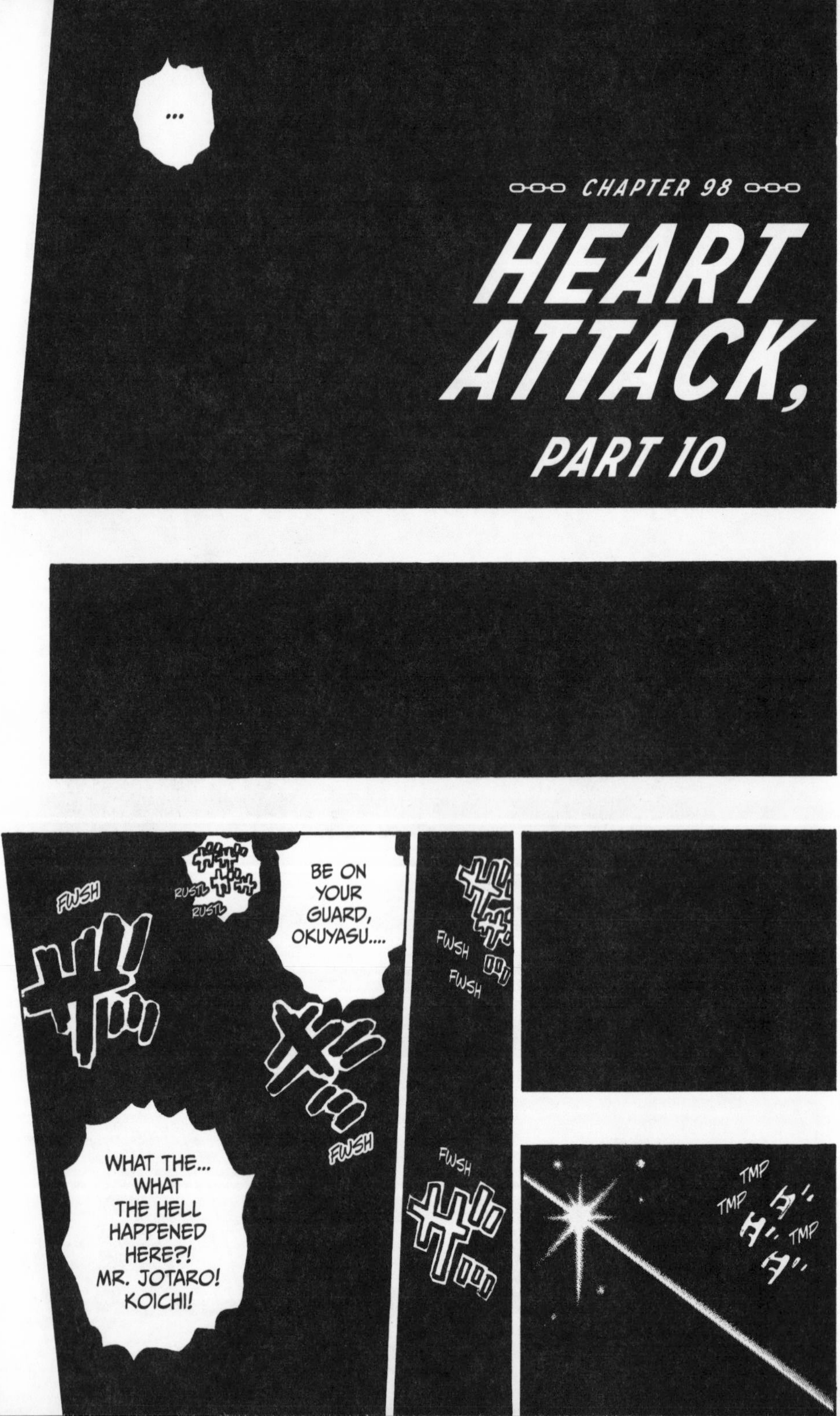
...
CHAPTER 98
HEART ATTACK, PART 10
TMP TMP TMP
FWSH FWSH
FWSH
BE ON YOUR GUARD, OKUYASU....
RUSTL RUSTL
FWSH
FWSH
WHAT THE... WHAT THE HELL HAPPENED HERE?! MR. JOTARO! KOICHI!

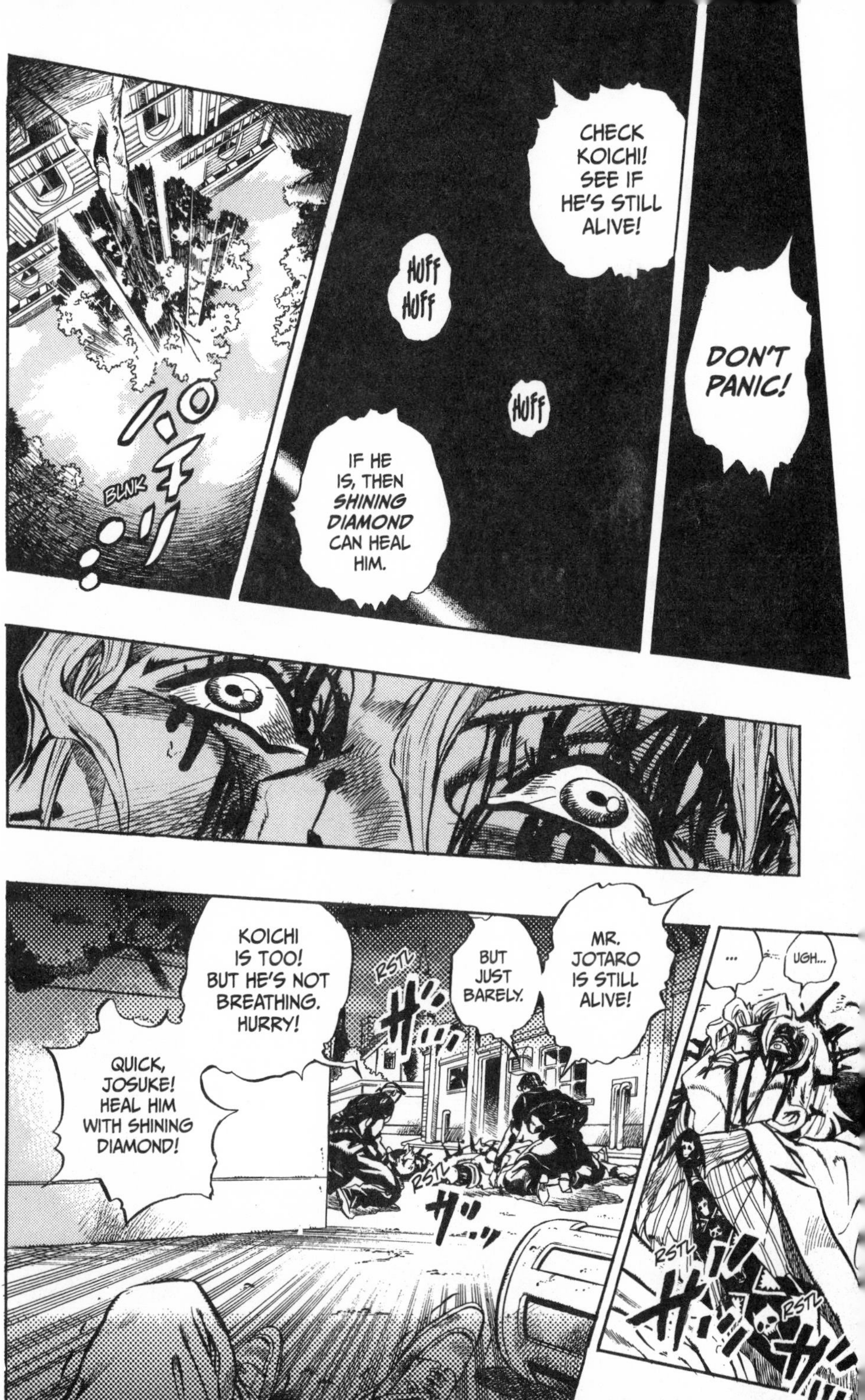
DON'T PANIC!
CHECK KOICHI! SEE IF HE'S STILL ALIVE!
HUFF HUFF
HUFF
IF HE IS, THEN SHINING DIAMOND CAN HEAL HIM.
BLNK
UGH...
...
RSTL
RSTL
MR. JOTARO IS STILL ALIVE!
BUT JUST BARELY.
KOICHI IS TOO! BUT HE'S NOT BREATHING. HURRY!
RSTL
QUICK, JOSUKE! HEAL HIM WITH SHINING DIAMOND!
RSTL

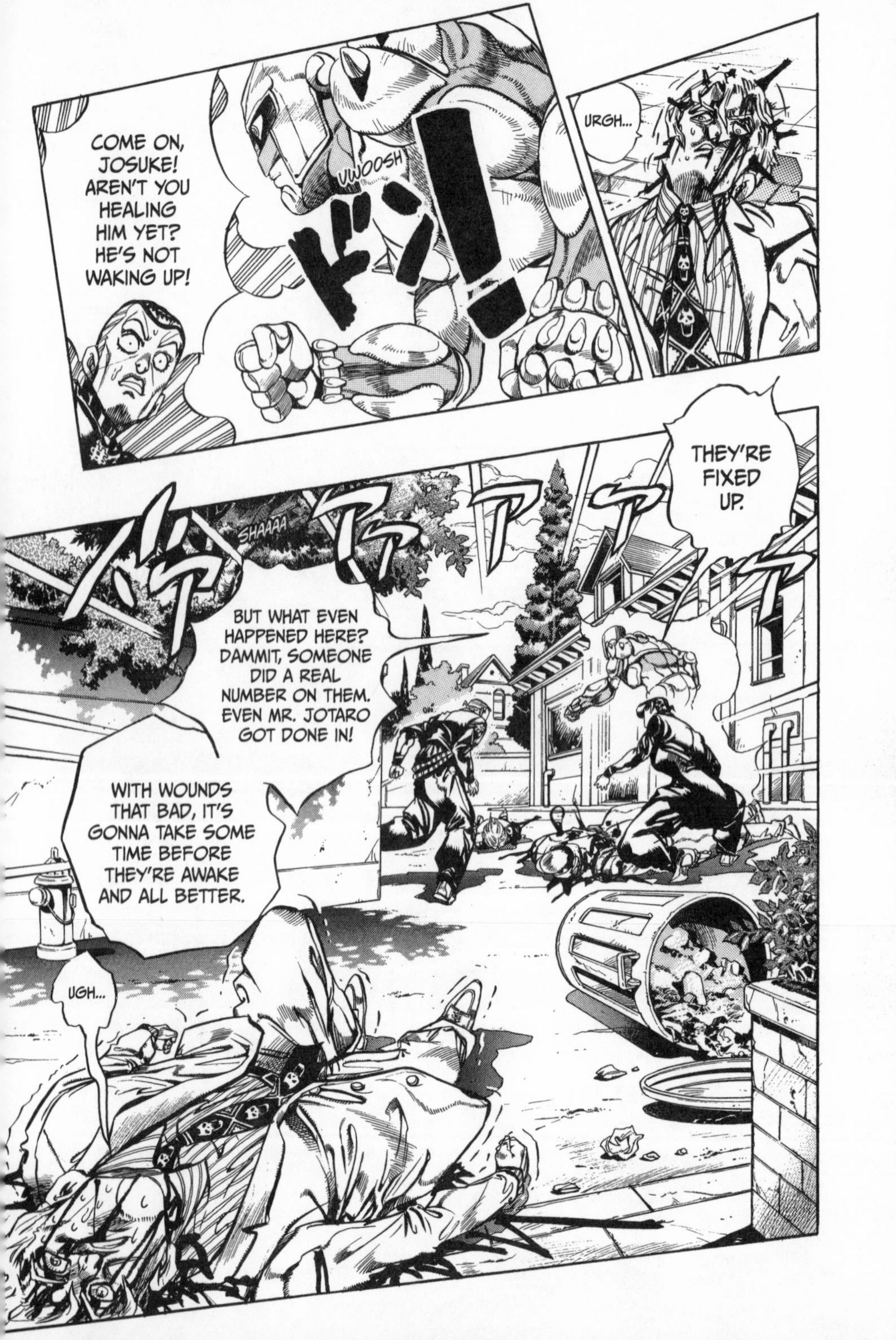
URGH...
COME ON, JOSUKE! AREN'T YOU HEALING HIM YET? HE'S NOT WAKING UP!
UWOOSH
ドン!
THEY'RE FIXED UP.
SHAAAA
BUT WHAT EVEN HAPPENED HERE? DAMMIT, SOMEONE DID A REAL NUMBER ON THEM. EVEN MR. JOTARO GOT DONE IN!
WITH WOUNDS THAT BAD, IT'S GONNA TAKE SOME TIME BEFORE THEY'RE AWAKE AND ALL BETTER.
UGH...

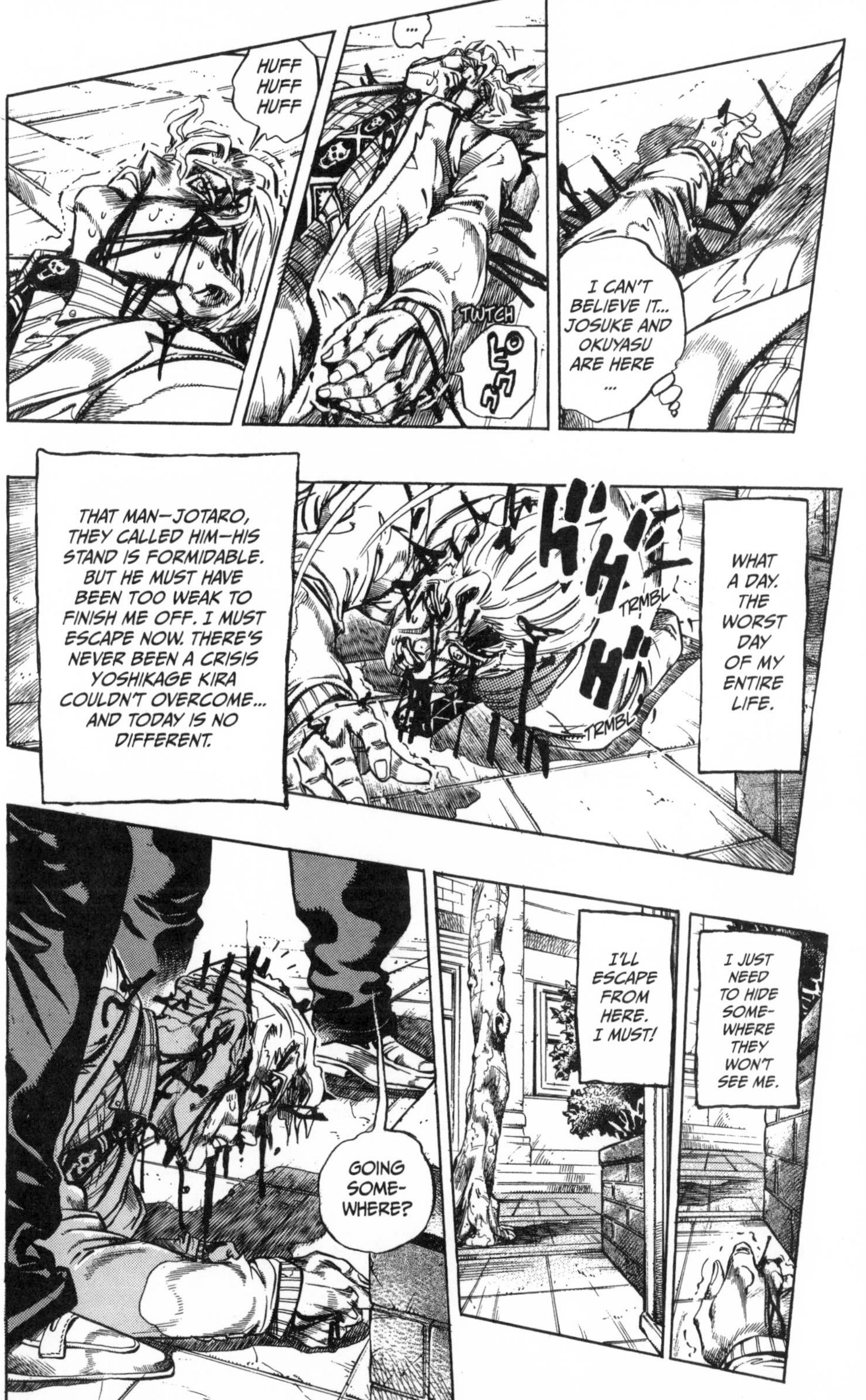
I CAN'T BELIEVE IT... JOSUKE AND OKUYASU ARE HERE ...
...
TWITCH
HUFF HUFF HUFF
WHAT A DAY. THE WORST DAY OF MY ENTIRE LIFE.
TRMBL
TRMBL
THAT MAN—JOTARO, THEY CALLED HIM—HIS STAND IS FORMIDABLE. BUT HE MUST HAVE BEEN TOO WEAK TO FINISH ME OFF. I MUST ESCAPE NOW. THERE'S NEVER BEEN A CRISIS YOSHIKAGE KIRA COULDN'T OVERCOME... AND TODAY IS NO DIFFERENT.
I JUST NEED TO HIDE SOME-WHERE THEY WON'T SEE ME.
I'LL ESCAPE FROM HERE. I MUST!
GOING SOME-WHERE?

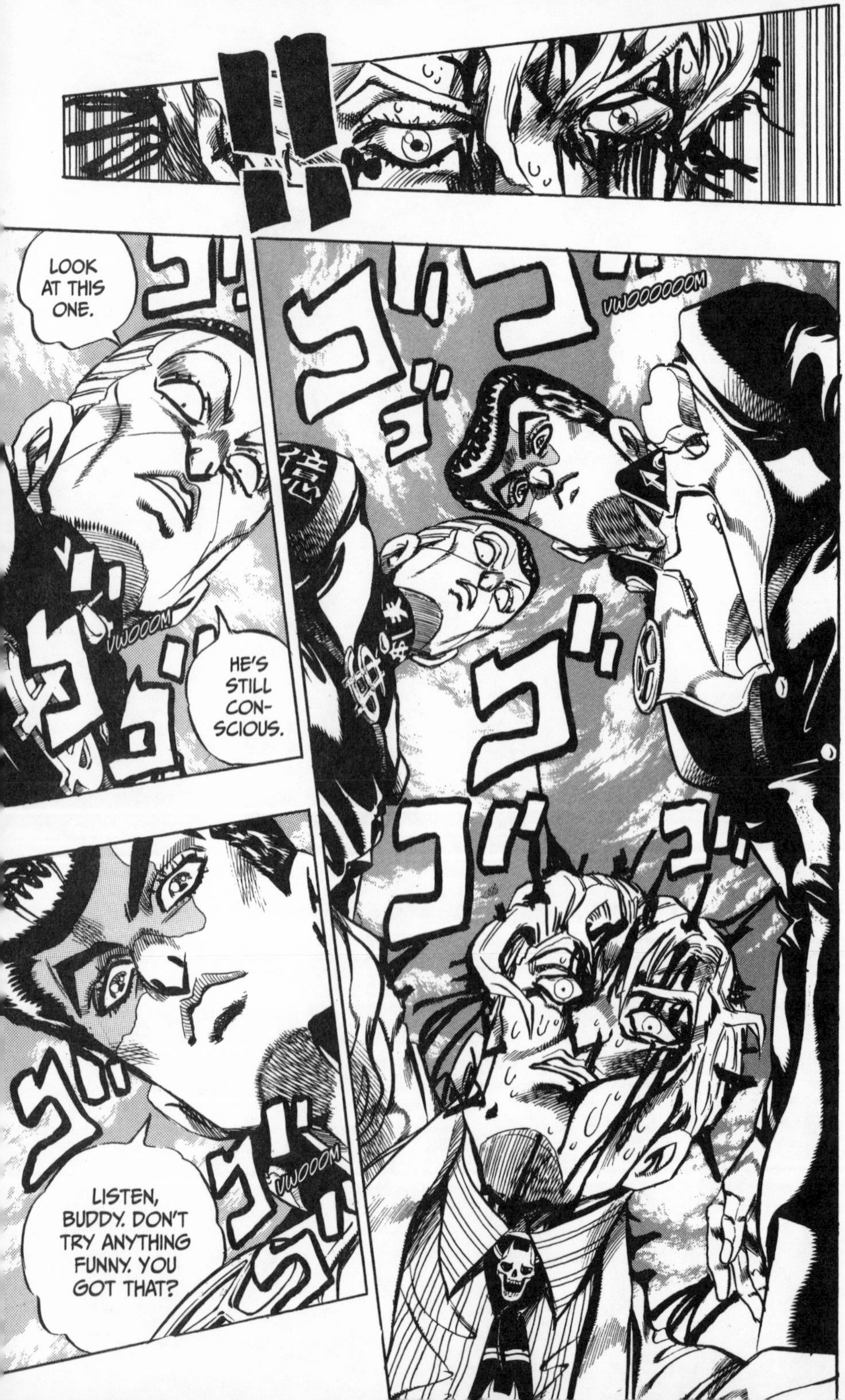
VWOOOOOOM
LOOK AT THIS ONE.
VWOOOM
HE'S STILL CON-SCIOUS.
VWOOOM
LISTEN, BUDDY. DON'T TRY ANYTHING FUNNY. YOU GOT THAT?

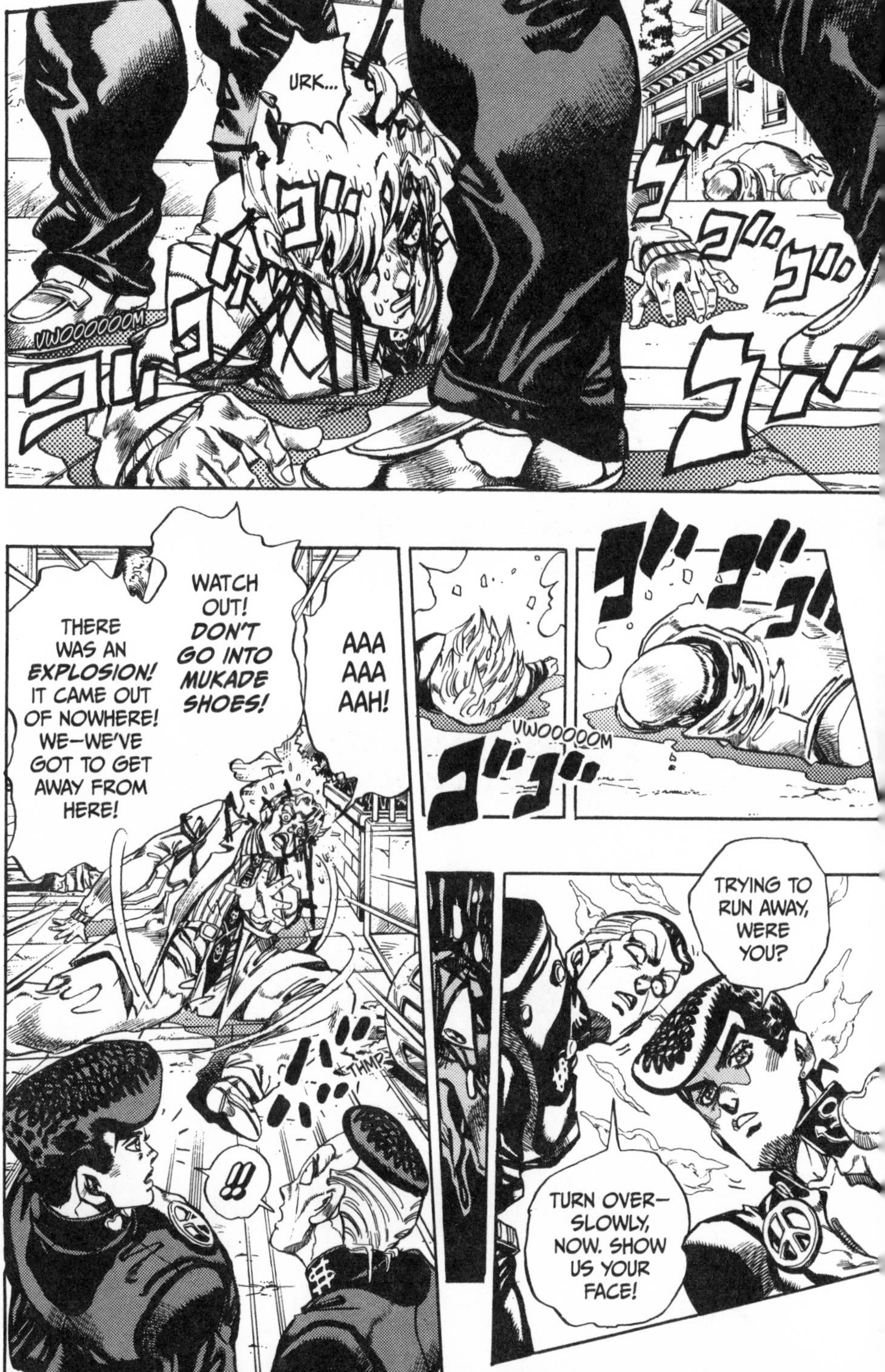
URK...
VWOOOOOOM
VWOOOOOM
TRYING TO RUN AWAY, WERE YOU?
TURN OVER—SLOWLY, NOW. SHOW US YOUR FACE!
AAA AAA AAH!
WATCH OUT! DON'T GO INTO MUKADE SHOES!
THERE WAS AN EXPLOSION! IT CAME OUT OF NOWHERE! WE—WE'VE GOT TO GET AWAY FROM HERE!
THMP
!!

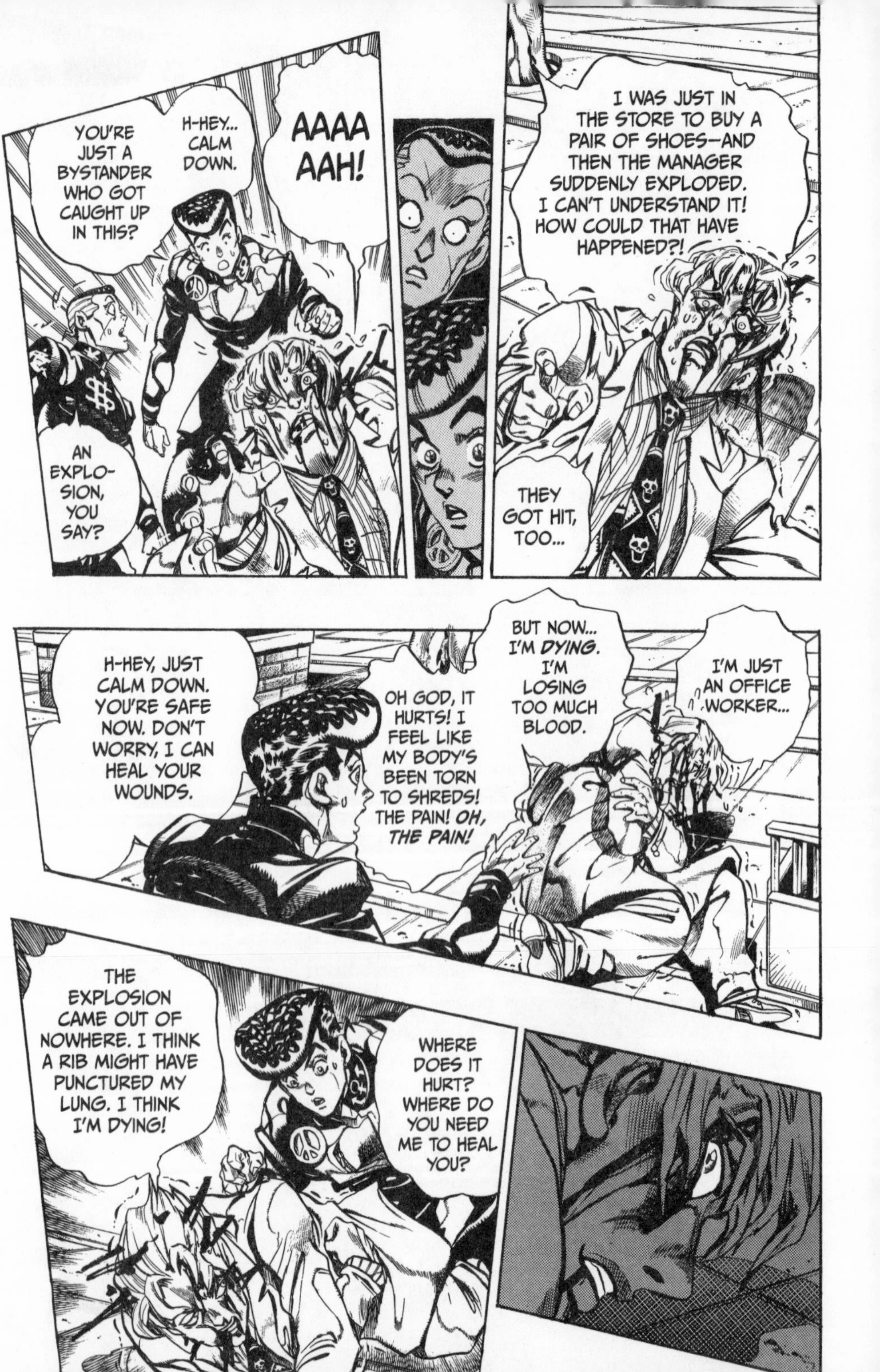
I WAS JUST IN THE STORE TO BUY A PAIR OF SHOES—AND THEN THE MANAGER SUDDENLY EXPLODED. I CAN'T UNDERSTAND IT! HOW COULD THAT HAVE HAPPENED?!
THEY GOT HIT, TOO...
AAAA AAH!
H-HEY... CALM DOWN.
YOU'RE JUST A BYSTANDER WHO GOT CAUGHT UP IN THIS?
AN EXPLOSION, YOU SAY?
I'M JUST AN OFFICE WORKER...
BUT NOW... I'M *DYING*. I'M LOSING TOO MUCH BLOOD.
OH GOD, IT HURTS! I FEEL LIKE MY BODY'S BEEN TORN TO SHREDS! THE PAIN! *OH, THE PAIN!*
H-HEY, JUST CALM DOWN. YOU'RE SAFE NOW. DON'T WORRY, I CAN HEAL YOUR WOUNDS.
WHERE DOES IT HURT? WHERE DO YOU NEED ME TO HEAL YOU?
THE EXPLOSION CAME OUT OF NOWHERE. I THINK A RIB MIGHT HAVE PUNCTURED MY LUNG. I THINK I'M DYING!

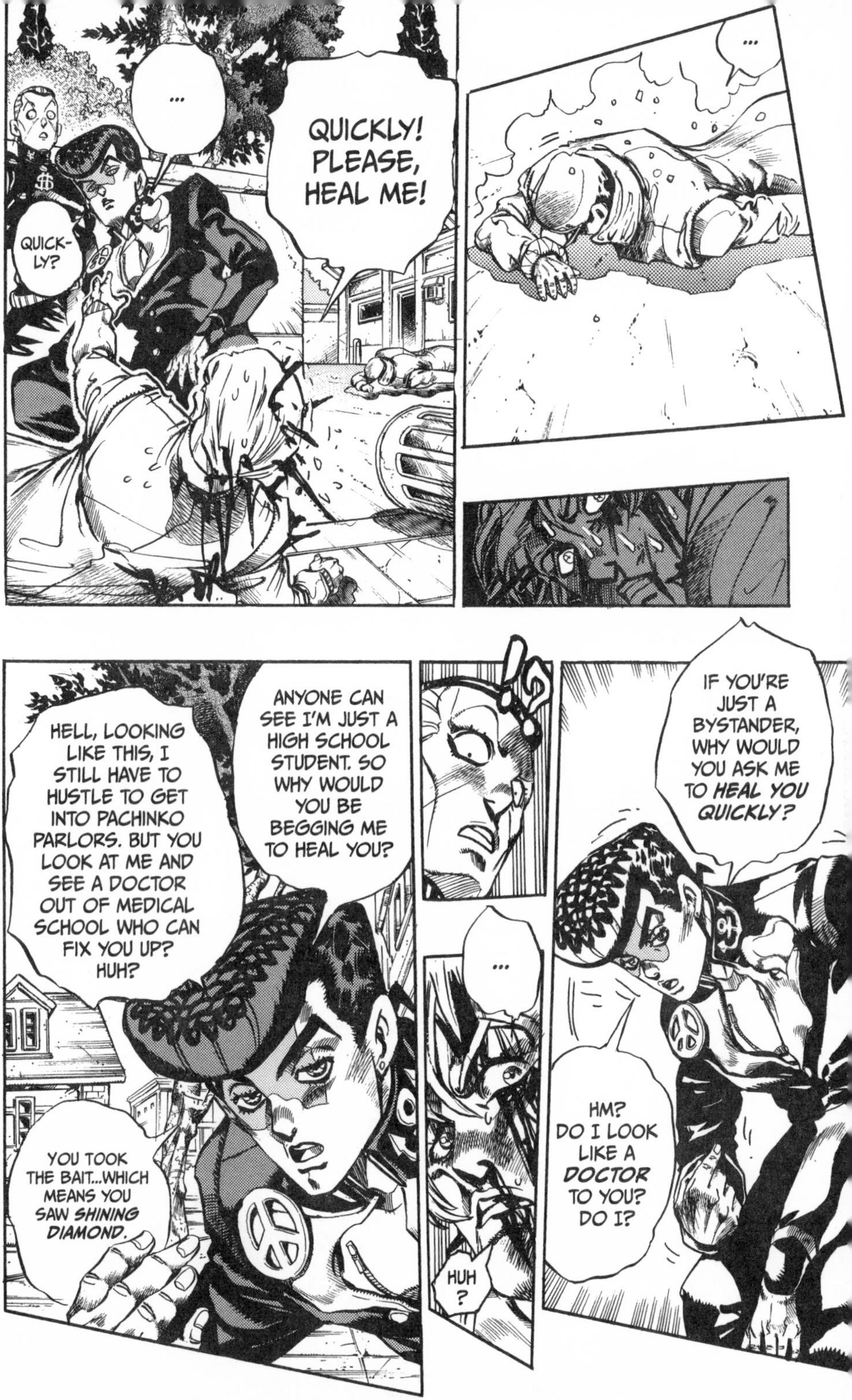
...
QUICKLY! PLEASE, HEAL ME!
...
QUICK-LY?
IF YOU'RE JUST A BYSTANDER, WHY WOULD YOU ASK ME TO *HEAL YOU QUICKLY?*
HM? DO I LOOK LIKE A *DOCTOR* TO YOU? DO I?
...
HUH?
ANYONE CAN SEE I'M JUST A HIGH SCHOOL STUDENT. SO WHY WOULD YOU BE BEGGING ME TO HEAL YOU?
HELL, LOOKING LIKE THIS, I STILL HAVE TO HUSTLE TO GET INTO PACHINKO PARLORS. BUT YOU LOOK AT ME AND SEE A DOCTOR OUT OF MEDICAL SCHOOL WHO CAN FIX YOU UP? HUH?
YOU TOOK THE BAIT...WHICH MEANS YOU SAW *SHINING DIAMOND*.

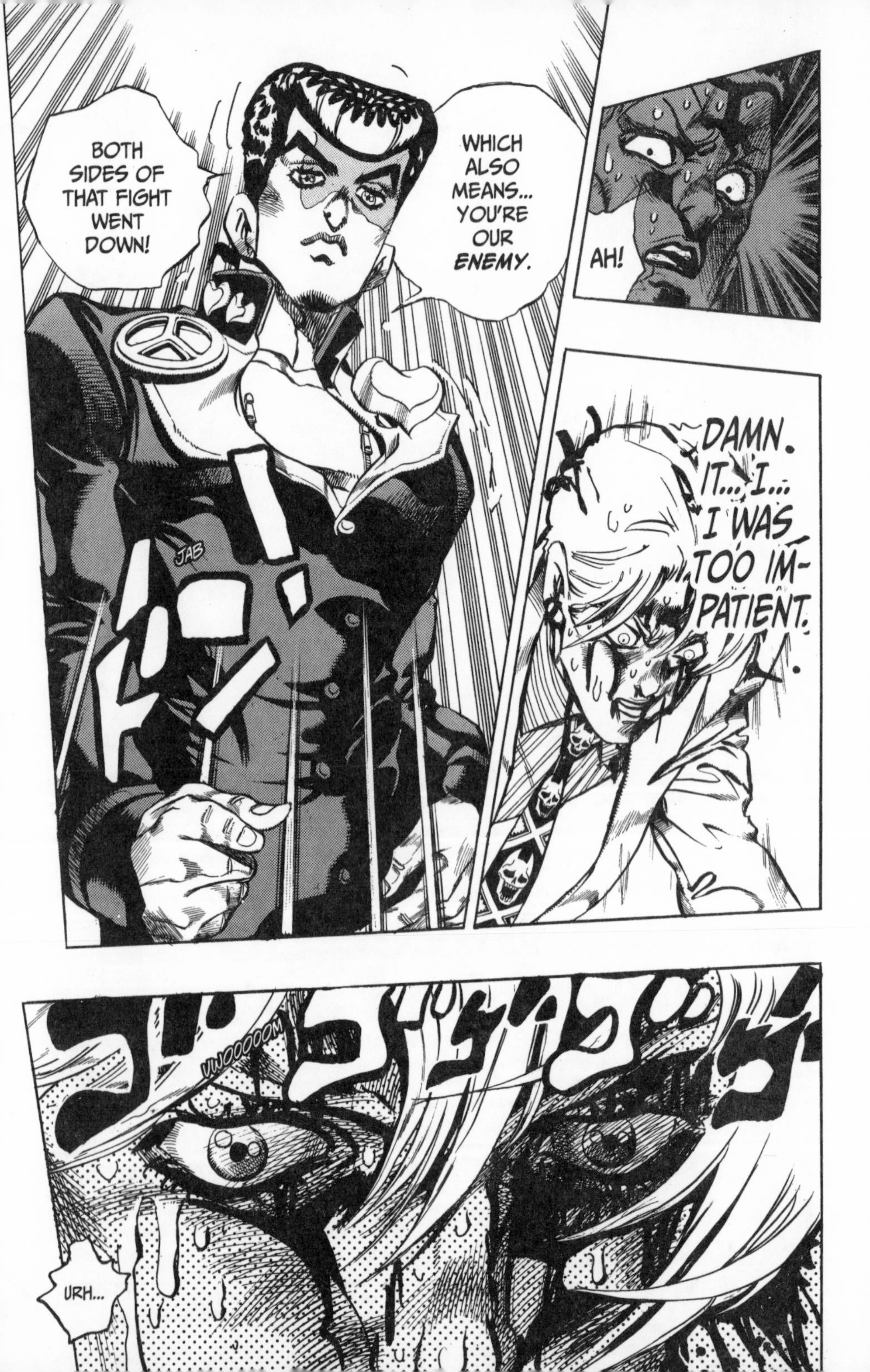
AH!
DAMN. IT... I... I WAS TOO IM-PATIENT.
WHICH ALSO MEANS... YOU'RE OUR ENEMY.
BOTH SIDES OF THAT FIGHT WENT DOWN!
JAB
VWOOOOOM
URH...

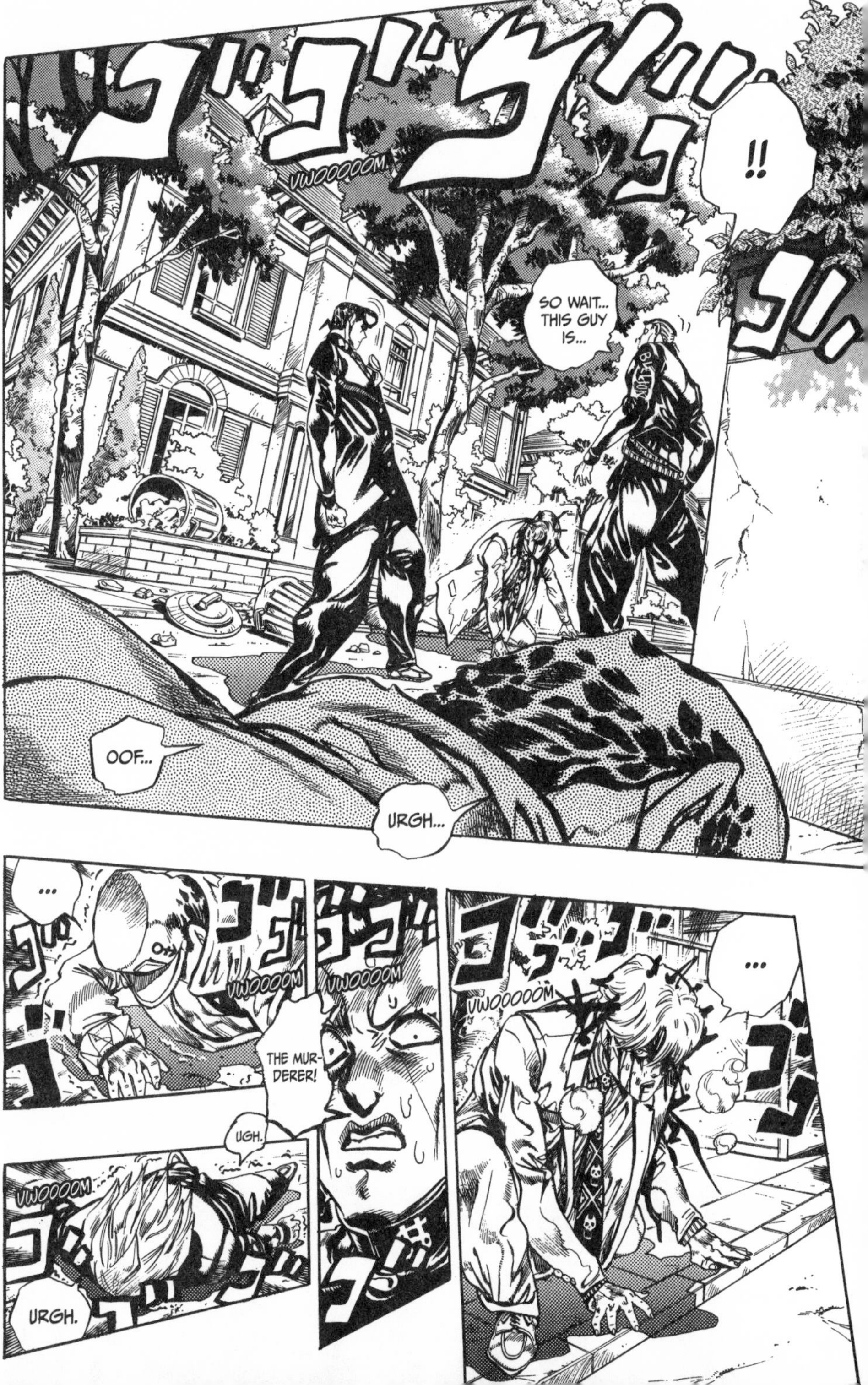
!!
SO WAIT... THIS GUY IS...
VWOOOOOM
OOF...
URGH...
...
VWOOOOOM
VWOOOOOM
THE MURDERER!
...
VWOOOOM
UGH.
VWOOOOM
URGH.

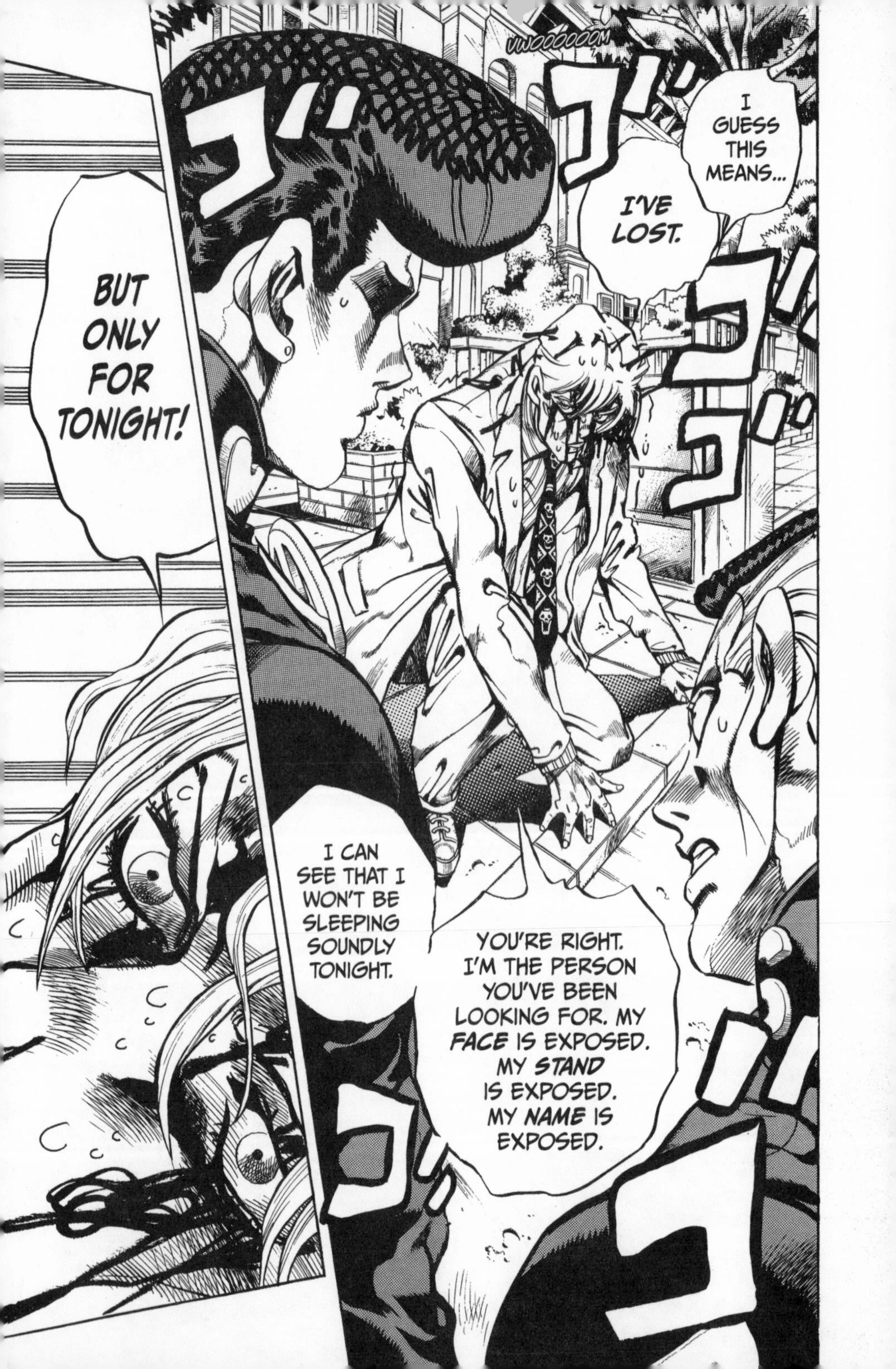
VWOOOOOOM
I GUESS THIS MEANS...
I'VE LOST.
YOU'RE RIGHT. I'M THE PERSON YOU'VE BEEN LOOKING FOR. MY FACE IS EXPOSED. MY STAND IS EXPOSED. MY NAME IS EXPOSED.
I CAN SEE THAT I WON'T BE SLEEPING SOUNDLY TONIGHT.
BUT ONLY FOR TONIGHT!

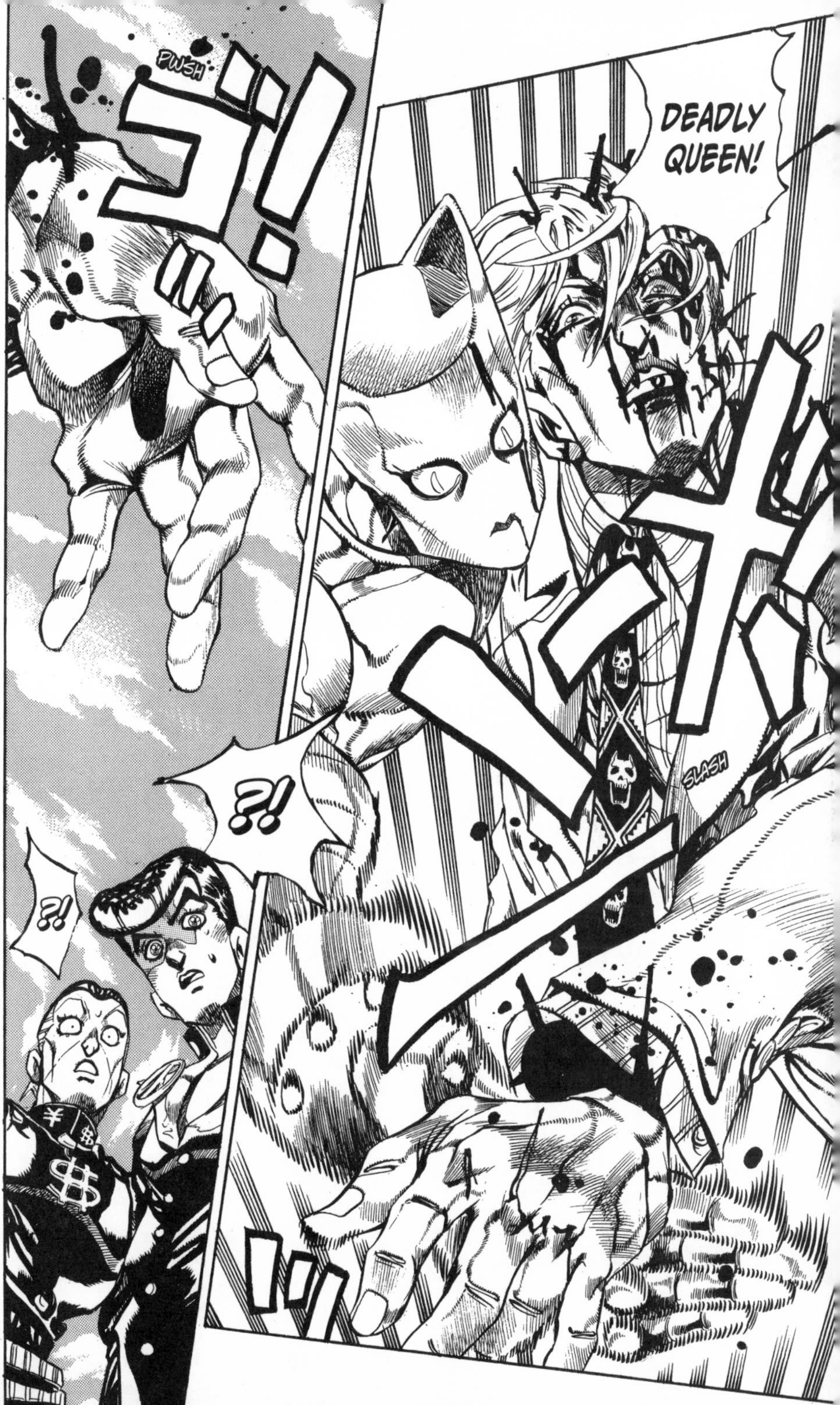
DEADLY QUEEN!
SLASH
?!
PWSH
?!

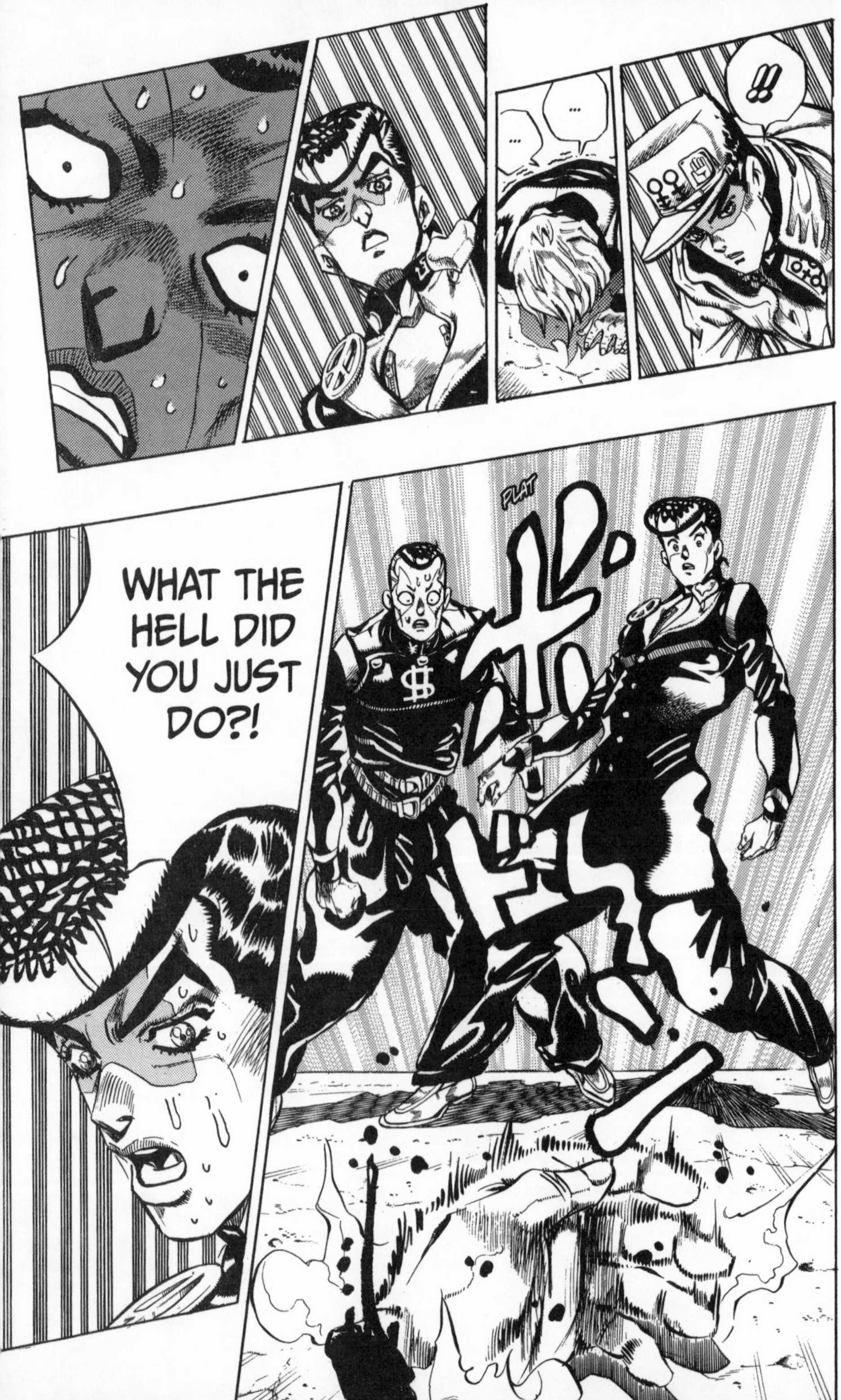
!!
...
...
PLAT
WHAT THE HELL DID YOU JUST DO?!

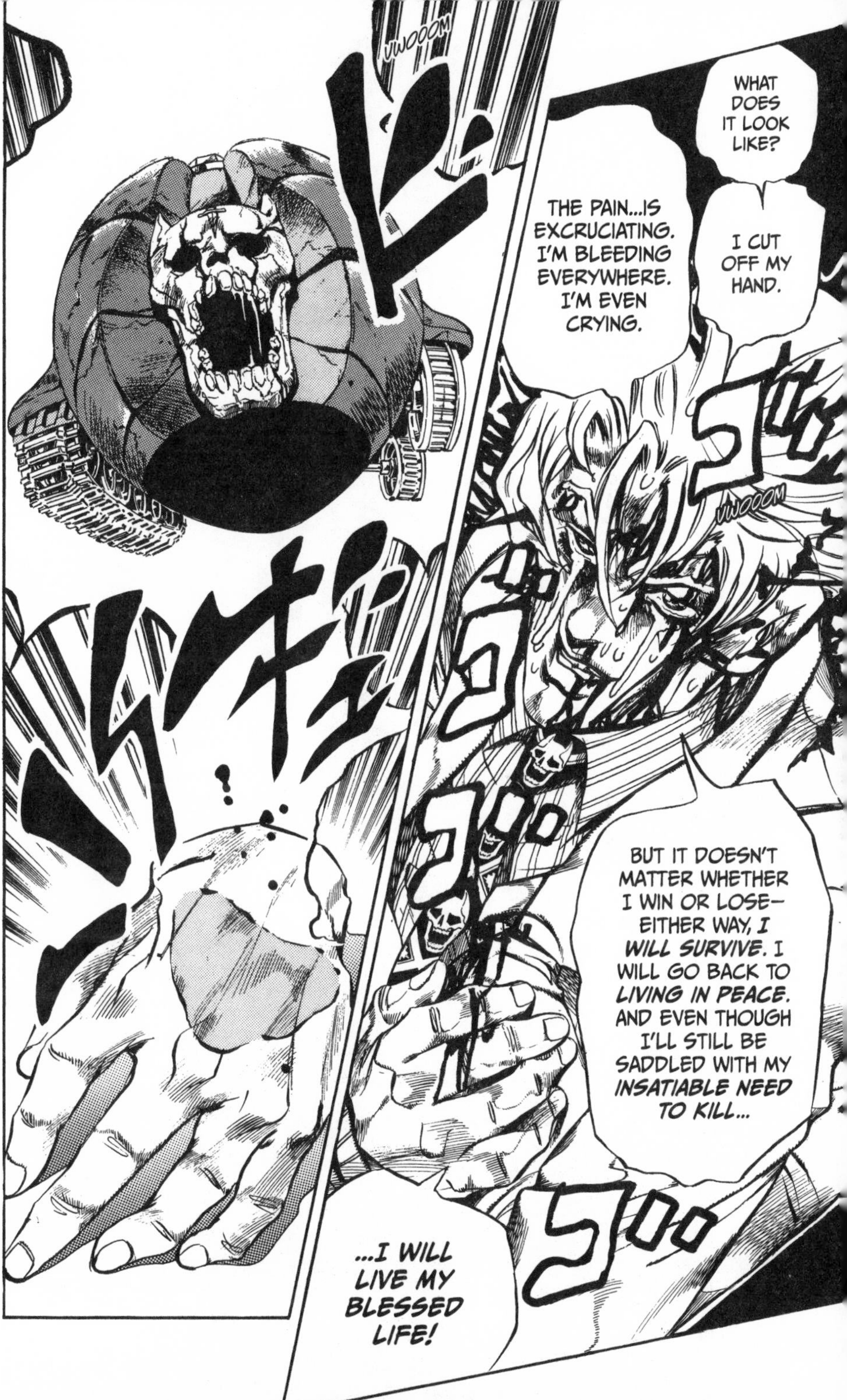
WHAT DOES IT LOOK LIKE?
I CUT OFF MY HAND.
THE PAIN...IS EXCRUCIATING. I'M BLEEDING EVERYWHERE. I'M EVEN CRYING.
UWOOOM
BUT IT DOESN'T MATTER WHETHER I WIN OR LOSE—EITHER WAY, *I WILL SURVIVE*. I WILL GO BACK TO *LIVING IN PEACE*. AND EVEN THOUGH I'LL STILL BE SADDLED WITH MY *INSATIABLE NEED TO KILL*...
...*I WILL LIVE MY BLESSED LIFE!*
UWOOOM

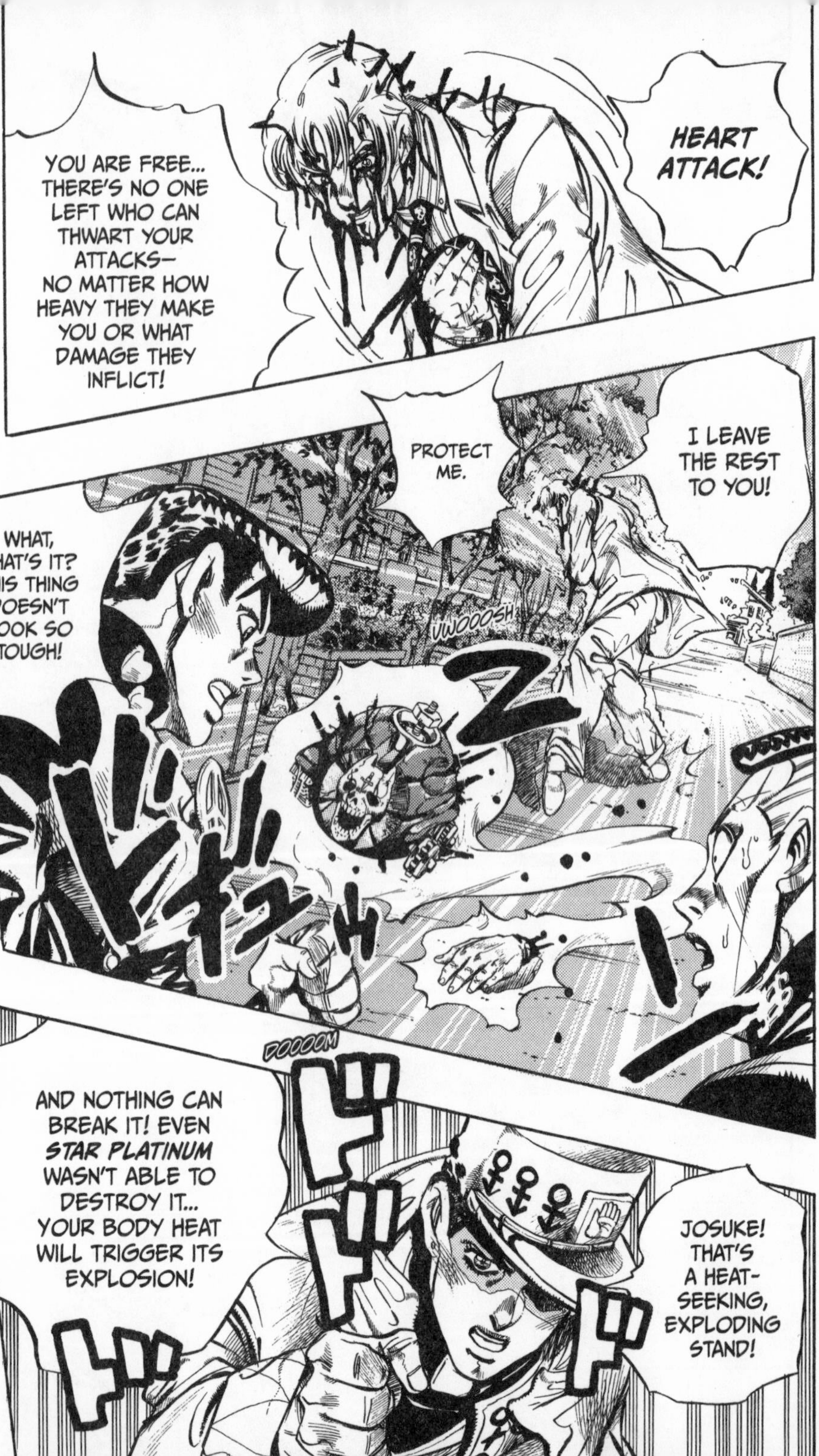
HEART ATTACK!
YOU ARE FREE... THERE'S NO ONE LEFT WHO CAN THWART YOUR ATTACKS— NO MATTER HOW HEAVY THEY MAKE YOU OR WHAT DAMAGE THEY INFLICT!
PROTECT ME.
I LEAVE THE REST TO YOU!
UWOOOSH
WHAT, THAT'S IT? THIS THING DOESN'T LOOK SO TOUGH!
DOOOOM
JOSUKE! THAT'S A HEAT-SEEKING, EXPLODING STAND!
AND NOTHING CAN BREAK IT! EVEN *STAR PLATINUM* WASN'T ABLE TO DESTROY IT... YOUR BODY HEAT WILL TRIGGER ITS EXPLOSION!

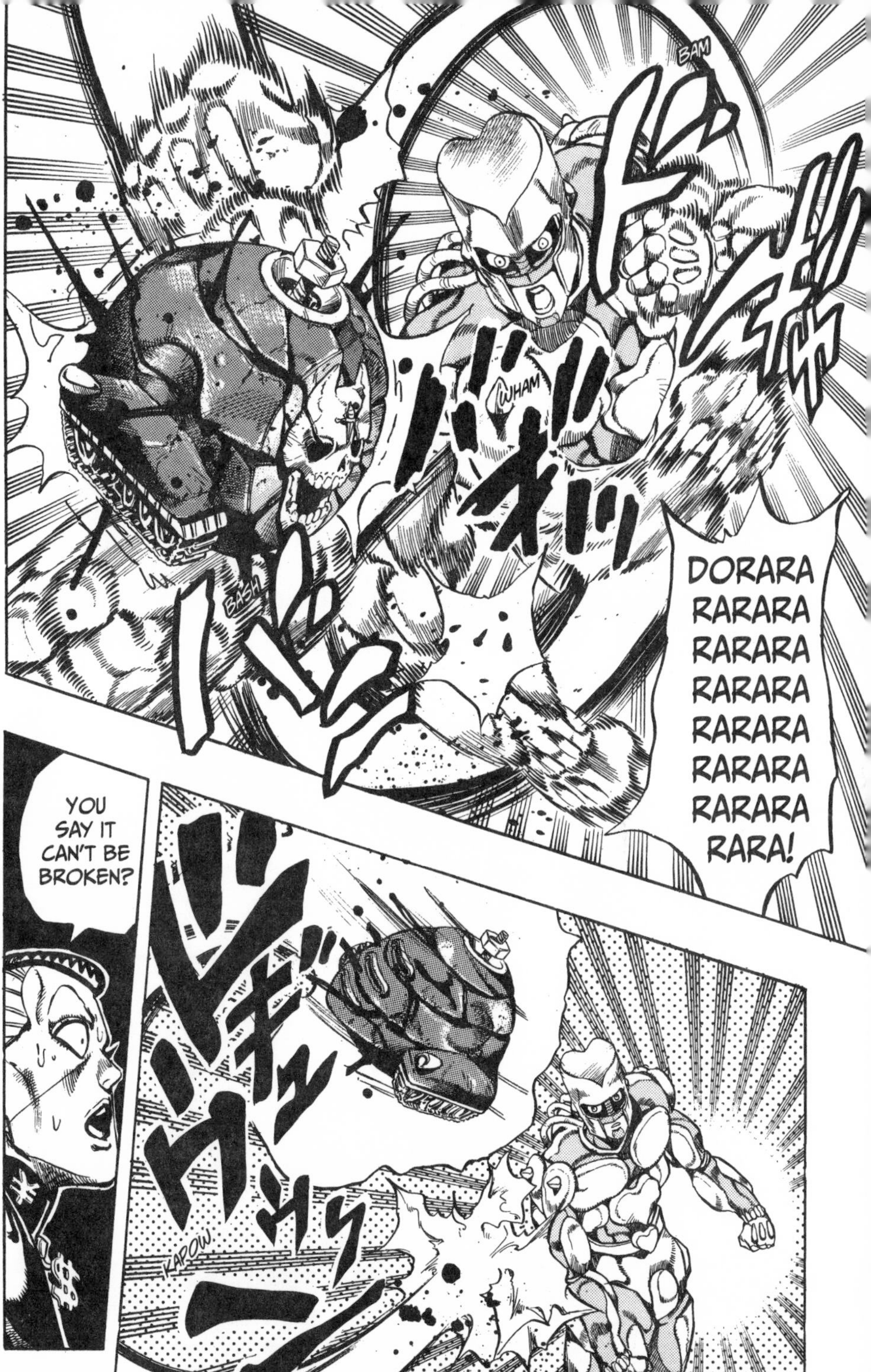
BAM
WHAM
DORARA RARARA RARARA RARARA RARARA RARARA RARARA RARA!
BASH
KAPOW
YOU SAY IT CAN'T BE BROKEN?

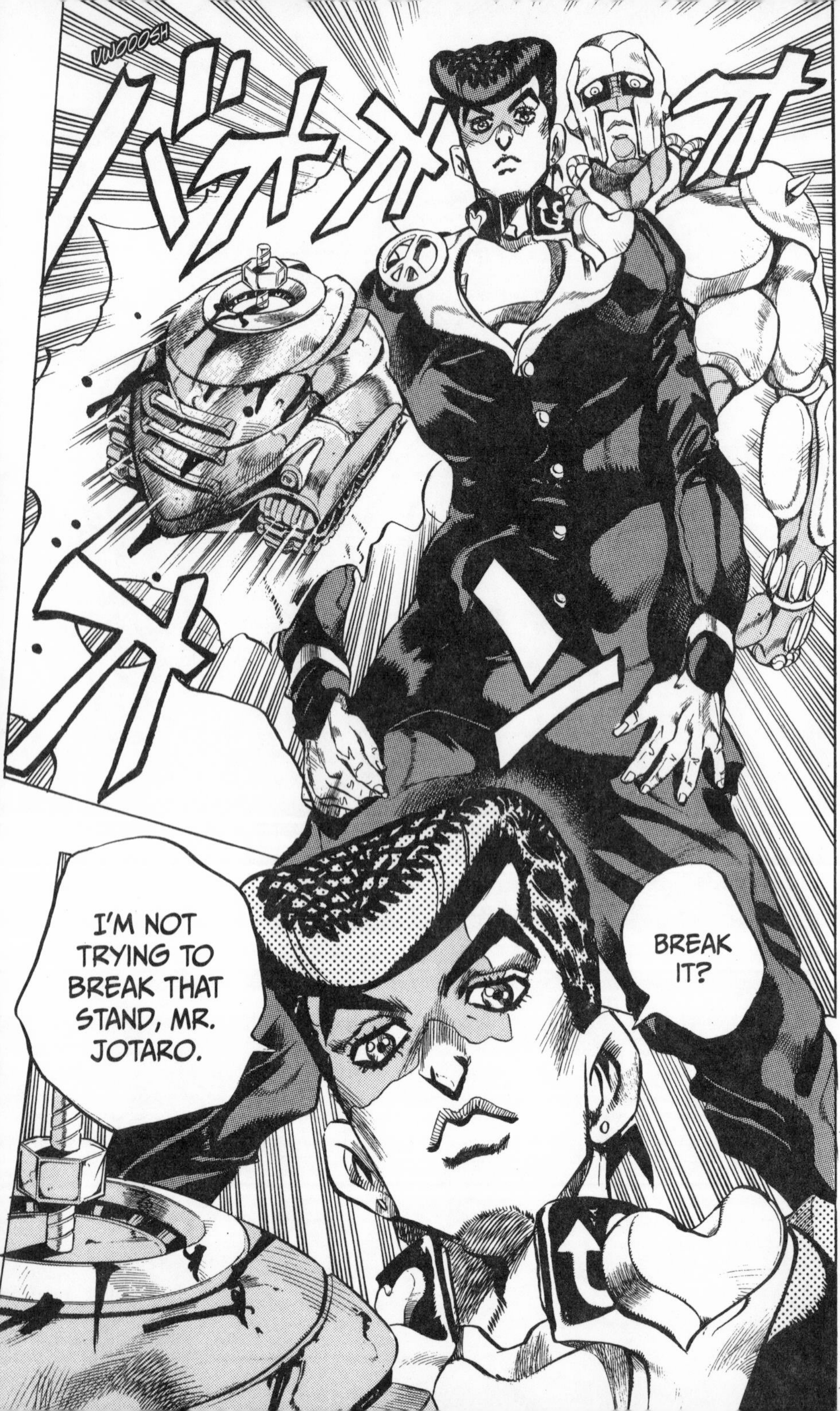
VWOOOSH
BREAK IT?
I'M NOT TRYING TO BREAK THAT STAND, MR. JOTARO.

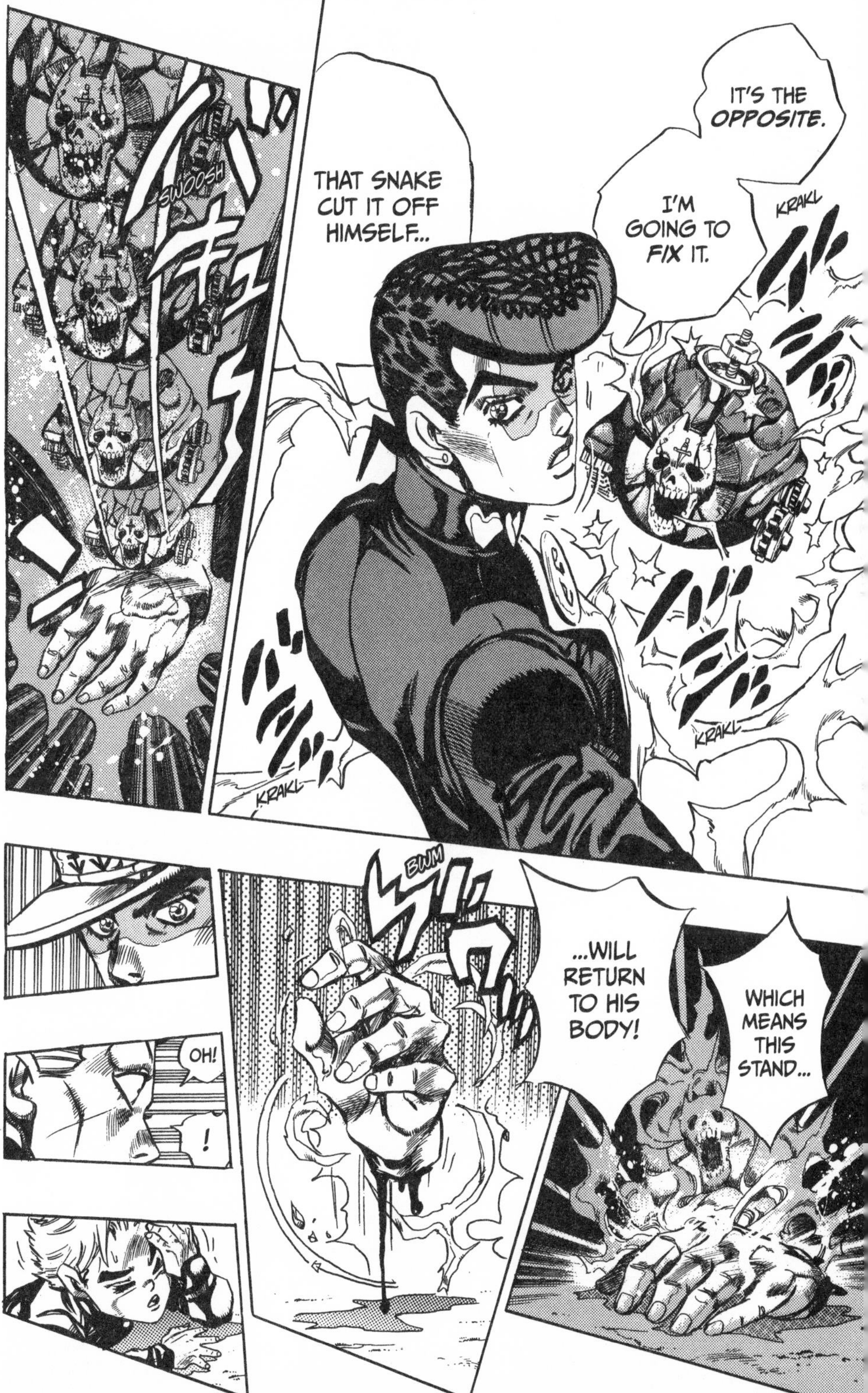
IT'S THE OPPOSITE.
I'M GOING TO FIX IT.
KRAKL
THAT SNAKE CUT IT OFF HIMSELF...
KRAKL
KRAKL
SWOOSH
WHICH MEANS THIS STAND...
...WILL RETURN TO HIS BODY!
BWM
OH!
!

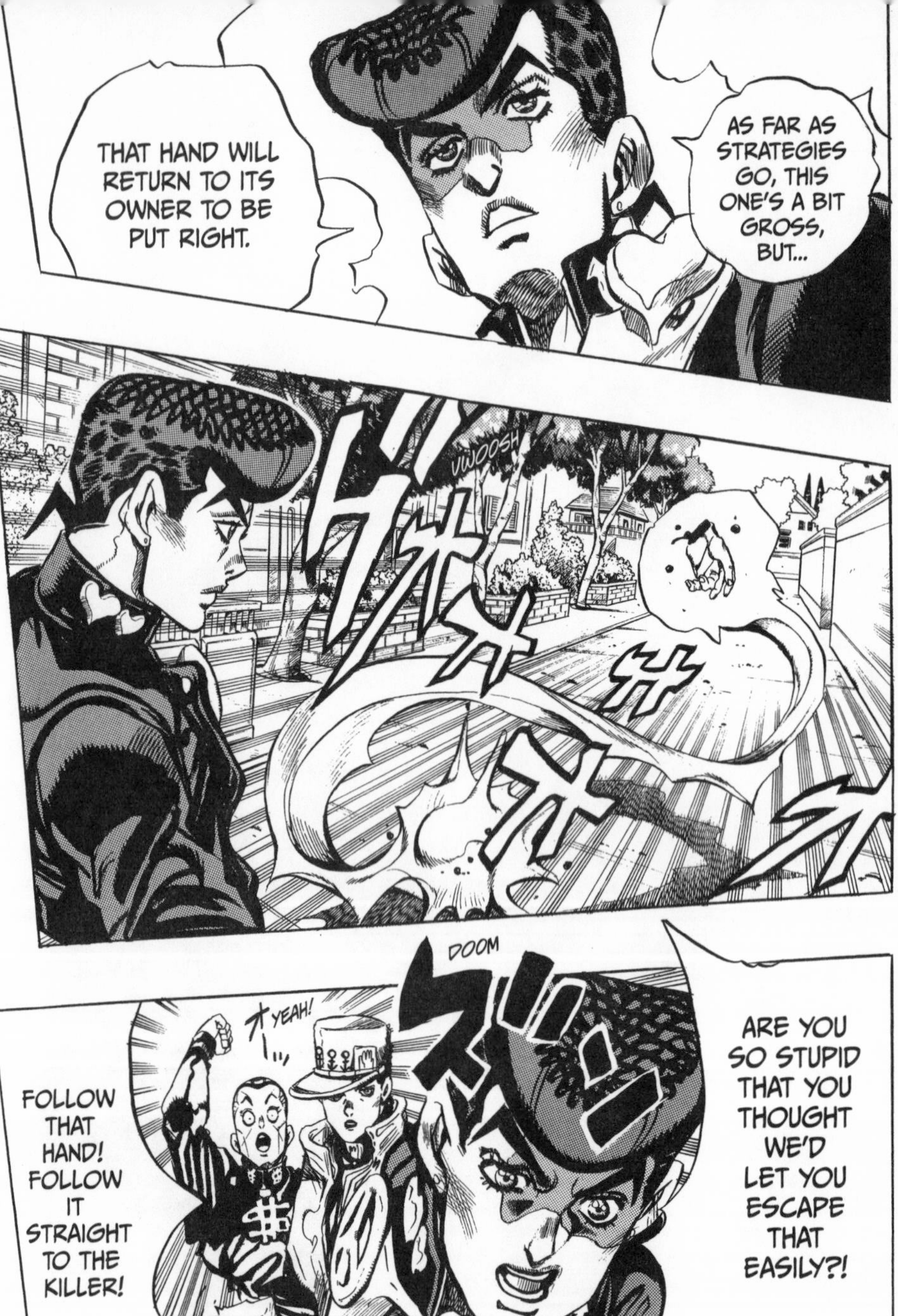
AS FAR AS STRATEGIES GO, THIS ONE'S A BIT GROSS, BUT...
THAT HAND WILL RETURN TO ITS OWNER TO BE PUT RIGHT.
VWOOSH
DOOM
ARE YOU SO STUPID THAT YOU THOUGHT WE'D LET YOU ESCAPE THAT EASILY?!
YEAH!
FOLLOW THAT HAND! FOLLOW IT STRAIGHT TO THE KILLER!

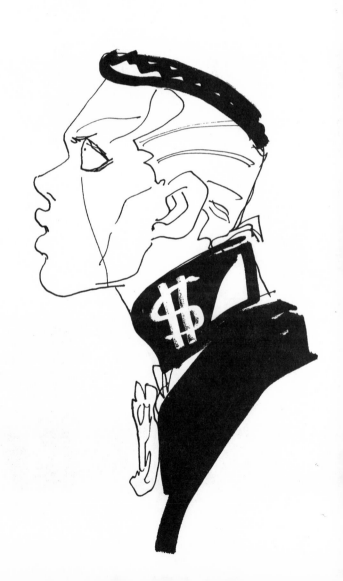

CHAPTER 99

HEART ATTACK, PART 11

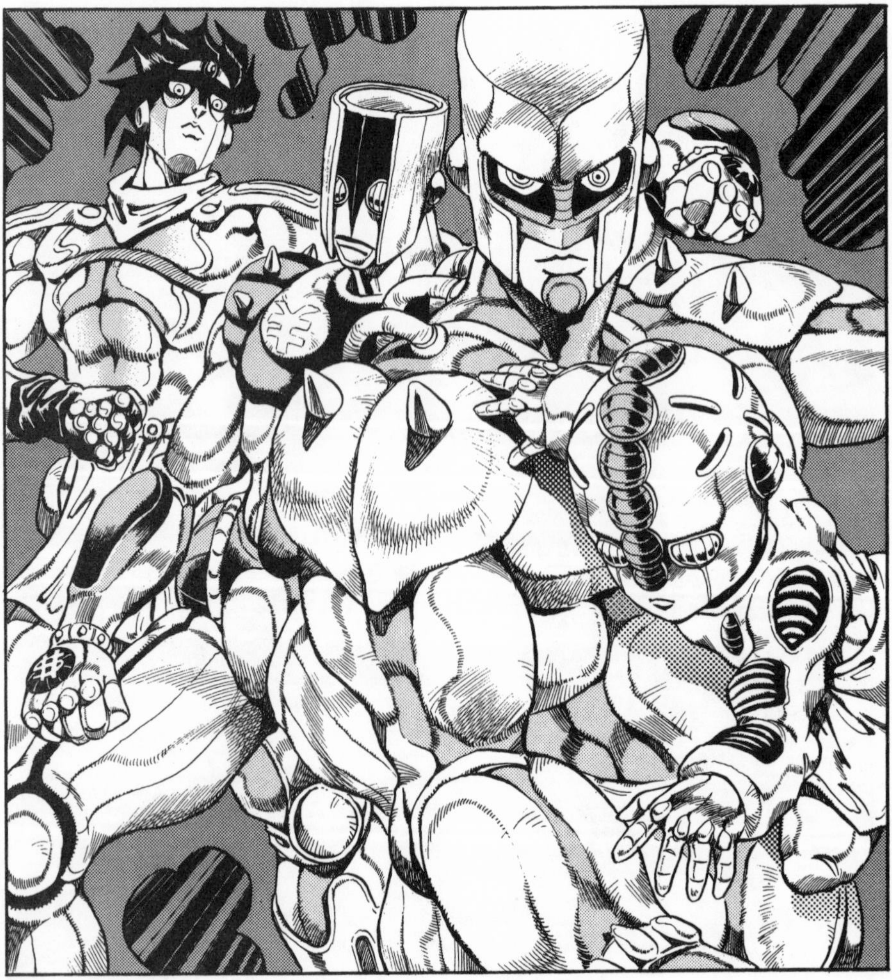

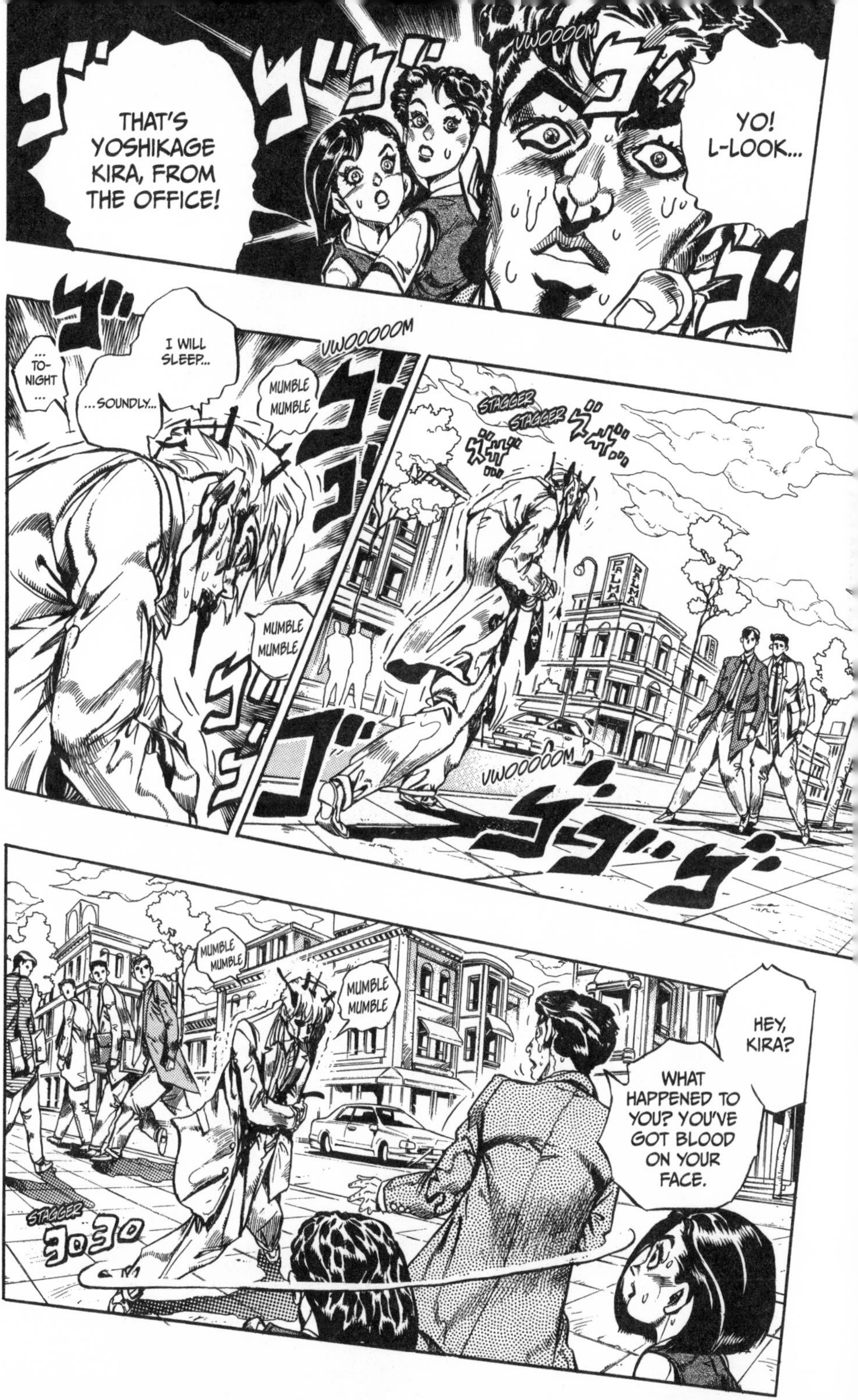
VWOOOOM
YO! L-LOOK...
THAT'S YOSHIKAGE KIRA, FROM THE OFFICE!
STAGGER
STAGGER
VWOOOOOM
VWOOOOOM
MUMBLE MUMBLE
I WILL SLEEP...
... TO-NIGHT ...
...SOUNDLY...
MUMBLE MUMBLE
HEY, KIRA?
WHAT HAPPENED TO YOU? YOU'VE GOT BLOOD ON YOUR FACE.
MUMBLE MUMBLE
MUMBLE MUMBLE
STAGGER

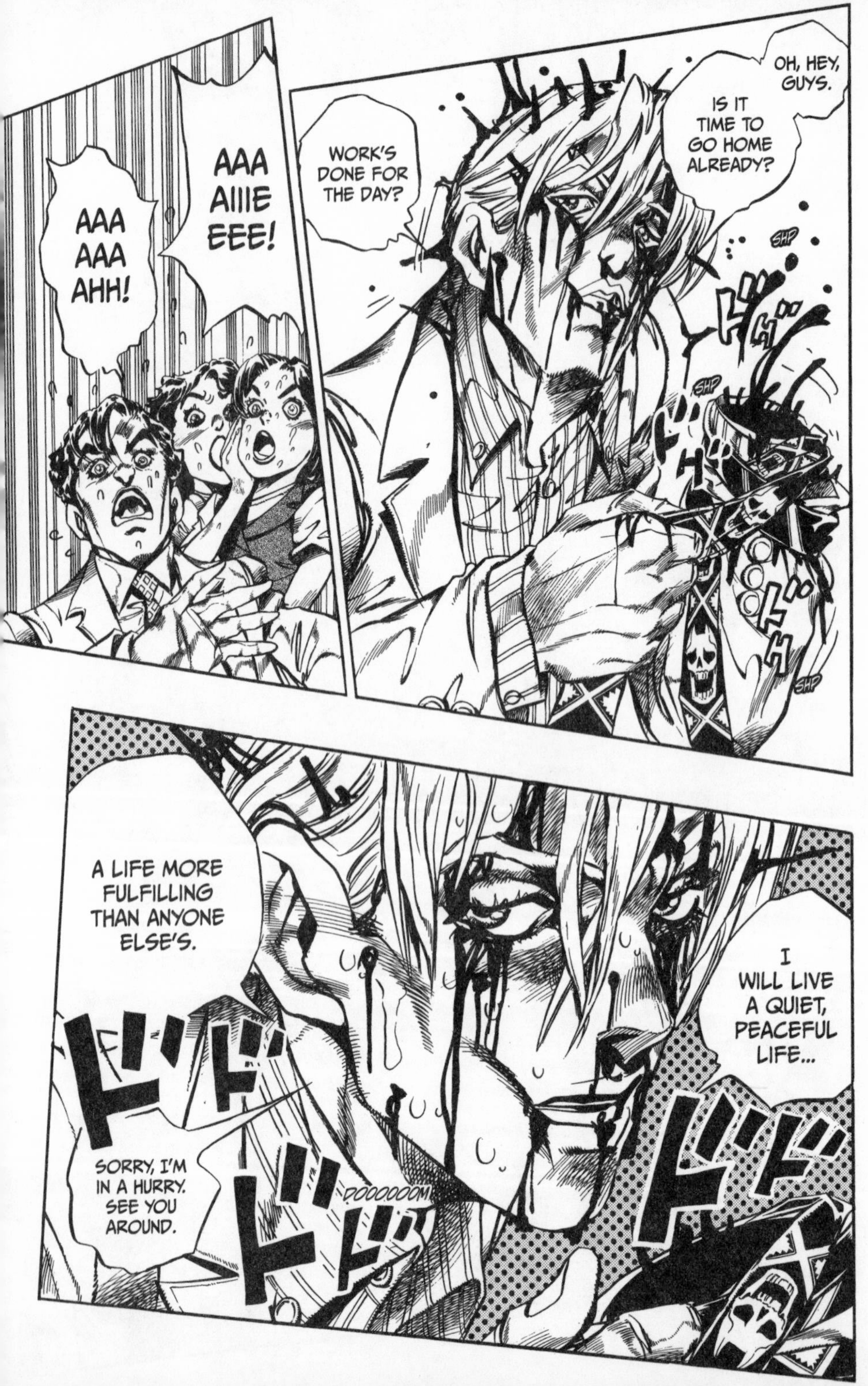
OH, HEY, GUYS.
IS IT TIME TO GO HOME ALREADY?
WORK'S DONE FOR THE DAY?
SHP
SHP
SHP
AAA AIIIE EEE!
AAA AAA AHH!
I WILL LIVE A QUIET, PEACEFUL LIFE...
A LIFE MORE FULFILLING THAN ANYONE ELSE'S.
DOOOOOOM
SORRY, I'M IN A HURRY. SEE YOU AROUND.

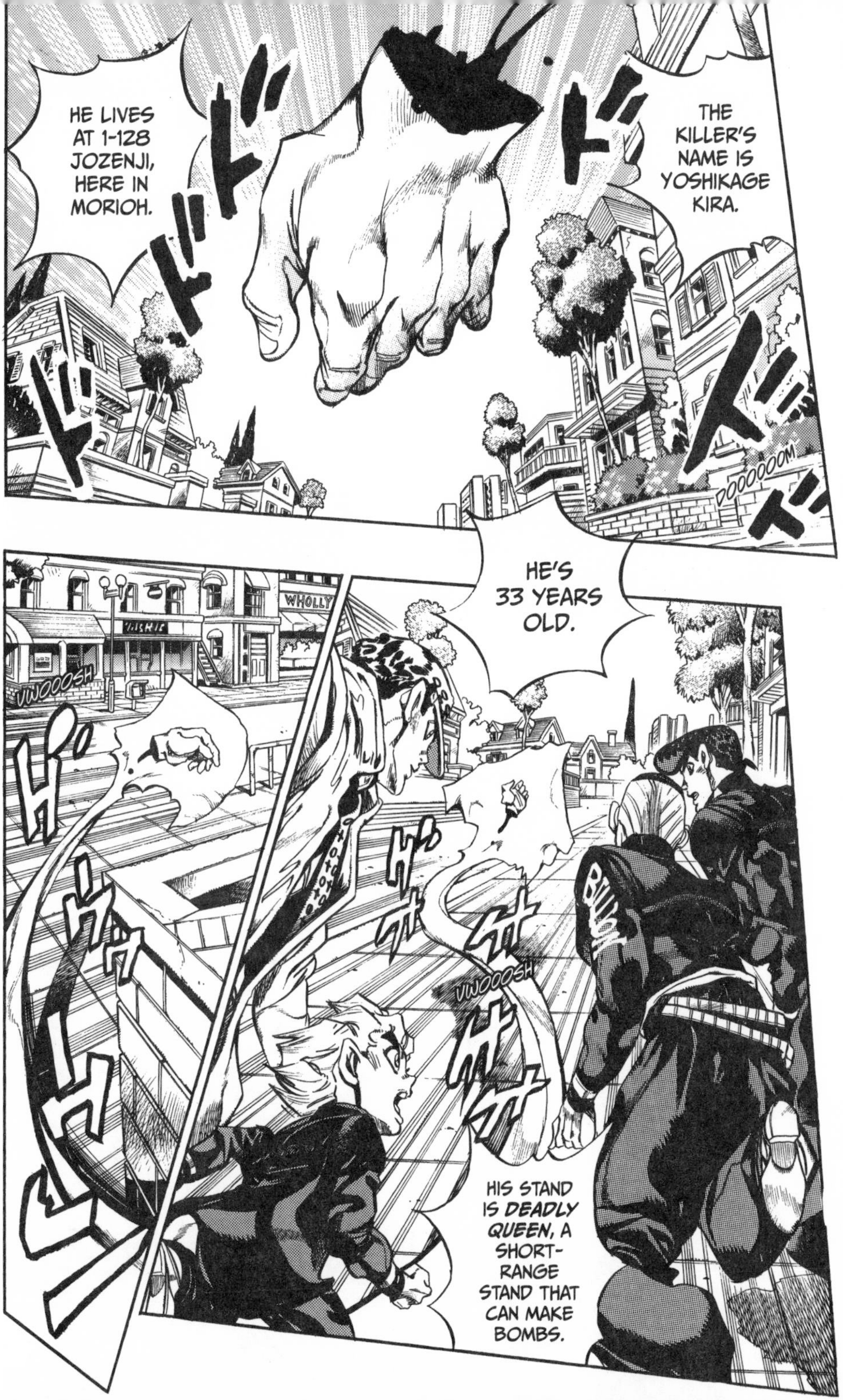
THE KILLER'S NAME IS YOSHIKAGE KIRA.
HE LIVES AT 1-128 JOZENJI, HERE IN MORIOH.
DOOOOOOOM
HE'S 33 YEARS OLD.
UWOOOSH
HIS STAND IS *DEADLY QUEEN*, A SHORT-RANGE STAND THAT CAN MAKE BOMBS.
WHOLLY
UWOOOSH

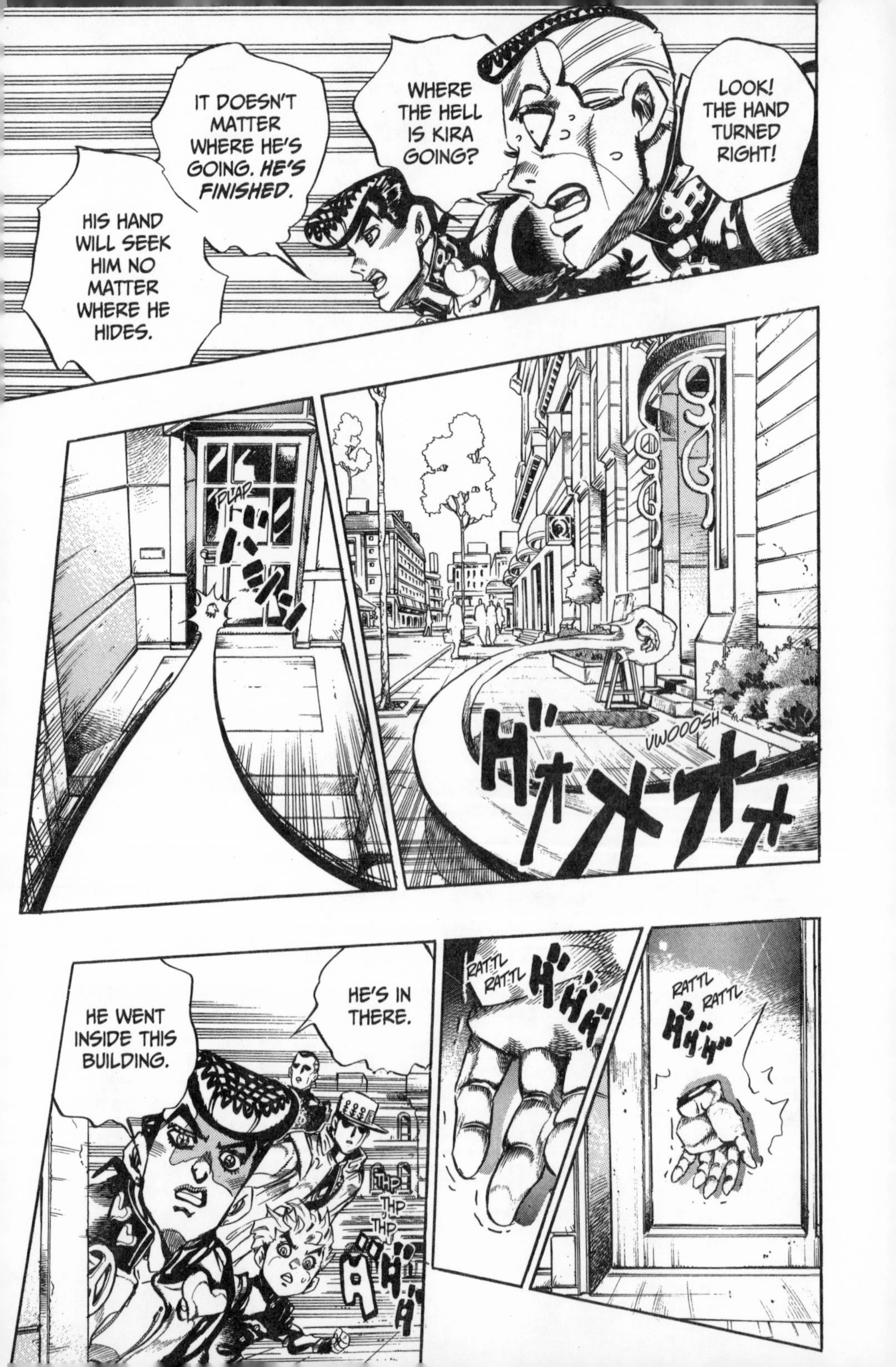
LOOK! THE HAND TURNED RIGHT!
WHERE THE HELL IS KIRA GOING?
IT DOESN'T MATTER WHERE HE'S GOING. *HE'S FINISHED.*
HIS HAND WILL SEEK HIM NO MATTER WHERE HE HIDES.
VWOOOSH
PLAP
RATTL RATTL
RATTL RATTL
HE'S IN THERE.
HE WENT INSIDE THIS BUILDING.
THP THP THP

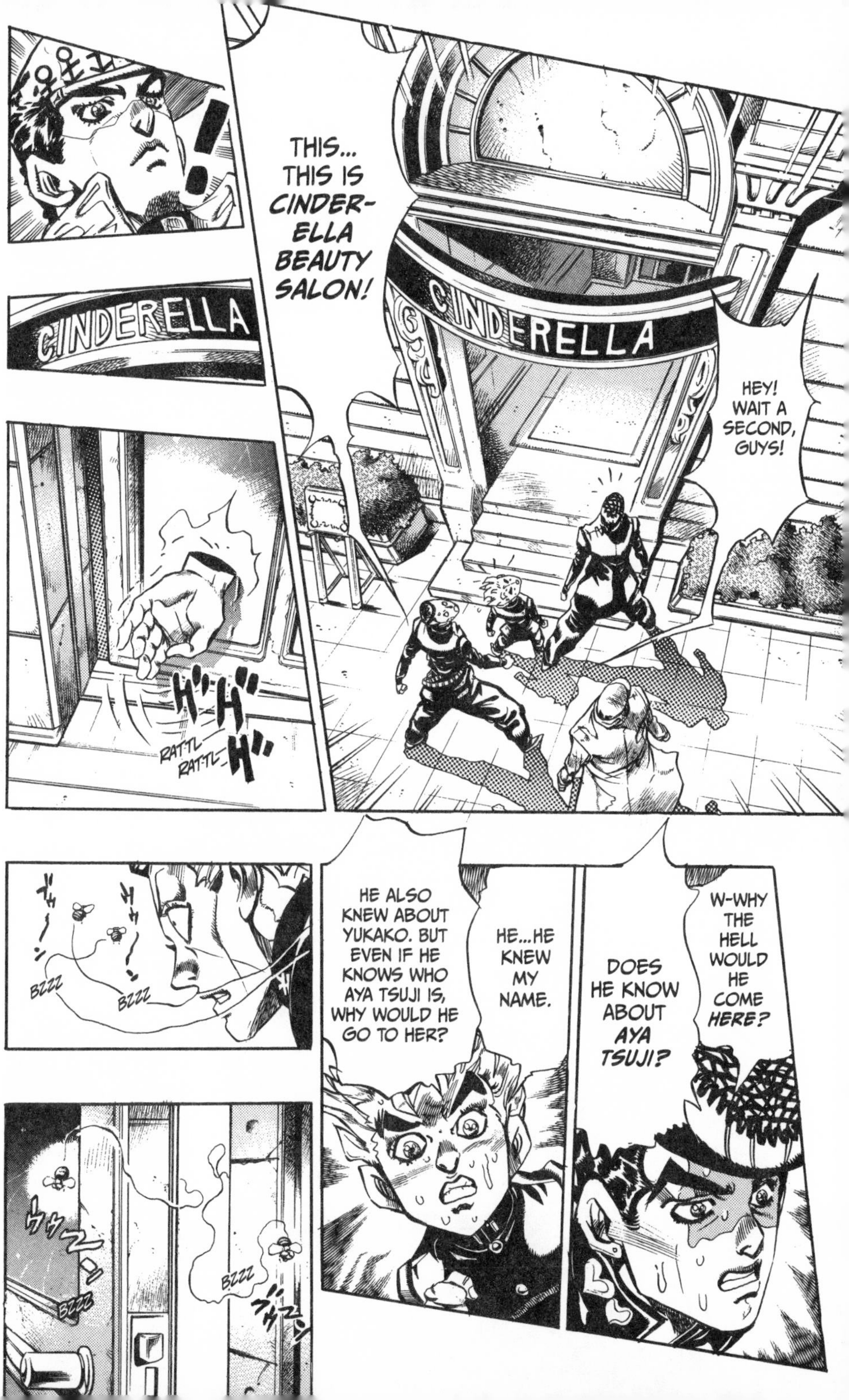
THIS... THIS IS CINDERELLA BEAUTY SALON!
CINDERELLA
HEY! WAIT A SECOND, GUYS!
!
CINDERELLA
RATTL RATTL
W-WHY THE HELL WOULD HE COME HERE?
DOES HE KNOW ABOUT AYA TSUJI?
HE...HE KNEW MY NAME.
HE ALSO KNEW ABOUT YUKAKO. BUT EVEN IF HE KNOWS WHO AYA TSUJI IS, WHY WOULD HE GO TO HER?
BZZZ
BZZZ
BZZZ
BZZZ

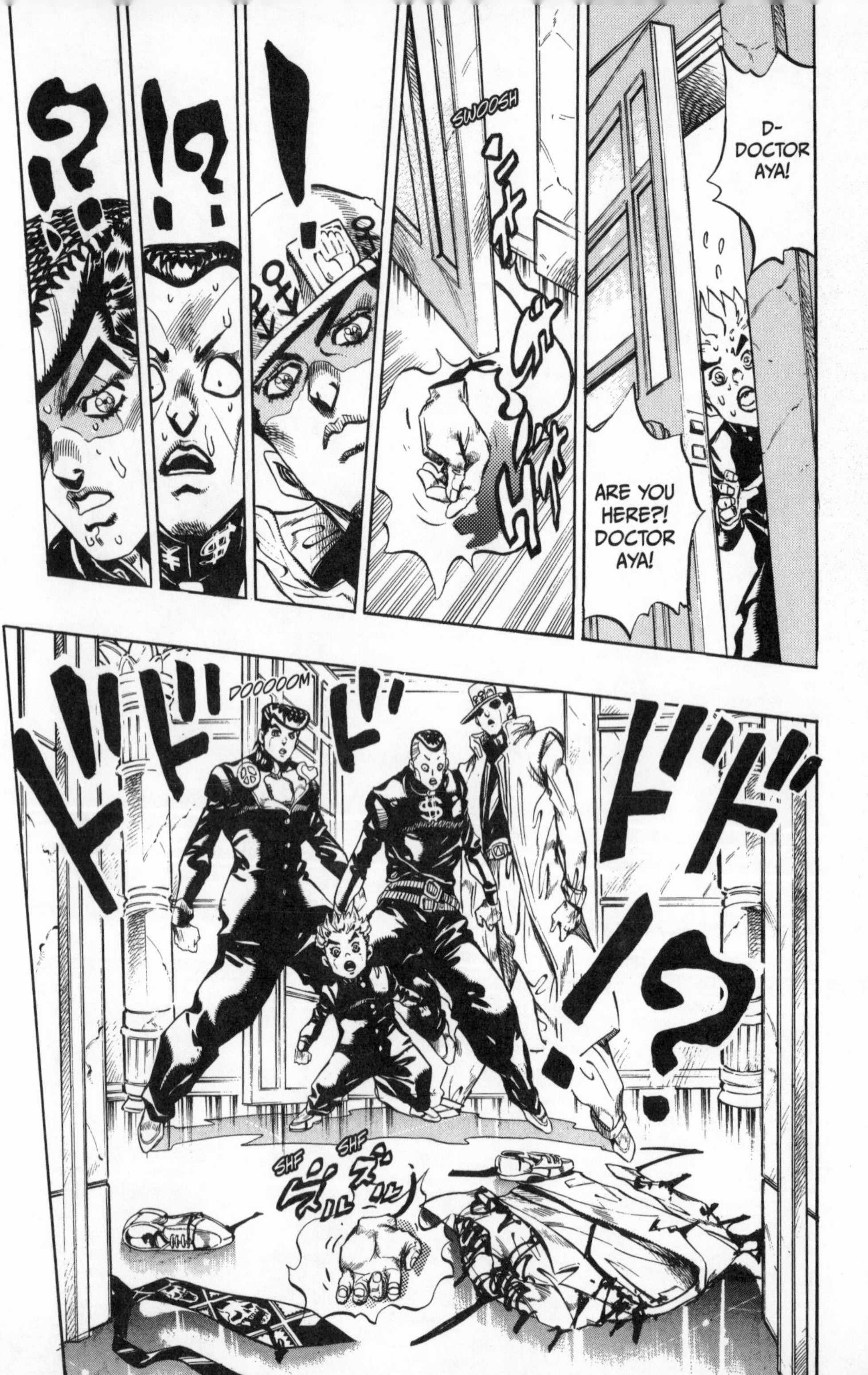
D- DOCTOR AYA!
ARE YOU HERE?! DOCTOR AYA!
SWOOSH
DOOOOOM
SHF
SHF

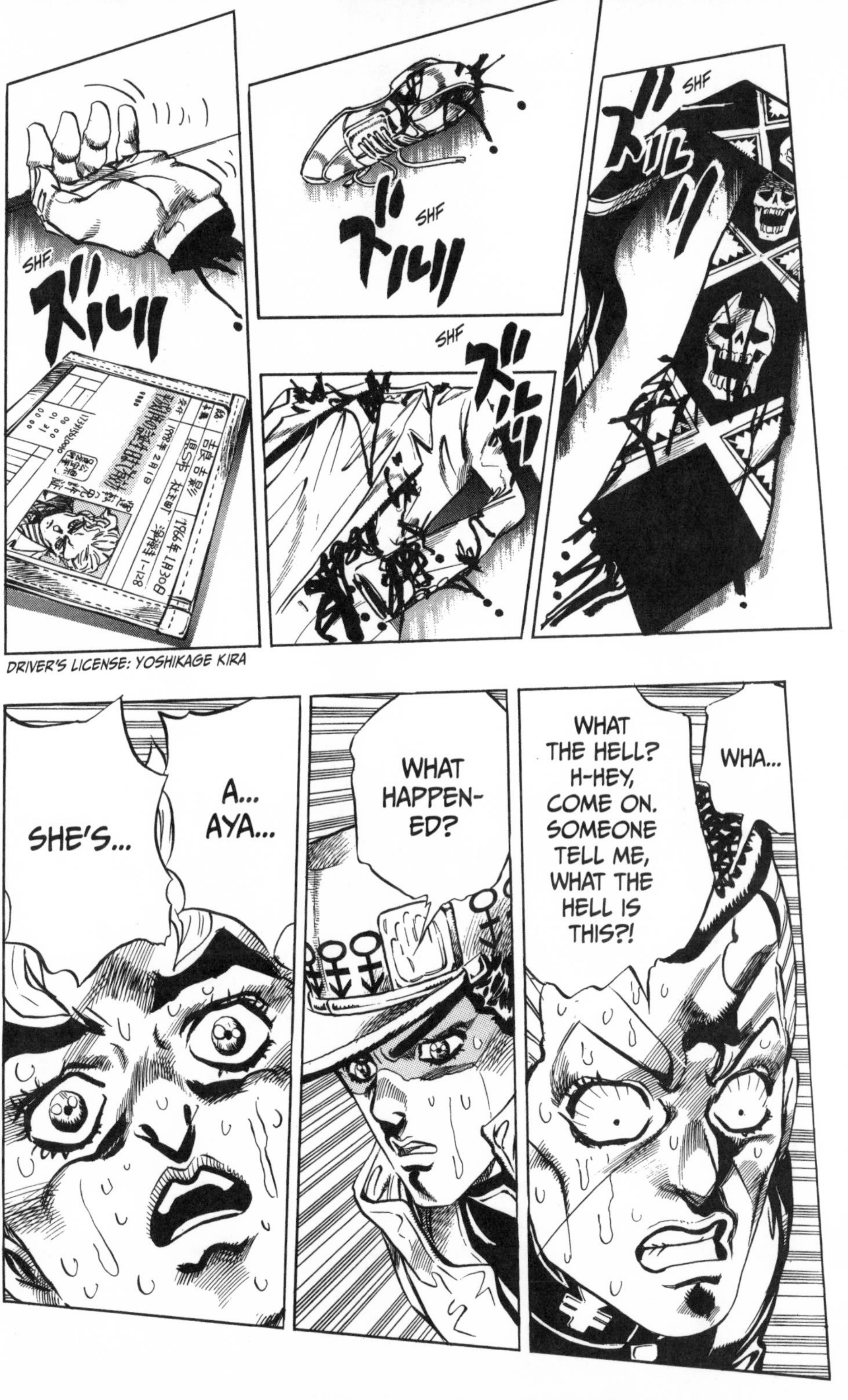
SHF
SHF
SHF
SHF
DRIVER'S LICENSE: YOSHIKAGE KIRA
WHA...
WHAT THE HELL? H-HEY, COME ON. SOMEONE TELL ME, WHAT THE HELL IS THIS?!
WHAT HAPPENED?
A... AYA...
SHE'S...

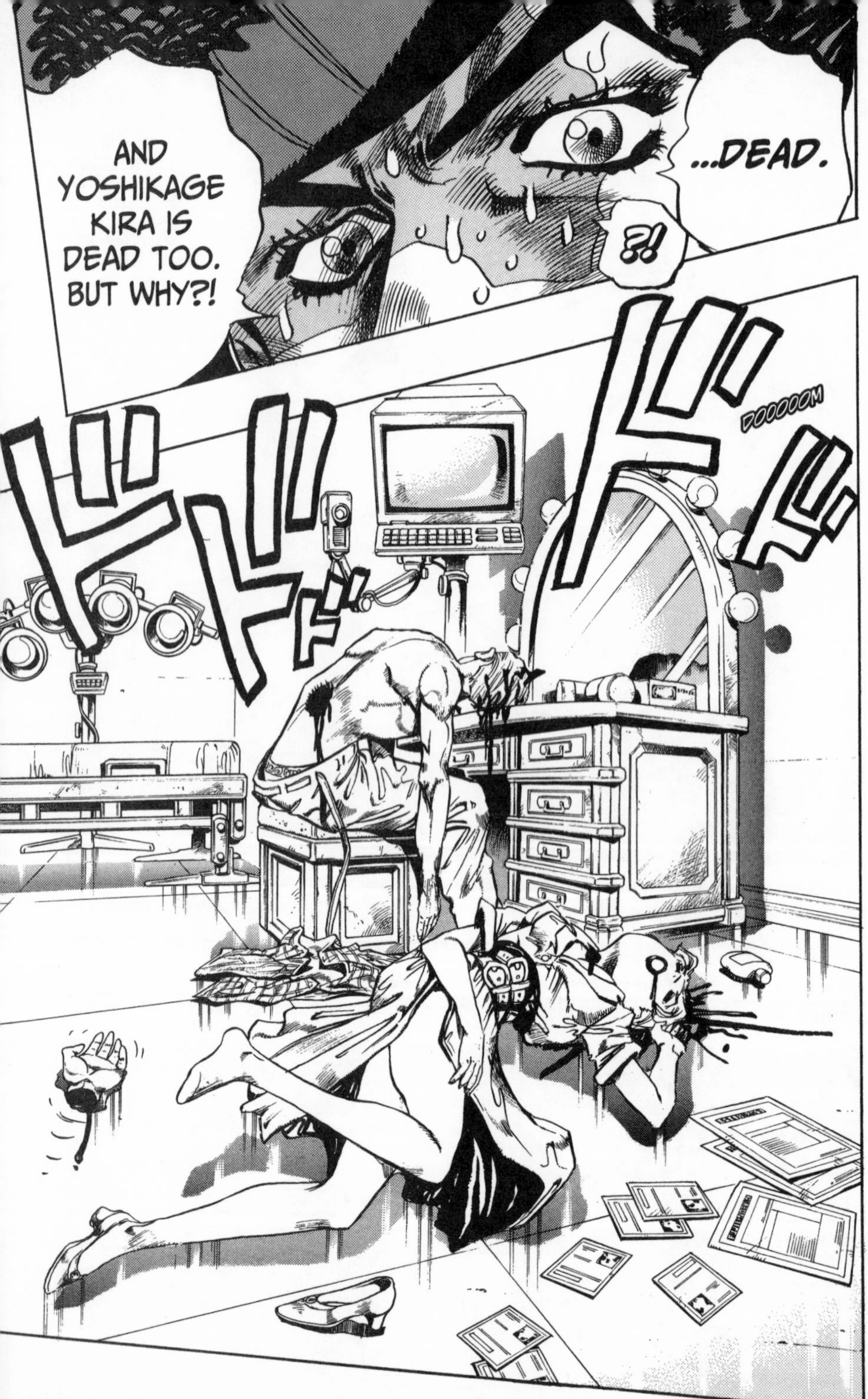
...DEAD.
?!
AND YOSHIKAGE KIRA IS DEAD TOO. BUT WHY?!
DOOOOOM

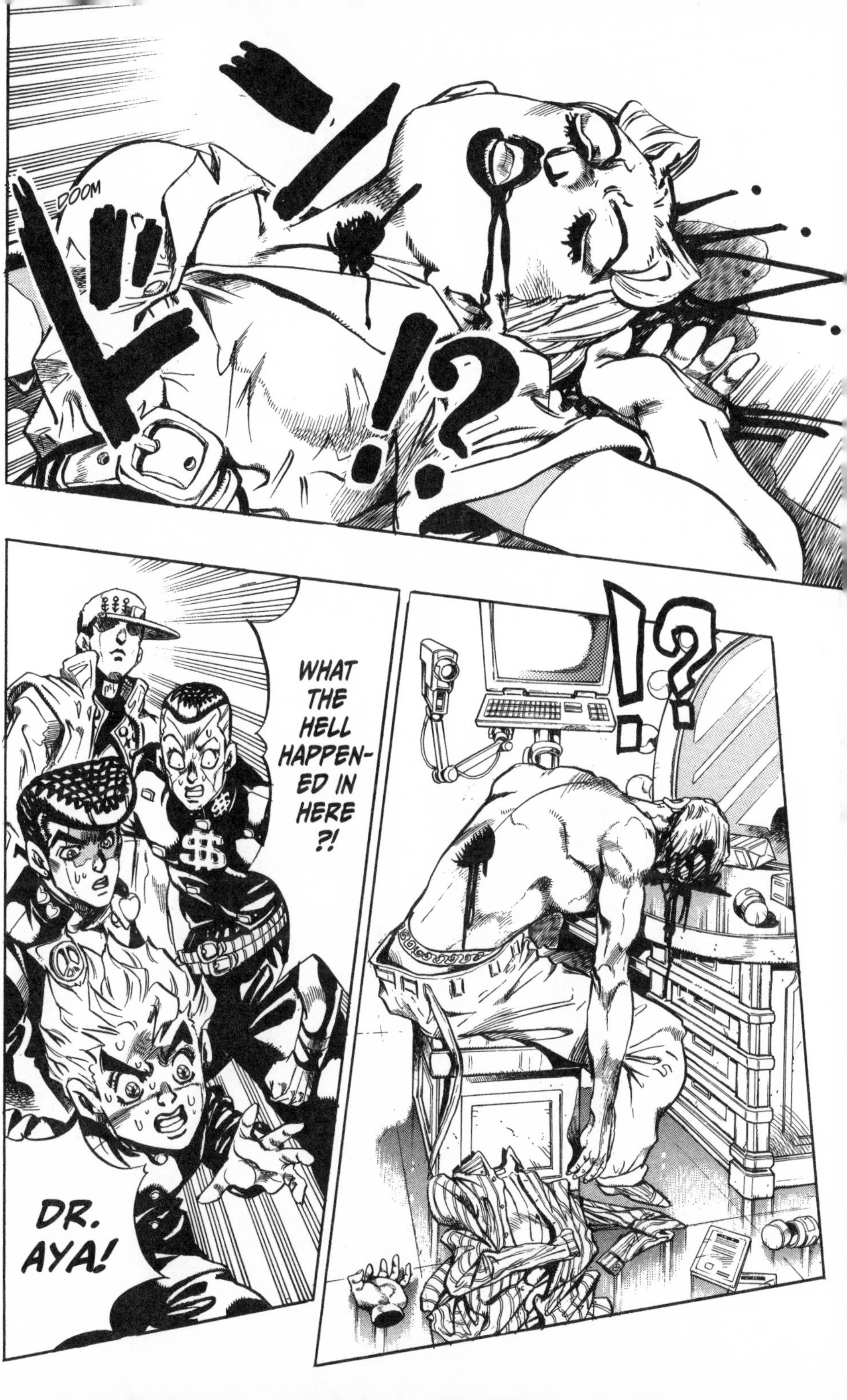
DOOM
!?
!?
WHAT THE HELL HAPPENED IN HERE?!
DR. AYA!

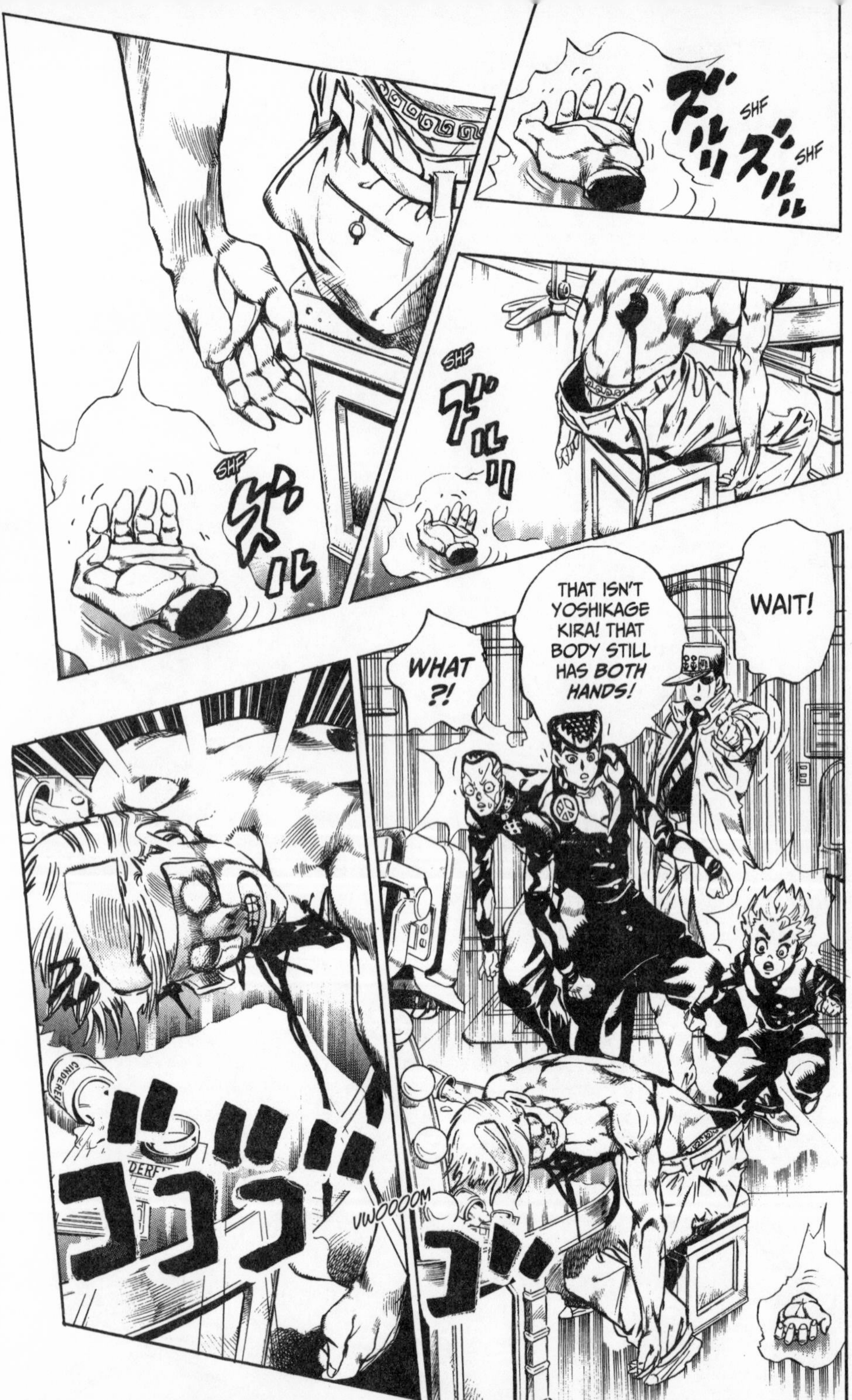

SHF
SHF
SHF
SHF
WAIT!
THAT ISN'T YOSHIKAGE KIRA! THAT BODY STILL HAS *BOTH HANDS!*
WHAT ?!
VWOOOOM

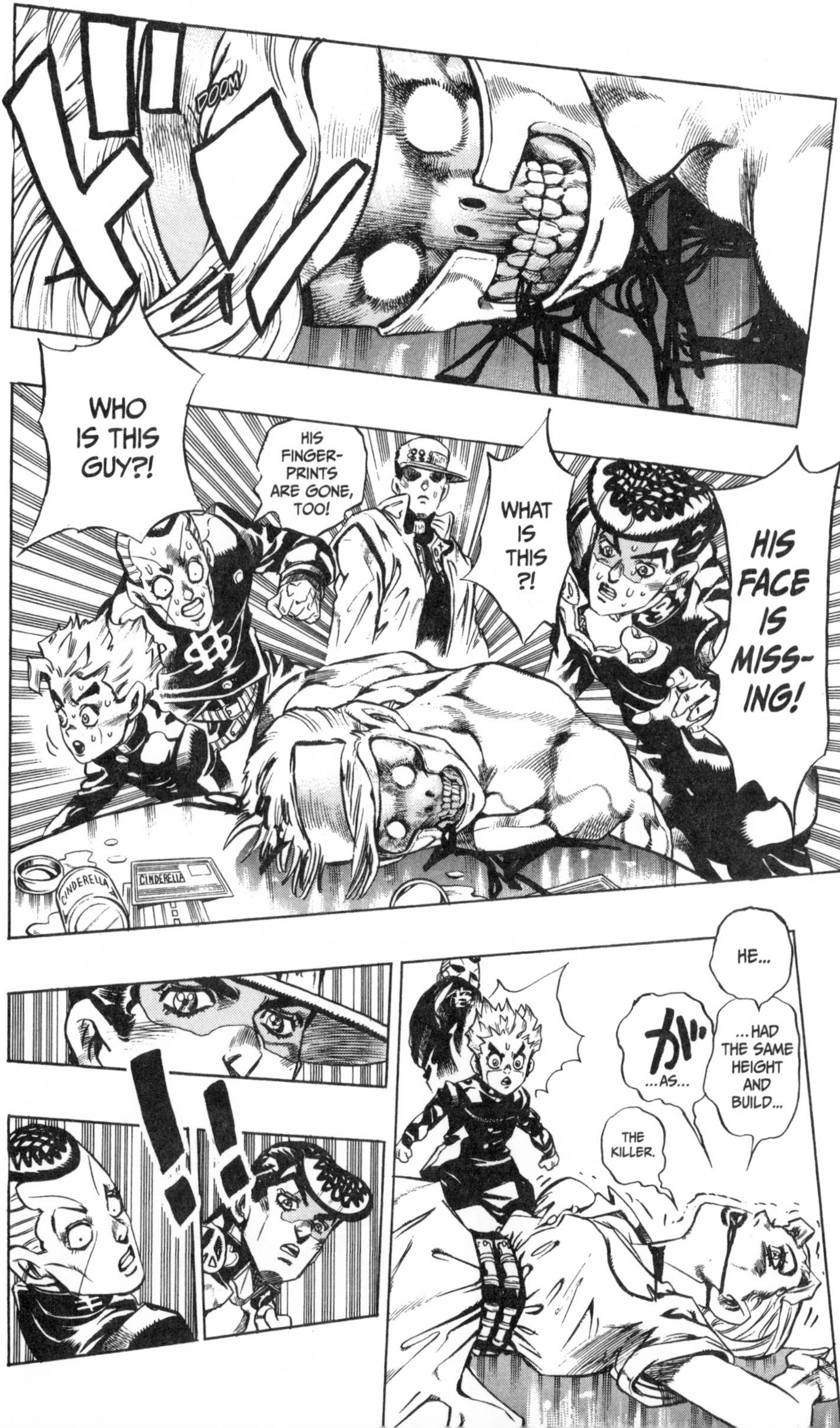

DOOM
HIS FACE IS MISSING!
WHAT IS THIS?!
HIS FINGER-PRINTS ARE GONE, TOO!
WHO IS THIS GUY?!
CINDERELLA
CINDERELLA
HE...
...HAD THE SAME HEIGHT AND BUILD...
が
...AS...
THE KILLER.
!!

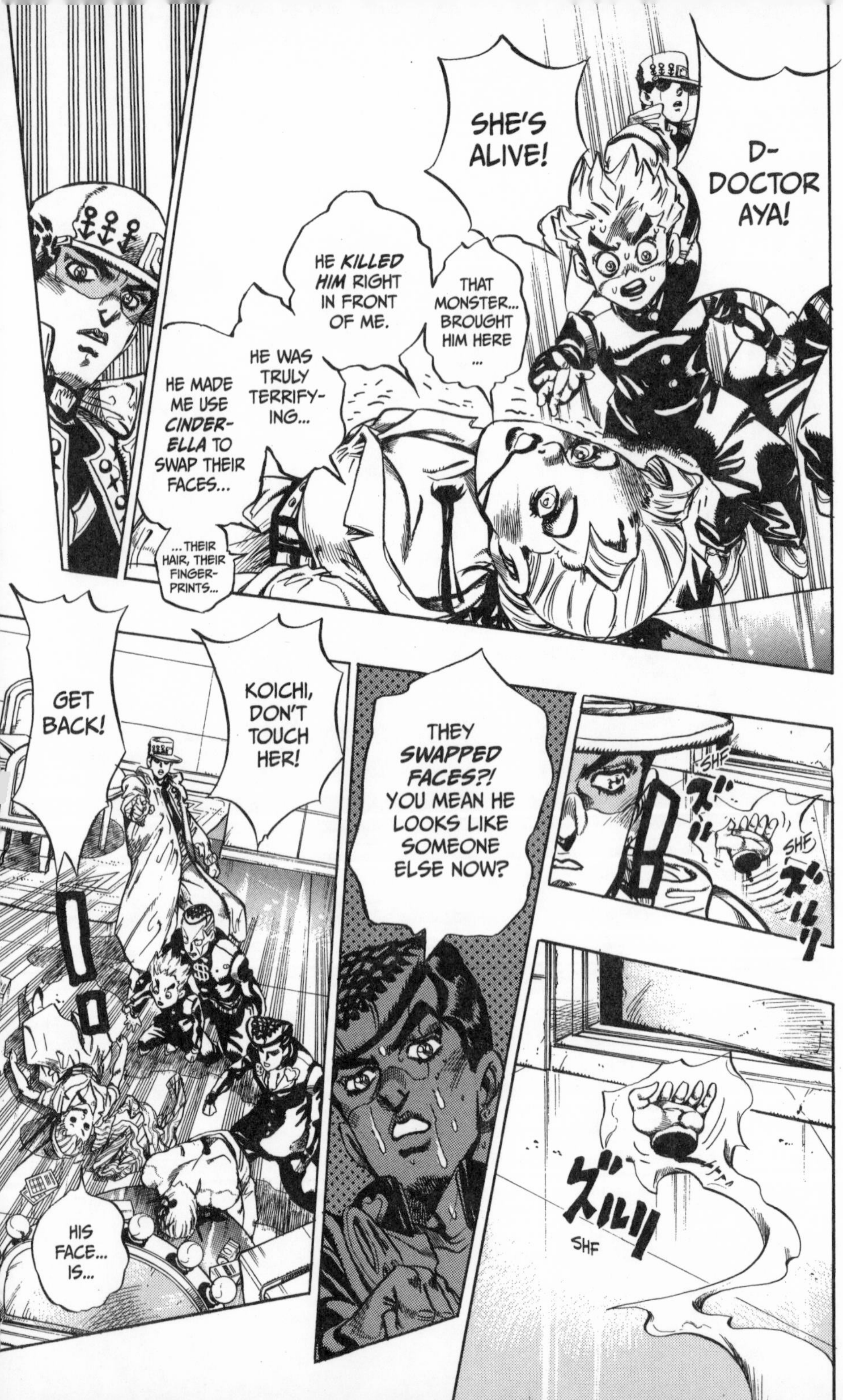
D-DOCTOR AYA!
SHE'S ALIVE!
THAT MONSTER... BROUGHT HIM HERE ...
HE *KILLED HIM* RIGHT IN FRONT OF ME.
HE WAS TRULY TERRIFYING...
HE MADE ME USE *CINDERELLA* TO SWAP THEIR FACES...
...THEIR HAIR, THEIR FINGERPRINTS...
SHF
ズル
SHF
ズルリ
ズルリ
SHF
THEY *SWAPPED FACES?!* YOU MEAN HE LOOKS LIKE SOMEONE ELSE NOW?
KOICHI, DON'T TOUCH HER!
GET BACK!
HIS FACE... IS...

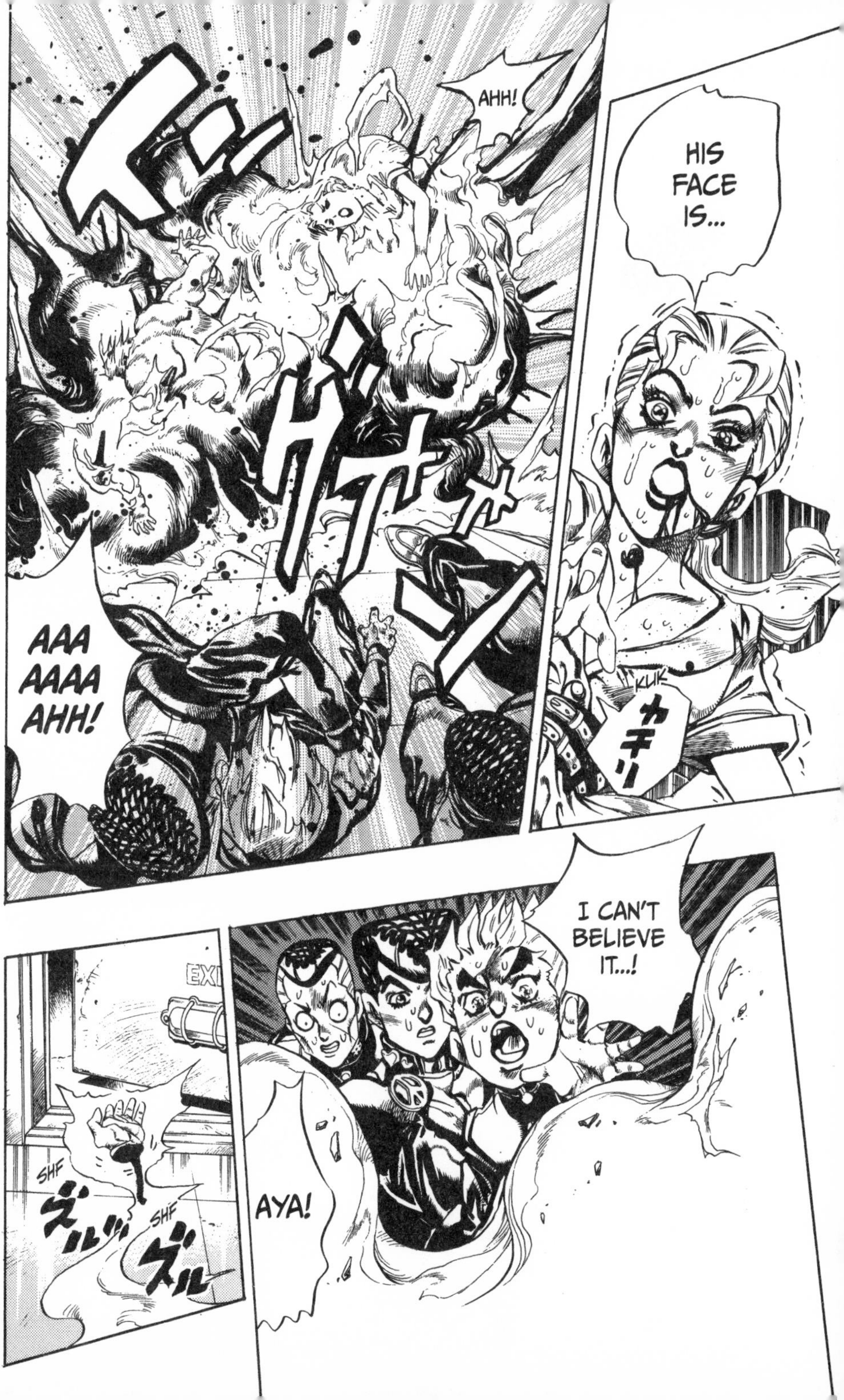
HIS FACE IS...
KUK
カチリ
AHH!
AAA AAAA AHH!
I CAN'T BELIEVE IT...!
AYA!
EXI
SHF
SHF

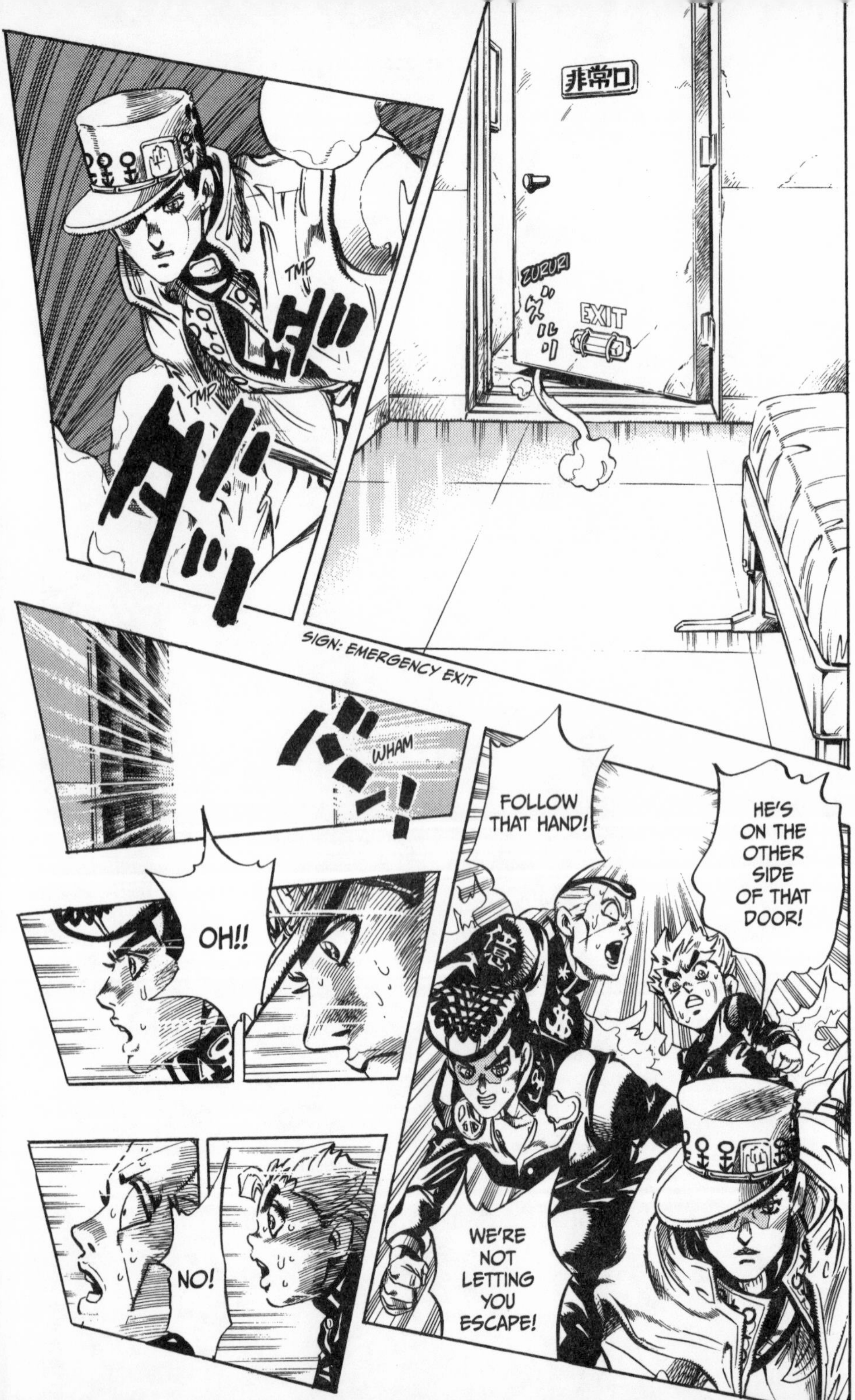

非常口
ZURURI
ズルリ
EXIT
SIGN: EMERGENCY EXIT
TMP
ダッ
TMP
ダッ
HE'S ON THE OTHER SIDE OF THAT DOOR!
FOLLOW THAT HAND!
WE'RE NOT LETTING YOU ESCAPE!
バーン
WHAM
OH!!
NO!

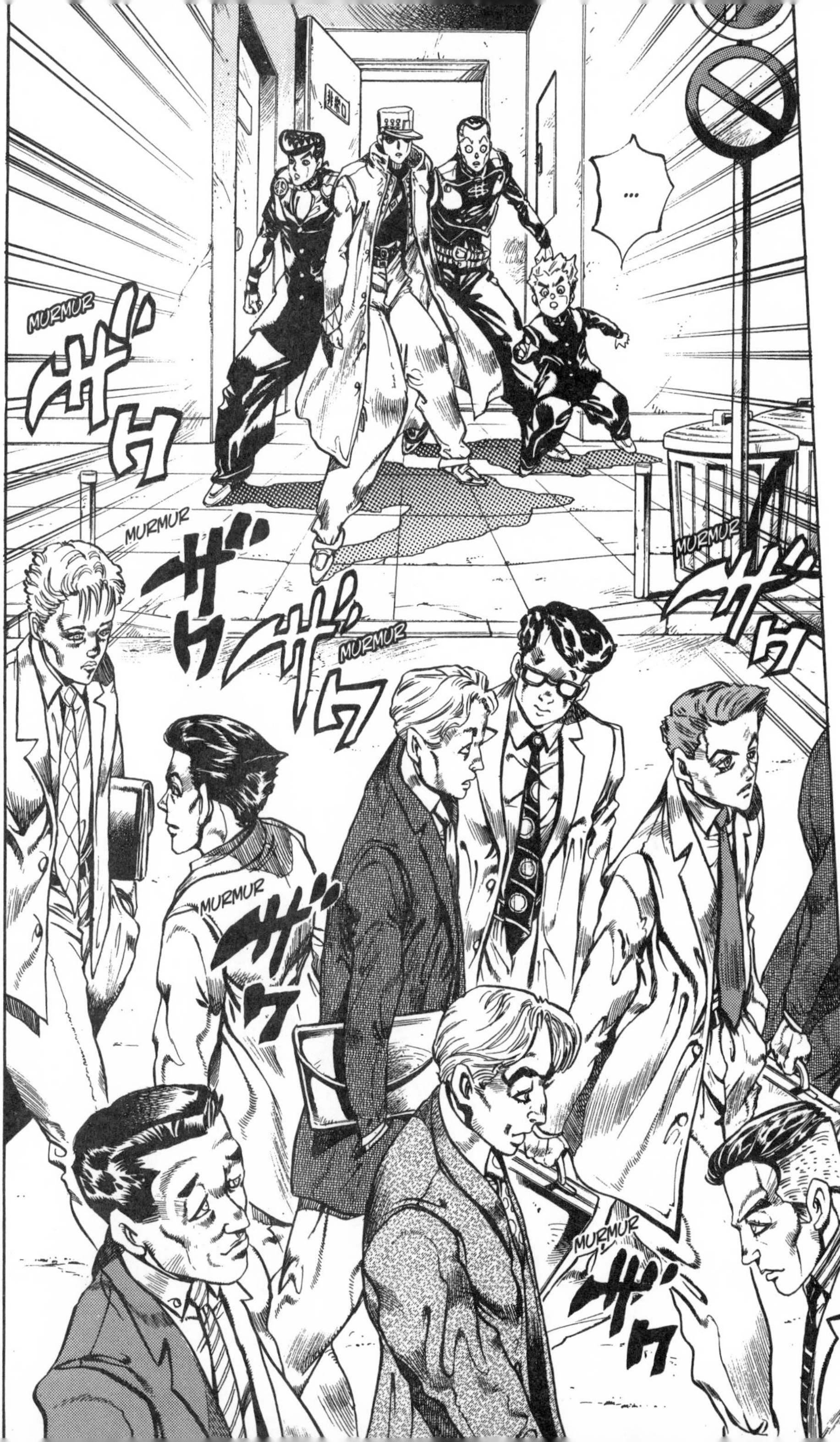

…
MURMUR
ザワ
MURMUR
ザワ
MURMUR
ザワ
MURMUR
ザワ
MURMUR
ザワ
MURMUR
ザワ

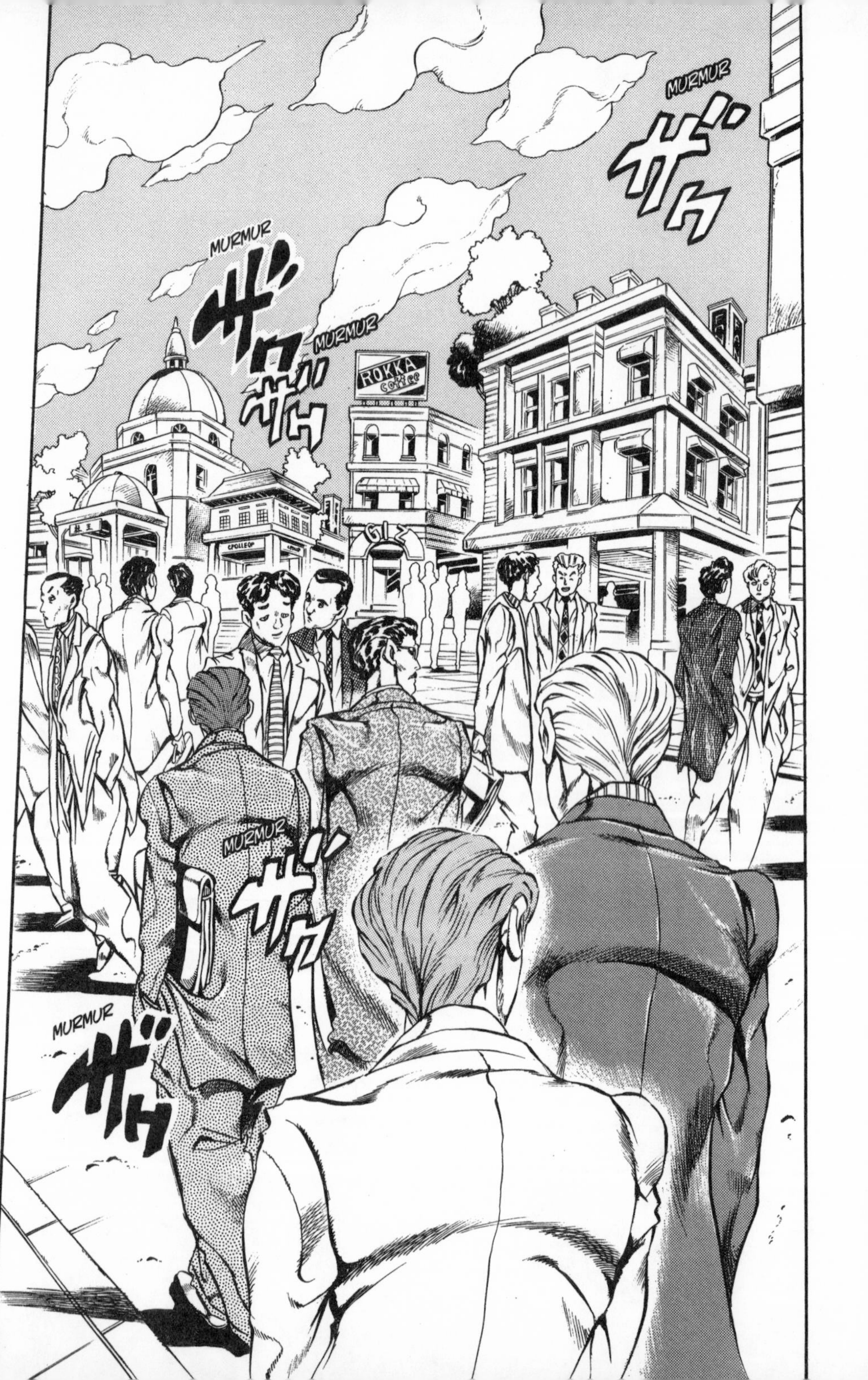
MURMUR
ザワ
MURMUR
ザワ
ROKKA coffee
MURMUR
ザワ
MURMUR
ザワ
MURMUR
ザワ

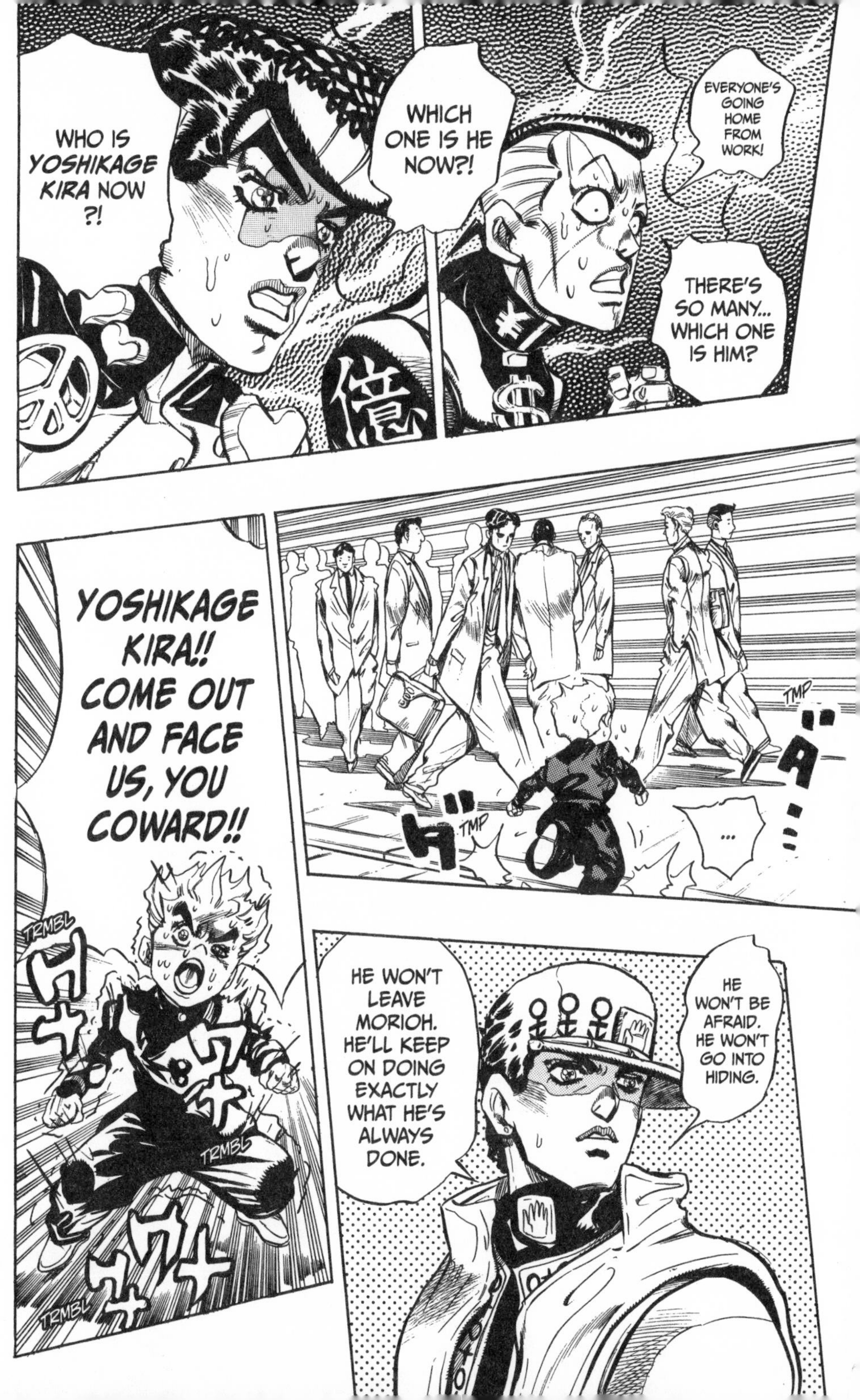
EVERYONE'S GOING HOME FROM WORK!
WHICH ONE IS HE NOW?!
THERE'S SO MANY... WHICH ONE IS HIM?
WHO IS YOSHIKAGE KIRA NOW ?!
TMP
...
TMP
HE WON'T BE AFRAID. HE WON'T GO INTO HIDING.
HE WON'T LEAVE MORIOH. HE'LL KEEP ON DOING EXACTLY WHAT HE'S ALWAYS DONE.
YOSHIKAGE KIRA!! COME OUT AND FACE US, YOU COWARD!!
TRMBL
TRMBL
TRMBL

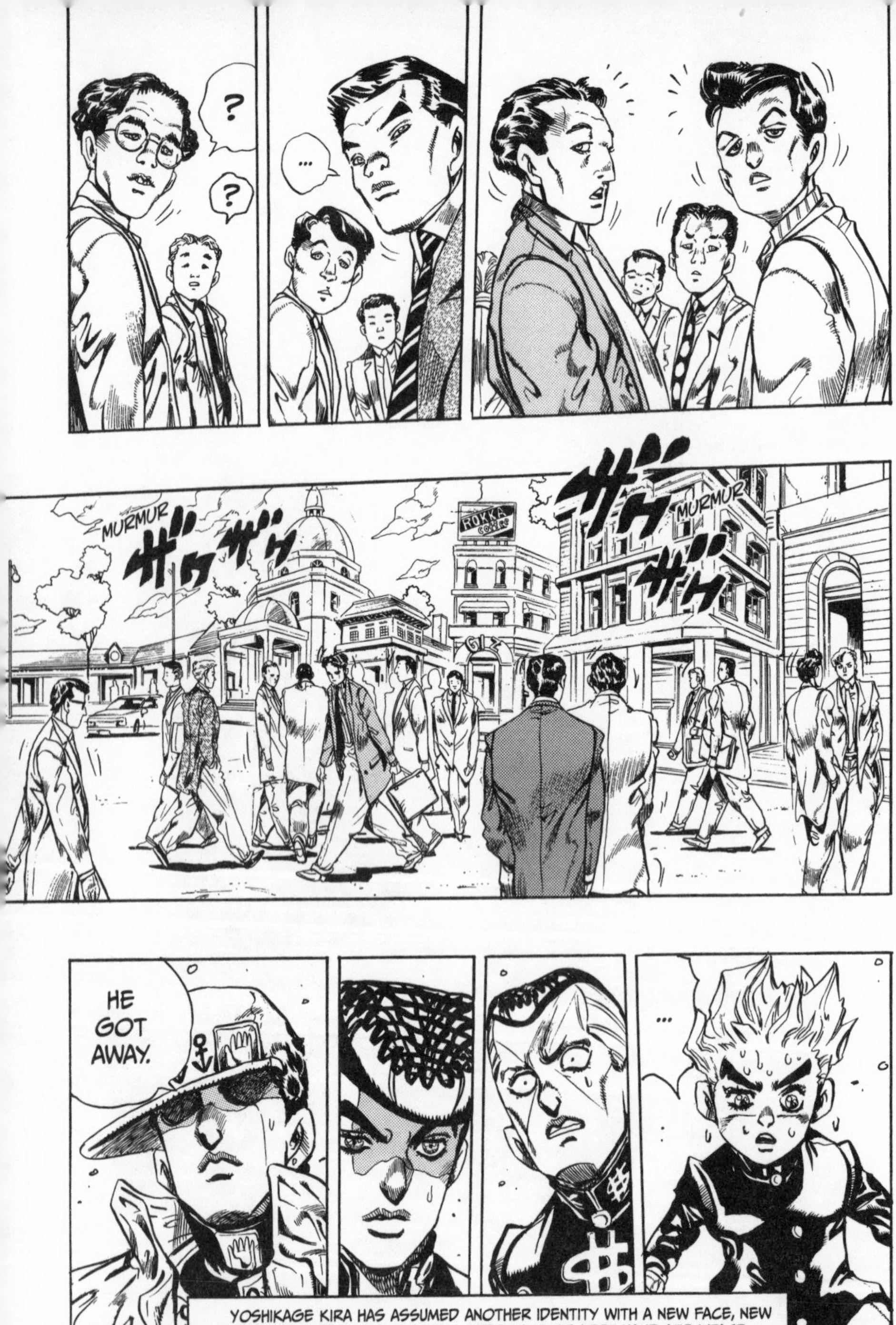
...
?
?
ザワ
MURMUR
ザワ
ザワ
MURMUR
ザワ
ザワ
ROKKA
...
HE GOT AWAY.
YOSHIKAGE KIRA HAS ASSUMED ANOTHER IDENTITY WITH A NEW FACE, NEW NAME AND NEW HOME. ***DEADLY QUEEN*** AND HIS LEFT HAND ARE INTACT.
AYA TSUJI—DECEASED.
TO BE CONTINUED...

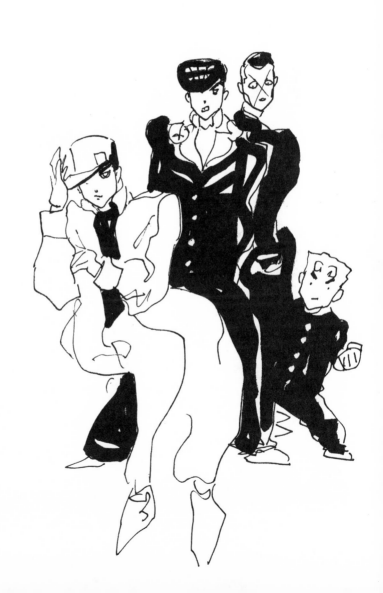

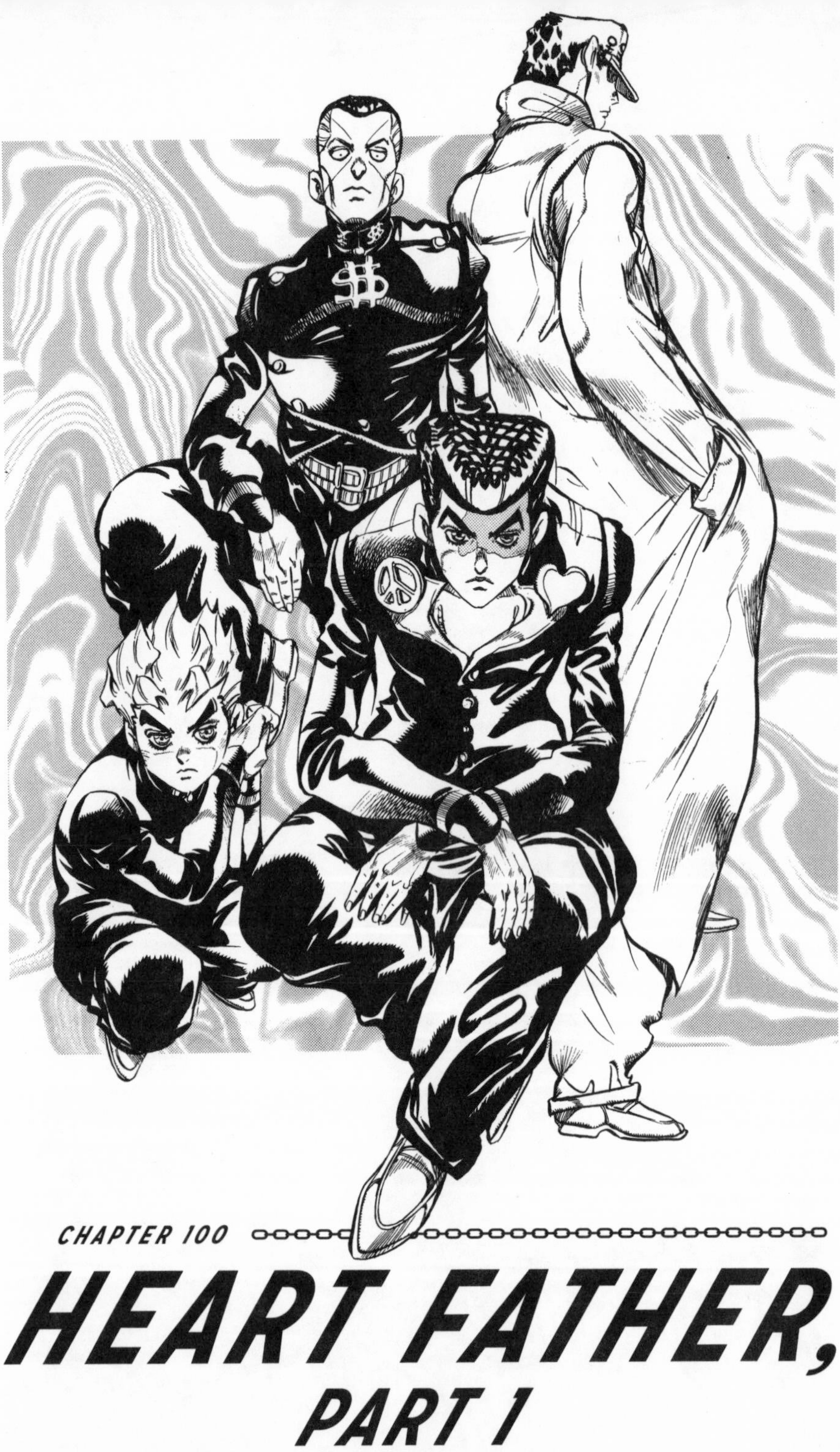

CHAPTER 100

HEART FATHER, PART 1

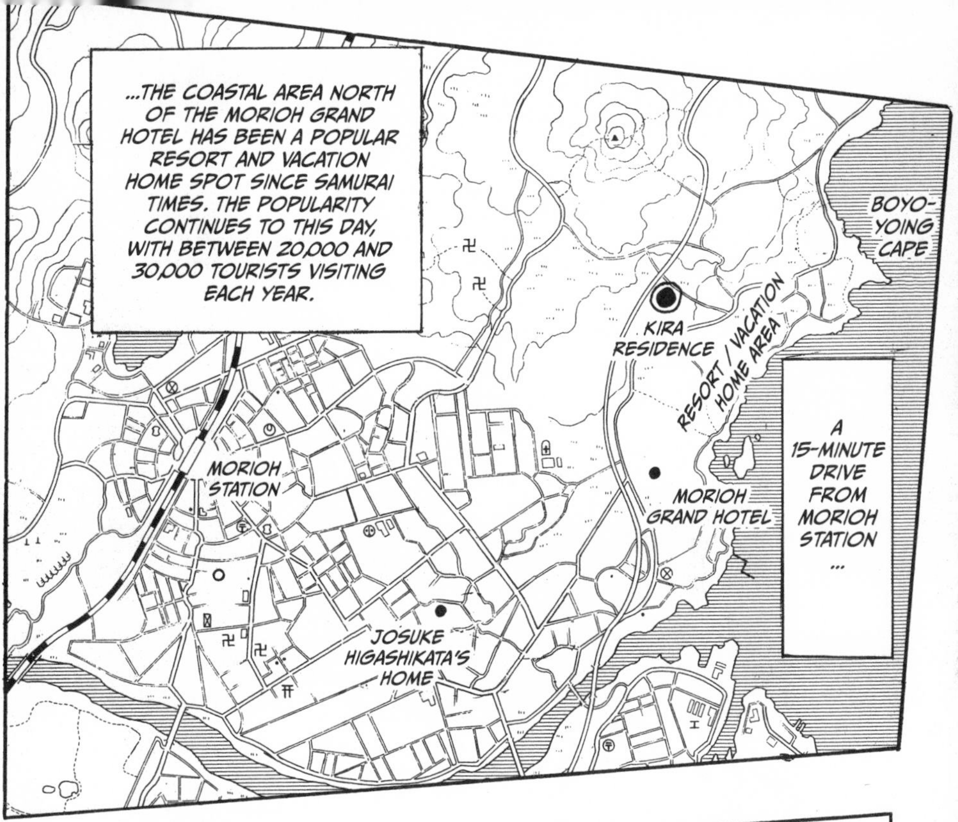
BOYO-YOING CAPE
A 15-MINUTE DRIVE FROM MORIOH STATION ...
KIRA RESIDENCE
RESORT / VACATION HOME AREA
MORIOH GRAND HOTEL
...THE COASTAL AREA NORTH OF THE MORIOH GRAND HOTEL HAS BEEN A POPULAR RESORT AND VACATION HOME SPOT SINCE SAMURAI TIMES. THE POPULARITY CONTINUES TO THIS DAY, WITH BETWEEN 20,000 AND 30,000 TOURISTS VISITING EACH YEAR.
MORIOH STATION
JOSUKE HIGASHIKATA'S HOME

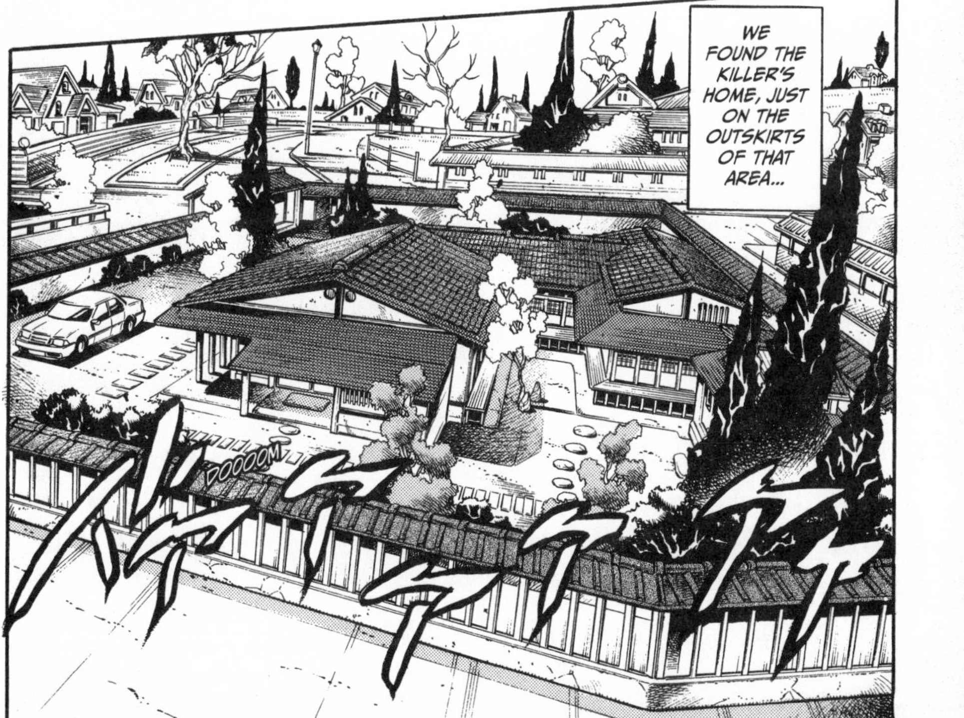
WE FOUND THE KILLER'S HOME, JUST ON THE OUTSKIRTS OF THAT AREA...
DOOOOM

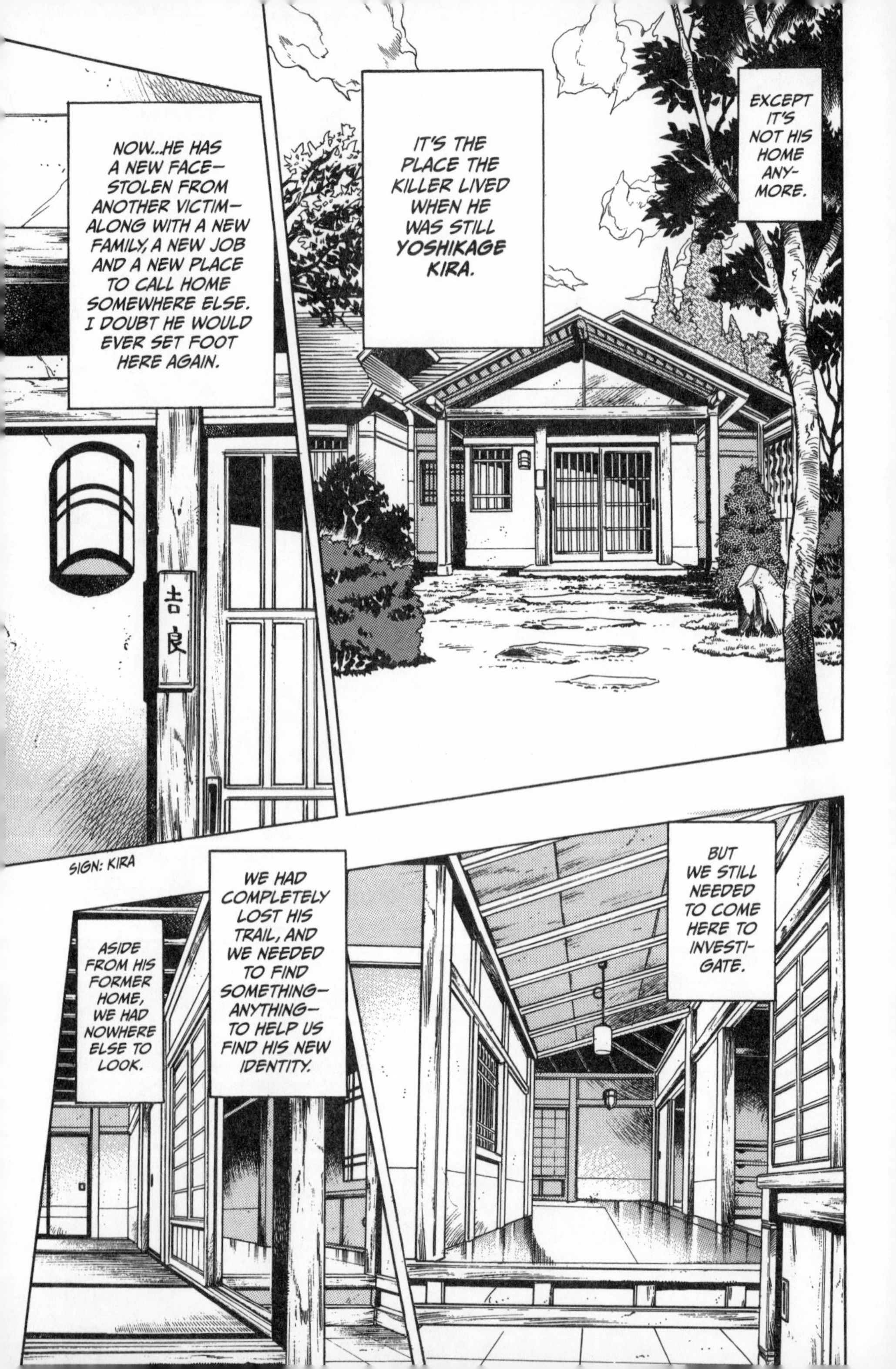
IT'S THE PLACE THE KILLER LIVED WHEN HE WAS STILL YOSHIKAGE KIRA.
EXCEPT IT'S NOT HIS HOME ANYMORE.
NOW...HE HAS A NEW FACE—STOLEN FROM ANOTHER VICTIM—ALONG WITH A NEW FAMILY, A NEW JOB AND A NEW PLACE TO CALL HOME SOMEWHERE ELSE. I DOUBT HE WOULD EVER SET FOOT HERE AGAIN.
吉良
SIGN: KIRA
BUT WE STILL NEEDED TO COME HERE TO INVESTIGATE.
WE HAD COMPLETELY LOST HIS TRAIL, AND WE NEEDED TO FIND SOMETHING—ANYTHING—TO HELP US FIND HIS NEW IDENTITY.
ASIDE FROM HIS FORMER HOME, WE HAD NOWHERE ELSE TO LOOK.

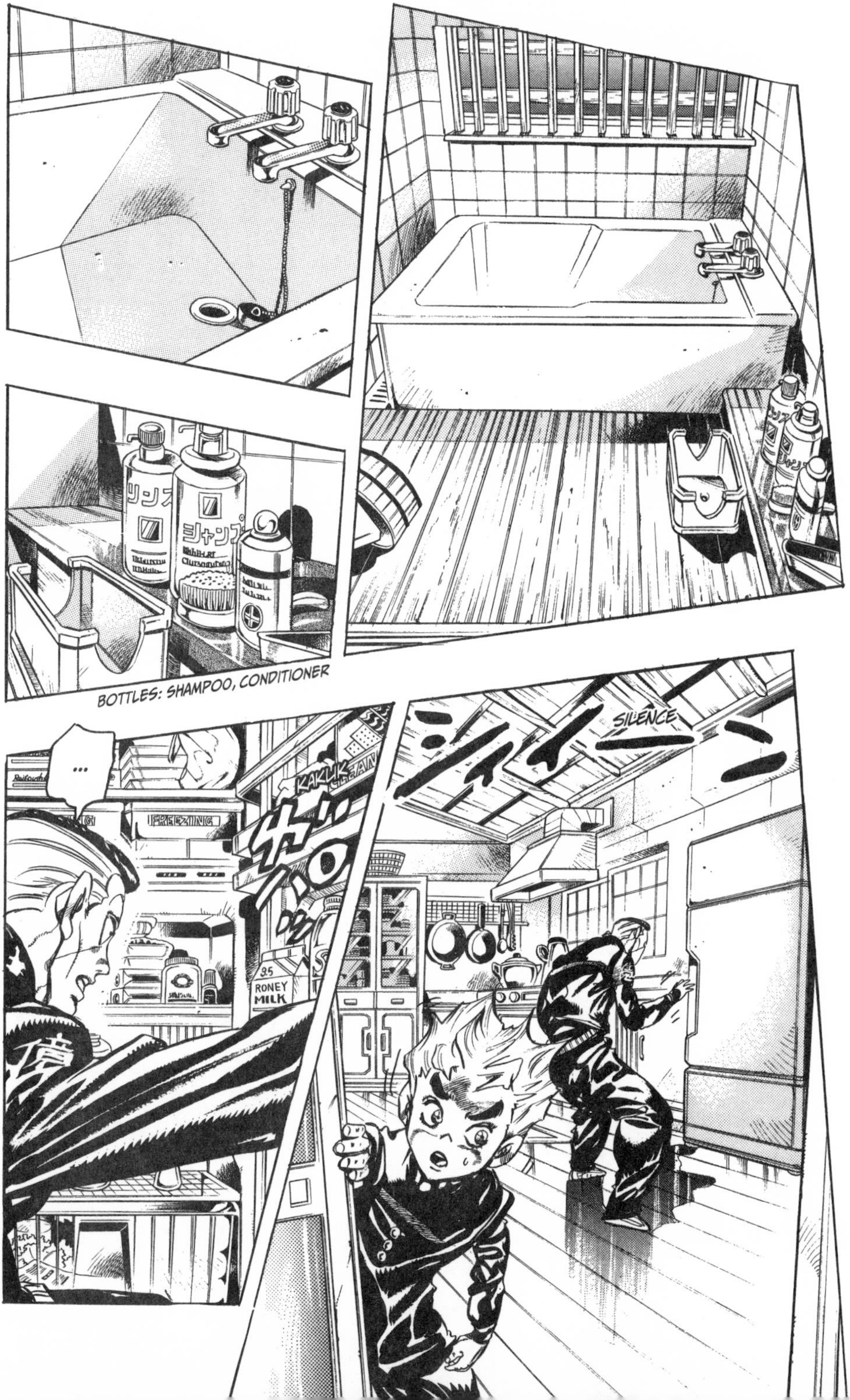
リンス
シャンプー
BOTTLES: SHAMPOO, CONDITIONER
SILENCE
...
KAKUK
FREEZING
RONEY
MILK

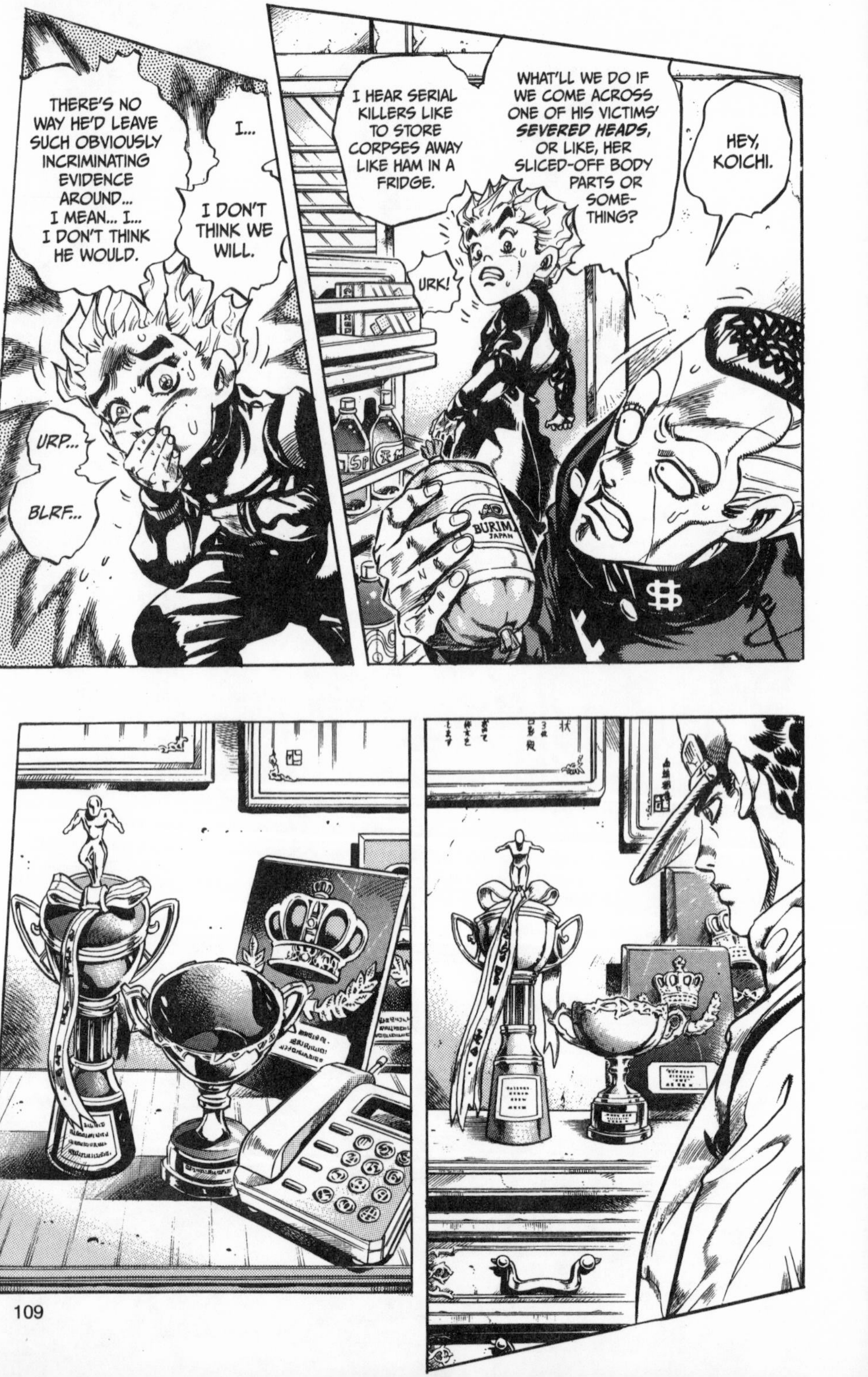
HEY, KOICHI.
WHAT'LL WE DO IF WE COME ACROSS ONE OF HIS VICTIMS' ***SEVERED HEADS***, OR LIKE, HER SLICED-OFF BODY PARTS OR SOME-THING?
I HEAR SERIAL KILLERS LIKE TO STORE CORPSES AWAY LIKE HAM IN A FRIDGE.
URK!
I...
I DON'T THINK WE WILL.
THERE'S NO WAY HE'D LEAVE SUCH OBVIOUSLY INCRIMINATING EVIDENCE AROUND... I MEAN... I... I DON'T THINK HE WOULD.
URP...
BLRF...
BURIMA
JAPAN

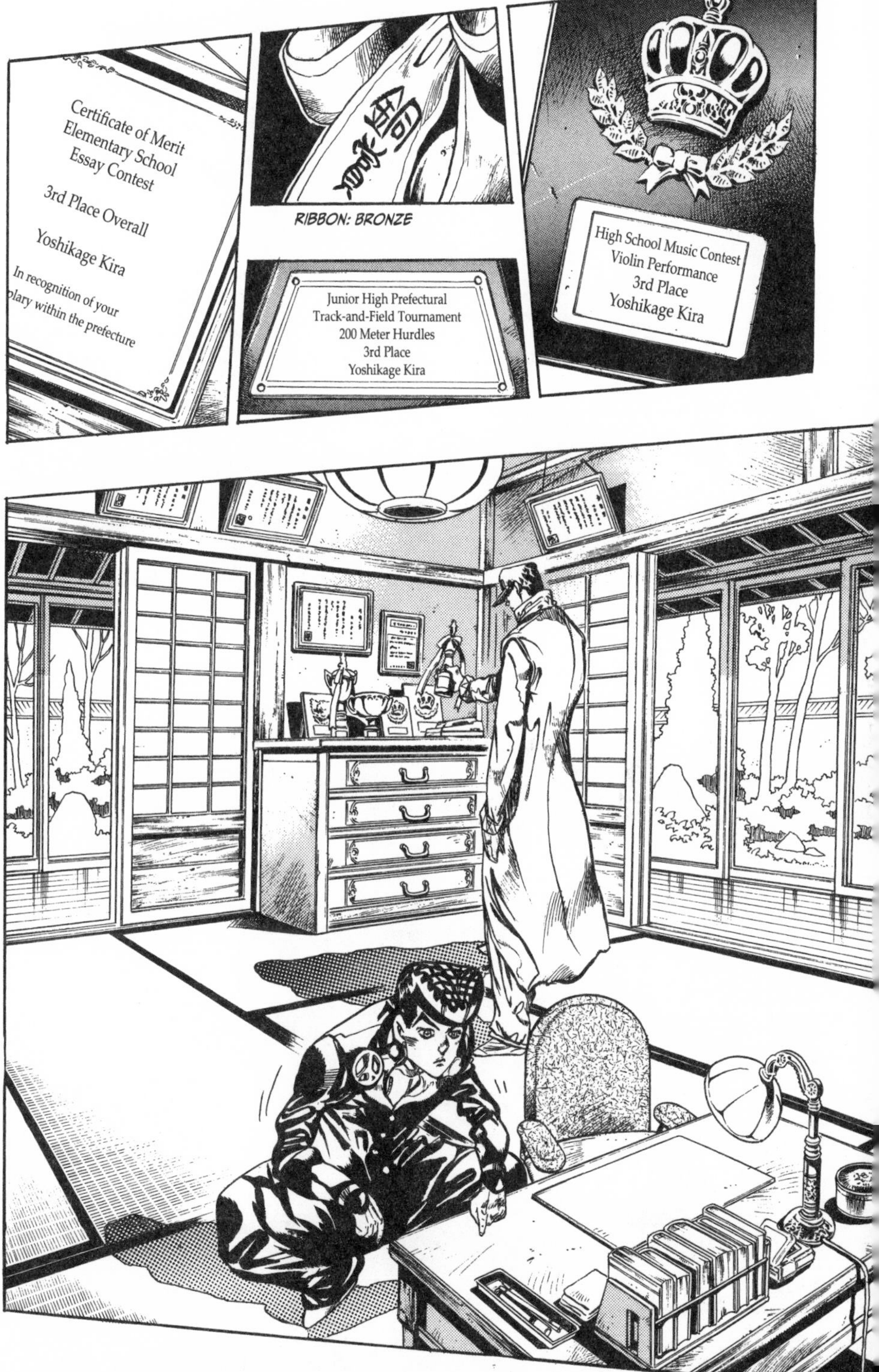
High School Music Contest
Violin Performance
3rd Place
Yoshikage Kira
RIBBON: BRONZE
Junior High Prefectural
Track-and-Field Tournament
200 Meter Hurdles
3rd Place
Yoshikage Kira
Certificate of Merit
Elementary School
Essay Contest
3rd Place Overall
Yoshikage Kira
In recognition of your
plary within the prefecture

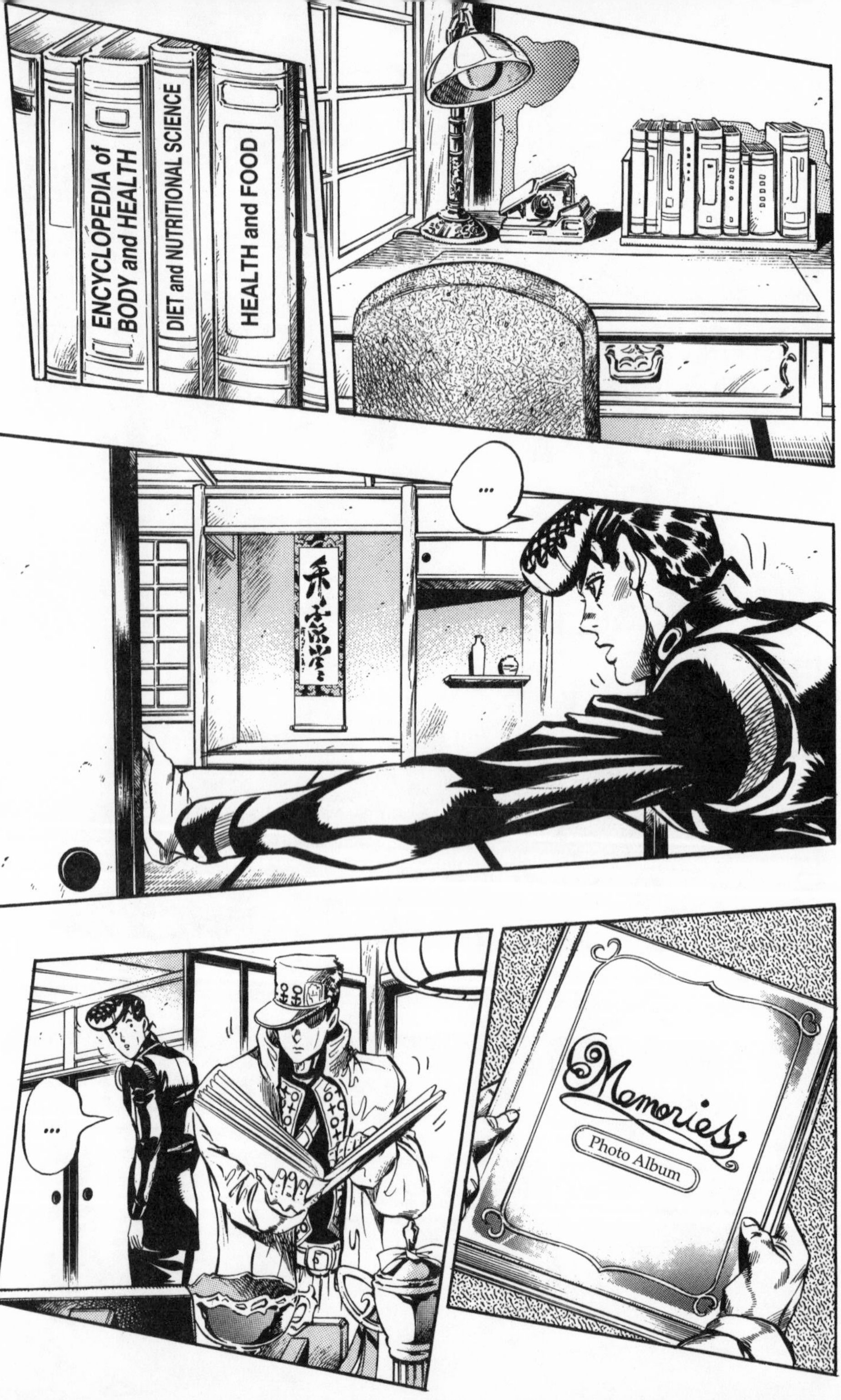
ENCYCLOPEDIA of BODY and HEALTH
DIET and NUTRITIONAL SCIENCE
HEALTH and FOOD
...
Memories
Photo Album
...

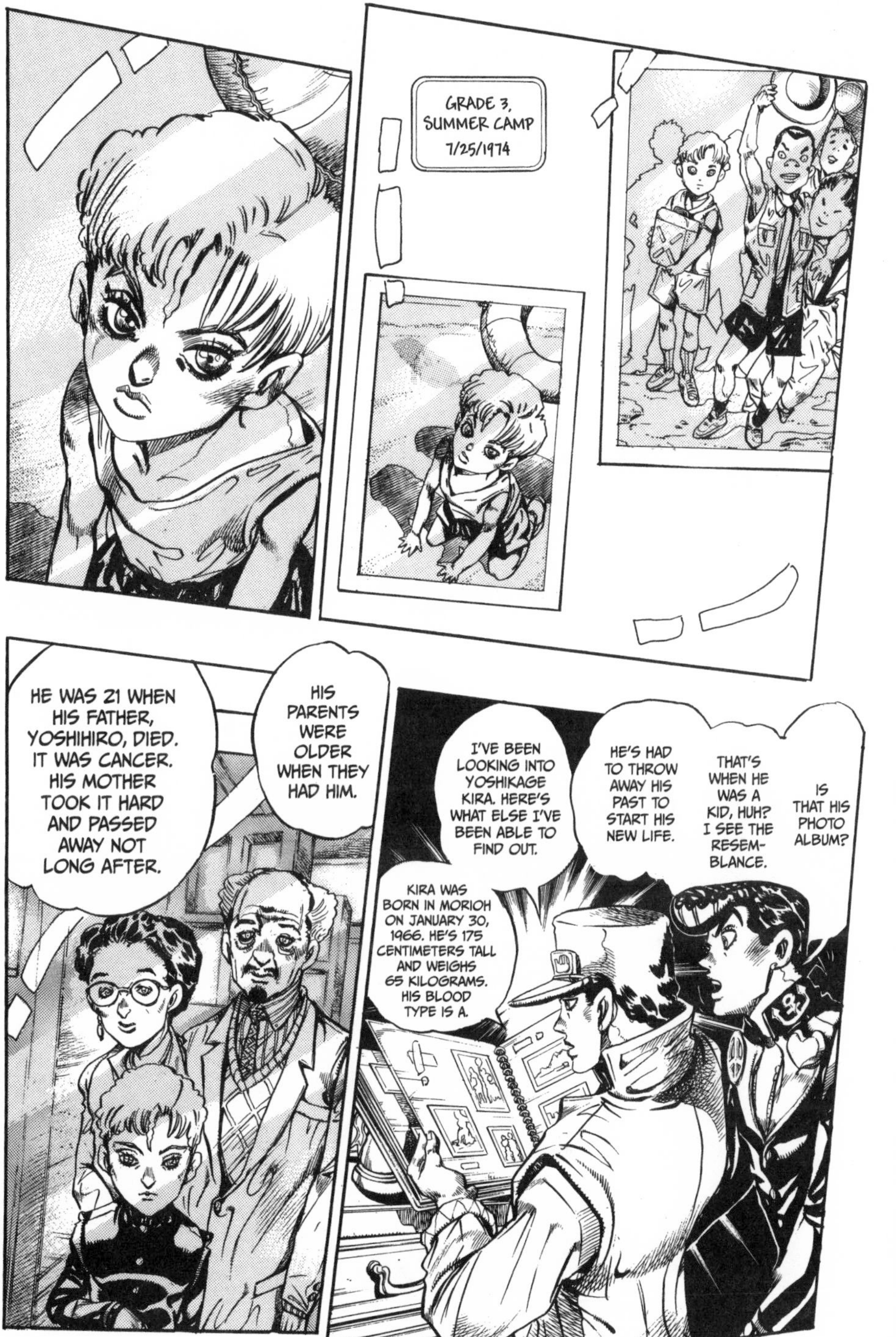
GRADE 3, SUMMER CAMP 7/25/1974
IS THAT HIS PHOTO ALBUM?
THAT'S WHEN HE WAS A KID, HUH? I SEE THE RESEMBLANCE.
HE'S HAD TO THROW AWAY HIS PAST TO START HIS NEW LIFE.
I'VE BEEN LOOKING INTO YOSHIKAGE KIRA. HERE'S WHAT ELSE I'VE BEEN ABLE TO FIND OUT.
KIRA WAS BORN IN MORIOH ON JANUARY 30, 1966. HE'S 175 CENTIMETERS TALL AND WEIGHS 65 KILOGRAMS. HIS BLOOD TYPE IS A.
HIS PARENTS WERE OLDER WHEN THEY HAD HIM.
HE WAS 21 WHEN HIS FATHER, YOSHIHIRO, DIED. IT WAS CANCER. HIS MOTHER TOOK IT HARD AND PASSED AWAY NOT LONG AFTER.

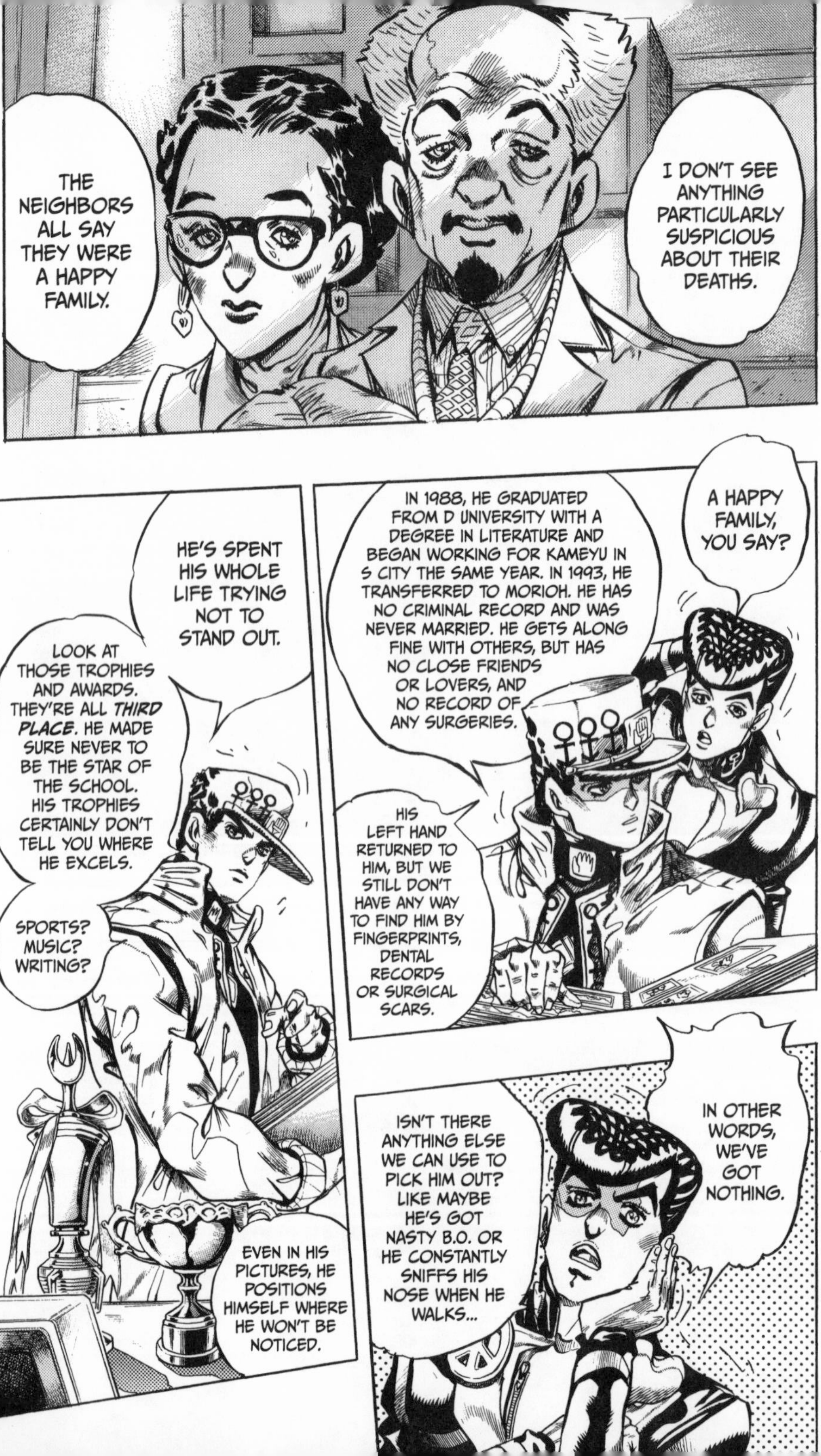
I DON'T SEE ANYTHING PARTICULARLY SUSPICIOUS ABOUT THEIR DEATHS.
THE NEIGHBORS ALL SAY THEY WERE A HAPPY FAMILY.
A HAPPY FAMILY, YOU SAY?
IN 1988, HE GRADUATED FROM D UNIVERSITY WITH A DEGREE IN LITERATURE AND BEGAN WORKING FOR KAMEYU IN S CITY THE SAME YEAR. IN 1993, HE TRANSFERRED TO MORIOH. HE HAS NO CRIMINAL RECORD AND WAS NEVER MARRIED. HE GETS ALONG FINE WITH OTHERS, BUT HAS NO CLOSE FRIENDS OR LOVERS, AND NO RECORD OF ANY SURGERIES.
HIS LEFT HAND RETURNED TO HIM, BUT WE STILL DON'T HAVE ANY WAY TO FIND HIM BY FINGERPRINTS, DENTAL RECORDS OR SURGICAL SCARS.
IN OTHER WORDS, WE'VE GOT NOTHING.
ISN'T THERE ANYTHING ELSE WE CAN USE TO PICK HIM OUT? LIKE MAYBE HE'S GOT NASTY B.O. OR HE CONSTANTLY SNIFFS HIS NOSE WHEN HE WALKS...
HE'S SPENT HIS WHOLE LIFE TRYING NOT TO STAND OUT.
LOOK AT THOSE TROPHIES AND AWARDS. THEY'RE ALL *THIRD PLACE*. HE MADE SURE NEVER TO BE THE STAR OF THE SCHOOL. HIS TROPHIES CERTAINLY DON'T TELL YOU WHERE HE EXCELS.
SPORTS? MUSIC? WRITING?
EVEN IN HIS PICTURES, HE POSITIONS HIMSELF WHERE HE WON'T BE NOTICED.

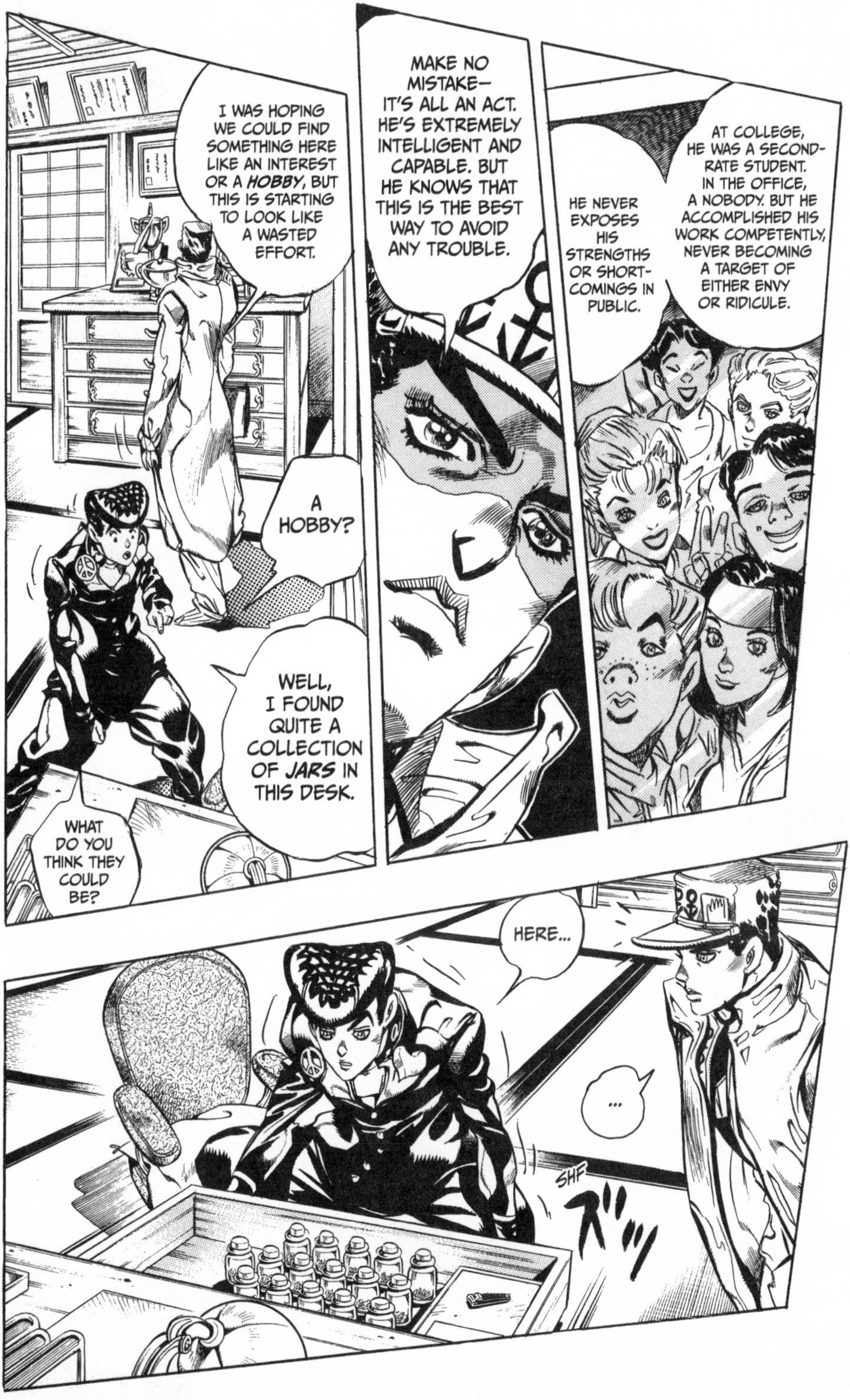
AT COLLEGE, HE WAS A SECOND-RATE STUDENT. IN THE OFFICE, A NOBODY. BUT HE ACCOMPLISHED HIS WORK COMPETENTLY, NEVER BECOMING A TARGET OF EITHER ENVY OR RIDICULE.
HE NEVER EXPOSES HIS STRENGTHS OR SHORT-COMINGS IN PUBLIC.
MAKE NO MISTAKE— IT'S ALL AN ACT. HE'S EXTREMELY INTELLIGENT AND CAPABLE. BUT HE KNOWS THAT THIS IS THE BEST WAY TO AVOID ANY TROUBLE.
I WAS HOPING WE COULD FIND SOMETHING HERE LIKE AN INTEREST OR A *HOBBY*, BUT THIS IS STARTING TO LOOK LIKE A WASTED EFFORT.
A HOBBY?
WELL, I FOUND QUITE A COLLECTION OF *JARS* IN THIS DESK.
WHAT DO YOU THINK THEY COULD BE?
HERE...
...
SHF

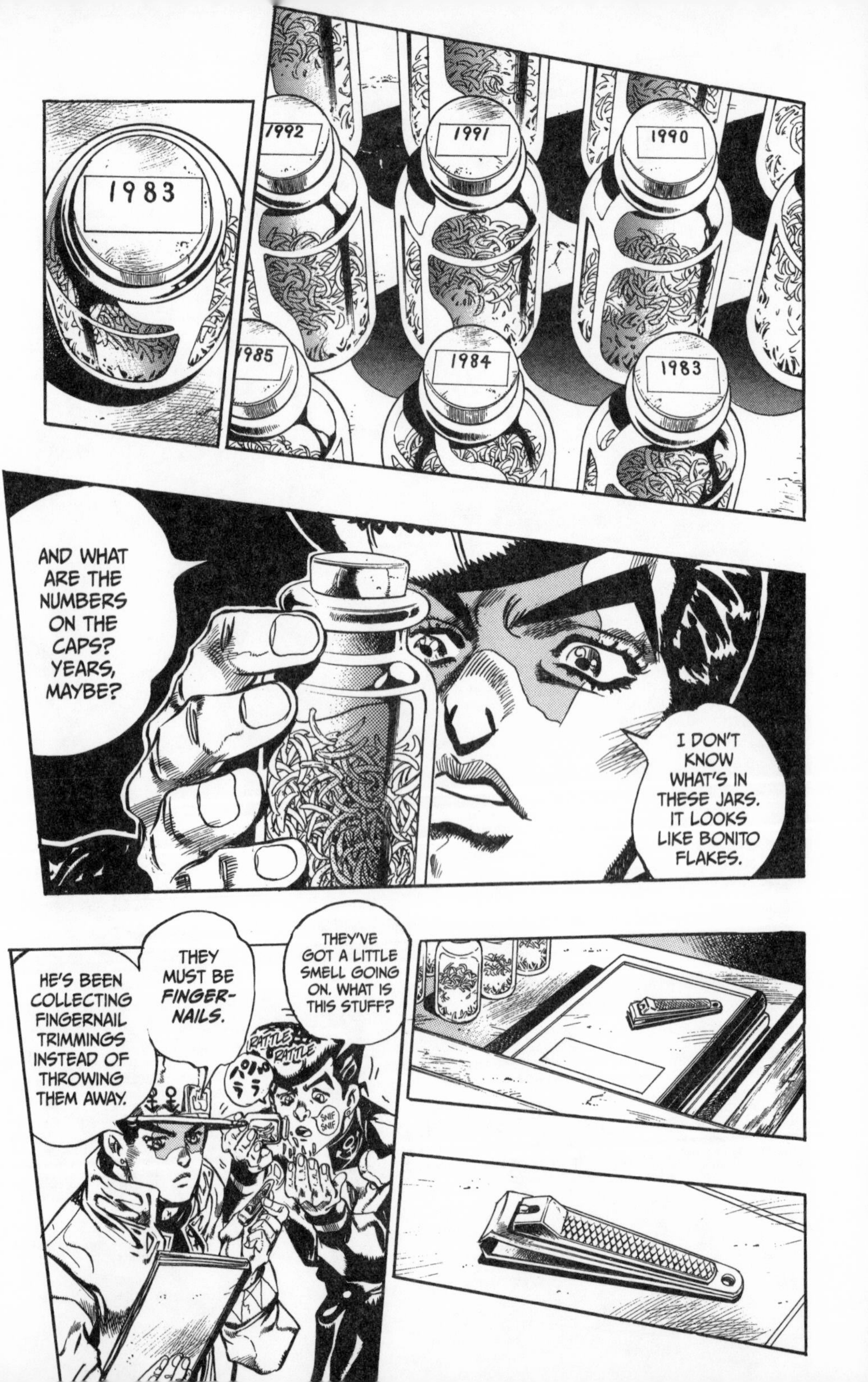
1992
1991
1990
1985
1984
1983
1983
I DON'T KNOW WHAT'S IN THESE JARS. IT LOOKS LIKE BONITO FLAKES.
AND WHAT ARE THE NUMBERS ON THE CAPS? YEARS, MAYBE?
THEY'VE GOT A LITTLE SMELL GOING ON. WHAT IS THIS STUFF?
RATTLE RATTLE
パラ パラ
SNIF SNIF
THEY MUST BE *FINGER-NAILS.*
HE'S BEEN COLLECTING FINGERNAIL TRIMMINGS INSTEAD OF THROWING THEM AWAY.

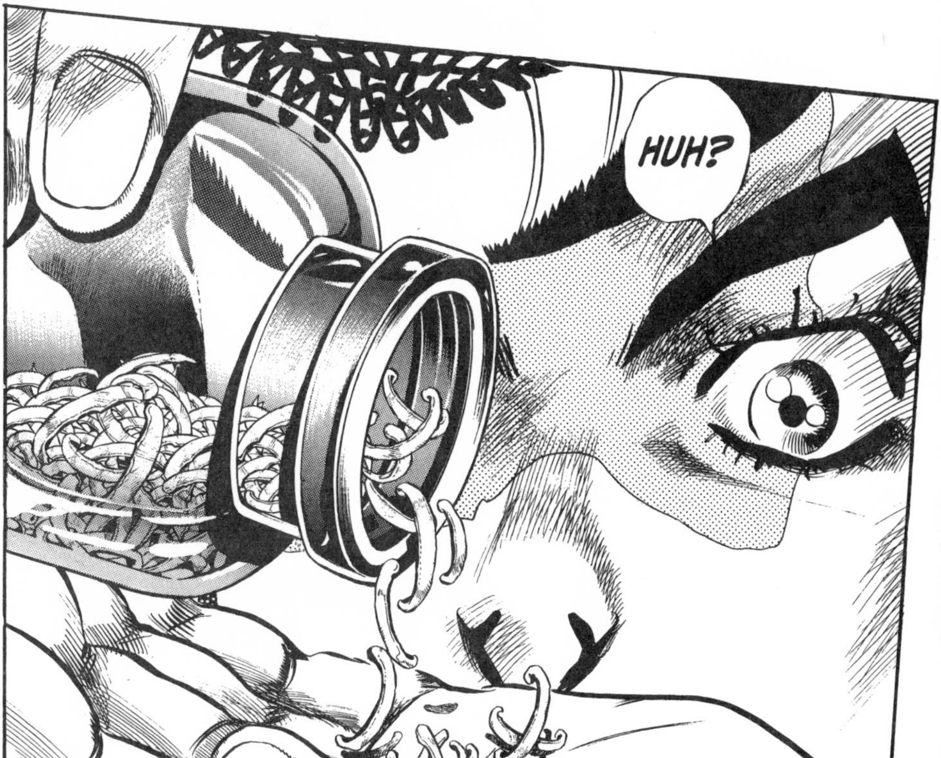
HUH?
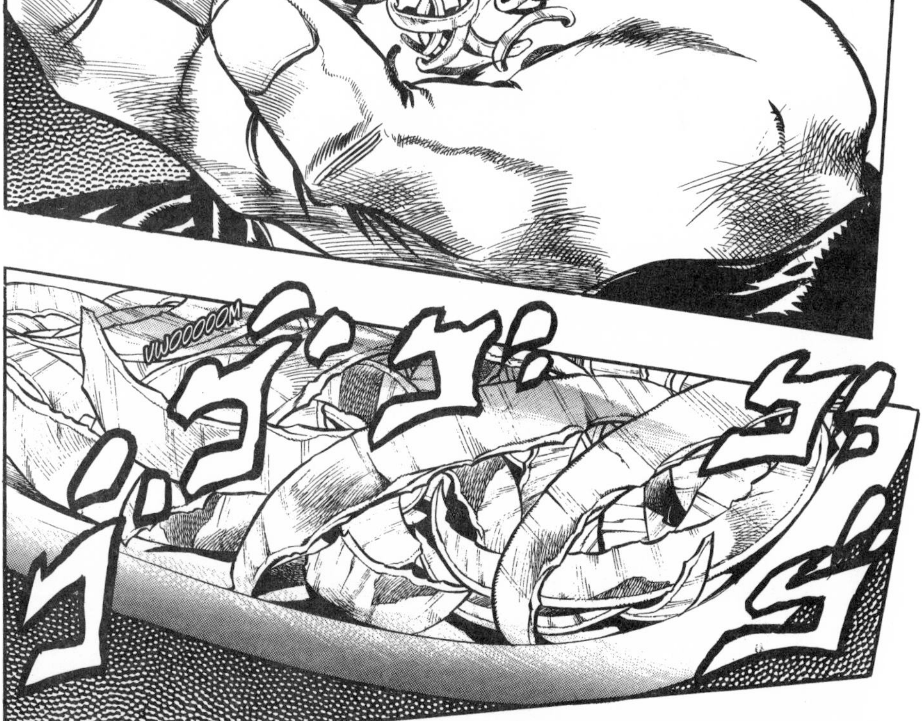
VWOOOOOM

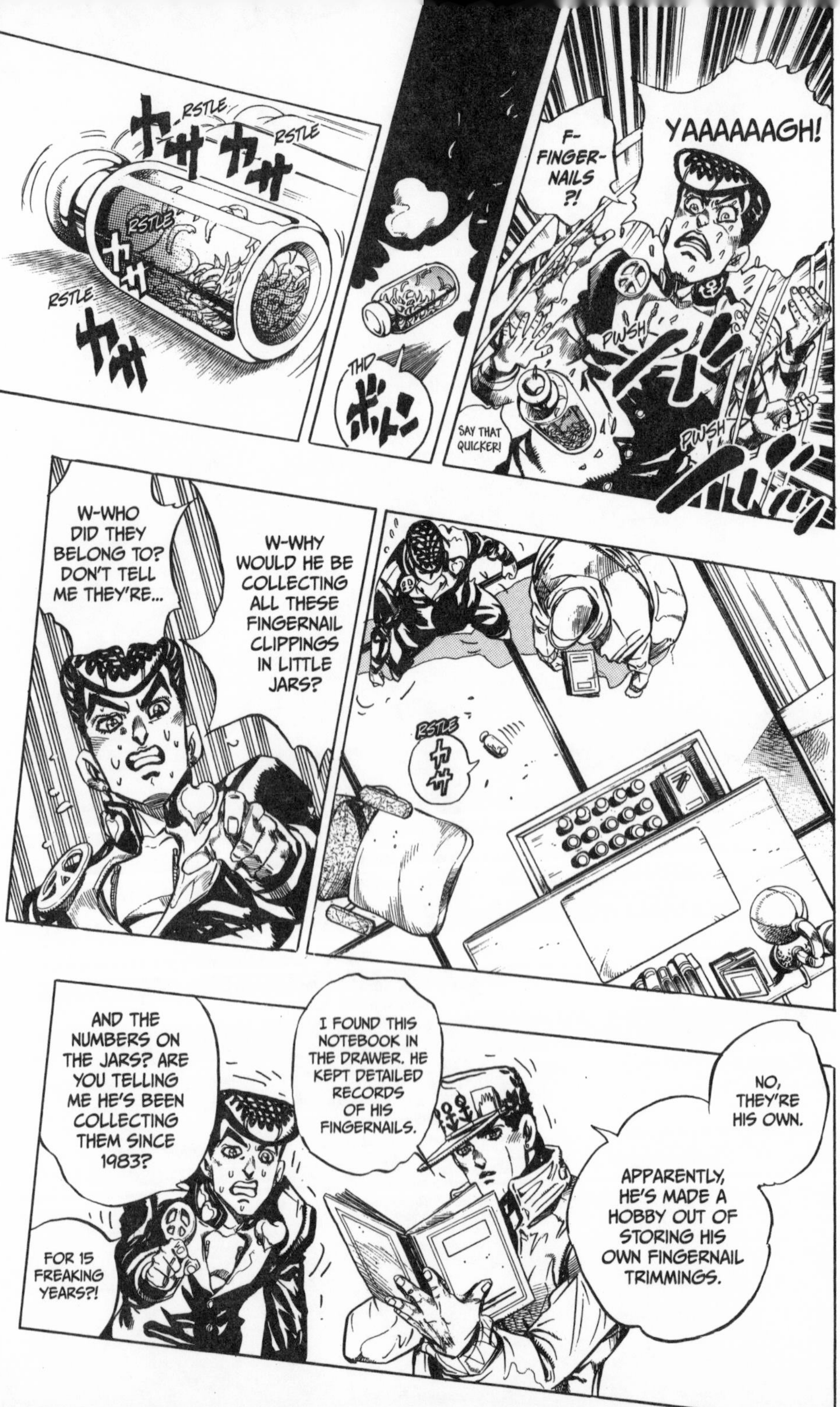
YAAAAAAGH!
F-FINGER-NAILS ?!
PWSH
PWSH
SAY THAT QUICKER!
THD
ボトン
RSTLE
カサ
RSTLE
カサ
RSTLE
カサ
RSTLE
カサ
RSTLE
カサ
W-WHY WOULD HE BE COLLECTING ALL THESE FINGERNAIL CLIPPINGS IN LITTLE JARS?
W-WHO DID THEY BELONG TO? DON'T TELL ME THEY'RE...
NO, THEY'RE HIS OWN.
APPARENTLY, HE'S MADE A HOBBY OUT OF STORING HIS OWN FINGERNAIL TRIMMINGS.
I FOUND THIS NOTEBOOK IN THE DRAWER. HE KEPT DETAILED RECORDS OF HIS FINGERNAILS.
AND THE NUMBERS ON THE JARS? ARE YOU TELLING ME HE'S BEEN COLLECTING THEM SINCE 1983?
FOR 15 FREAKING YEARS?!

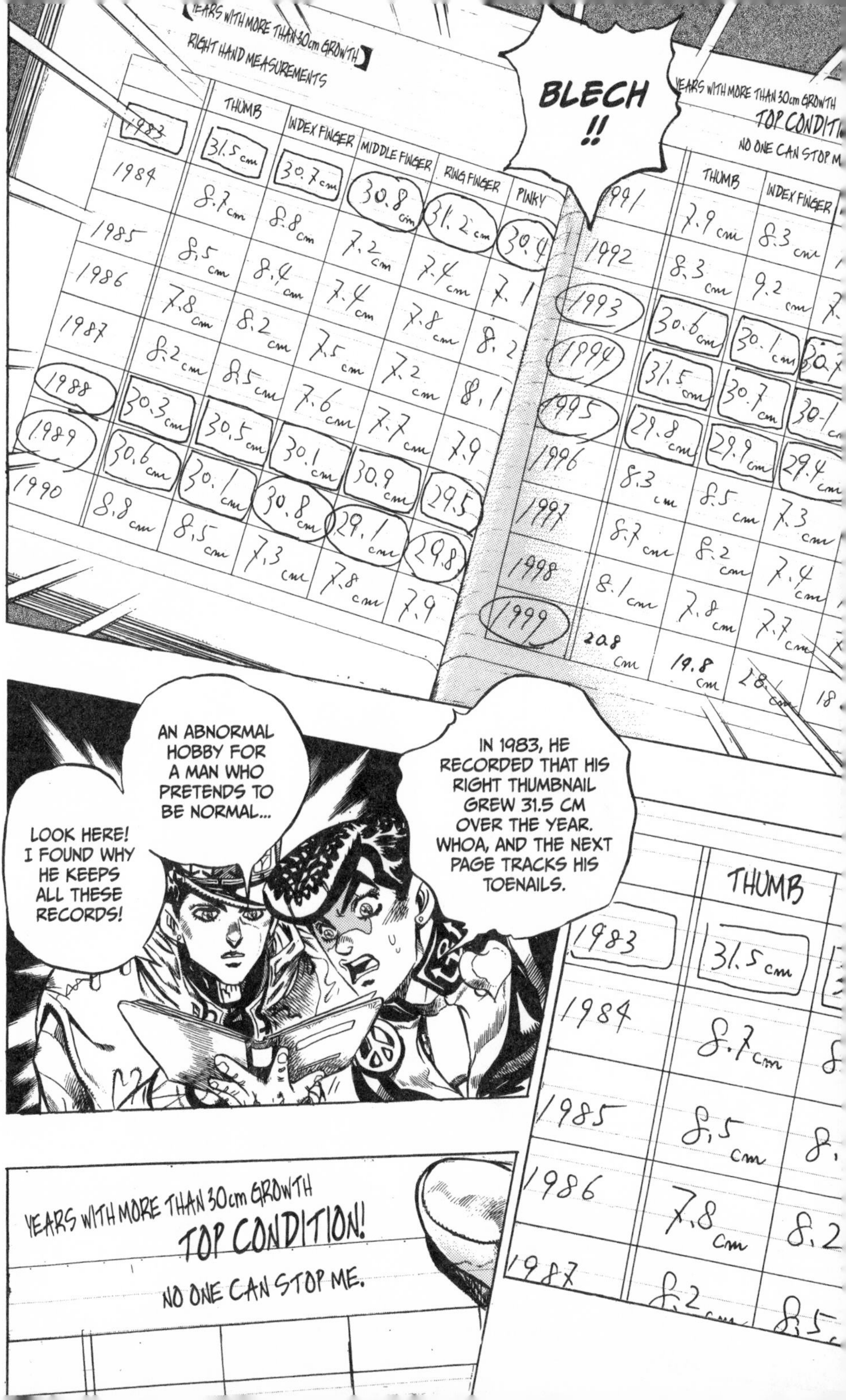

BLECH!!
YEARS WITH MORE THAN 30cm GROWTH
RIGHT HAND MEASUREMENTS
THUMB
INDEX FINGER
MIDDLE FINGER
RING FINGER
PINKY
YEARS WITH MORE THAN 30cm GROWTH
TOP CONDITI
NO ONE CAN STOP M
IN 1983, HE RECORDED THAT HIS RIGHT THUMBNAIL GREW 31.5 CM OVER THE YEAR. WHOA, AND THE NEXT PAGE TRACKS HIS TOENAILS.
AN ABNORMAL HOBBY FOR A MAN WHO PRETENDS TO BE NORMAL...
LOOK HERE! I FOUND WHY HE KEEPS ALL THESE RECORDS!
THUMB
YEARS WITH MORE THAN 30cm GROWTH
TOP CONDITION!
NO ONE CAN STOP ME.

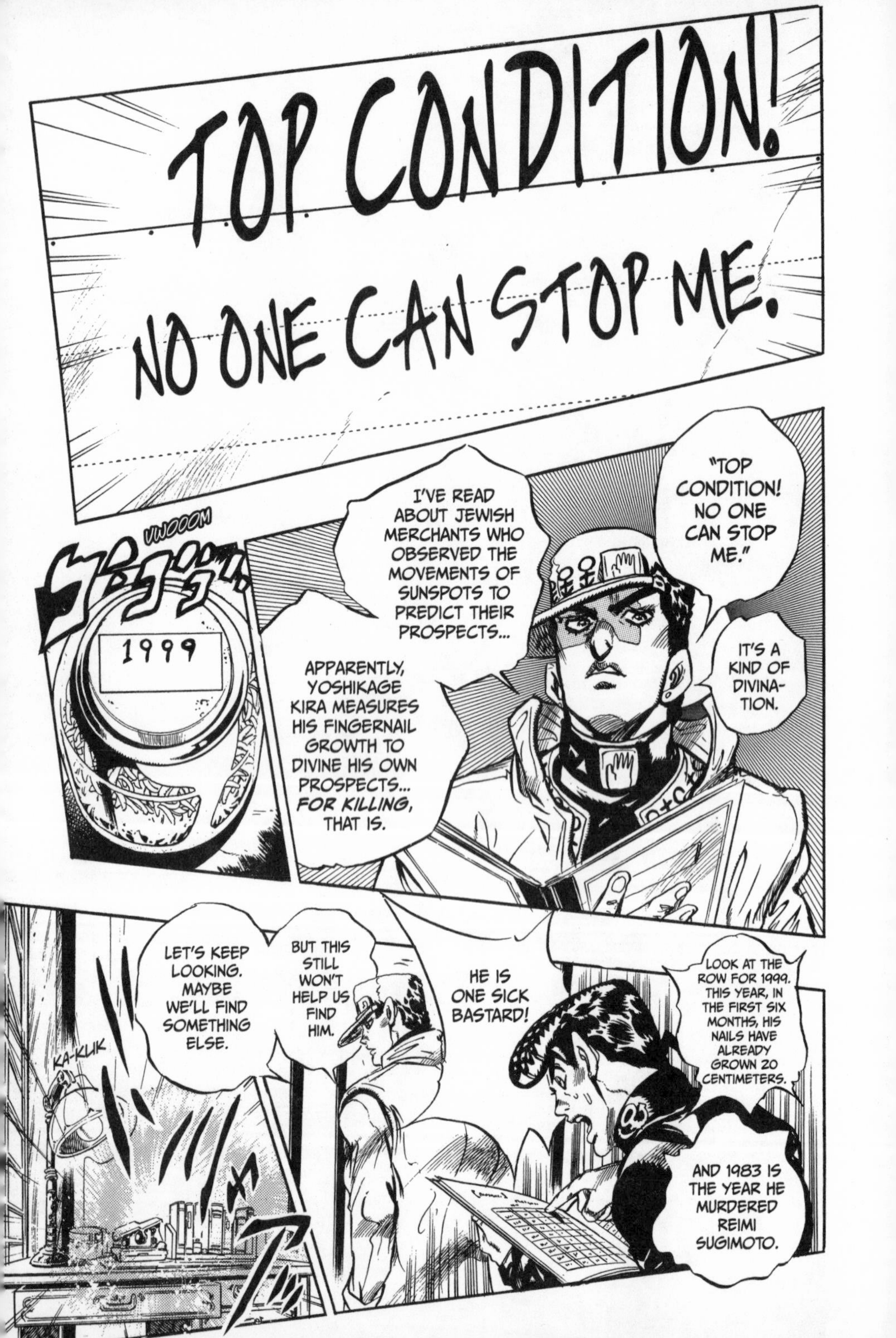
TOP CONDITION!
NO ONE CAN STOP ME.
"TOP CONDITION! NO ONE CAN STOP ME."
IT'S A KIND OF DIVINATION.
I'VE READ ABOUT JEWISH MERCHANTS WHO OBSERVED THE MOVEMENTS OF SUNSPOTS TO PREDICT THEIR PROSPECTS...
APPARENTLY, YOSHIKAGE KIRA MEASURES HIS FINGERNAIL GROWTH TO DIVINE HIS OWN PROSPECTS... *FOR KILLING*, THAT IS.
VWOOOM
1999
LOOK AT THE ROW FOR 1999. THIS YEAR, IN THE FIRST SIX MONTHS, HIS NAILS HAVE ALREADY GROWN 20 CENTIMETERS.
AND 1983 IS THE YEAR HE MURDERED REIMI SUGIMOTO.
HE IS ONE SICK BASTARD!
BUT THIS STILL WON'T HELP US FIND HIM.
LET'S KEEP LOOKING. MAYBE WE'LL FIND SOMETHING ELSE.
KA-KUK

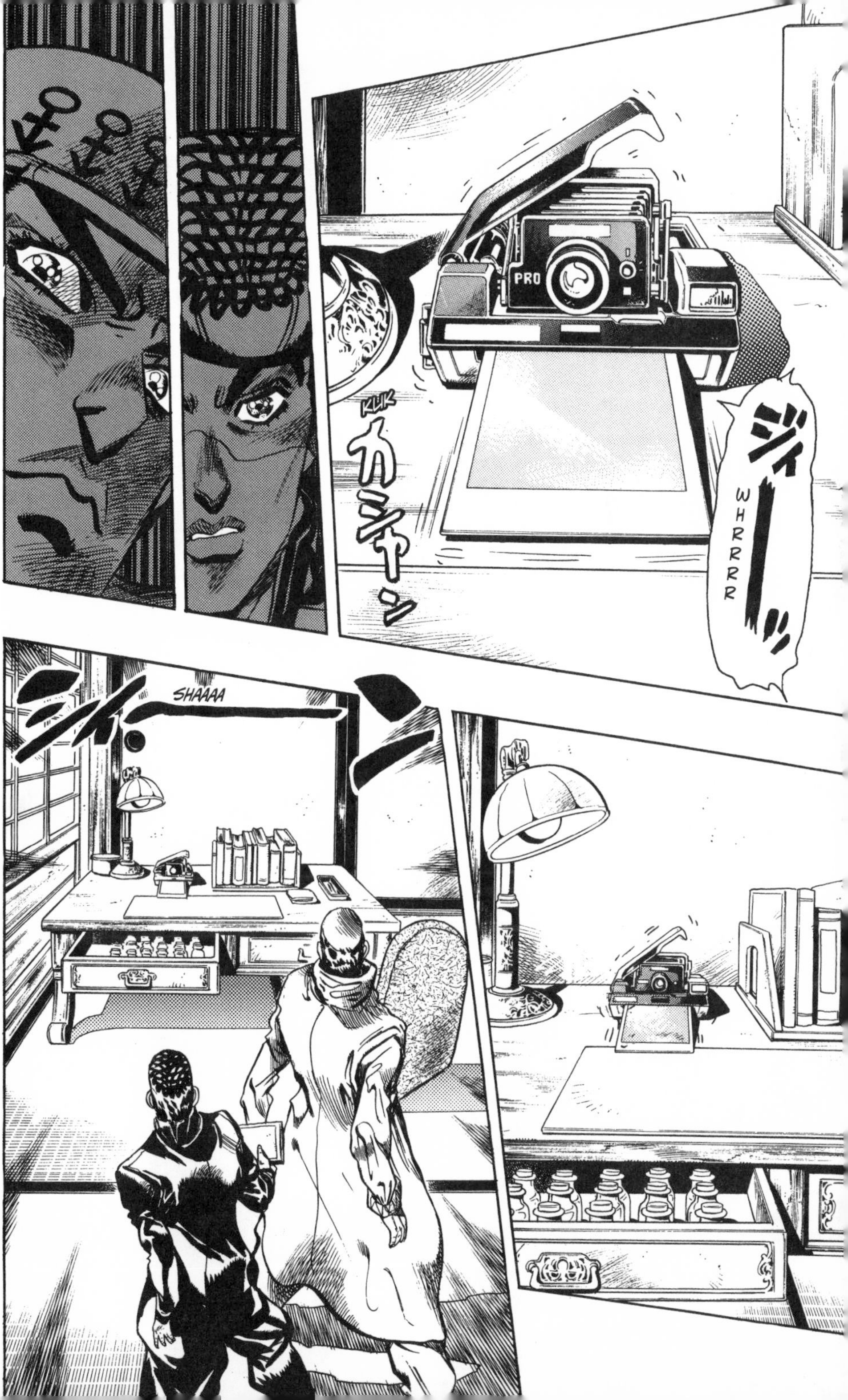
ジィーーッ
WHRRRR
KUK
カシャーン
シィーーン
SHAAAA

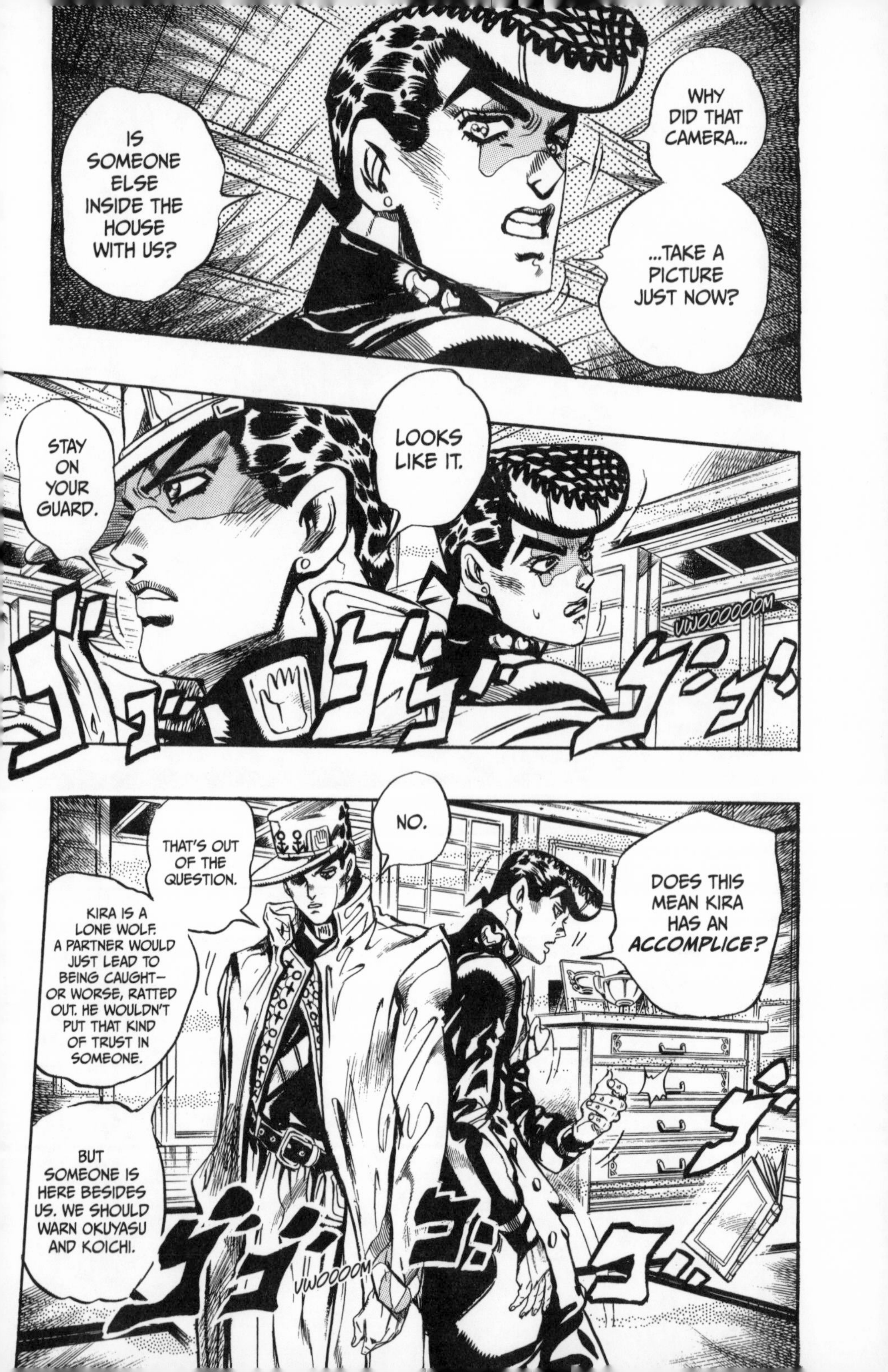
WHY DID THAT CAMERA...
...TAKE A PICTURE JUST NOW?
IS SOMEONE ELSE INSIDE THE HOUSE WITH US?
UWOOOOOOM
LOOKS LIKE IT.
STAY ON YOUR GUARD.
DOES THIS MEAN KIRA HAS AN *ACCOMPLICE?*
NO.
THAT'S OUT OF THE QUESTION.
KIRA IS A LONE WOLF. A PARTNER WOULD JUST LEAD TO BEING CAUGHT— OR WORSE, RATTED OUT. HE WOULDN'T PUT THAT KIND OF TRUST IN SOMEONE.
BUT SOMEONE IS HERE BESIDES US. WE SHOULD WARN OKUYASU AND KOICHI.
UWOOOOM

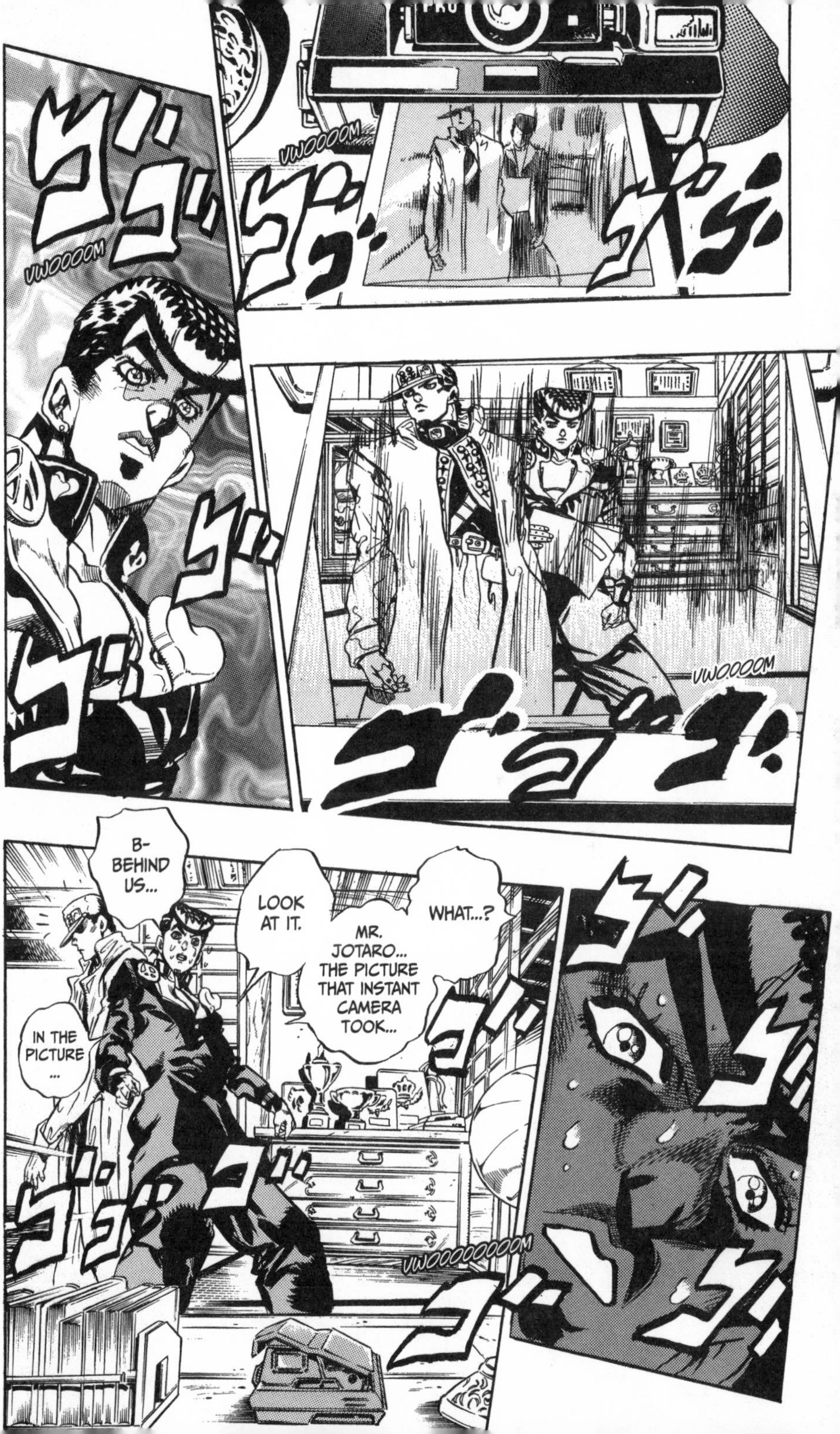
VWOOOOM
VWOOOOM
VWOOOOM
WHAT...?
MR. JOTARO... THE PICTURE THAT INSTANT CAMERA TOOK...
LOOK AT IT.
B-BEHIND US...
IN THE PICTURE ...
VWOOOOOOOOOM

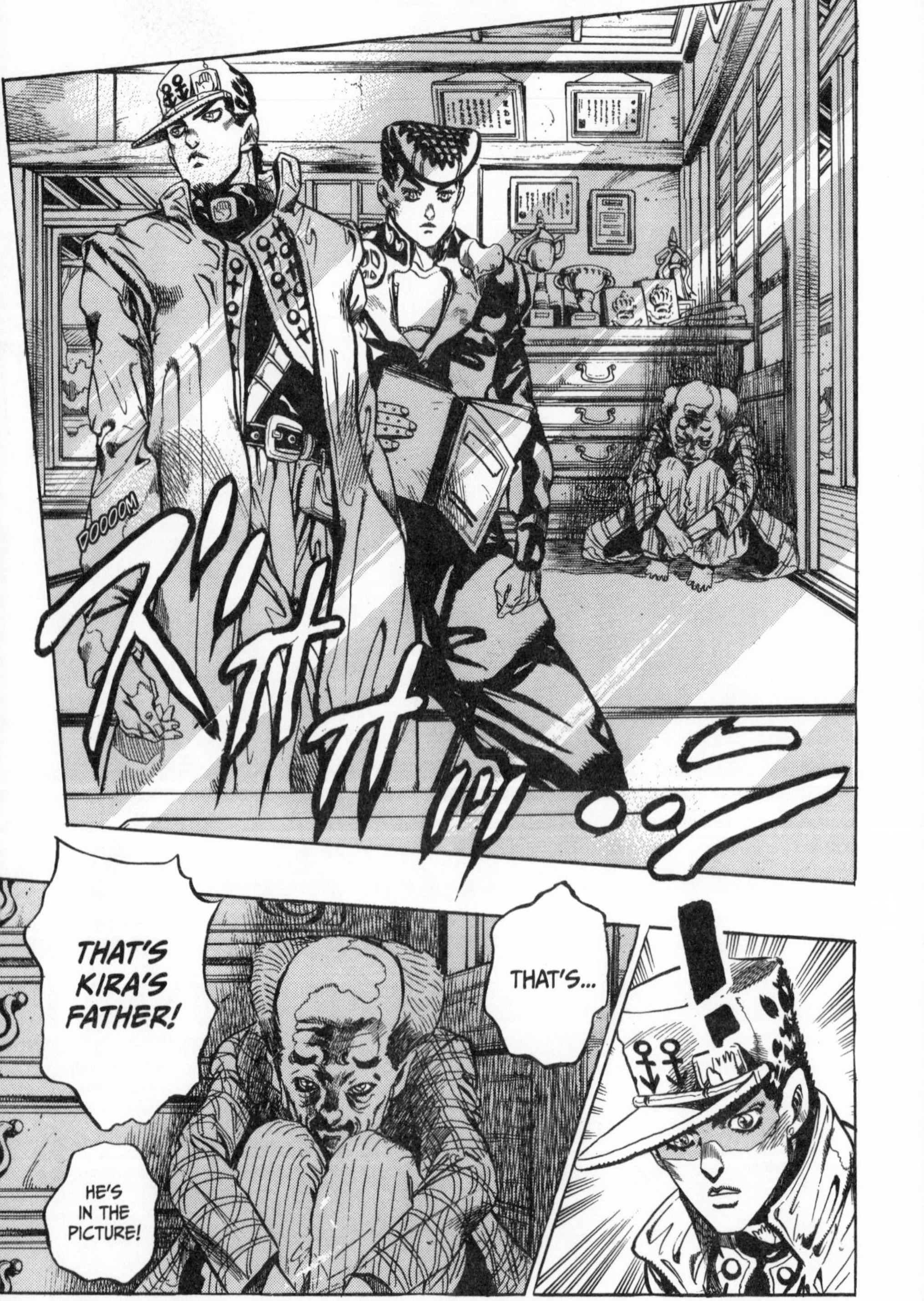
DOOOOM
THAT'S...
THAT'S KIRA'S FATHER!
HE'S IN THE PICTURE!

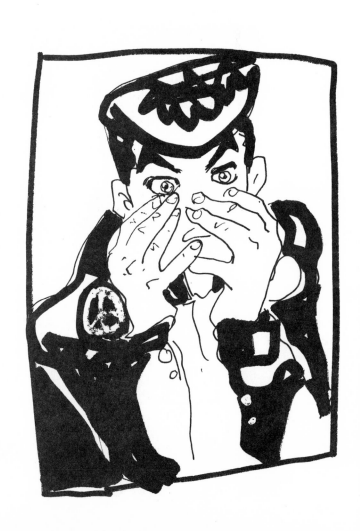

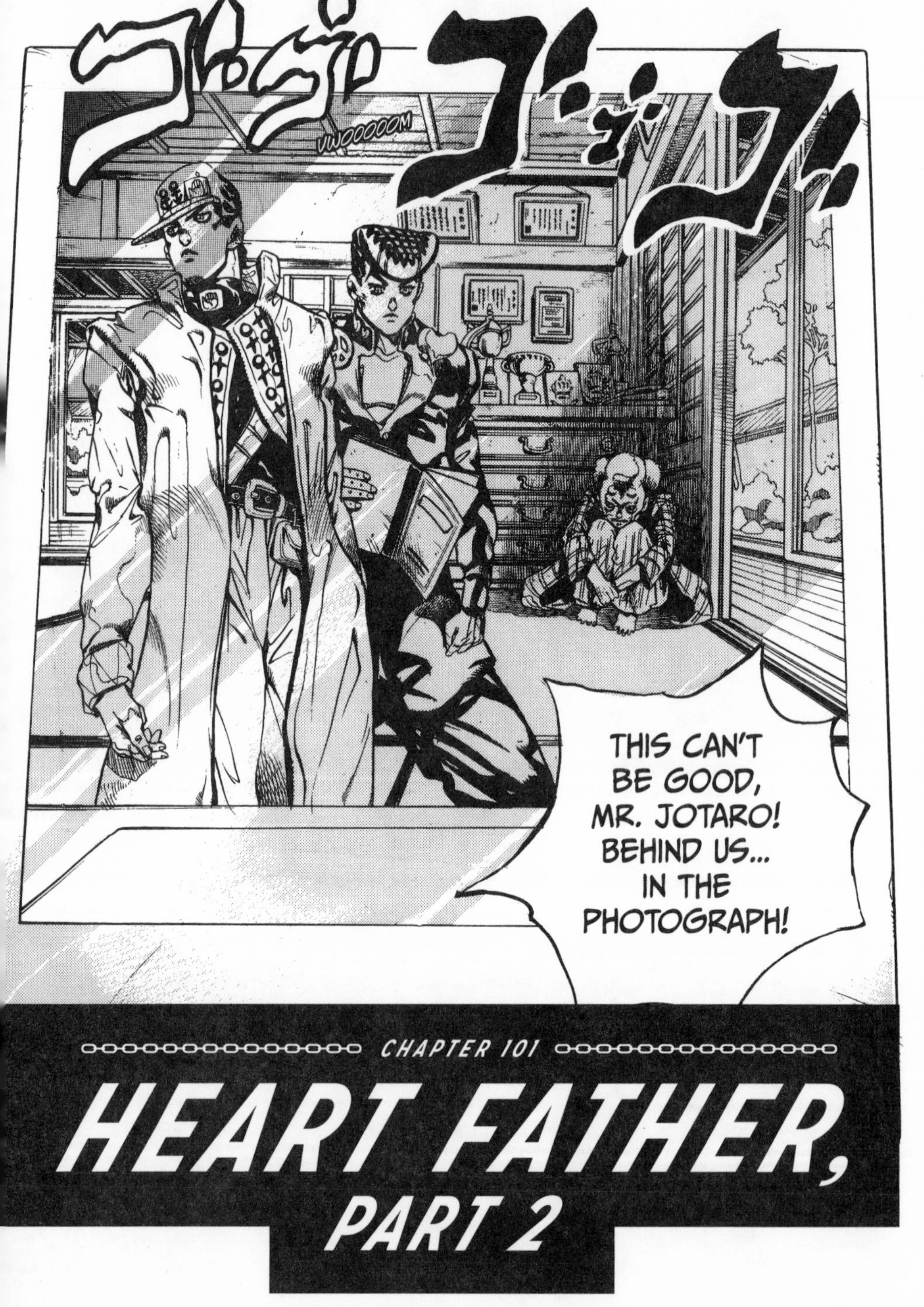
VWOOOOOM
THIS CAN'T BE GOOD, MR. JOTARO! BEHIND US... IN THE PHOTOGRAPH!

CHAPTER 101

HEART FATHER, PART 2

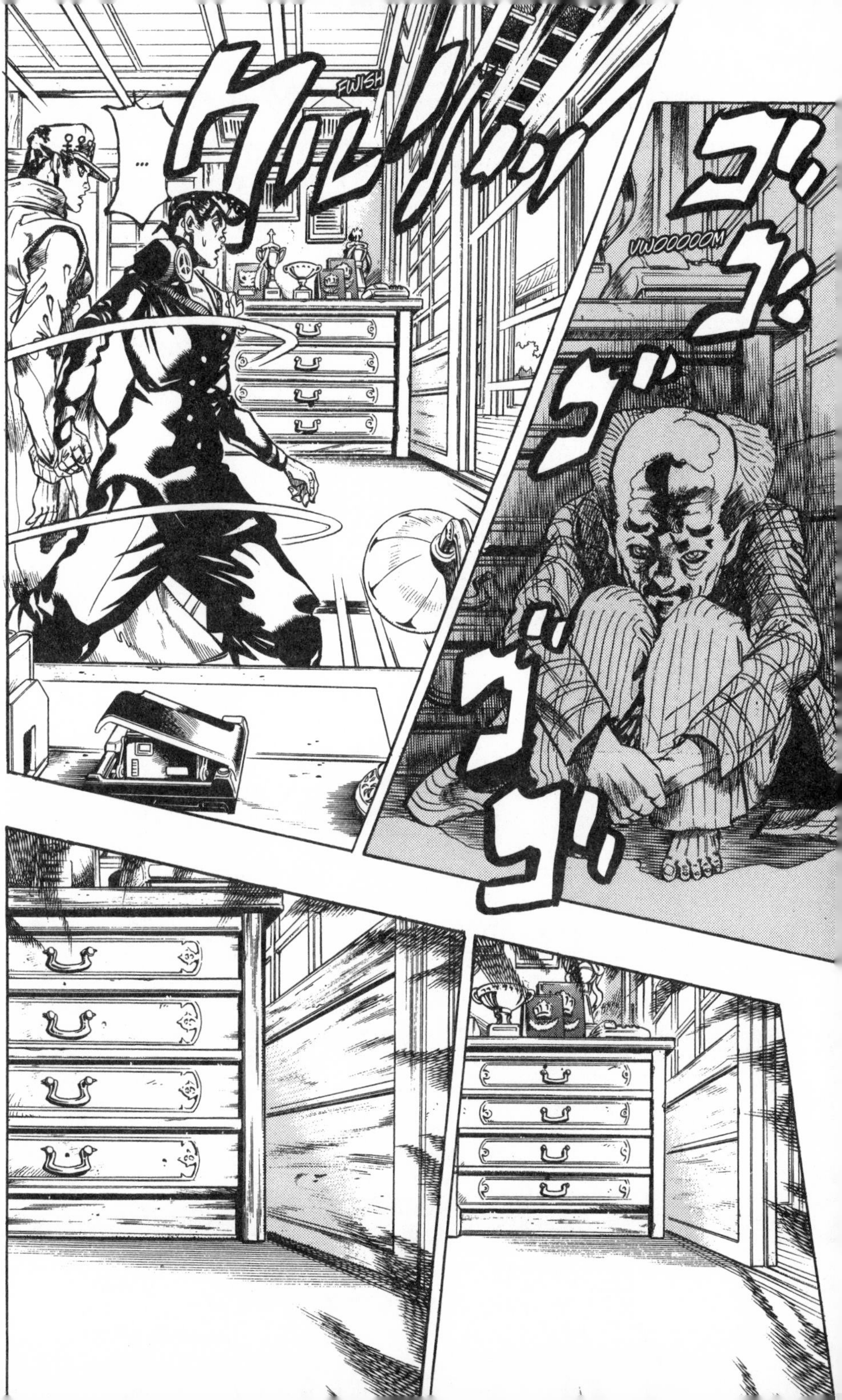
VWOOOOOM
FWISH
...

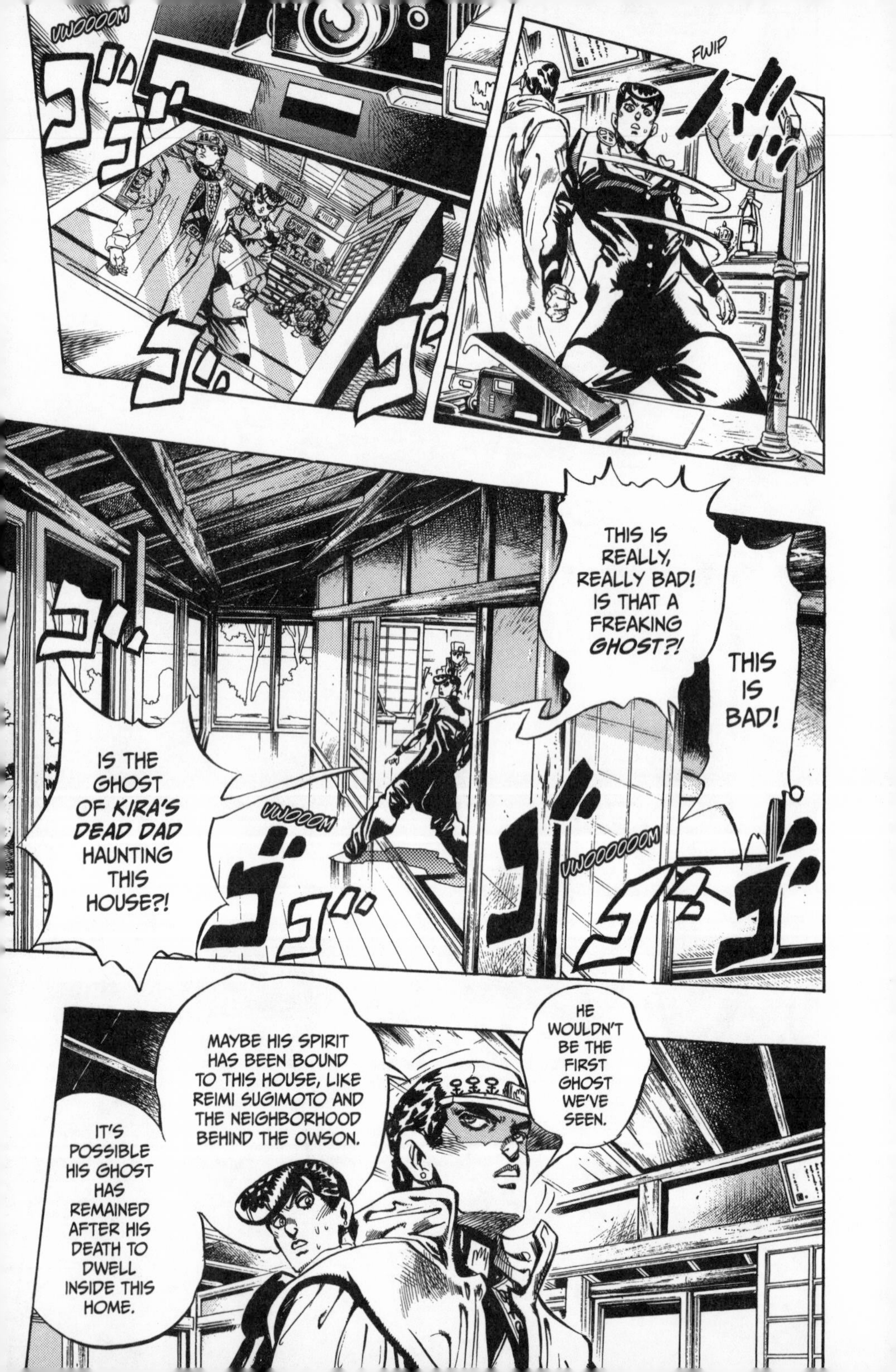
FWIP
VWOOOOM
THIS IS REALLY, REALLY BAD! IS THAT A FREAKING GHOST?!
THIS IS BAD!
VWOOOOOOOM
VWOOOM
IS THE GHOST OF KIRA'S DEAD DAD HAUNTING THIS HOUSE?!
HE WOULDN'T BE THE FIRST GHOST WE'VE SEEN.
MAYBE HIS SPIRIT HAS BEEN BOUND TO THIS HOUSE, LIKE REIMI SUGIMOTO AND THE NEIGHBORHOOD BEHIND THE OWSON.
IT'S POSSIBLE HIS GHOST HAS REMAINED AFTER HIS DEATH TO DWELL INSIDE THIS HOME.

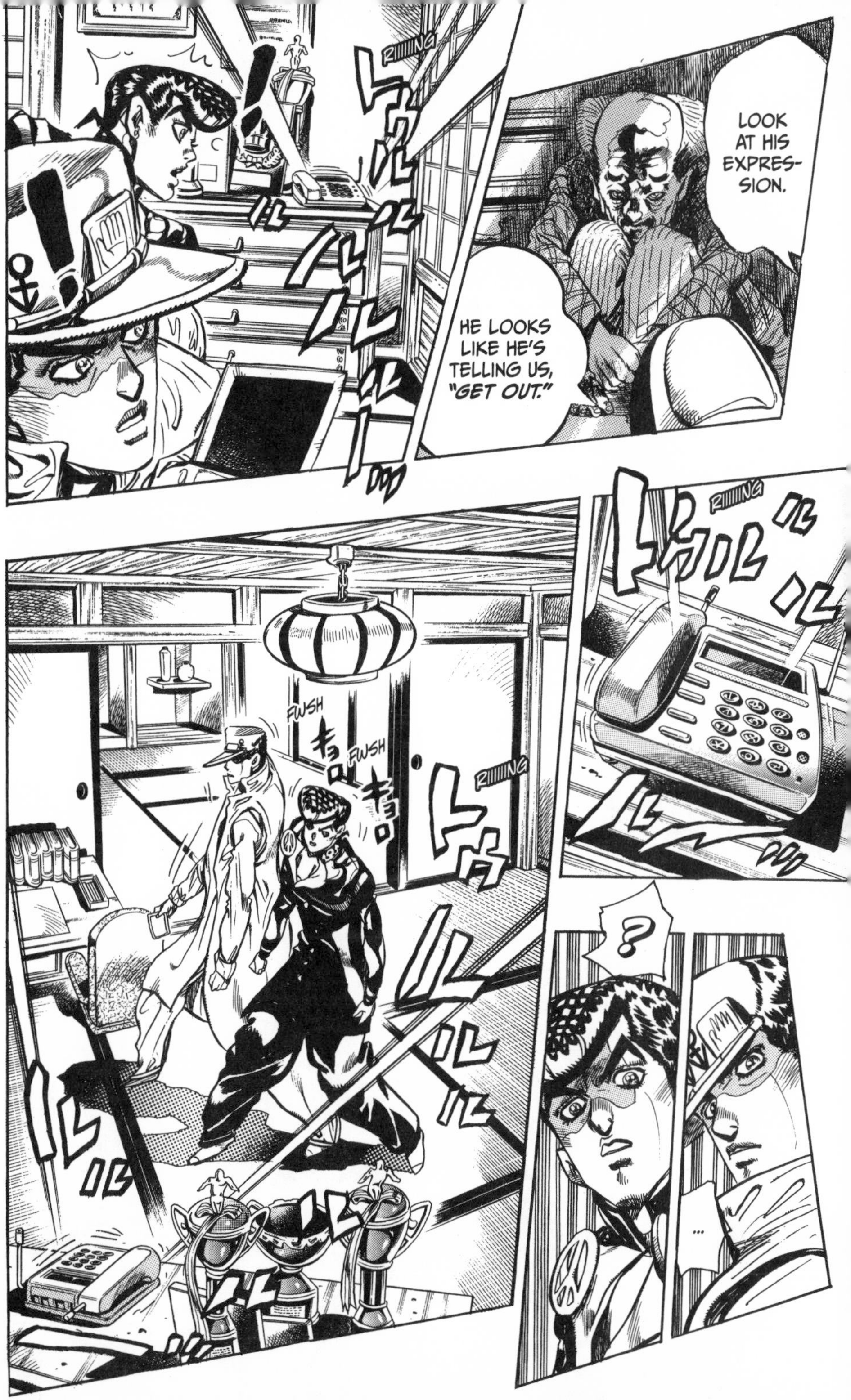
LOOK AT HIS EXPRESSION.
HE LOOKS LIKE HE'S TELLING US, "GET OUT."
RIIIING
RIIIING
RIIIING
FWSH
FWSH
?
...

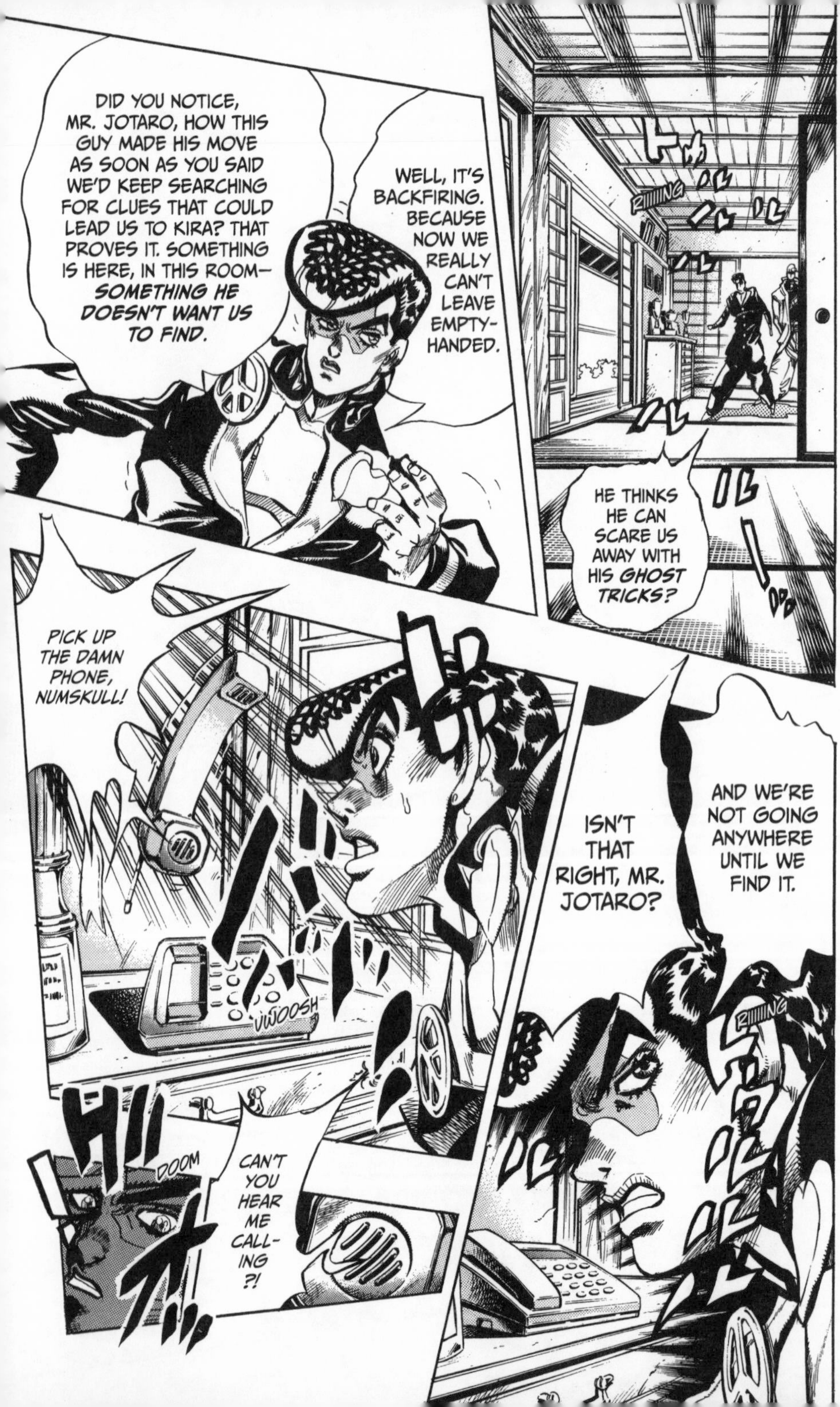
RIIING
HE THINKS HE CAN SCARE US AWAY WITH HIS GHOST TRICKS?
DID YOU NOTICE, MR. JOTARO, HOW THIS GUY MADE HIS MOVE AS SOON AS YOU SAID WE'D KEEP SEARCHING FOR CLUES THAT COULD LEAD US TO KIRA? THAT PROVES IT. SOMETHING IS HERE, IN THIS ROOM—SOMETHING HE DOESN'T WANT US TO FIND.
WELL, IT'S BACKFIRING. BECAUSE NOW WE REALLY CAN'T LEAVE EMPTY-HANDED.
AND WE'RE NOT GOING ANYWHERE UNTIL WE FIND IT.
ISN'T THAT RIGHT, MR. JOTARO?
RIIING
PICK UP THE DAMN PHONE, NUMSKULL!
VWOOSH
CAN'T YOU HEAR ME CALLING?!
DOOM

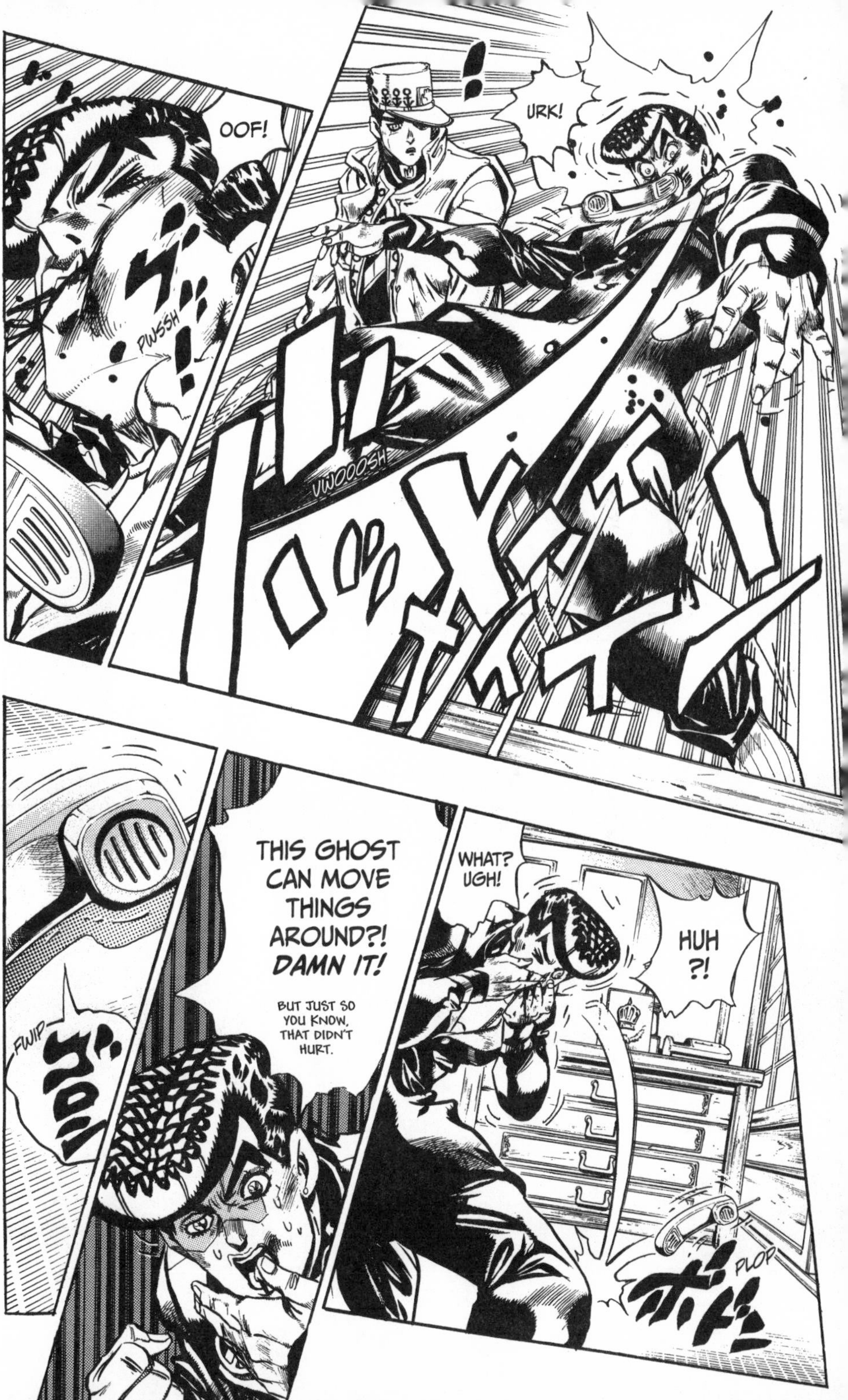
URK!
VWOOOSH
OOF!
PWSSH
WHAT? UGH!
HUH ?!
PLOP
THIS GHOST CAN MOVE THINGS AROUND?! DAMN IT!
BUT JUST SO YOU KNOW, THAT DIDN'T HURT.
FWIP

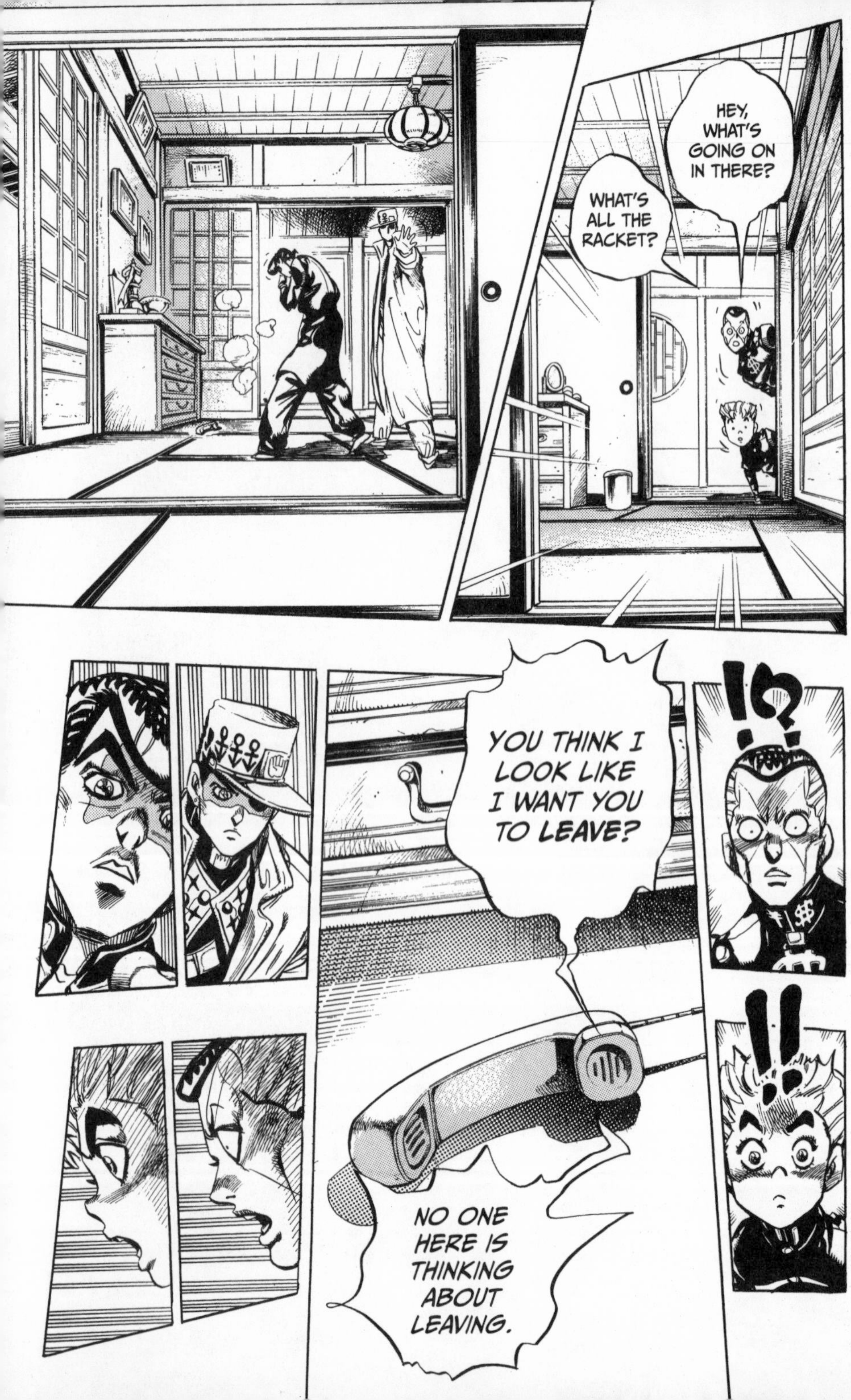
HEY, WHAT'S GOING ON IN THERE?
WHAT'S ALL THE RACKET?
!?
!!
YOU THINK I LOOK LIKE I WANT YOU TO ***LEAVE***?
NO ONE HERE IS THINKING ABOUT LEAVING.

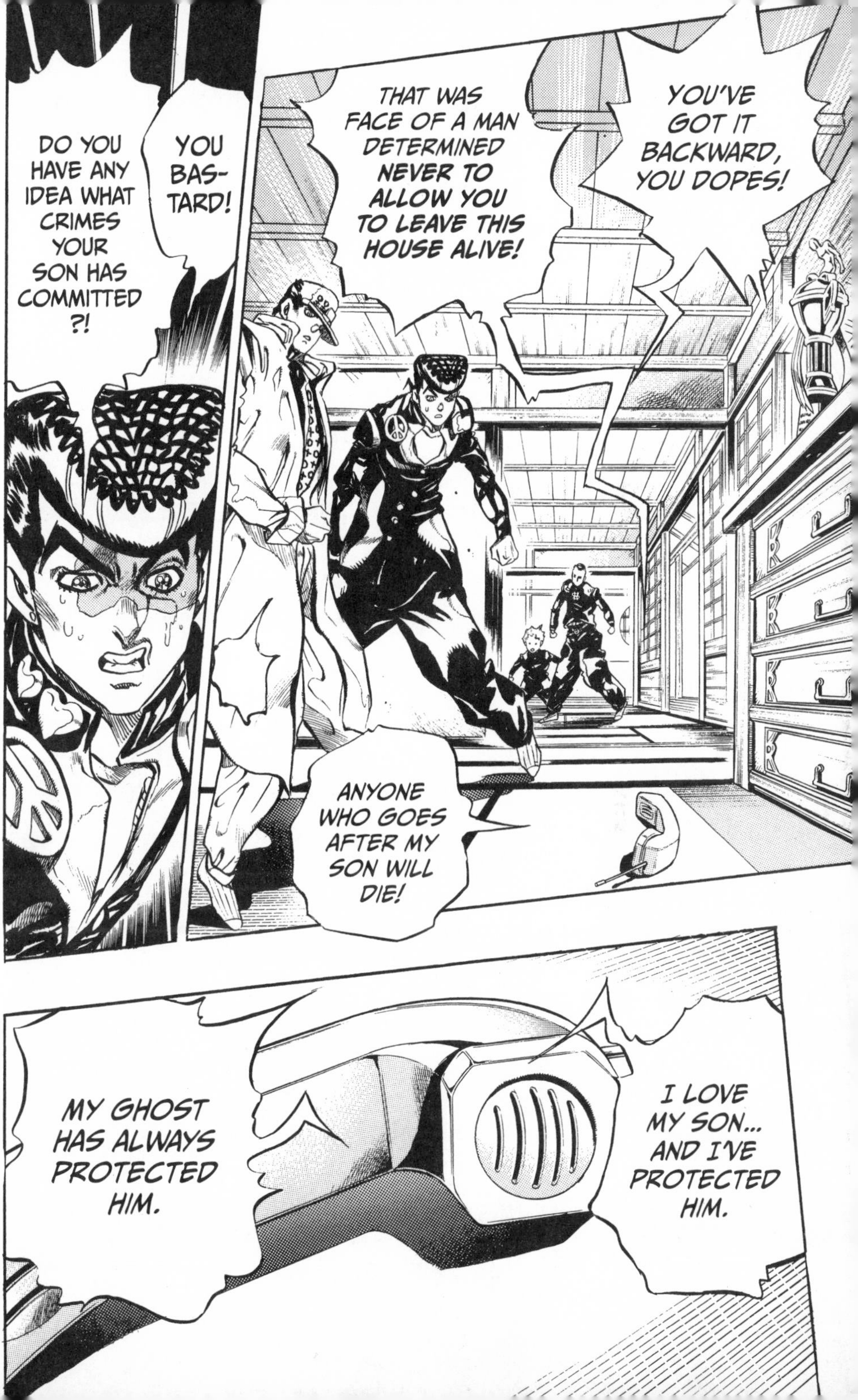
YOU'VE GOT IT BACKWARD, YOU DOPES!
THAT WAS FACE OF A MAN DETERMINED NEVER TO ALLOW YOU TO LEAVE THIS HOUSE ALIVE!
ANYONE WHO GOES AFTER MY SON WILL DIE!
YOU BAS-TARD!
DO YOU HAVE ANY IDEA WHAT CRIMES YOUR SON HAS COMMITTED ?!
I LOVE MY SON... AND I'VE PROTECTED HIM.
MY GHOST HAS ALWAYS PROTECTED HIM.

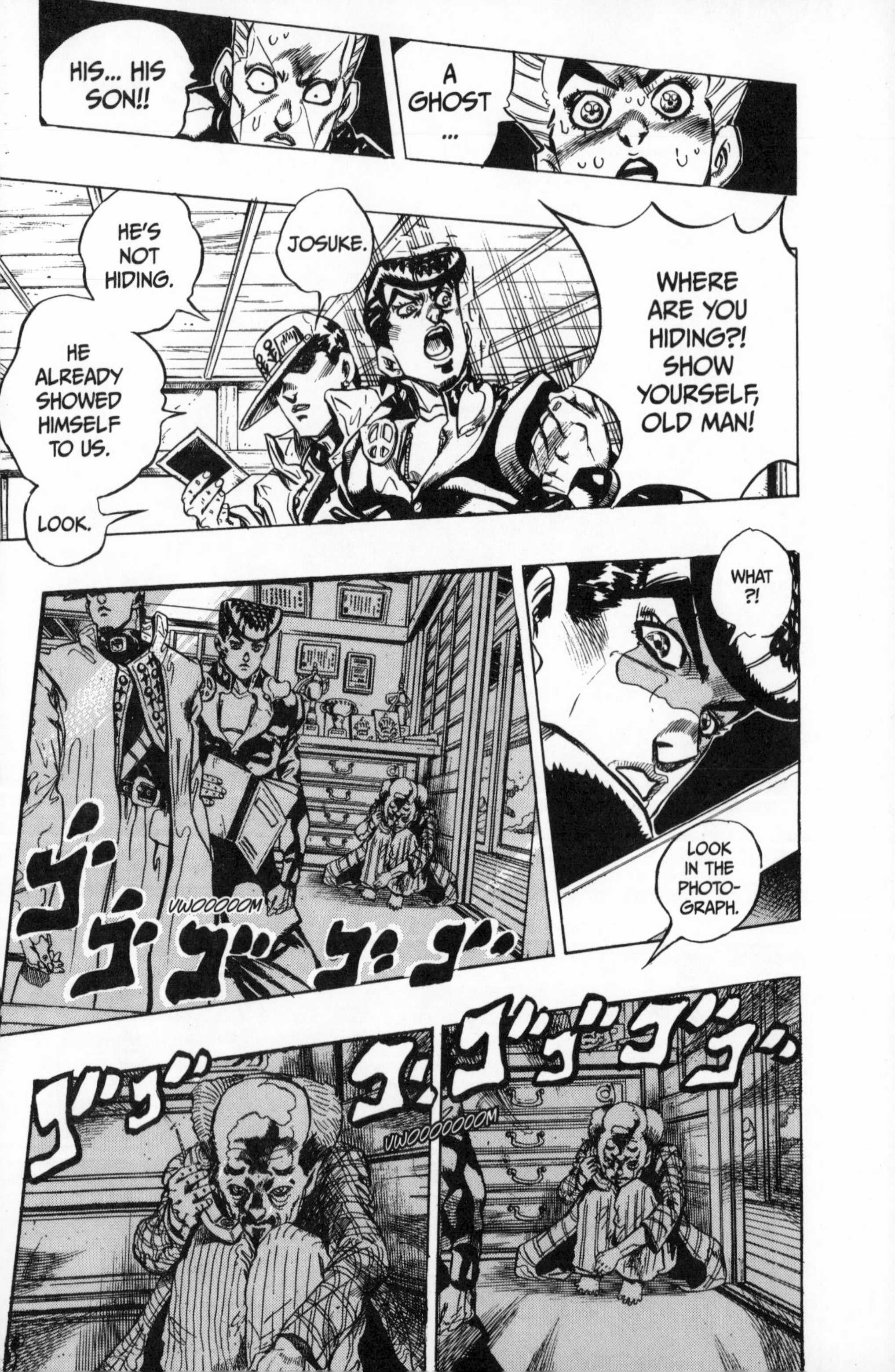
A GHOST ...
HIS... HIS SON!!
WHERE ARE YOU HIDING?! SHOW YOURSELF, OLD MAN!
JOSUKE.
HE'S NOT HIDING.
HE ALREADY SHOWED HIMSELF TO US.
LOOK.
WHAT?!
LOOK IN THE PHOTOGRAPH.
VWOOOOOM
VWOOOOOOOM

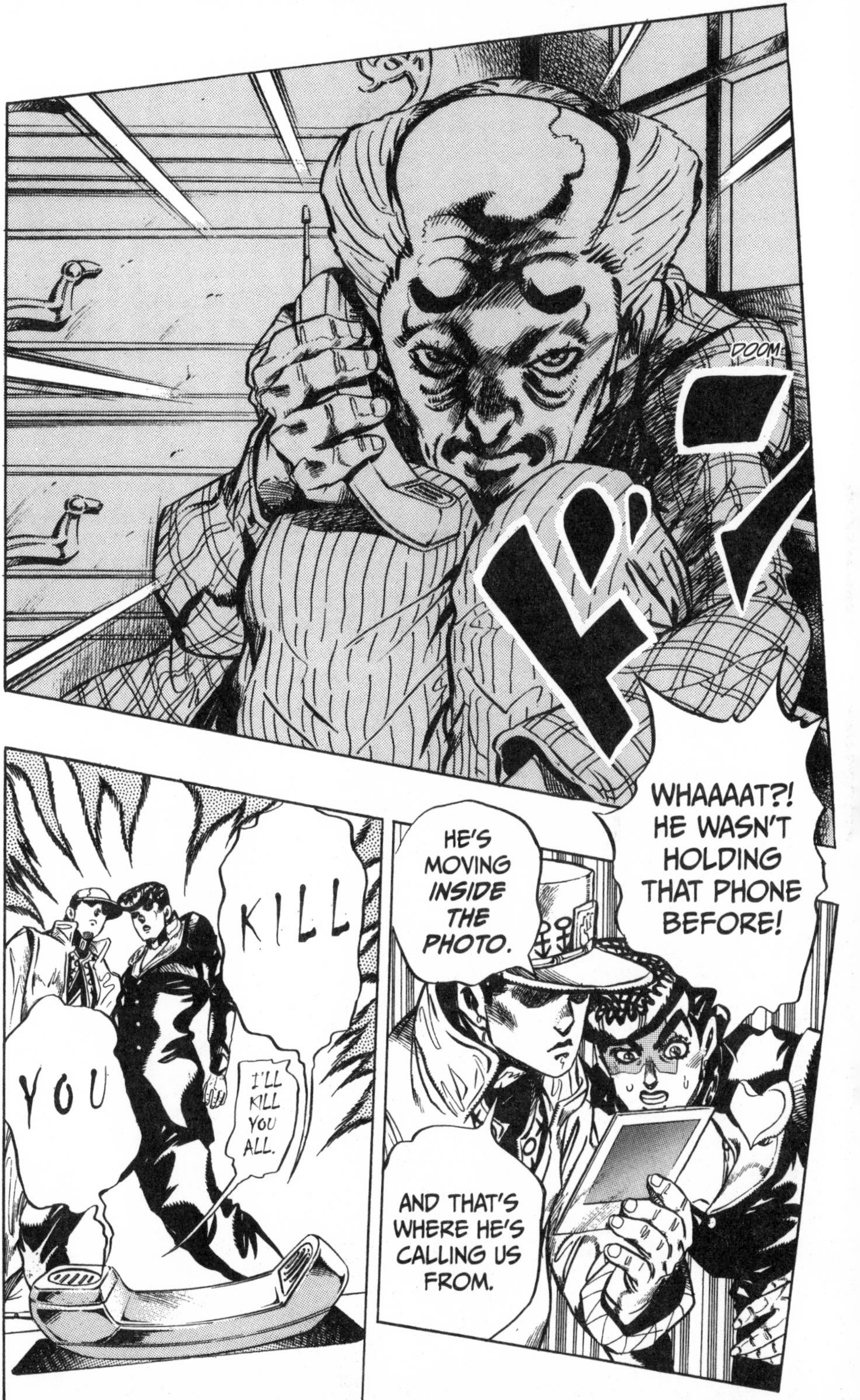
DOOM
WHAAAAT?! HE WASN'T HOLDING THAT PHONE BEFORE!
HE'S MOVING INSIDE THE PHOTO.
AND THAT'S WHERE HE'S CALLING US FROM.
KILL
YOU
I'LL KILL YOU ALL.

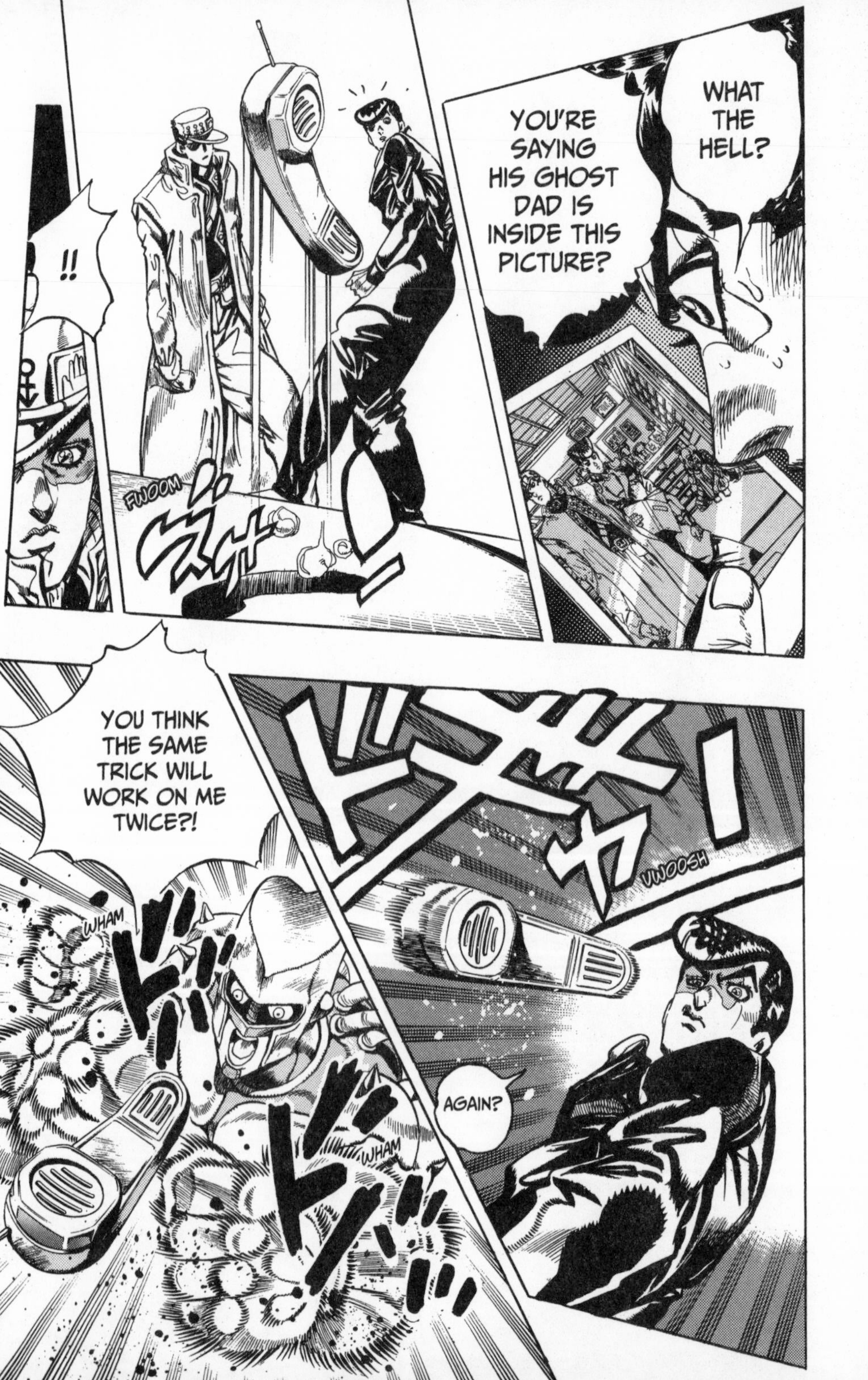

WHAT THE HELL?
YOU'RE SAYING HIS GHOST DAD IS INSIDE THIS PICTURE?
FWOOM
!!
VWOOSH
AGAIN?
YOU THINK THE SAME TRICK WILL WORK ON ME TWICE?!
WHAM
WHAM

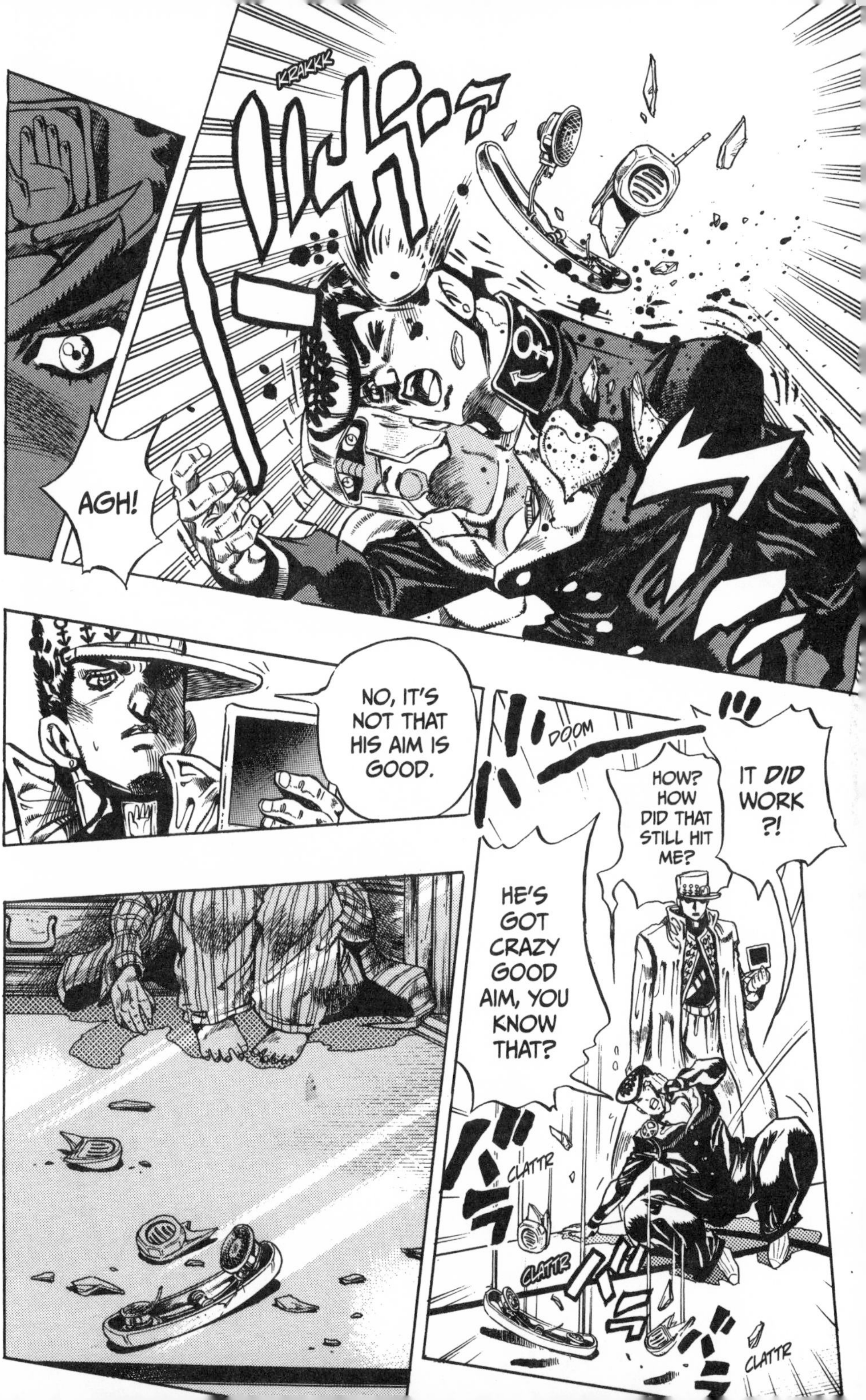
KRAKKK
AGH!
DOOM
IT DID WORK ?!
HOW? HOW DID THAT STILL HIT ME?
HE'S GOT CRAZY GOOD AIM, YOU KNOW THAT?
CLATTR
CLATTR
CLATTR
NO, IT'S NOT THAT HIS AIM IS GOOD.

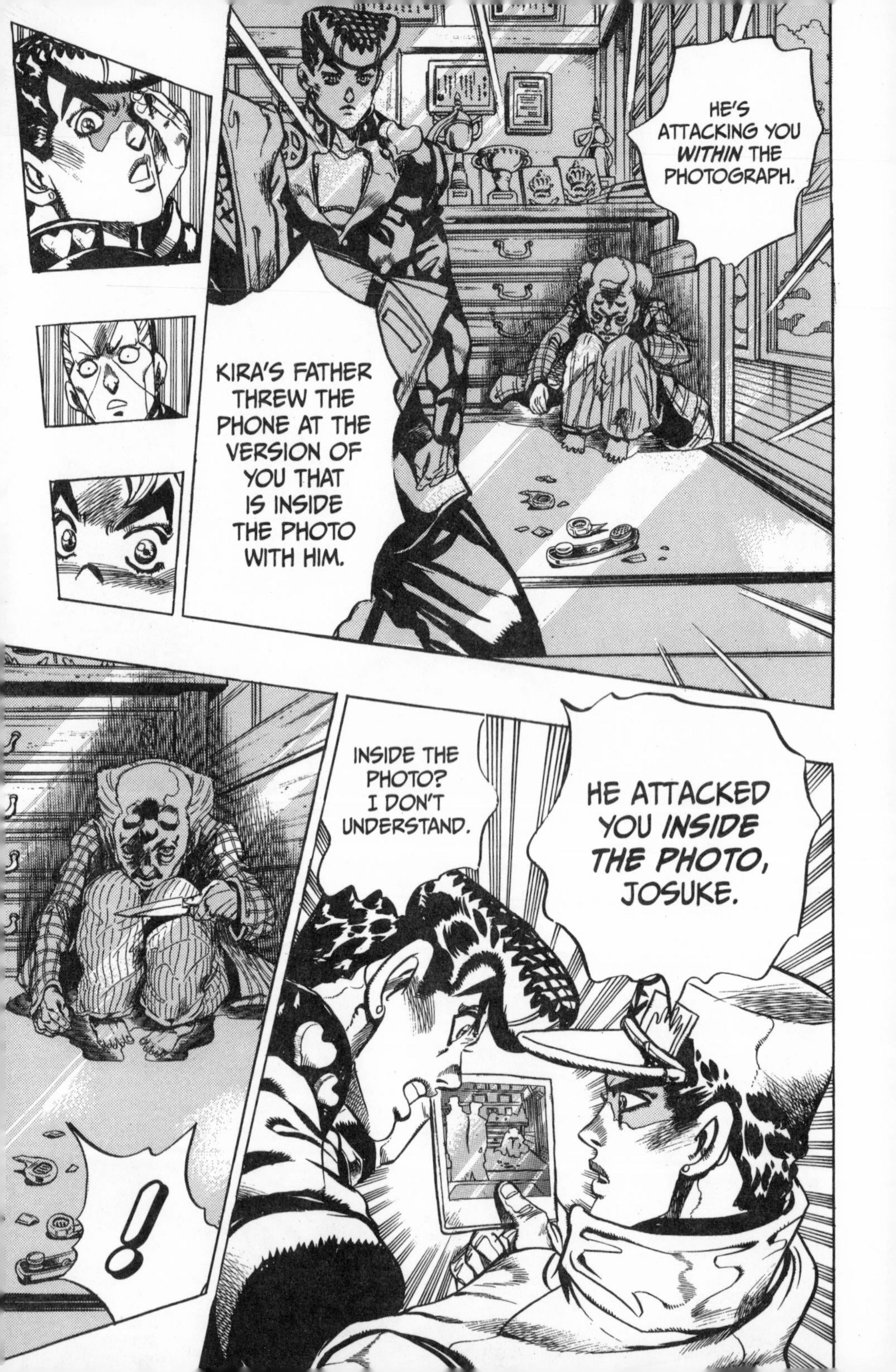

HE'S ATTACKING YOU *WITHIN* THE PHOTOGRAPH.
KIRA'S FATHER THREW THE PHONE AT THE VERSION OF YOU THAT IS INSIDE THE PHOTO WITH HIM.
HE ATTACKED YOU *INSIDE THE PHOTO,* JOSUKE.
INSIDE THE PHOTO? I DON'T UNDERSTAND.
!

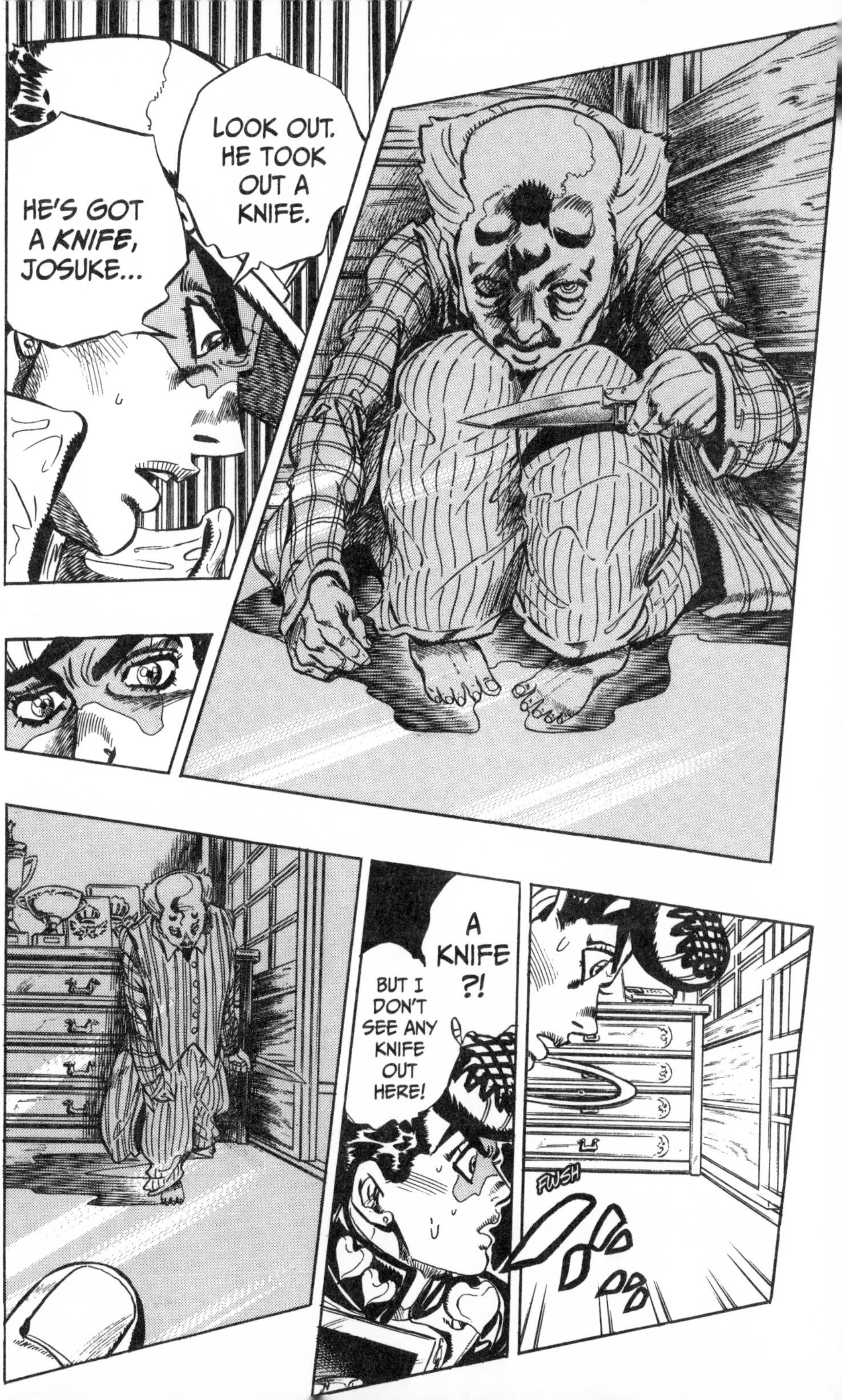

LOOK OUT. HE TOOK OUT A KNIFE.
HE'S GOT A *KNIFE*, JOSUKE...
FWSH
A KNIFE ?!
BUT I DON'T SEE ANY KNIFE OUT HERE!

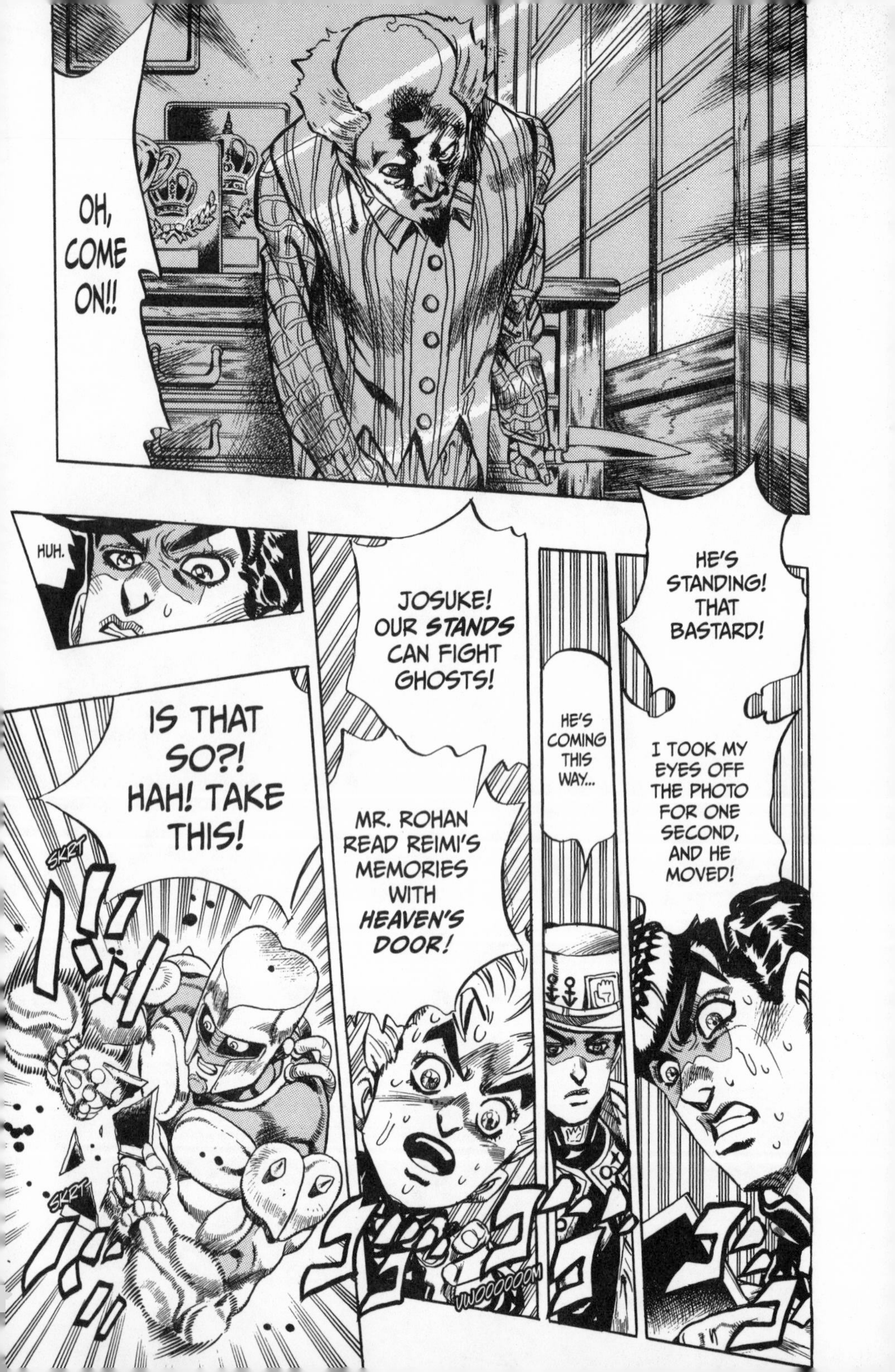
OH, COME ON!!
HE'S STANDING! THAT BASTARD!
JOSUKE! OUR STANDS CAN FIGHT GHOSTS!
HUH.
I TOOK MY EYES OFF THE PHOTO FOR ONE SECOND, AND HE MOVED!
HE'S COMING THIS WAY...
MR. ROHAN READ REIMI'S MEMORIES WITH HEAVEN'S DOOR!
VWOOOOOOM
IS THAT SO?! HAH! TAKE THIS!
SKRT
SKRT

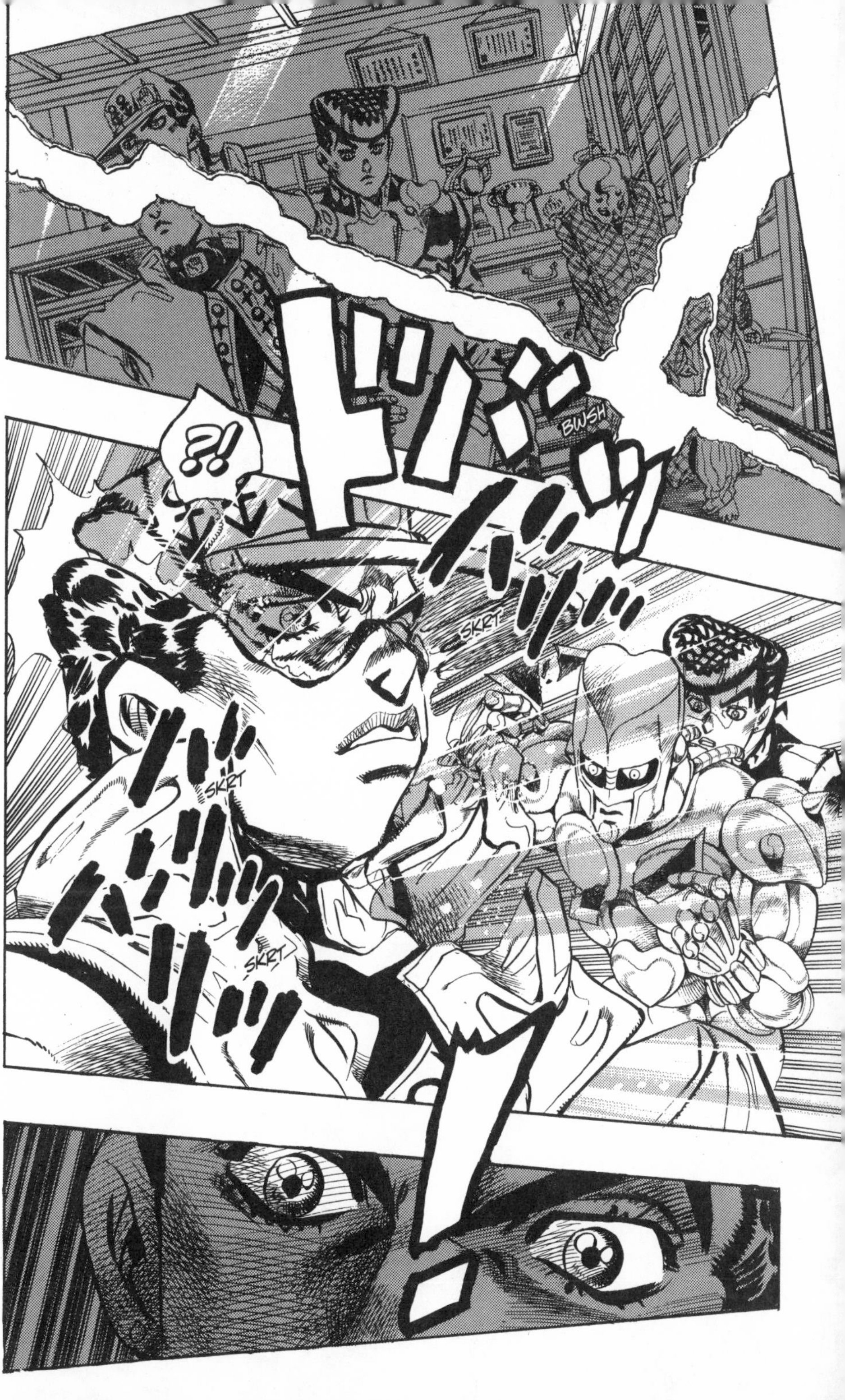
BWSH
SKRT
?!
SKRT
SKRT

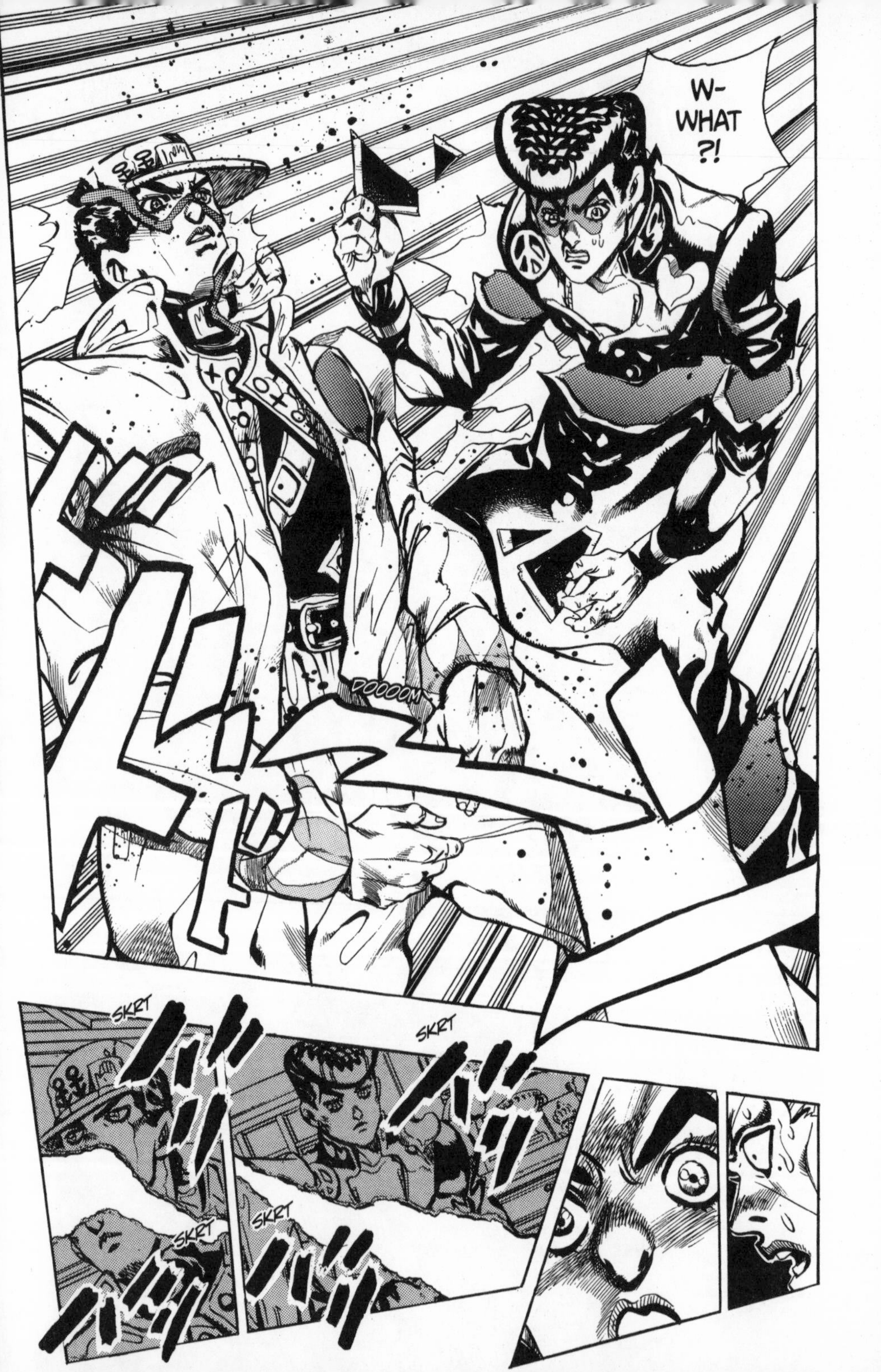
W-WHAT ?!
DOOOOM
SKRT
SKRT
SKRT
SKRT

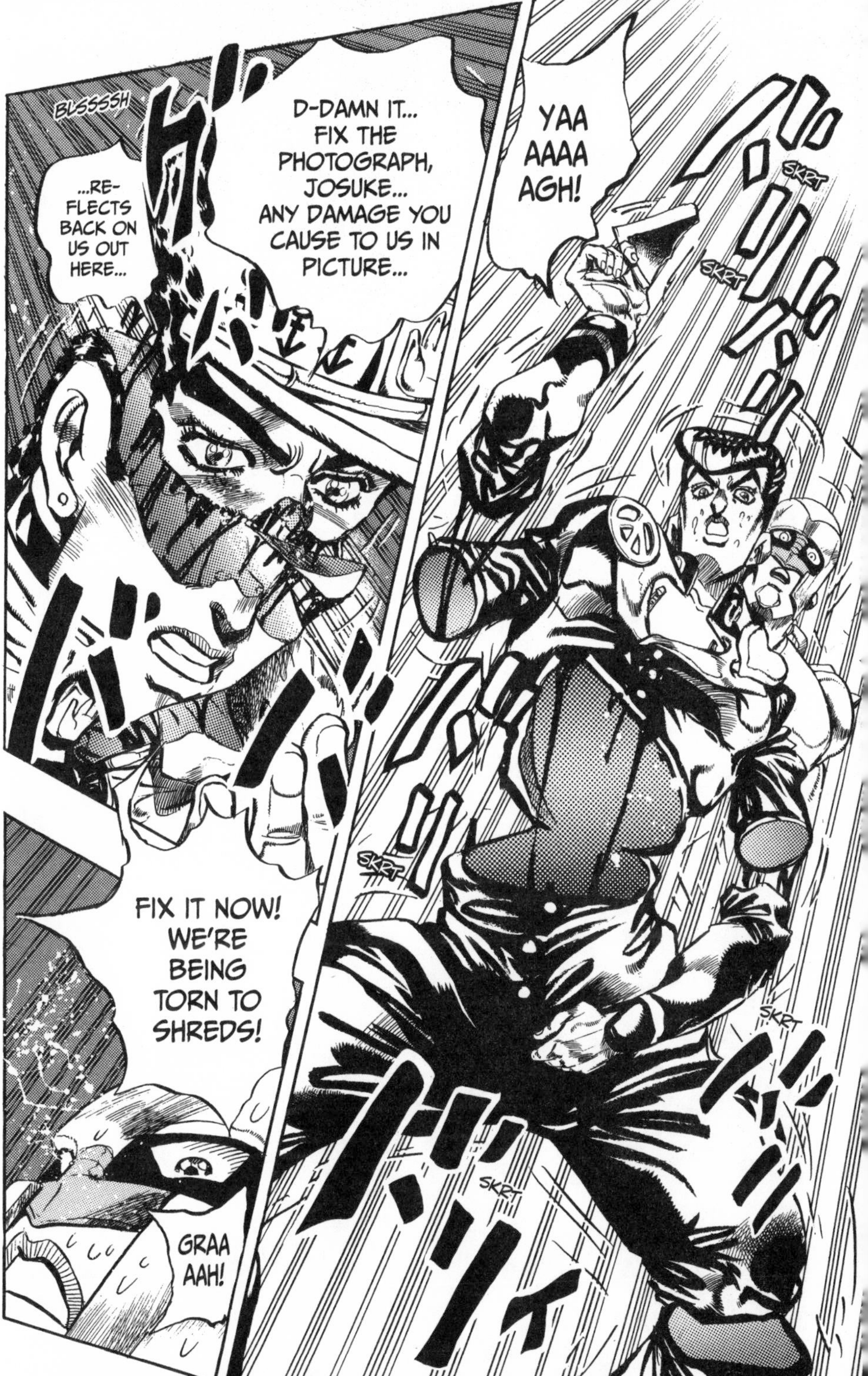
YAA AAAA AGH!
SKRT
SKRT
SKRT
SKRT
SKRT
BLSSSSH
D-DAMN IT... FIX THE PHOTOGRAPH, JOSUKE... ANY DAMAGE YOU CAUSE TO US IN PICTURE...
...RE-FLECTS BACK ON US OUT HERE...
FIX IT NOW! WE'RE BEING TORN TO SHREDS!
GRAA AAH!

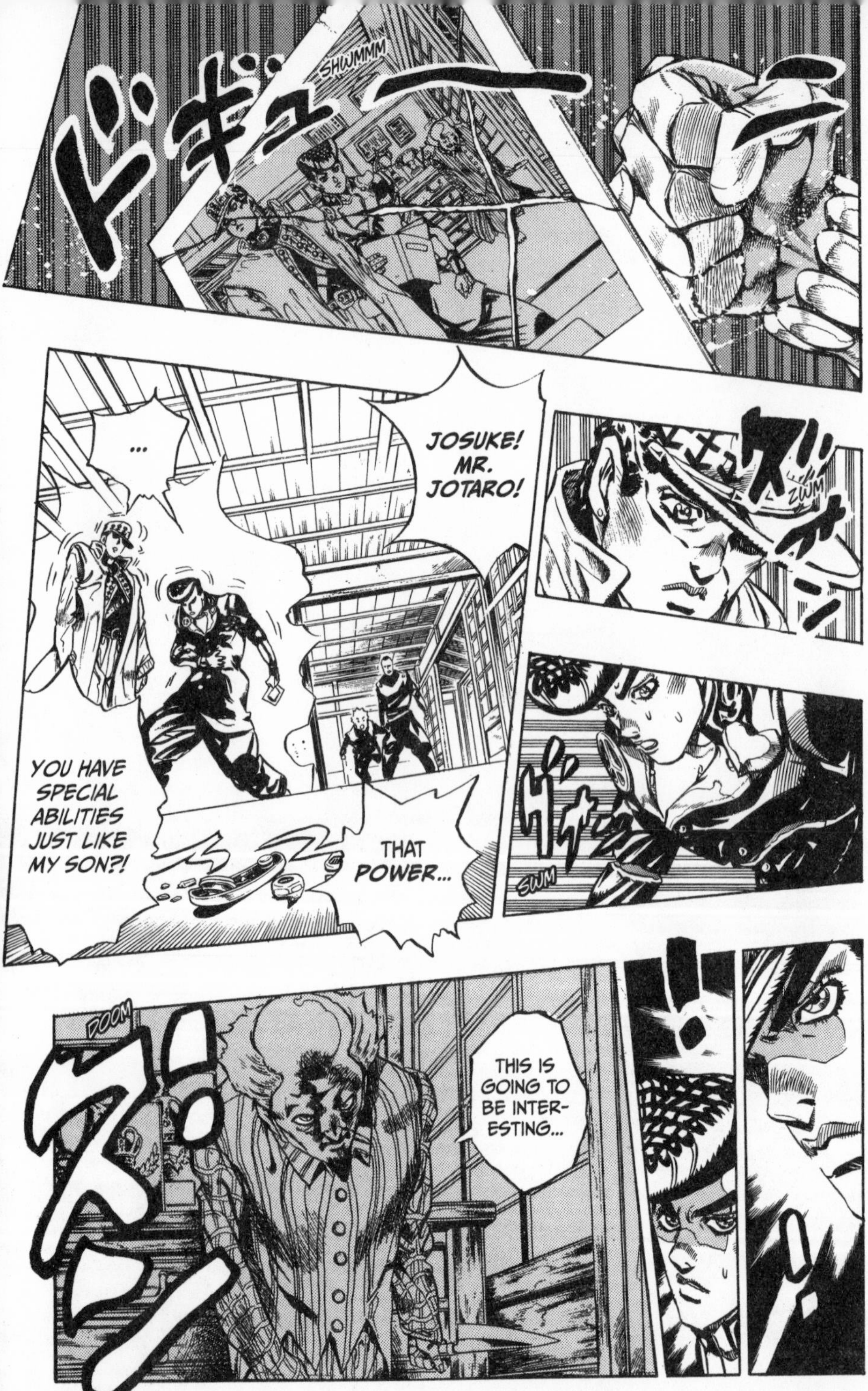
SHWUMMM
ZWM
SWM
JOSUKE! MR. JOTARO!
...
THAT POWER...
YOU HAVE SPECIAL ABILITIES JUST LIKE MY SON?!
!
THIS IS GOING TO BE INTER- ESTING...
DOOM

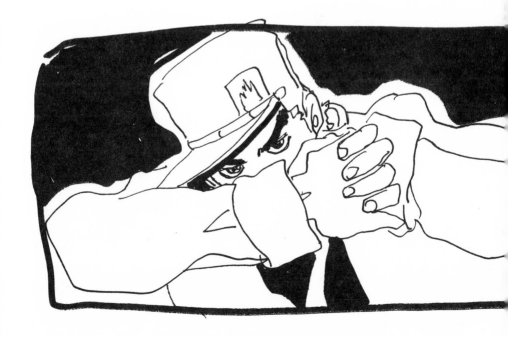

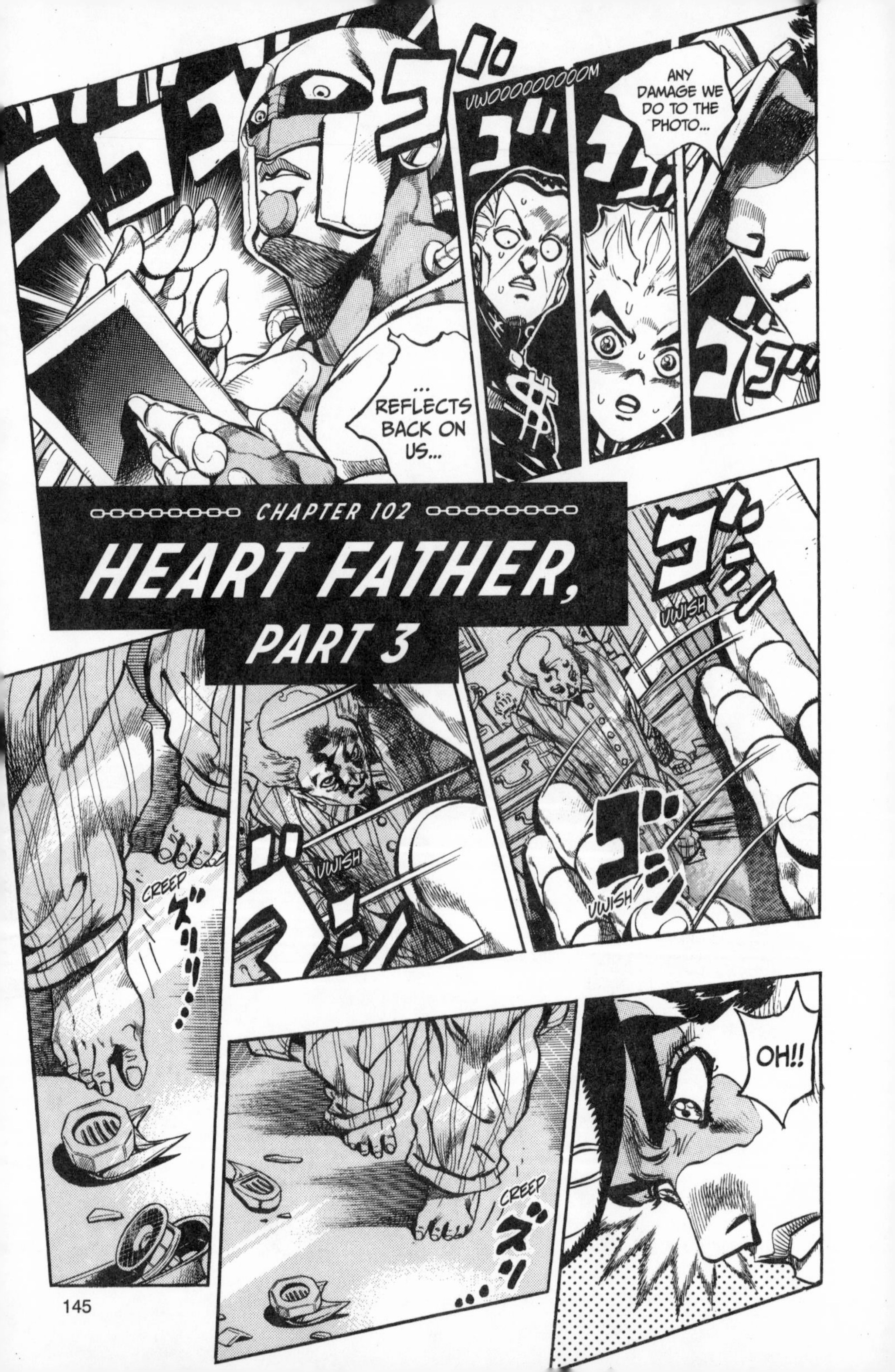
ANY DAMAGE WE DO TO THE PHOTO...
VWOOOOOOOOOOM
...REFLECTS BACK ON US...
CHAPTER 102
HEART FATHER, PART 3
UWISH
UWISH
UWISH
CREEP
OH!!
CREEP

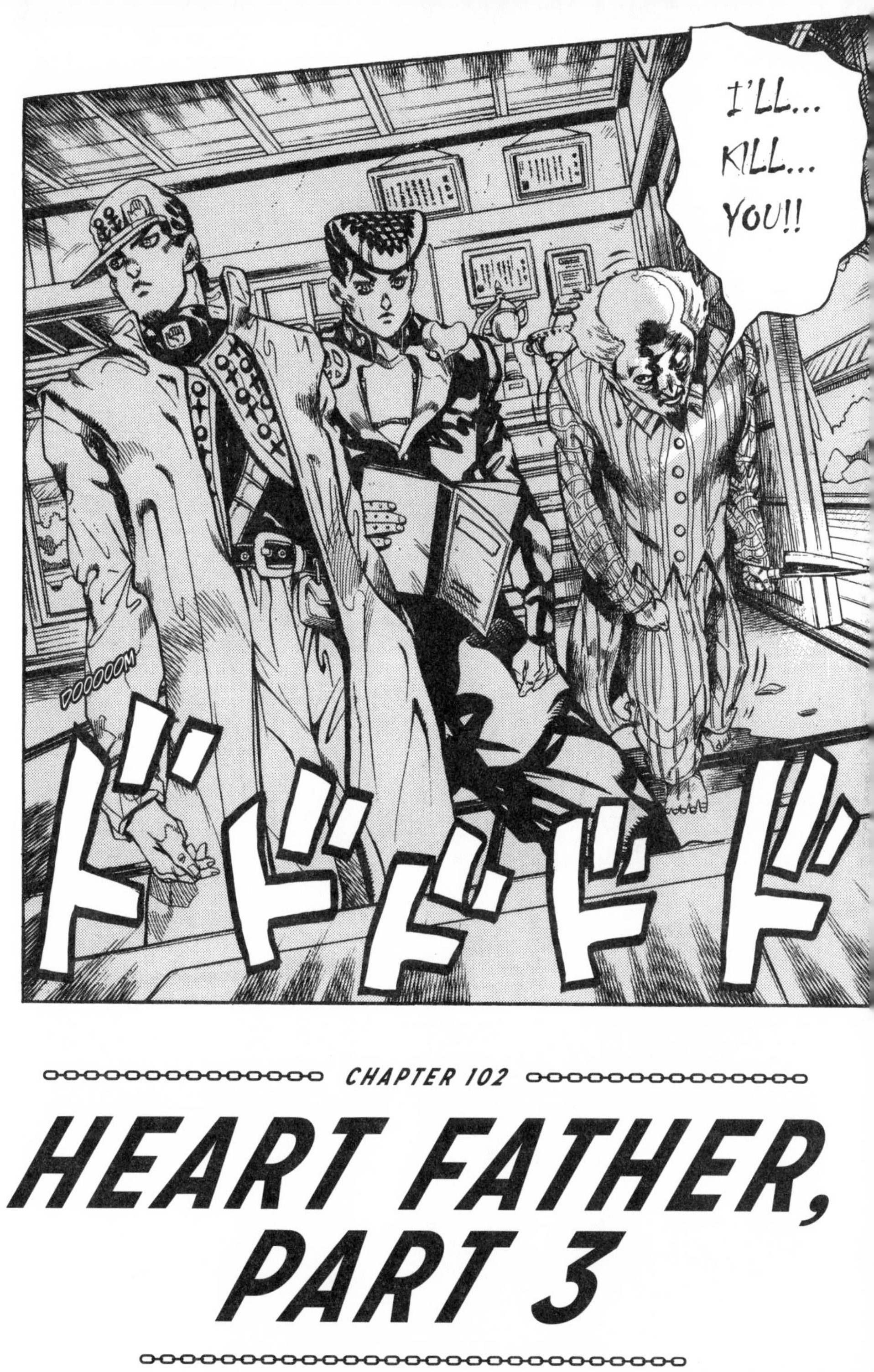
I'LL... KILL... YOU!!
DOOOOOM
ドドドドドド

CHAPTER 102

HEART FATHER, PART 3

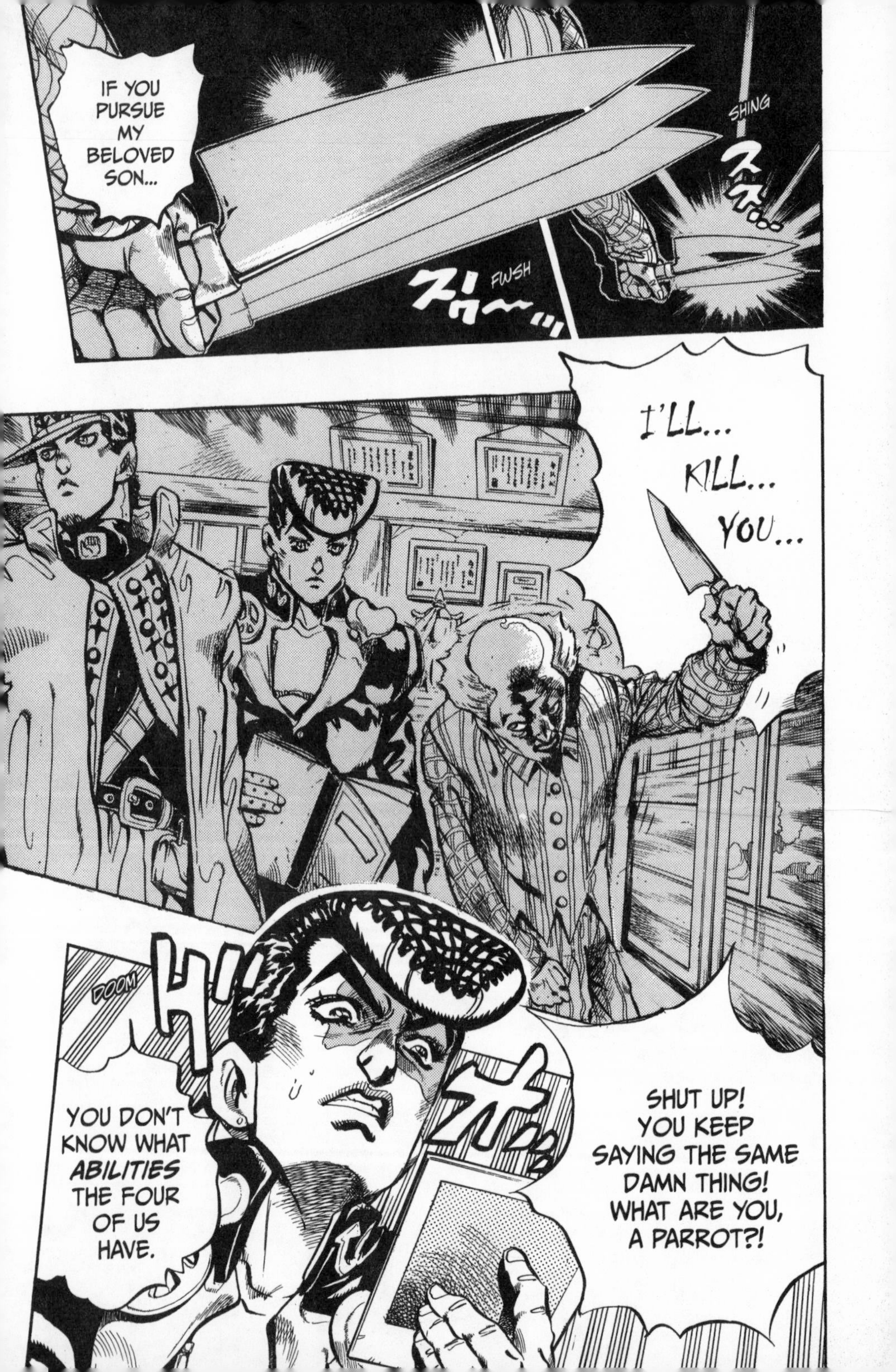
SHING
IF YOU PURSUE MY BELOVED SON...
FWSH
I'LL... KILL... YOU...
SHUT UP! YOU KEEP SAYING THE SAME DAMN THING! WHAT ARE YOU, A PARROT?!
DOOM
YOU DON'T KNOW WHAT *ABILITIES* THE FOUR OF US HAVE.

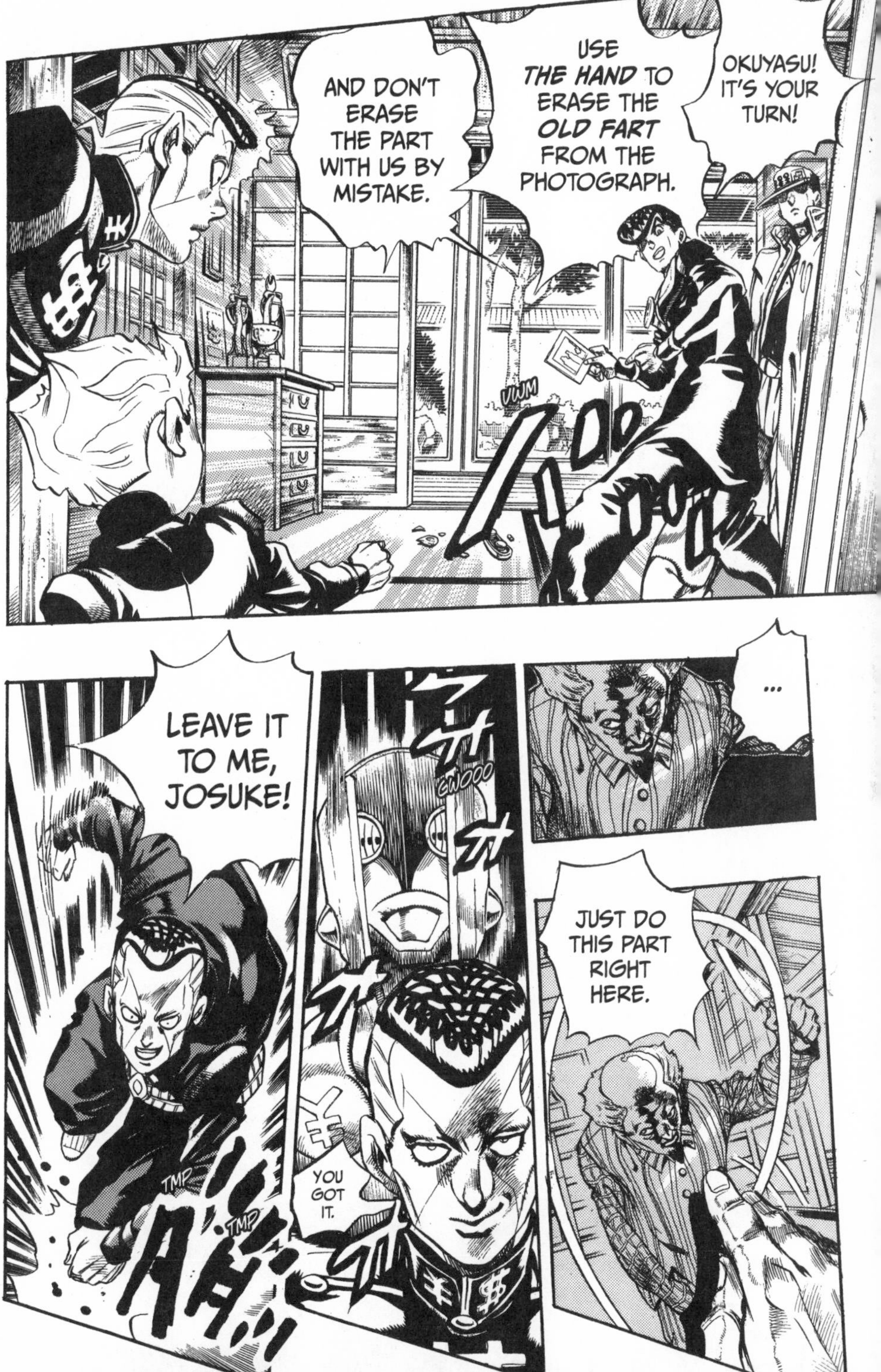
OKUYASU! IT'S YOUR TURN!
USE THE HAND TO ERASE THE OLD FART FROM THE PHOTOGRAPH.
AND DON'T ERASE THE PART WITH US BY MISTAKE.
VWM
...
JUST DO THIS PART RIGHT HERE.
GWOOO
YOU GOT IT.
LEAVE IT TO ME, JOSUKE!
TMP
TMP

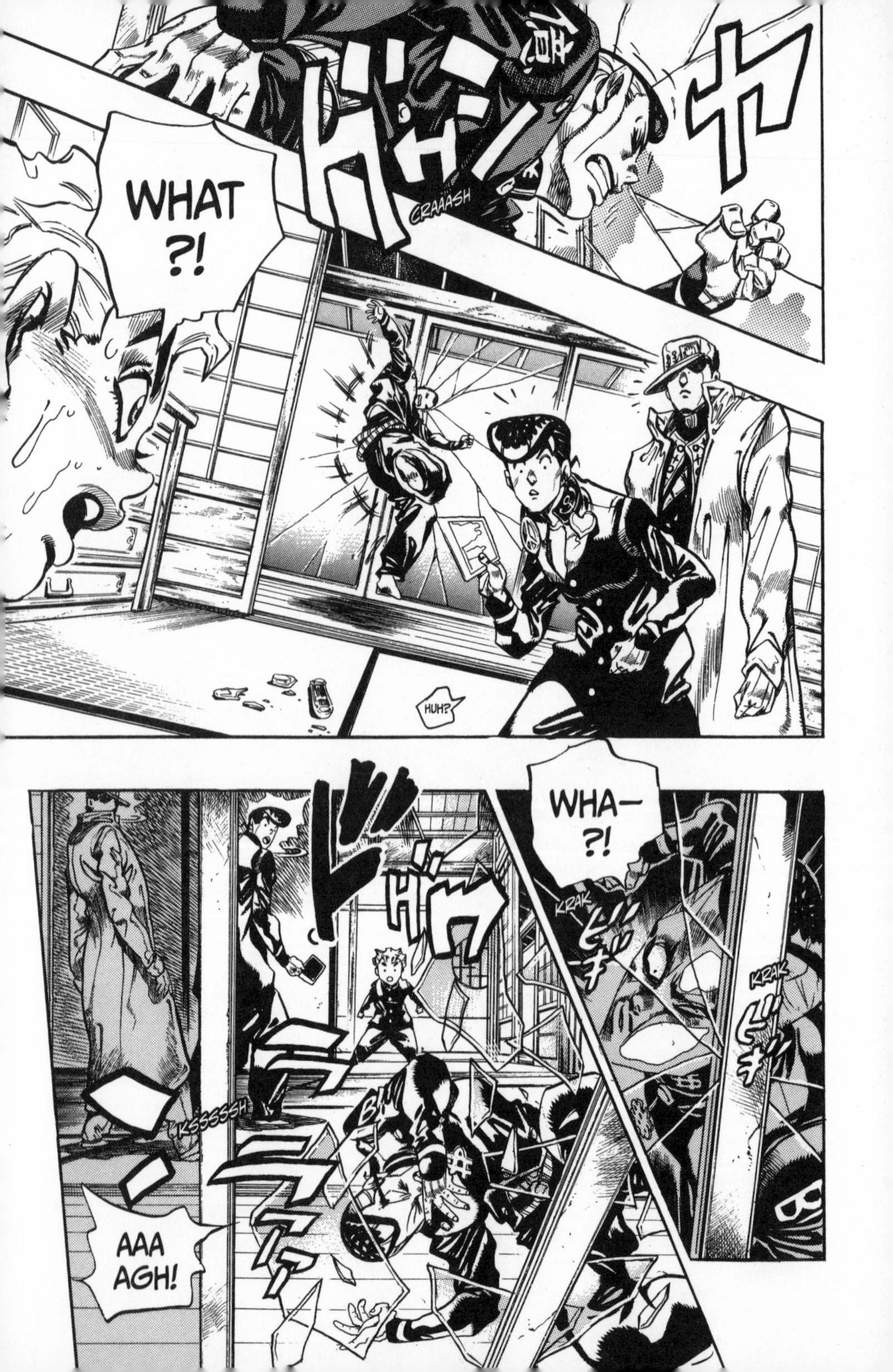
CRAAASH
WHAT ?!
HUH?
WHA— ?!
KRAK
KRAK
KSSSSSH
AAA AGH!

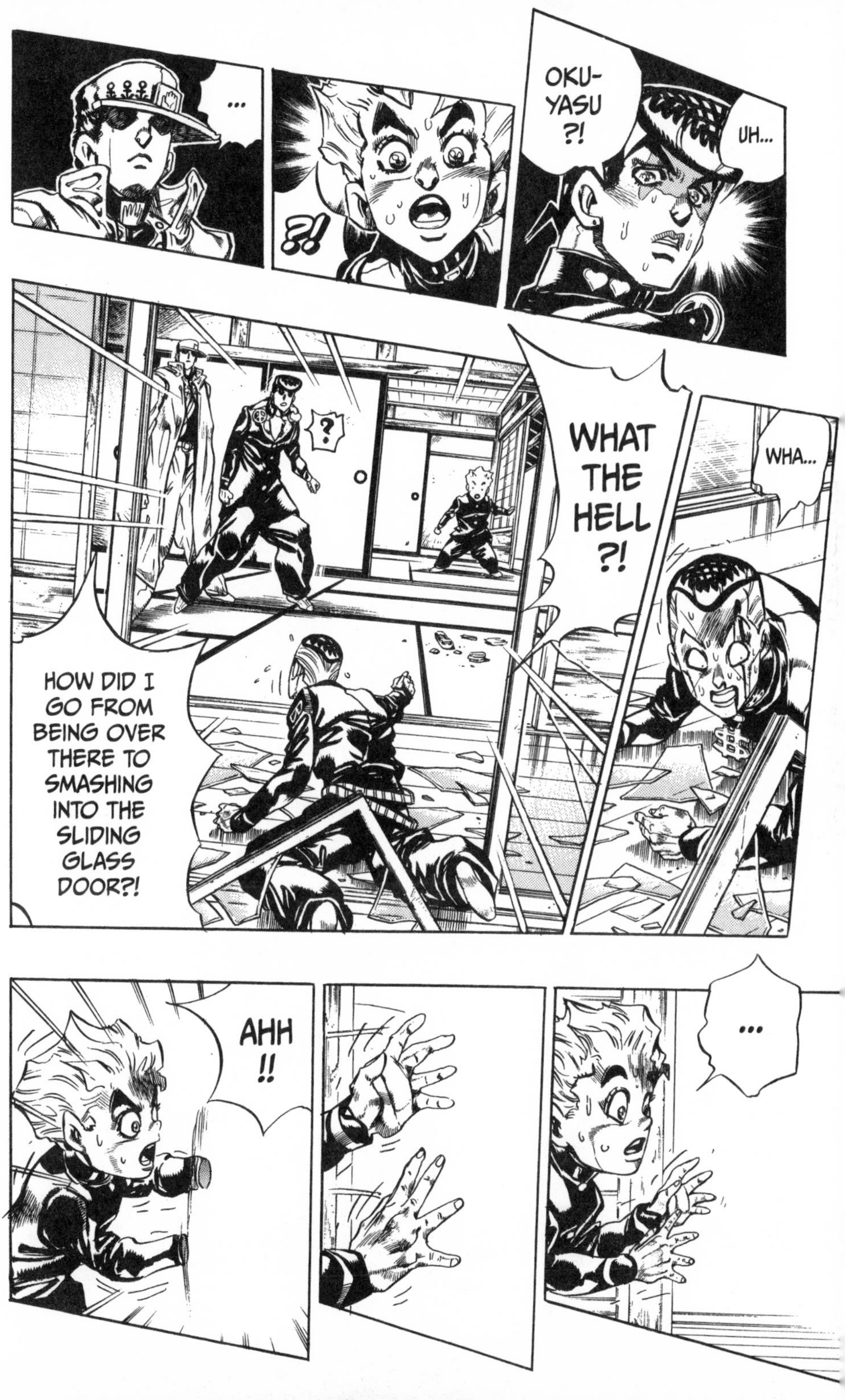
OKU-YASU ?!
UH...
?!
...
WHA...
WHAT THE HELL ?!
HOW DID I GO FROM BEING OVER THERE TO SMASHING INTO THE SLIDING GLASS DOOR?!
?
...
AHH !!

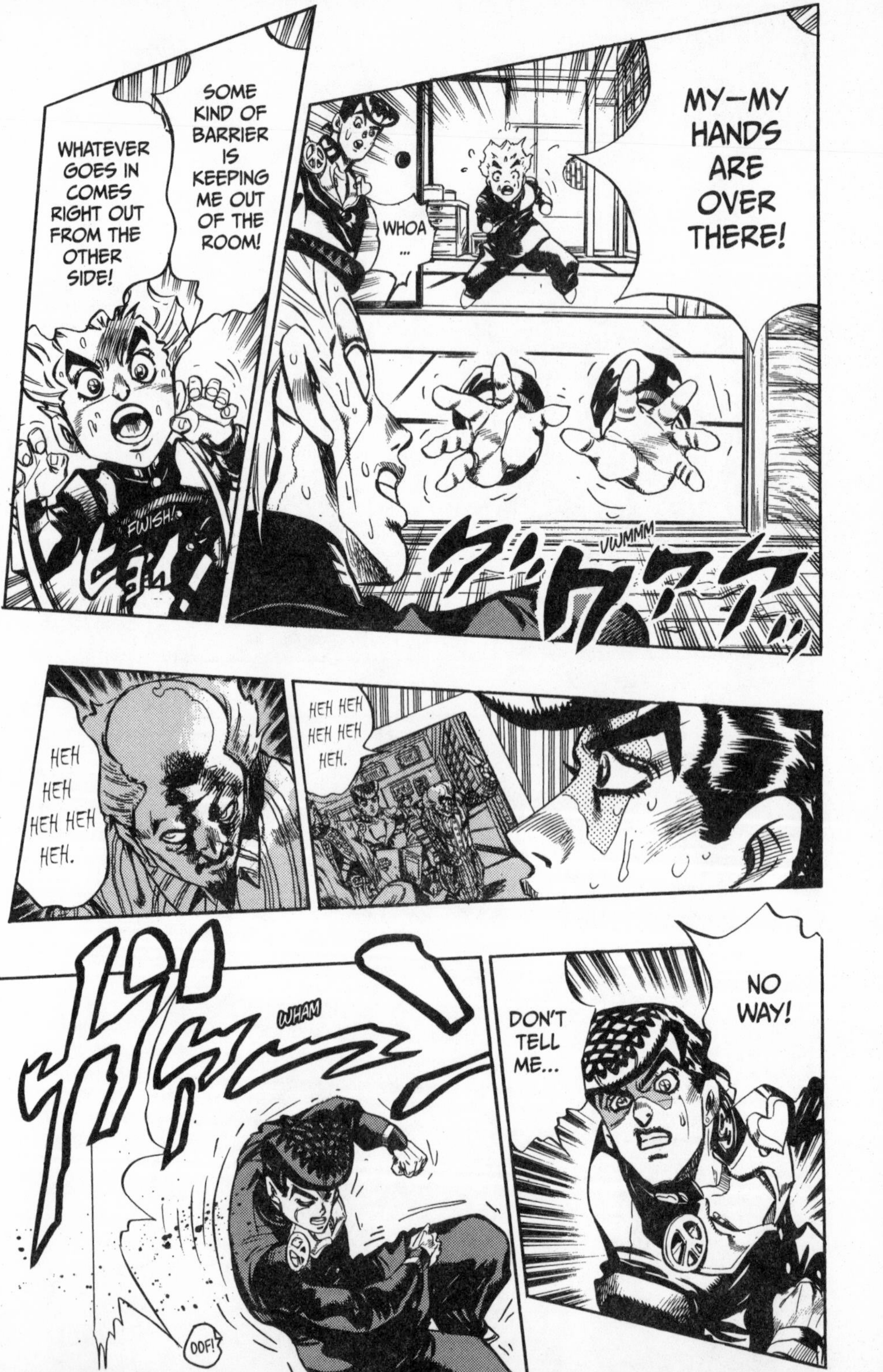
MY—MY HANDS ARE OVER THERE!
WHOA ...
VWMMM
SOME KIND OF BARRIER IS KEEPING ME OUT OF THE ROOM!
WHATEVER GOES IN COMES RIGHT OUT FROM THE OTHER SIDE!
FWISH!
HEH HEH HEH HEH HEH.
HEH HEH HEH HEH HEH.
NO WAY!
DON'T TELL ME...
WHAM
OOF!

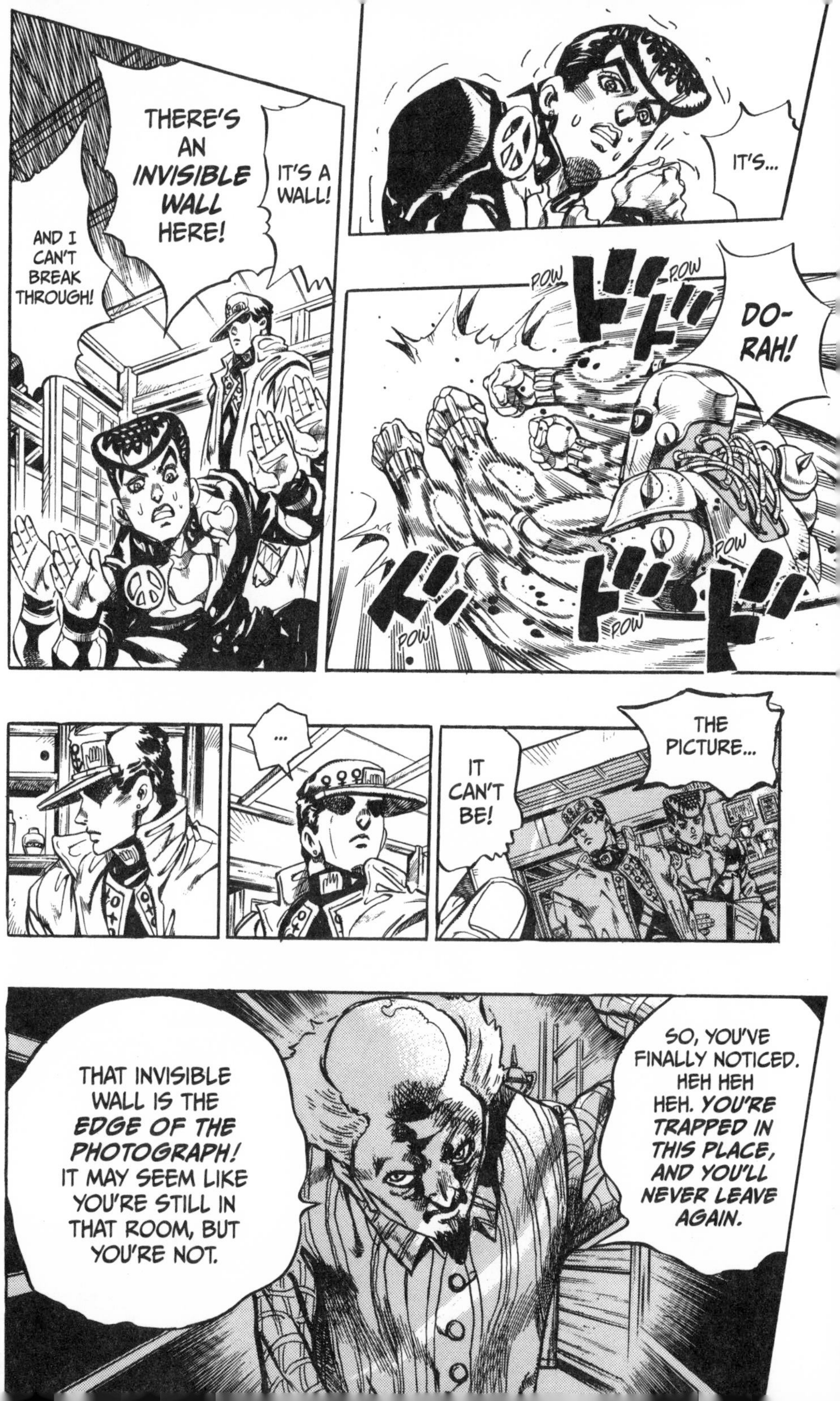

IT'S...
POW POW
DO-RAH!
POW POW POW
IT'S A WALL!
THERE'S AN INVISIBLE WALL HERE!
AND I CAN'T BREAK THROUGH!
THE PICTURE...
IT CAN'T BE!
...
SO, YOU'VE FINALLY NOTICED. HEH HEH HEH. YOU'RE TRAPPED IN THIS PLACE, AND YOU'LL NEVER LEAVE AGAIN.
THAT INVISIBLE WALL IS THE EDGE OF THE PHOTOGRAPH! IT MAY SEEM LIKE YOU'RE STILL IN THAT ROOM, BUT YOU'RE NOT.

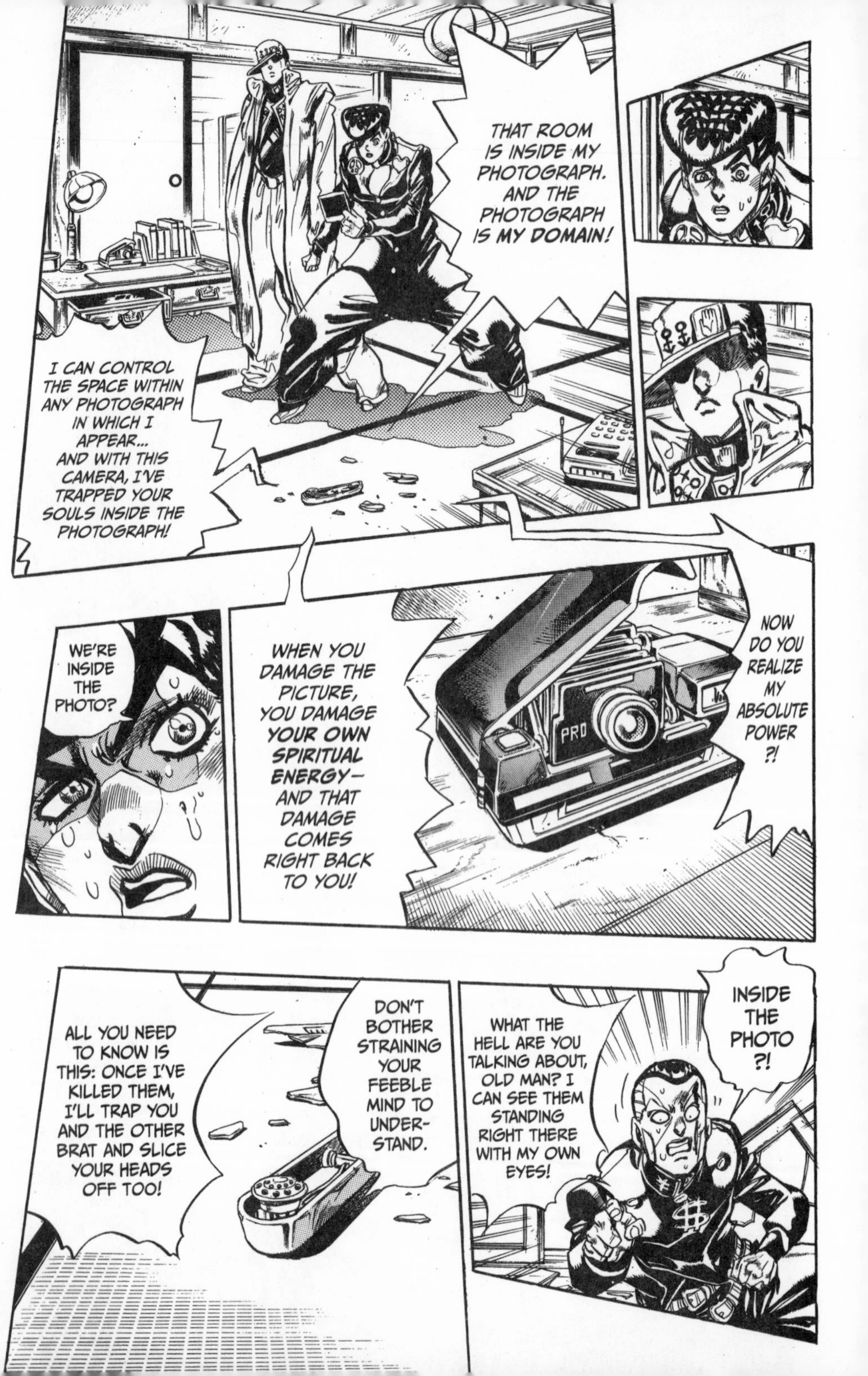

THAT ROOM IS INSIDE MY PHOTOGRAPH. AND THE PHOTOGRAPH IS MY DOMAIN!
I CAN CONTROL THE SPACE WITHIN ANY PHOTOGRAPH IN WHICH I APPEAR... AND WITH THIS CAMERA, I'VE TRAPPED YOUR SOULS INSIDE THE PHOTOGRAPH!
NOW DO YOU REALIZE MY ABSOLUTE POWER ?!
PRO
WHEN YOU DAMAGE THE PICTURE, YOU DAMAGE YOUR OWN SPIRITUAL ENERGY— AND THAT DAMAGE COMES RIGHT BACK TO YOU!
WE'RE INSIDE THE PHOTO?
INSIDE THE PHOTO ?!
WHAT THE HELL ARE YOU TALKING ABOUT, OLD MAN? I CAN SEE THEM STANDING RIGHT THERE WITH MY OWN EYES!
DON'T BOTHER STRAINING YOUR FEEBLE MIND TO UNDER- STAND.
ALL YOU NEED TO KNOW IS THIS: ONCE I'VE KILLED THEM, I'LL TRAP YOU AND THE OTHER BRAT AND SLICE YOUR HEADS OFF TOO!

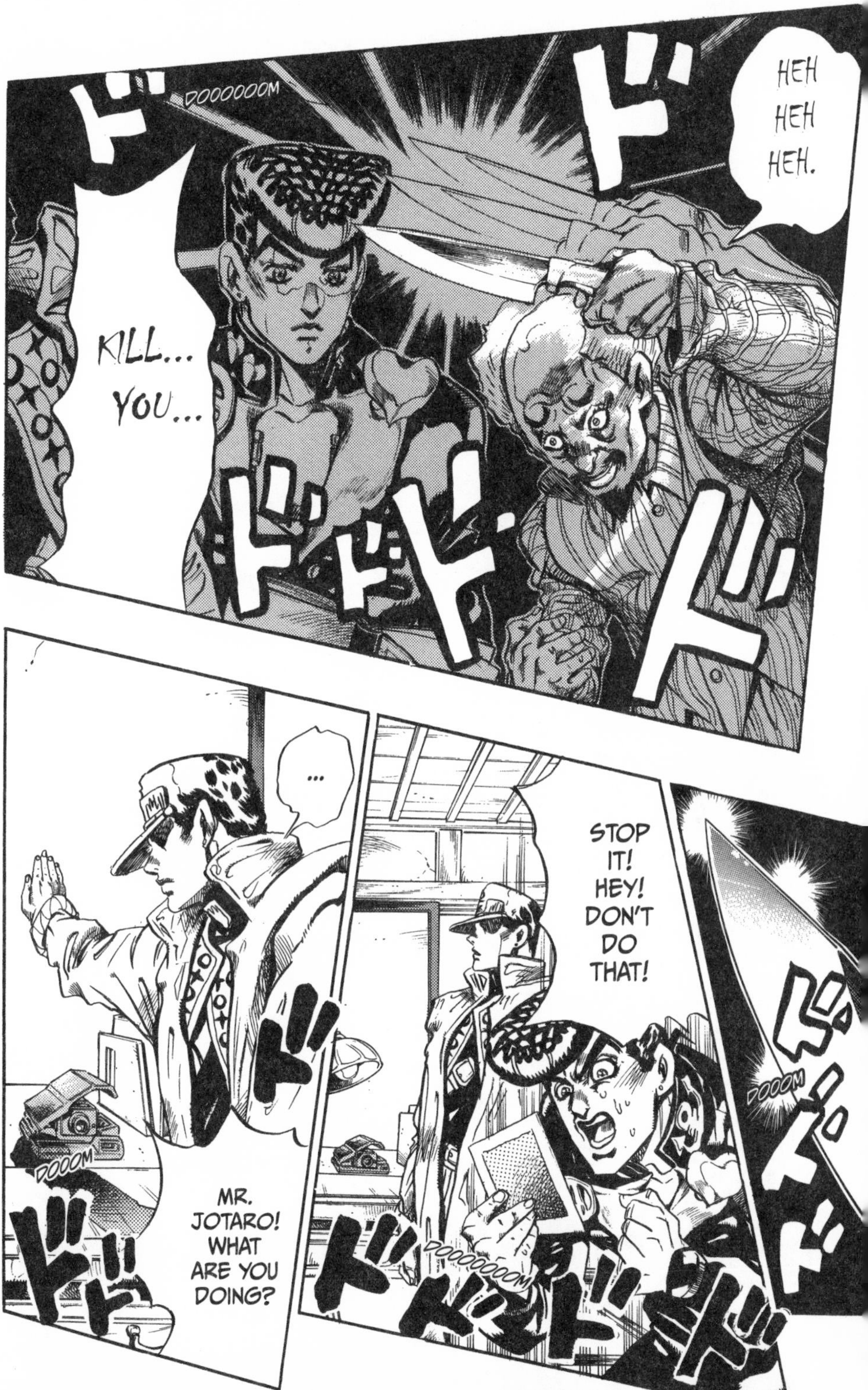
HEH HEH HEH.
DOOOOOOM
KILL... YOU...
DOOOM
STOP IT! HEY! DON'T DO THAT!
DOOOOOOOM
...
MR. JOTARO! WHAT ARE YOU DOING?
DOOOM

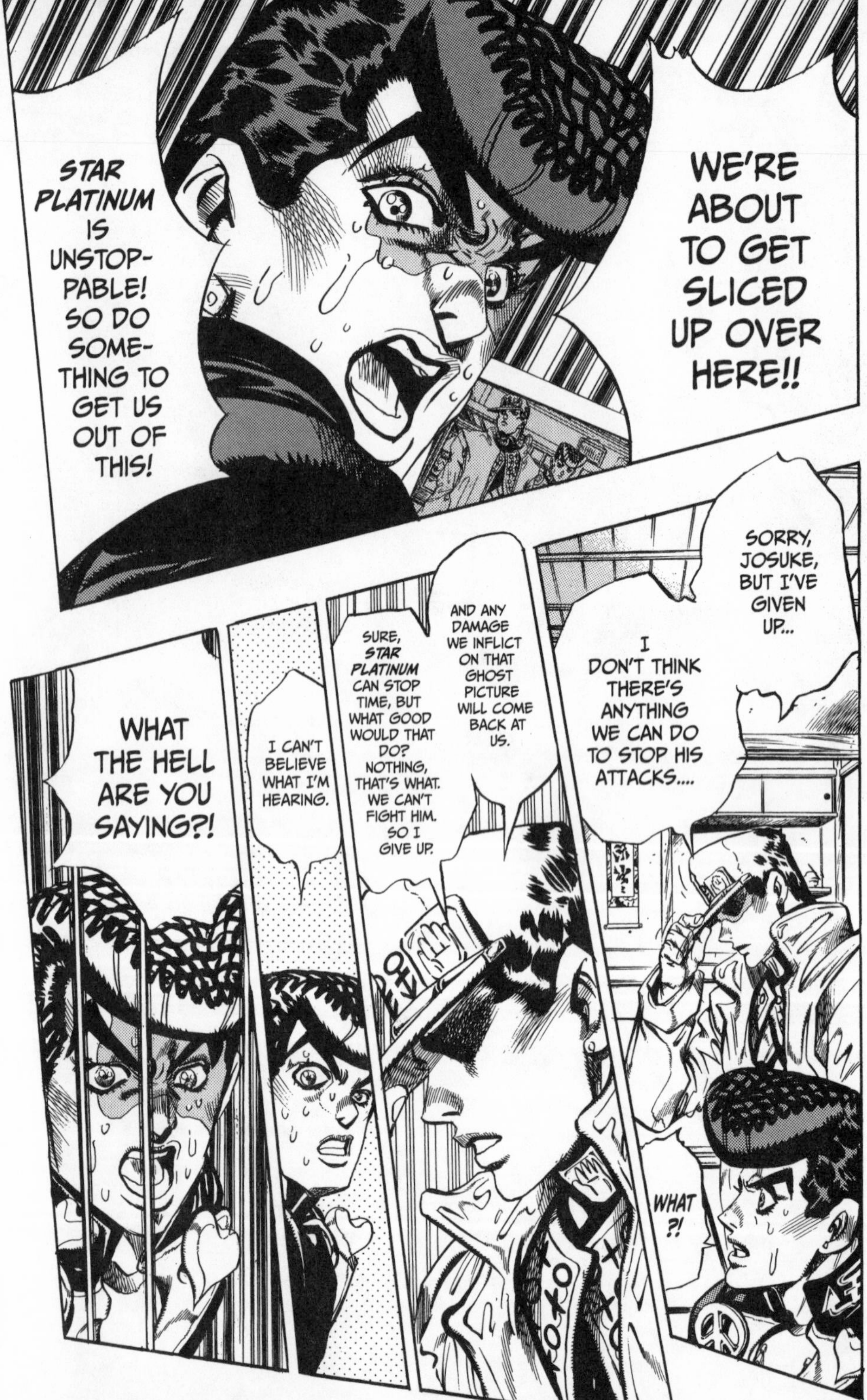

WE'RE ABOUT TO GET SLICED UP OVER HERE!!
STAR PLATINUM IS UNSTOP-PABLE! SO DO SOME-THING TO GET US OUT OF THIS!
SORRY, JOSUKE, BUT I'VE GIVEN UP...
I DON'T THINK THERE'S ANYTHING WE CAN DO TO STOP HIS ATTACKS....
WHAT ?!
AND ANY DAMAGE WE INFLICT ON THAT GHOST PICTURE WILL COME BACK AT US.
SURE, STAR PLATINUM CAN STOP TIME, BUT WHAT GOOD WOULD THAT DO? NOTHING, THAT'S WHAT. WE CAN'T FIGHT HIM. SO I GIVE UP.
I CAN'T BELIEVE WHAT I'M HEARING.
WHAT THE HELL ARE YOU SAYING?!

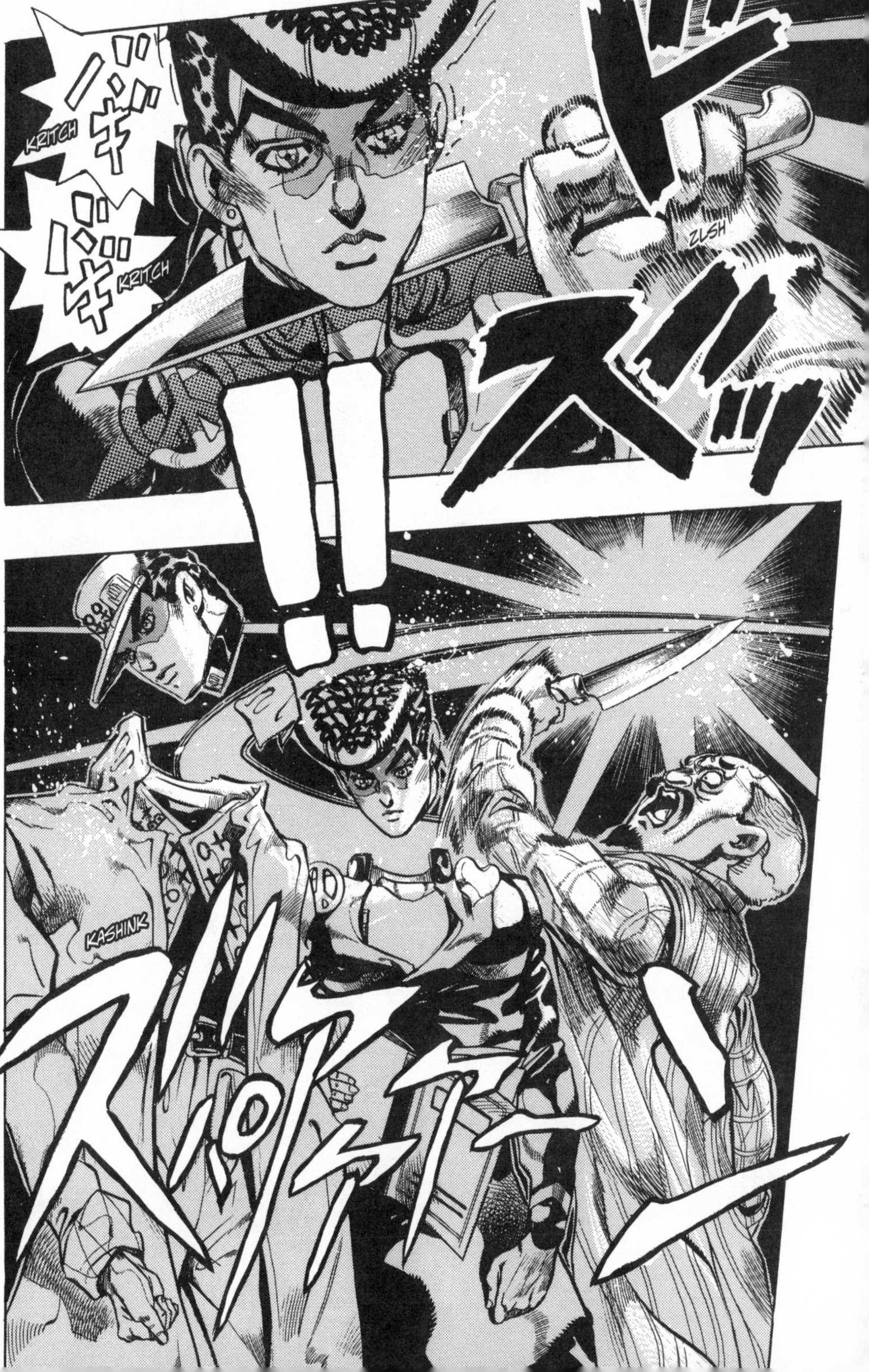
ドズッ
ZLSH
KRITCH
KRITCH
!!
KASHINK

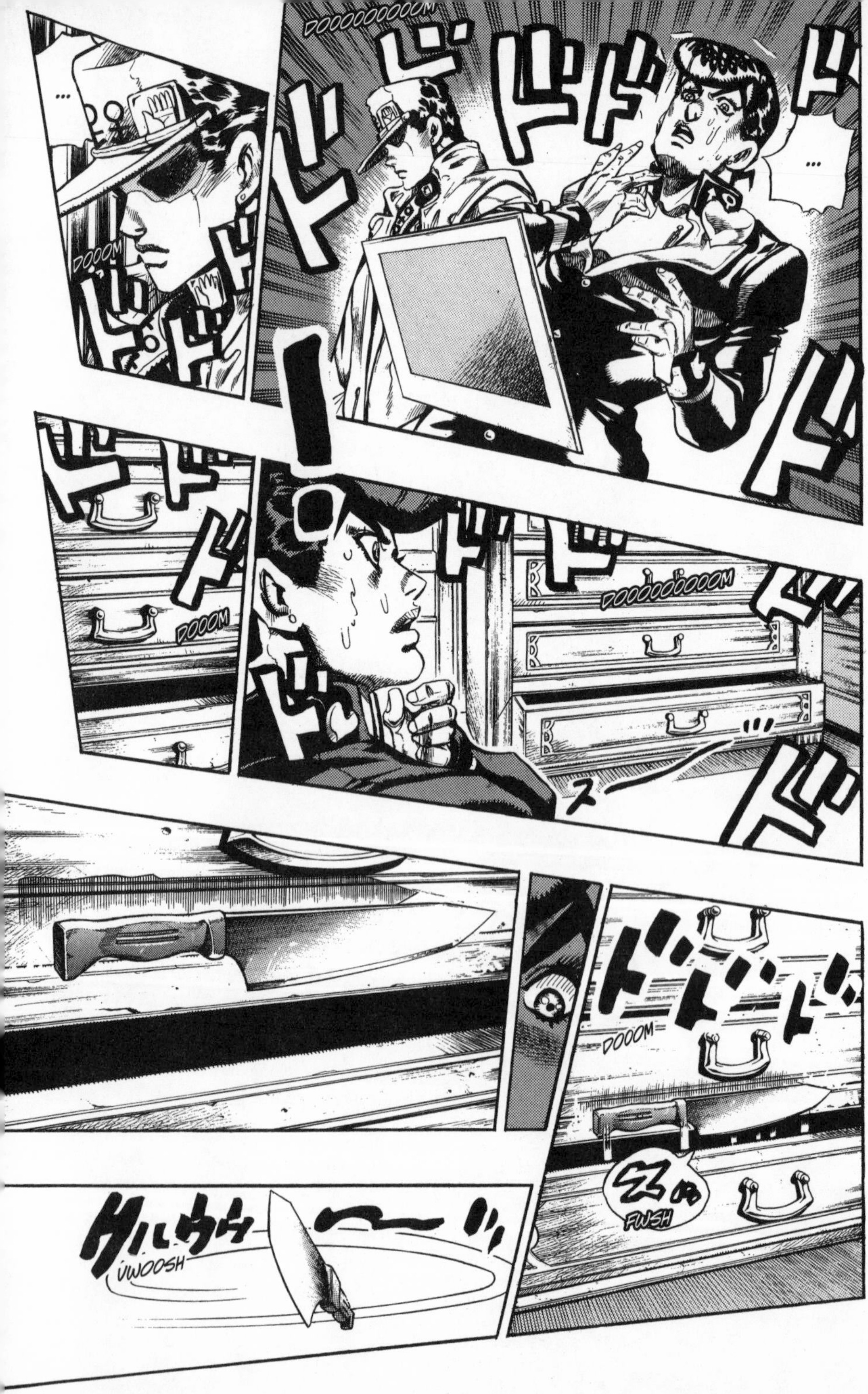
DOOOOOOOOOM
...
...
DOOOM
DOOOOOOOOOM
DOOOM
DOOOM
FWSH
VWOOSH

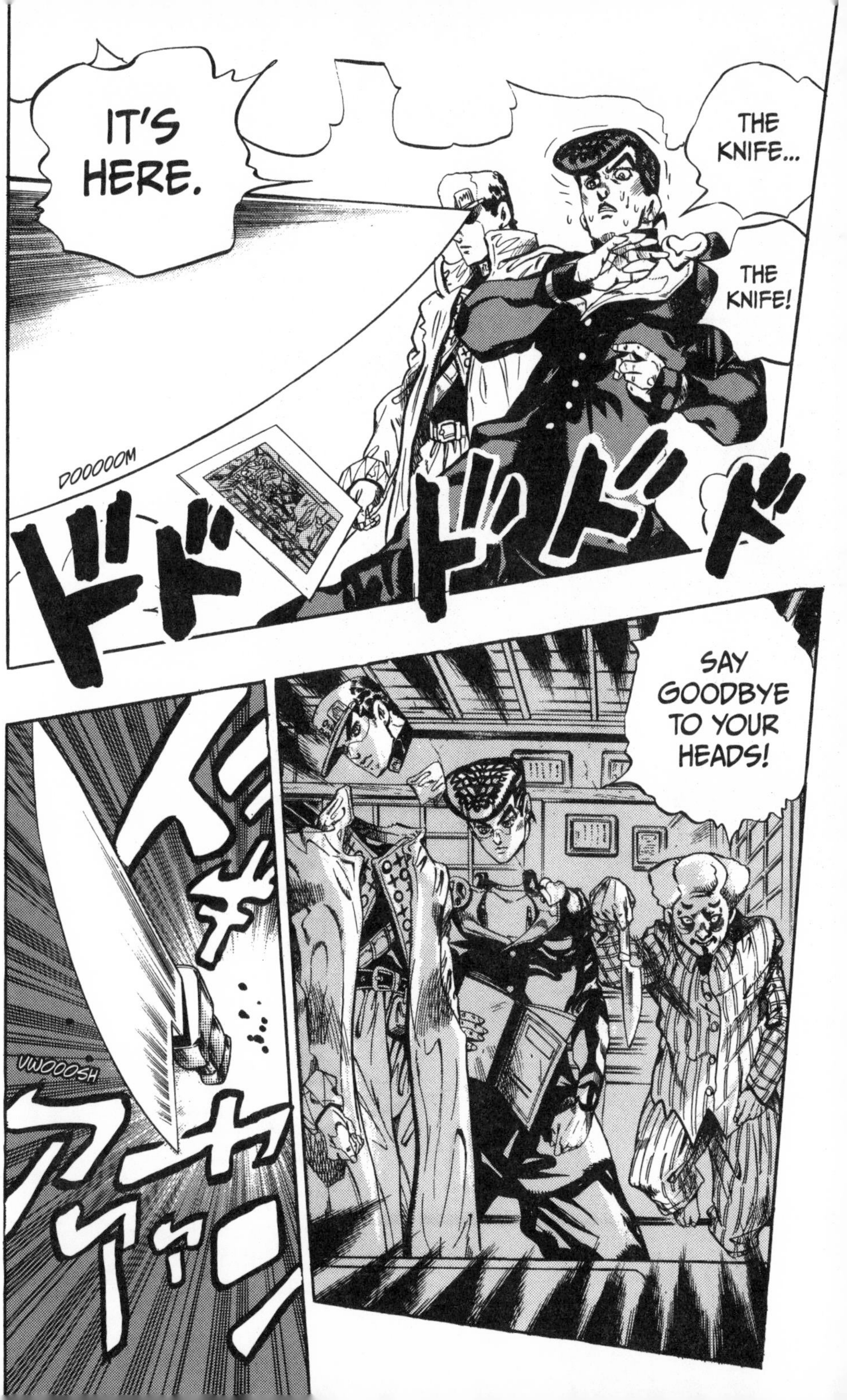
THE KNIFE...
THE KNIFE!
IT'S HERE.
DOOOOOM
SAY GOODBYE TO YOUR HEADS!
VWOOOSH

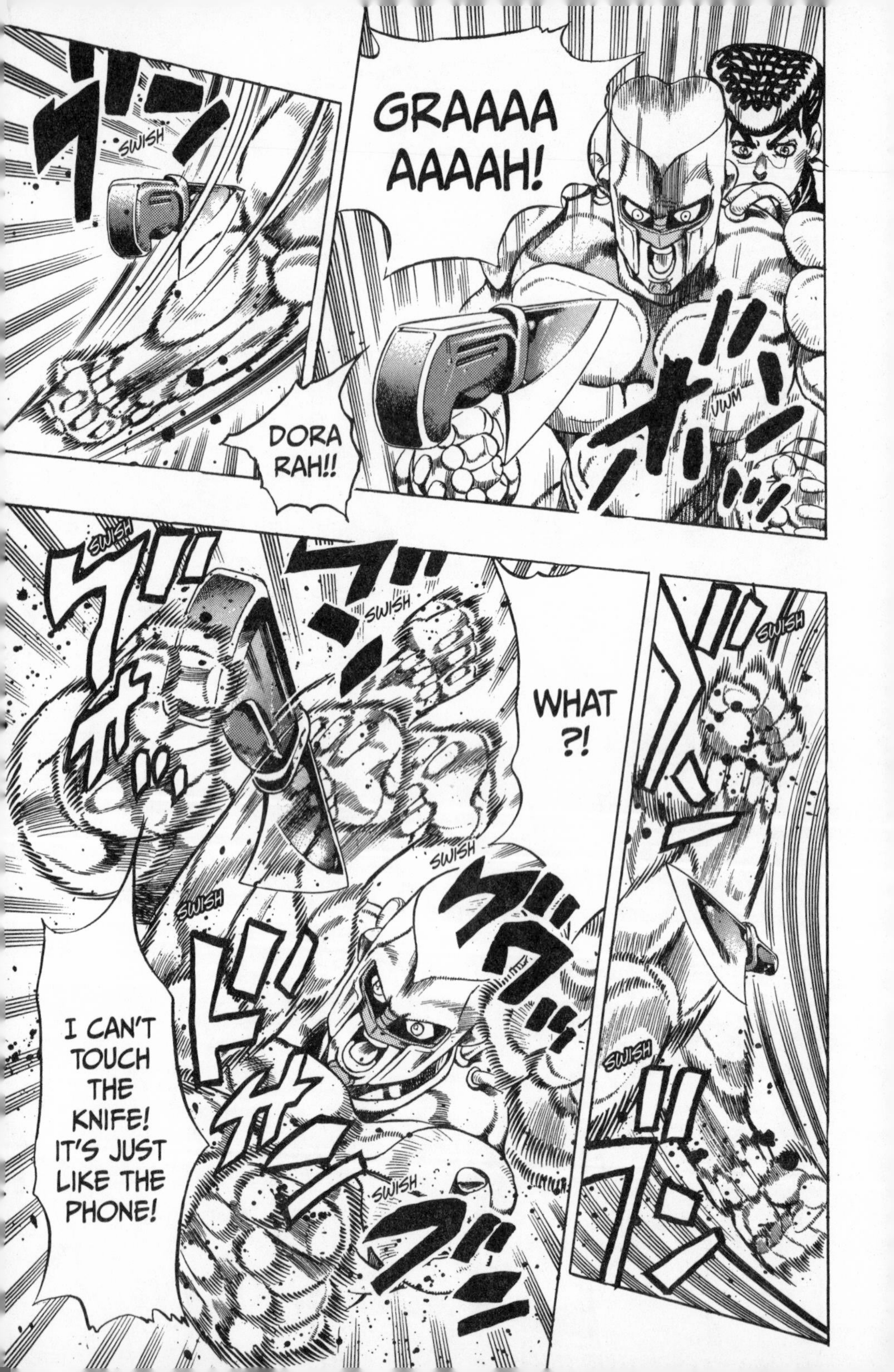
GRAAAA AAAAH!
VWM
DORA RAH!!
SWISH
SWISH
SWISH
WHAT ?!
SWISH
SWISH
SWISH
I CAN'T TOUCH THE KNIFE! IT'S JUST LIKE THE PHONE!
SWISH

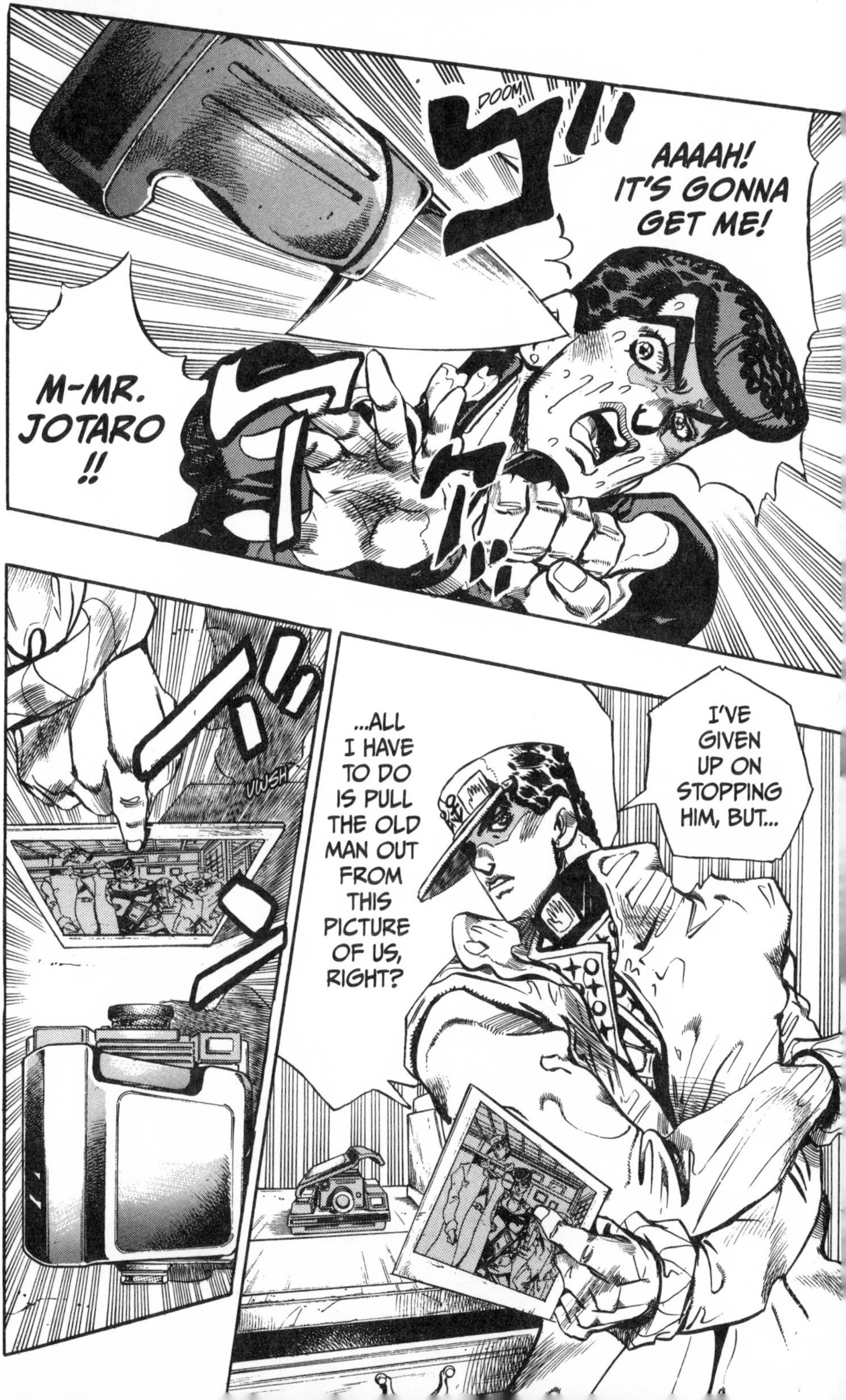
DOOM
AAAAH! IT'S GONNA GET ME!
M-MR. JOTARO !!
I'VE GIVEN UP ON STOPPING HIM, BUT...
...ALL I HAVE TO DO IS PULL THE OLD MAN OUT FROM THIS PICTURE OF US, RIGHT?
VWSH

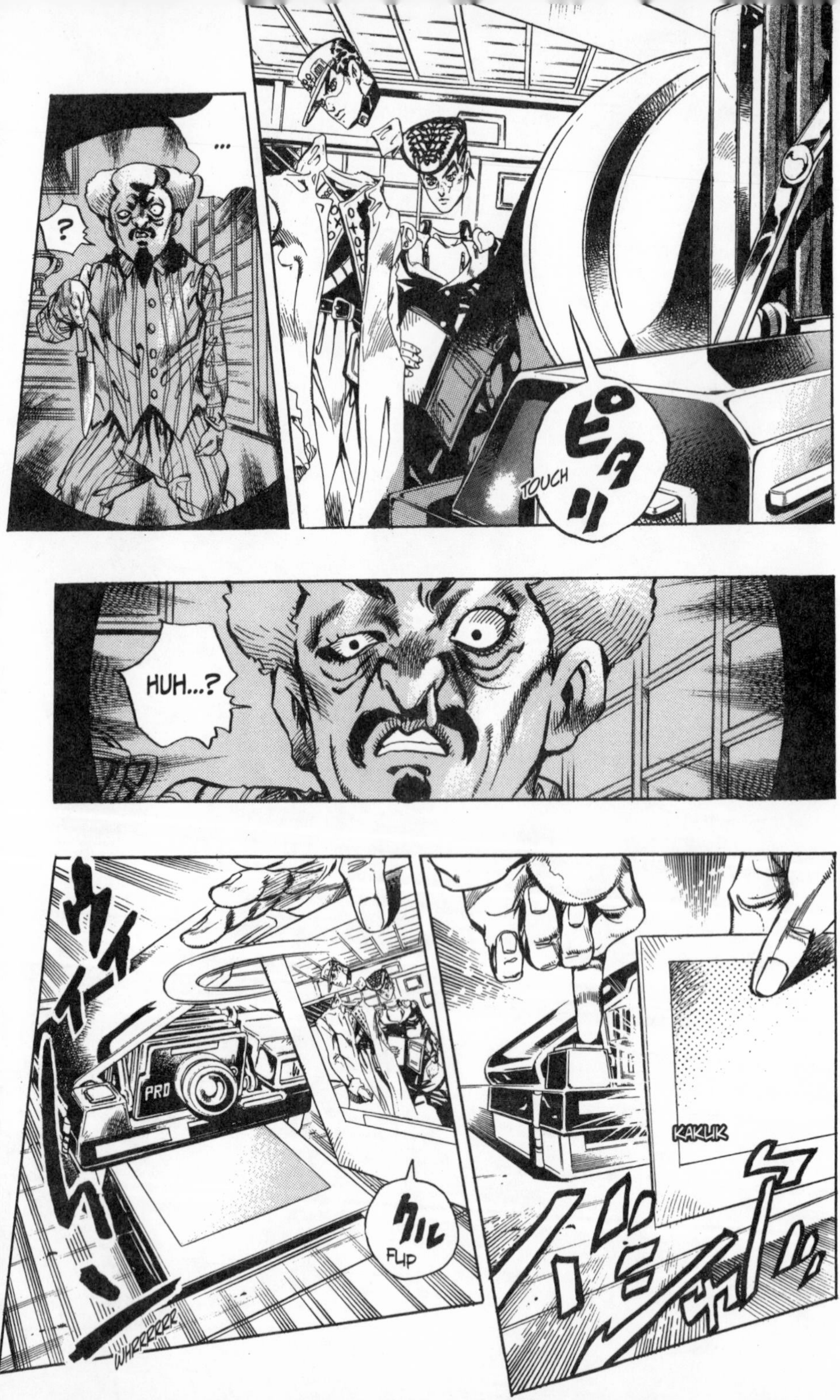

ピタッ
TOUCH
...
?
HUH...?
KAKUK
パシャ
クル
FLIP
WHRRRRR

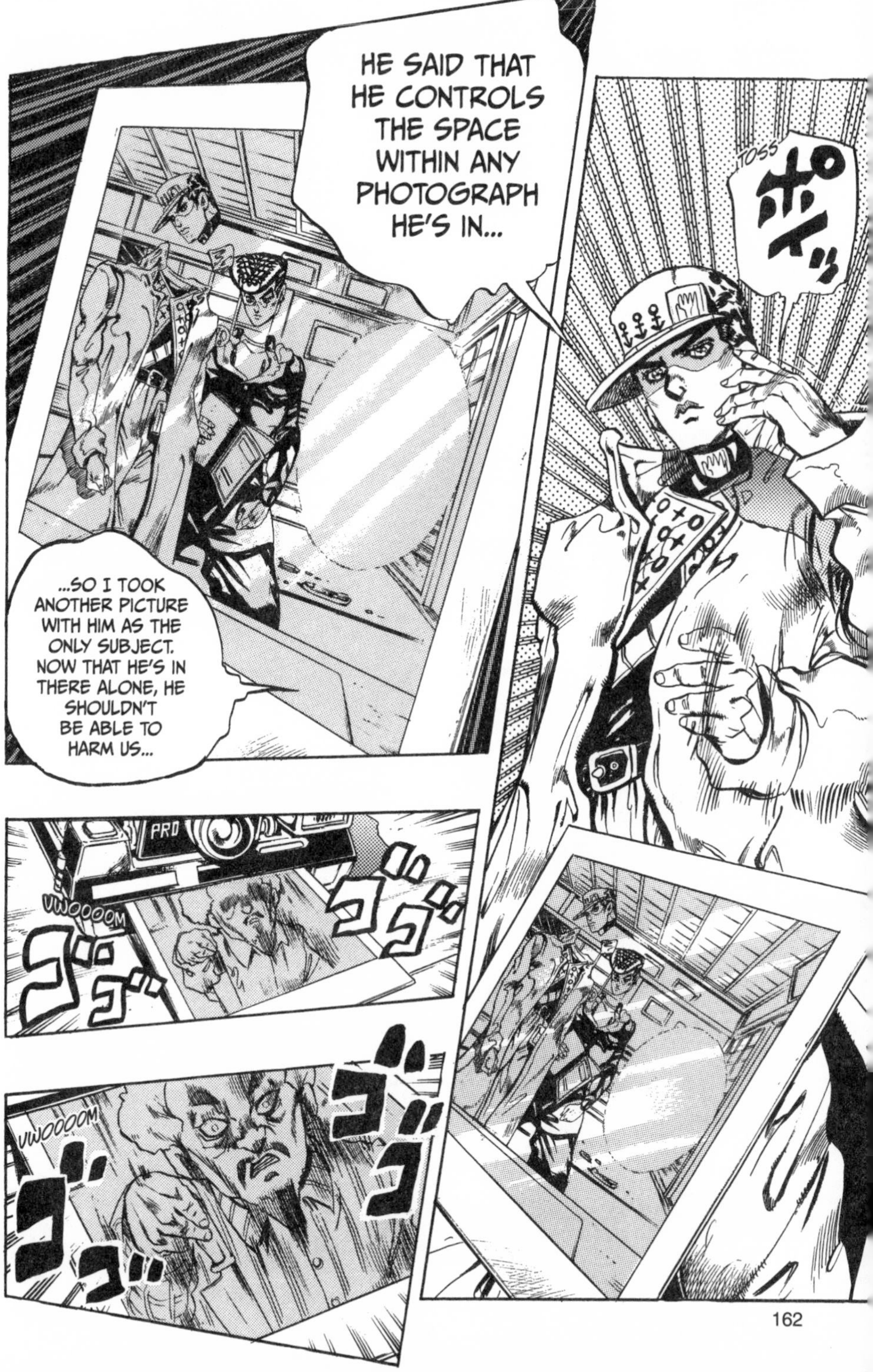
TOSS
HE SAID THAT HE CONTROLS THE SPACE WITHIN ANY PHOTOGRAPH HE'S IN...
...SO I TOOK ANOTHER PICTURE WITH HIM AS THE ONLY SUBJECT. NOW THAT HE'S IN THERE ALONE, HE SHOULDN'T BE ABLE TO HARM US...
PRO
VWOOOOM
VWOOOOM

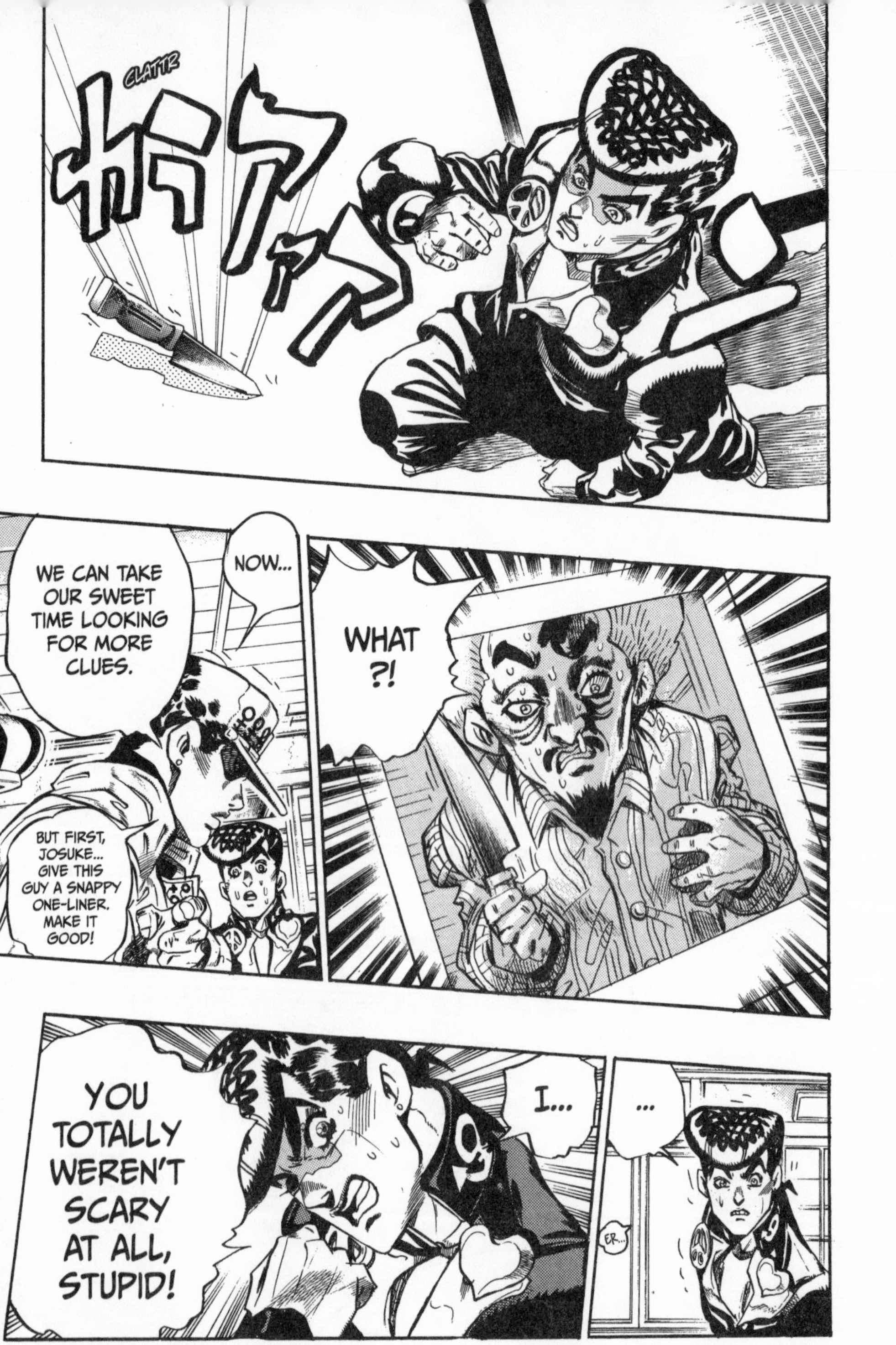
CLATTR
WHAT ?!
NOW...
WE CAN TAKE OUR SWEET TIME LOOKING FOR MORE CLUES.
BUT FIRST, JOSUKE... GIVE THIS GUY A SNAPPY ONE-LINER. MAKE IT GOOD!
...
ER...
I...
YOU TOTALLY WEREN'T SCARY AT ALL, STUPID!

AW, CRUD. I TOTALLY SOUNDED LIKE A LITTLE KID!

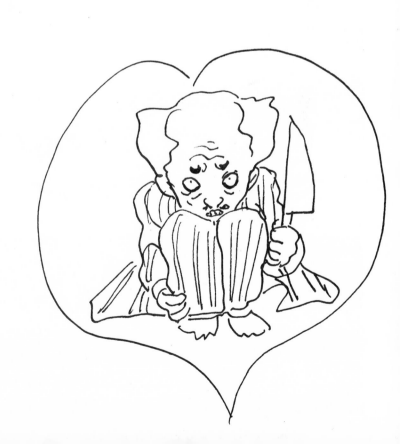

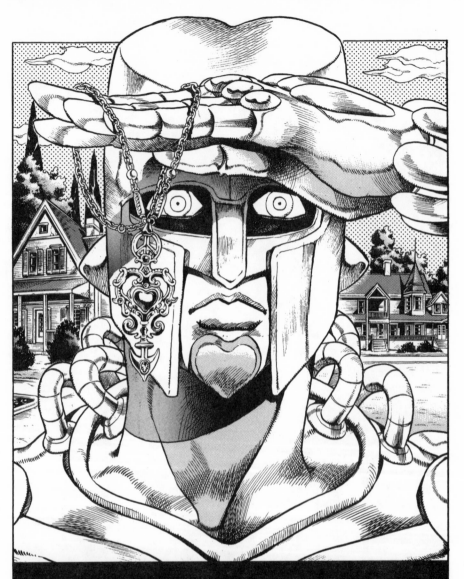

CHAPTER 103

HEART FATHER,
PART 4

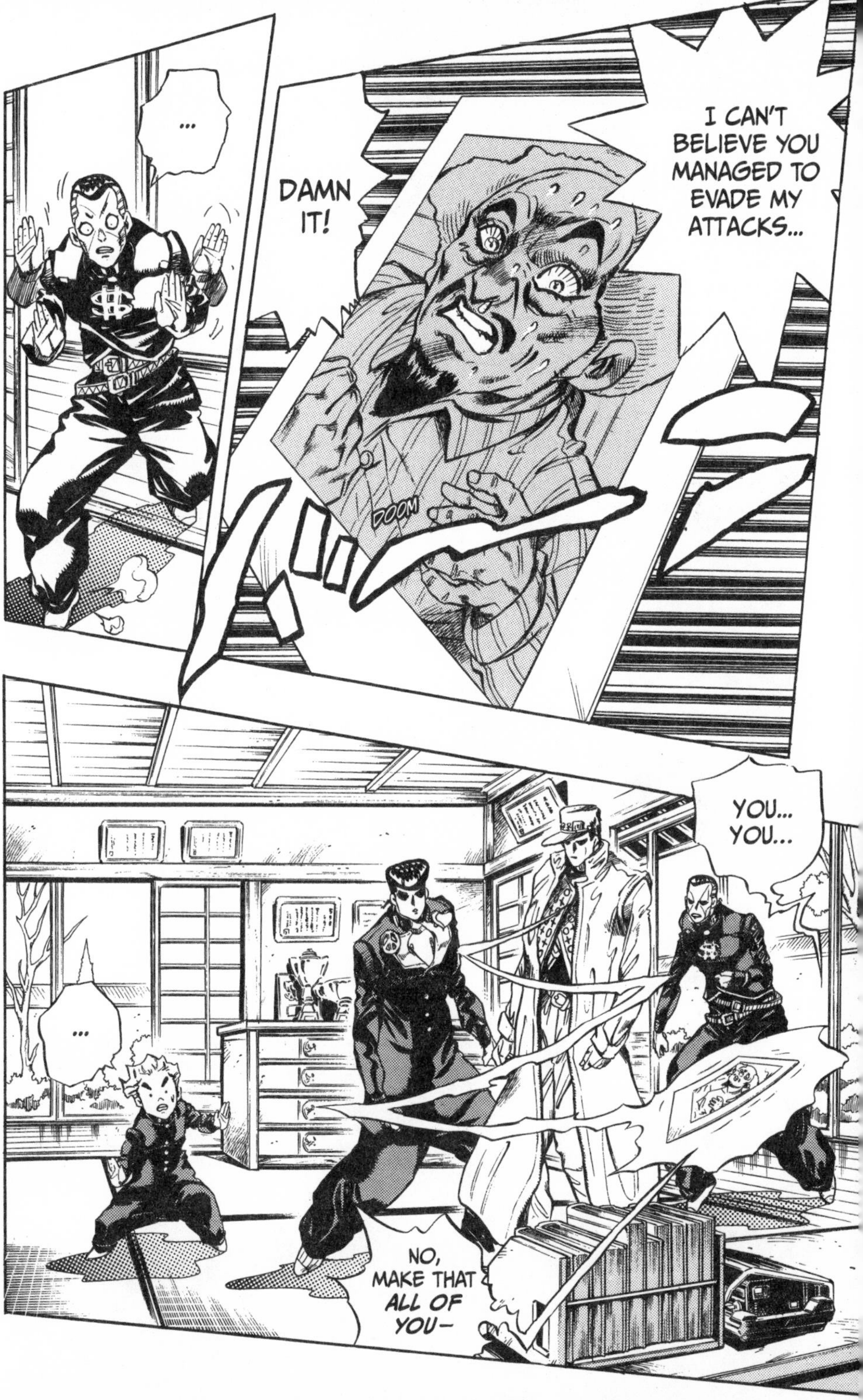
I CAN'T BELIEVE YOU MANAGED TO EVADE MY ATTACKS...
DAMN IT!
DOOM
...
YOU... YOU...
NO, MAKE THAT ALL OF YOU—
...

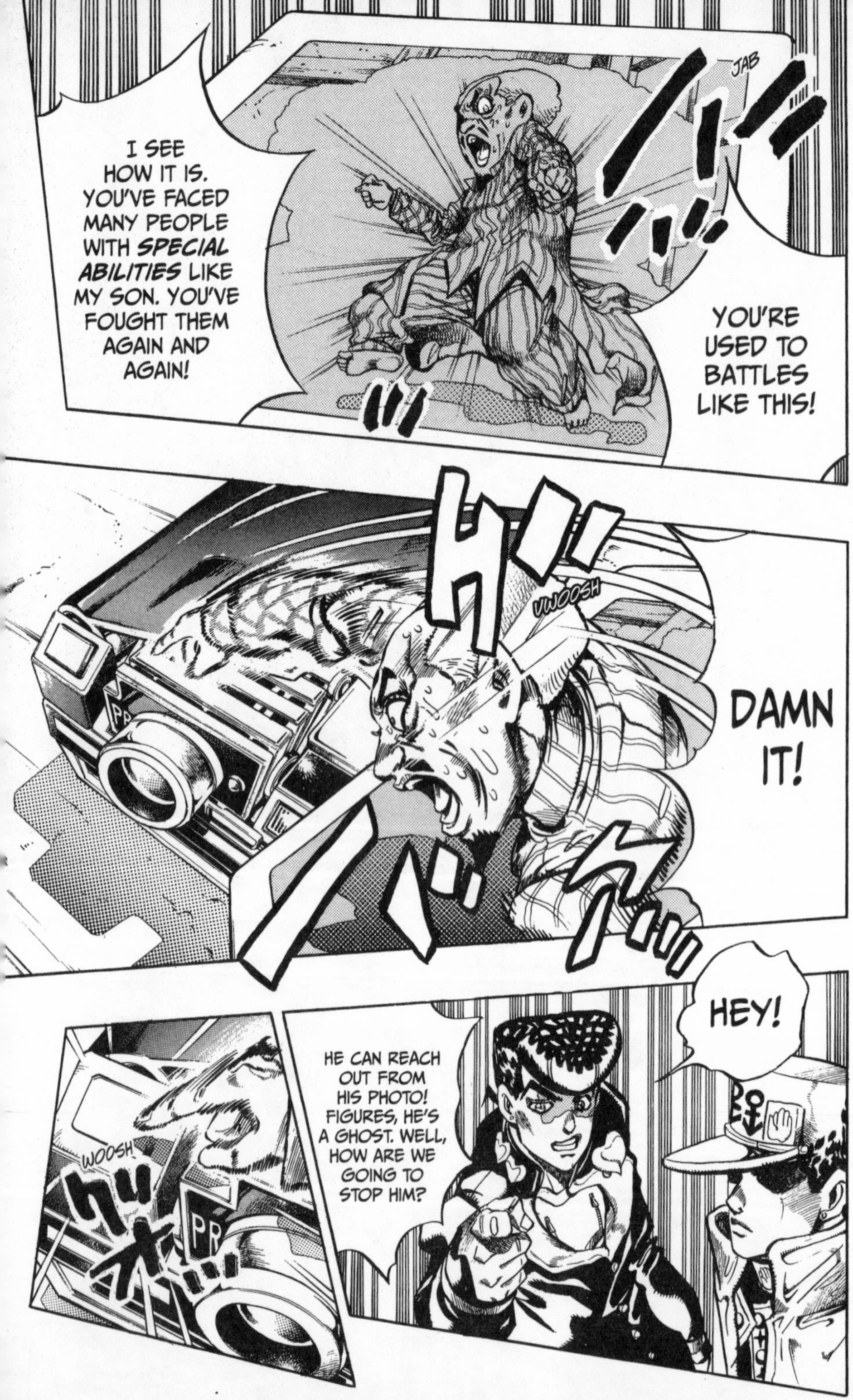
JAB
YOU'RE USED TO BATTLES LIKE THIS!
I SEE HOW IT IS. YOU'VE FACED MANY PEOPLE WITH *SPECIAL ABILITIES* LIKE MY SON. YOU'VE FOUGHT THEM AGAIN AND AGAIN!
VWOOSH
DAMN IT!
HEY!
HE CAN REACH OUT FROM HIS PHOTO! FIGURES, HE'S A GHOST. WELL, HOW ARE WE GOING TO STOP HIM?
WOOSH

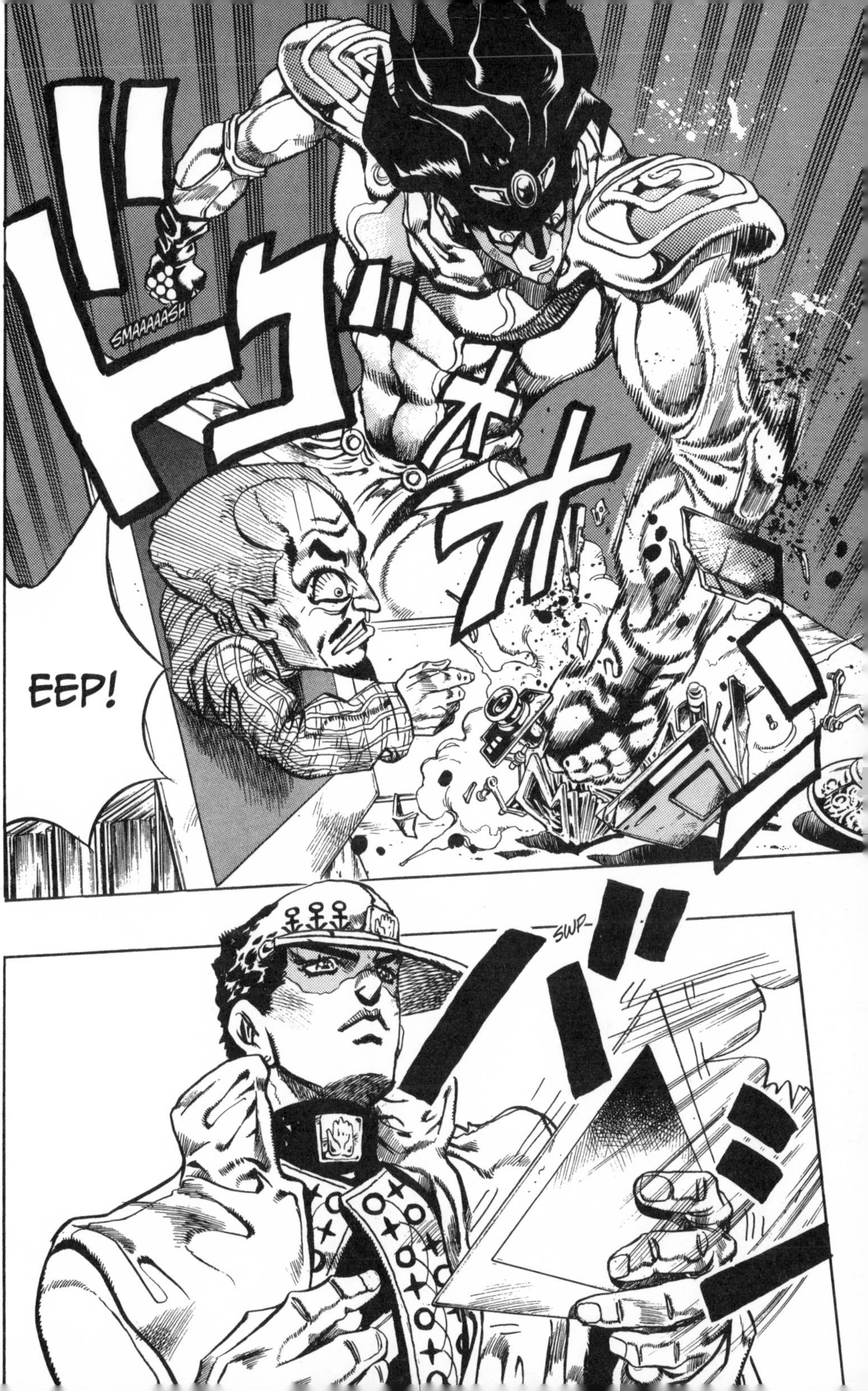
SMAAAAASH
EEP!
SWP

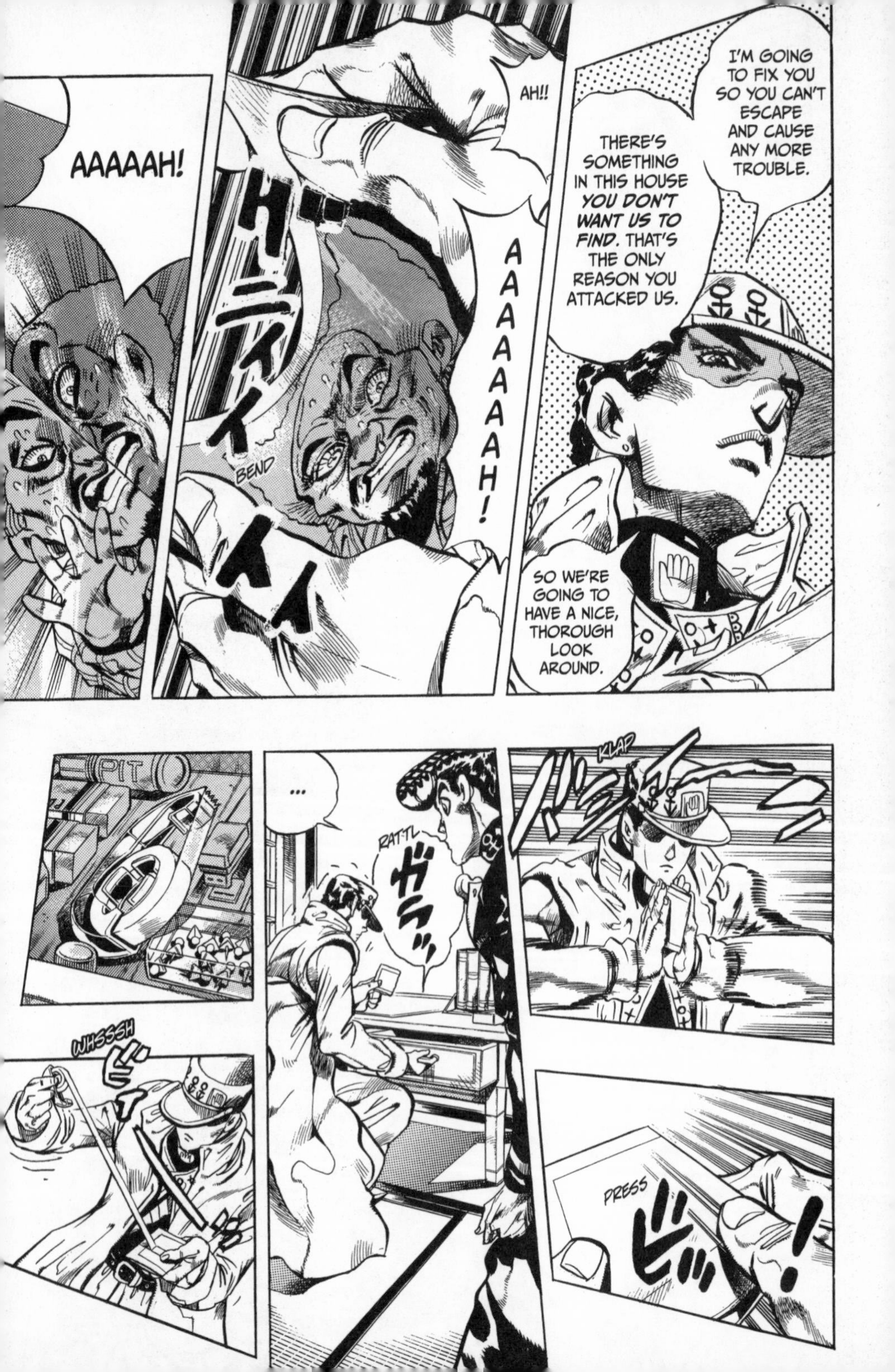
I'M GOING TO FIX YOU SO YOU CAN'T ESCAPE AND CAUSE ANY MORE TROUBLE.
THERE'S SOMETHING IN THIS HOUSE *YOU DON'T WANT US TO FIND*. THAT'S THE ONLY REASON YOU ATTACKED US.
SO WE'RE GOING TO HAVE A NICE, THOROUGH LOOK AROUND.
AH!!
AAAAAAAAAH!
BEND
AAAAAH!
KLAP
PRESS
...
RAT-TL
ガラッ
PIT
WHSSSH

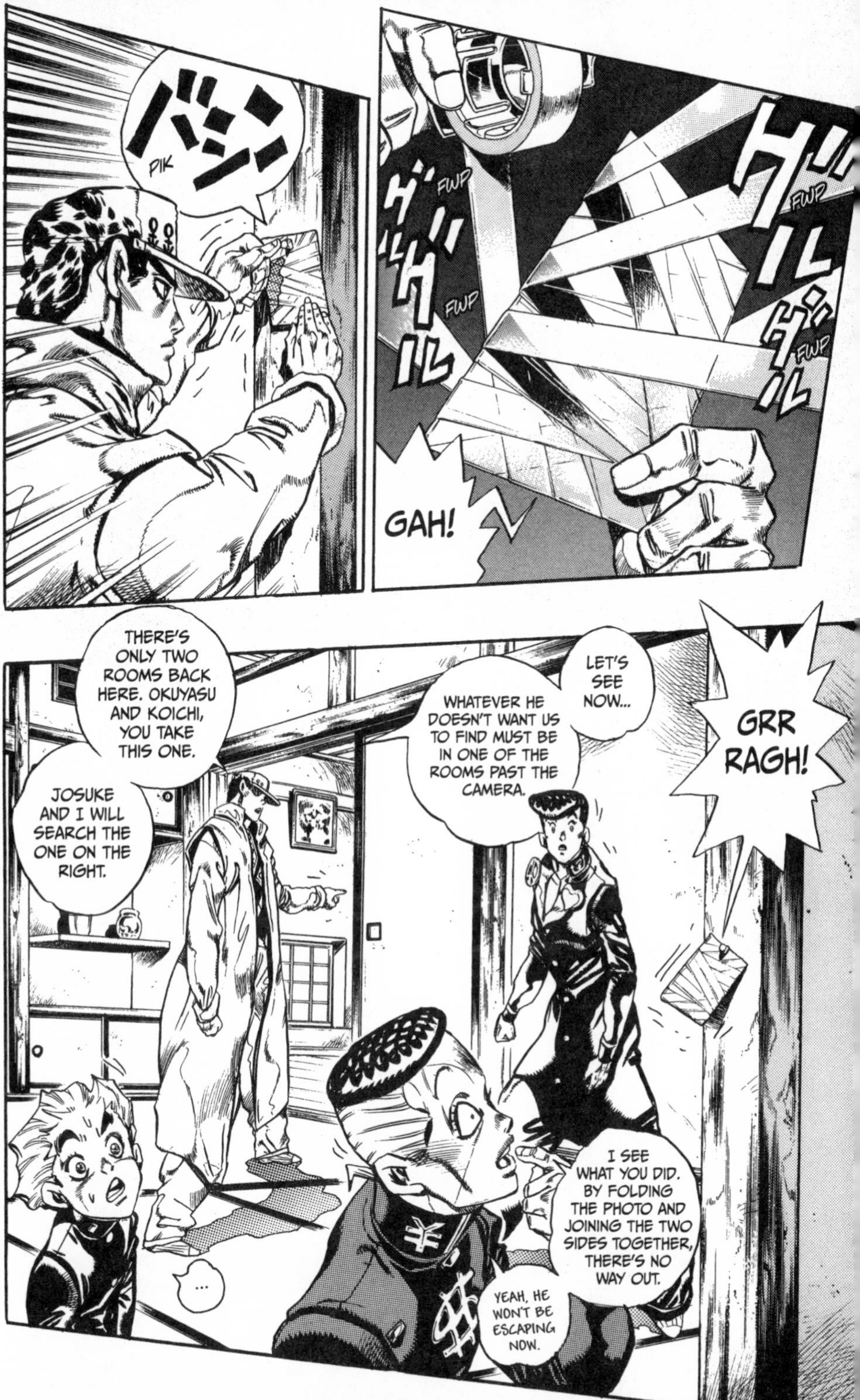
FWP
FWP
FWP
FWP
GAH!
バシン
PIK
GRR RAGH!
LET'S SEE NOW...
WHATEVER HE DOESN'T WANT US TO FIND MUST BE IN ONE OF THE ROOMS PAST THE CAMERA.
THERE'S ONLY TWO ROOMS BACK HERE. OKUYASU AND KOICHI, YOU TAKE THIS ONE.
JOSUKE AND I WILL SEARCH THE ONE ON THE RIGHT.
I SEE WHAT YOU DID. BY FOLDING THE PHOTO AND JOINING THE TWO SIDES TOGETHER, THERE'S NO WAY OUT.
YEAH, HE WON'T BE ESCAPING NOW.
...

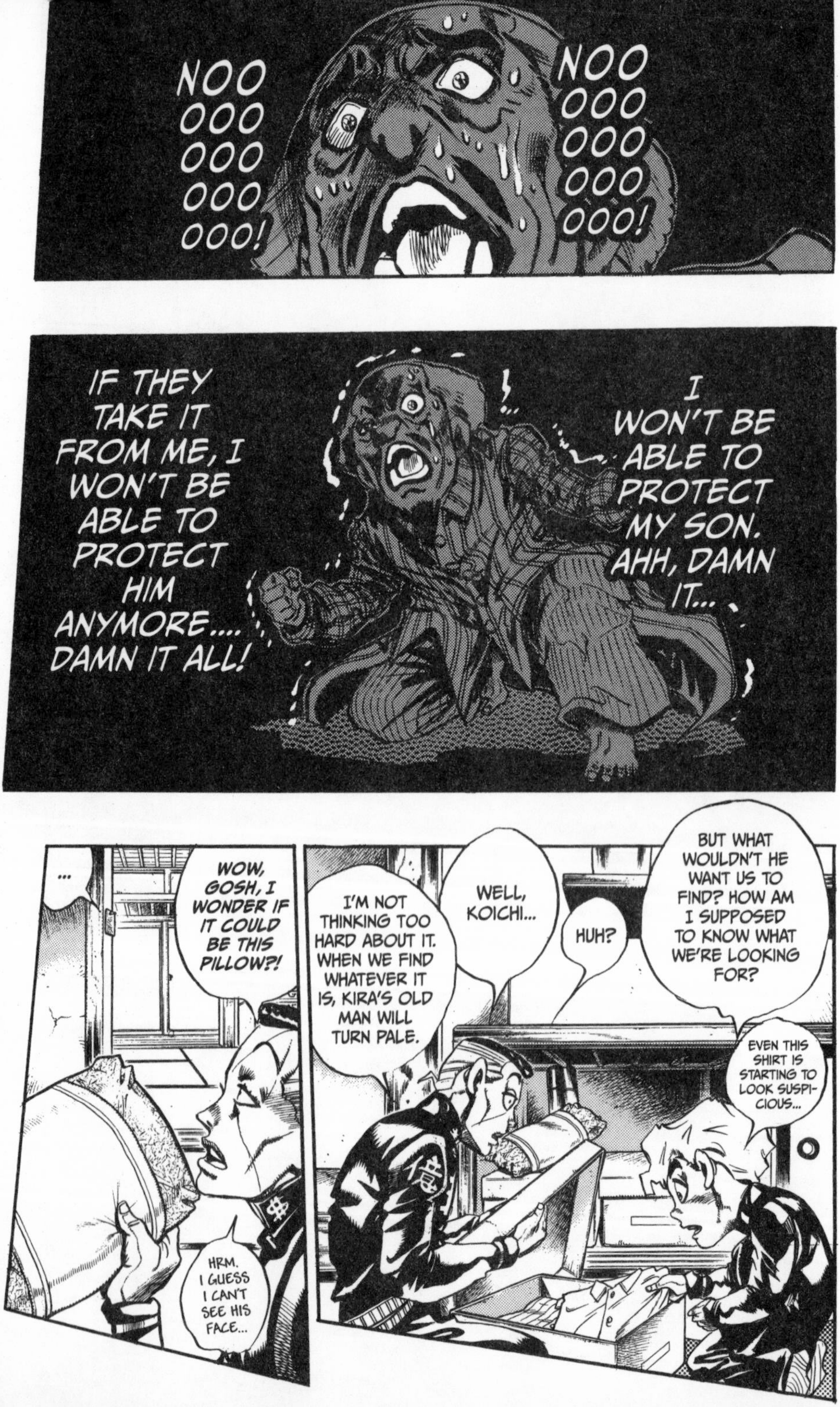
NOO OOO OOO OOO OOO!
NOO OOO OOO OOO OOO!
I WON'T BE ABLE TO PROTECT MY SON. AHH, DAMN IT...
IF THEY TAKE IT FROM ME, I WON'T BE ABLE TO PROTECT HIM ANYMORE.... DAMN IT ALL!
BUT WHAT WOULDN'T HE WANT US TO FIND? HOW AM I SUPPOSED TO KNOW WHAT WE'RE LOOKING FOR?
EVEN THIS SHIRT IS STARTING TO LOOK SUSPI-CIOUS...
HUH?
WELL, KOICHI...
I'M NOT THINKING TOO HARD ABOUT IT. WHEN WE FIND WHATEVER IT IS, KIRA'S OLD MAN WILL TURN PALE.
WOW, GOSH, I WONDER IF IT COULD BE THIS PILLOW?!
...
HRM. I GUESS I CAN'T SEE HIS FACE...

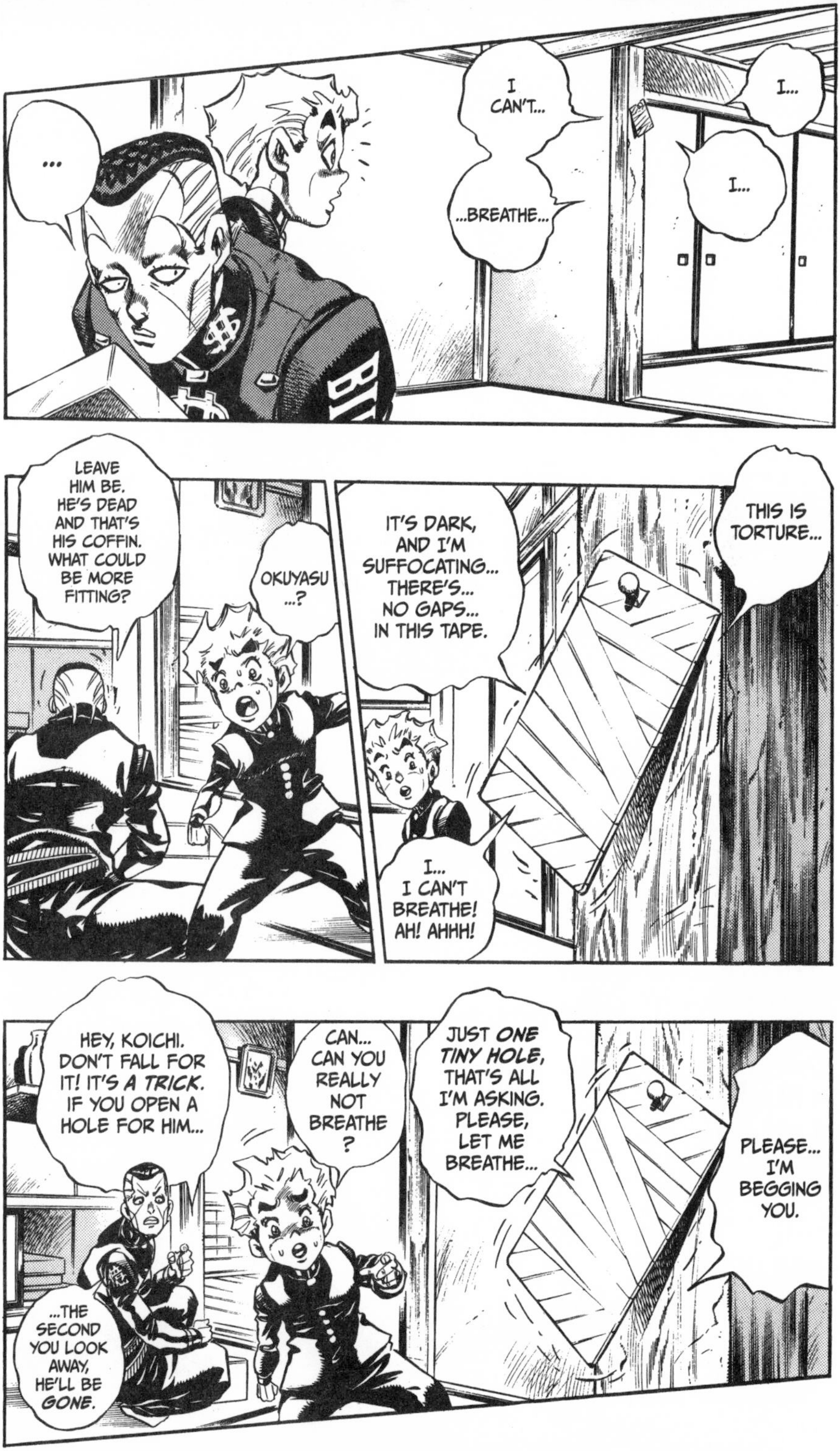
I...
I CAN'T...
I...
...BREATHE...
...
THIS IS TORTURE...
IT'S DARK, AND I'M SUFFOCATING... THERE'S... NO GAPS... IN THIS TAPE.
I... I CAN'T BREATHE! AH! AHHH!
OKUYASU ...?
LEAVE HIM BE. HE'S DEAD AND THAT'S HIS COFFIN. WHAT COULD BE MORE FITTING?
JUST *ONE TINY HOLE*, THAT'S ALL I'M ASKING. PLEASE, LET ME BREATHE...
PLEASE... I'M BEGGING YOU.
CAN... CAN YOU REALLY NOT BREATHE ?
HEY, KOICHI. DON'T FALL FOR IT! IT'S *A TRICK*. IF YOU OPEN A HOLE FOR HIM...
...THE SECOND YOU LOOK AWAY, HE'LL BE *GONE*.

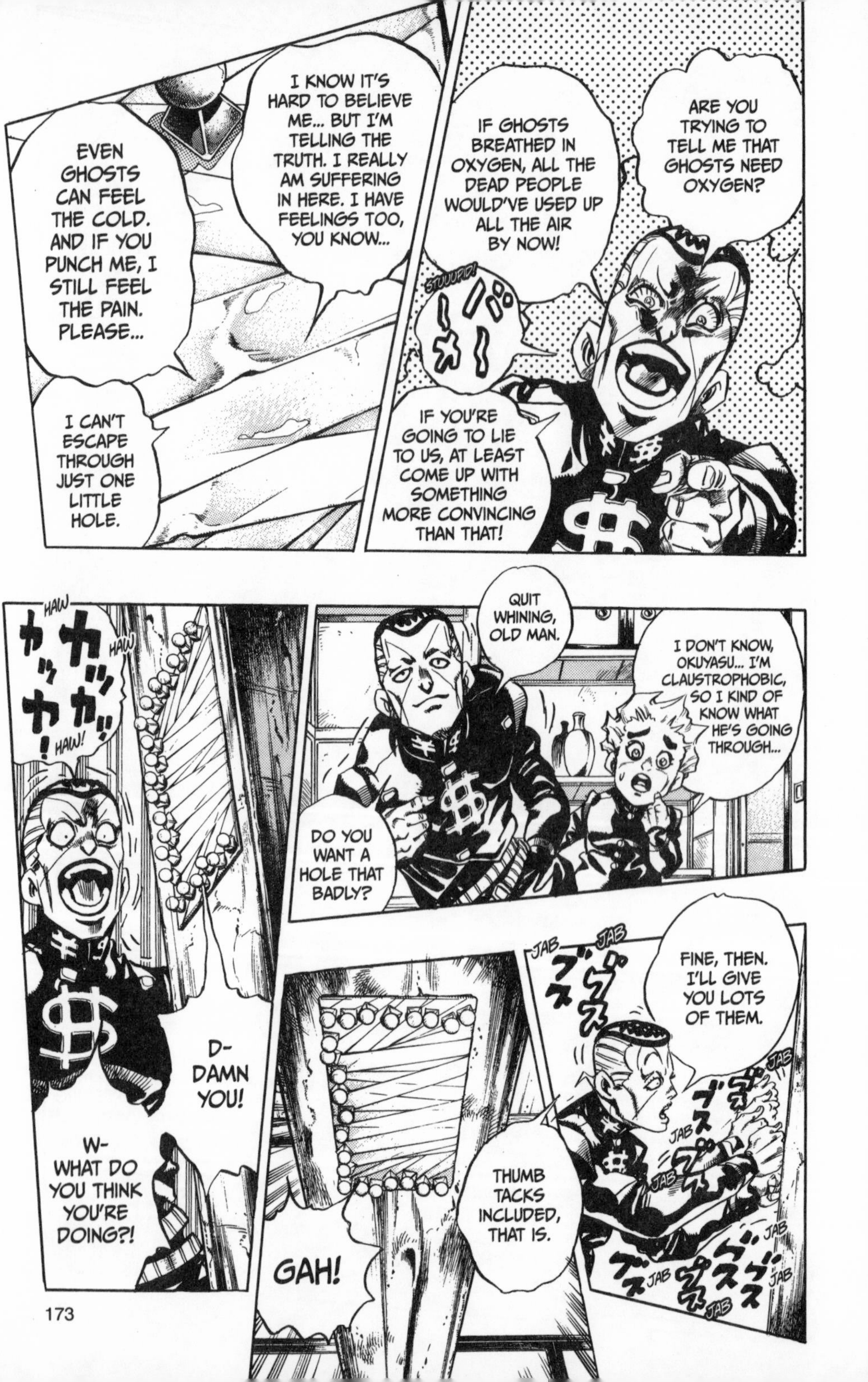
ARE YOU TRYING TO TELL ME THAT GHOSTS NEED OXYGEN?
IF GHOSTS BREATHED IN OXYGEN, ALL THE DEAD PEOPLE WOULD'VE USED UP ALL THE AIR BY NOW!
STUUUPID!
IF YOU'RE GOING TO LIE TO US, AT LEAST COME UP WITH SOMETHING MORE CONVINCING THAN THAT!
I KNOW IT'S HARD TO BELIEVE ME... BUT I'M TELLING THE TRUTH. I REALLY AM SUFFERING IN HERE. I HAVE FEELINGS TOO, YOU KNOW...
EVEN GHOSTS CAN FEEL THE COLD. AND IF YOU PUNCH ME, I STILL FEEL THE PAIN. PLEASE...
I CAN'T ESCAPE THROUGH JUST ONE LITTLE HOLE.
QUIT WHINING, OLD MAN.
DO YOU WANT A HOLE THAT BADLY?
I DON'T KNOW, OKUYASU... I'M CLAUSTROPHOBIC, SO I KIND OF KNOW WHAT HE'S GOING THROUGH...
JAB JAB
FINE, THEN. I'LL GIVE YOU LOTS OF THEM.
JAB JAB JAB
THUMB TACKS INCLUDED, THAT IS.
JAB JAB JAB JAB
GAH!
HAW HAW HAW!
D-DAMN YOU!
W-WHAT DO YOU THINK YOU'RE DOING?!

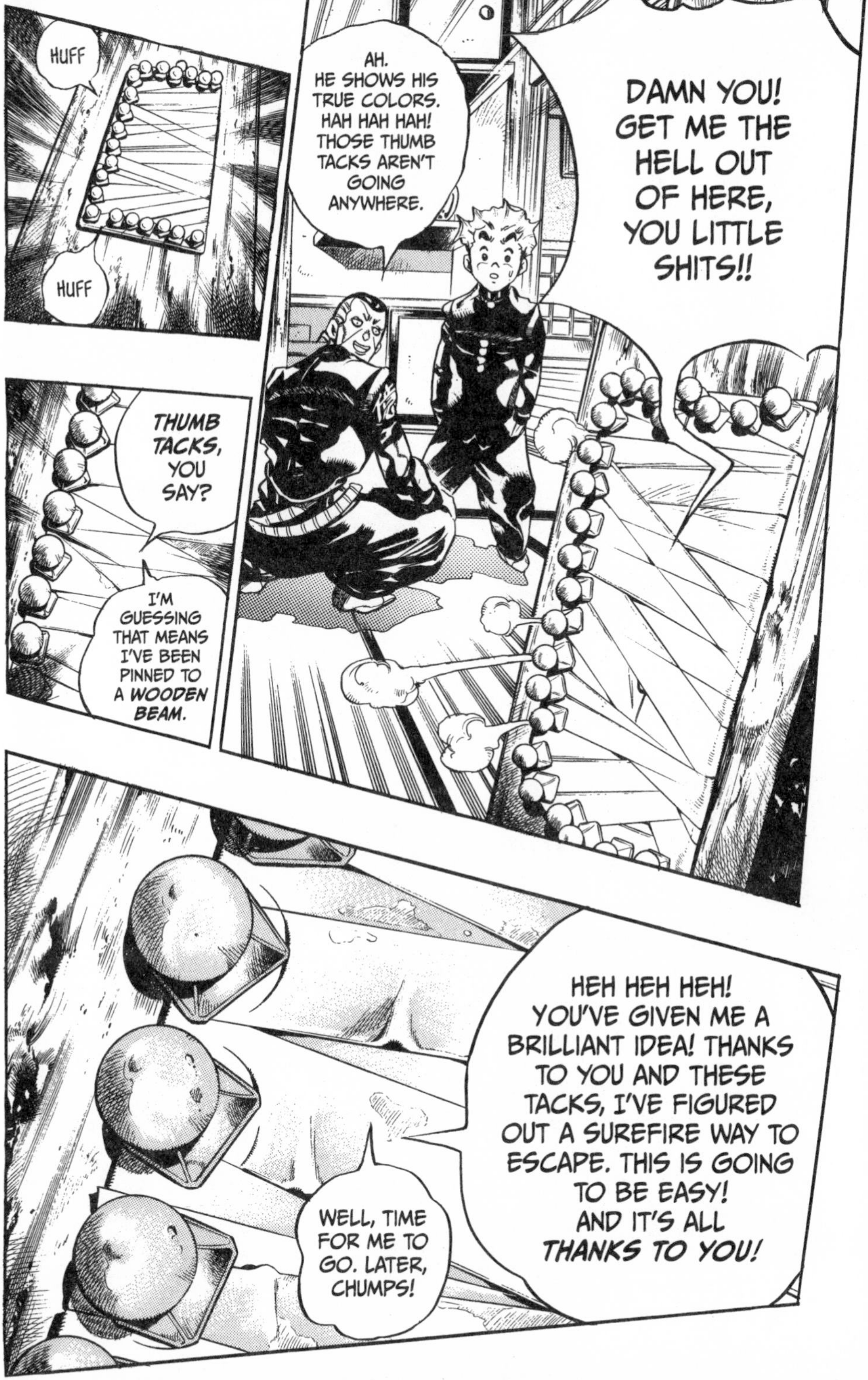
DAMN YOU! GET ME THE HELL OUT OF HERE, YOU LITTLE SHITS!!
AH. HE SHOWS HIS TRUE COLORS. HAH HAH HAH! THOSE THUMB TACKS AREN'T GOING ANYWHERE.
HUFF
HUFF
THUMB TACKS, YOU SAY?
I'M GUESSING THAT MEANS I'VE BEEN PINNED TO A *WOODEN BEAM.*
HEH HEH HEH! YOU'VE GIVEN ME A BRILLIANT IDEA! THANKS TO YOU AND THESE TACKS, I'VE FIGURED OUT A SUREFIRE WAY TO ESCAPE. THIS IS GOING TO BE EASY! AND IT'S ALL *THANKS TO YOU!*
WELL, TIME FOR ME TO GO. LATER, CHUMPS!

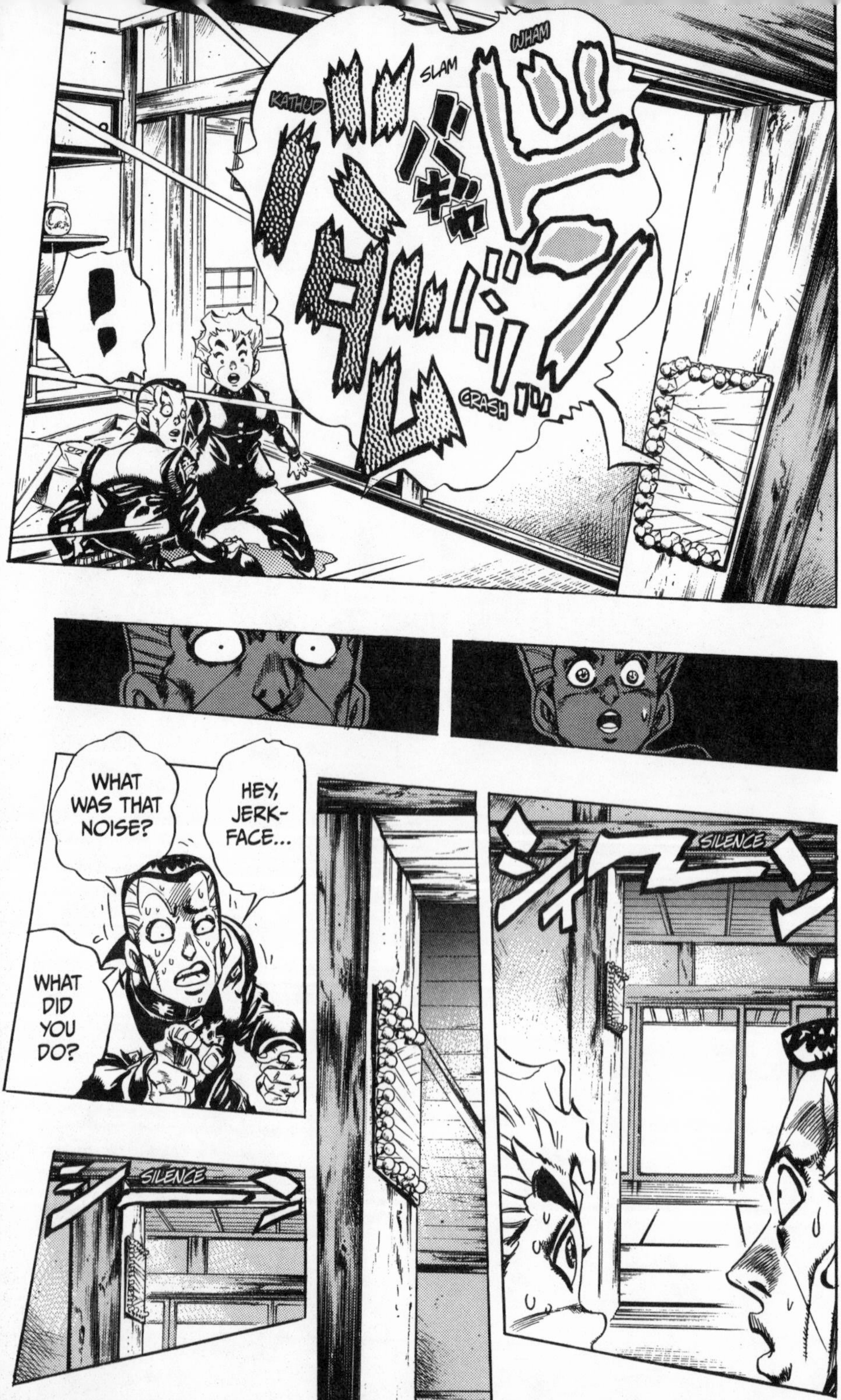
WHAM
SLAM
KATHUD
CRASH
!
SILENCE
HEY, JERK-FACE...
WHAT WAS THAT NOISE?
WHAT DID YOU DO?
SILENCE

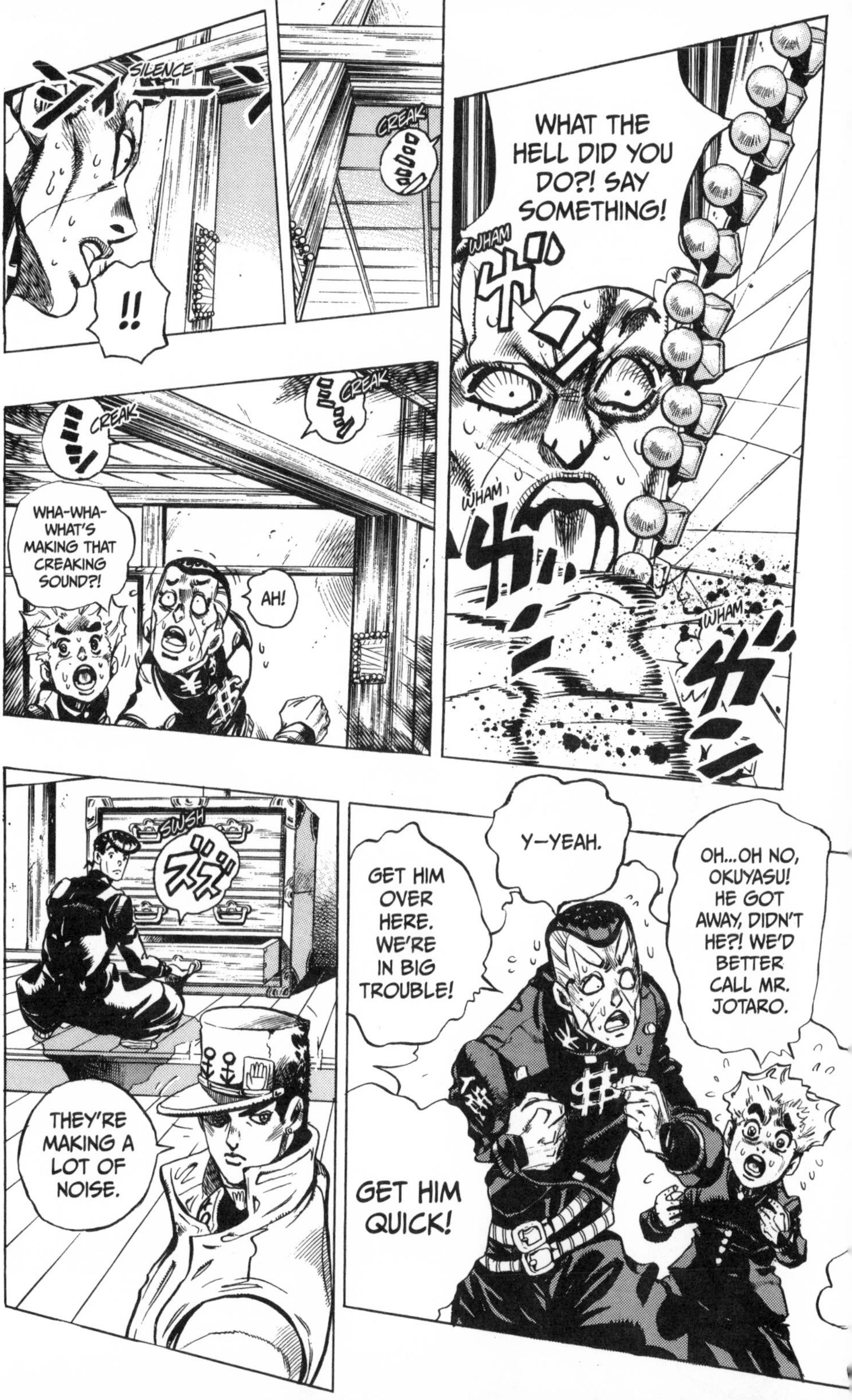
WHAT THE HELL DID YOU DO?! SAY SOMETHING!
WHAM
WHAM
WHAM
CREAK
SILENCE
!!
CREAK
CREAK
WHA-WHA-WHAT'S MAKING THAT CREAKING SOUND?!
AH!
OH...OH NO, OKUYASU! HE GOT AWAY, DIDN'T HE?! WE'D BETTER CALL MR. JOTARO.
Y-YEAH.
GET HIM OVER HERE. WE'RE IN BIG TROUBLE!
GET HIM QUICK!
SWSH
THEY'RE MAKING A LOT OF NOISE.

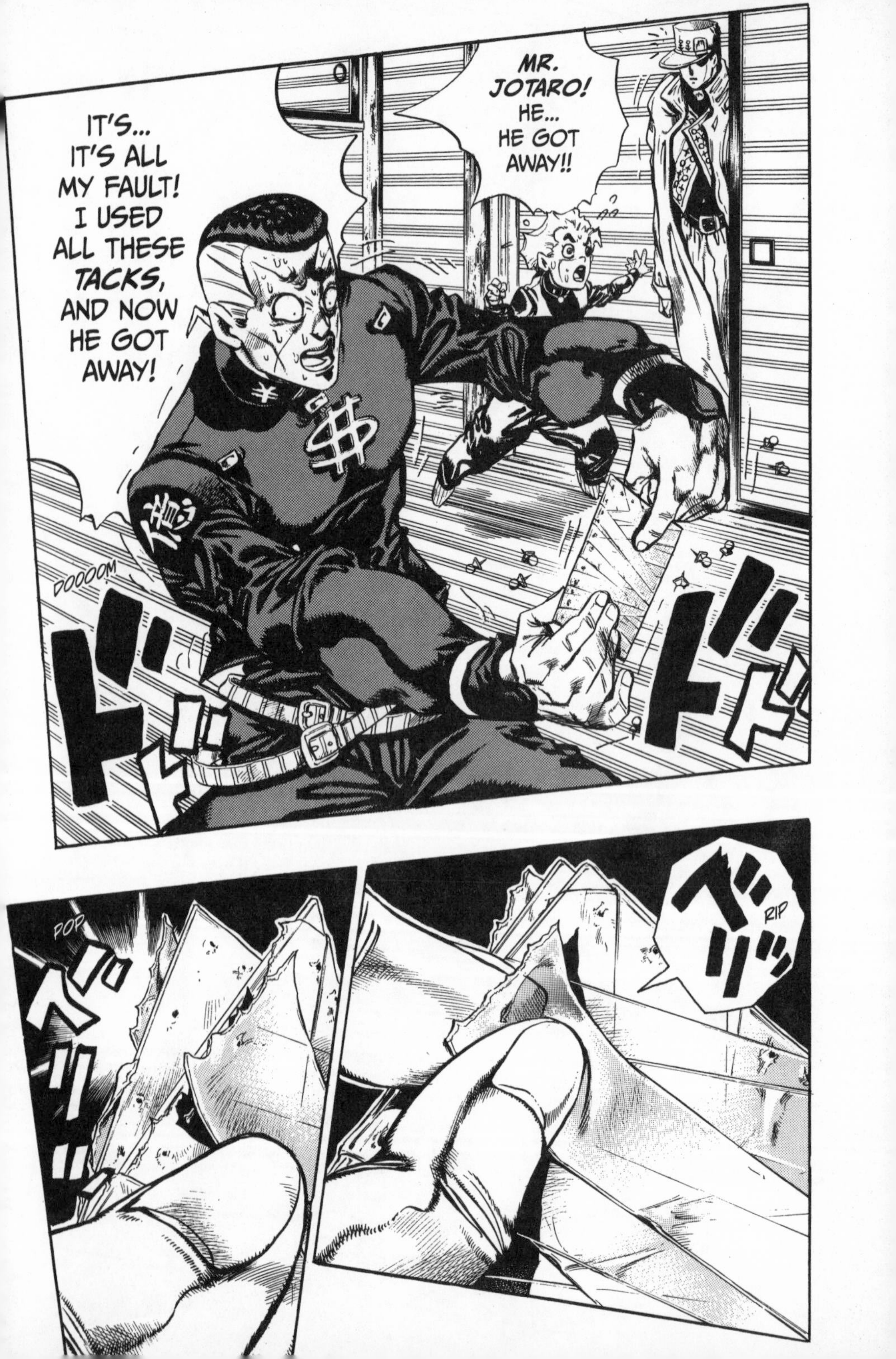
MR. JOTARO! HE... HE GOT AWAY!!
IT'S... IT'S ALL MY FAULT! I USED ALL THESE *TACKS*, AND NOW HE GOT AWAY!
DOOOOM
RIP
POP

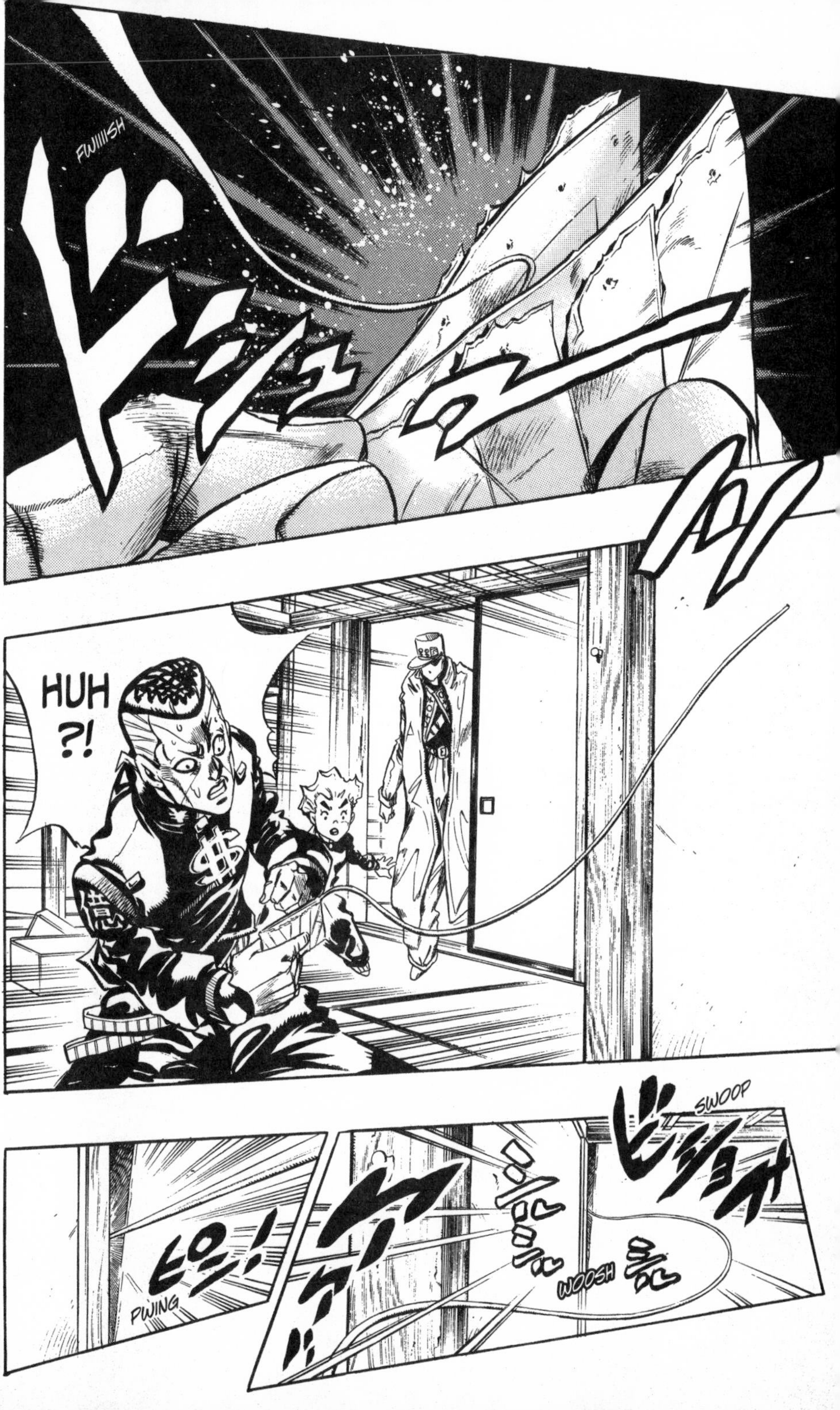
FWIIIISH
HUH ?!
SWOOP
WOOSH
PWING

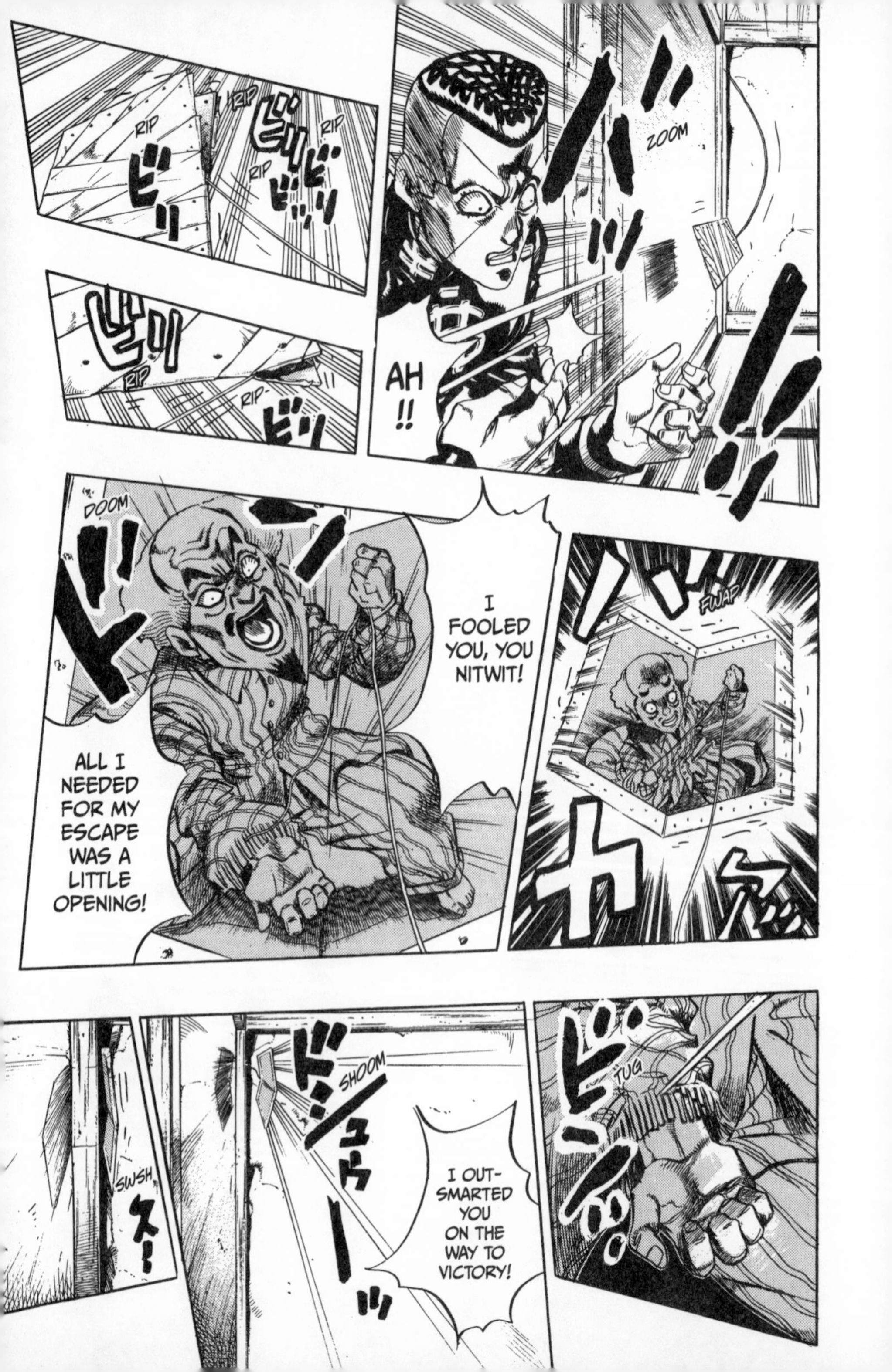
ZOOM
AH!!
RIP
RIP
RIP
RIP
RIP
RIP
RIP-
FWAP
DOOM
I FOOLED YOU, YOU NITWIT!
ALL I NEEDED FOR MY ESCAPE WAS A LITTLE OPENING!
TUG
SHOOM
I OUT-SMARTED YOU ON THE WAY TO VICTORY!
SWSH

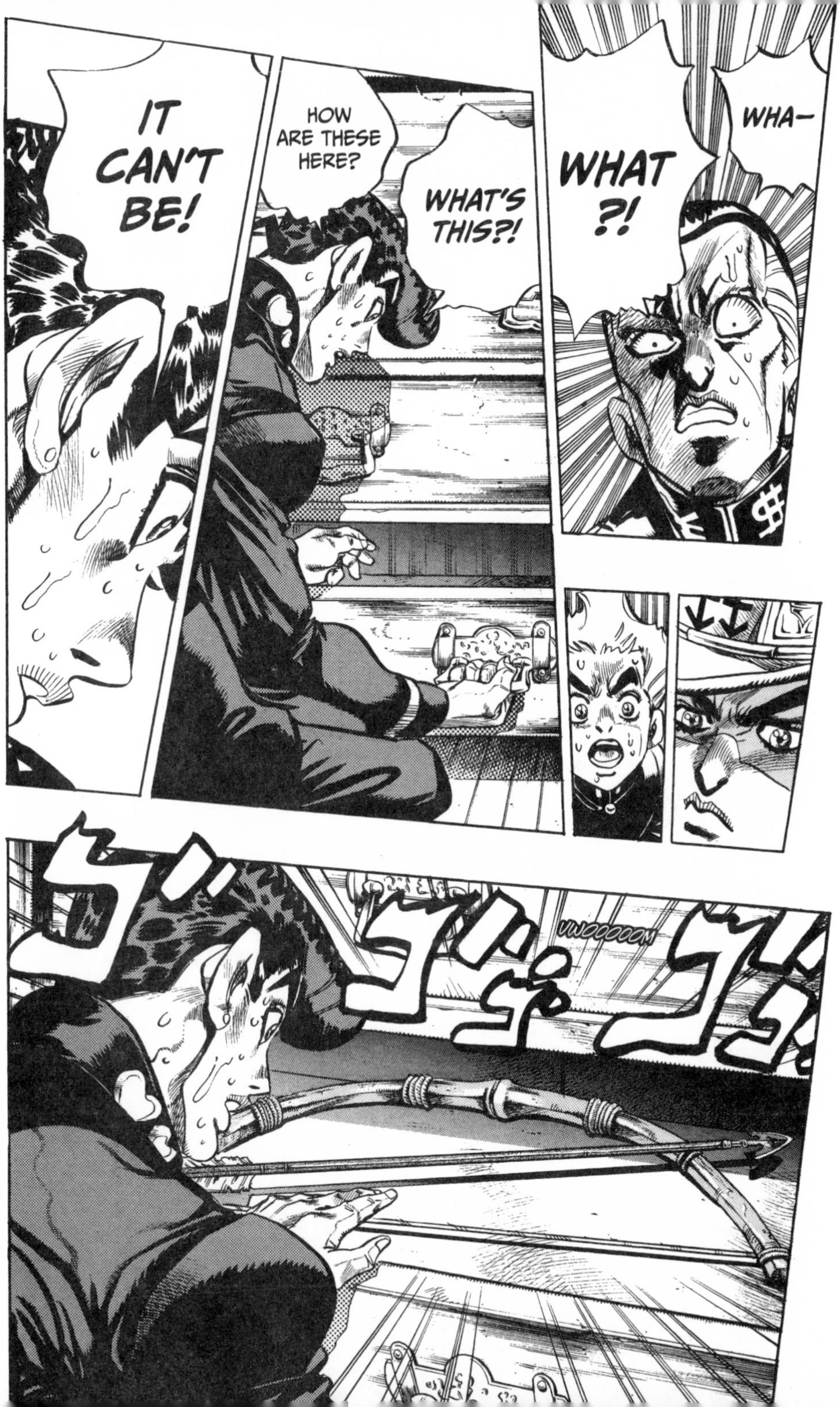
WHA-
WHAT?!
WHAT'S THIS?!
HOW ARE THESE HERE?
IT CAN'T BE!
VWOOOOOM

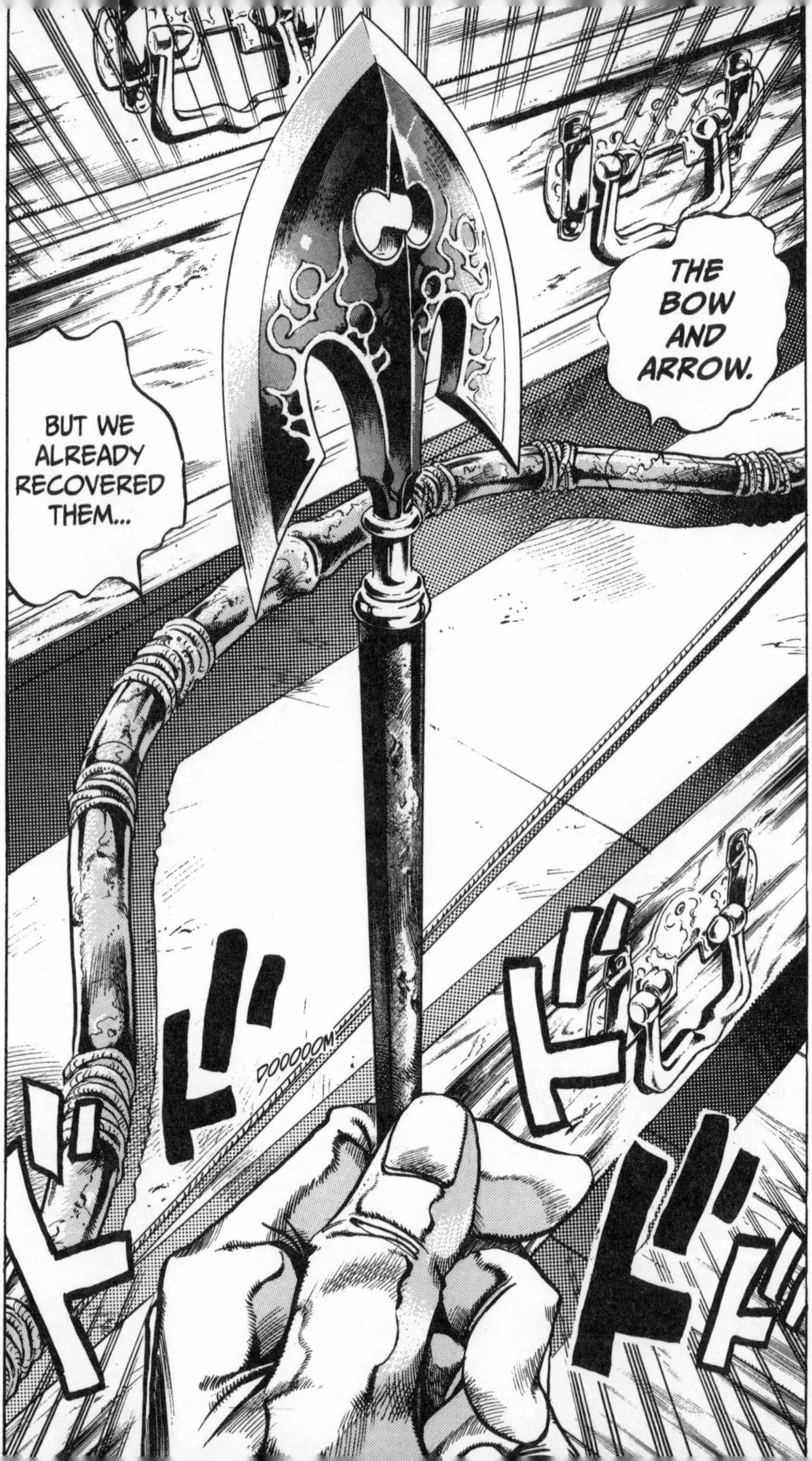
THE BOW AND ARROW.
BUT WE ALREADY RECOVERED THEM...
DOOOOOM

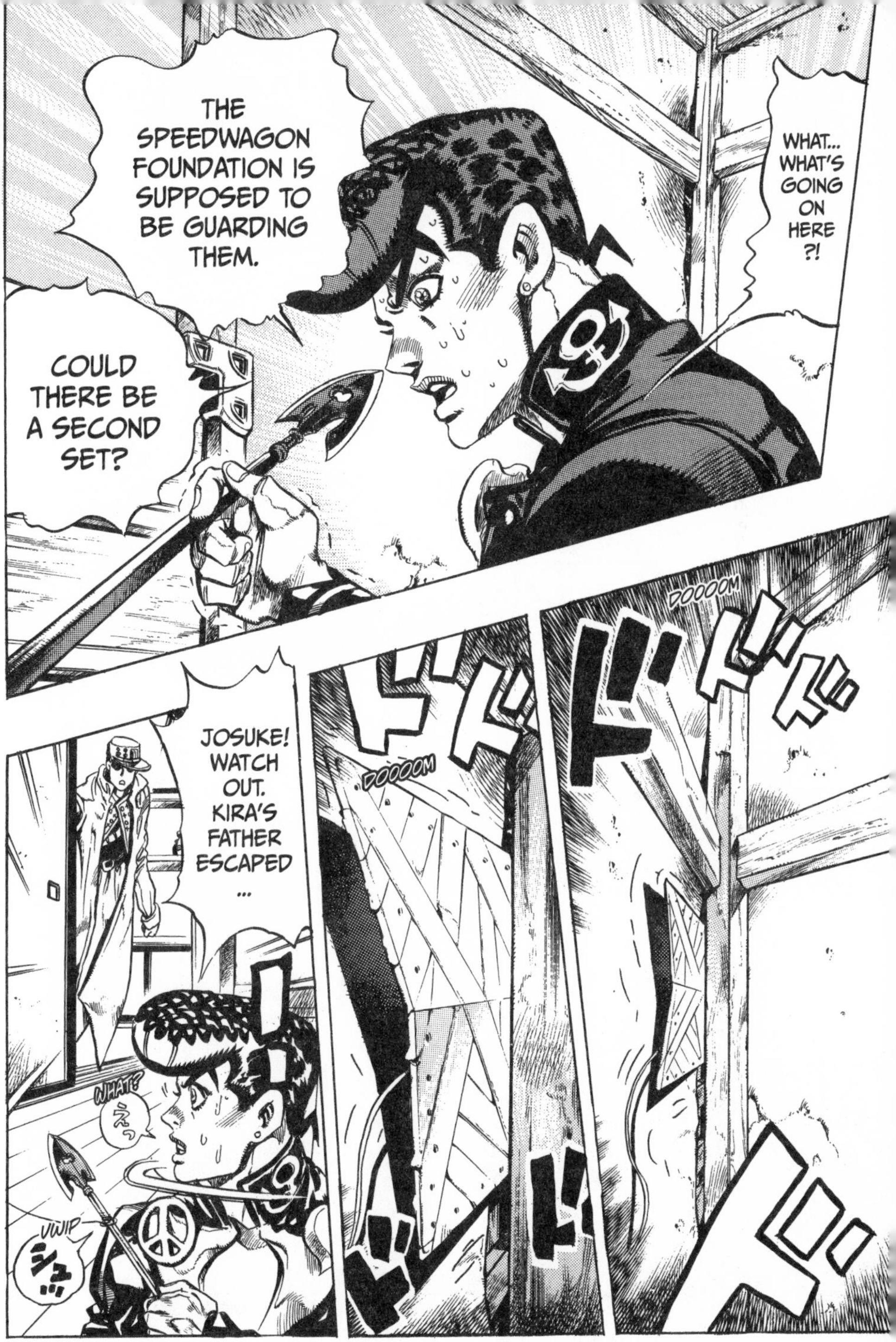

WHAT... WHAT'S GOING ON HERE ?!
THE SPEEDWAGON FOUNDATION IS SUPPOSED TO BE GUARDING THEM.
COULD THERE BE A SECOND SET?
DOOOOM
DOOOOM
JOSUKE! WATCH OUT. KIRA'S FATHER ESCAPED ...
WHAT?
えっ
VWIP

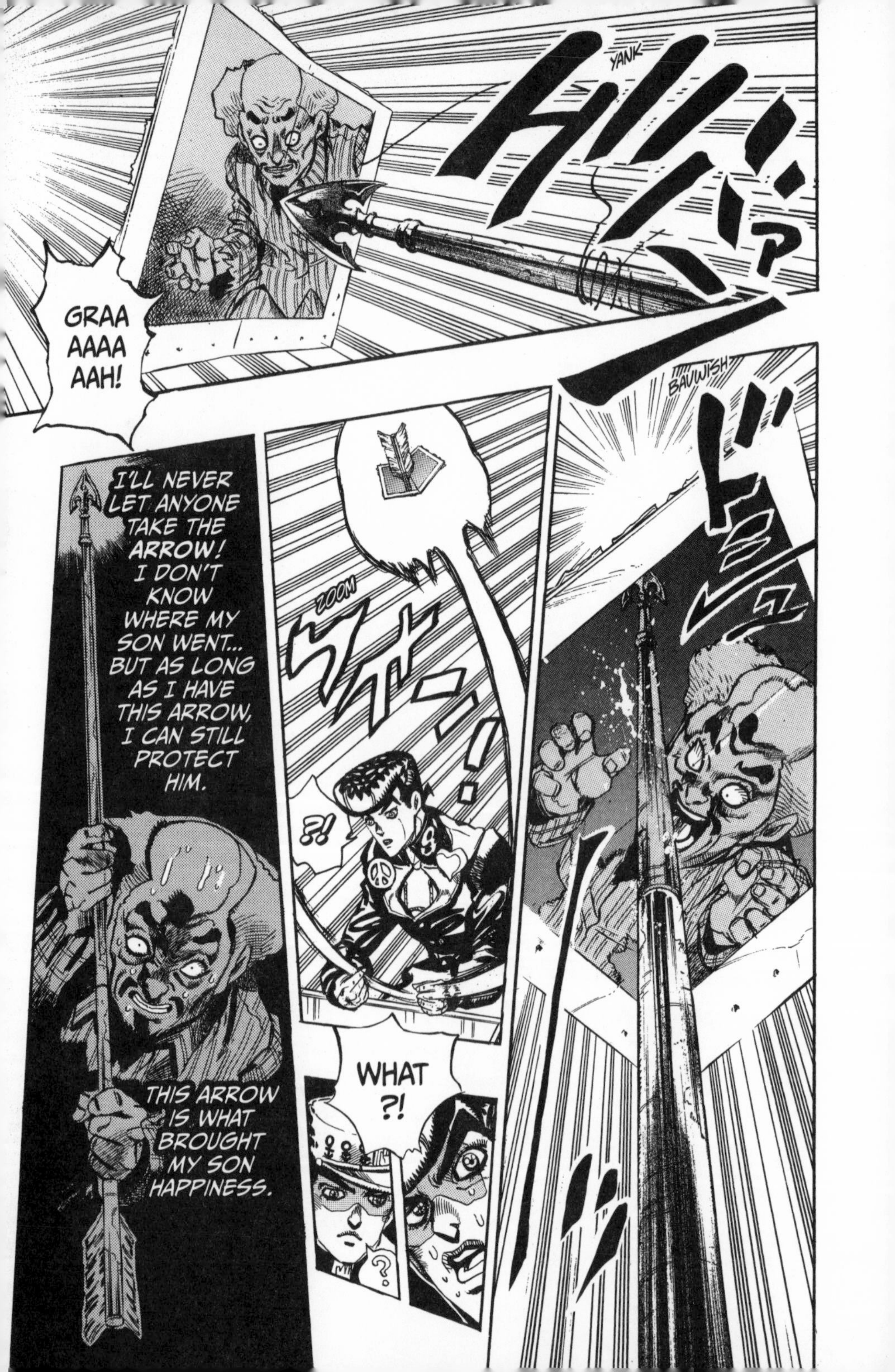

YANK
GRAA AAAA AAH!
BAUWISH
ZOOM
?!
WHAT ?!
?
I'LL NEVER LET ANYONE TAKE THE ARROW! I DON'T KNOW WHERE MY SON WENT... BUT AS LONG AS I HAVE THIS ARROW, I CAN STILL PROTECT HIM.
THIS ARROW IS WHAT BROUGHT MY SON HAPPINESS.

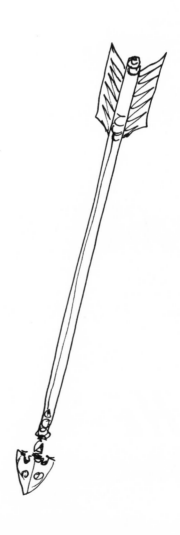

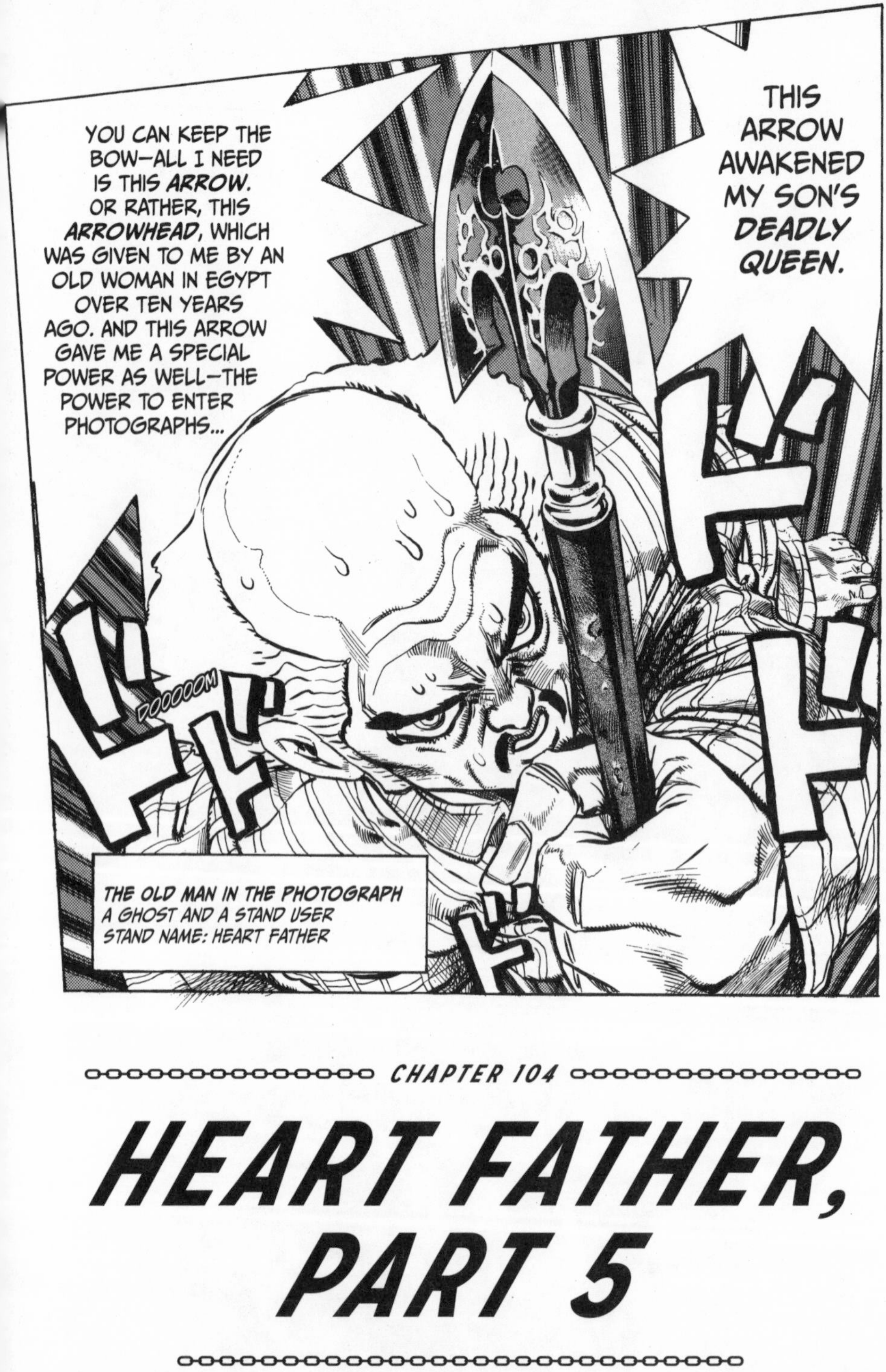
THIS ARROW AWAKENED MY SON'S DEADLY QUEEN.
YOU CAN KEEP THE BOW—ALL I NEED IS THIS ARROW. OR RATHER, THIS ARROWHEAD, WHICH WAS GIVEN TO ME BY AN OLD WOMAN IN EGYPT OVER TEN YEARS AGO. AND THIS ARROW GAVE ME A SPECIAL POWER AS WELL—THE POWER TO ENTER PHOTOGRAPHS...
DOOOOOM
THE OLD MAN IN THE PHOTOGRAPH
A GHOST AND A STAND USER
STAND NAME: HEART FATHER

CHAPTER 104

HEART FATHER, PART 5

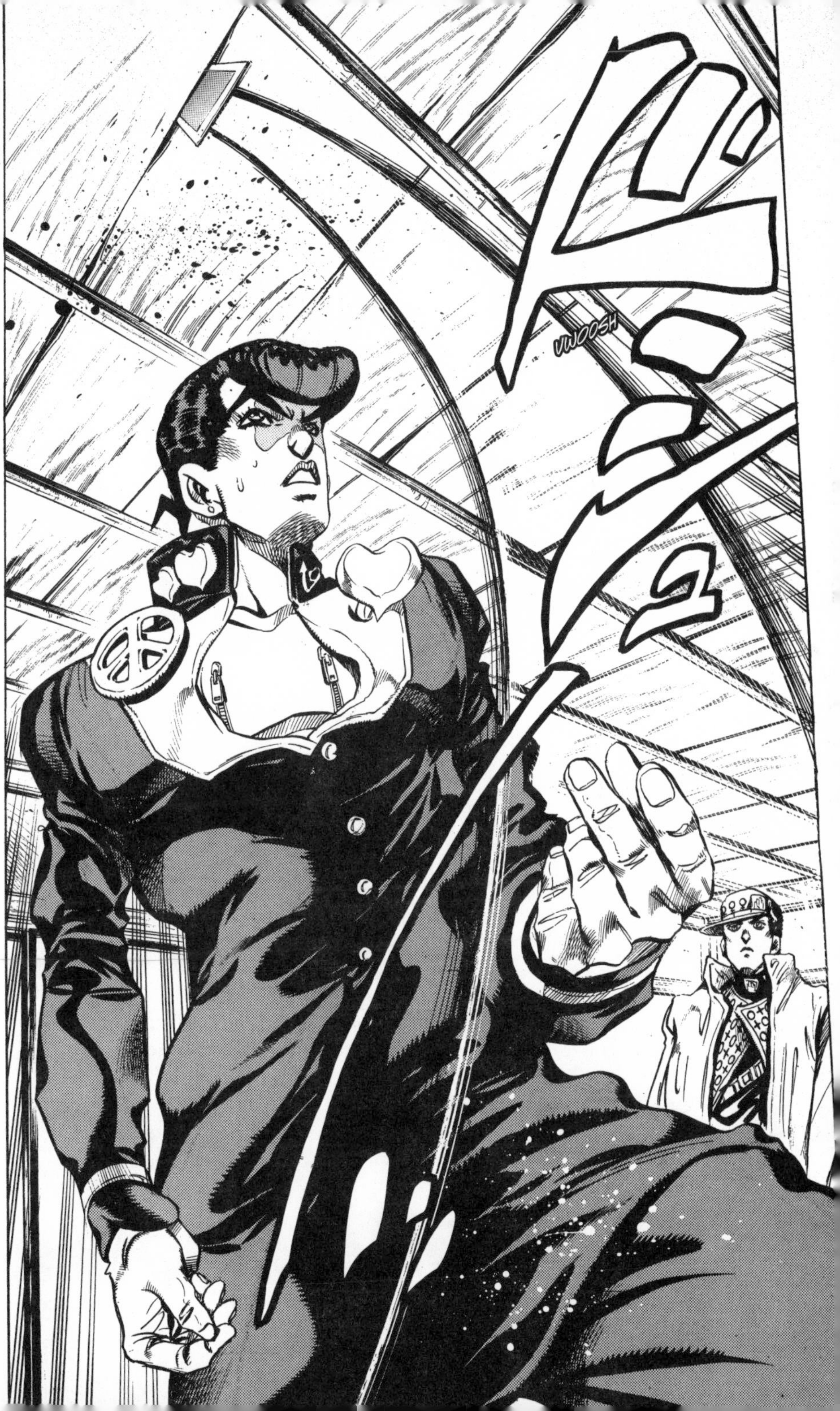
VWOOSH

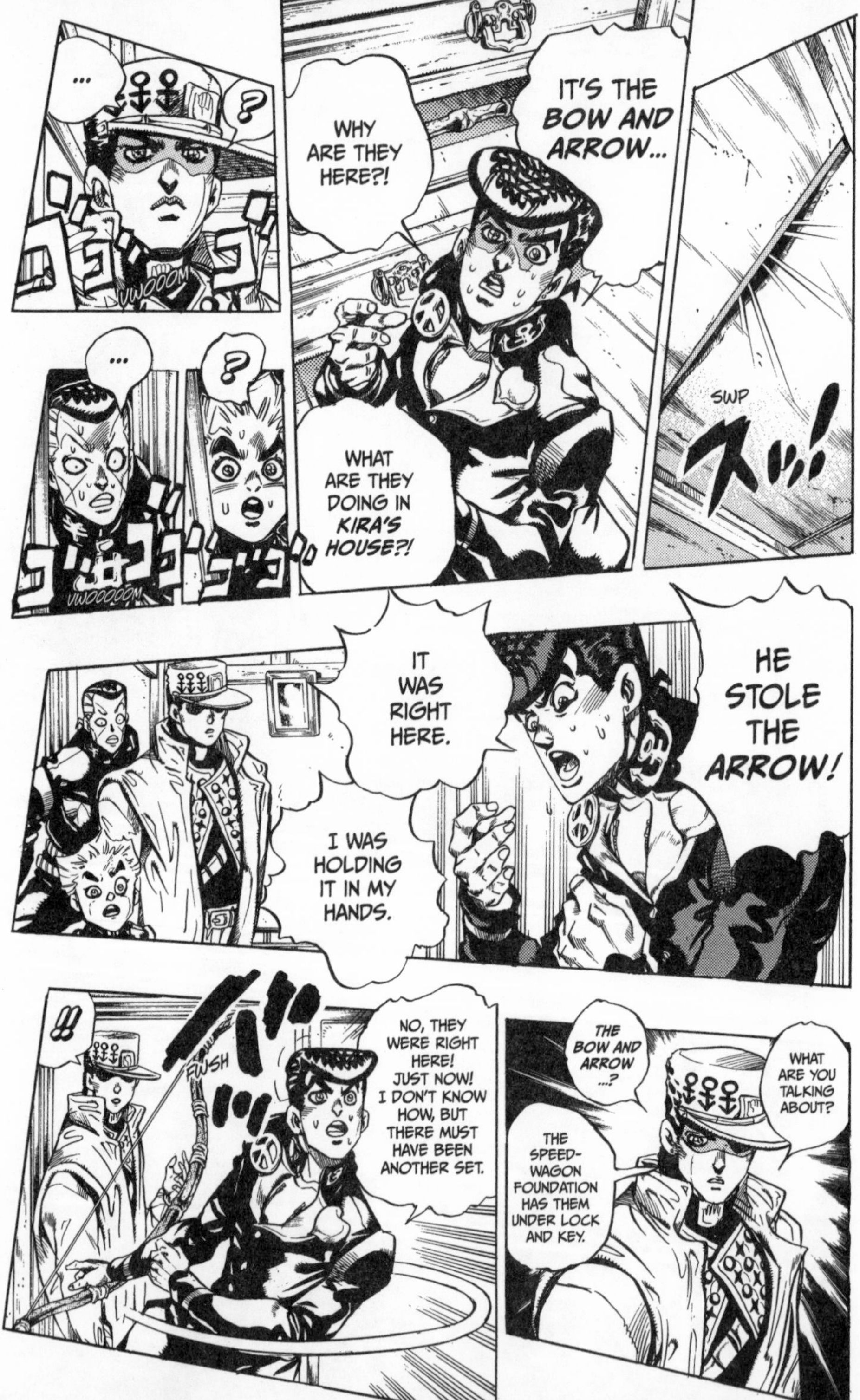
SWP
IT'S THE BOW AND ARROW...
WHY ARE THEY HERE?!
WHAT ARE THEY DOING IN KIRA'S HOUSE?!
...
?
VWOOOM
...
?
VWOOOOOM
HE STOLE THE ARROW!
IT WAS RIGHT HERE.
I WAS HOLDING IT IN MY HANDS.
THE BOW AND ARROW ...?
WHAT ARE YOU TALKING ABOUT?
THE SPEED-WAGON FOUNDATION HAS THEM UNDER LOCK AND KEY.
NO, THEY WERE RIGHT HERE! JUST NOW! I DON'T KNOW HOW, BUT THERE MUST HAVE BEEN ANOTHER SET.
FWSH
!!

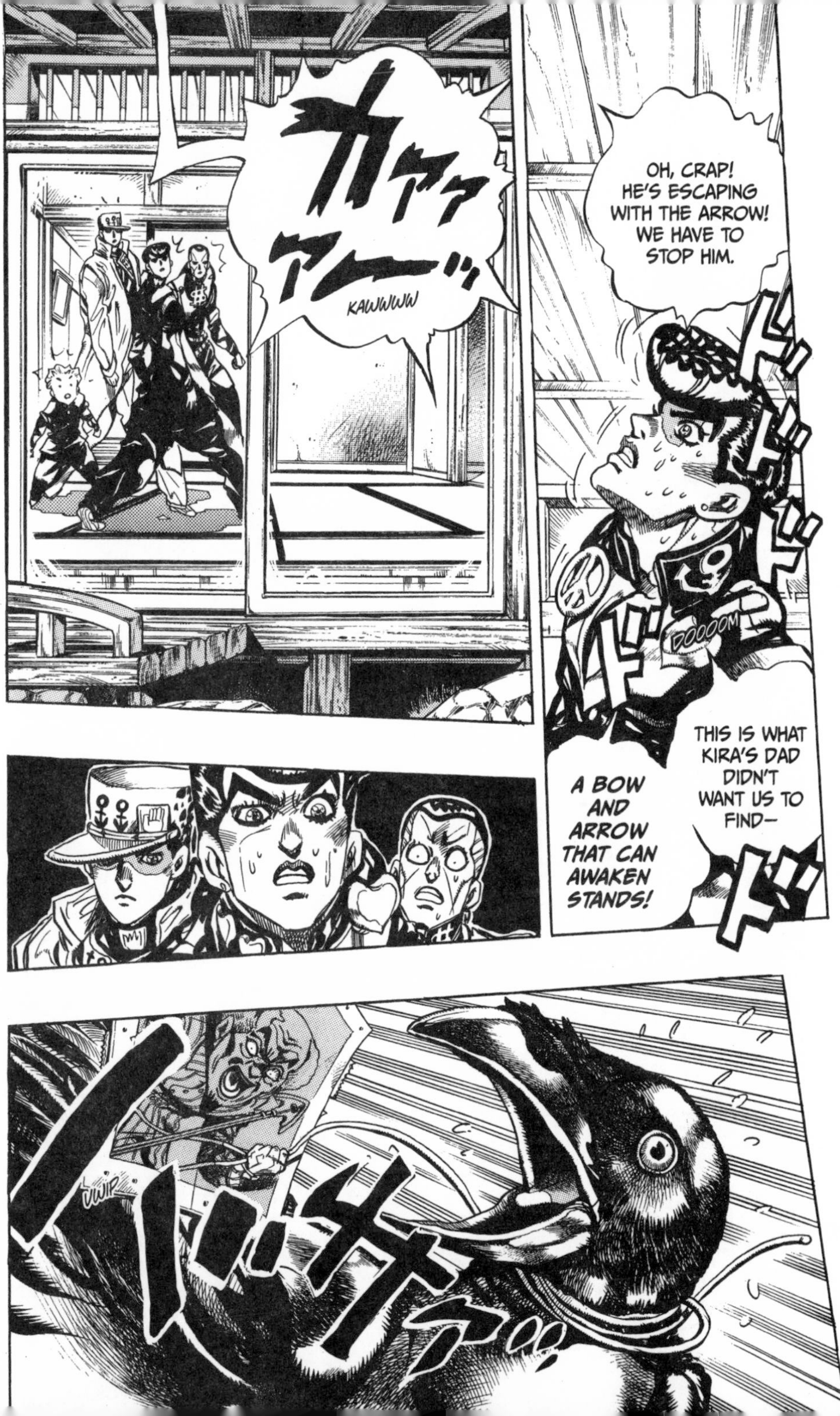
OH, CRAP! HE'S ESCAPING WITH THE ARROW! WE HAVE TO STOP HIM.
DOOOOM
THIS IS WHAT KIRA'S DAD DIDN'T WANT US TO FIND—
A BOW AND ARROW THAT CAN AWAKEN STANDS!
KAWWWW
VWIP

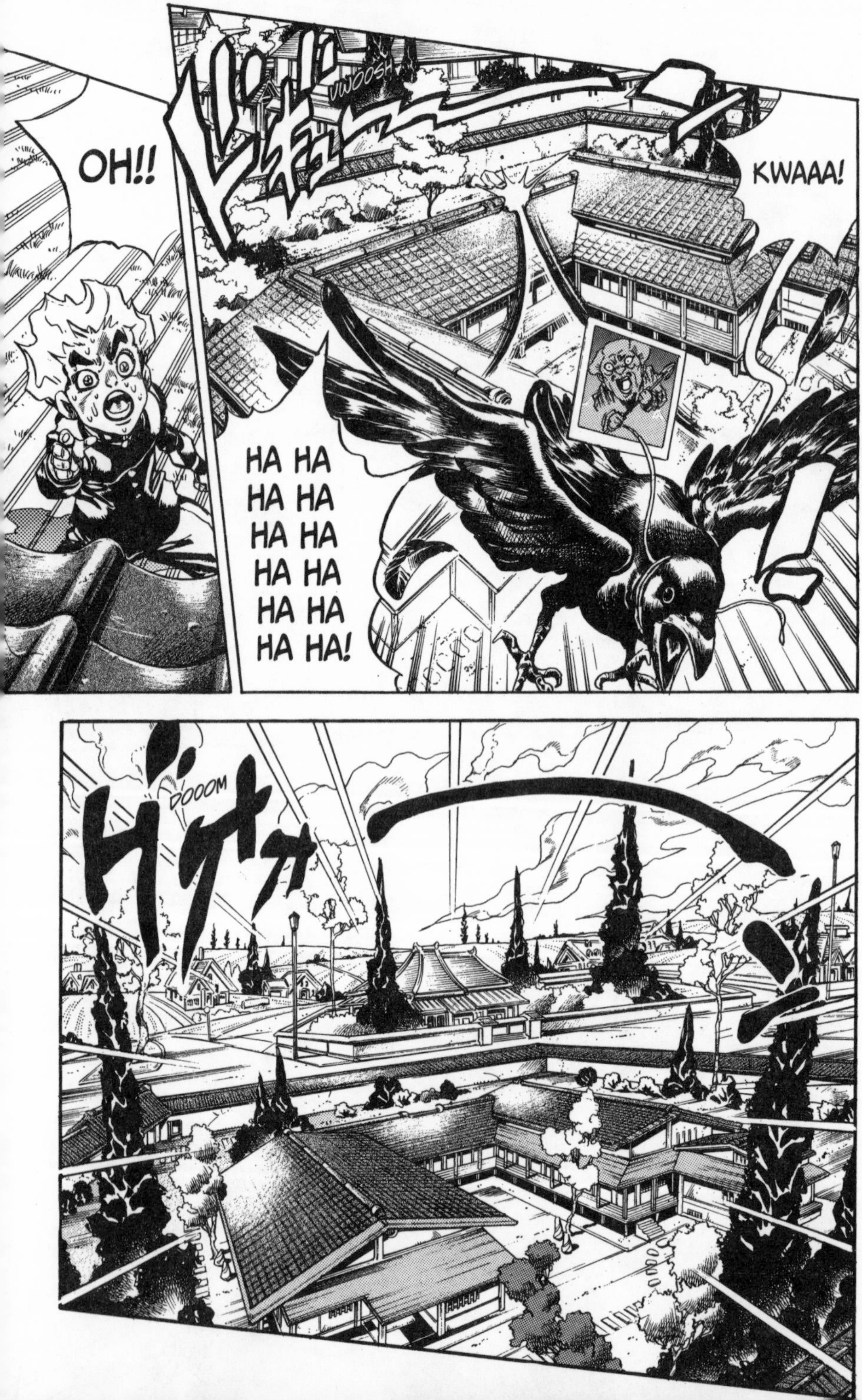
VWOOSH
KWAAA!
HA HA
HA HA
HA HA
HA HA
HA HA
HA HA!
OH!!
DOOOM

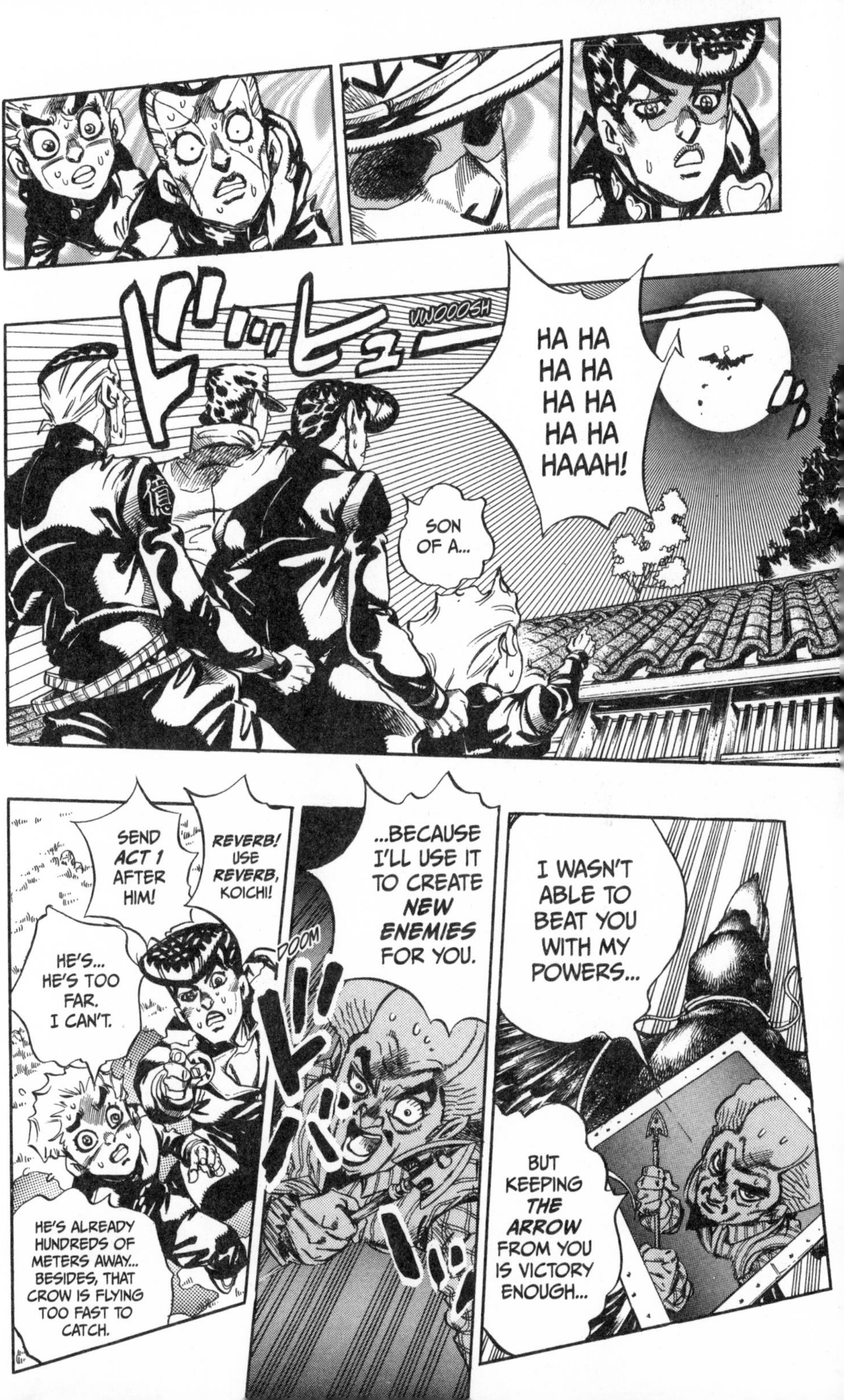
HA HA HA HA HA HA HA HA HAAAH!
VWOOOSH
SON OF A...
I WASN'T ABLE TO BEAT YOU WITH MY POWERS...
BUT KEEPING *THE ARROW* FROM YOU IS VICTORY ENOUGH...
...BECAUSE I'LL USE IT TO CREATE *NEW ENEMIES* FOR YOU.
DOOM
REVERB! USE *REVERB,* KOICHI!
SEND *ACT 1* AFTER HIM!
HE'S... HE'S TOO FAR. I CAN'T.
HE'S ALREADY HUNDREDS OF METERS AWAY... BESIDES, THAT CROW IS FLYING TOO FAST TO CATCH.

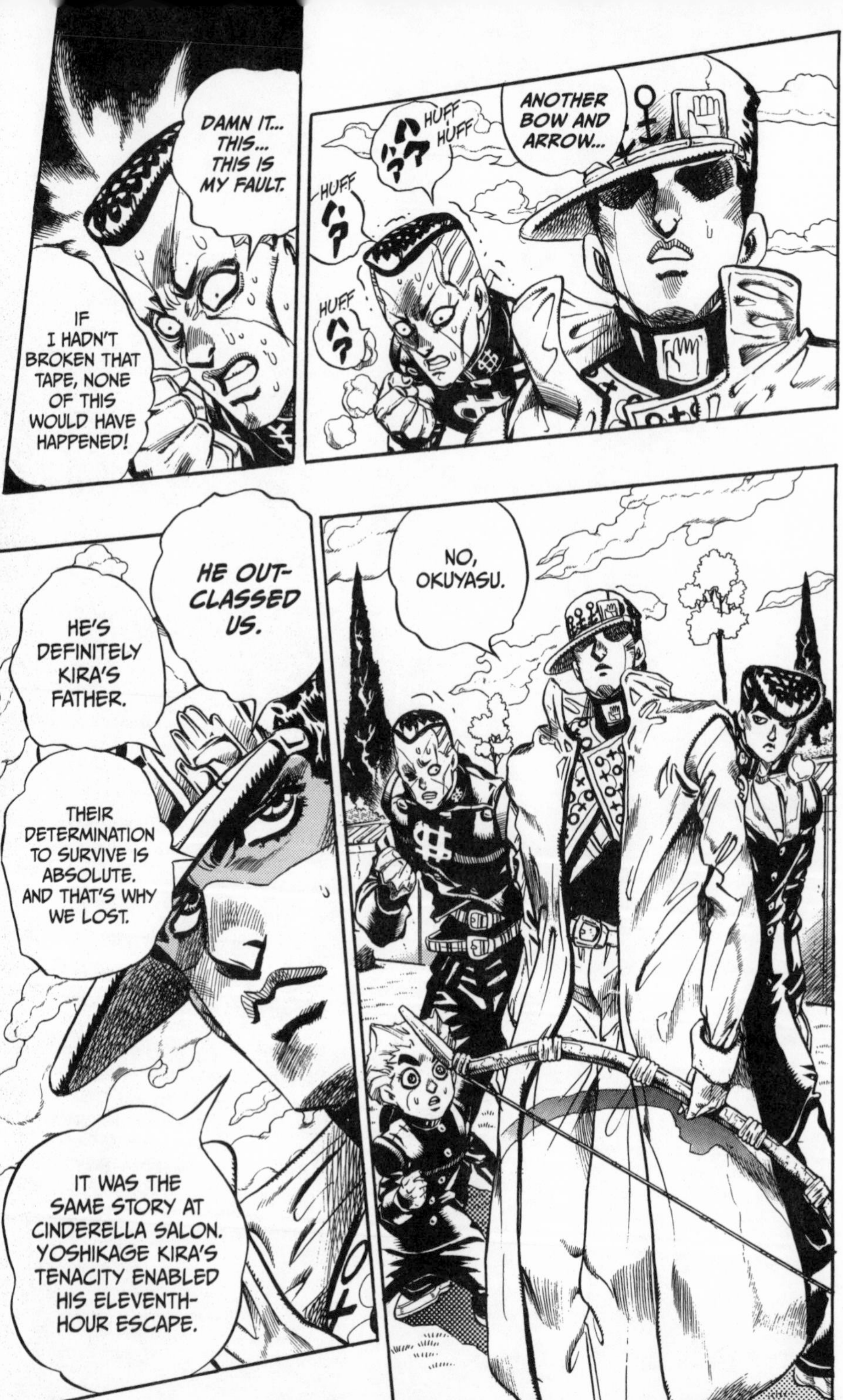
ANOTHER BOW AND ARROW...
ハァ HUFF HUFF
ハァ HUFF
ハァ HUFF
DAMN IT... THIS... THIS IS MY FAULT.
IF I HADN'T BROKEN THAT TAPE, NONE OF THIS WOULD HAVE HAPPENED!
NO, OKUYASU.
HE OUT-CLASSED US.
HE'S DEFINITELY KIRA'S FATHER.
THEIR DETERMINATION TO SURVIVE IS ABSOLUTE. AND THAT'S WHY WE LOST.
IT WAS THE SAME STORY AT CINDERELLA SALON. YOSHIKAGE KIRA'S TENACITY ENABLED HIS ELEVENTH-HOUR ESCAPE.

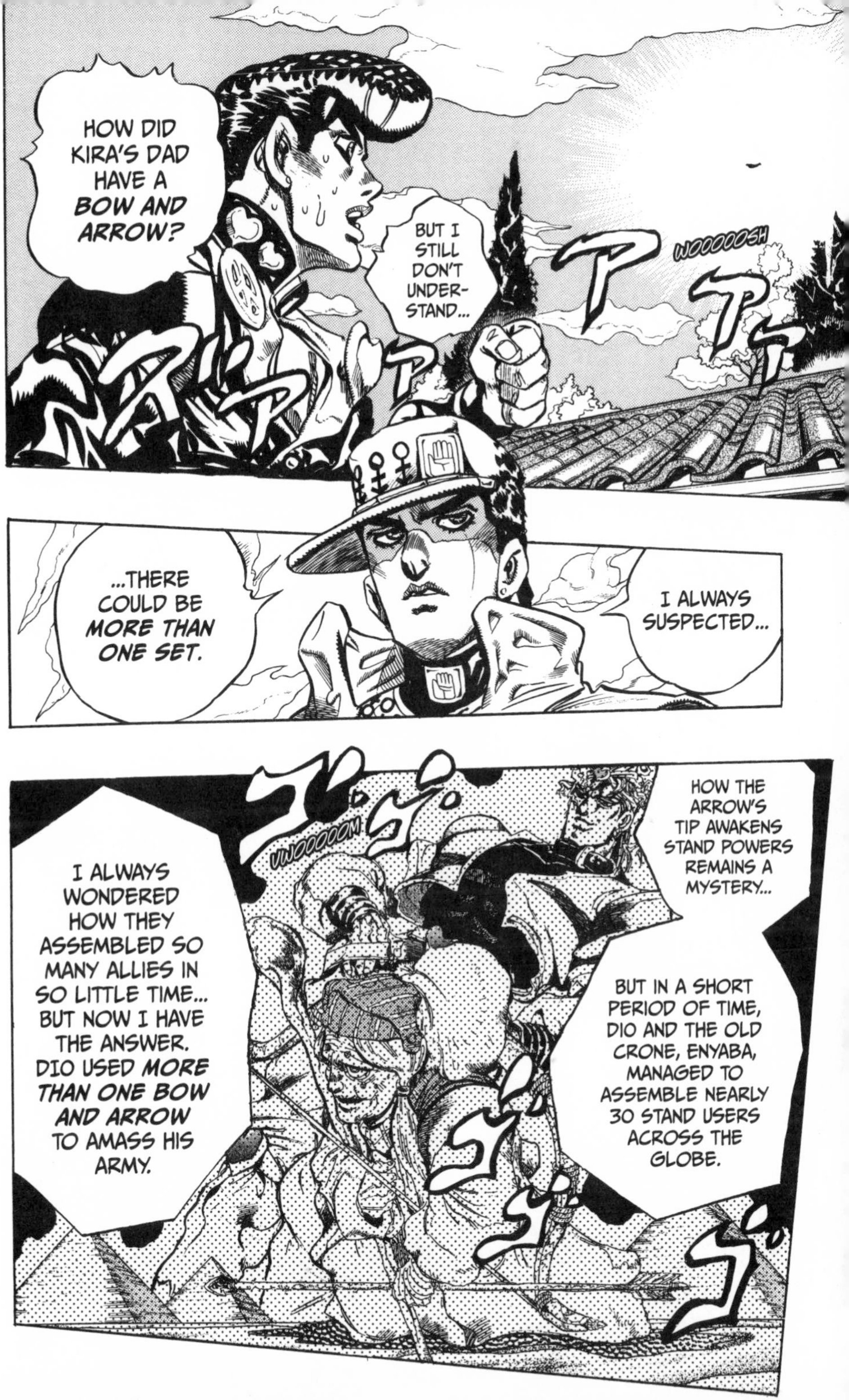
WOOOOOOSH
BUT I STILL DON'T UNDER-STAND...
HOW DID KIRA'S DAD HAVE A *BOW AND ARROW?*
I ALWAYS SUSPECTED...
...THERE COULD BE *MORE THAN ONE SET.*
UWOOOOOM
HOW THE ARROW'S TIP AWAKENS STAND POWERS REMAINS A MYSTERY...
BUT IN A SHORT PERIOD OF TIME, DIO AND THE OLD CRONE, ENYABA, MANAGED TO ASSEMBLE NEARLY 30 STAND USERS ACROSS THE GLOBE.
I ALWAYS WONDERED HOW THEY ASSEMBLED SO MANY ALLIES IN SO LITTLE TIME... BUT NOW I HAVE THE ANSWER. DIO USED *MORE THAN ONE BOW AND ARROW* TO AMASS HIS ARMY.

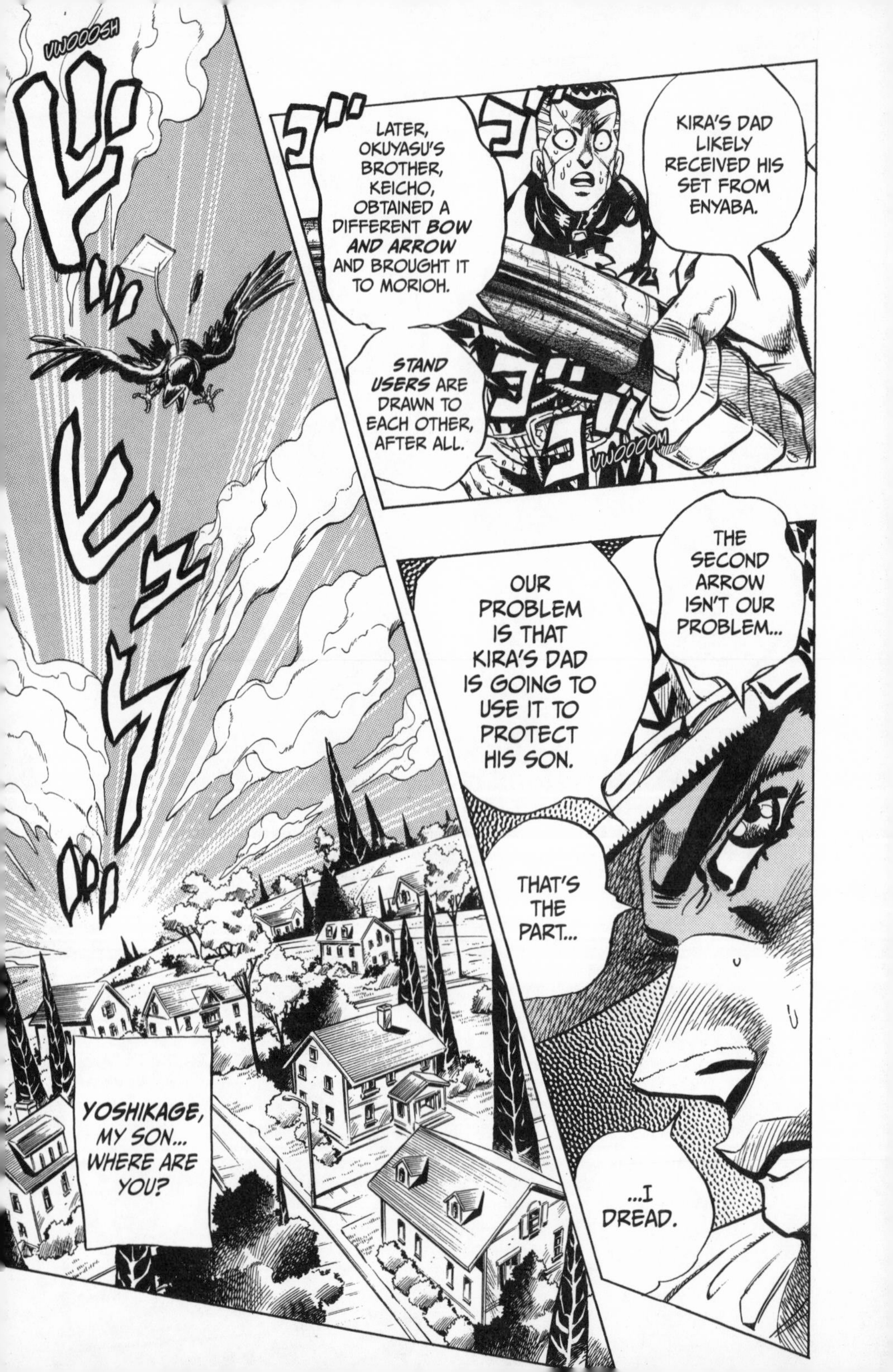
KIRA'S DAD LIKELY RECEIVED HIS SET FROM ENYABA.
LATER, OKUYASU'S BROTHER, KEICHO, OBTAINED A DIFFERENT *BOW AND ARROW* AND BROUGHT IT TO MORIOH.
STAND USERS ARE DRAWN TO EACH OTHER, AFTER ALL.
VWOOOOM
THE SECOND ARROW ISN'T OUR PROBLEM...
OUR PROBLEM IS THAT KIRA'S DAD IS GOING TO USE IT TO PROTECT HIS SON.
THAT'S THE PART...
...I DREAD.
VWOOOSH
YOSHIKAGE, MY SON... WHERE ARE YOU?

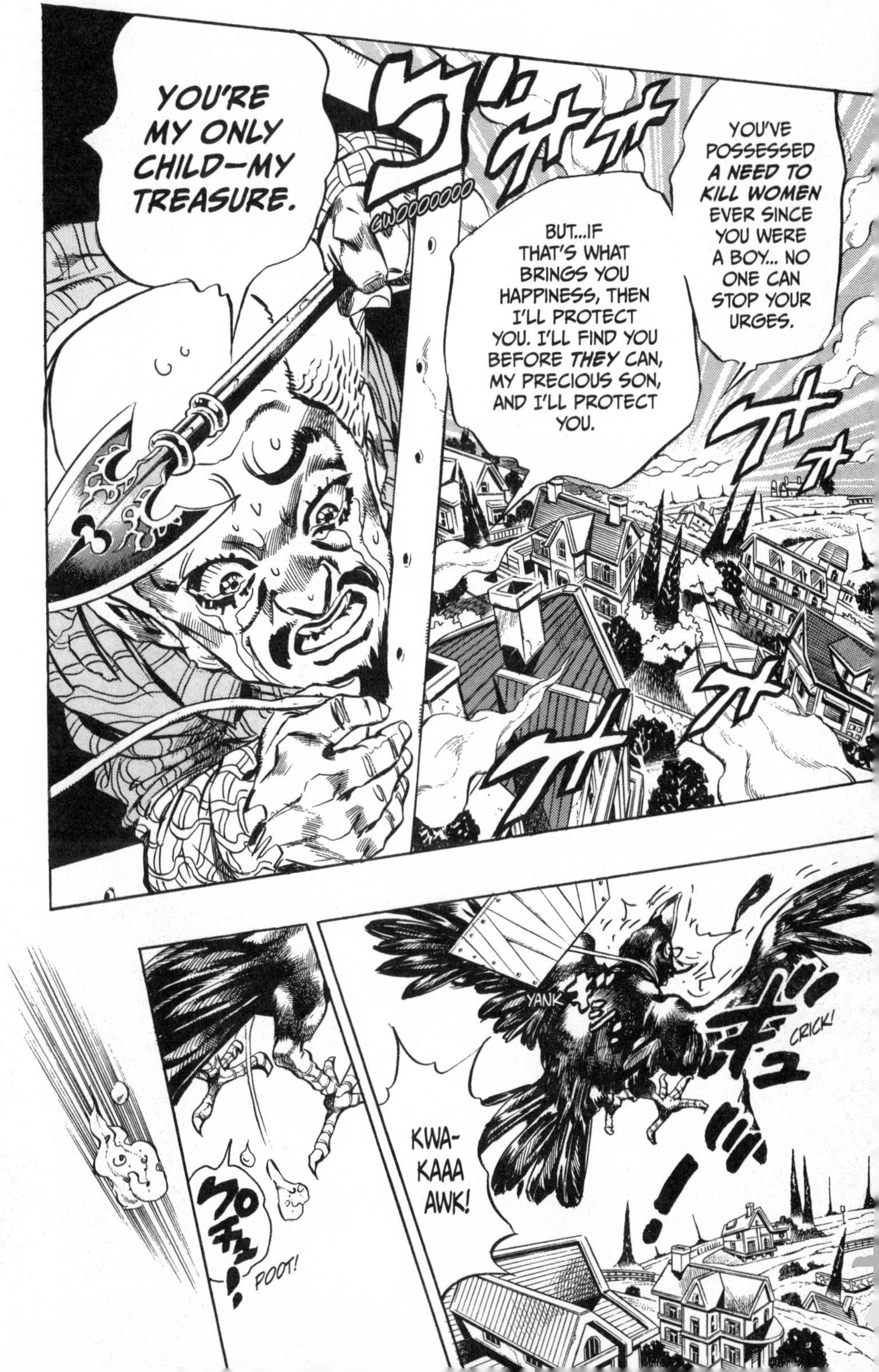
YOU'VE POSSESSED A NEED TO KILL WOMEN EVER SINCE YOU WERE A BOY... NO ONE CAN STOP YOUR URGES.
BUT...IF THAT'S WHAT BRINGS YOU HAPPINESS, THEN I'LL PROTECT YOU. I'LL FIND YOU BEFORE THEY CAN, MY PRECIOUS SON, AND I'LL PROTECT YOU.
GWOOOOOOOO
YOU'RE MY ONLY CHILD—MY TREASURE.
CRICK!
YANK
KWA-KAAA AWK!
POOT!

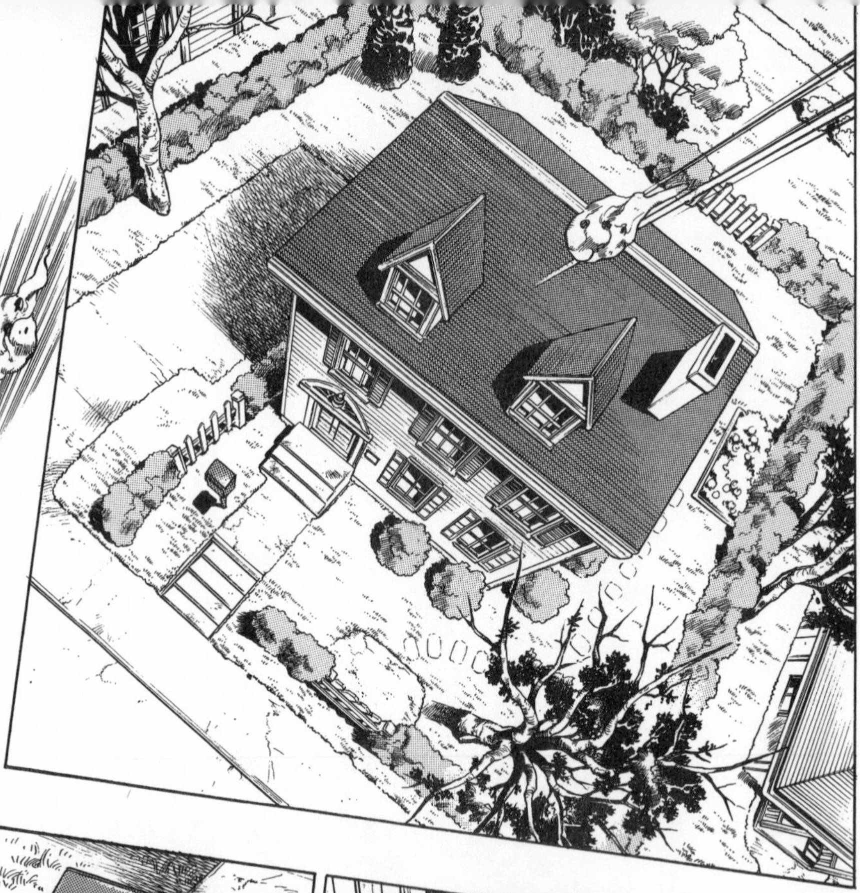

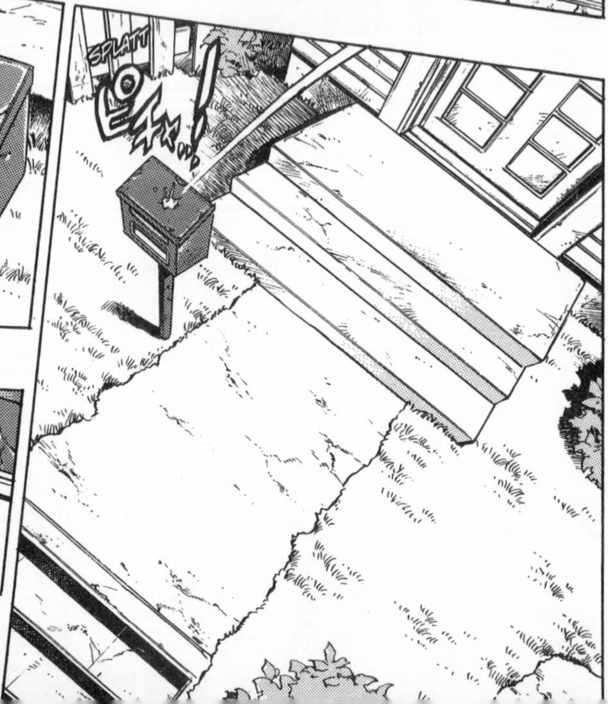
SPLATT
ピチャッ!!

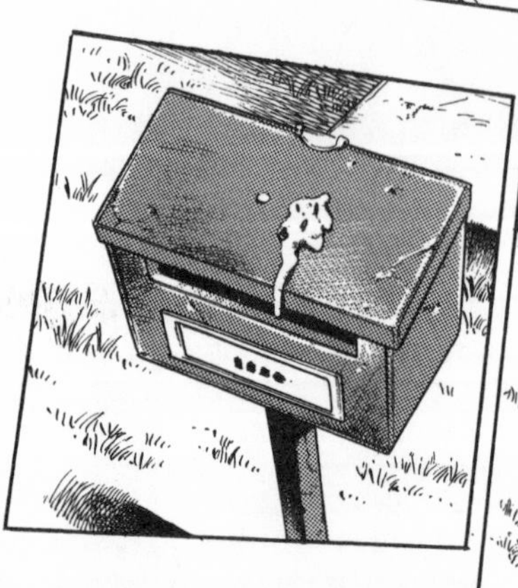

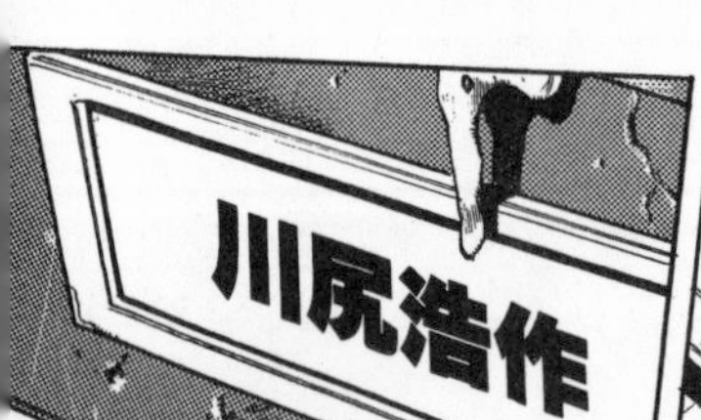
川尻浩作

MAILBOX: KOSAKU KAWAJIRI

JINGL
チャラ
JINGL
チャラ
JINGL
チャラ
...
川尻浩作
SWSH
ズ
RATTL
ガッ
RATTL
ガッ
...
ズョ
SWSH
JINGL
チャラ
SWSH
ズズズッ
KAKLIK
カチャ
!

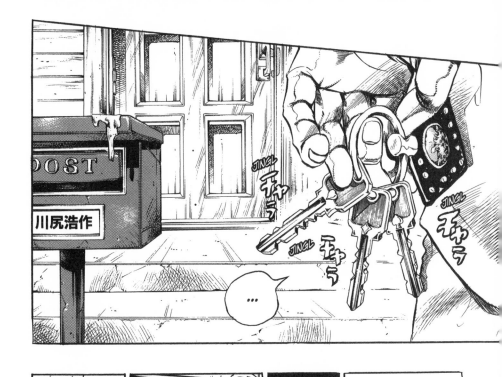

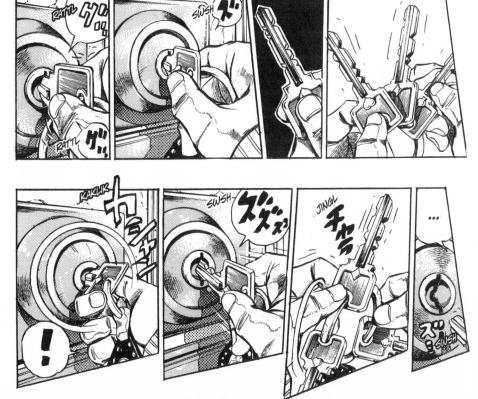

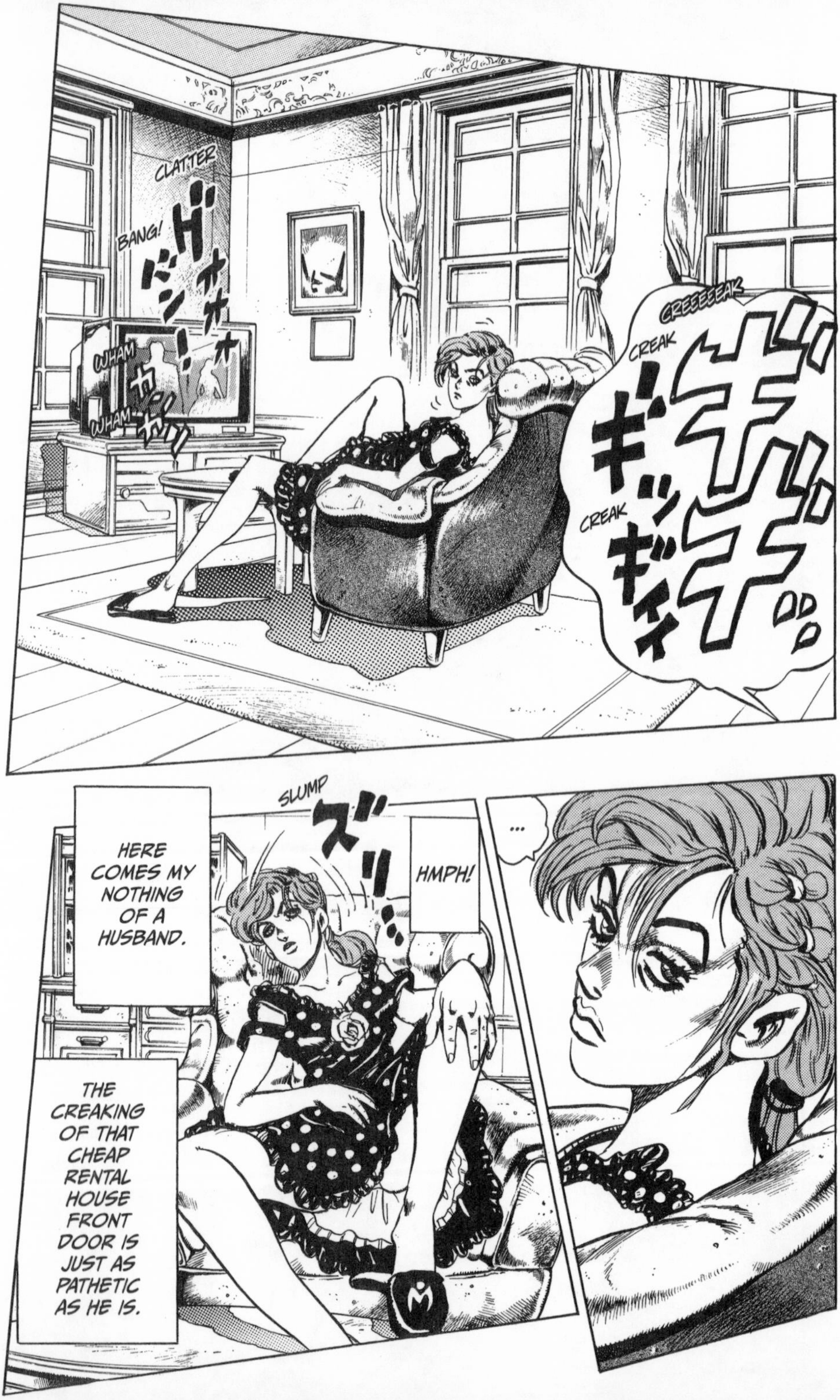
CREEEEEAK
CREAK
CREAK
CLATTER
BANG!
WHAM
WHAM
...
SLUMP
HMPH!
HERE COMES MY NOTHING OF A HUSBAND.
THE CREAKING OF THAT CHEAP RENTAL HOUSE FRONT DOOR IS JUST AS PATHETIC AS HE IS.

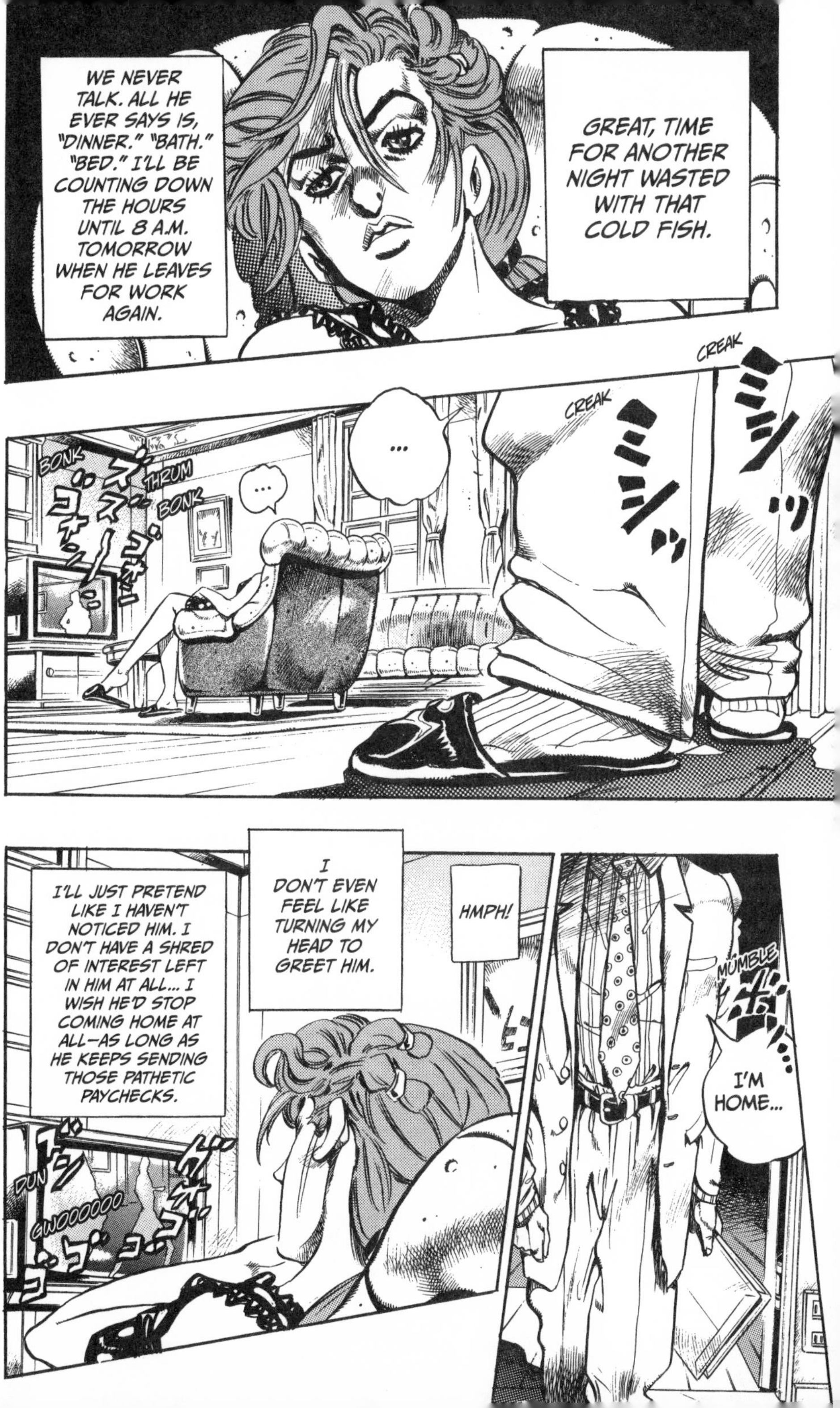
GREAT, TIME FOR ANOTHER NIGHT WASTED WITH THAT COLD FISH.
WE NEVER TALK. ALL HE EVER SAYS IS, "DINNER." "BATH." "BED." I'LL BE COUNTING DOWN THE HOURS UNTIL 8 A.M. TOMORROW WHEN HE LEAVES FOR WORK AGAIN.
CREAK
CREAK
...
...
BONK
THRUM
BONK
MUMBLE
I'M HOME...
HMPH!
I DON'T EVEN FEEL LIKE TURNING MY HEAD TO GREET HIM.
I'LL JUST PRETEND LIKE I HAVEN'T NOTICED HIM. I DON'T HAVE A SHRED OF INTEREST LEFT IN HIM AT ALL... I WISH HE'D STOP COMING HOME AT ALL—AS LONG AS HE KEEPS SENDING THOSE PATHETIC PAYCHECKS.
DUN
GWOOOOOO

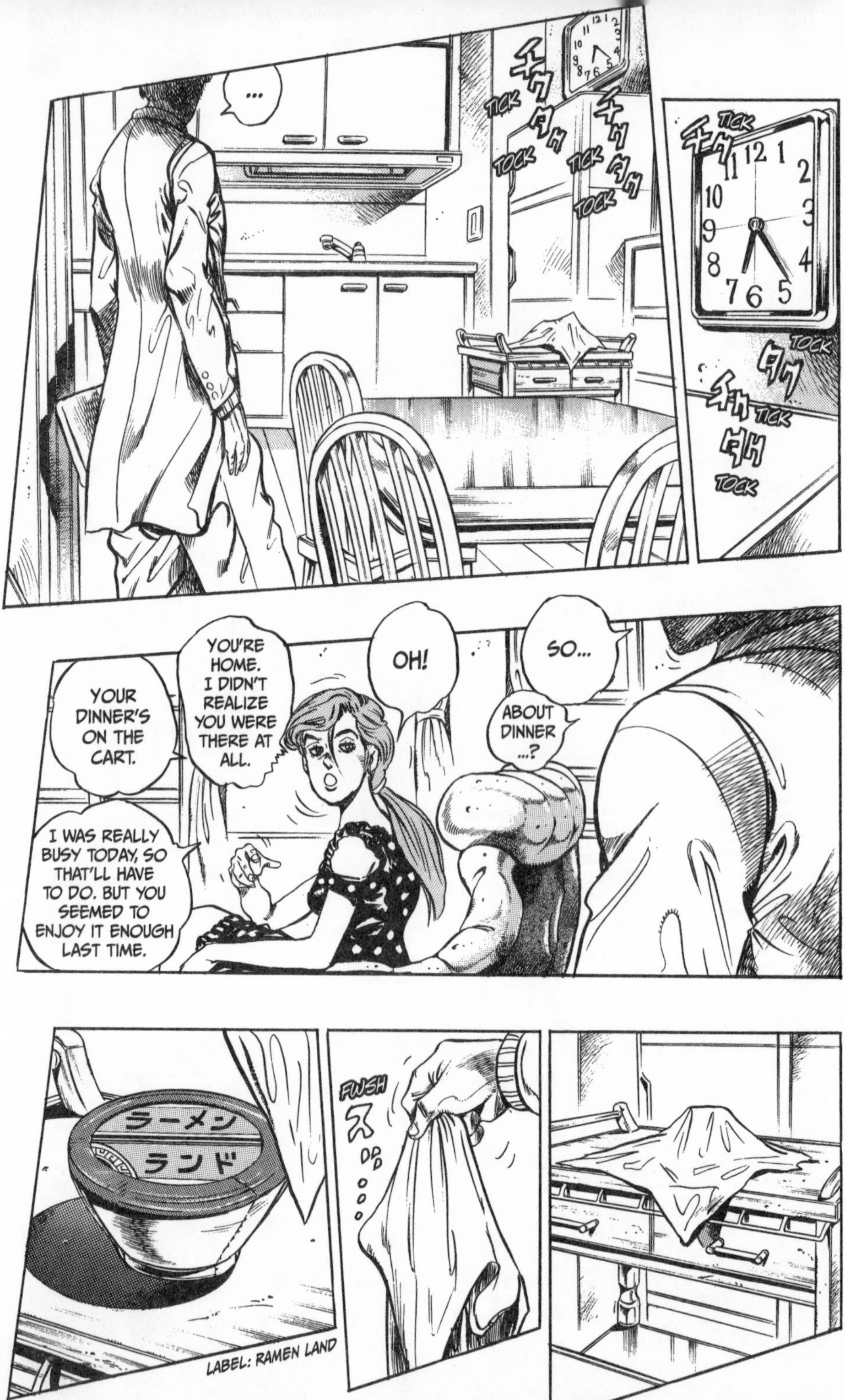

チク
TICK
タク
TOCK
チク
TICK
タク
TOCK
...
チク
TICK
タク
TOCK
チク
TICK
タク
TOCK
SO...
ABOUT DINNER ...?
OH!
YOU'RE HOME. I DIDN'T REALIZE YOU WERE THERE AT ALL.
YOUR DINNER'S ON THE CART.
I WAS REALLY BUSY TODAY, SO THAT'LL HAVE TO DO. BUT YOU SEEMED TO ENJOY IT ENOUGH LAST TIME.
FWSH
ス
ラーメン
ランド
LABEL: RAMEN LAND

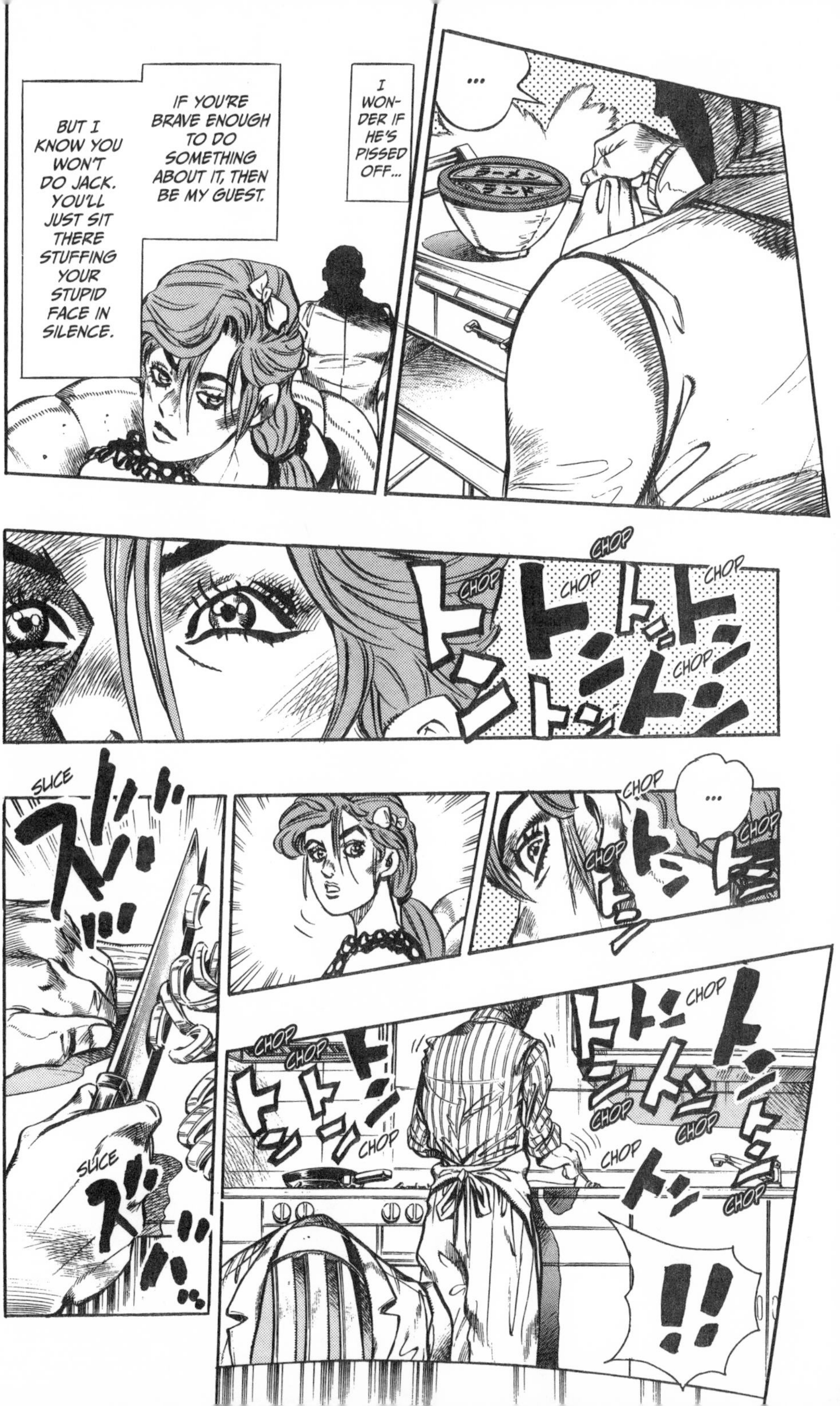
...
I WONDER IF HE'S PISSED OFF...
IF YOU'RE BRAVE ENOUGH TO DO SOMETHING ABOUT IT, THEN BE MY GUEST.
BUT I KNOW YOU WON'T DO JACK. YOU'LL JUST SIT THERE STUFFING YOUR STUPID FACE IN SILENCE.
CHOP
CHOP
CHOP
CHOP
CHOP
...
CHOP
CHOP
CHOP
SLICE
SLICE
CHOP
CHOP
CHOP
CHOP
CHOP
CHOP
CHOP
CHOP
!!

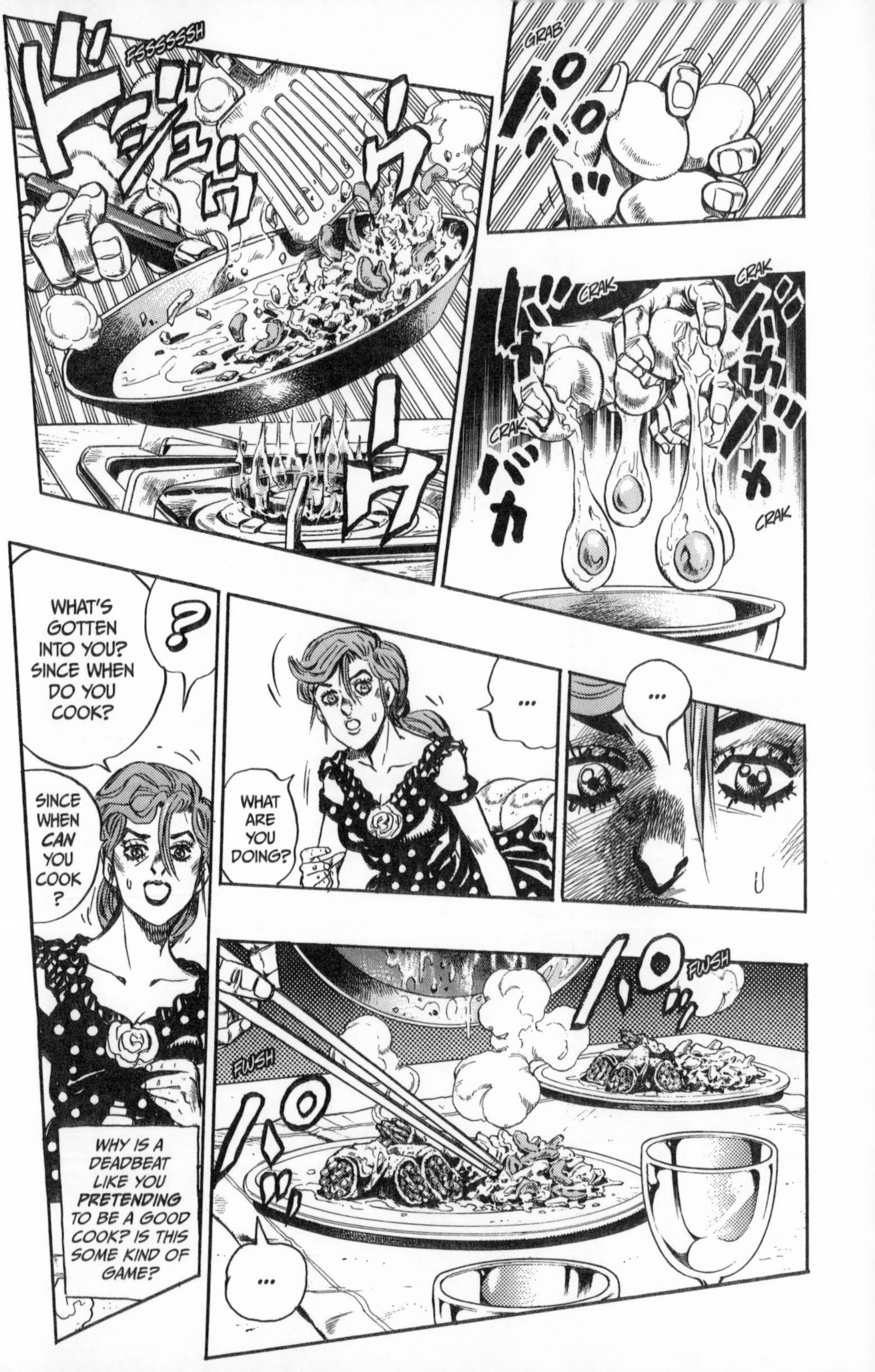
GRAB
CRAK
CRAK
CRAK
CRAK
PSSSSSSH
...
...
WHAT ARE YOU DOING?
FWSH
FWSH
...
?
WHAT'S GOTTEN INTO YOU? SINCE WHEN DO YOU COOK?
SINCE WHEN CAN YOU COOK?
WHY IS A DEADBEAT LIKE YOU PRETENDING TO BE A GOOD COOK? IS THIS SOME KIND OF GAME?

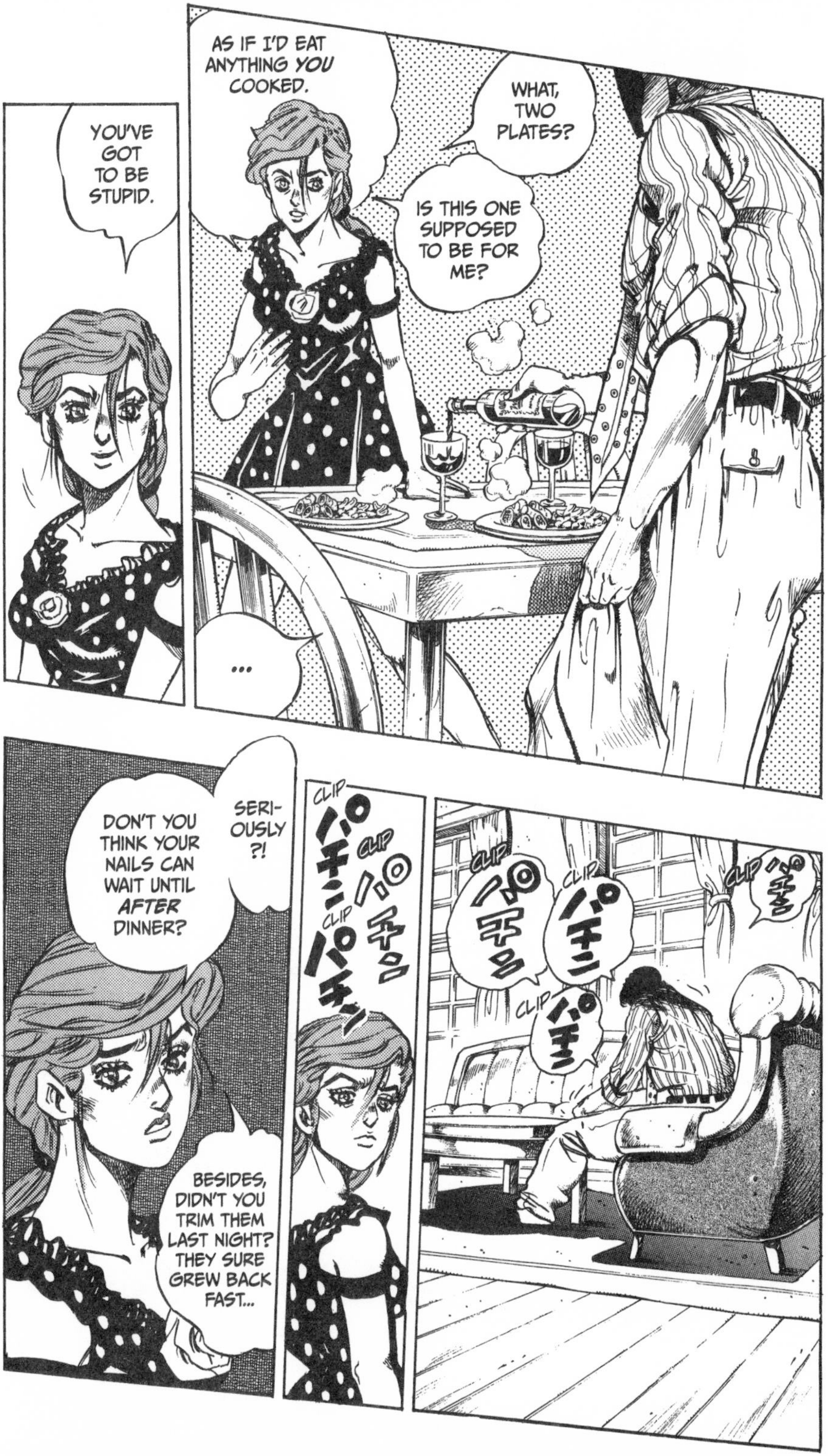
AS IF I'D EAT ANYTHING *YOU* COOKED.
WHAT, TWO PLATES?
IS THIS ONE SUPPOSED TO BE FOR ME?
...
YOU'VE GOT TO BE STUPID.
CLIP
CLIP
CLIP
CLIP
CLIP
CLIP
CLIP
SERIOUSLY?!
DON'T YOU THINK YOUR NAILS CAN WAIT UNTIL *AFTER* DINNER?
BESIDES, DIDN'T YOU TRIM THEM LAST NIGHT? THEY SURE GREW BACK FAST...

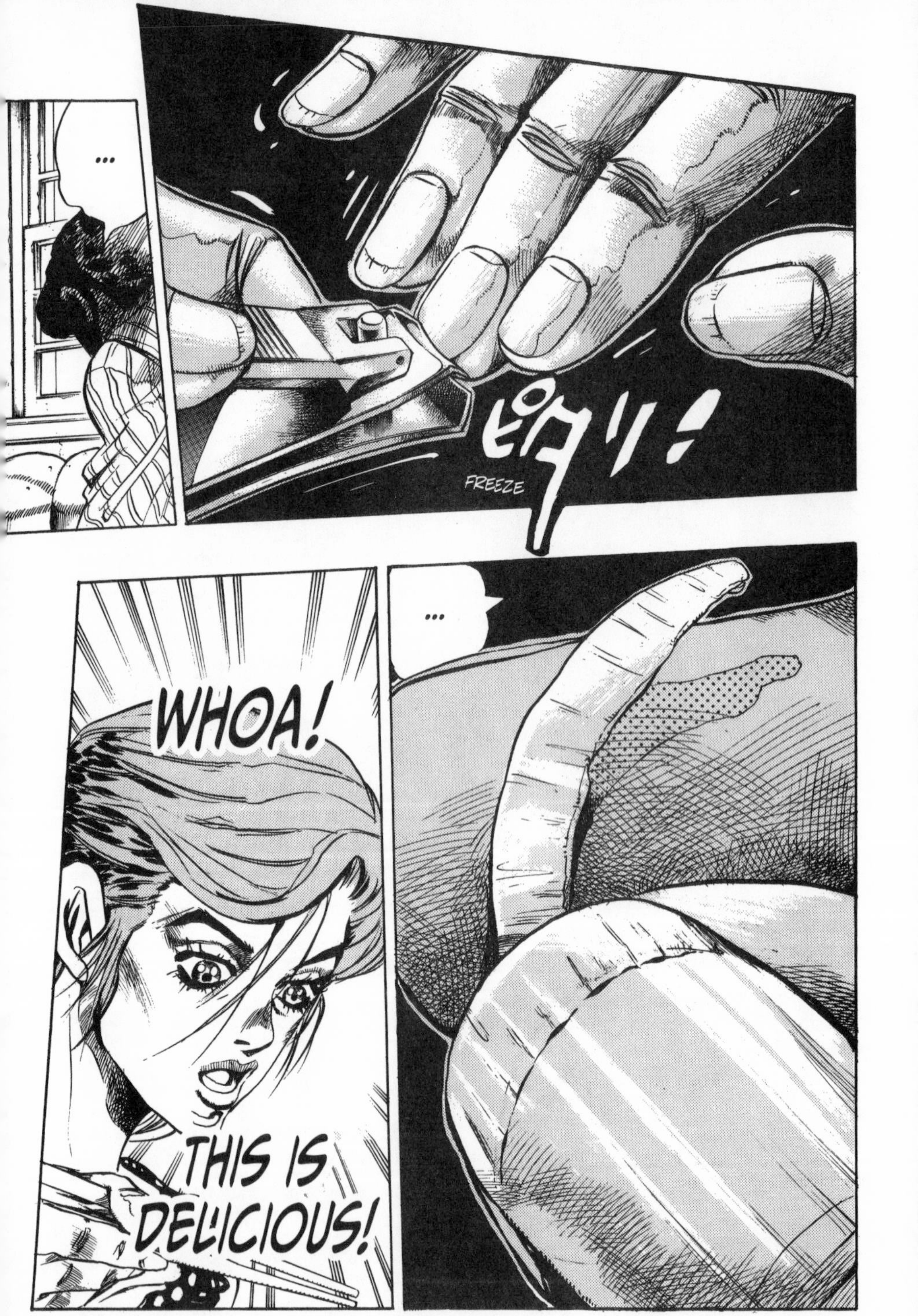
ピタリ!
FREEZE
...
...
WHOA!
THIS IS DELICIOUS!

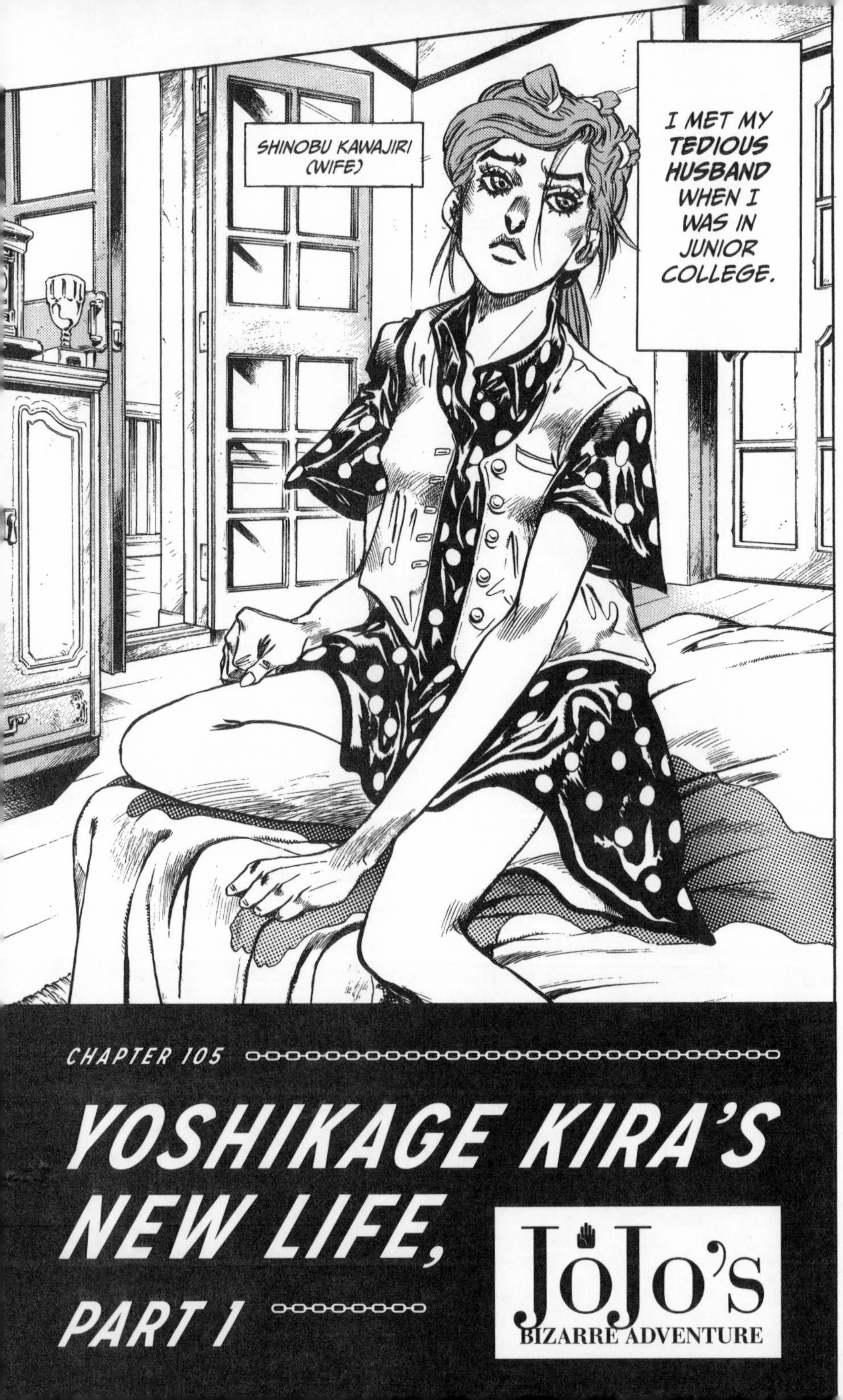
I MET MY TEDIOUS HUSBAND WHEN I WAS IN JUNIOR COLLEGE.
SHINOBU KAWAJIRI (WIFE)

CHAPTER 105

YOSHIKAGE KIRA'S NEW LIFE, PART 1

JoJo's
BIZARRE ADVENTURE

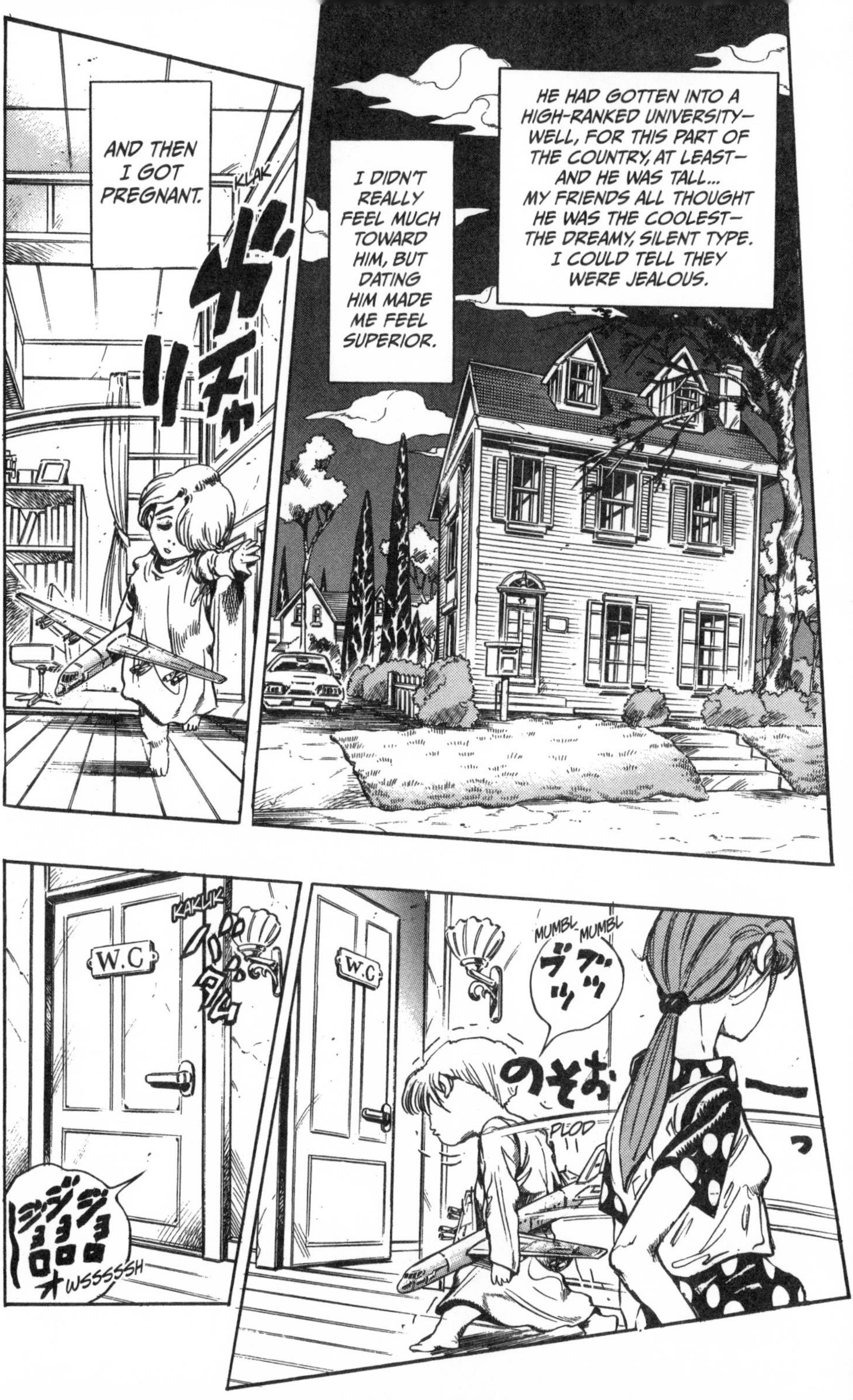
HE HAD GOTTEN INTO A HIGH-RANKED UNIVERSITY— WELL, FOR THIS PART OF THE COUNTRY, AT LEAST— AND HE WAS TALL... MY FRIENDS ALL THOUGHT HE WAS THE COOLEST— THE DREAMY, SILENT TYPE. I COULD TELL THEY WERE JEALOUS.
I DIDN'T REALLY FEEL MUCH TOWARD HIM, BUT DATING HIM MADE ME FEEL SUPERIOR.
AND THEN I GOT PREGNANT.
KLAK
MUMBL MUMBL
PLOD
W.C
W.C
KAKUK
WSSSSSH

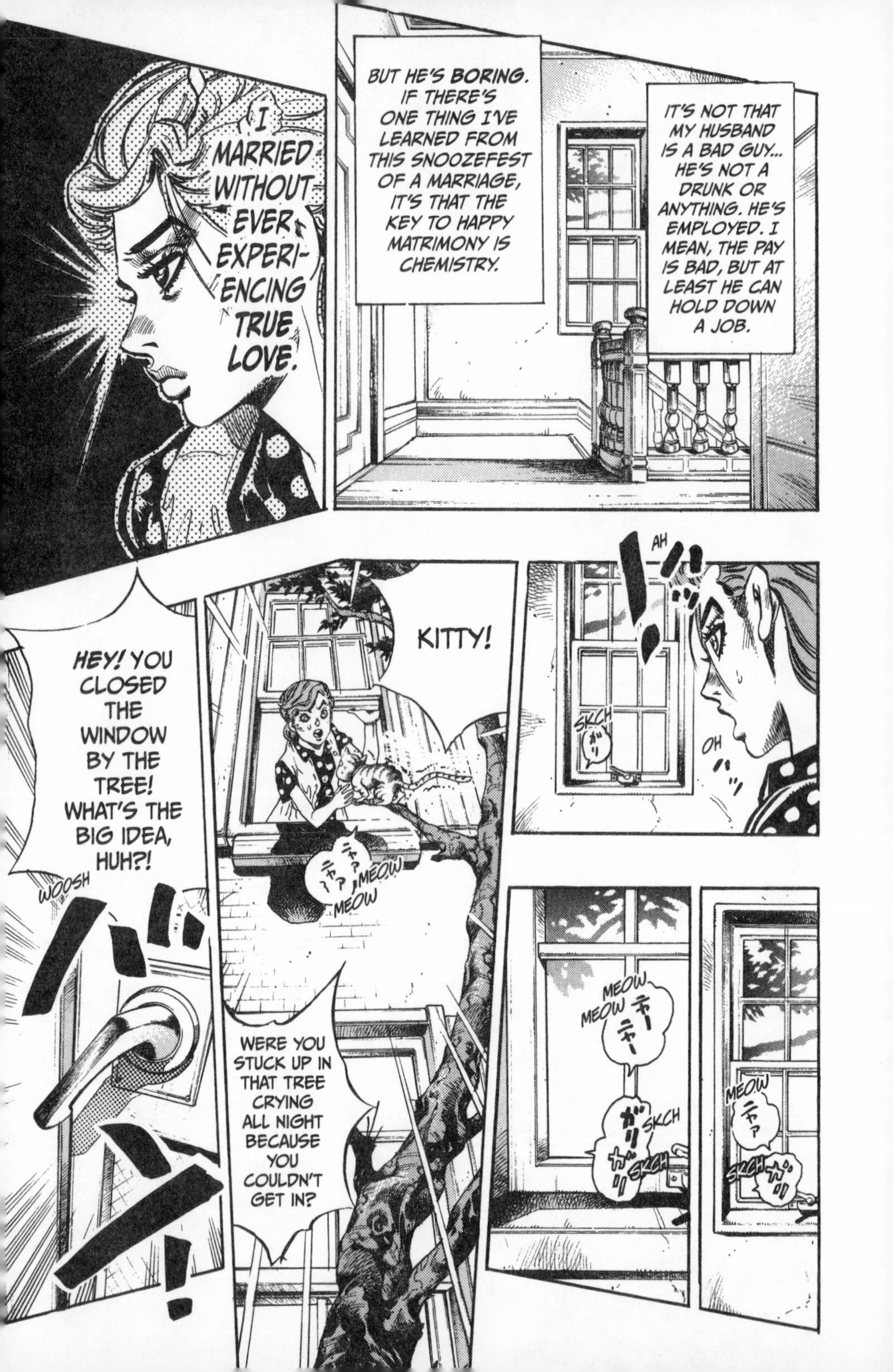
IT'S NOT THAT MY HUSBAND IS A BAD GUY... HE'S NOT A DRUNK OR ANYTHING. HE'S EMPLOYED. I MEAN, THE PAY IS BAD, BUT AT LEAST HE CAN HOLD DOWN A JOB.
BUT HE'S BORING. IF THERE'S ONE THING I'VE LEARNED FROM THIS SNOOZEFEST OF A MARRIAGE, IT'S THAT THE KEY TO HAPPY MATRIMONY IS CHEMISTRY.
I MARRIED WITHOUT EVER EXPERIENCING TRUE LOVE.
AH
SKCH
ガリ
OH
MEOW
ニャア
SKCH
ガリ
MEOW
MEOW
ニャー
ニャー
SKCH
ガリ
SKCH
ガリ
KITTY!
ニャア
ニャア~
MEOW
MEOW
WERE YOU STUCK UP IN THAT TREE CRYING ALL NIGHT BECAUSE YOU COULDN'T GET IN?
HEY! YOU CLOSED THE WINDOW BY THE TREE! WHAT'S THE BIG IDEA, HUH?!
WOOSH

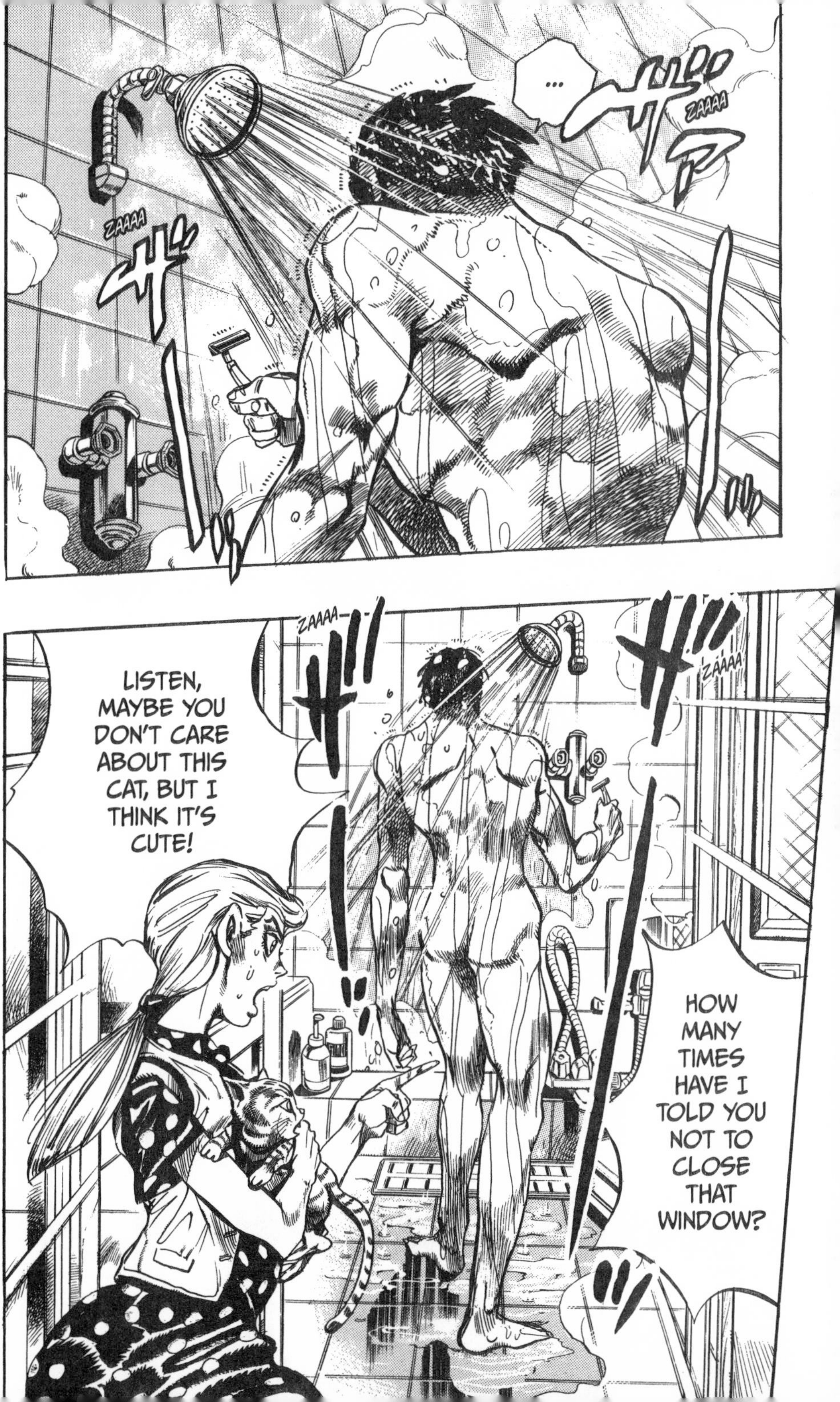

...
ZAAAA
ZAAAA
ZAAAA
ZAAAA
HOW MANY TIMES HAVE I TOLD YOU NOT TO CLOSE THAT WINDOW?
LISTEN, MAYBE YOU DON'T CARE ABOUT THIS CAT, BUT I THINK IT'S CUTE!

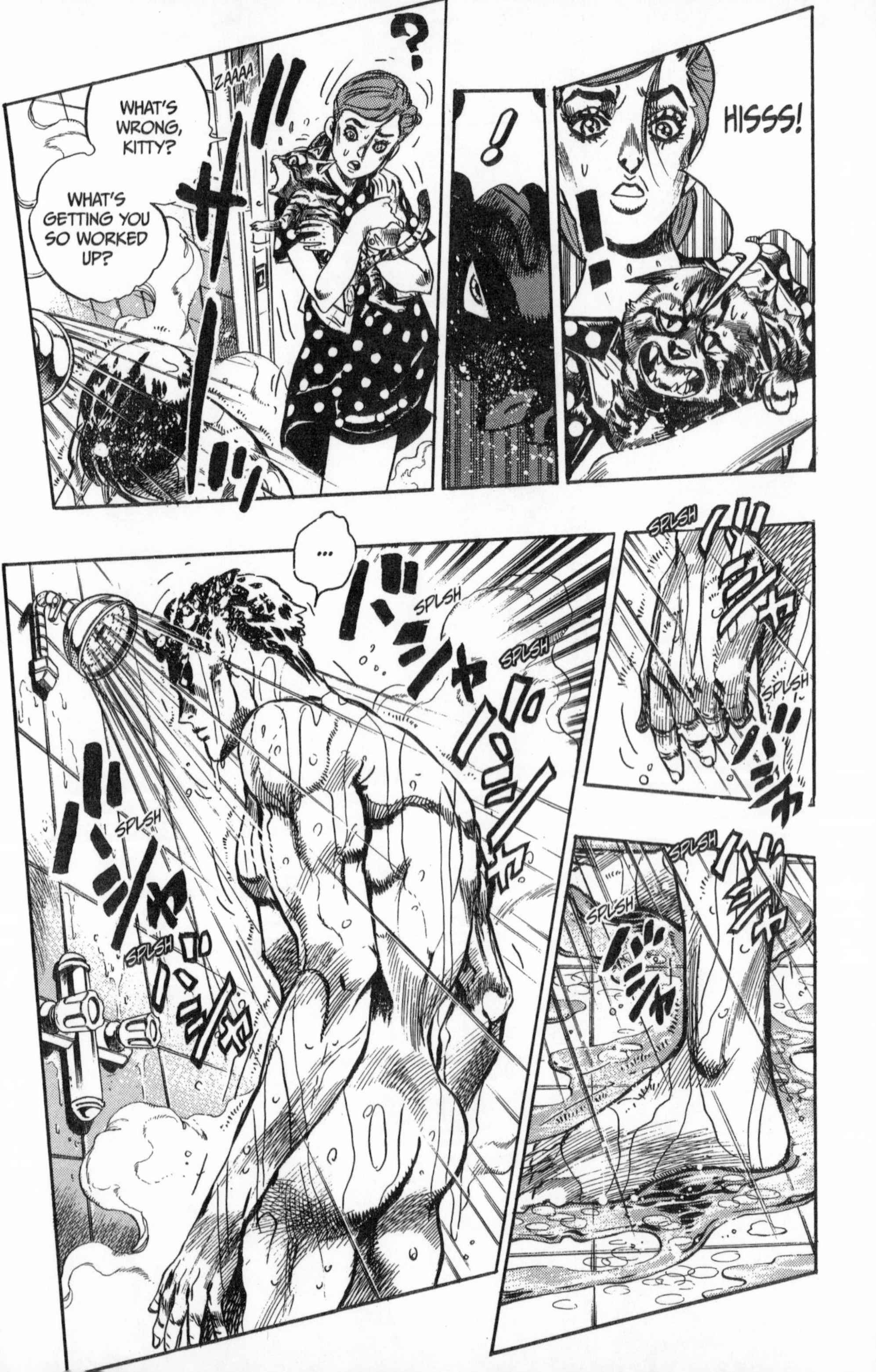
HISSS!
!
?
ZAAAA
WHAT'S WRONG, KITTY?
WHAT'S GETTING YOU SO WORKED UP?
SPLSH
SPLSH
SPLSH
SPLSH
...
SPLSH
SPLSH
SPLSH
SPLSH

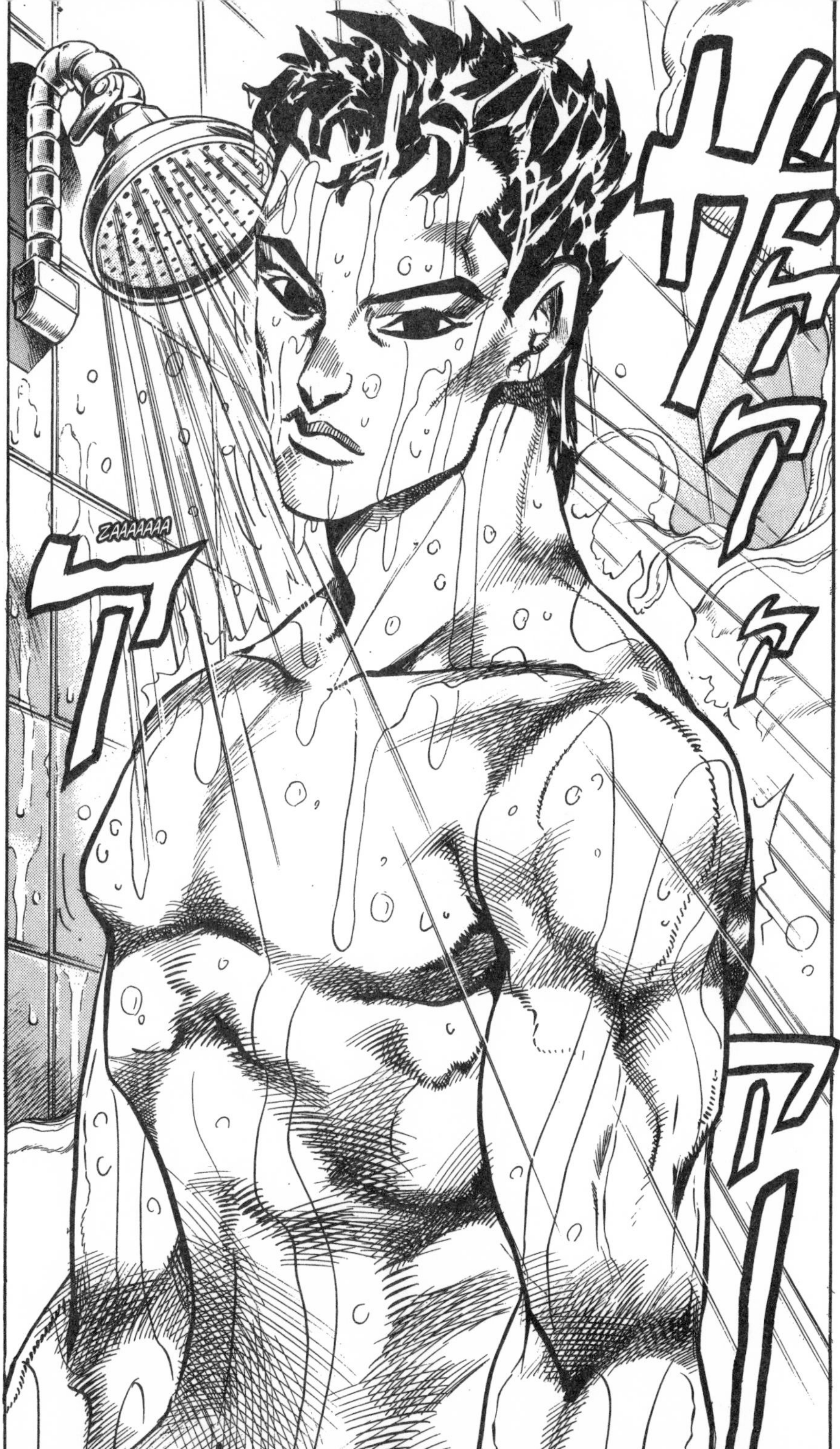

ZAAAAAAA

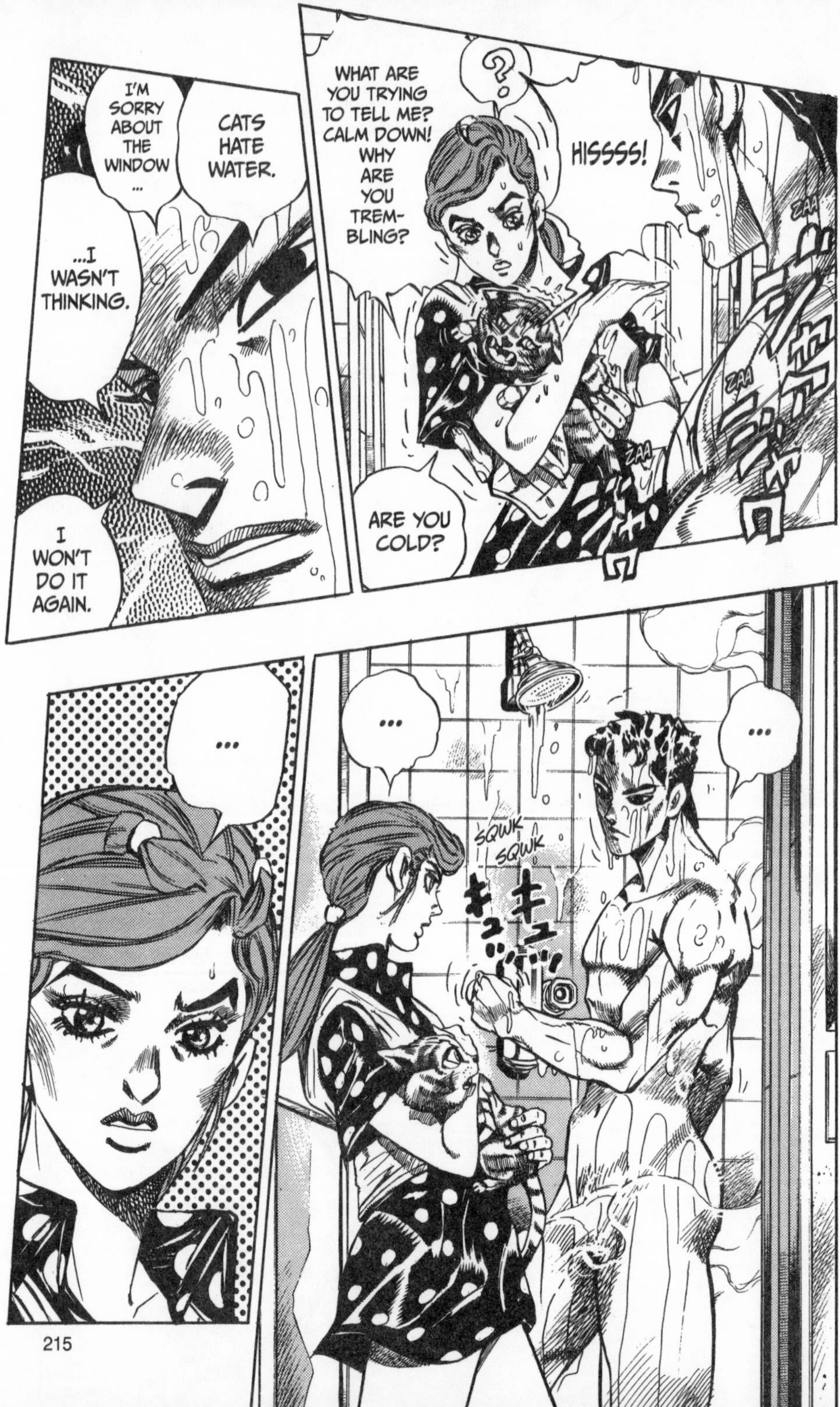
?
WHAT ARE YOU TRYING TO TELL ME? CALM DOWN! WHY ARE YOU TREMBLING?
HISSSS!
ZAA
ZAA
ZAA
ARE YOU COLD?
CATS HATE WATER.
I'M SORRY ABOUT THE WINDOW ...
...I WASN'T THINKING.
I WON'T DO IT AGAIN.
...
...
SQWK SQWK
...

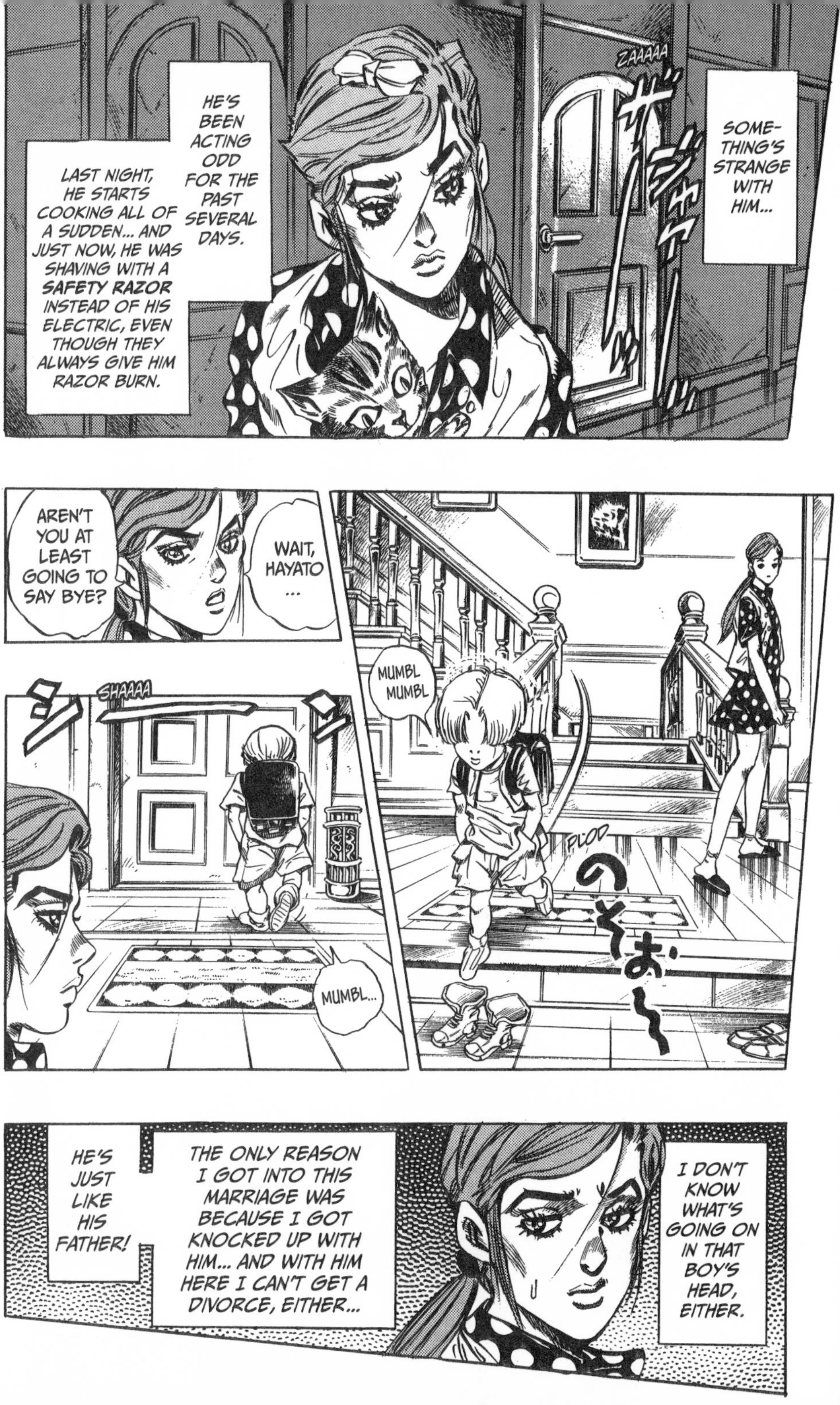
ZAAAAA
SOME-THING'S STRANGE WITH HIM...
HE'S BEEN ACTING ODD FOR THE PAST SEVERAL DAYS.
LAST NIGHT, HE STARTS COOKING ALL OF A SUDDEN... AND JUST NOW, HE WAS SHAVING WITH A **SAFETY RAZOR** INSTEAD OF HIS ELECTRIC, EVEN THOUGH THEY ALWAYS GIVE HIM RAZOR BURN.
MUMBL MUMBL
PLOD
WAIT, HAYATO ...
AREN'T YOU AT LEAST GOING TO SAY BYE?
SHAAAA
MUMBL...
I DON'T KNOW WHAT'S GOING ON IN THAT BOY'S HEAD, EITHER.
THE ONLY REASON I GOT INTO THIS MARRIAGE WAS BECAUSE I GOT KNOCKED UP WITH HIM... AND WITH HIM HERE I CAN'T GET A DIVORCE, EITHER...
HE'S JUST LIKE HIS FATHER!

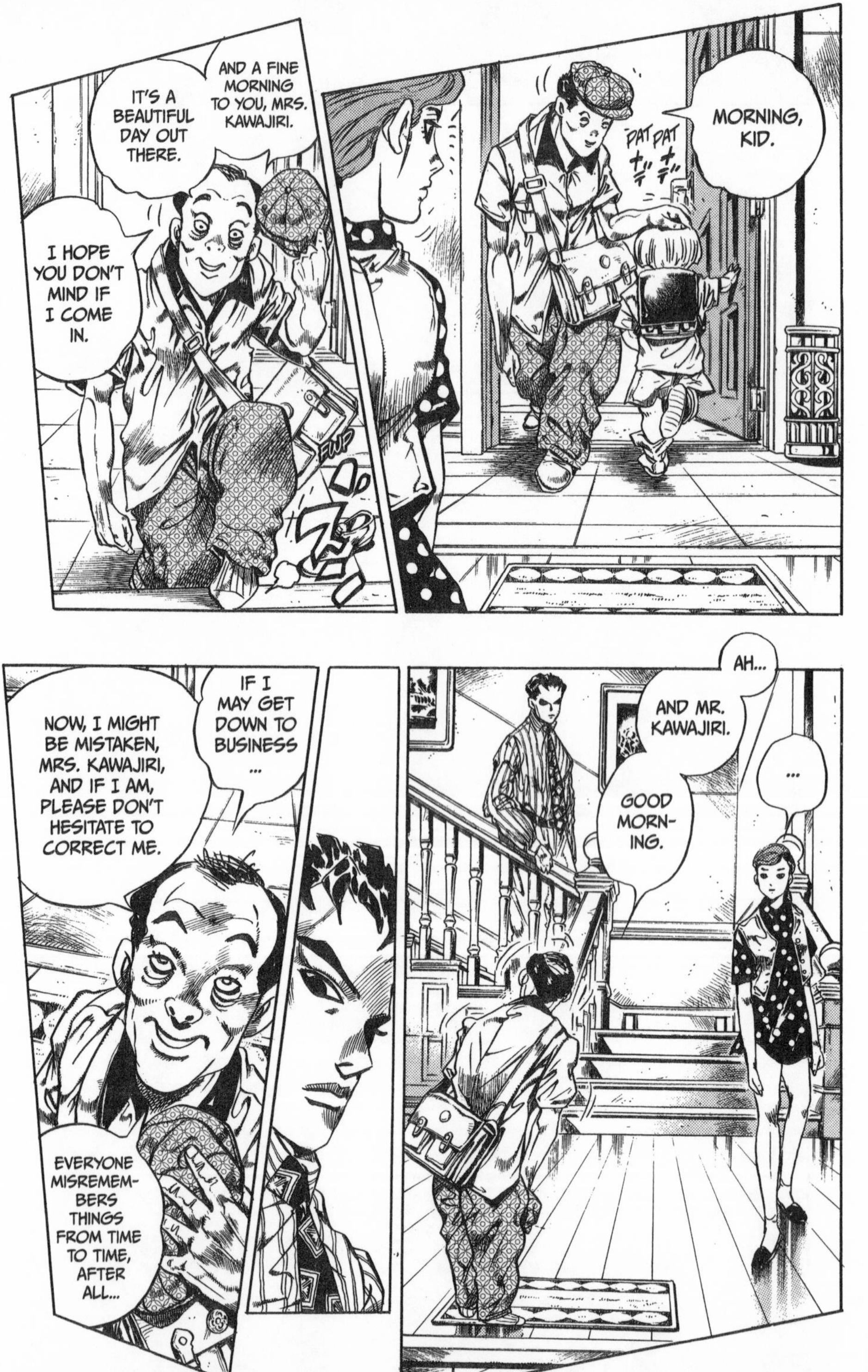
MORNING, KID.
PAT PAT
ナデ ナデ
AND A FINE MORNING TO YOU, MRS. KAWAJIRI.
IT'S A BEAUTIFUL DAY OUT THERE.
I HOPE YOU DON'T MIND IF I COME IN.
FWP
AH...
AND MR. KAWAJIRI.
GOOD MORNING.
...
IF I MAY GET DOWN TO BUSINESS...
NOW, I MIGHT BE MISTAKEN, MRS. KAWAJIRI, AND IF I AM, PLEASE DON'T HESITATE TO CORRECT ME.
EVERYONE MISREMEMBERS THINGS FROM TIME TO TIME, AFTER ALL...

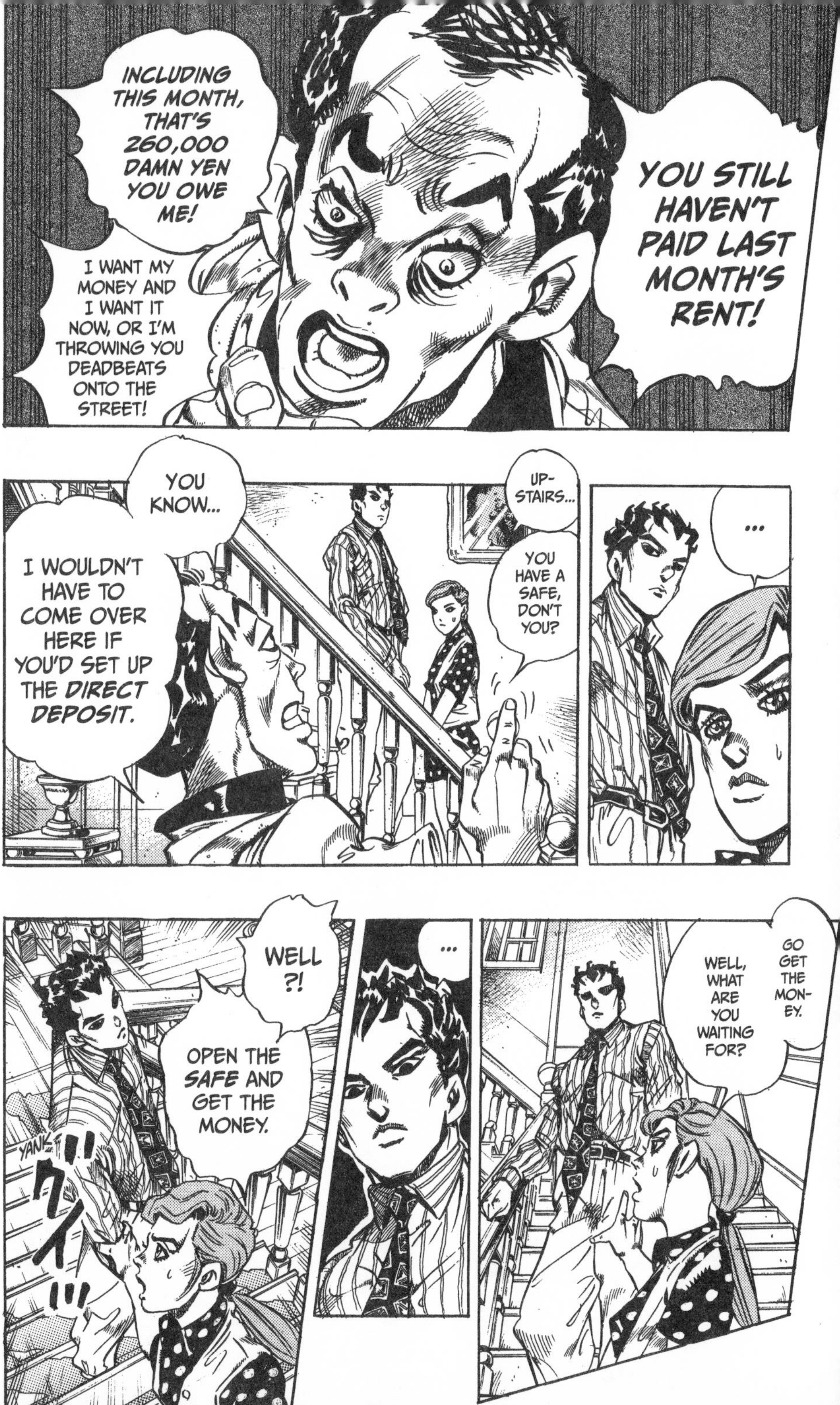

YOU STILL HAVEN'T PAID LAST MONTH'S RENT!
INCLUDING THIS MONTH, THAT'S 260,000 DAMN YEN YOU OWE ME!
I WANT MY MONEY AND I WANT IT NOW, OR I'M THROWING YOU DEADBEATS ONTO THE STREET!
...
UP-STAIRS...
YOU HAVE A SAFE, DON'T YOU?
YOU KNOW...
I WOULDN'T HAVE TO COME OVER HERE IF YOU'D SET UP THE DIRECT DEPOSIT.
GO GET THE MON-EY.
WELL, WHAT ARE YOU WAITING FOR?
...
WELL ?!
OPEN THE SAFE AND GET THE MONEY.
YANK

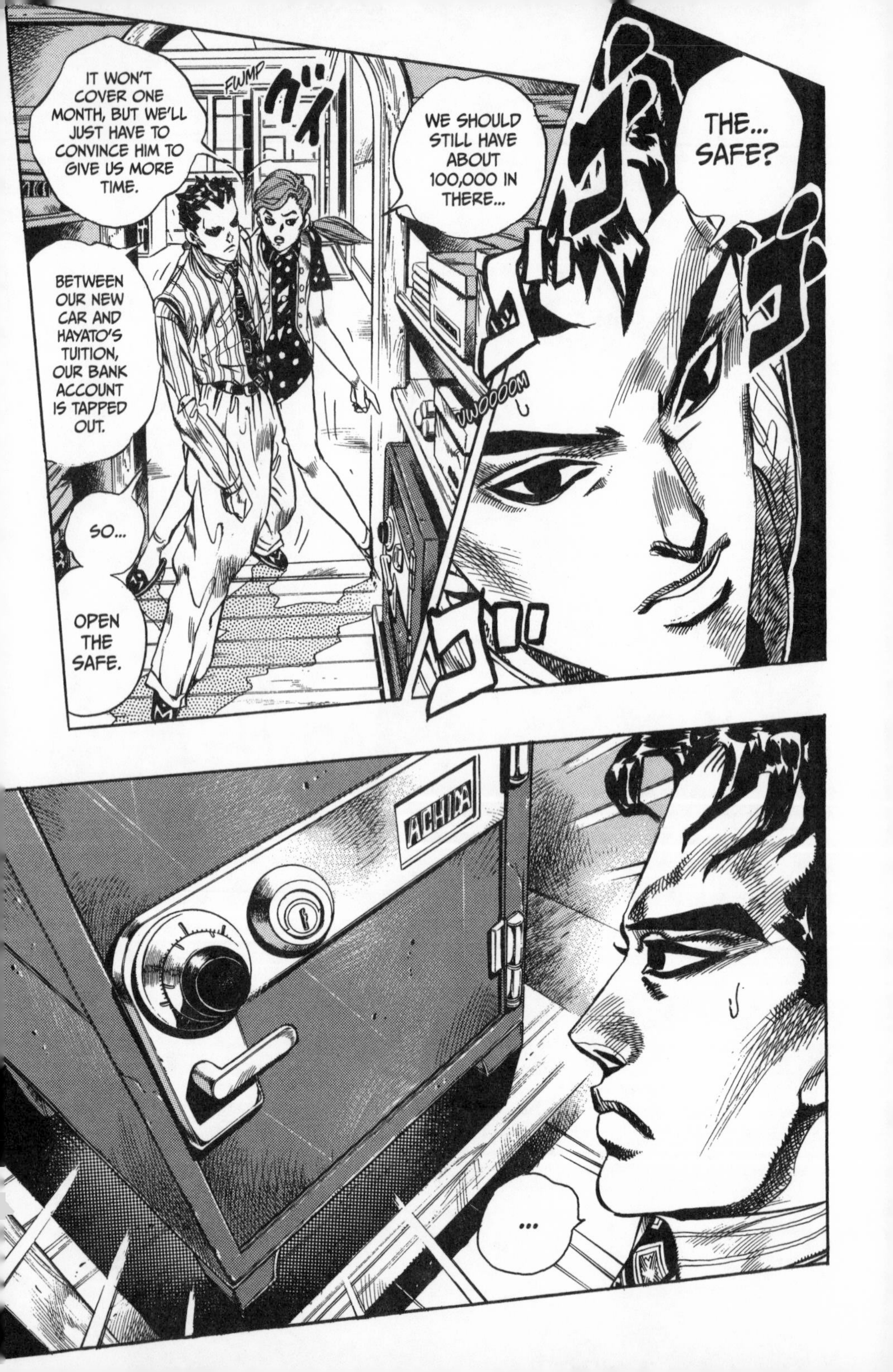
THE... SAFE?
WE SHOULD STILL HAVE ABOUT 100,000 IN THERE...
FWUMP
IT WON'T COVER ONE MONTH, BUT WE'LL JUST HAVE TO CONVINCE HIM TO GIVE US MORE TIME.
BETWEEN OUR NEW CAR AND HAYATO'S TUITION, OUR BANK ACCOUNT IS TAPPED OUT.
SO...
OPEN THE SAFE.
ACHIDA
...

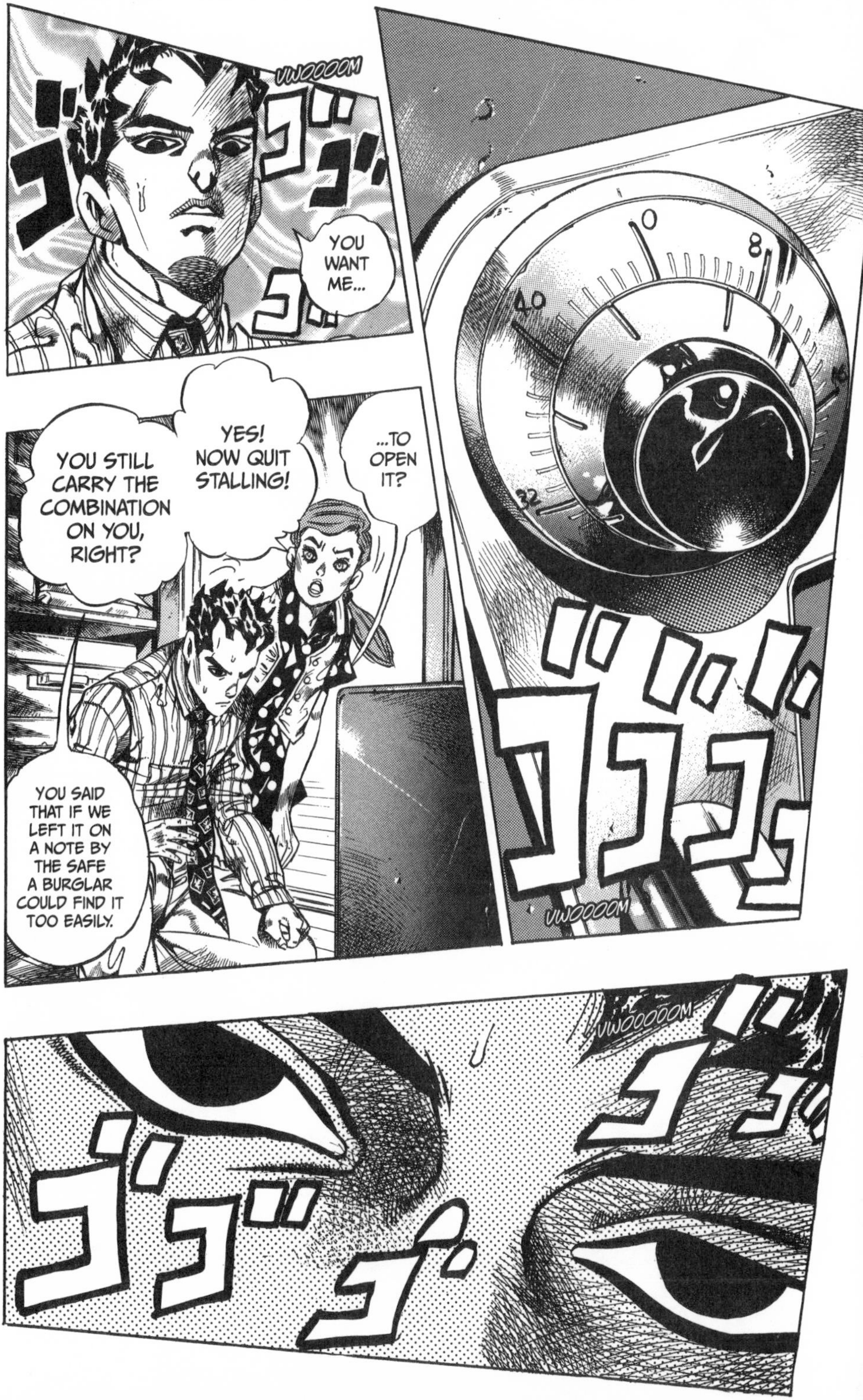
VWOOOOM
VWOOOOM
YOU WANT ME...
...TO OPEN IT?
YES! NOW QUIT STALLING!
YOU STILL CARRY THE COMBINATION ON YOU, RIGHT?
YOU SAID THAT IF WE LEFT IT ON A NOTE BY THE SAFE A BURGLAR COULD FIND IT TOO EASILY.
VWOOOOOM

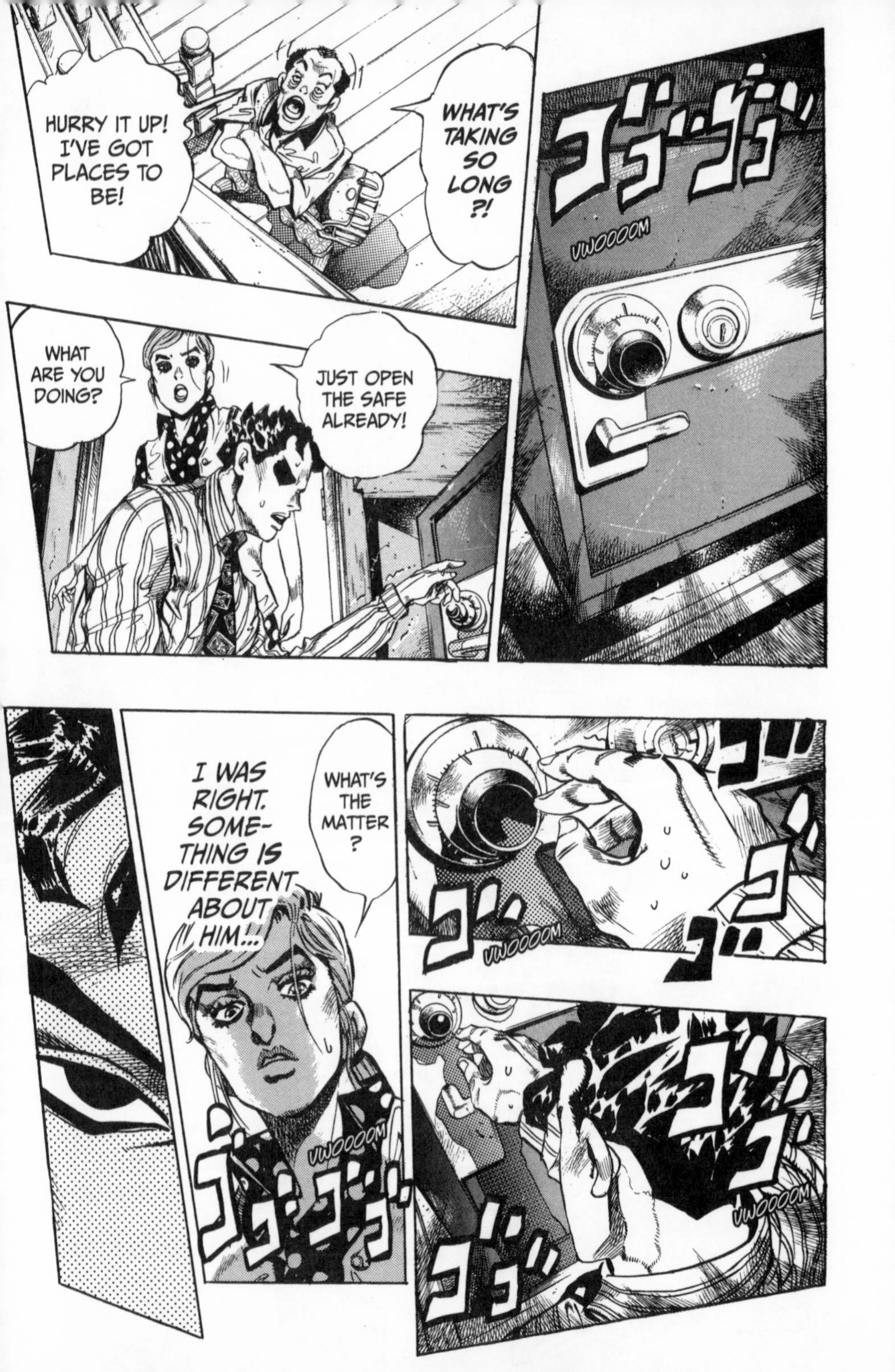
UWOOOOM
WHAT'S TAKING SO LONG ?!
HURRY IT UP! I'VE GOT PLACES TO BE!
JUST OPEN THE SAFE ALREADY!
WHAT ARE YOU DOING?
UWOOOOM
UWOOOOM
WHAT'S THE MATTER ?
I WAS RIGHT. SOME-THING IS DIFFERENT ABOUT HIM...
UWOOOOM

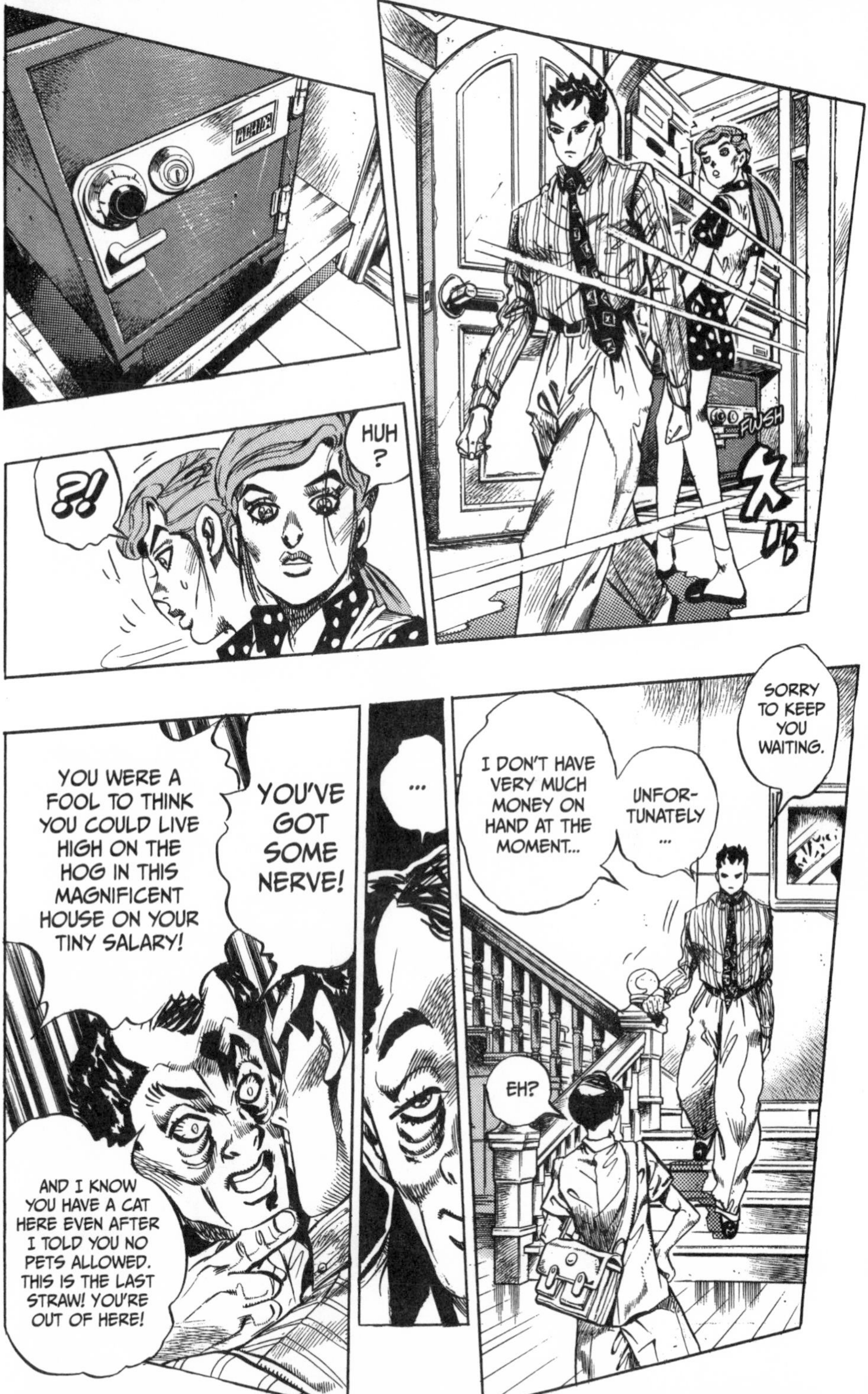
FLUSH
HUH?
?!
SORRY TO KEEP YOU WAITING.
UNFORTUNATELY...
I DON'T HAVE VERY MUCH MONEY ON HAND AT THE MOMENT...
EH?
...
YOU'VE GOT SOME NERVE!
YOU WERE A FOOL TO THINK YOU COULD LIVE HIGH ON THE HOG IN THIS MAGNIFICENT HOUSE ON YOUR TINY SALARY!
AND I KNOW YOU HAVE A CAT HERE EVEN AFTER I TOLD YOU NO PETS ALLOWED. THIS IS THE LAST STRAW! YOU'RE OUT OF HERE!

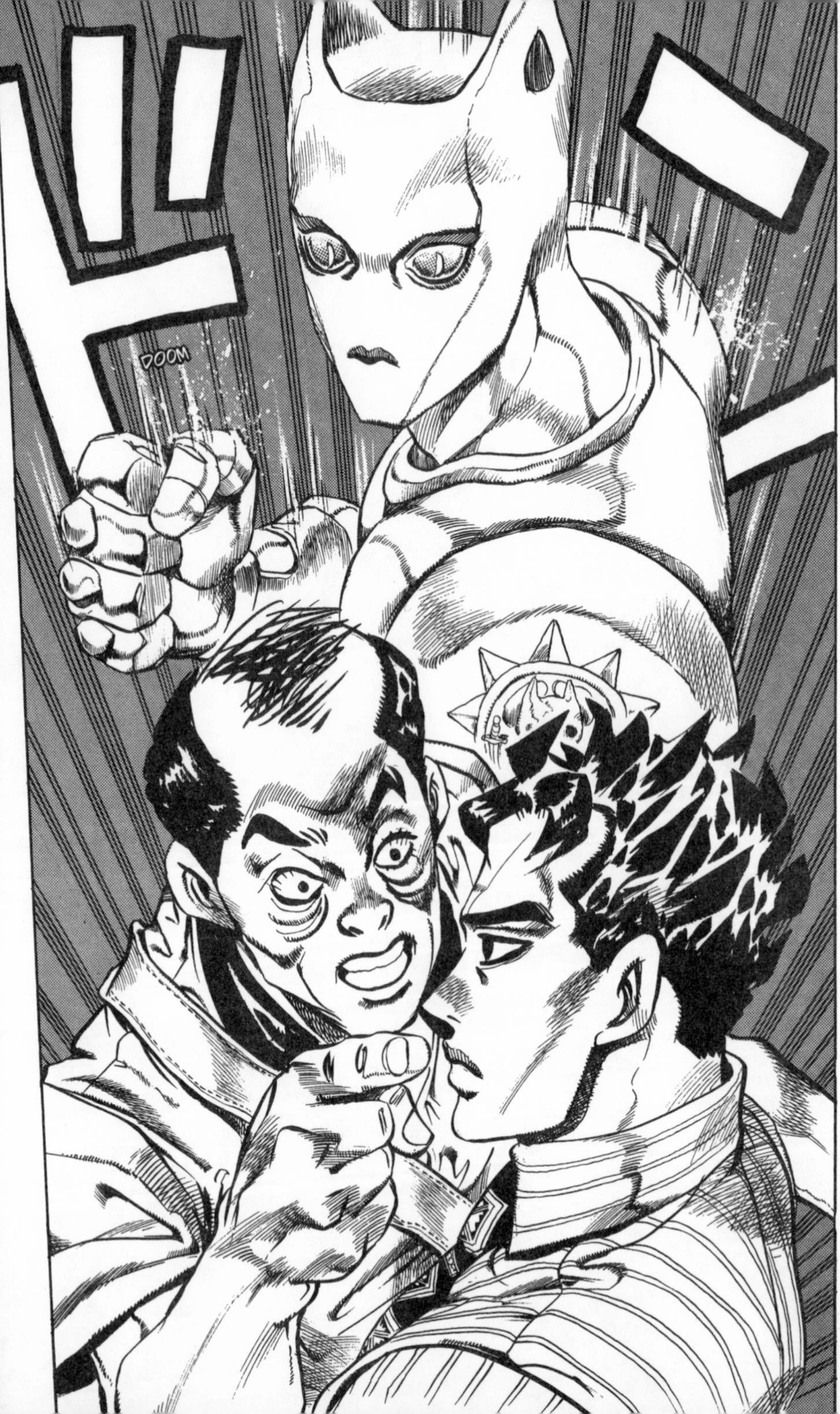
DOOM

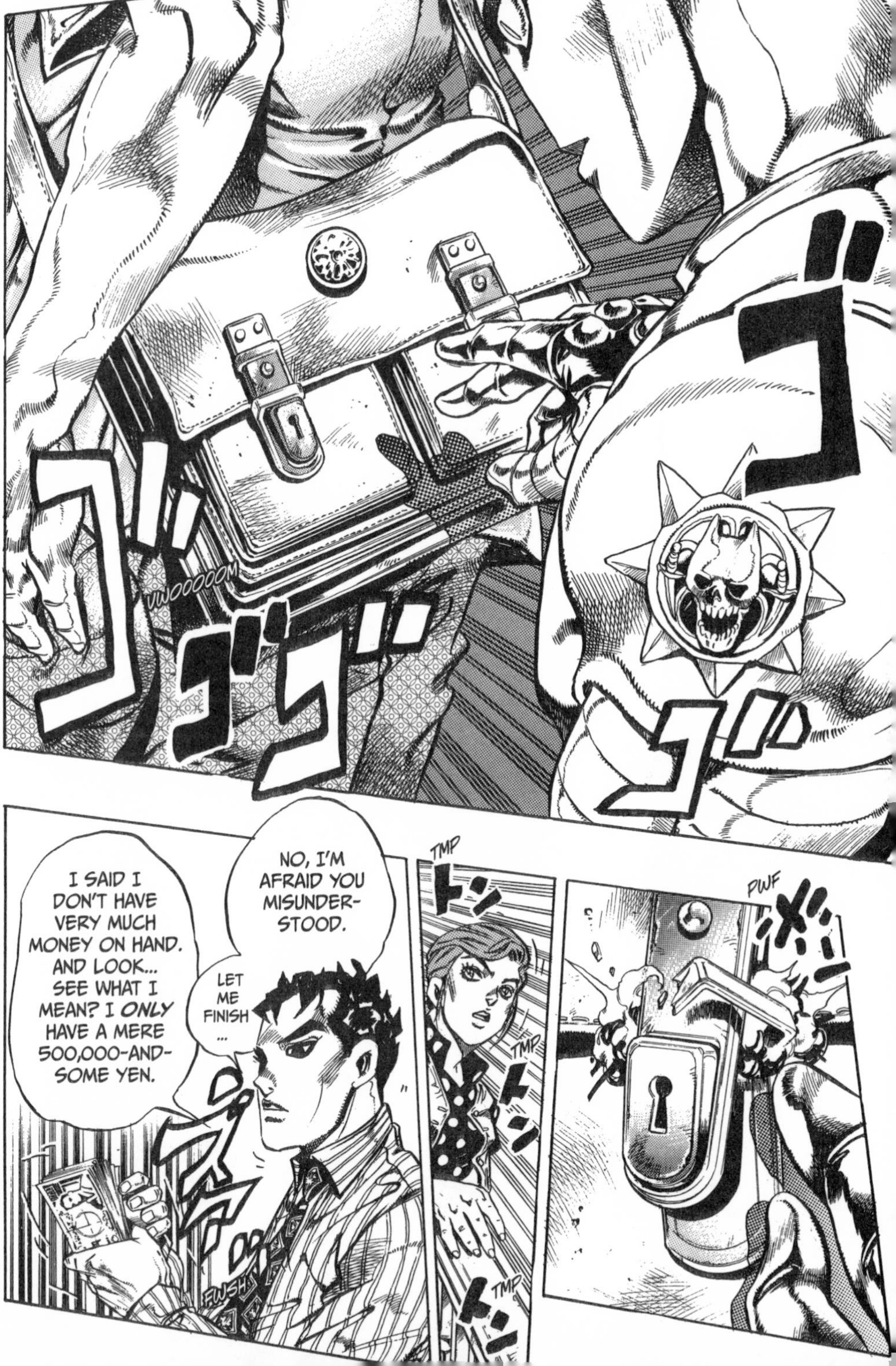
VWOOOOOM
PWF
TMP
TMP
TMP
NO, I'M AFRAID YOU MISUNDER-STOOD.
I SAID I DON'T HAVE VERY MUCH MONEY ON HAND. AND LOOK... SEE WHAT I MEAN? I *ONLY* HAVE A MERE 500,000-AND-SOME YEN.
LET ME FINISH ...
FWSH

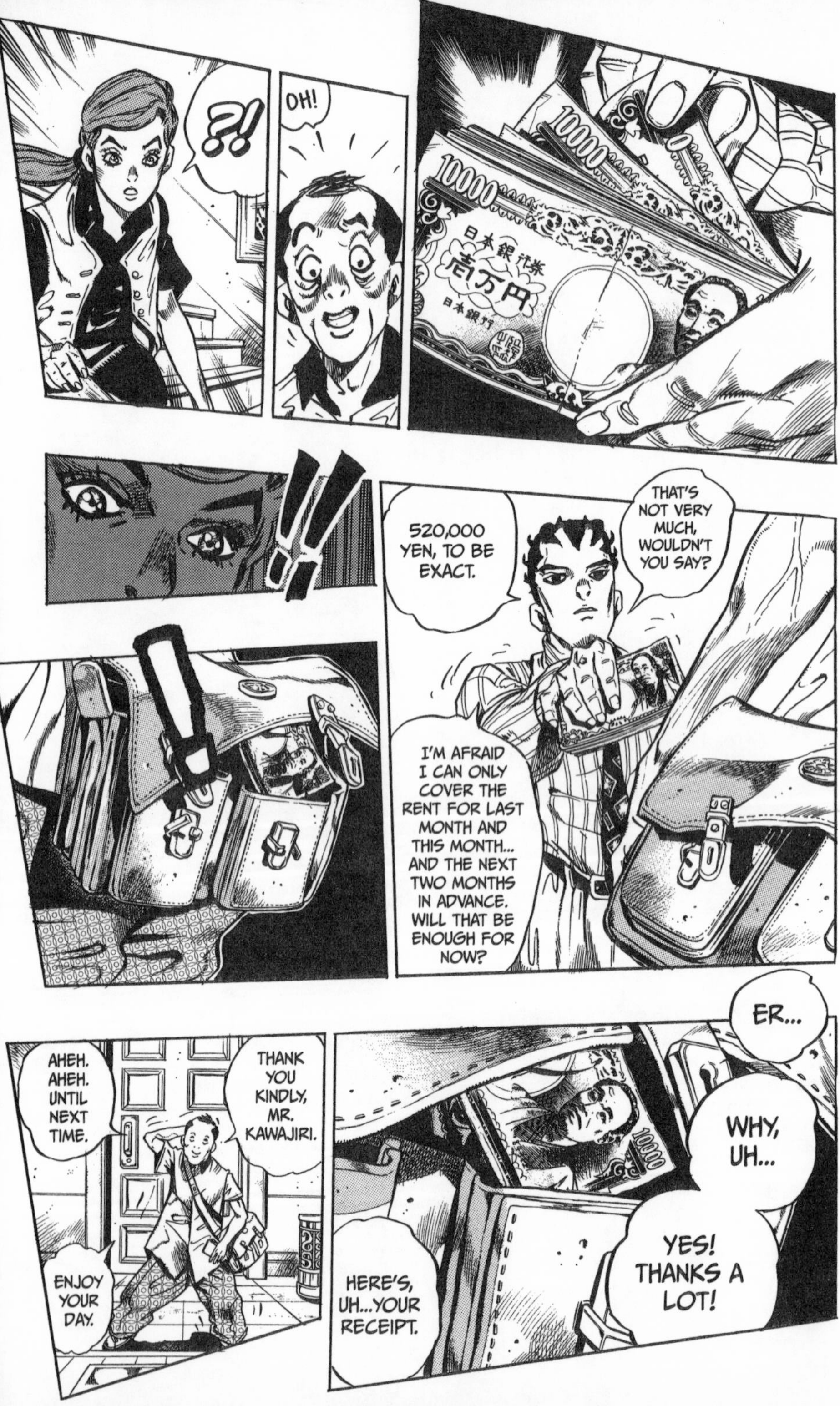
OH!
?!
THAT'S NOT VERY MUCH, WOULDN'T YOU SAY?
520,000 YEN, TO BE EXACT.
I'M AFRAID I CAN ONLY COVER THE RENT FOR LAST MONTH AND THIS MONTH... AND THE NEXT TWO MONTHS IN ADVANCE. WILL THAT BE ENOUGH FOR NOW?
!!
!
ER...
WHY, UH...
YES! THANKS A LOT!
HERE'S, UH...YOUR RECEIPT.
THANK YOU KINDLY, MR. KAWAJIRI.
AHEH. AHEH. UNTIL NEXT TIME.
ENJOY YOUR DAY.

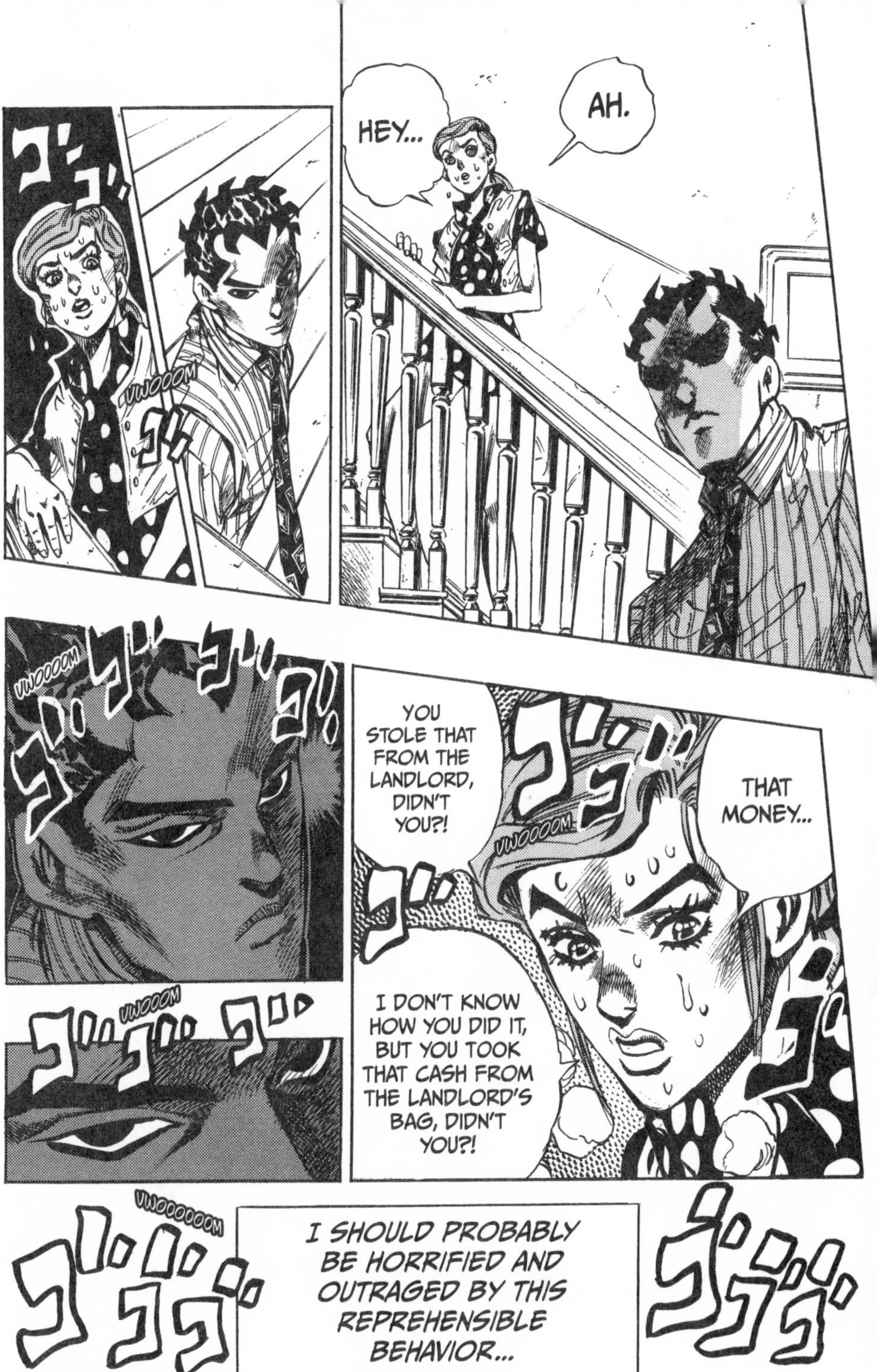
AH.
HEY...
VWOOOM
THAT MONEY...
YOU STOLE THAT FROM THE LANDLORD, DIDN'T YOU?!
VWOOOOM
I DON'T KNOW HOW YOU DID IT, BUT YOU TOOK THAT CASH FROM THE LANDLORD'S BAG, DIDN'T YOU?!
VWOOOOM
VWOOOM
I SHOULD PROBABLY BE HORRIFIED AND OUTRAGED BY THIS REPREHENSIBLE BEHAVIOR...
VWOOOOOOOM

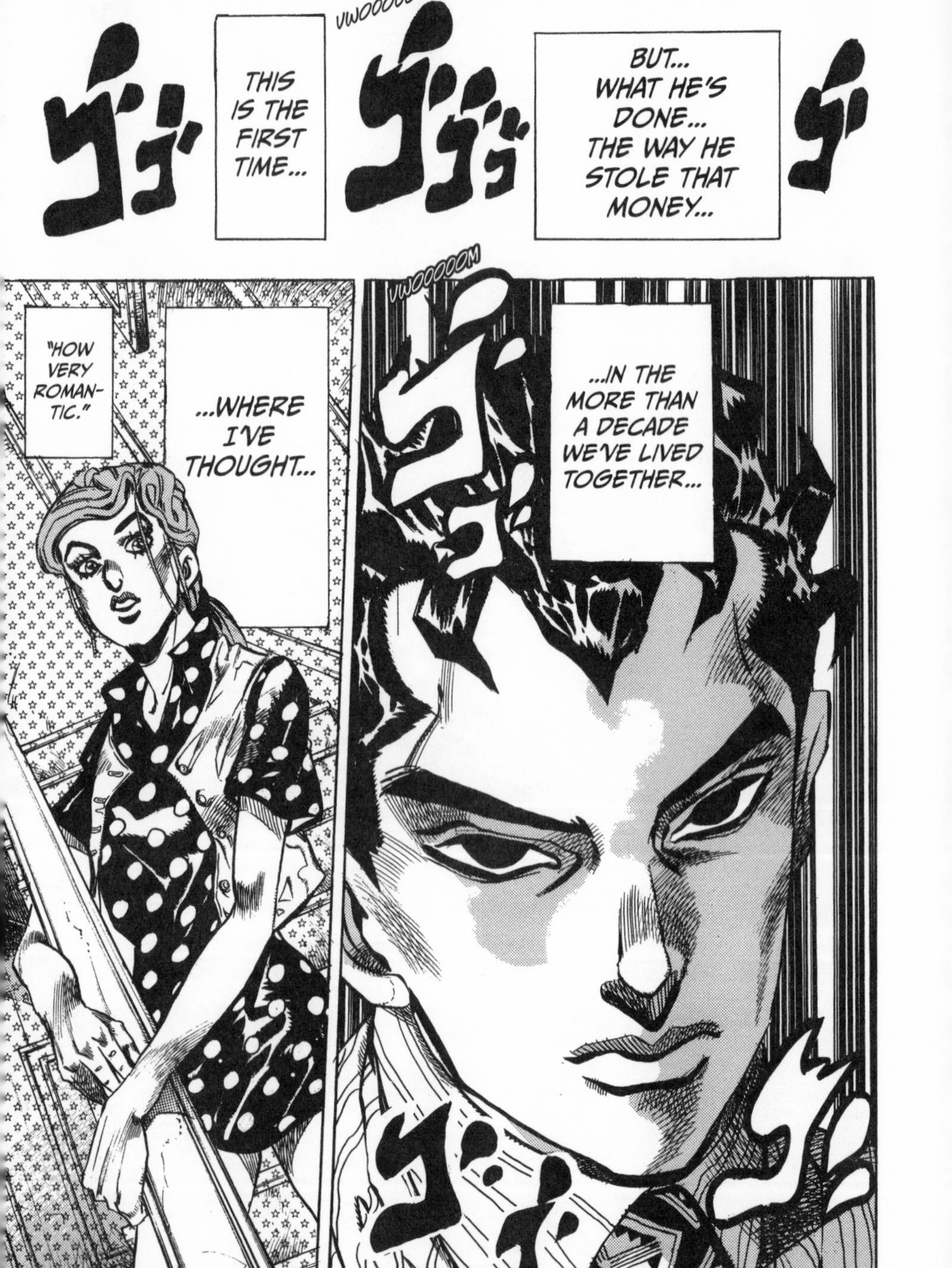
BUT... WHAT HE'S DONE... THE WAY HE STOLE THAT MONEY...
VWOOOOOOM
THIS IS THE FIRST TIME...
VWOOOOOOM
...IN THE MORE THAN A DECADE WE'VE LIVED TOGETHER...
...WHERE I'VE THOUGHT...
"HOW VERY ROMANTIC."

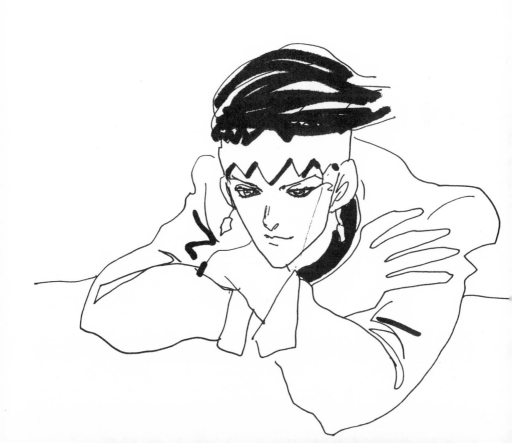

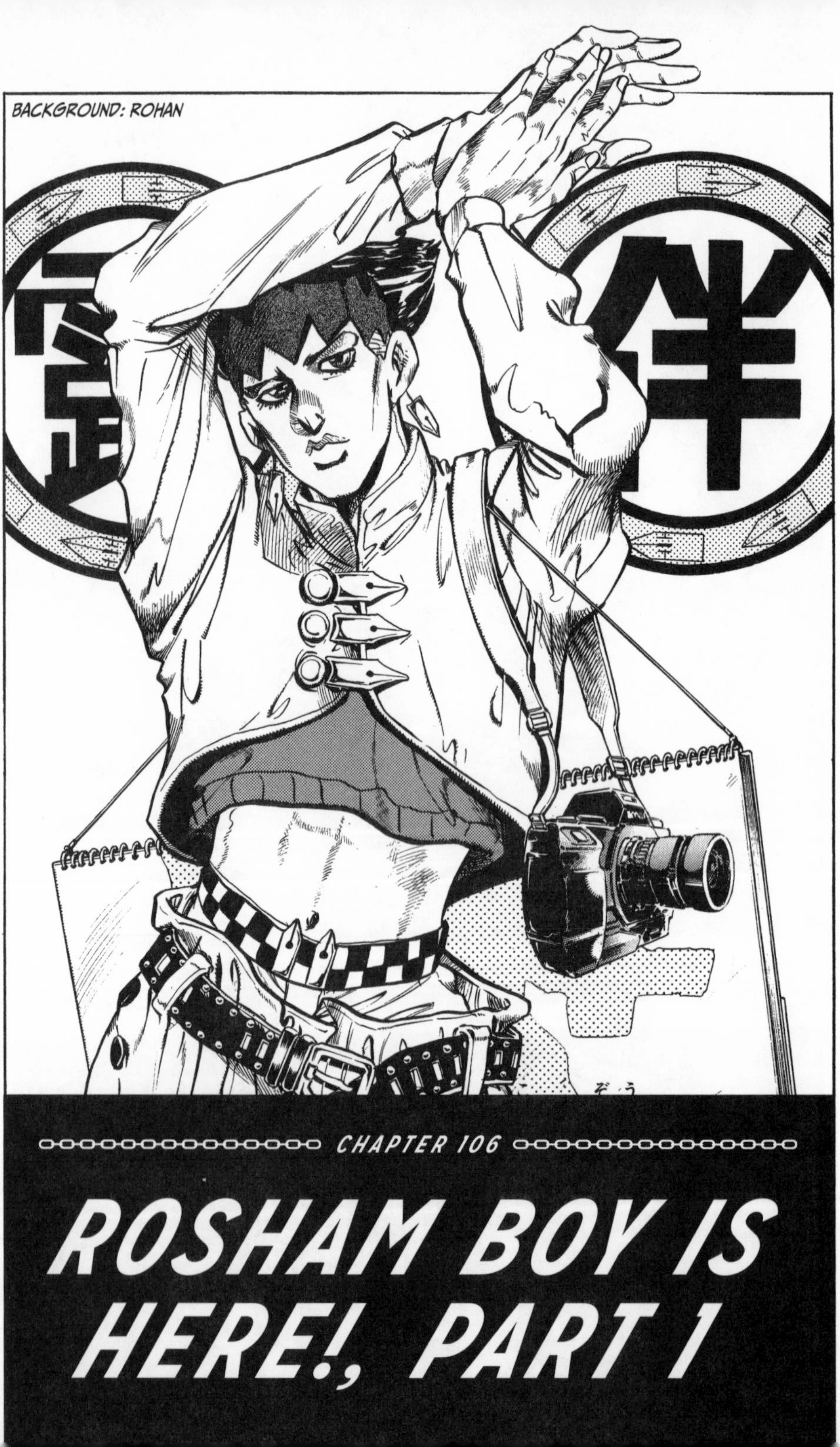
BACKGROUND: ROHAN

CHAPTER 106

ROSHAM BOY IS HERE!, PART 1

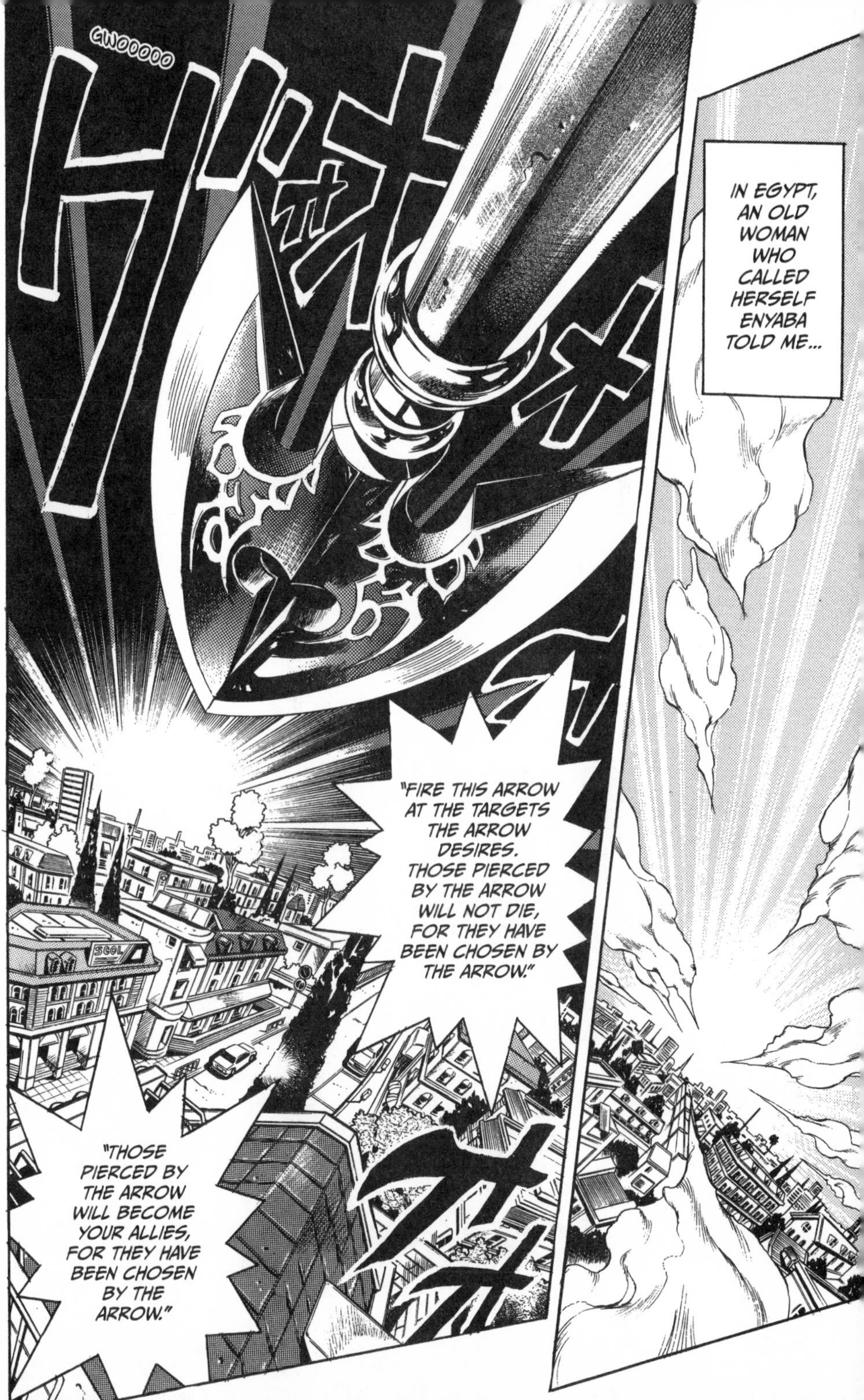
IN EGYPT, AN OLD WOMAN WHO CALLED HERSELF ENYABA TOLD ME...
GWOOOOO
"FIRE THIS ARROW AT THE TARGETS THE ARROW DESIRES. THOSE PIERCED BY THE ARROW WILL NOT DIE, FOR THEY HAVE BEEN CHOSEN BY THE ARROW."
"THOSE PIERCED BY THE ARROW WILL BECOME YOUR ALLIES, FOR THEY HAVE BEEN CHOSEN BY THE ARROW."

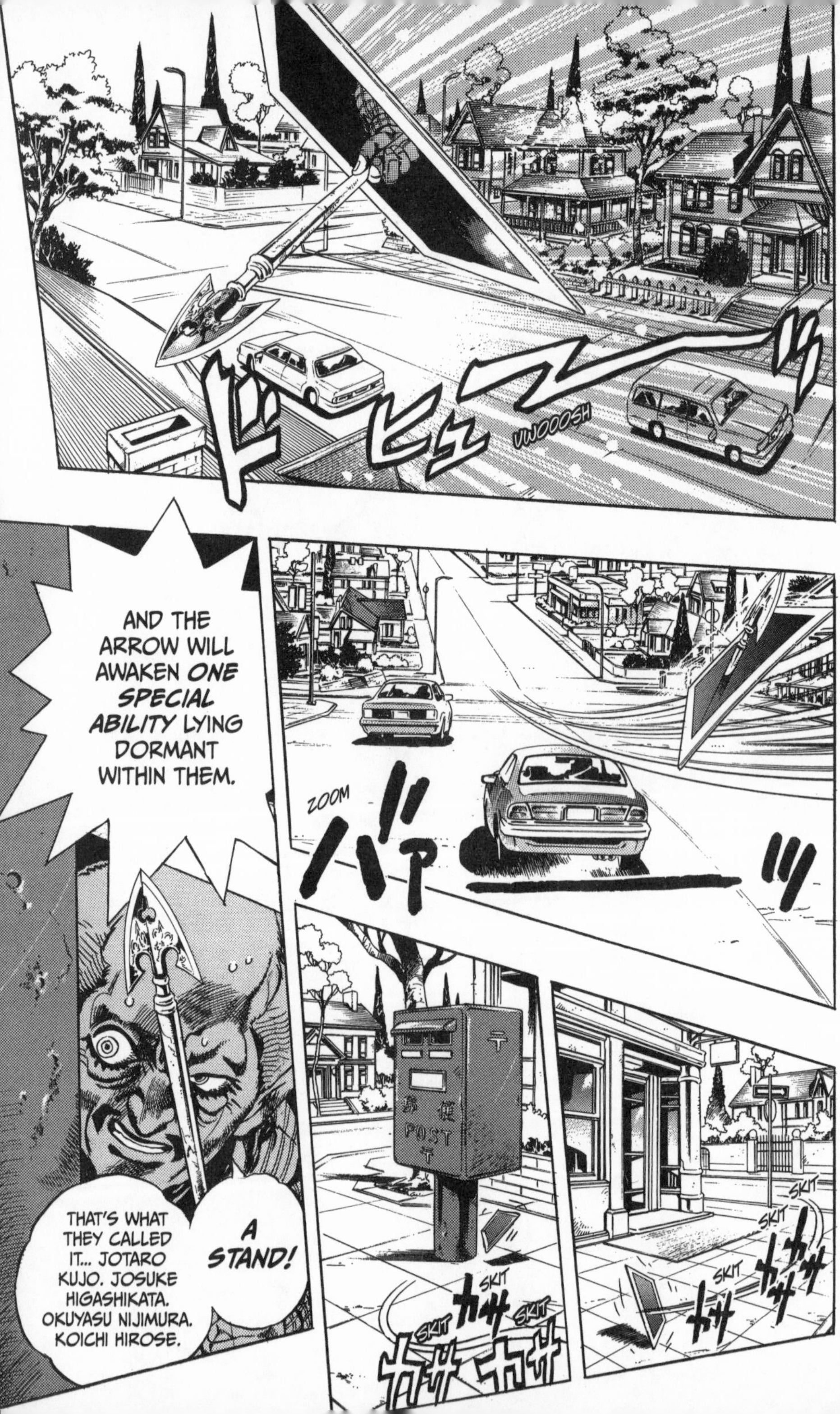

VWOOOSH
ZOOM
SKIT
SKIT
SKIT
POST
SKIT
SKIT
SKIT
AND THE ARROW WILL AWAKEN ONE SPECIAL ABILITY LYING DORMANT WITHIN THEM.
A STAND!
THAT'S WHAT THEY CALLED IT... JOTARO KUJO. JOSUKE HIGASHIKATA. OKUYASU NIJIMURA. KOICHI HIROSE.

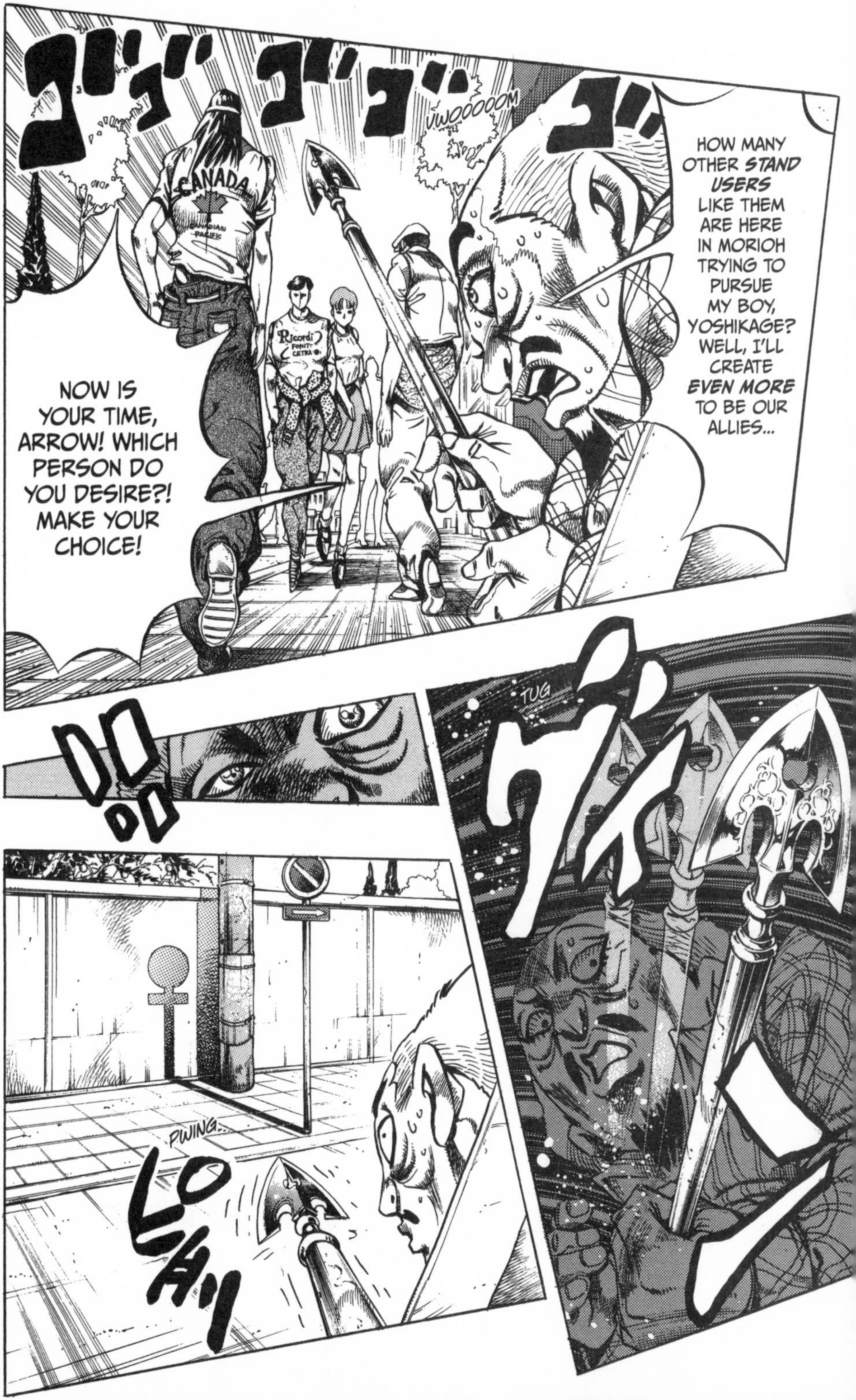
HOW MANY OTHER STAND USERS LIKE THEM ARE HERE IN MORIOH TRYING TO PURSUE MY BOY, YOSHIKAGE? WELL, I'LL CREATE EVEN MORE TO BE OUR ALLIES...
VWOOOOOM
NOW IS YOUR TIME, ARROW! WHICH PERSON DO YOU DESIRE?! MAKE YOUR CHOICE!
TUG
PWING...

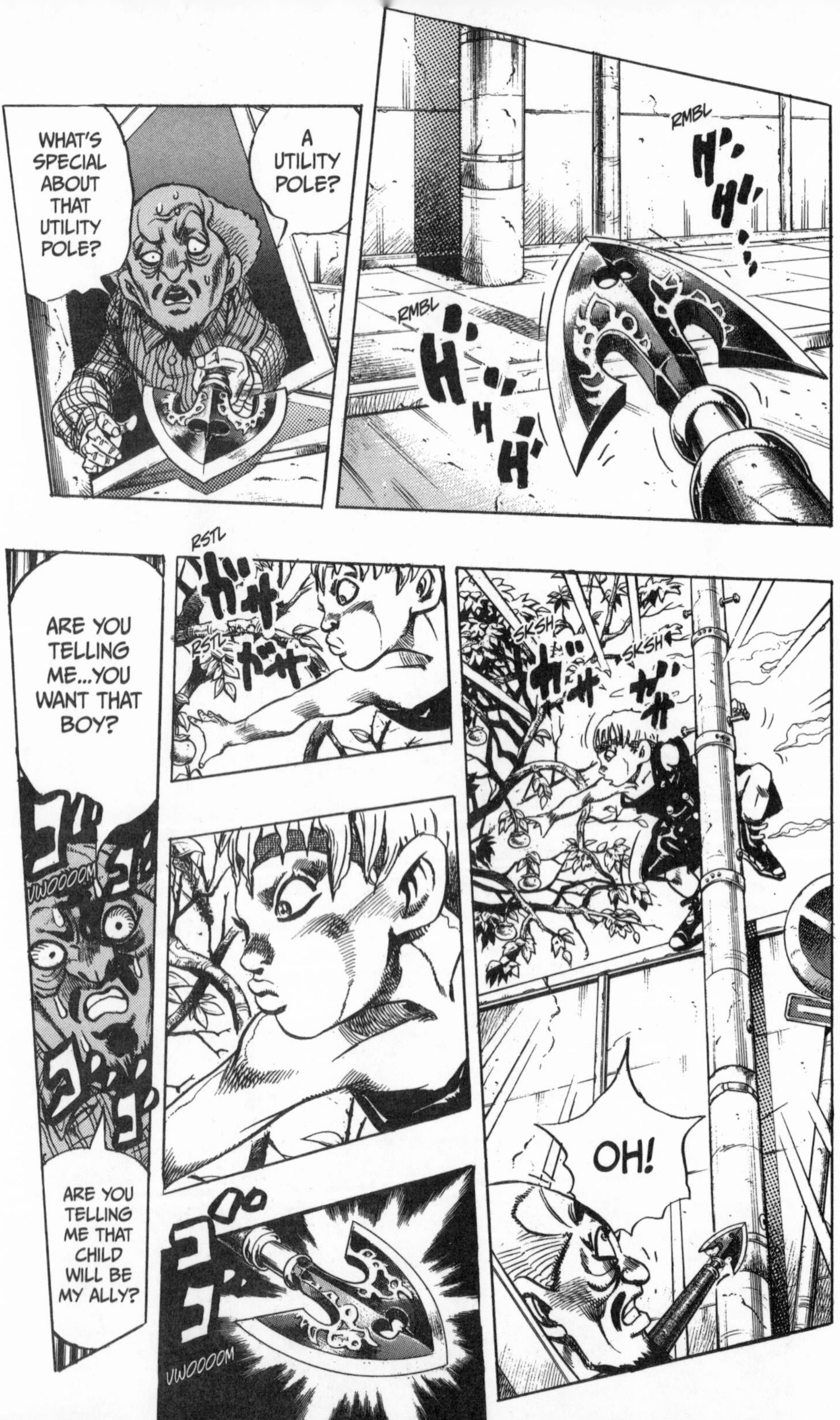

RMBL
RMBL
A UTILITY POLE?
WHAT'S SPECIAL ABOUT THAT UTILITY POLE?
SKSH
SKSH
OH!
RSTL
RSTL
VWOOOOM
ARE YOU TELLING ME...YOU WANT THAT BOY?
UWOOOOM
ARE YOU TELLING ME THAT CHILD WILL BE MY ALLY?

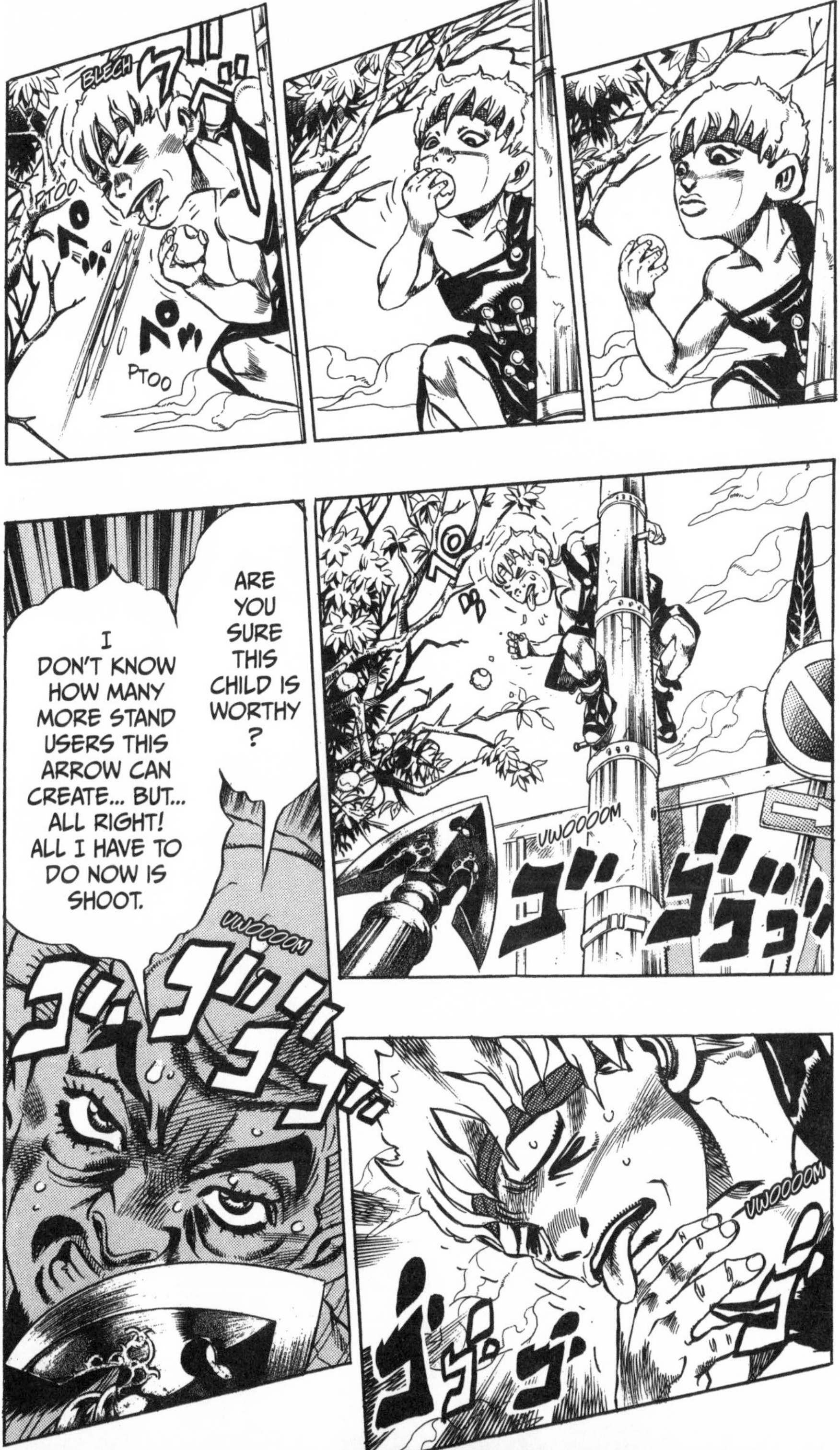
BLECH
PTOO
PTOO
VWOOOOM
ARE YOU SURE THIS CHILD IS WORTHY?
I DON'T KNOW HOW MANY MORE STAND USERS THIS ARROW CAN CREATE... BUT... ALL RIGHT! ALL I HAVE TO DO NOW IS SHOOT.
VWOOOOM
VWOOOOM

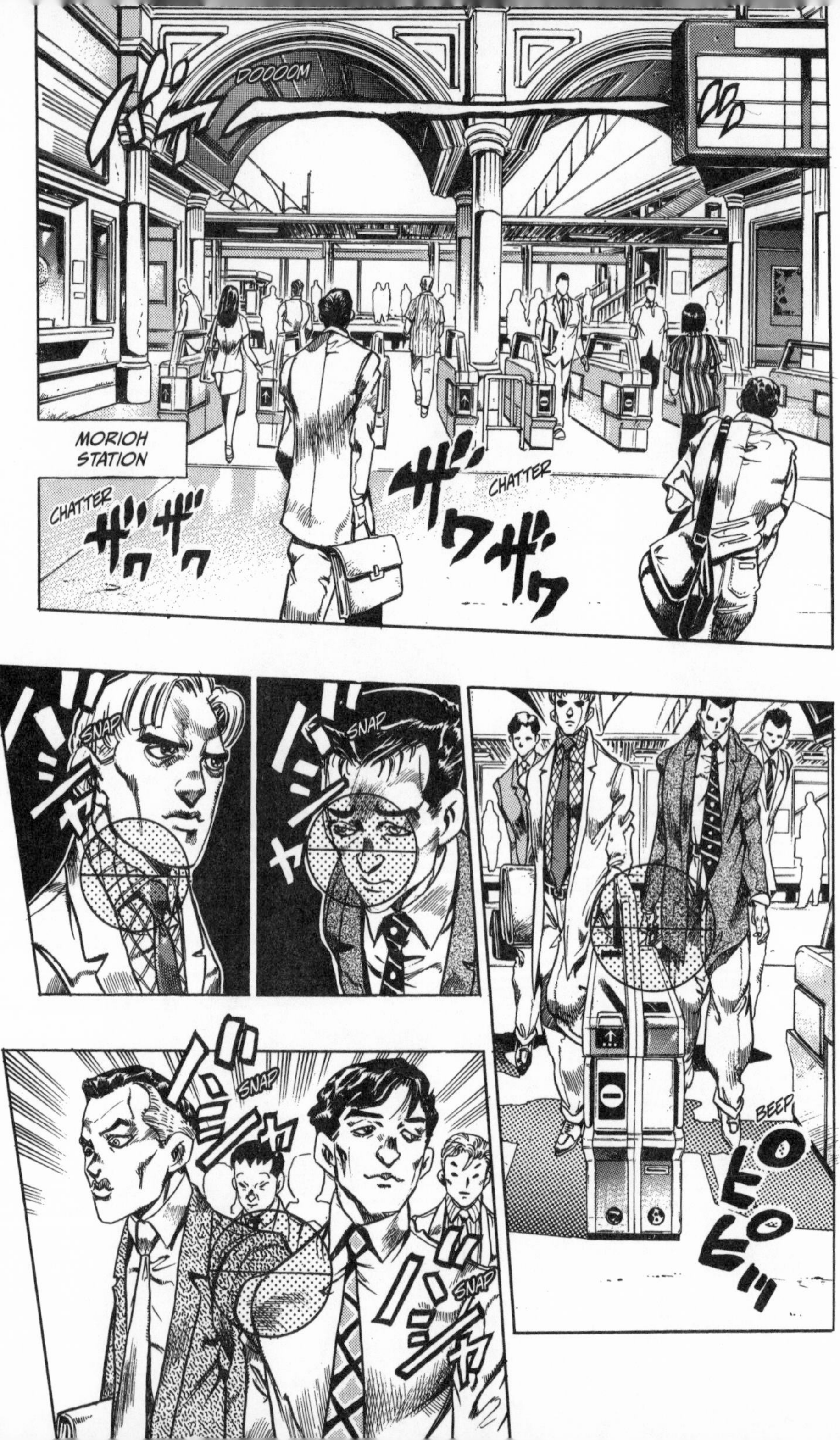
DOOOOM
CHATTER
MORIOH STATION
CHATTER
BEEP
SNAP
SNAP
SNAP
SNAP

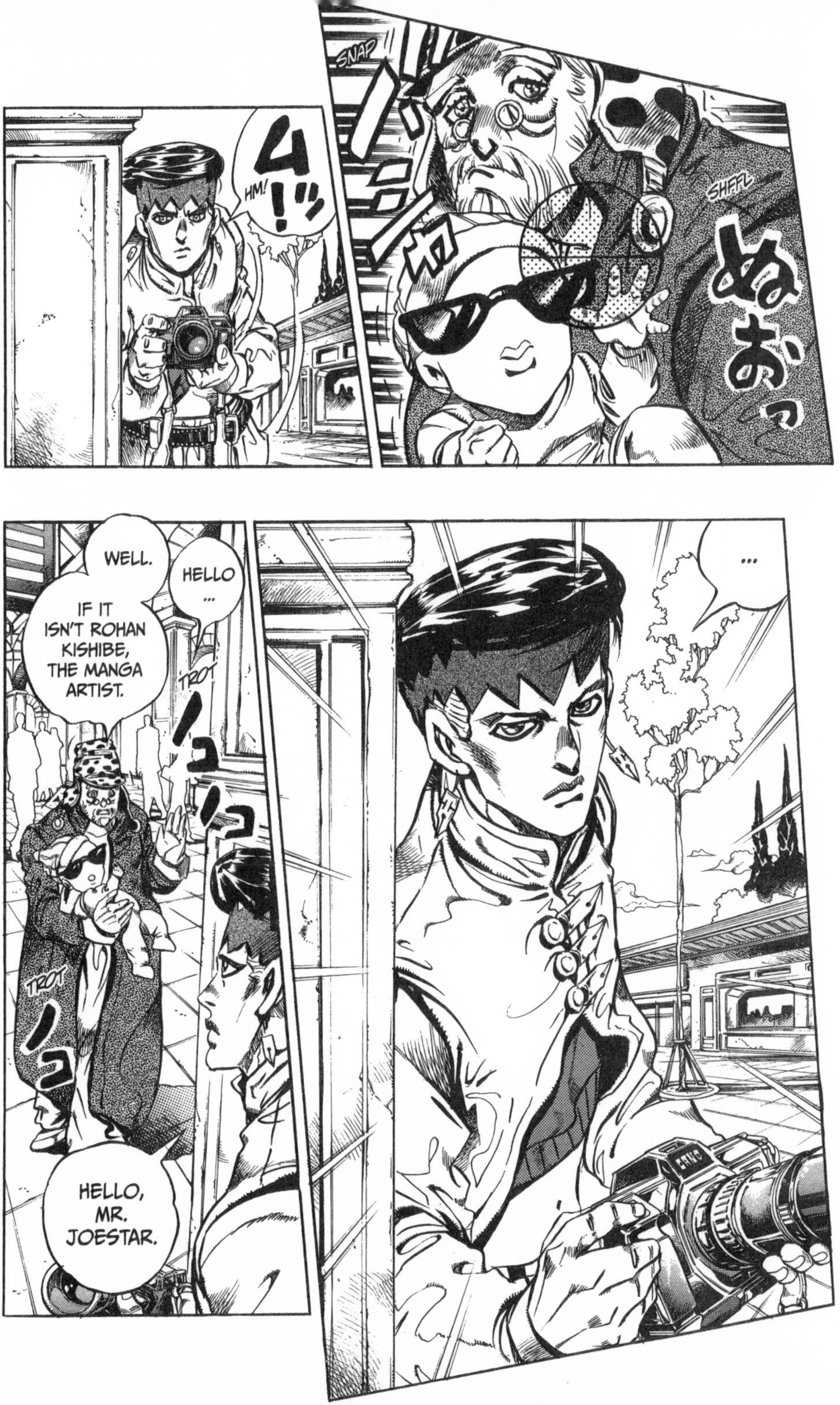
SNAP
SHFFL
ぬおっ
HM!
ム!ッ
...
HELLO ...
WELL.
IF IT ISN'T ROHAN KISHIBE, THE MANGA ARTIST.
TROT
ノコノコ
TROT
ノコ
HELLO, MR. JOESTAR.

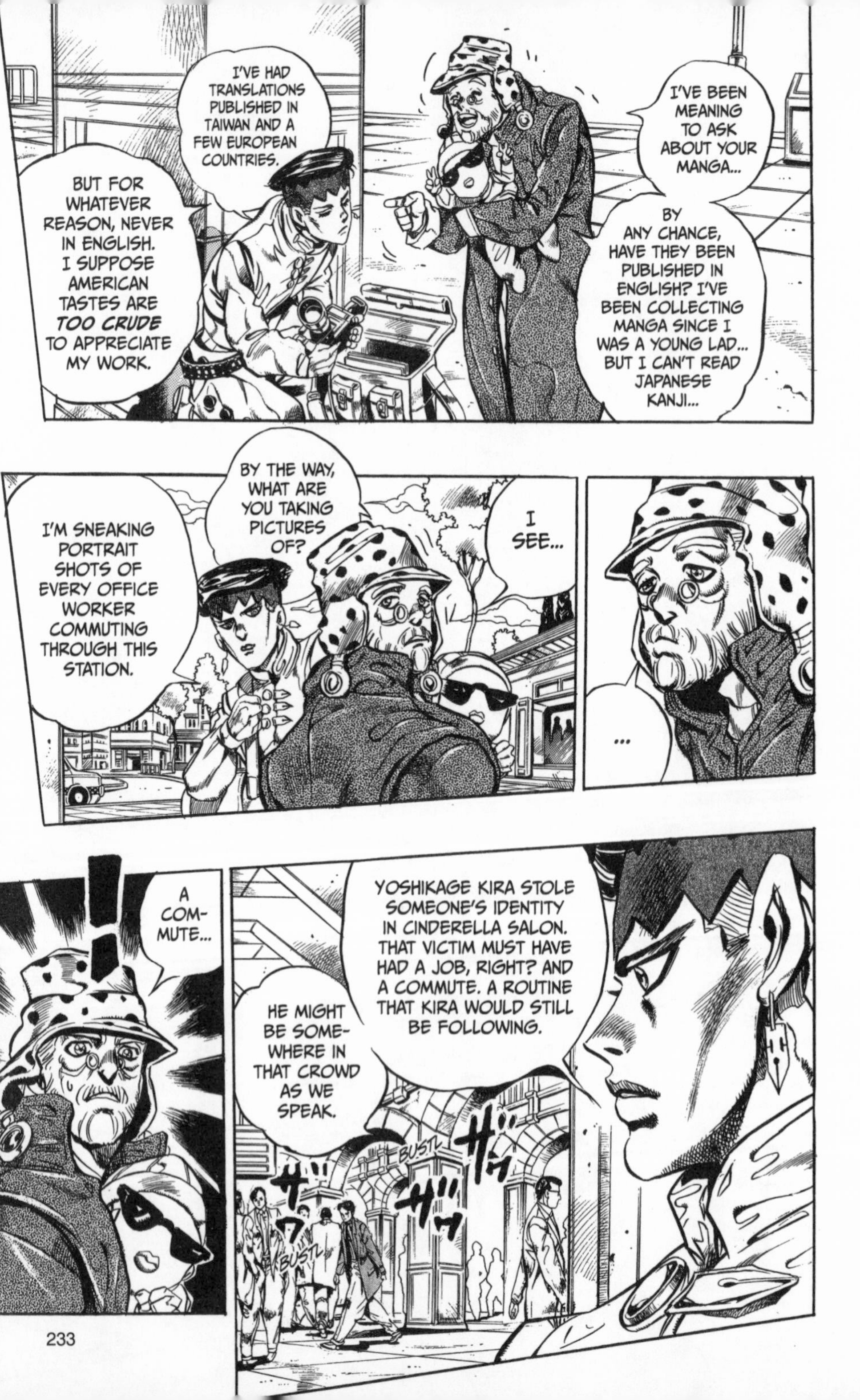
I'VE BEEN MEANING TO ASK ABOUT YOUR MANGA...
BY ANY CHANCE, HAVE THEY BEEN PUBLISHED IN ENGLISH? I'VE BEEN COLLECTING MANGA SINCE I WAS A YOUNG LAD... BUT I CAN'T READ JAPANESE KANJI...
I'VE HAD TRANSLATIONS PUBLISHED IN TAIWAN AND A FEW EUROPEAN COUNTRIES.
BUT FOR WHATEVER REASON, NEVER IN ENGLISH. I SUPPOSE AMERICAN TASTES ARE *TOO CRUDE* TO APPRECIATE MY WORK.
...
I SEE...
BY THE WAY, WHAT ARE YOU TAKING PICTURES OF?
I'M SNEAKING PORTRAIT SHOTS OF EVERY OFFICE WORKER COMMUTING THROUGH THIS STATION.
YOSHIKAGE KIRA STOLE SOMEONE'S IDENTITY IN CINDERELLA SALON. THAT VICTIM MUST HAVE HAD A JOB, RIGHT? AND A COMMUTE. A ROUTINE THAT KIRA WOULD STILL BE FOLLOWING.
HE MIGHT BE SOME-WHERE IN THAT CROWD AS WE SPEAK.
BUSTL
BUSTL
!
A COM-MUTE...

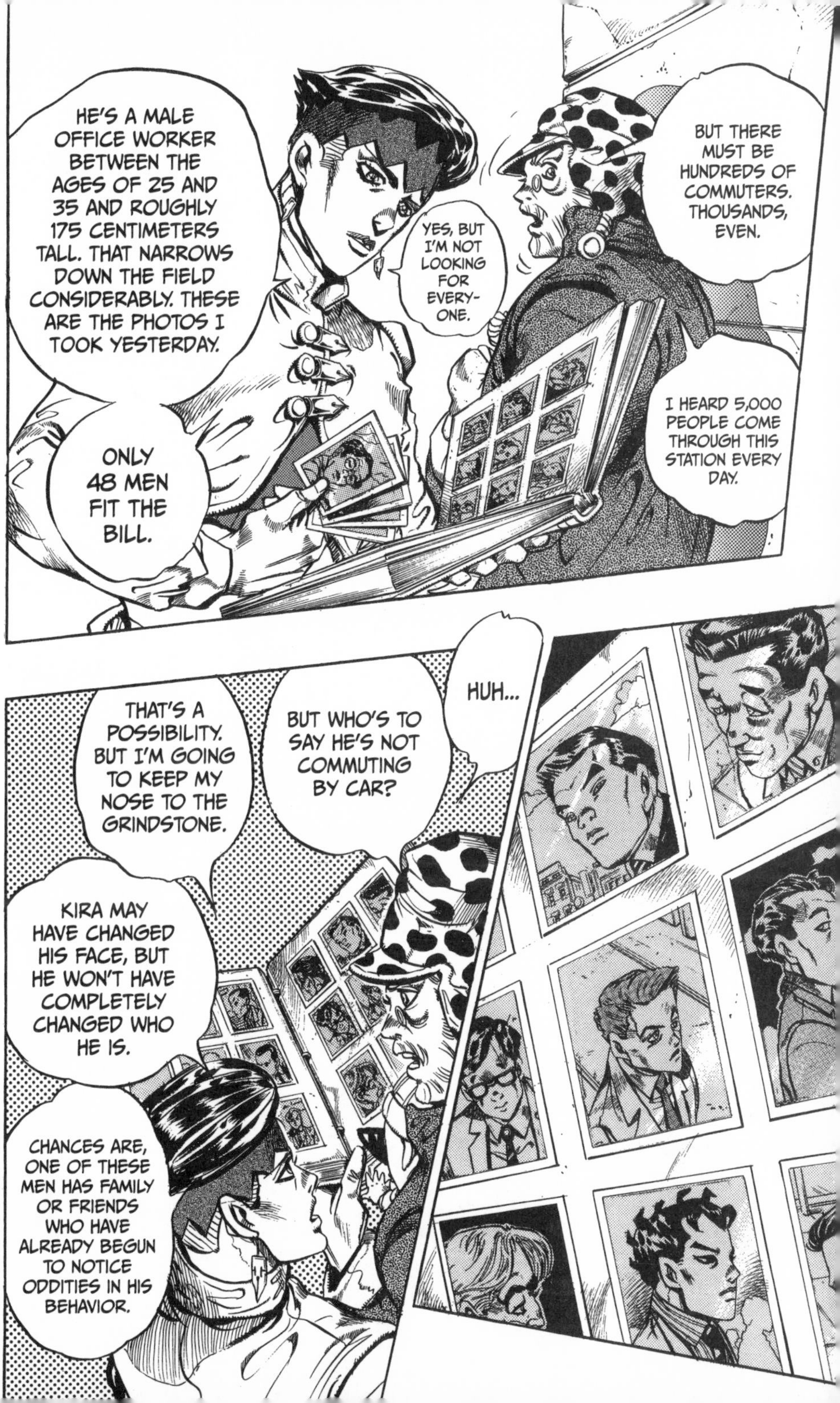
BUT THERE MUST BE HUNDREDS OF COMMUTERS. THOUSANDS, EVEN.
I HEARD 5,000 PEOPLE COME THROUGH THIS STATION EVERY DAY.
YES, BUT I'M NOT LOOKING FOR EVERY-ONE.
HE'S A MALE OFFICE WORKER BETWEEN THE AGES OF 25 AND 35 AND ROUGHLY 175 CENTIMETERS TALL. THAT NARROWS DOWN THE FIELD CONSIDERABLY. THESE ARE THE PHOTOS I TOOK YESTERDAY.
ONLY 48 MEN FIT THE BILL.
HUH...
BUT WHO'S TO SAY HE'S NOT COMMUTING BY CAR?
THAT'S A POSSIBILITY. BUT I'M GOING TO KEEP MY NOSE TO THE GRINDSTONE.
KIRA MAY HAVE CHANGED HIS FACE, BUT HE WON'T HAVE COMPLETELY CHANGED WHO HE IS.
CHANCES ARE, ONE OF THESE MEN HAS FAMILY OR FRIENDS WHO HAVE ALREADY BEGUN TO NOTICE ODDITIES IN HIS BEHAVIOR.

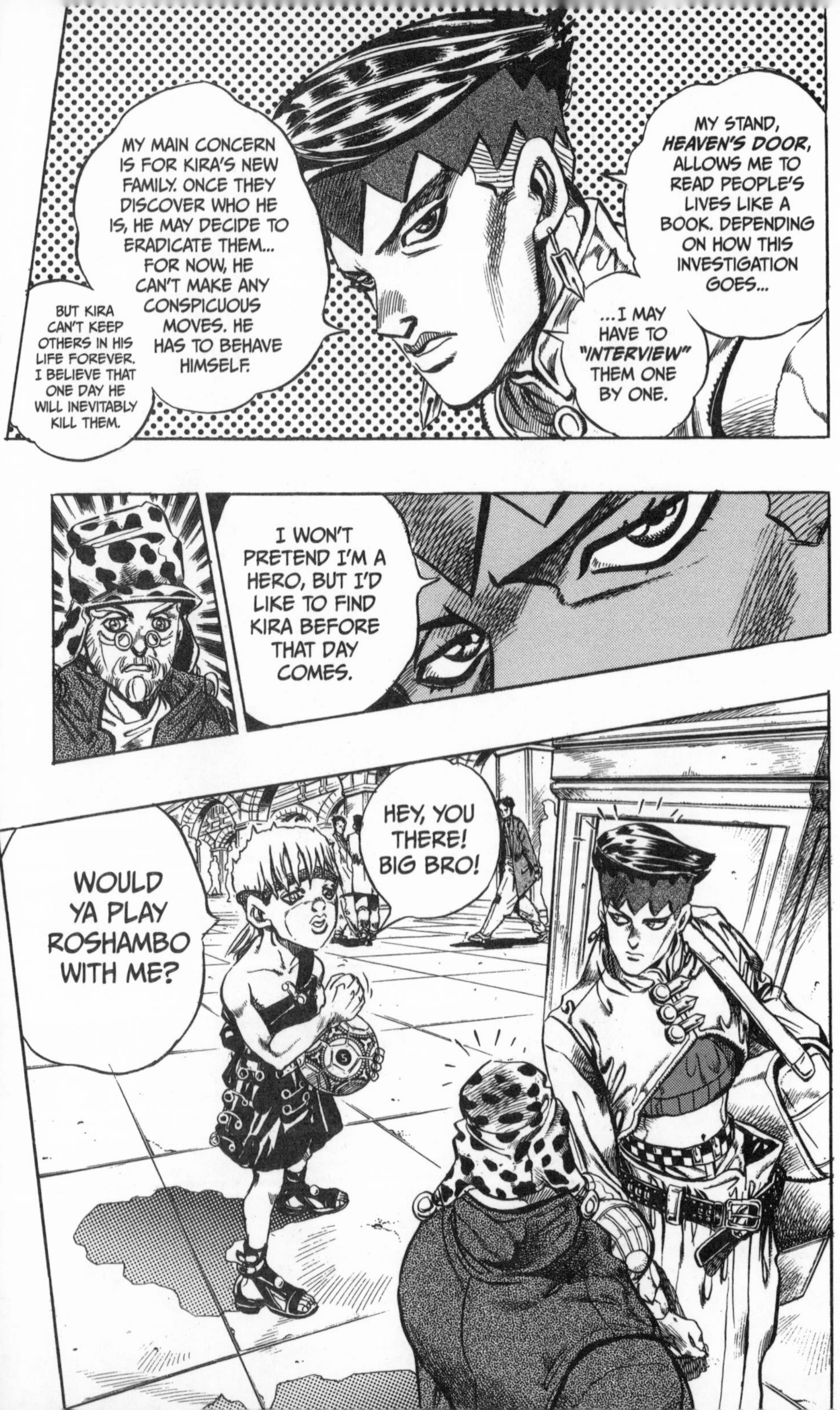
MY STAND, *HEAVEN'S DOOR*, ALLOWS ME TO READ PEOPLE'S LIVES LIKE A BOOK. DEPENDING ON HOW THIS INVESTIGATION GOES...
...I MAY HAVE TO *"INTERVIEW"* THEM ONE BY ONE.
MY MAIN CONCERN IS FOR KIRA'S NEW FAMILY. ONCE THEY DISCOVER WHO HE IS, HE MAY DECIDE TO ERADICATE THEM... FOR NOW, HE CAN'T MAKE ANY CONSPICUOUS MOVES. HE HAS TO BEHAVE HIMSELF.
BUT KIRA CAN'T KEEP OTHERS IN HIS LIFE FOREVER. I BELIEVE THAT ONE DAY HE WILL INEVITABLY KILL THEM.
I WON'T PRETEND I'M A HERO, BUT I'D LIKE TO FIND KIRA BEFORE THAT DAY COMES.
HEY, YOU THERE! BIG BRO!
WOULD YA PLAY ROSHAMBO WITH ME?

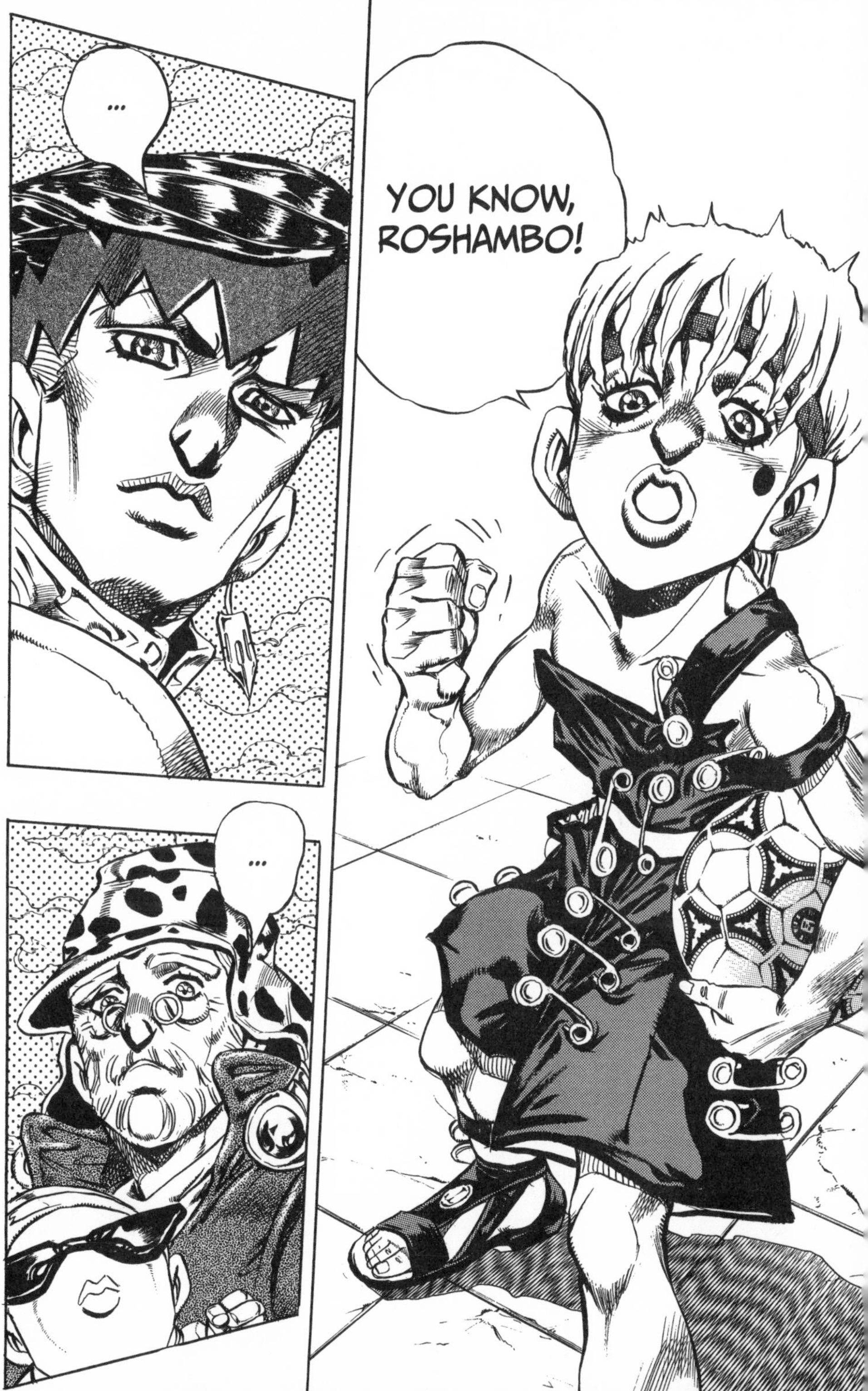
YOU KNOW, ROSHAMBO!
...
...

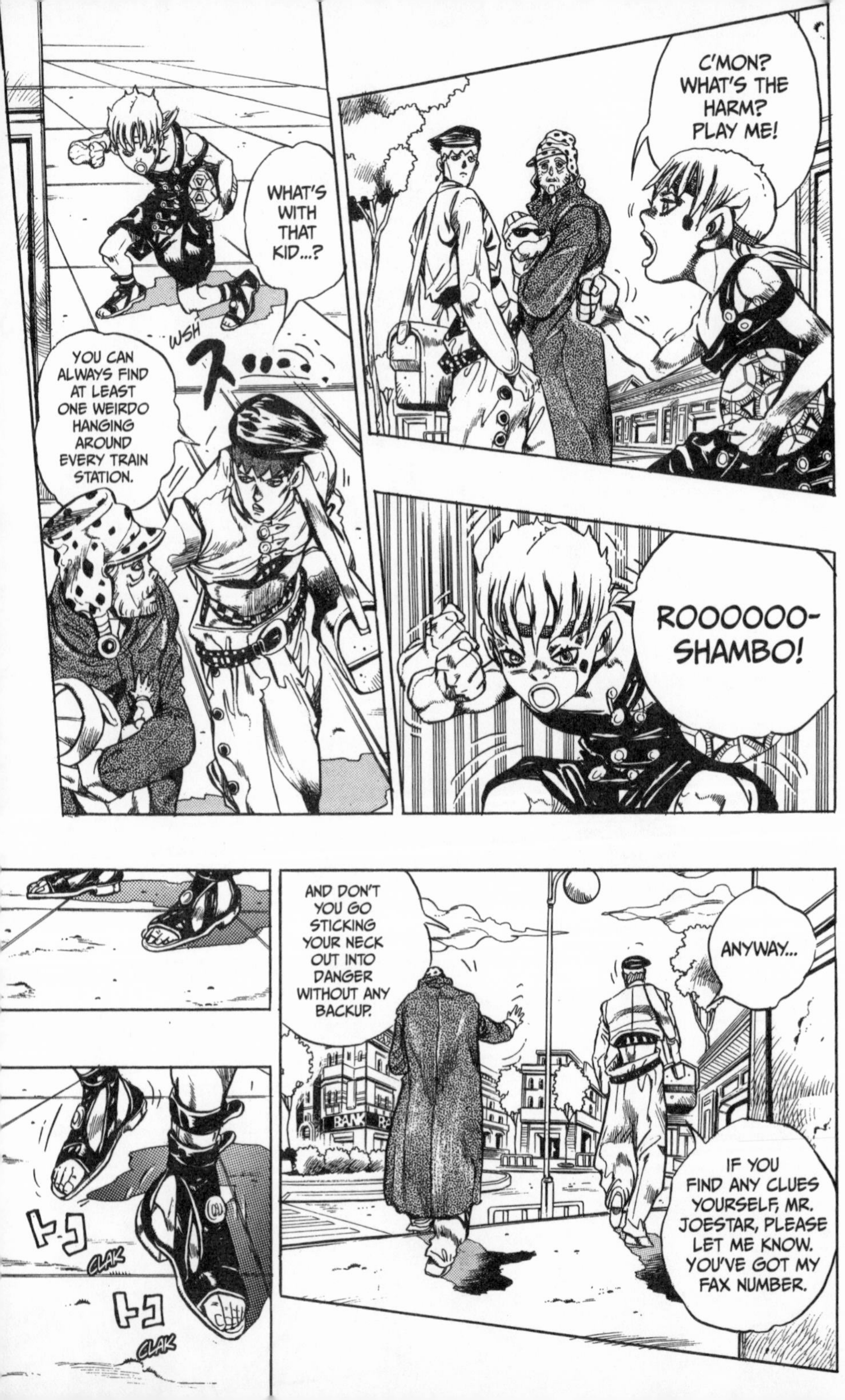

C'MON? WHAT'S THE HARM? PLAY ME!
ROOOOOO-SHAMBO!
WHAT'S WITH THAT KID...?
WSH
YOU CAN ALWAYS FIND AT LEAST ONE WEIRDO HANGING AROUND EVERY TRAIN STATION.
ANYWAY...
IF YOU FIND ANY CLUES YOURSELF, MR. JOESTAR, PLEASE LET ME KNOW. YOU'VE GOT MY FAX NUMBER.
AND DON'T YOU GO STICKING YOUR NECK OUT INTO DANGER WITHOUT ANY BACKUP.
BANK
トコ
CLAK
トコ
CLAK

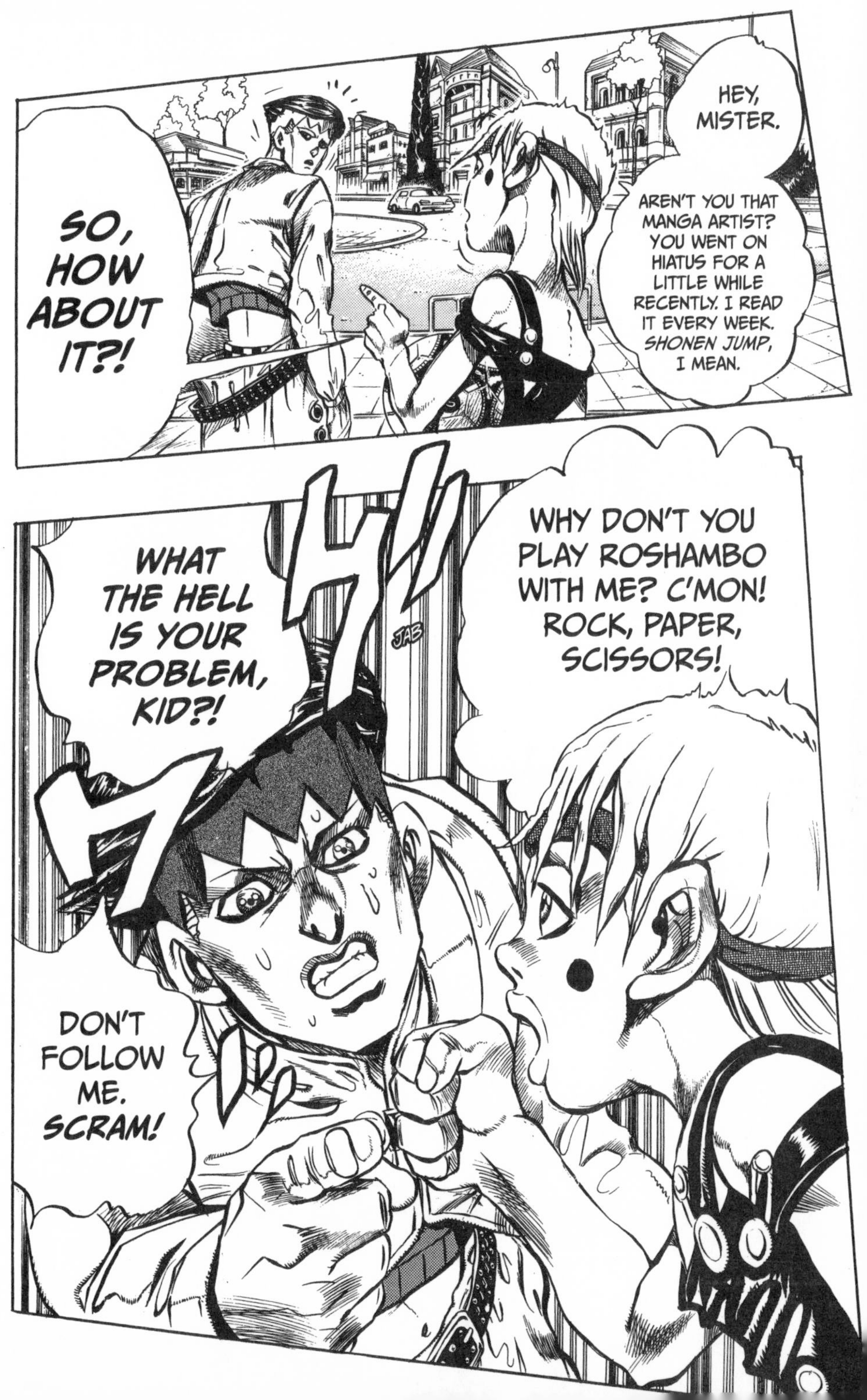
HEY, MISTER.
AREN'T YOU THAT MANGA ARTIST? YOU WENT ON HIATUS FOR A LITTLE WHILE RECENTLY. I READ IT EVERY WEEK. SHONEN JUMP, I MEAN.
SO, HOW ABOUT IT?!
WHY DON'T YOU PLAY ROSHAMBO WITH ME? C'MON! ROCK, PAPER, SCISSORS!
JAB
WHAT THE HELL IS YOUR PROBLEM, KID?!
DON'T FOLLOW ME. SCRAM!

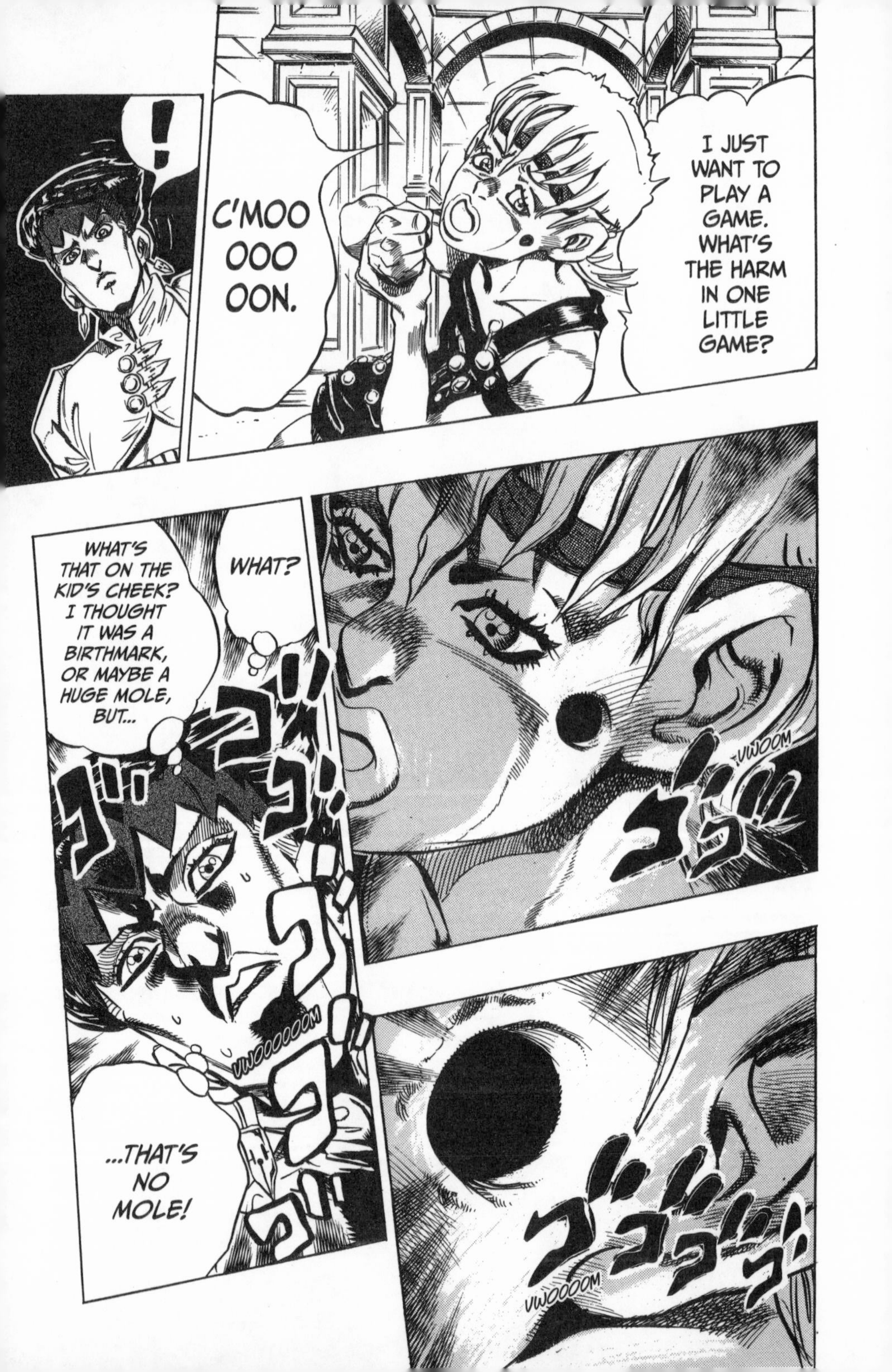

I JUST WANT TO PLAY A GAME. WHAT'S THE HARM IN ONE LITTLE GAME?
C'MOOOOOOOON.
!
VWOOM
VWOOOOM
WHAT?
WHAT'S THAT ON THE KID'S CHEEK? I THOUGHT IT WAS A BIRTHMARK, OR MAYBE A HUGE MOLE, BUT...
VWOOOOOOM
...THAT'S NO MOLE!

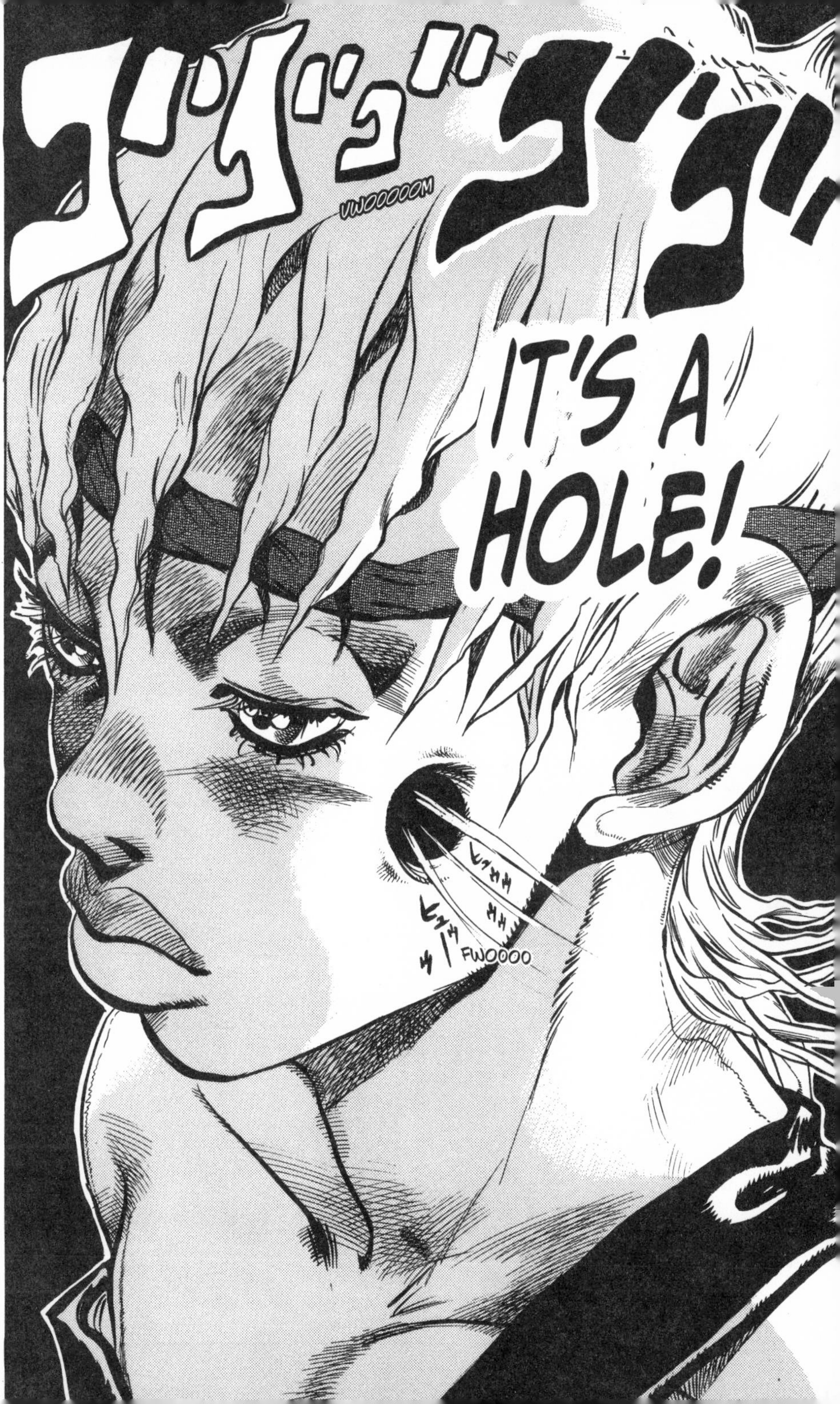
VWOOOOOM
IT'S A HOLE!
FWOOOO

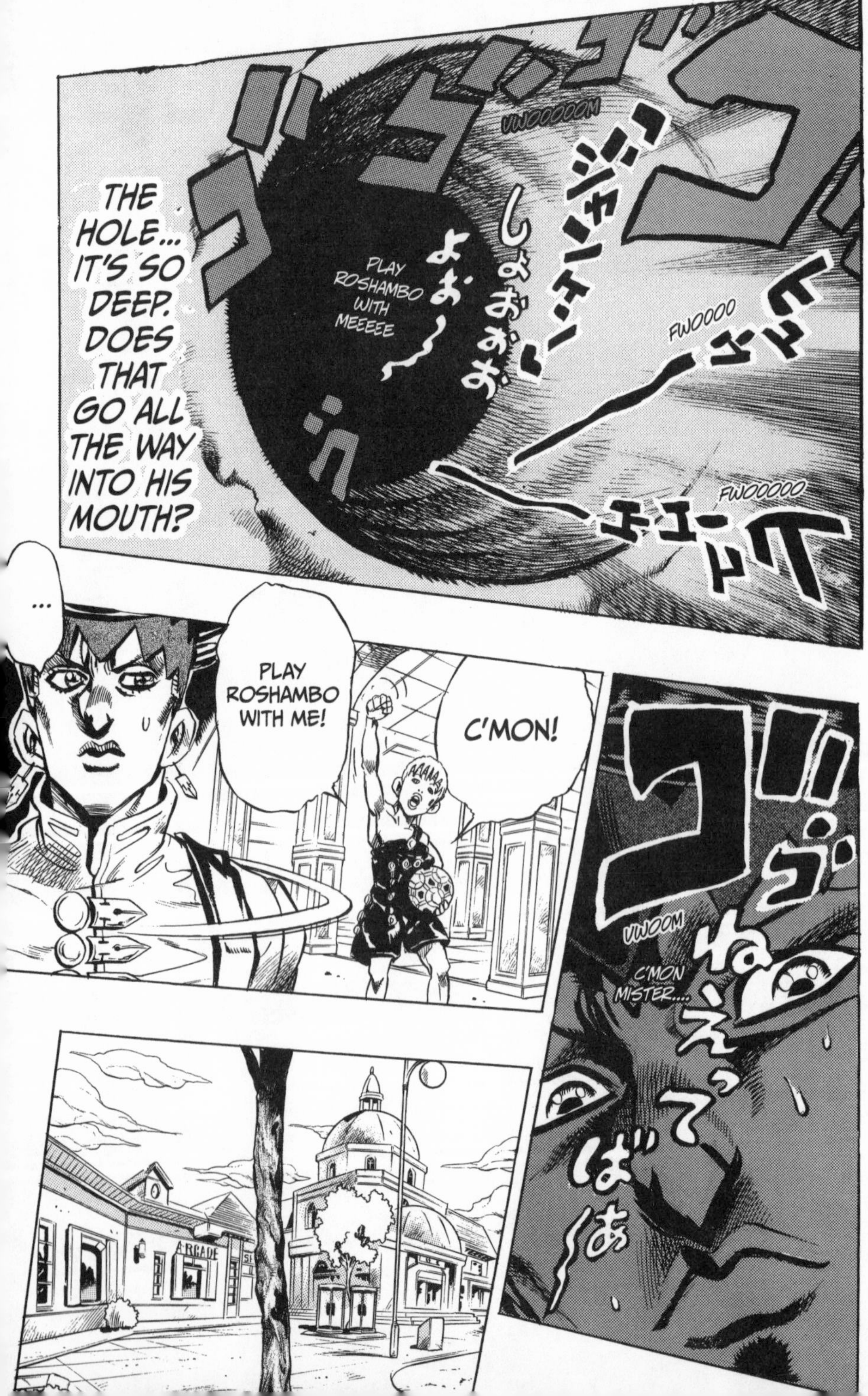

VWOOOOOM
FWOOOO
PLAY ROSHAMBO WITH MEEEEE
FWOOOOO
THE HOLE... IT'S SO DEEP. DOES THAT GO ALL THE WAY INTO HIS MOUTH?
VWOOM
C'MON MISTER...
C'MON!
PLAY ROSHAMBO WITH ME!
...
ARCADE

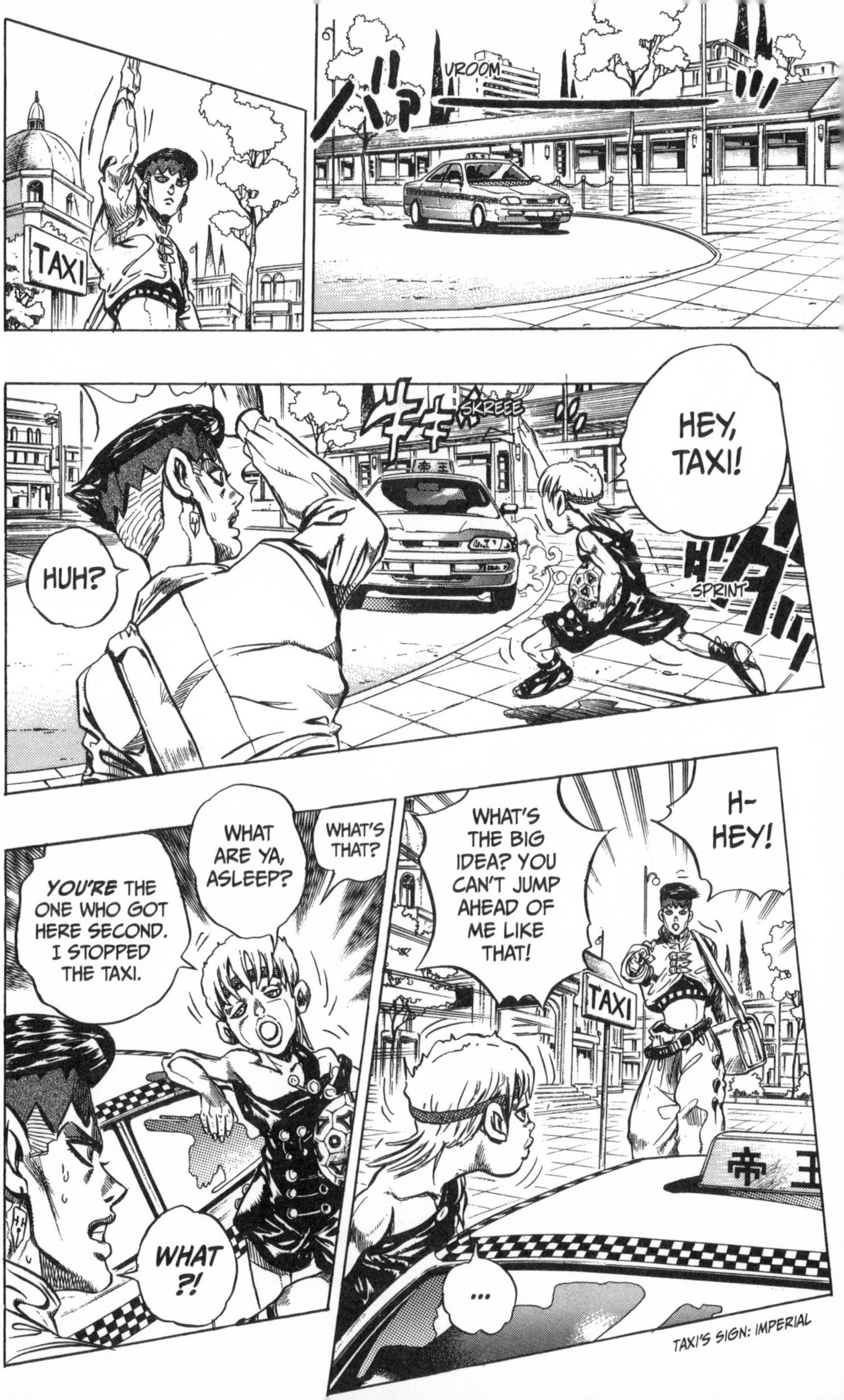
UROOM
TAXI
HEY, TAXI!
SKREEE
SPRINT
HUH?
H-HEY!
WHAT'S THE BIG IDEA? YOU CAN'T JUMP AHEAD OF ME LIKE THAT!
TAXI
帝王
...
WHAT'S THAT?
WHAT ARE YA, ASLEEP?
YOU'RE THE ONE WHO GOT HERE SECOND. I STOPPED THE TAXI.
WHAT?!

TAXI'S SIGN: IMPERIAL

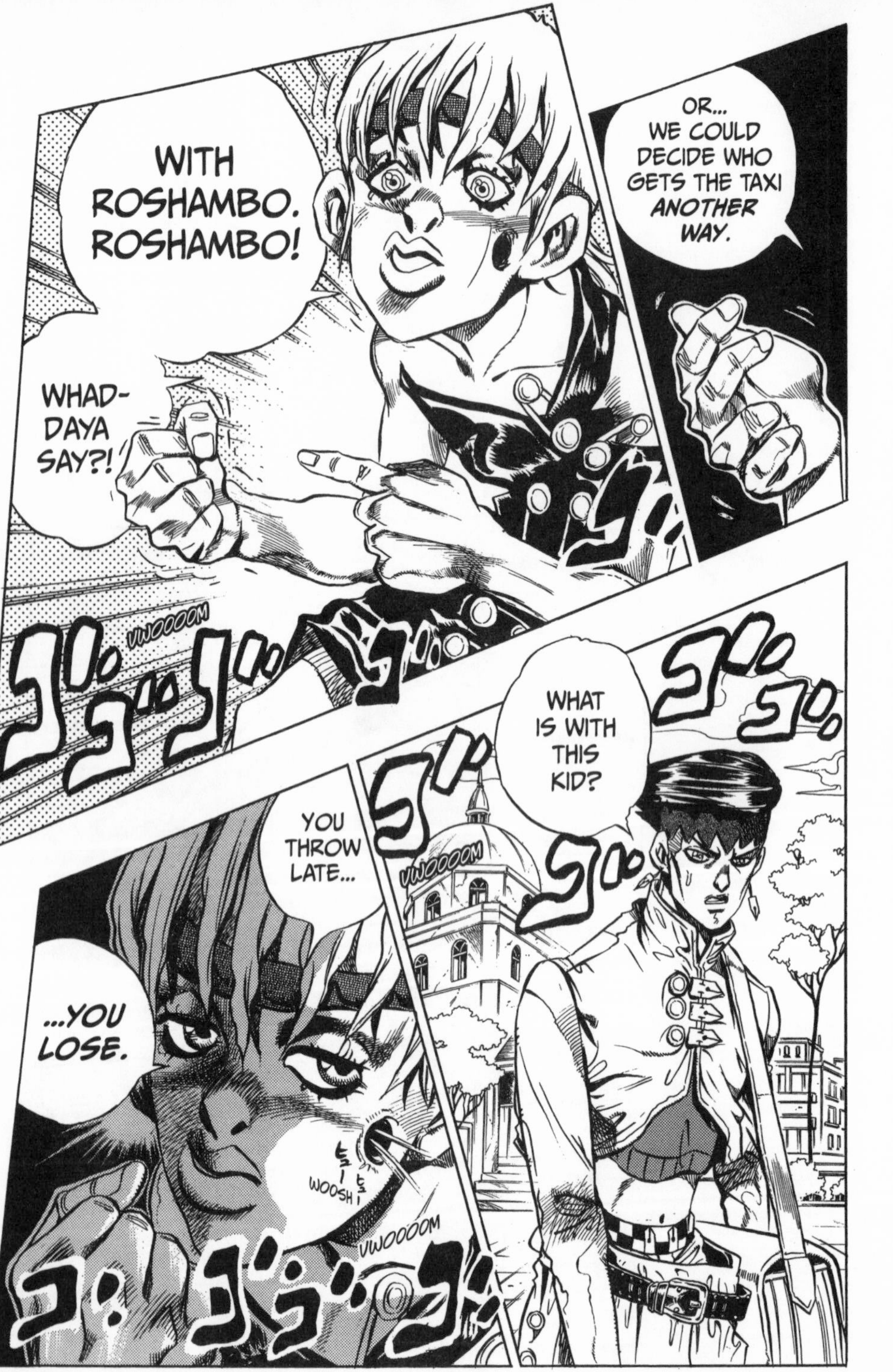
OR... WE COULD DECIDE WHO GETS THE TAXI *ANOTHER* WAY.
WITH ROSHAMBO. ROSHAMBO!
WHAD-DAYA SAY?!
VWOOOOM
WHAT IS WITH THIS KID?
VWOOOOM
YOU THROW LATE...
...YOU LOSE.
WOOSH
VWOOOOM

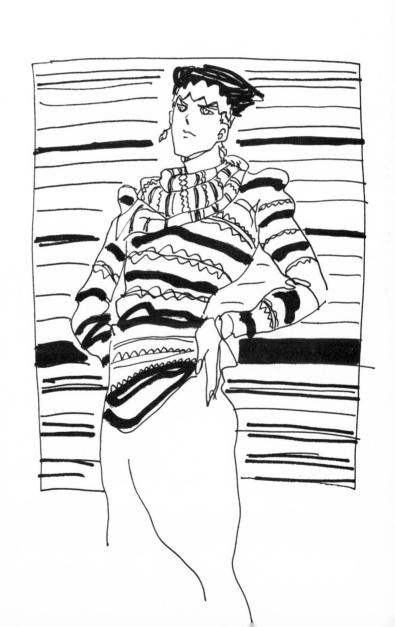

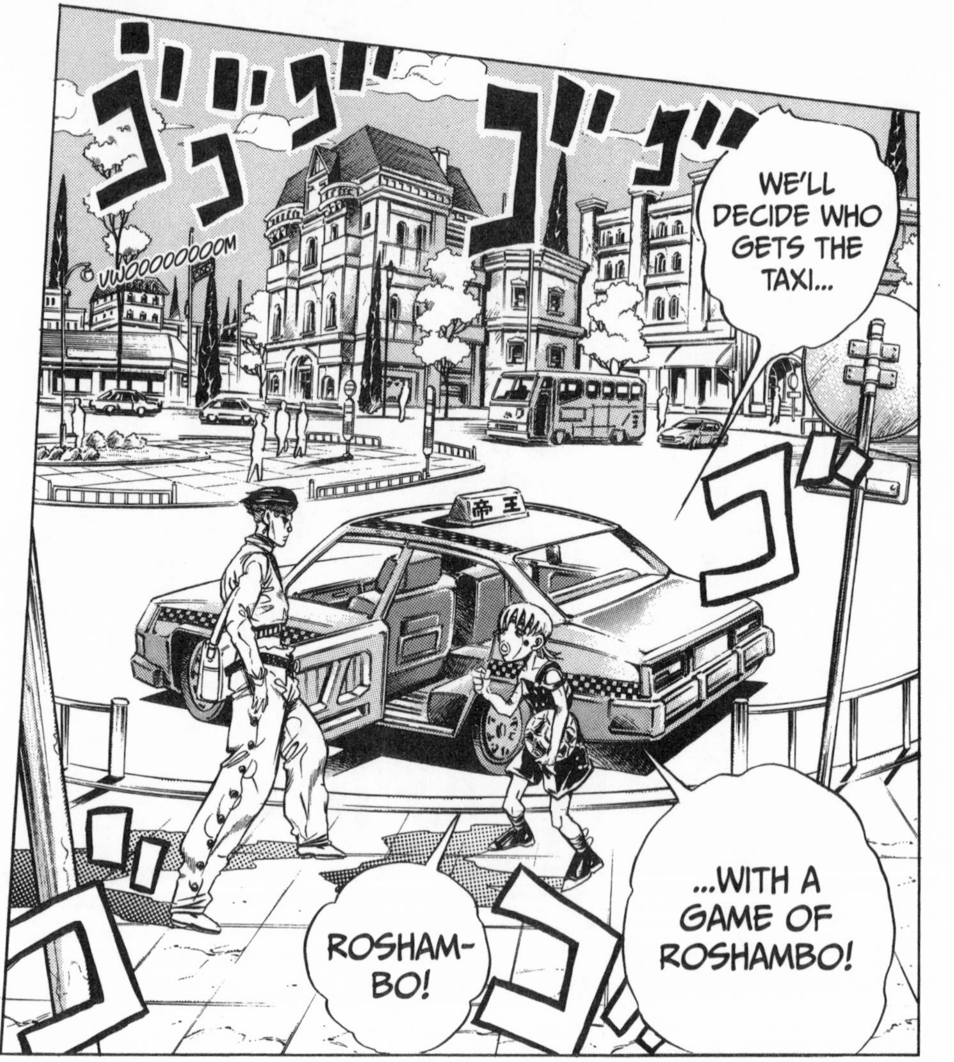

CHAPTER 107

ROSHAM BOY IS HERE!, PART 2

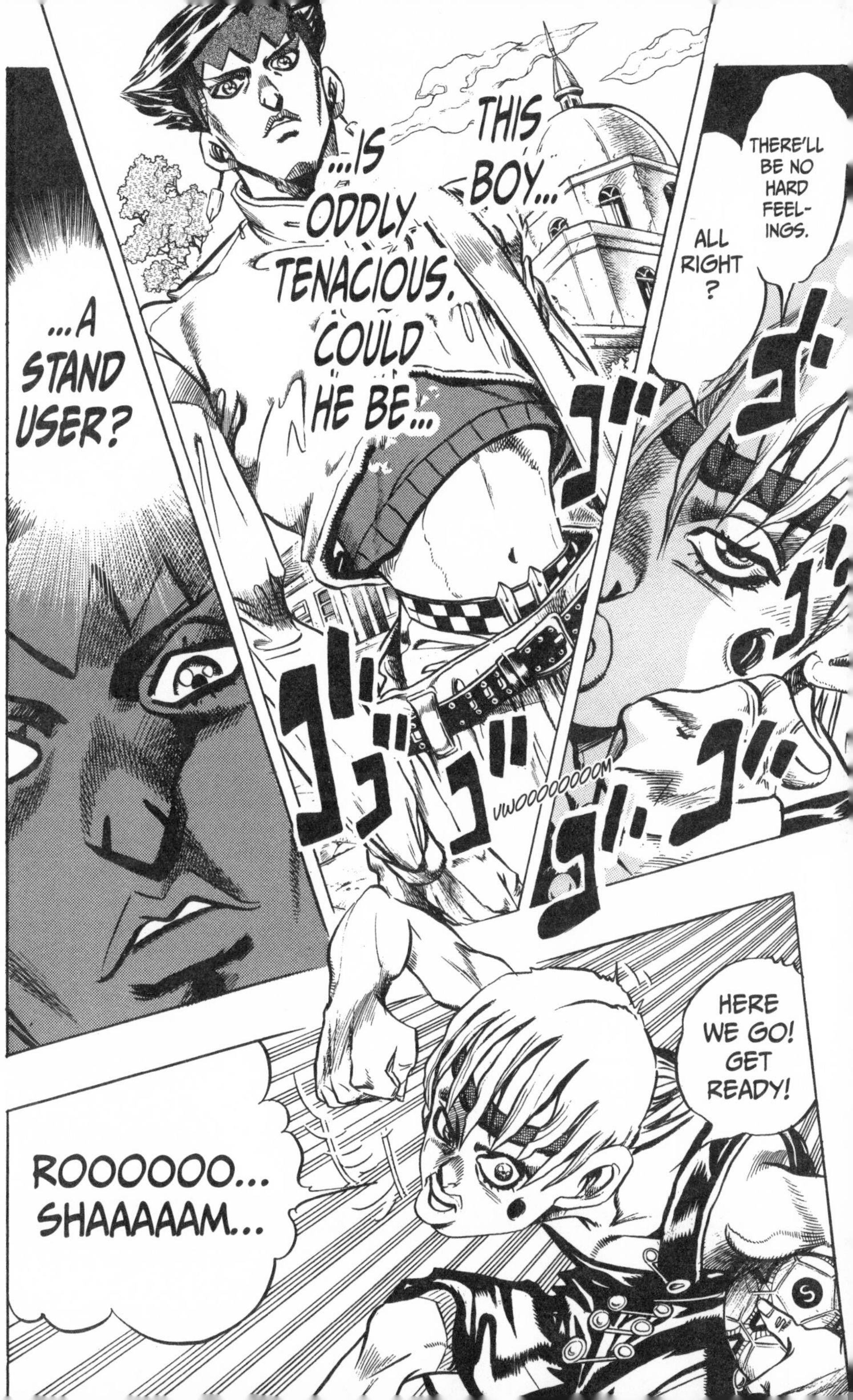
THERE'LL BE NO HARD FEELINGS.
ALL RIGHT?
THIS BOY...
...IS ODDLY TENACIOUS. COULD HE BE...
...A STAND USER?
VWOOOOOOOOOM
HERE WE GO! GET READY!
ROOOOOO... SHAAAAAM...

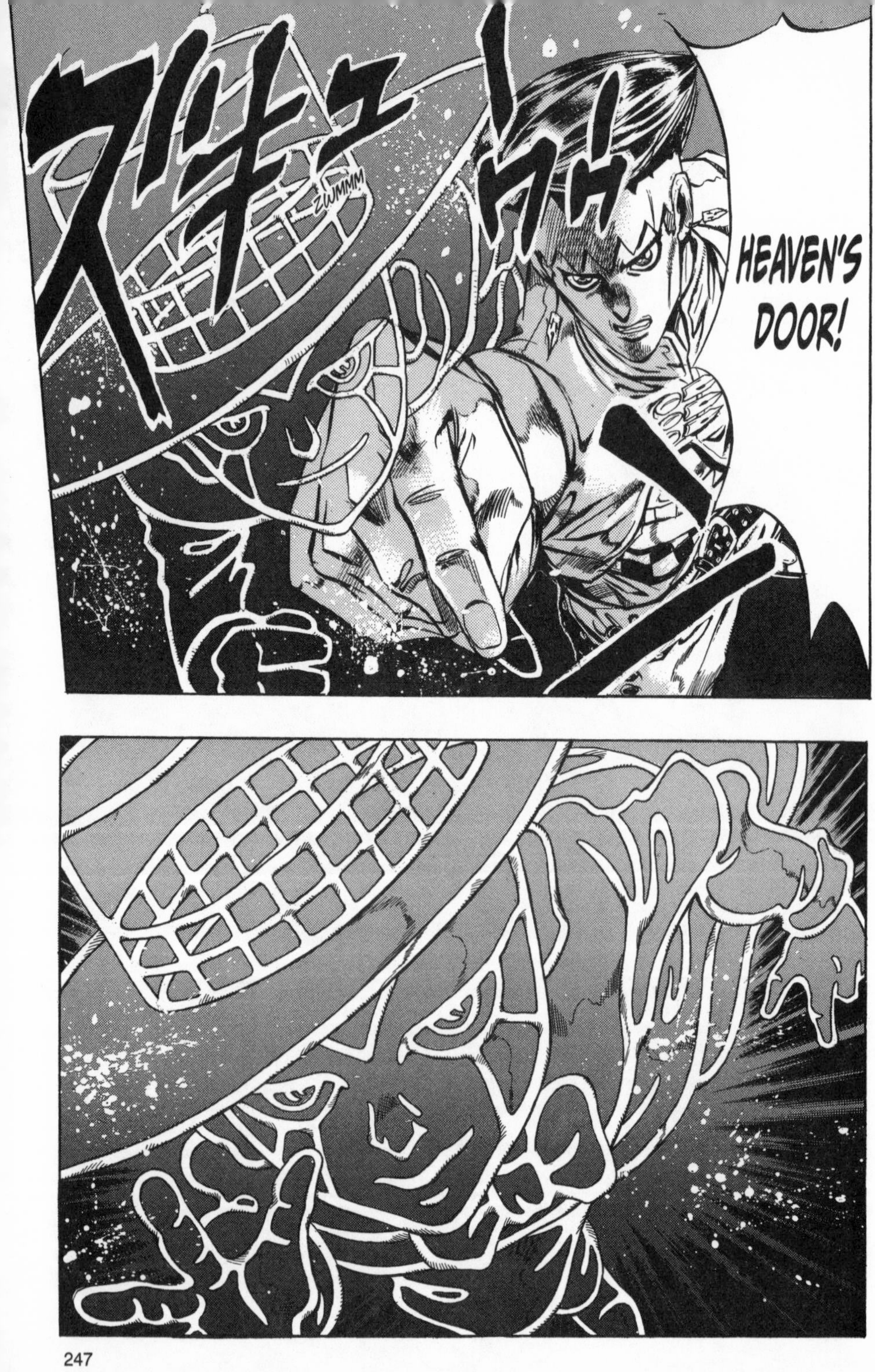
ZWMMM
HEAVEN'S DOOR!

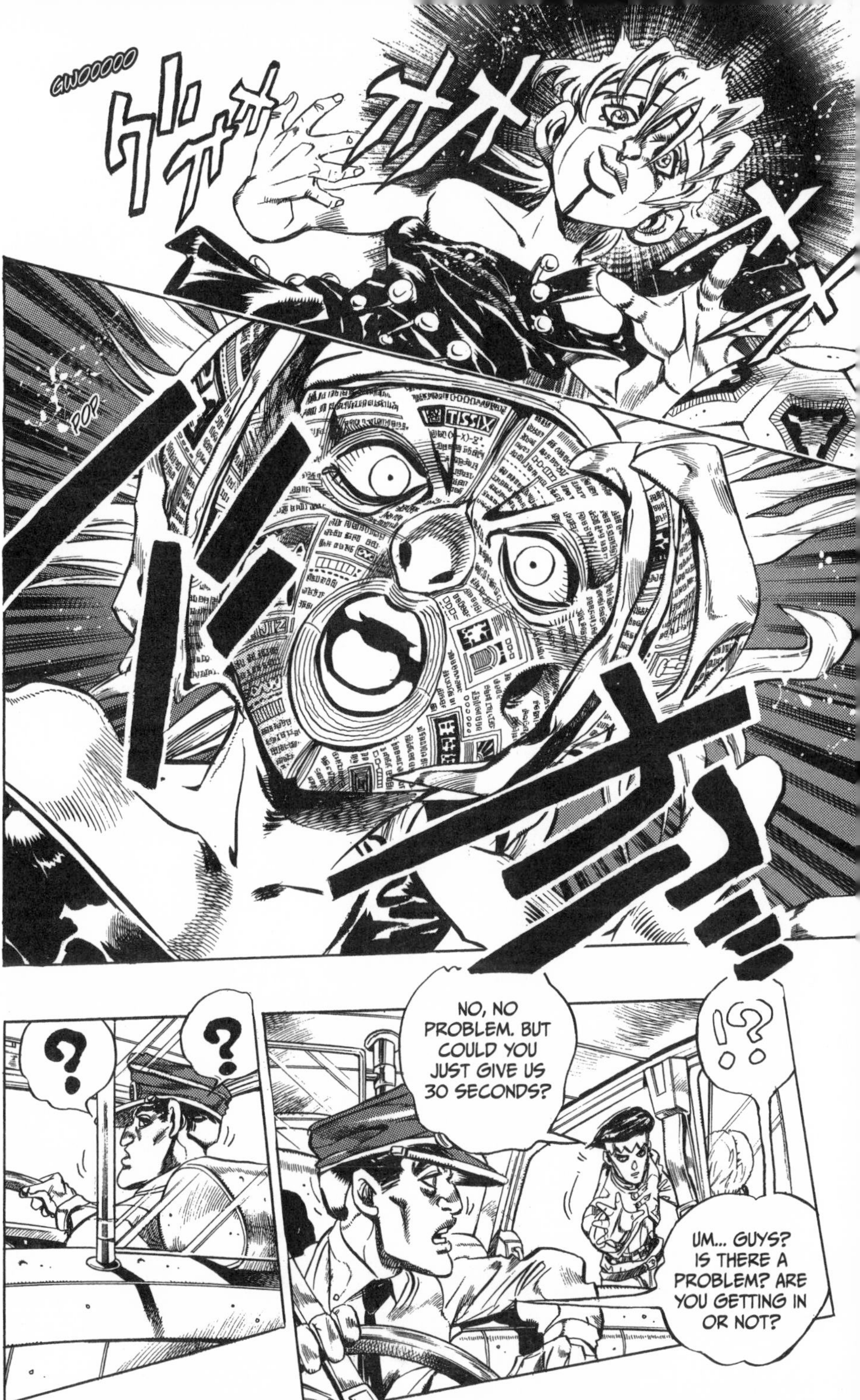
GWOOOOO
POP
NO, NO PROBLEM. BUT COULD YOU JUST GIVE US 30 SECONDS?
!?
UM... GUYS? IS THERE A PROBLEM? ARE YOU GETTING IN OR NOT?
?
?

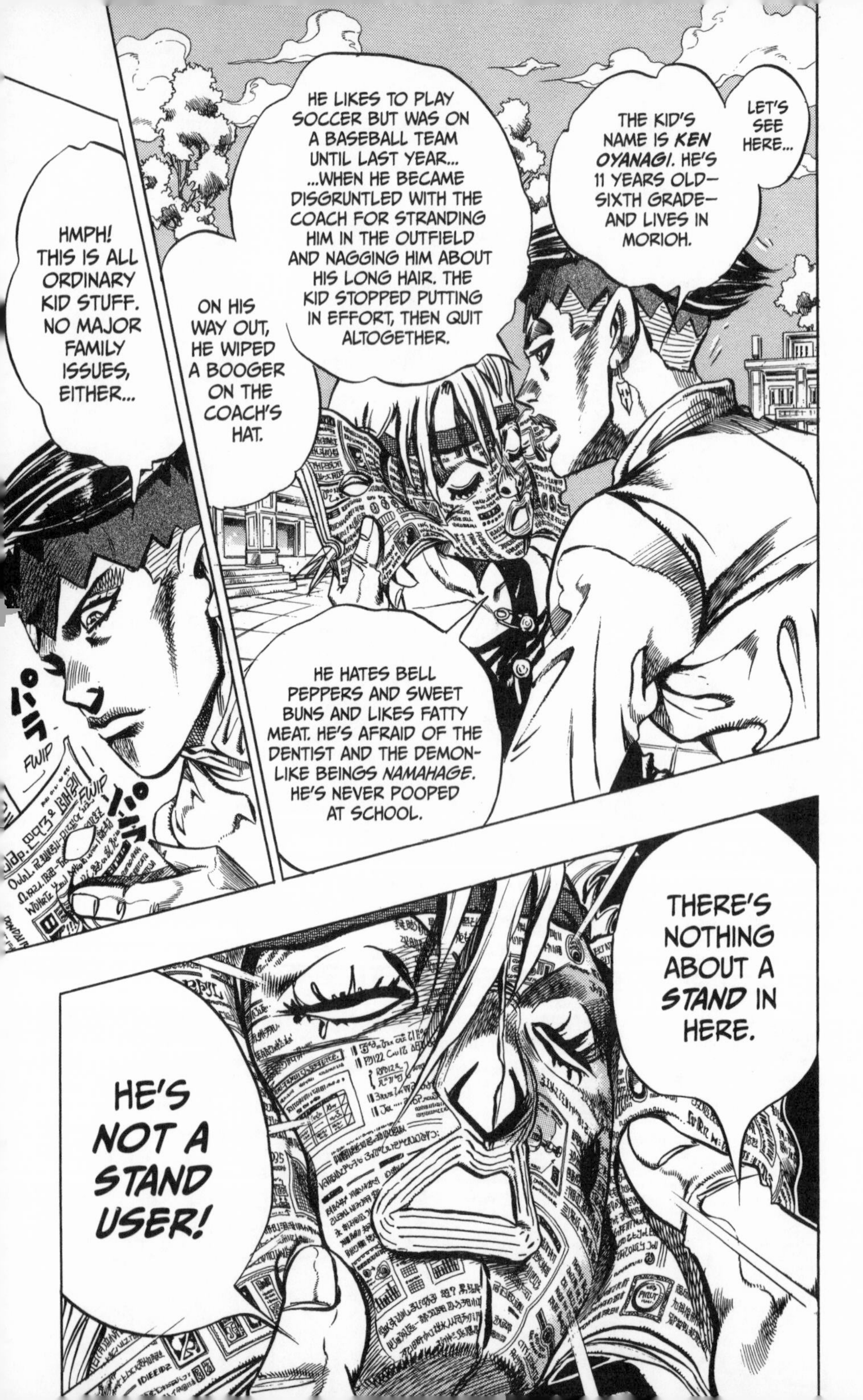
LET'S SEE HERE...
THE KID'S NAME IS KEN OYANAGI. HE'S 11 YEARS OLD— SIXTH GRADE— AND LIVES IN MORIOH.
HE LIKES TO PLAY SOCCER BUT WAS ON A BASEBALL TEAM UNTIL LAST YEAR... ...WHEN HE BECAME DISGRUNTLED WITH THE COACH FOR STRANDING HIM IN THE OUTFIELD AND NAGGING HIM ABOUT HIS LONG HAIR. THE KID STOPPED PUTTING IN EFFORT, THEN QUIT ALTOGETHER.
ON HIS WAY OUT, HE WIPED A BOOGER ON THE COACH'S HAT.
HE HATES BELL PEPPERS AND SWEET BUNS AND LIKES FATTY MEAT. HE'S AFRAID OF THE DENTIST AND THE DEMON-LIKE BEINGS NAMAHAGE. HE'S NEVER POOPED AT SCHOOL.
HMPH! THIS IS ALL ORDINARY KID STUFF. NO MAJOR FAMILY ISSUES, EITHER...
FWIP
FWIP
THERE'S NOTHING ABOUT A STAND IN HERE.
HE'S NOT A STAND USER!

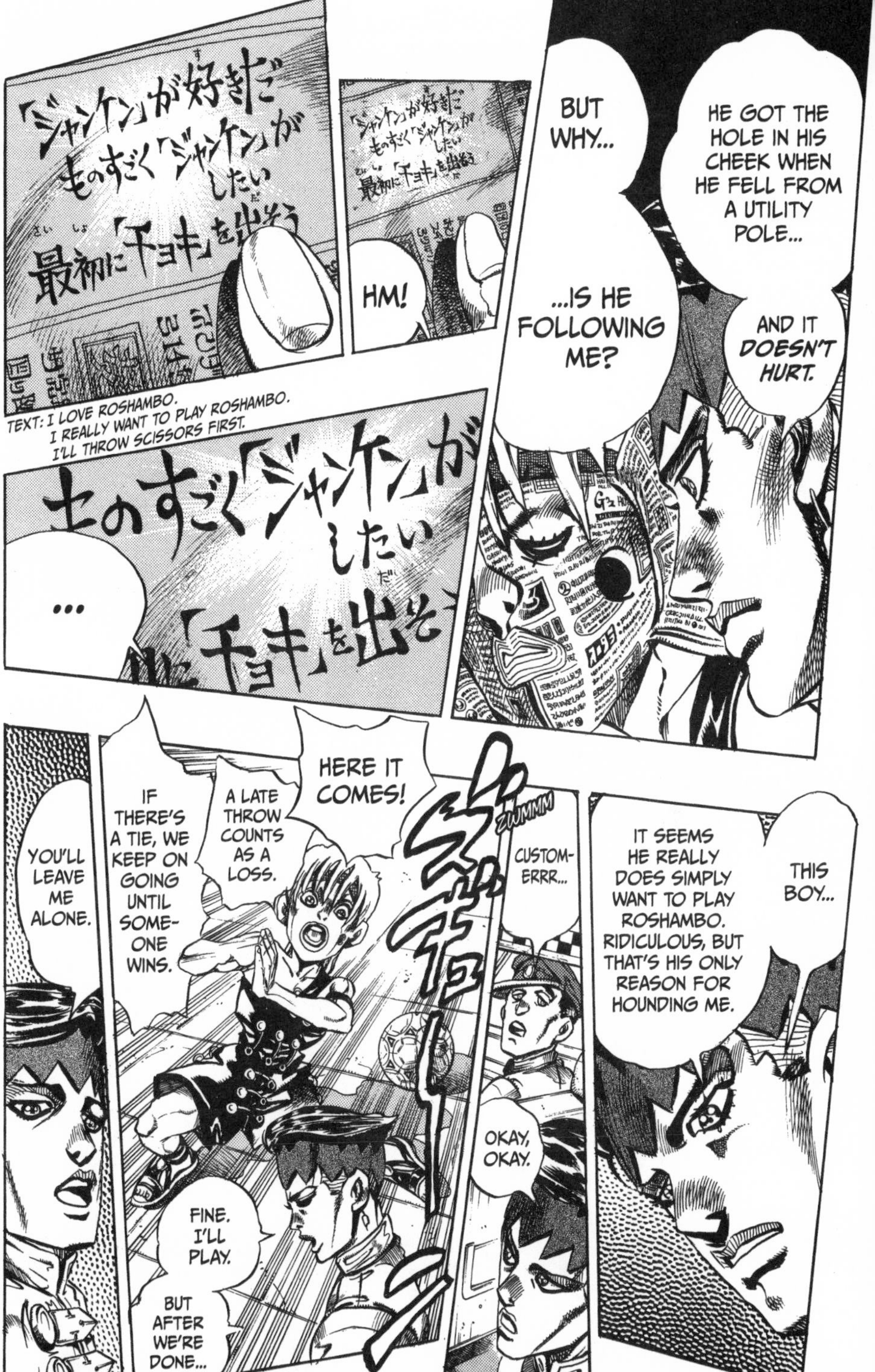
HE GOT THE HOLE IN HIS CHEEK WHEN HE FELL FROM A UTILITY POLE...
AND IT DOESN'T HURT.
BUT WHY...
...IS HE FOLLOWING ME?
「ジャンケン」が好きだ ものすごく「ジャンケン」がしたい 最初に「チョキ」を出そう
HM!
「ジャンケン」が好きだ ものすごく「ジャンケン」がしたい 最初に「チョキ」を出そう
TEXT: I LOVE ROSHAMBO. I REALLY WANT TO PLAY ROSHAMBO. I'LL THROW SCISSORS FIRST.
...
THIS BOY...
IT SEEMS HE REALLY DOES SIMPLY WANT TO PLAY ROSHAMBO. RIDICULOUS, BUT THAT'S HIS ONLY REASON FOR HOUNDING ME.
OKAY, OKAY.
ZUMMM
CUSTOM-ERRR...
HERE IT COMES!
A LATE THROW COUNTS AS A LOSS.
IF THERE'S A TIE, WE KEEP ON GOING UNTIL SOMEONE WINS.
FINE. I'LL PLAY.
BUT AFTER WE'RE DONE...
YOU'LL LEAVE ME ALONE.

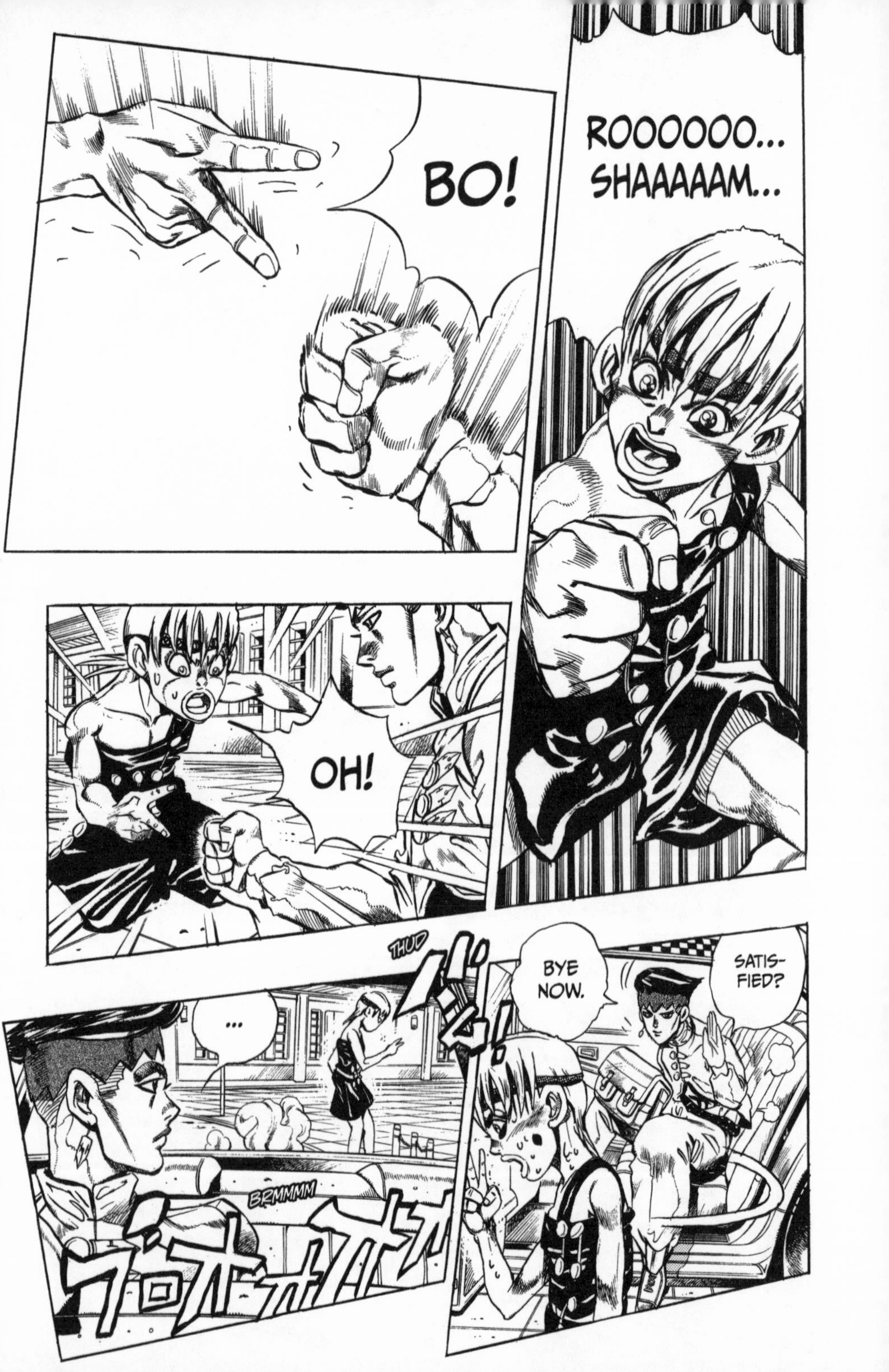
ROOOOOO... SHAAAAAM...
BO!
OH!
SATIS-FIED?
BYE NOW.
THUD
...
BRMMMM

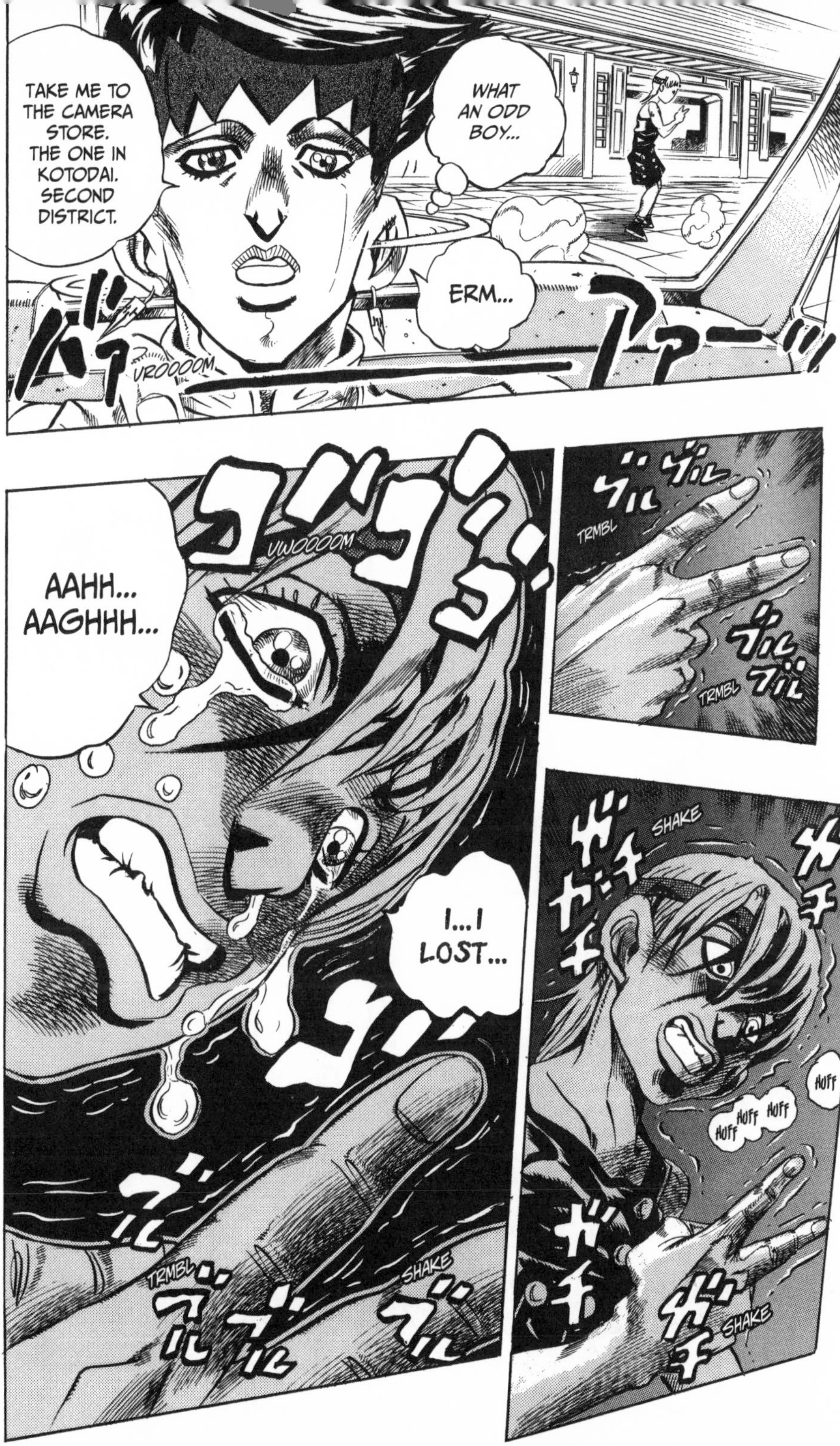

WHAT AN ODD BOY...
TAKE ME TO THE CAMERA STORE. THE ONE IN KOTODAI. SECOND DISTRICT.
ERM...
VROOOOM
TRMBL
TRMBL
SHAKE
HUFF
HUFF HUFF HUFF HUFF
SHAKE
VWOOOOM
AAHH... AAGHHH...
I...I LOST...
TRMBL
SHAKE

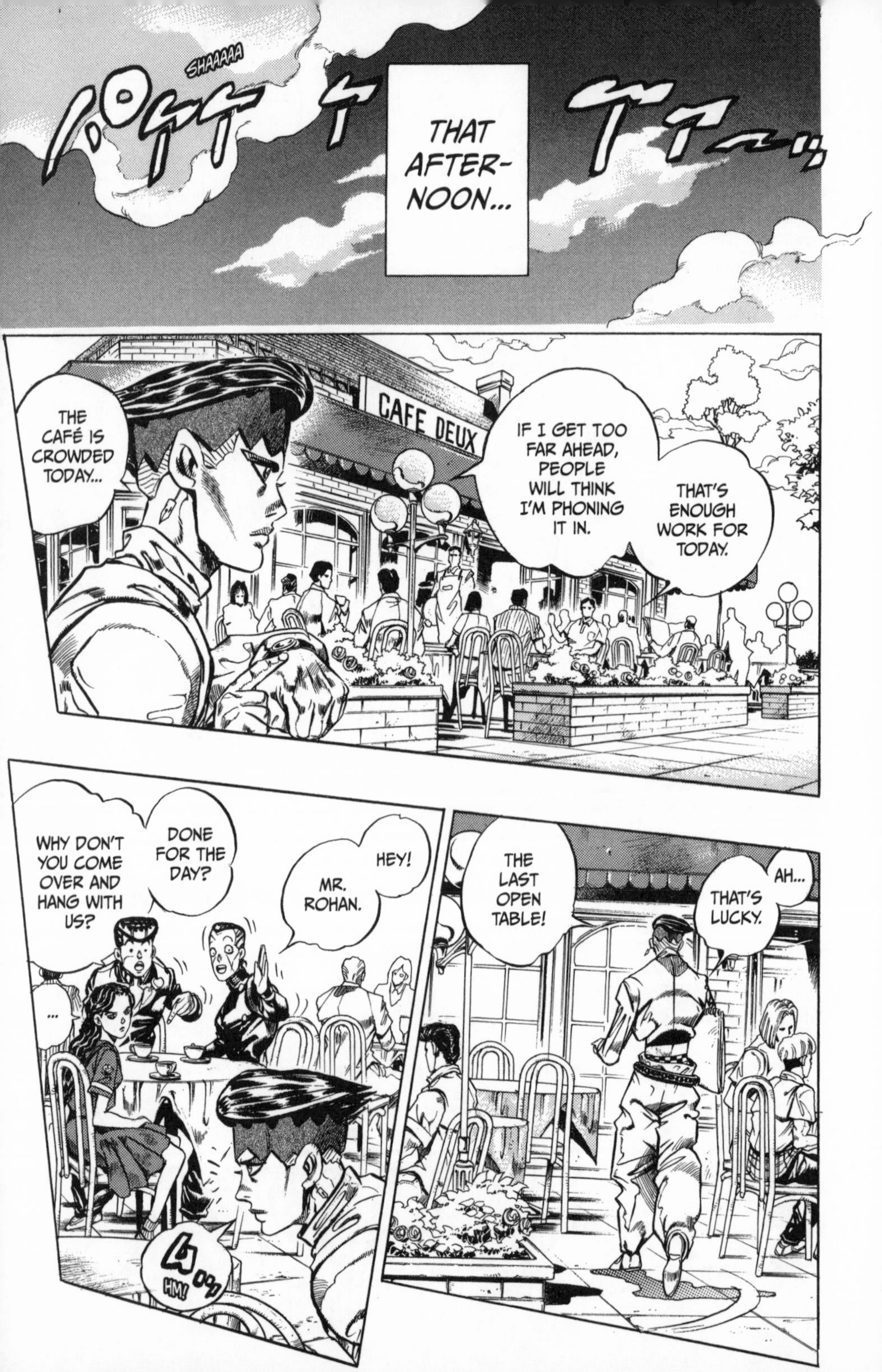
THAT AFTER-NOON...
SHAAAAA
THAT'S ENOUGH WORK FOR TODAY.
IF I GET TOO FAR AHEAD, PEOPLE WILL THINK I'M PHONING IT IN.
THE CAFÉ IS CROWDED TODAY...
CAFE DEUX
AH... THAT'S LUCKY.
THE LAST OPEN TABLE!
HEY!
MR. ROHAN.
DONE FOR THE DAY?
WHY DON'T YOU COME OVER AND HANG WITH US?
...
HM!

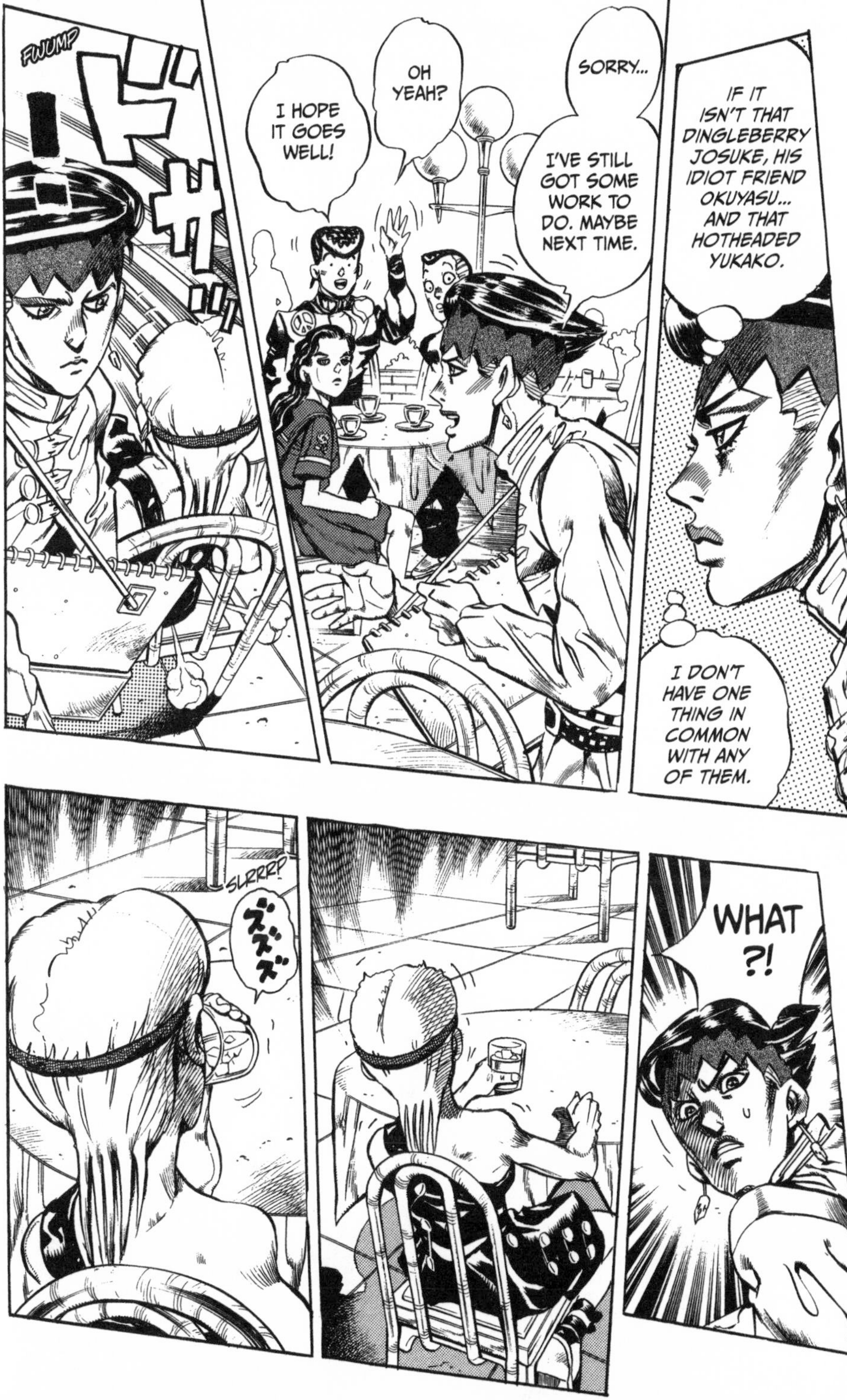
IF IT ISN'T THAT DINGLEBERRY JOSUKE, HIS IDIOT FRIEND OKUYASU... AND THAT HOTHEADED YUKAKO.
I DON'T HAVE ONE THING IN COMMON WITH ANY OF THEM.
SORRY...
I'VE STILL GOT SOME WORK TO DO. MAYBE NEXT TIME.
OH YEAH?
I HOPE IT GOES WELL!
FWUMP
ドサッ
WHAT ?!
SLRRRP
ズズズ

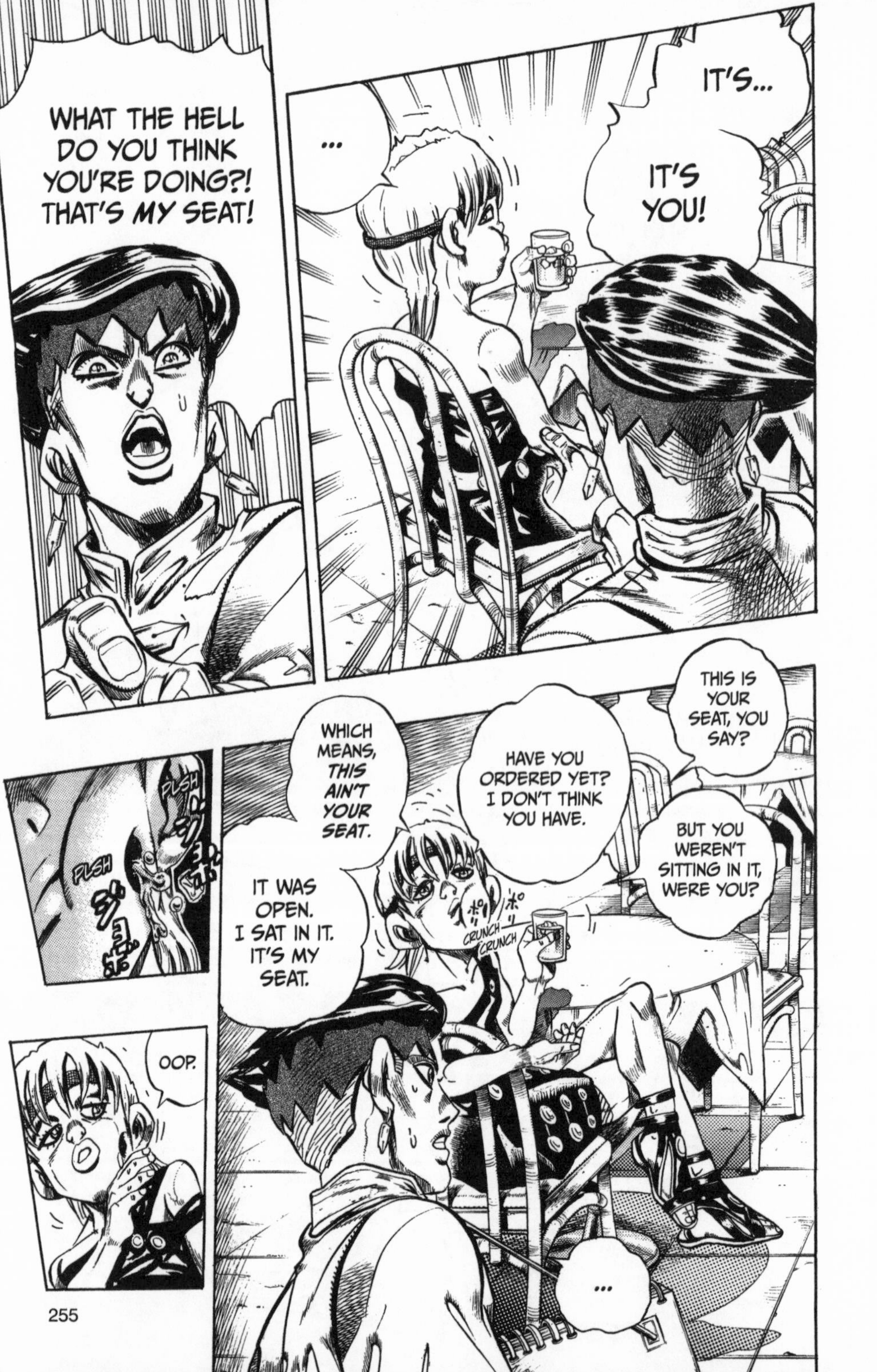
IT'S...
IT'S YOU!
...
WHAT THE HELL DO YOU THINK YOU'RE DOING?! THAT'S *MY* SEAT!
THIS IS YOUR SEAT, YOU SAY?
BUT YOU WEREN'T SITTING IN IT, WERE YOU?
HAVE YOU ORDERED YET? I DON'T THINK YOU HAVE.
WHICH MEANS, *THIS AIN'T YOUR SEAT.*
CRUNCH CRUNCH
IT WAS OPEN. I SAT IN IT. IT'S MY SEAT.
...
PLSH
PLSH
OOP.

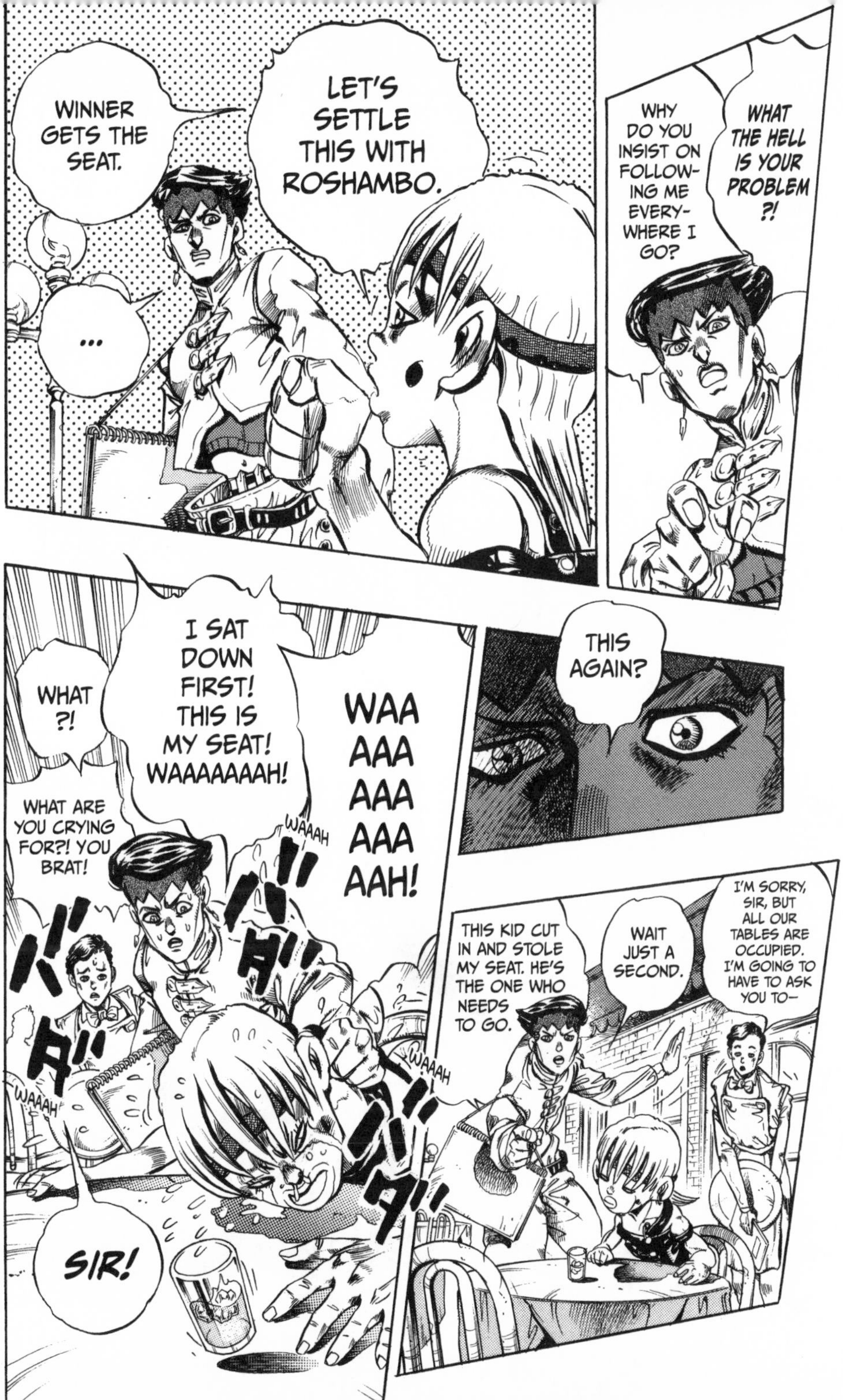
WHAT THE HELL IS YOUR PROBLEM?!
WHY DO YOU INSIST ON FOLLOWING ME EVERYWHERE I GO?
LET'S SETTLE THIS WITH ROSHAMBO.
WINNER GETS THE SEAT.
...
THIS AGAIN?
I'M SORRY, SIR, BUT ALL OUR TABLES ARE OCCUPIED. I'M GOING TO HAVE TO ASK YOU TO—
WAIT JUST A SECOND.
THIS KID CUT IN AND STOLE MY SEAT. HE'S THE ONE WHO NEEDS TO GO.
WAA AAA AAA AAA AAH!
I SAT DOWN FIRST! THIS IS MY SEAT! WAAAAAAAH!
WHAT?!
WHAT ARE YOU CRYING FOR?! YOU BRAT!
WAAAH
WAAAH
WAAAH
SIR!

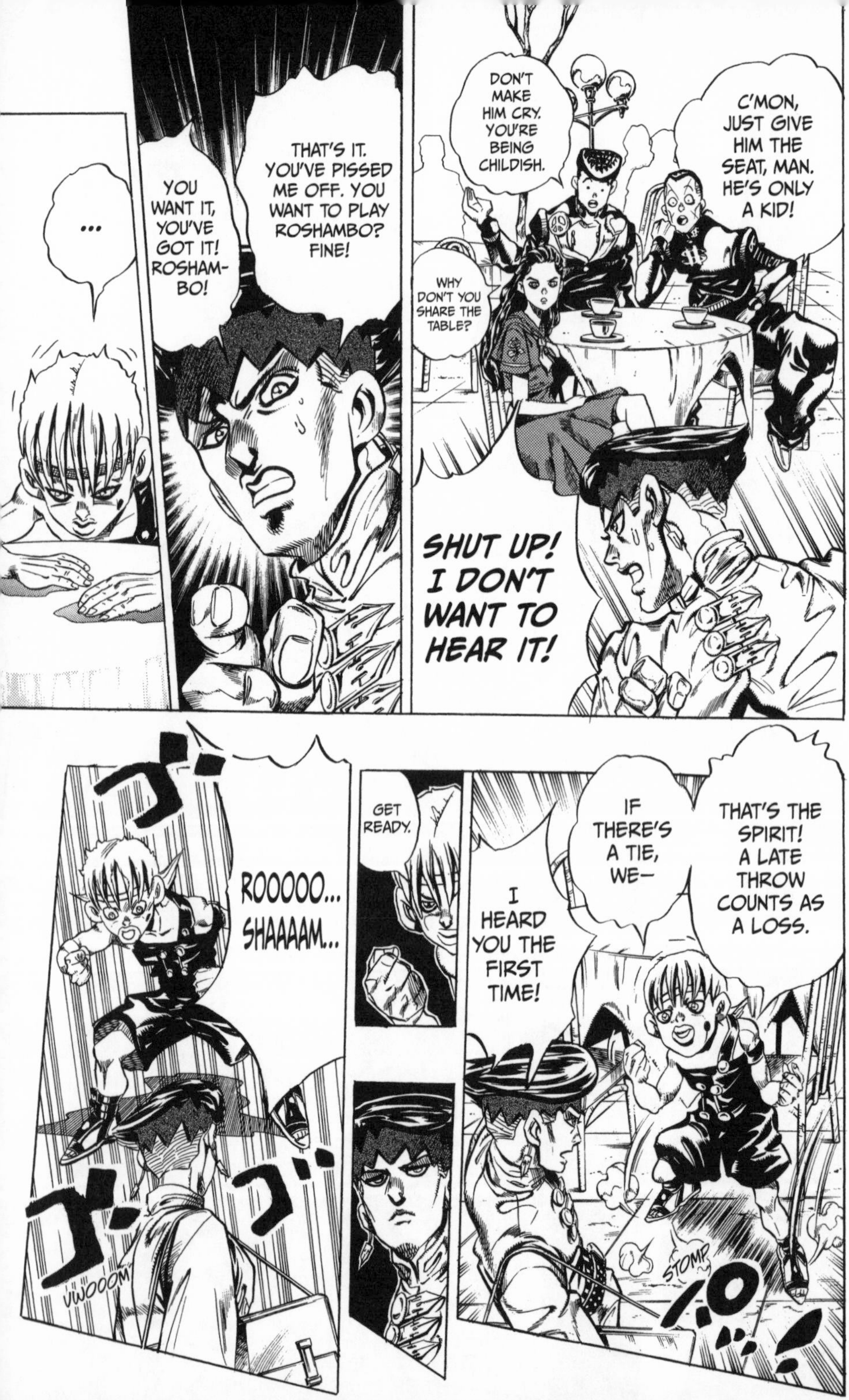
C'MON, JUST GIVE HIM THE SEAT, MAN. HE'S ONLY A KID!
DON'T MAKE HIM CRY. YOU'RE BEING CHILDISH.
WHY DON'T YOU SHARE THE TABLE?
SHUT UP! I DON'T WANT TO HEAR IT!
THAT'S IT. YOU'VE PISSED ME OFF. YOU WANT TO PLAY ROSHAMBO? FINE!
YOU WANT IT, YOU'VE GOT IT! ROSHAMBO!
...
THAT'S THE SPIRIT! A LATE THROW COUNTS AS A LOSS.
IF THERE'S A TIE, WE—
I HEARD YOU THE FIRST TIME!
STOMP
GET READY.
ROOOOO... SHAAAAM...
VWOOOM

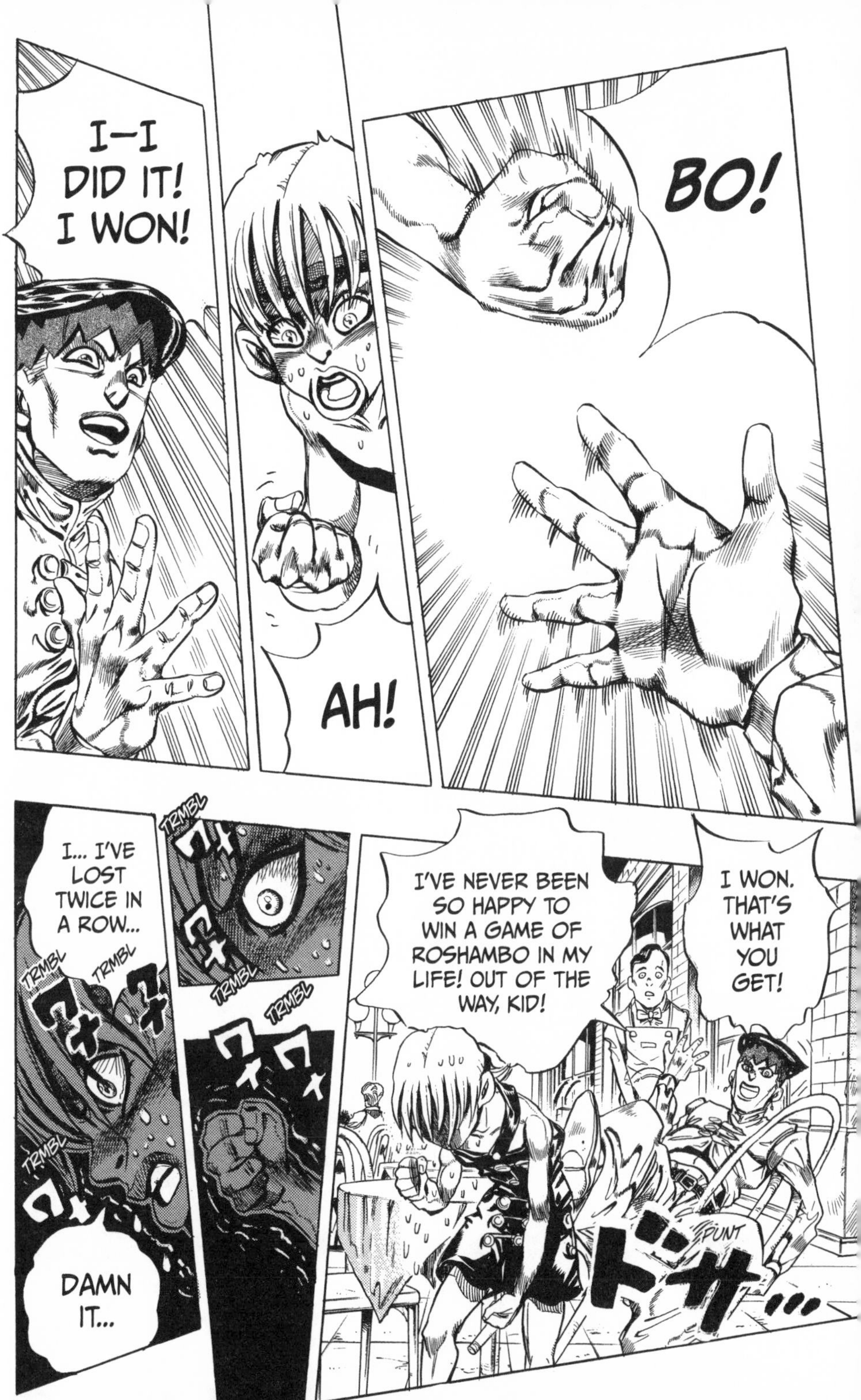
BO!
AH!
I—I DID IT! I WON!
I WON. THAT'S WHAT YOU GET!
I'VE NEVER BEEN SO HAPPY TO WIN A GAME OF ROSHAMBO IN MY LIFE! OUT OF THE WAY, KID!
PUNT
TRMBL
TRMBL
TRMBL
I... I'VE LOST TWICE IN A ROW...
TRMBL
TRMBL
TRMBL
DAMN IT...

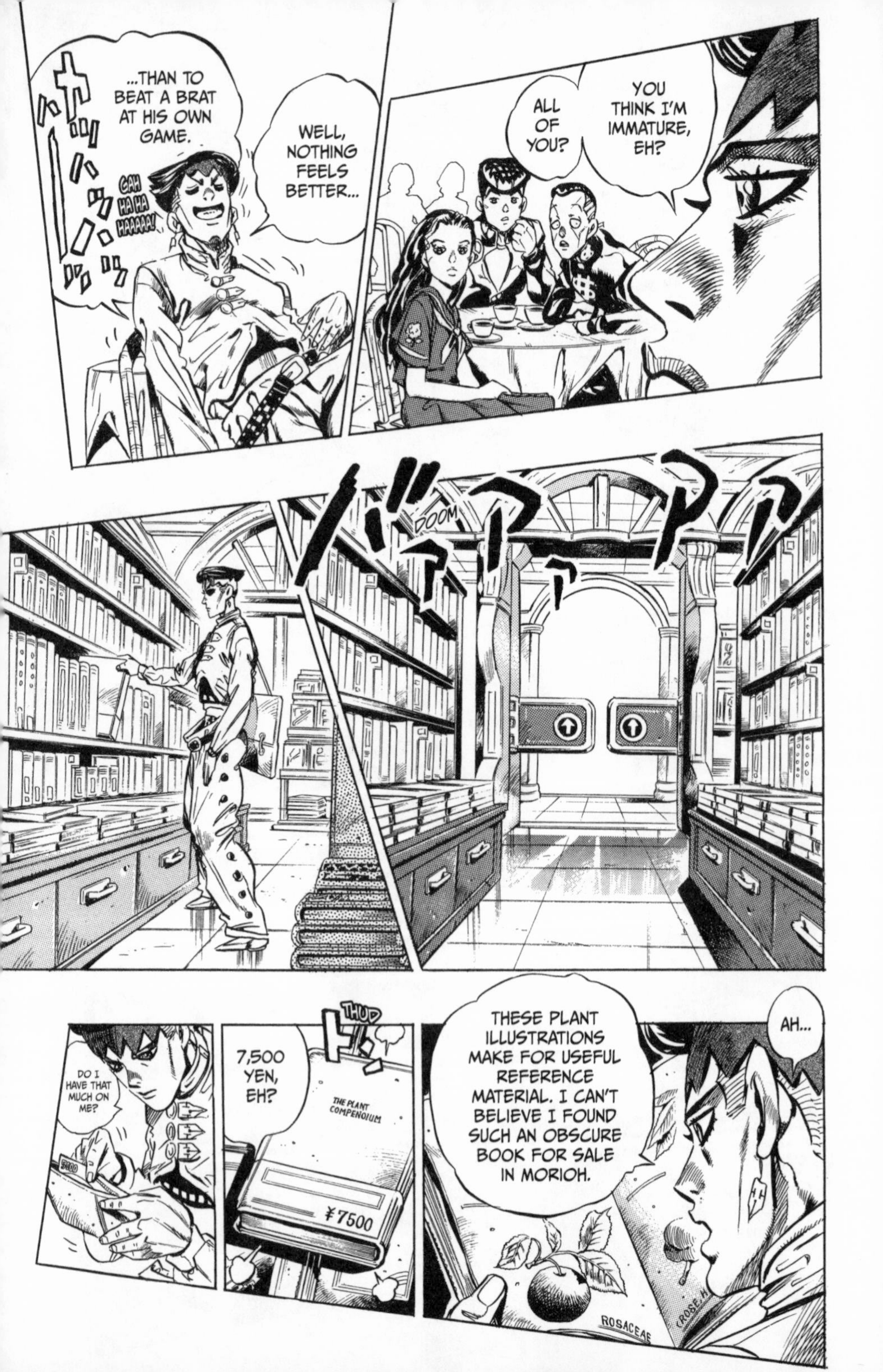
YOU THINK I'M IMMATURE, EH?
ALL OF YOU?
WELL, NOTHING FEELS BETTER...
...THAN TO BEAT A BRAT AT HIS OWN GAME.
GAH HA HA HAAAAA!
DOOM
AH...
THESE PLANT ILLUSTRATIONS MAKE FOR USEFUL REFERENCE MATERIAL. I CAN'T BELIEVE I FOUND SUCH AN OBSCURE BOOK FOR SALE IN MORIOH.
ROSACEAE
THUD
7,500 YEN, EH?
THE PLANT COMPENDIUM
¥7500
DO I HAVE THAT MUCH ON ME?

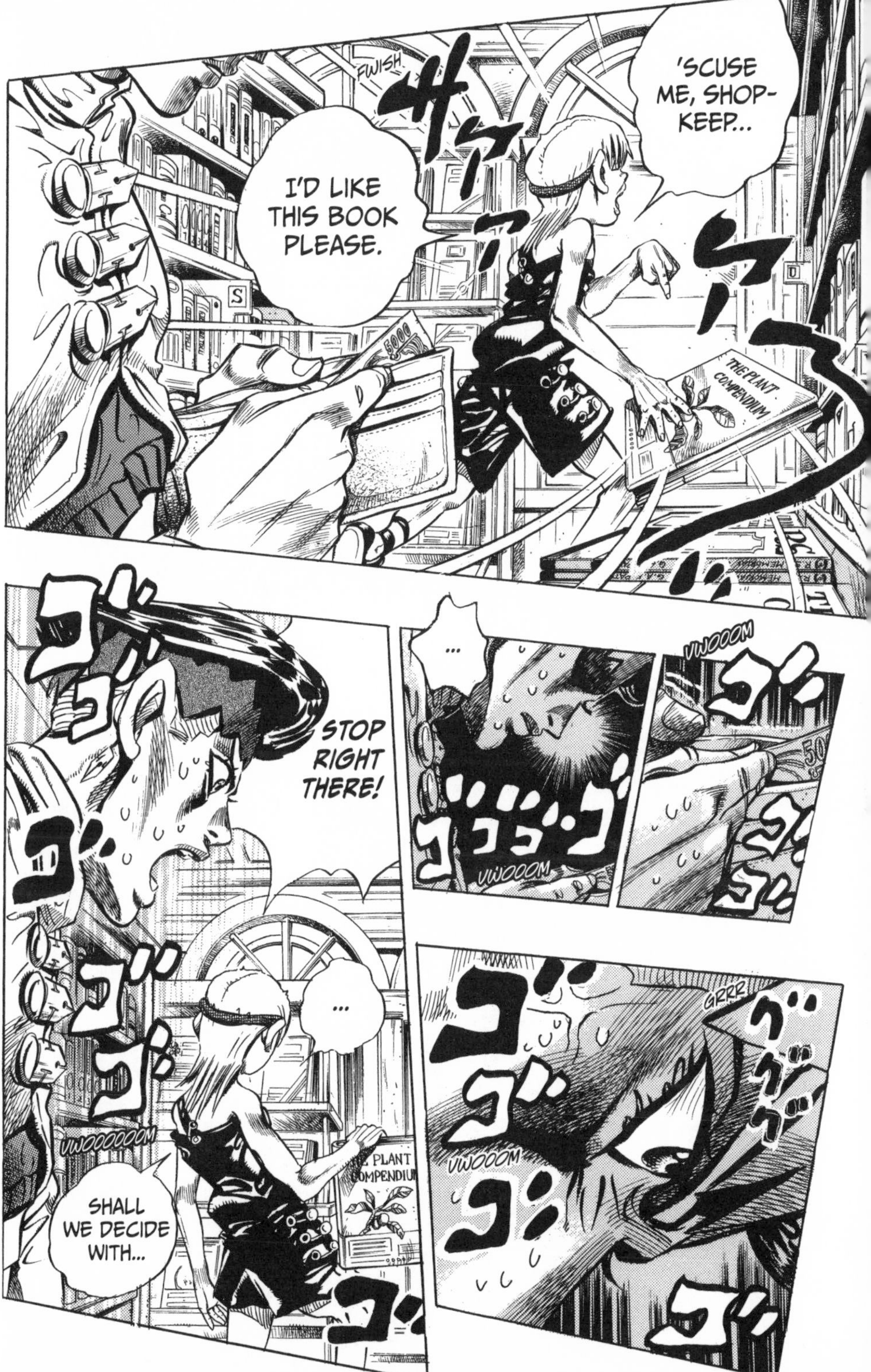
'SCUSE ME, SHOP-KEEP...
FWISH
I'D LIKE THIS BOOK PLEASE.
THE PLANT COMPENDIUM
VWOOOM
...
VWOOOM
GRRR
VWOOOM
STOP RIGHT THERE!
...
VWOOOOOOM
SHALL WE DECIDE WITH...
THE PLANT COMPENDIUM

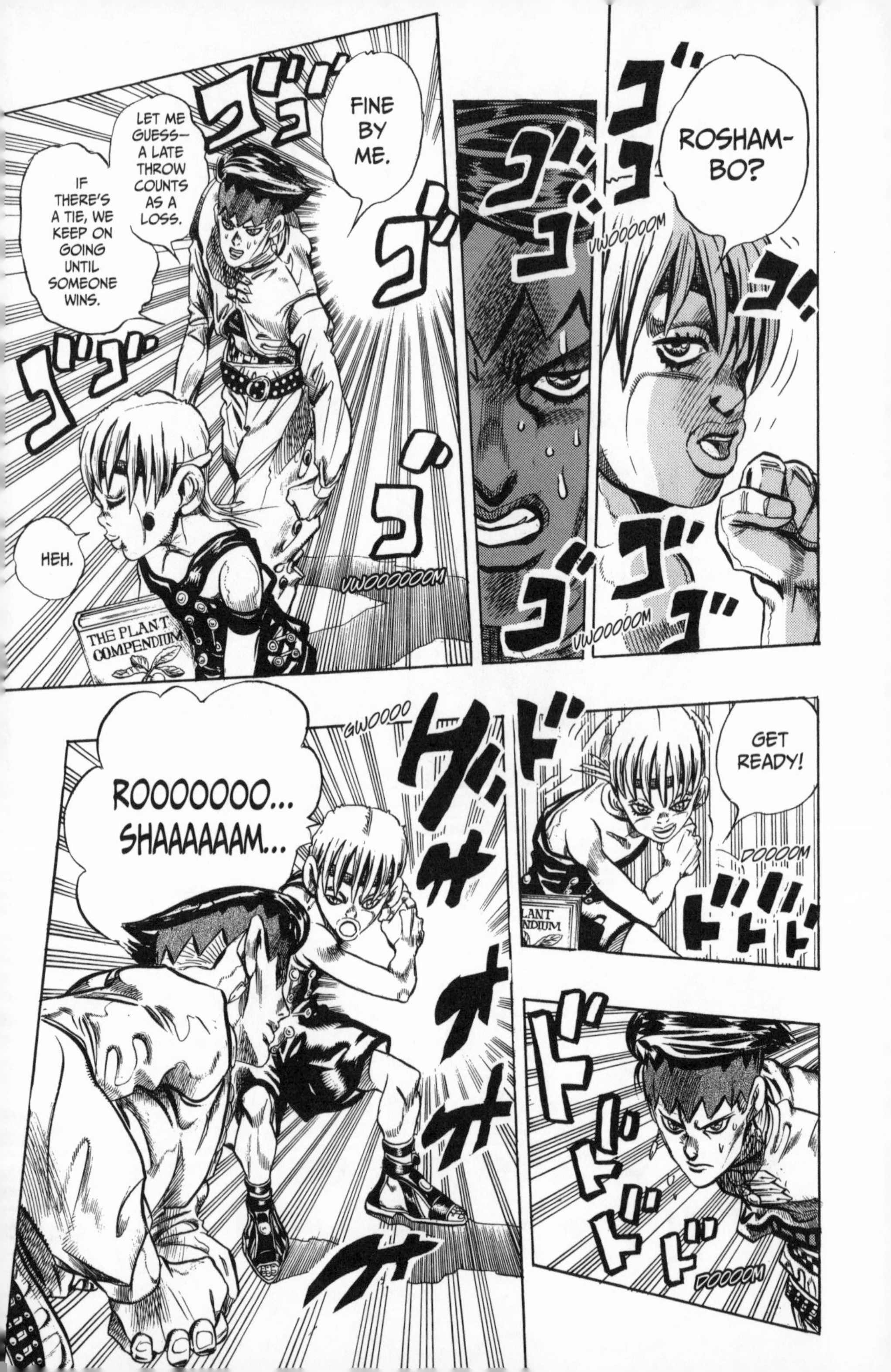
ROSHAMBO?
VWOOOOOM
VWOOOOOM
FINE BY ME.
LET ME GUESS—A LATE THROW COUNTS AS A LOSS.
IF THERE'S A TIE, WE KEEP ON GOING UNTIL SOMEONE WINS.
HEH.
VWOOOOOOM
THE PLANT COMPENDIUM
GET READY!
DOOOOM
DOOOOM
GWOOOO
ROOOOOOO... SHAAAAAM...

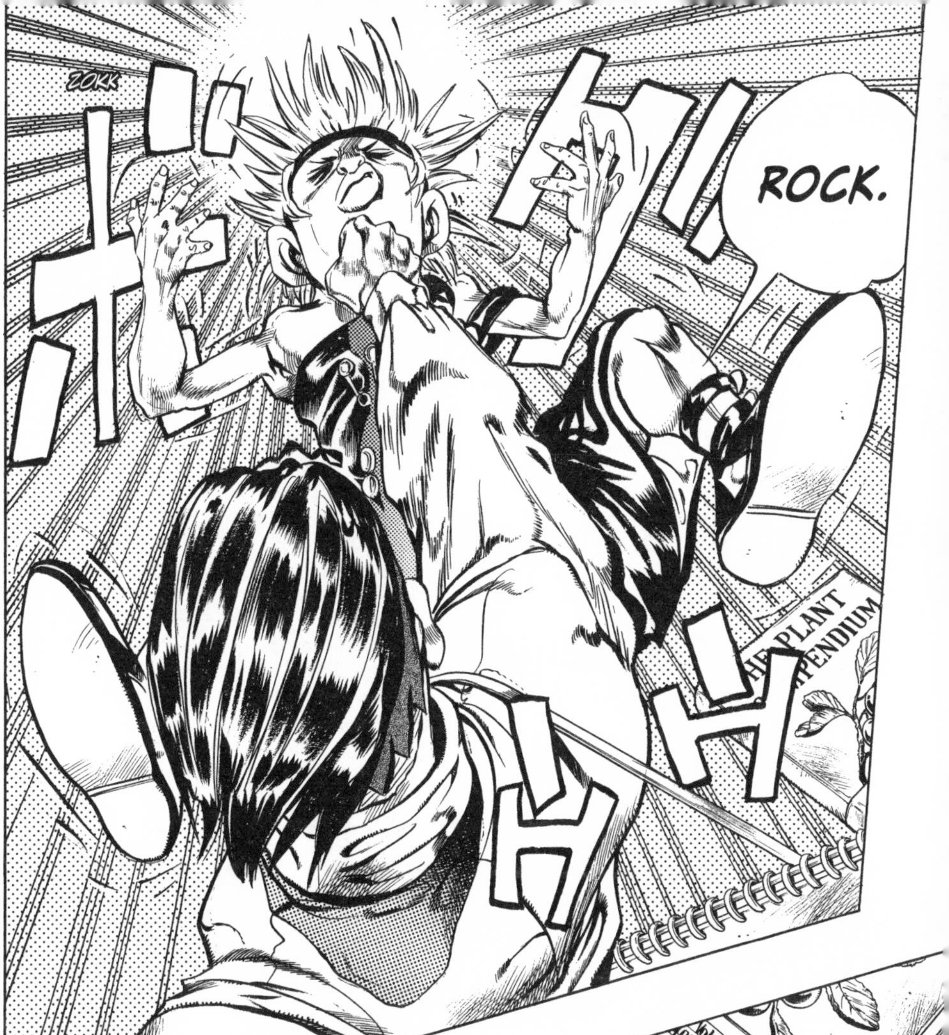
ZOKK
ROCK.
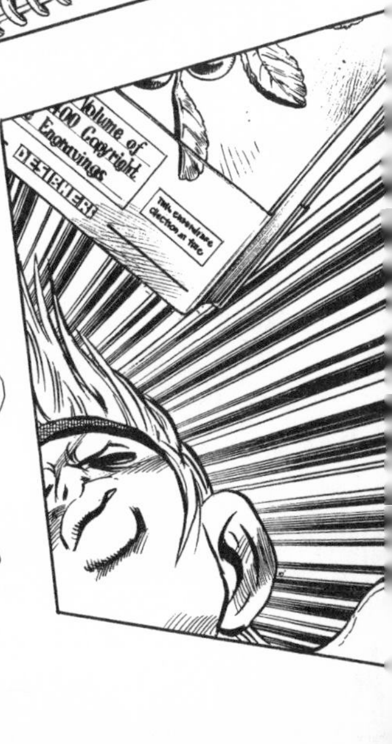
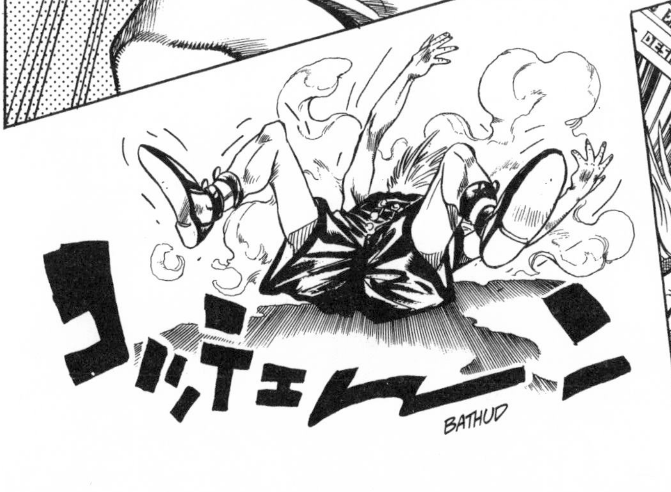
BATHUD

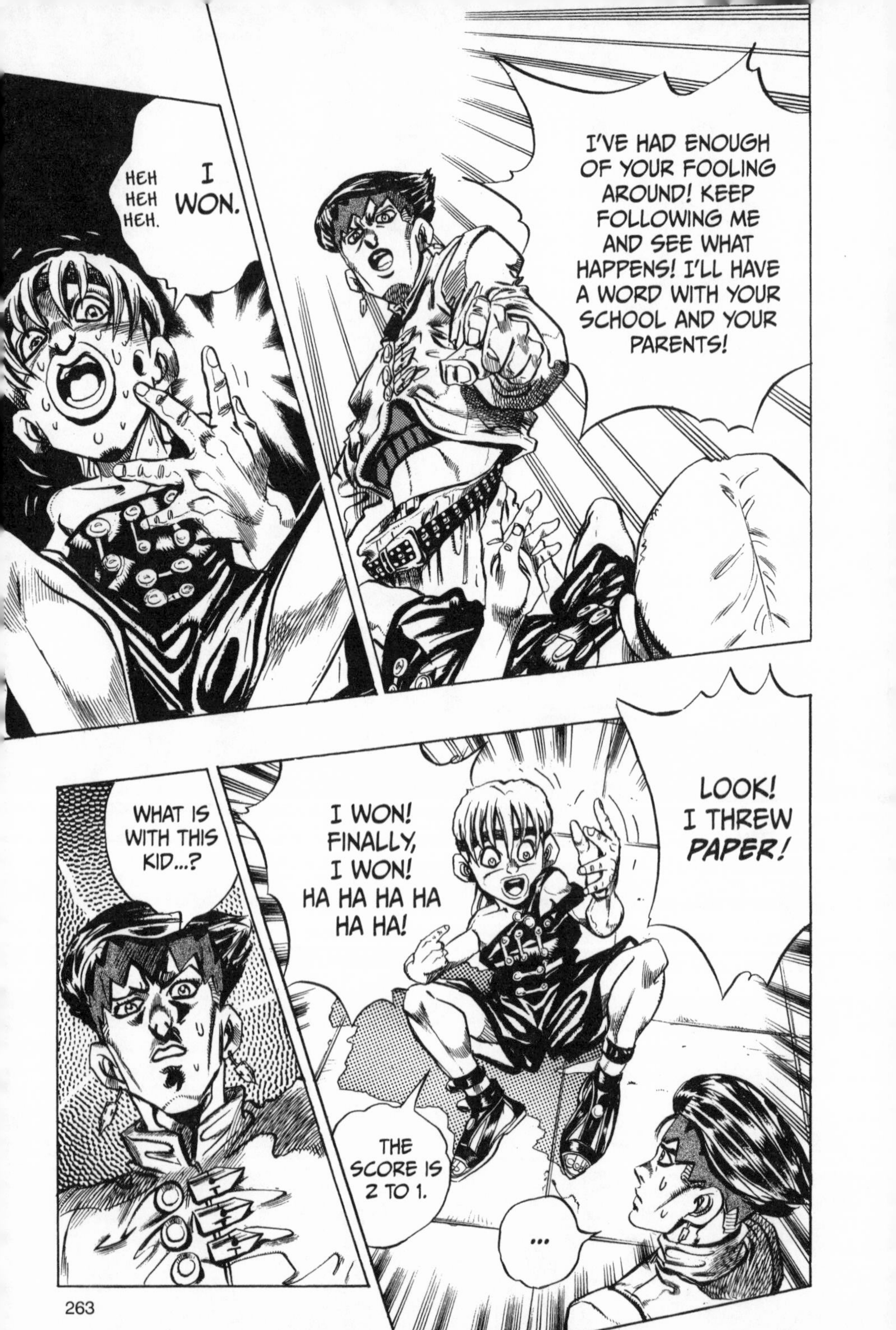
I'VE HAD ENOUGH OF YOUR FOOLING AROUND! KEEP FOLLOWING ME AND SEE WHAT HAPPENS! I'LL HAVE A WORD WITH YOUR SCHOOL AND YOUR PARENTS!
HEH HEH HEH. I WON.
LOOK! I THREW *PAPER!*
I WON! FINALLY, I WON! HA HA HA HA HA HA!
THE SCORE IS 2 TO 1.
...
WHAT IS WITH THIS KID...?

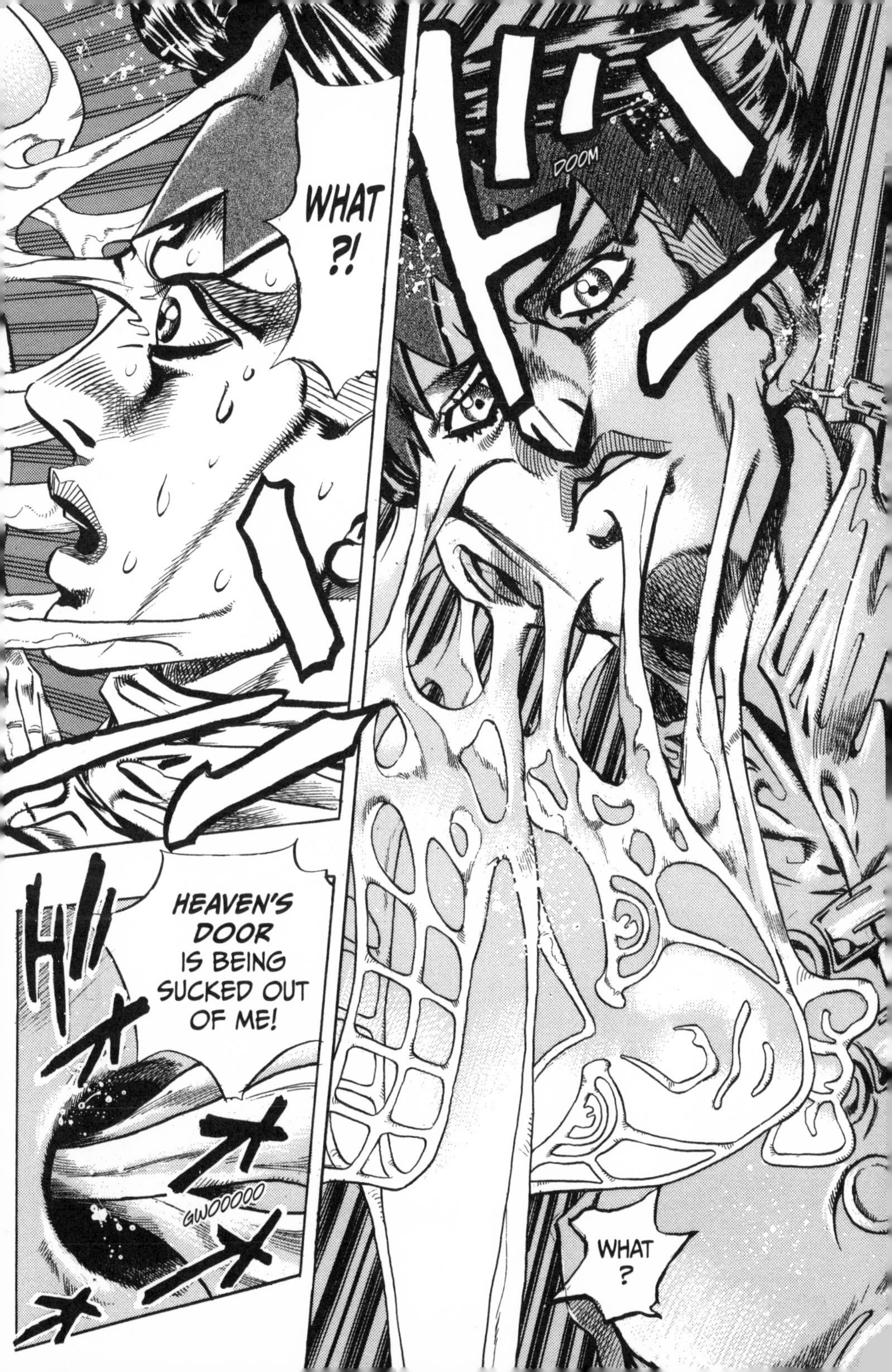
DOOM
WHAT ?
WHAT ?!
HEAVEN'S DOOR IS BEING SUCKED OUT OF ME!
GWOOOOO

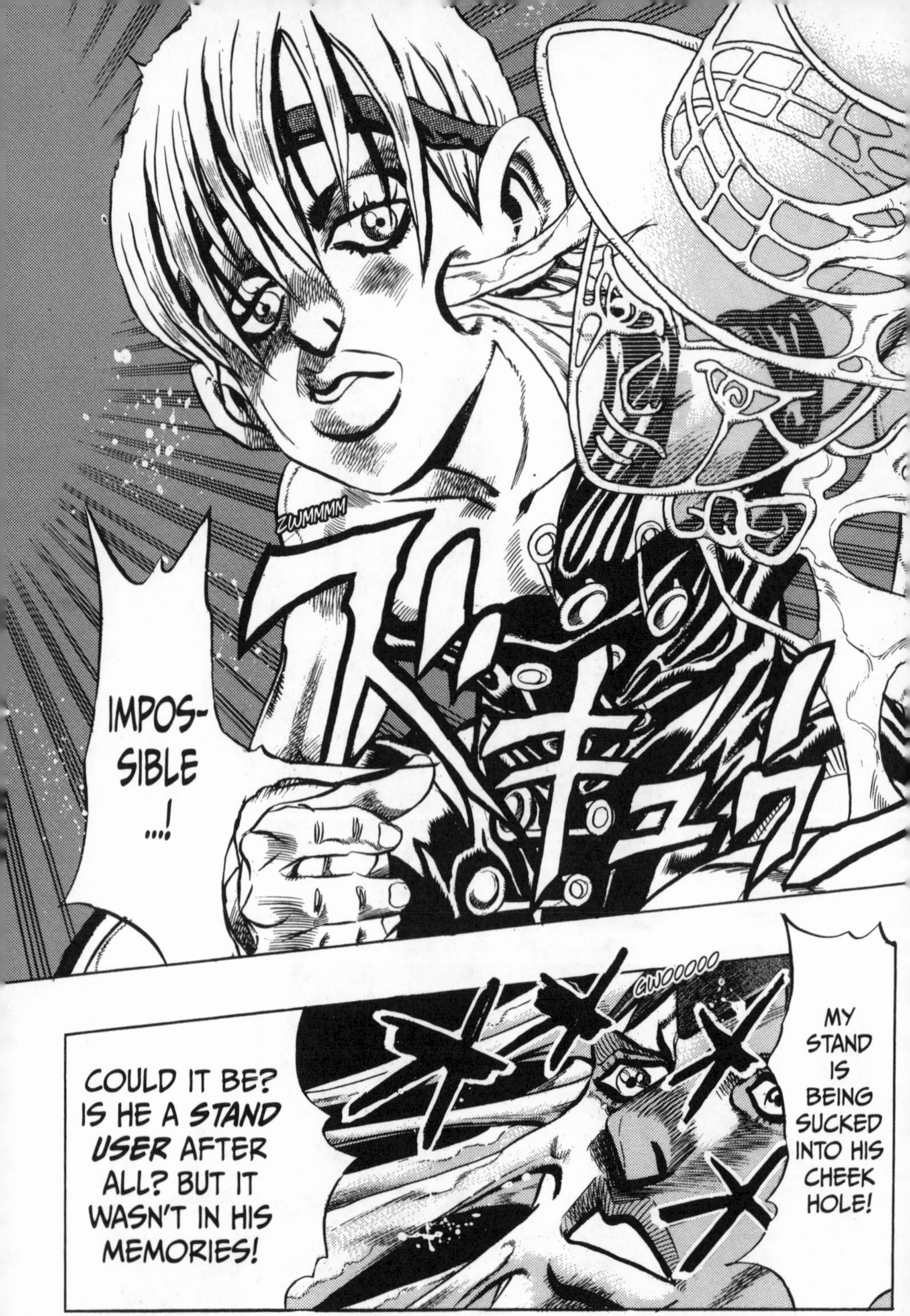
ZWMMMM
IMPOS-SIBLE ...!
MY STAND IS BEING SUCKED INTO HIS CHEEK HOLE!
GWOOOOO
COULD IT BE? IS HE A STAND USER AFTER ALL? BUT IT WASN'T IN HIS MEMORIES!

CHAPTER 108

ROSHAM BOY IS HERE!, PART 3

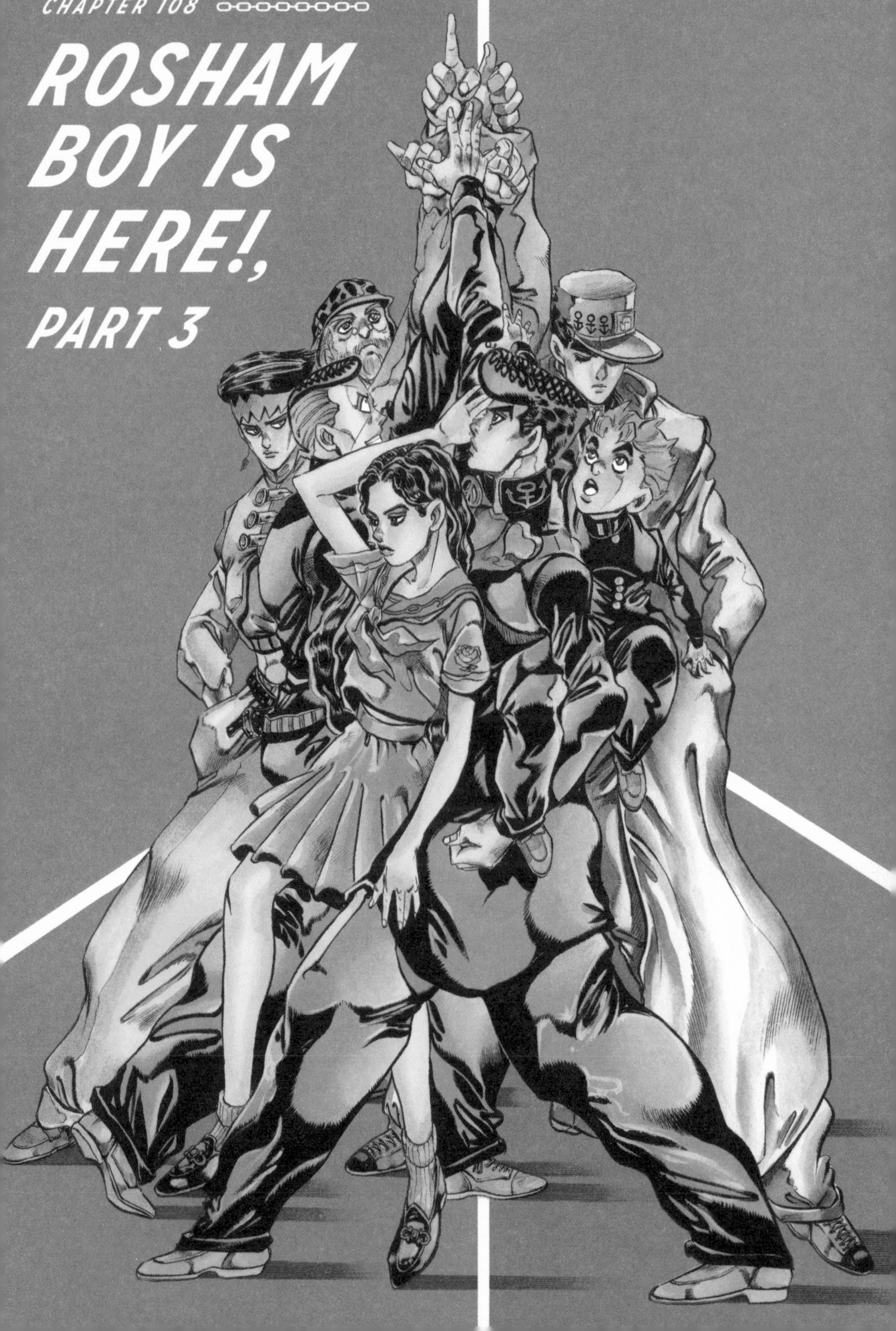

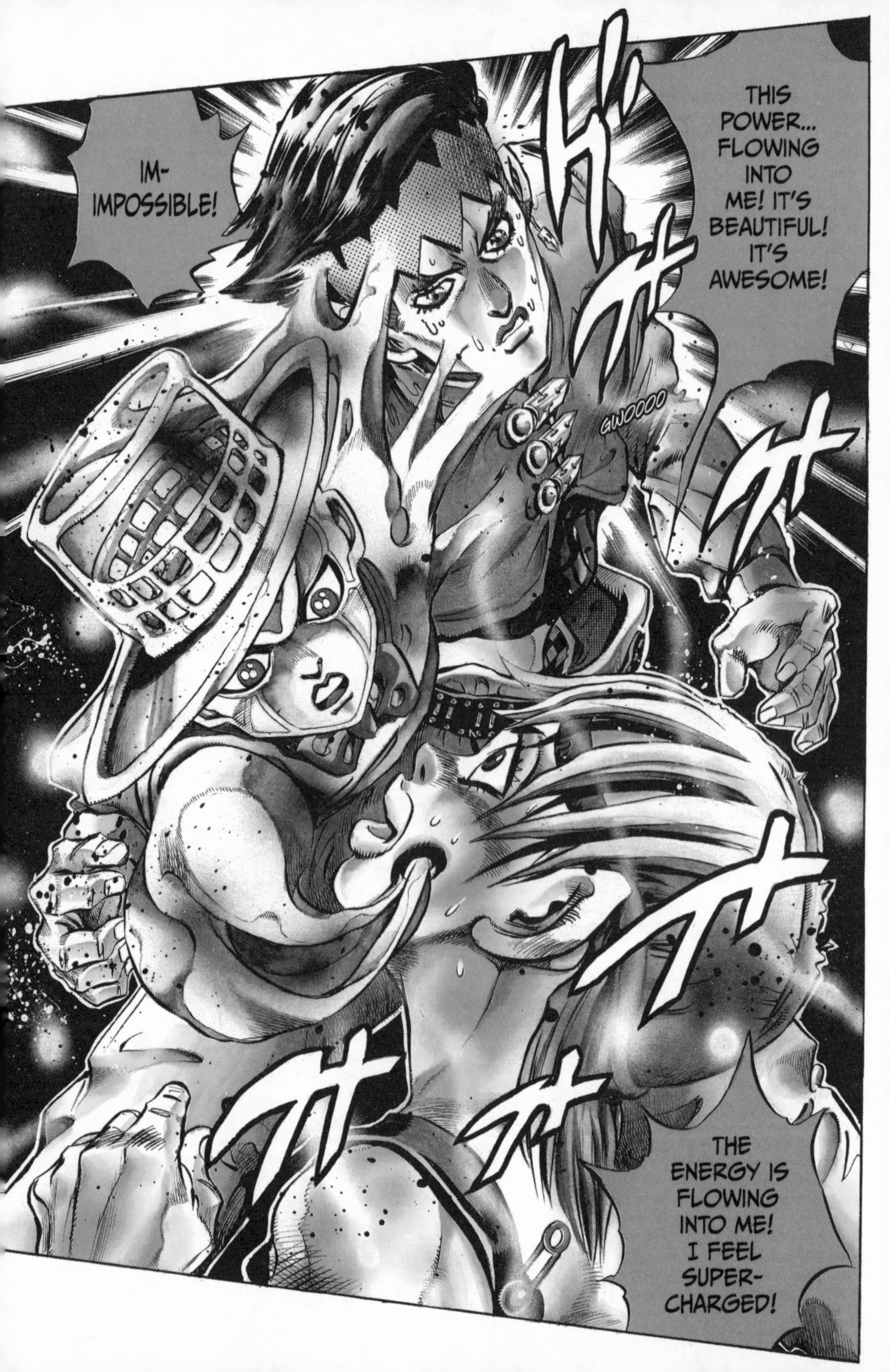
THIS POWER... FLOWING INTO ME! IT'S BEAUTIFUL! IT'S AWESOME!
IM-IMPOSSIBLE!
GWOOOO
THE ENERGY IS FLOWING INTO ME! I FEEL SUPER-CHARGED!

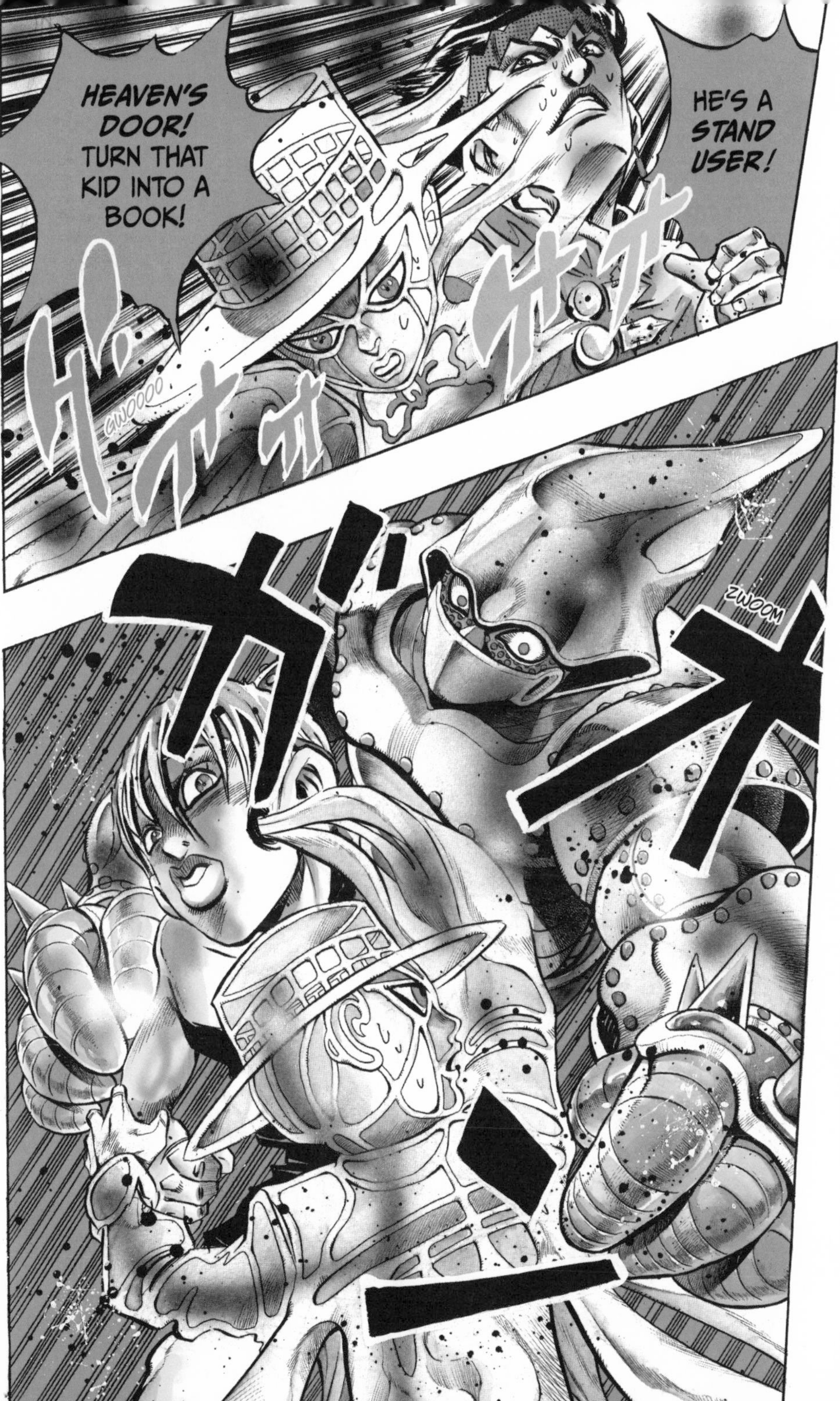
HE'S A STAND USER!
HEAVEN'S DOOR! TURN THAT KID INTO A BOOK!
GWOOOO
ZWOOM

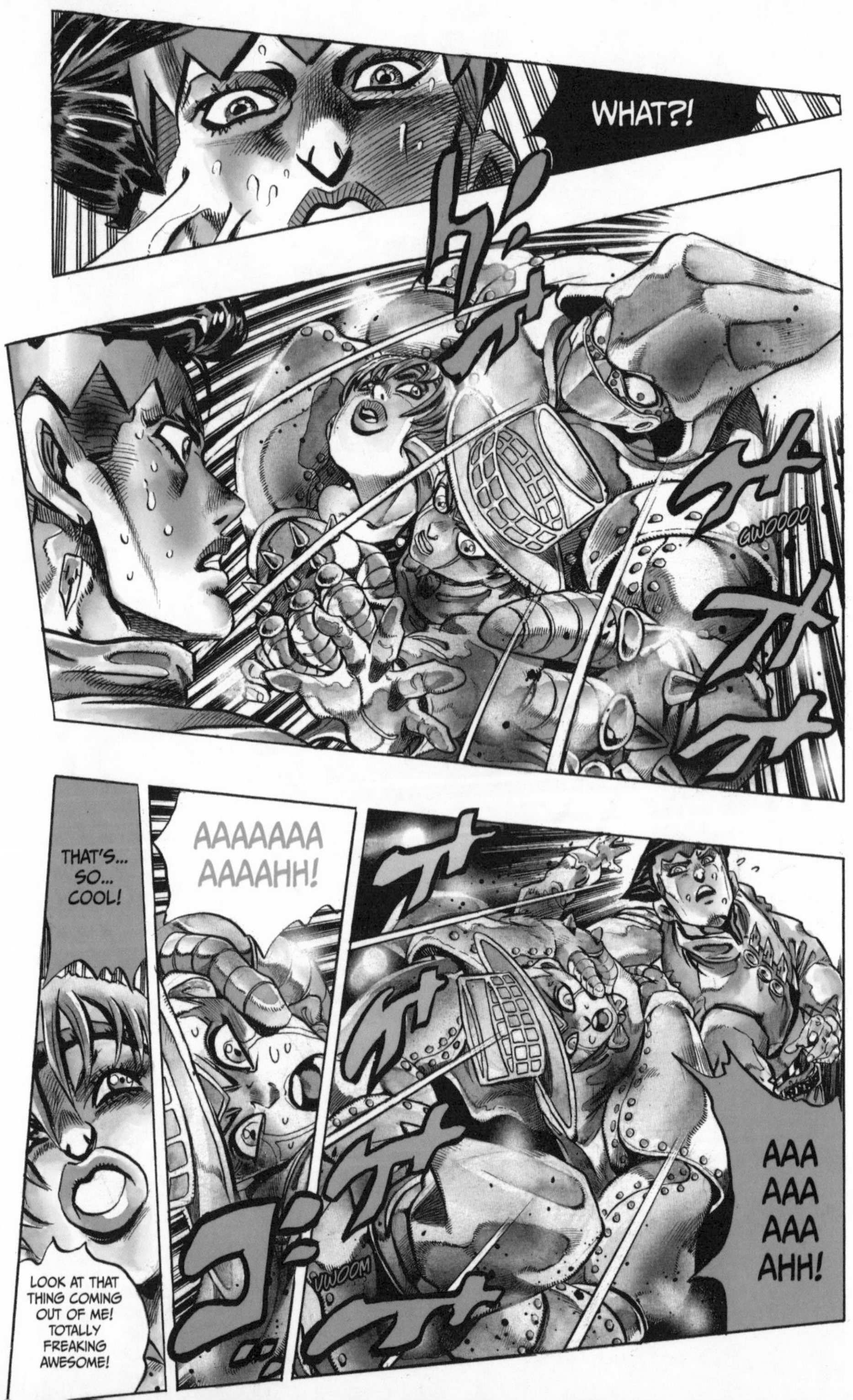
WHAT?!
GWOOOO
AAA
AAA
AAA
AHH!
VWOOM
AAAAAAA
AAAAAHH!
THAT'S... SO... COOL!
LOOK AT THAT THING COMING OUT OF ME! TOTALLY FREAKING AWESOME!

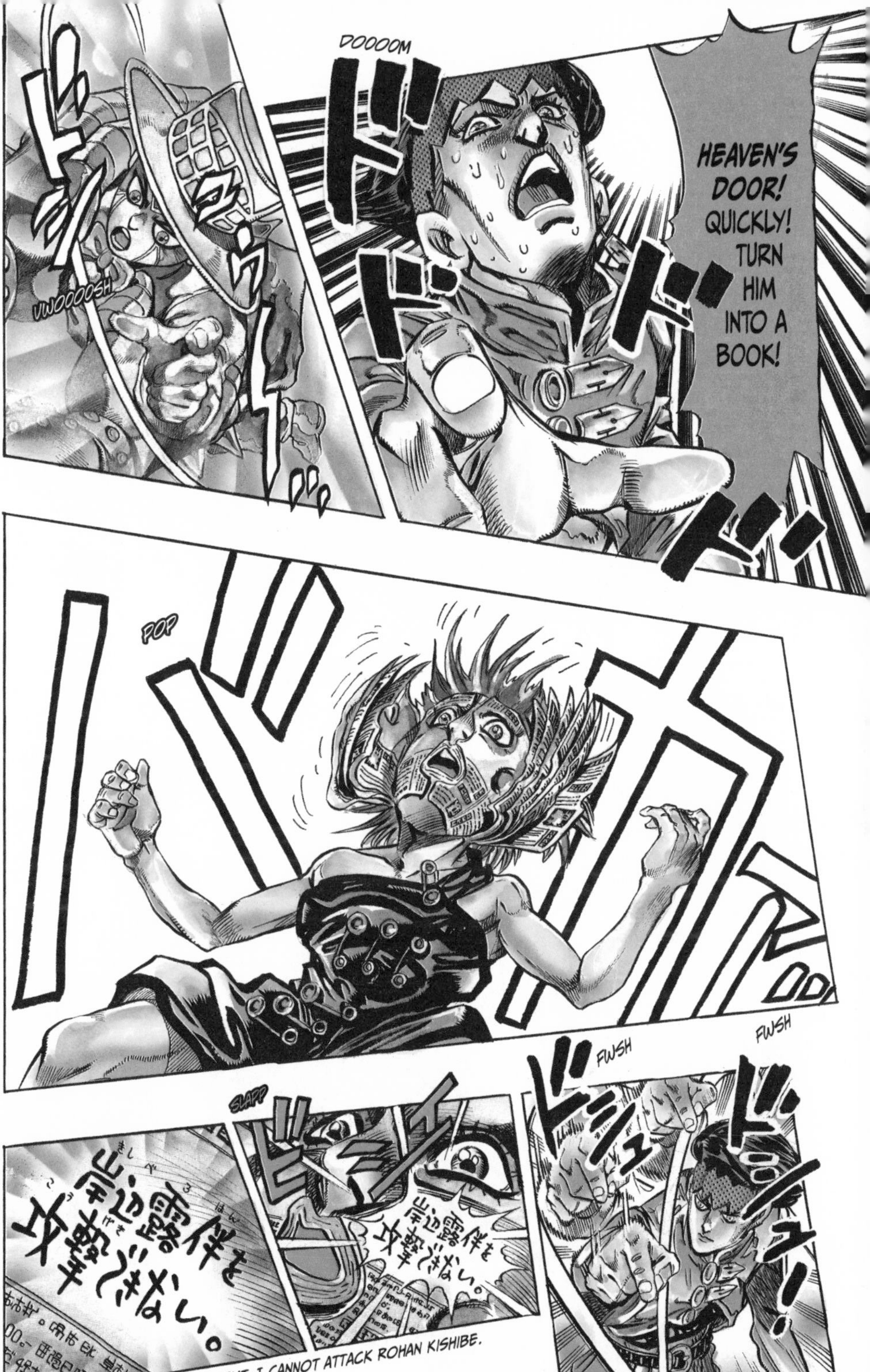
DOOOOM
HEAVEN'S DOOR! QUICKLY! TURN HIM INTO A BOOK!
VWOOOOSH
POP
FWSH
FWSH
SLAPP
岸辺露伴を攻撃できない。
岸辺露伴を攻撃できない。
TEXT: I CANNOT ATTACK ROHAN KISHIBE.

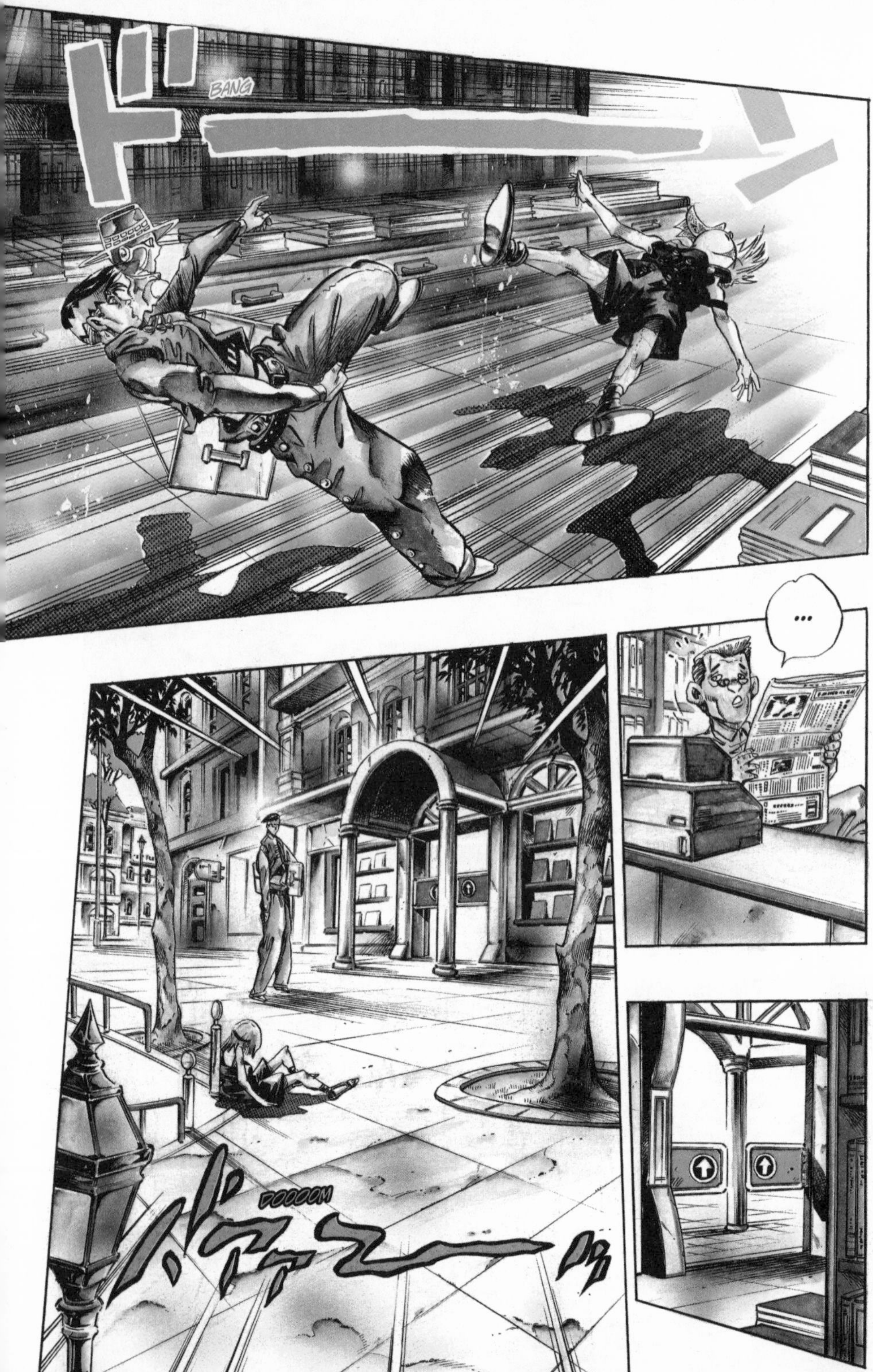
BANG
...
DOOOOM

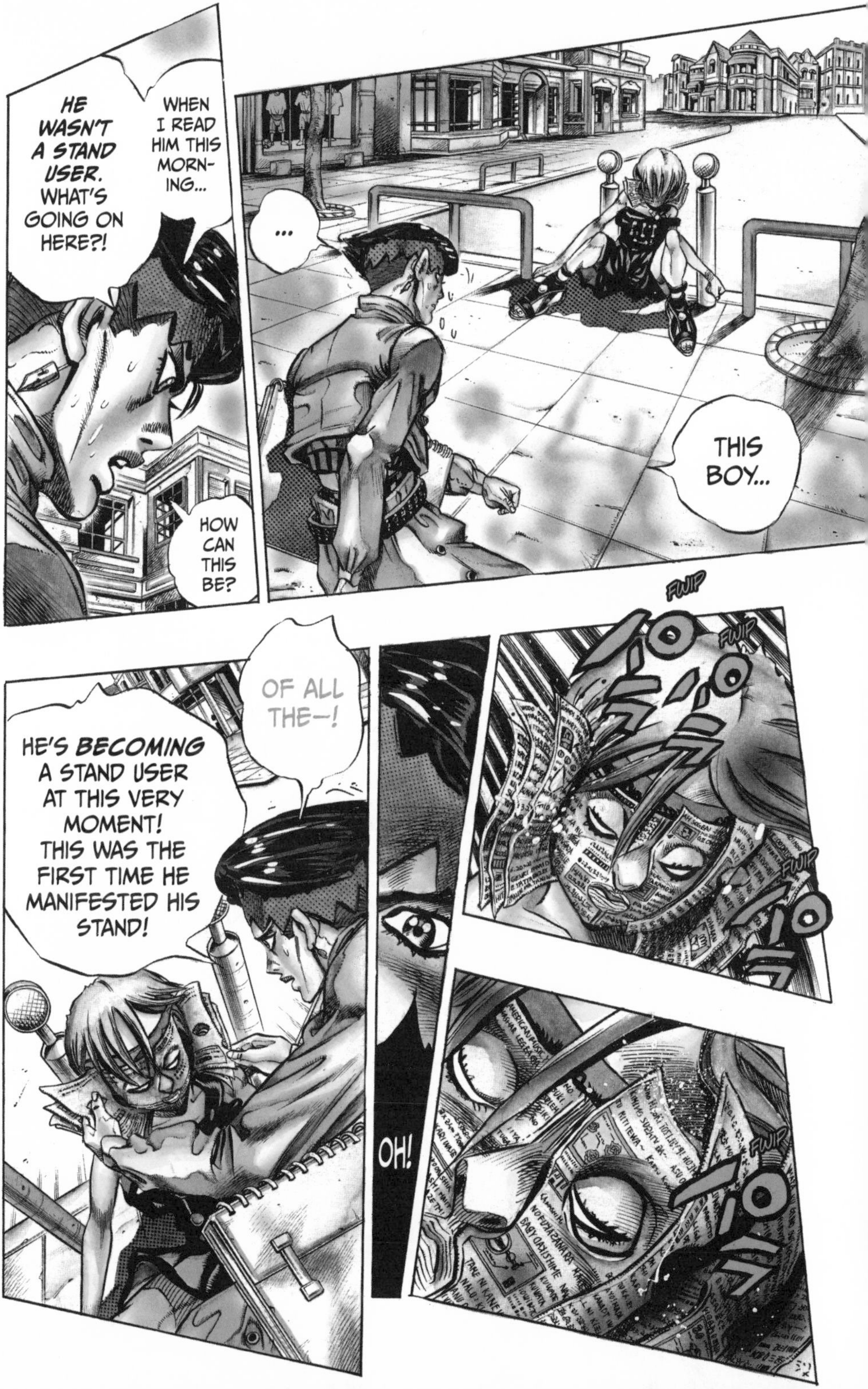

...
THIS BOY...
WHEN I READ HIM THIS MORNING...
HE WASN'T A STAND USER. WHAT'S GOING ON HERE?!
HOW CAN THIS BE?
FWIP
FWIP
FWIP
FWIP
OH!
OF ALL THE—!
HE'S BECOMING A STAND USER AT THIS VERY MOMENT! THIS WAS THE FIRST TIME HE MANIFESTED HIS STAND!

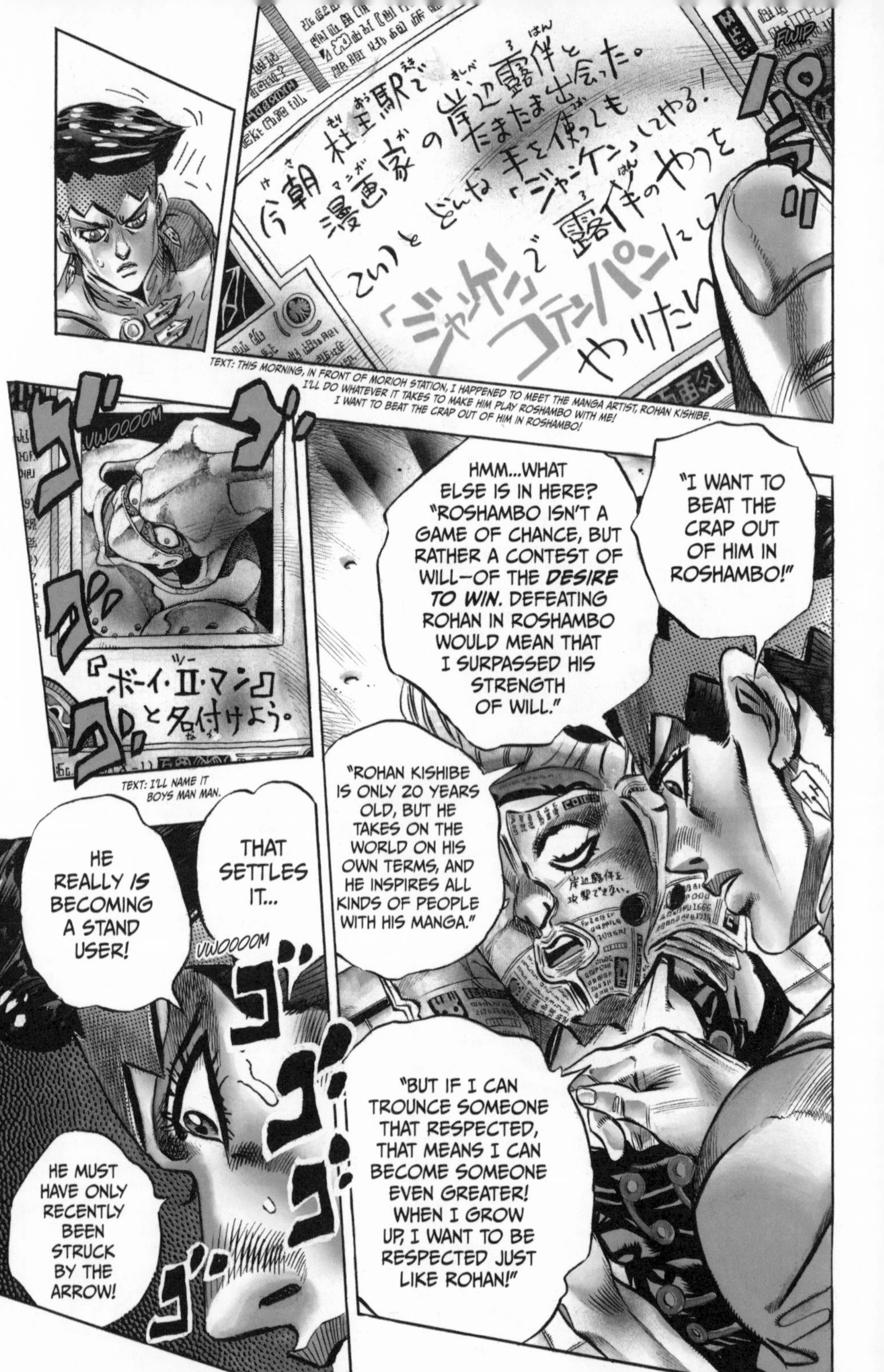
パラ
FWIP
今朝杜王駅で漫画家の岸辺露伴とたまたま出会った。
こいつとどんな手を使っても「ジャンケン」してやる！
露伴のやつを「ジャンケン」でコテンパンにしてやりたい
TEXT: THIS MORNING, IN FRONT OF MORIOH STATION, I HAPPENED TO MEET THE MANGA ARTIST, ROHAN KISHIBE.
I'LL DO WHATEVER IT TAKES TO MAKE HIM PLAY ROSHAMBO WITH ME!
I WANT TO BEAT THE CRAP OUT OF HIM IN ROSHAMBO!
"I WANT TO BEAT THE CRAP OUT OF HIM IN ROSHAMBO!"
HMM...WHAT ELSE IS IN HERE? "ROSHAMBO ISN'T A GAME OF CHANCE, BUT RATHER A CONTEST OF WILL—OF THE *DESIRE TO WIN*. DEFEATING ROHAN IN ROSHAMBO WOULD MEAN THAT I SURPASSED HIS STRENGTH OF WILL."
岸辺露伴を攻撃できない。
"ROHAN KISHIBE IS ONLY 20 YEARS OLD, BUT HE TAKES ON THE WORLD ON HIS OWN TERMS, AND HE INSPIRES ALL KINDS OF PEOPLE WITH HIS MANGA."
"BUT IF I CAN TROUNCE SOMEONE THAT RESPECTED, THAT MEANS I CAN BECOME SOMEONE EVEN GREATER! WHEN I GROW UP, I WANT TO BE RESPECTED JUST LIKE ROHAN!"
ゴゴ
VWOOOOM
ゴゴ
『ボーイ・II・マン』と名付けよう。
TEXT: I'LL NAME IT BOYS MAN MAN.
THAT SETTLES IT...
HE REALLY *IS* BECOMING A STAND USER!
VWOOOOM
ゴゴゴゴ
HE MUST HAVE ONLY RECENTLY BEEN STRUCK BY THE ARROW!

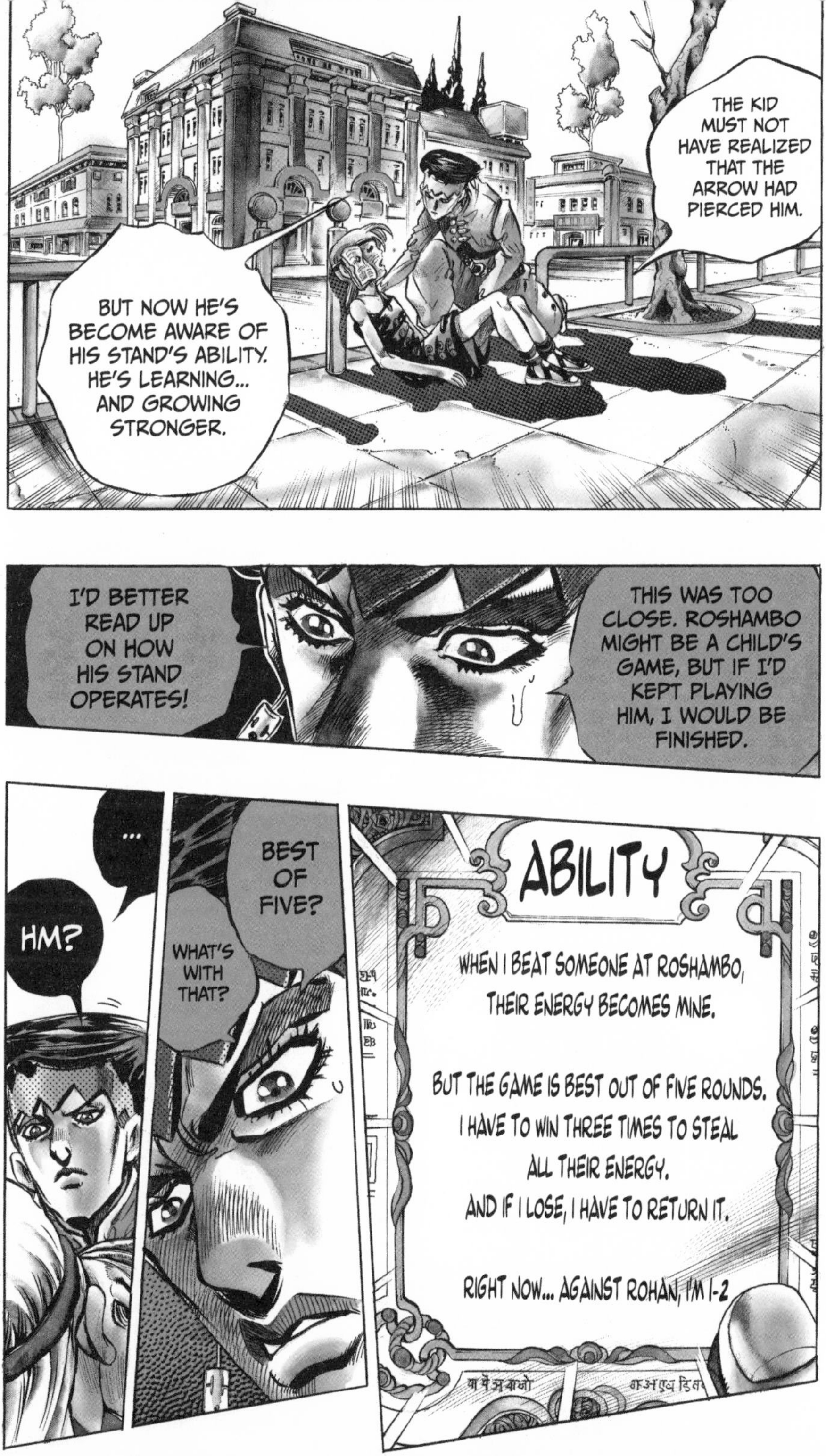
THE KID MUST NOT HAVE REALIZED THAT THE ARROW HAD PIERCED HIM.
BUT NOW HE'S BECOME AWARE OF HIS STAND'S ABILITY. HE'S LEARNING... AND GROWING STRONGER.
THIS WAS TOO CLOSE. ROSHAMBO MIGHT BE A CHILD'S GAME, BUT IF I'D KEPT PLAYING HIM, I WOULD BE FINISHED.
I'D BETTER READ UP ON HOW HIS STAND OPERATES!
ABILITY
WHEN I BEAT SOMEONE AT ROSHAMBO, THEIR ENERGY BECOMES MINE.
BUT THE GAME IS BEST OUT OF FIVE ROUNDS. I HAVE TO WIN THREE TIMES TO STEAL ALL THEIR ENERGY. AND IF I LOSE, I HAVE TO RETURN IT.
RIGHT NOW... AGAINST ROHAN, I'M 1-2
BEST OF FIVE?
WHAT'S WITH THAT?
...
HM?

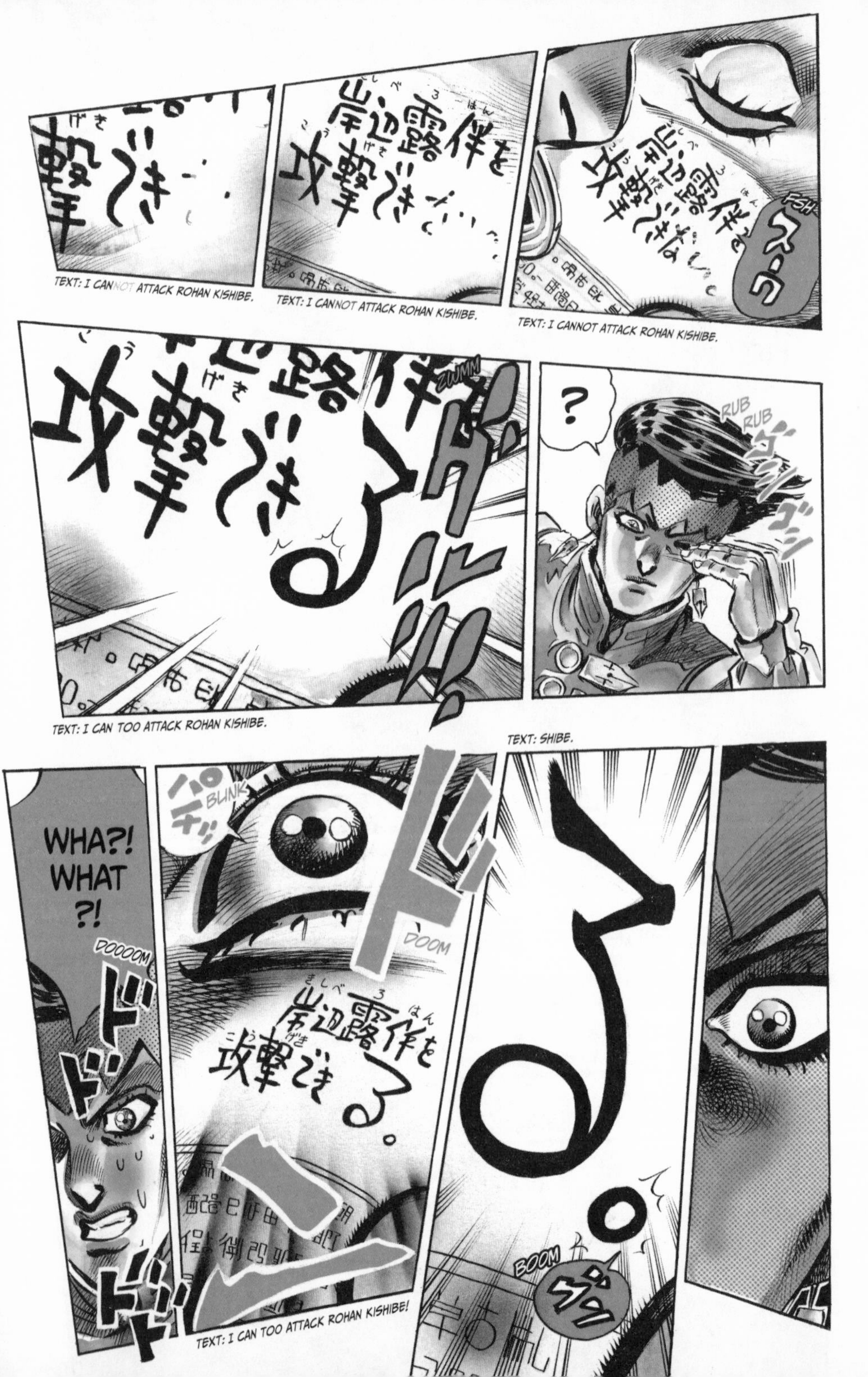

岸辺露伴を攻撃できない。
FSH
スーッ
TEXT: I CANNOT ATTACK ROHAN KISHIBE.
岸辺露伴を攻撃できない
TEXT: I CANNOT ATTACK ROHAN KISHIBE.
攻撃でき
TEXT: I CANNOT ATTACK ROHAN KISHIBE.
?
RUB RUB
ゴシゴシ
TEXT: SHIBE.
攻撃できる
ZWMM
TEXT: I CAN TOO ATTACK ROHAN KISHIBE.
る。
BOOM
ボン
BLINK
パチッ
DOOM
岸辺露伴を攻撃できる。
WHA?! WHAT ?!
DOOOOM
TEXT: I CAN TOO ATTACK ROHAN KISHIBE!

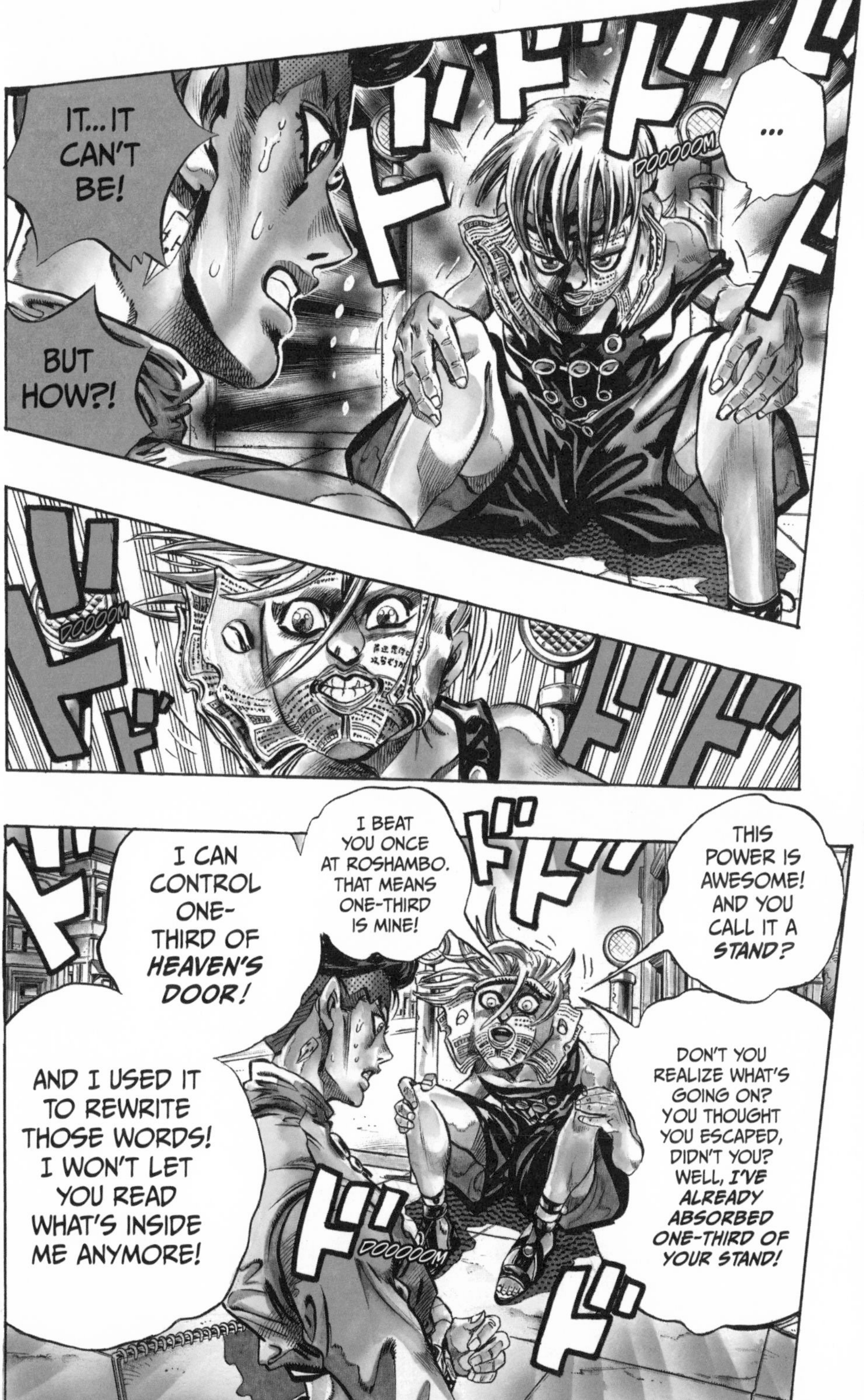
...
DOOOOOM
IT...IT CAN'T BE!
BUT HOW?!
DOOOOM
THIS POWER IS AWESOME! AND YOU CALL IT A *STAND?*
I BEAT YOU ONCE AT ROSHAMBO. THAT MEANS ONE-THIRD IS MINE!
I CAN CONTROL ONE-THIRD OF ***HEAVEN'S DOOR!***
DON'T YOU REALIZE WHAT'S GOING ON? YOU THOUGHT YOU ESCAPED, DIDN'T YOU? WELL, *I'VE* ***ALREADY ABSORBED ONE-THIRD OF YOUR STAND!***
AND I USED IT TO REWRITE THOSE WORDS! I WON'T LET YOU READ WHAT'S INSIDE ME ANYMORE!
DOOOOOM

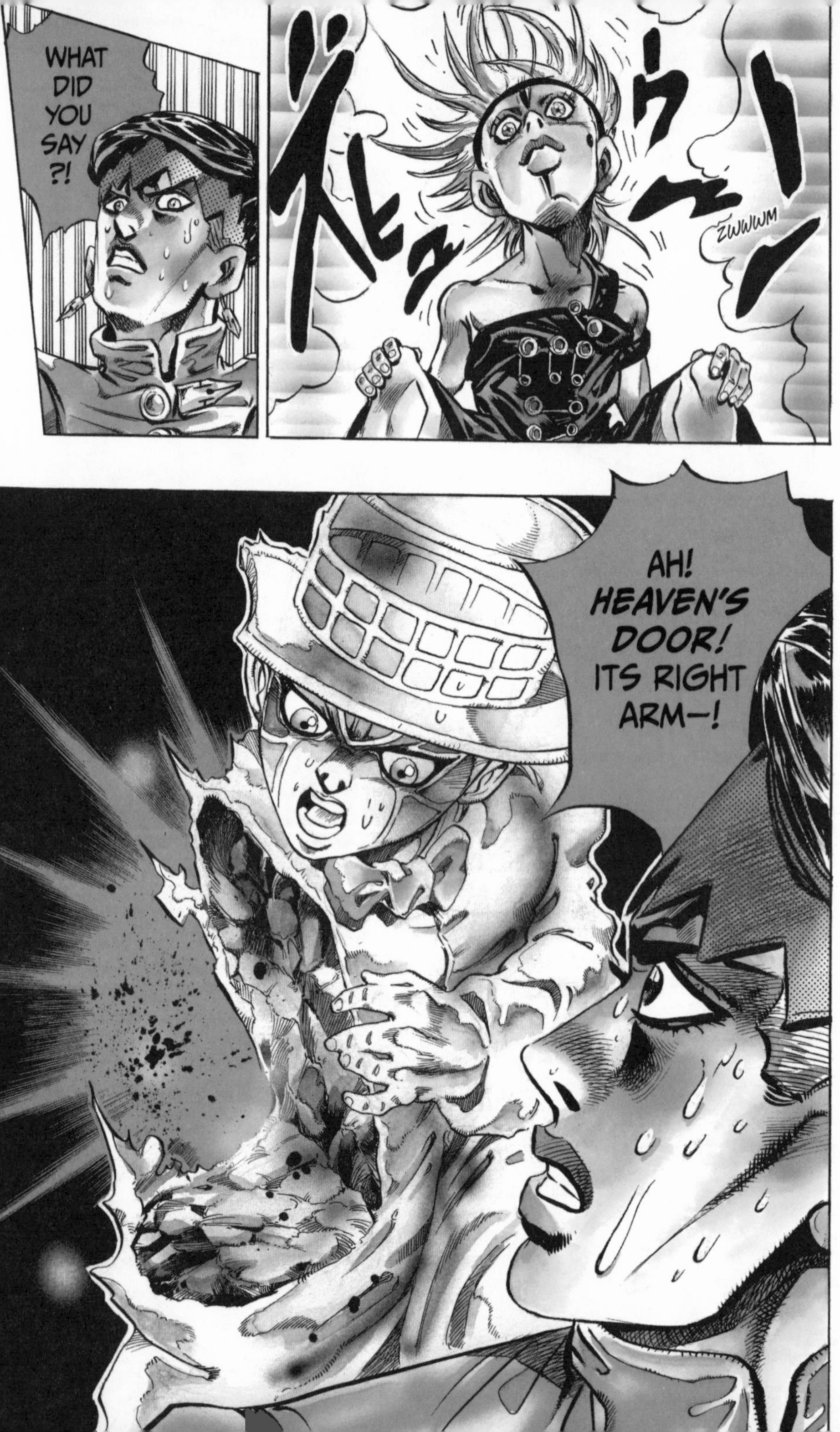
ZWWWM
WHAT DID YOU SAY?!
AH! HEAVEN'S DOOR! ITS RIGHT ARM—!

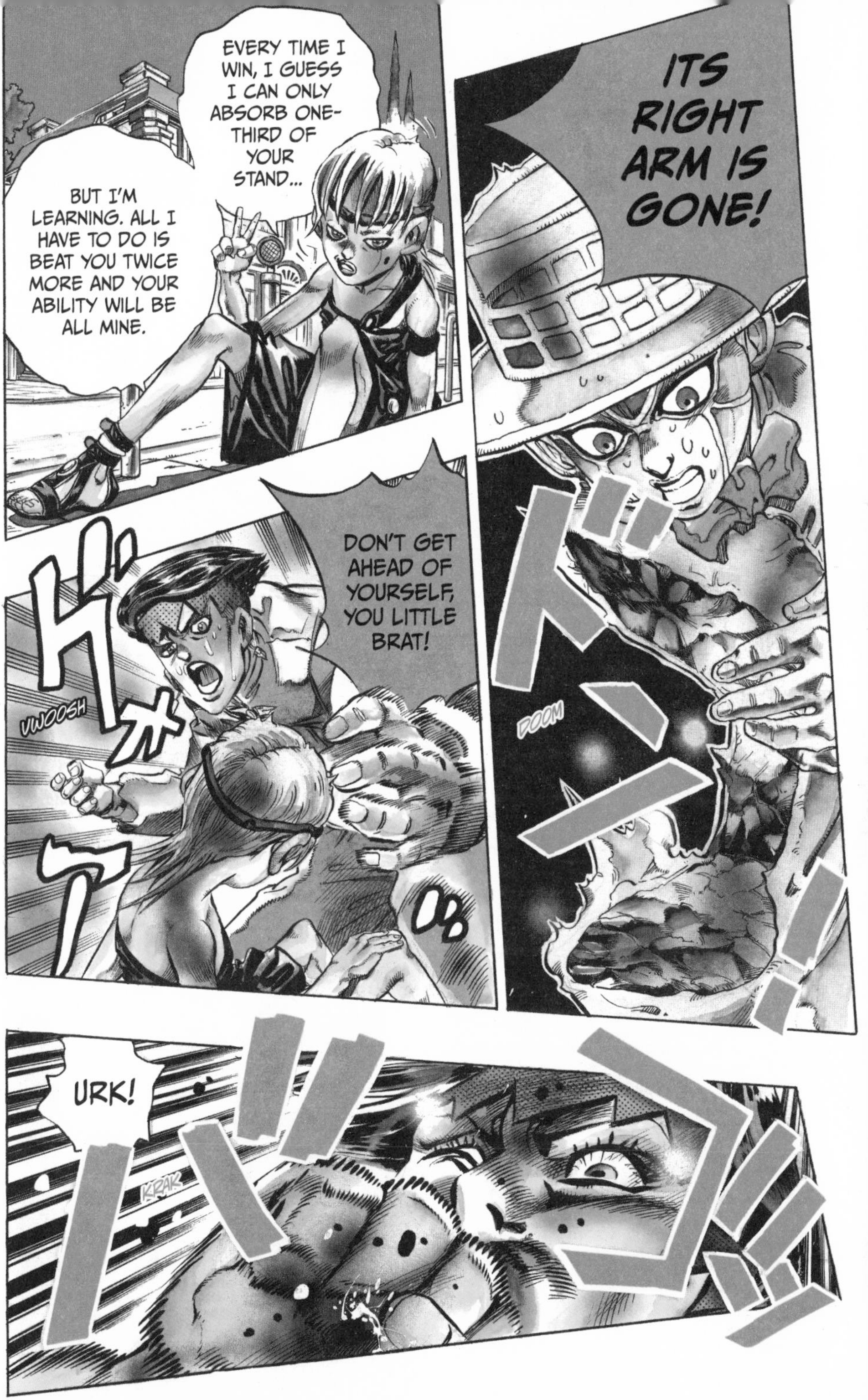
ITS RIGHT ARM IS GONE!
DOOM
EVERY TIME I WIN, I GUESS I CAN ONLY ABSORB ONE-THIRD OF YOUR STAND...
BUT I'M LEARNING. ALL I HAVE TO DO IS BEAT YOU TWICE MORE AND YOUR ABILITY WILL BE ALL MINE.
DON'T GET AHEAD OF YOURSELF, YOU LITTLE BRAT!
VWOOSH
URK!
KRAK

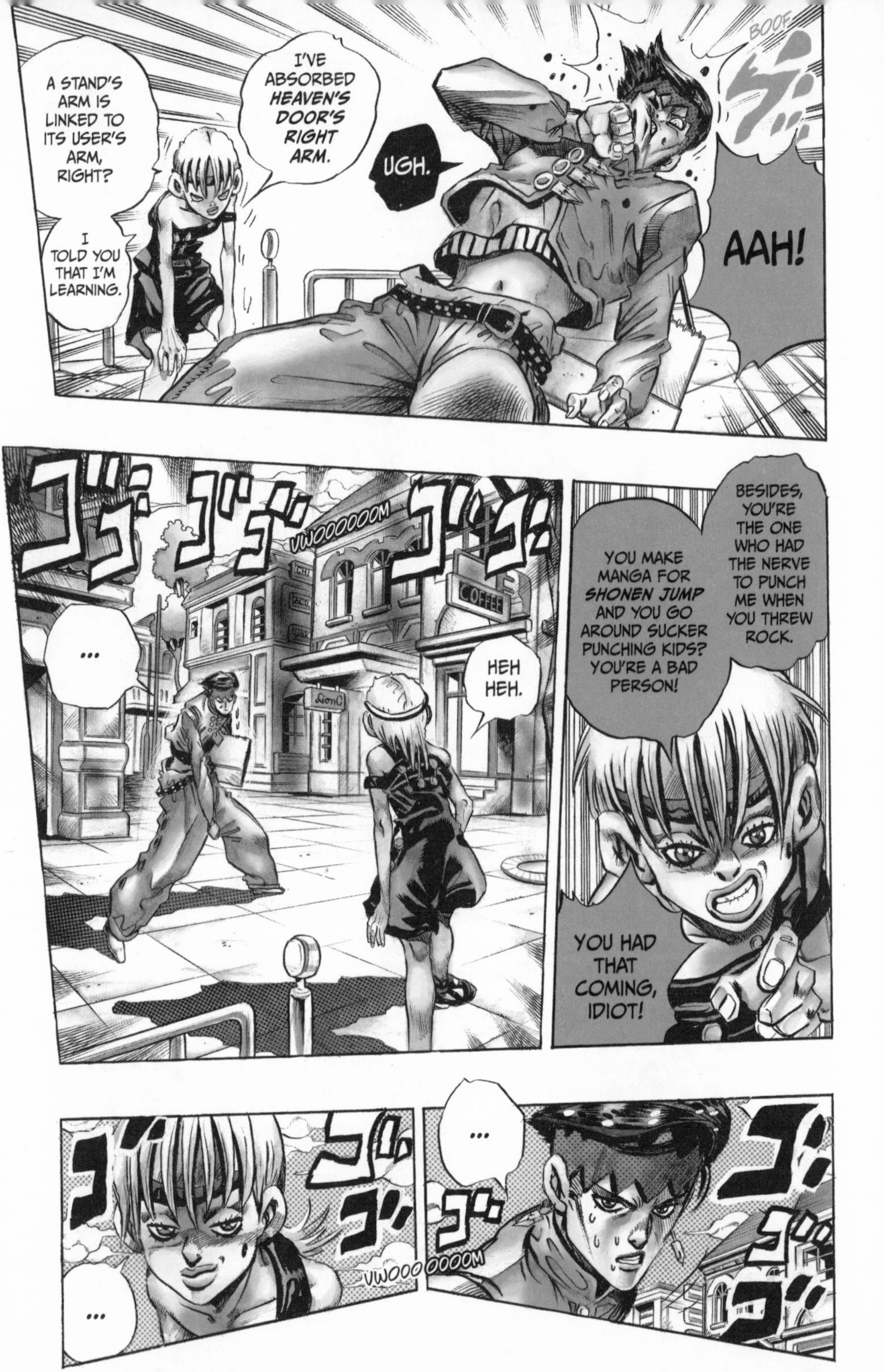
BOOF
AAH!
UGH.
I'VE ABSORBED HEAVEN'S DOOR'S RIGHT ARM.
A STAND'S ARM IS LINKED TO ITS USER'S ARM, RIGHT?
I TOLD YOU THAT I'M LEARNING.
BESIDES, YOU'RE THE ONE WHO HAD THE NERVE TO PUNCH ME WHEN YOU THREW ROCK.
YOU MAKE MANGA FOR SHONEN JUMP AND YOU GO AROUND SUCKER PUNCHING KIDS? YOU'RE A BAD PERSON!
YOU HAD THAT COMING, IDIOT!
VWOOOOOOOM
COFFEE
HEH HEH.
...
...
VWOOO OOOOM
...

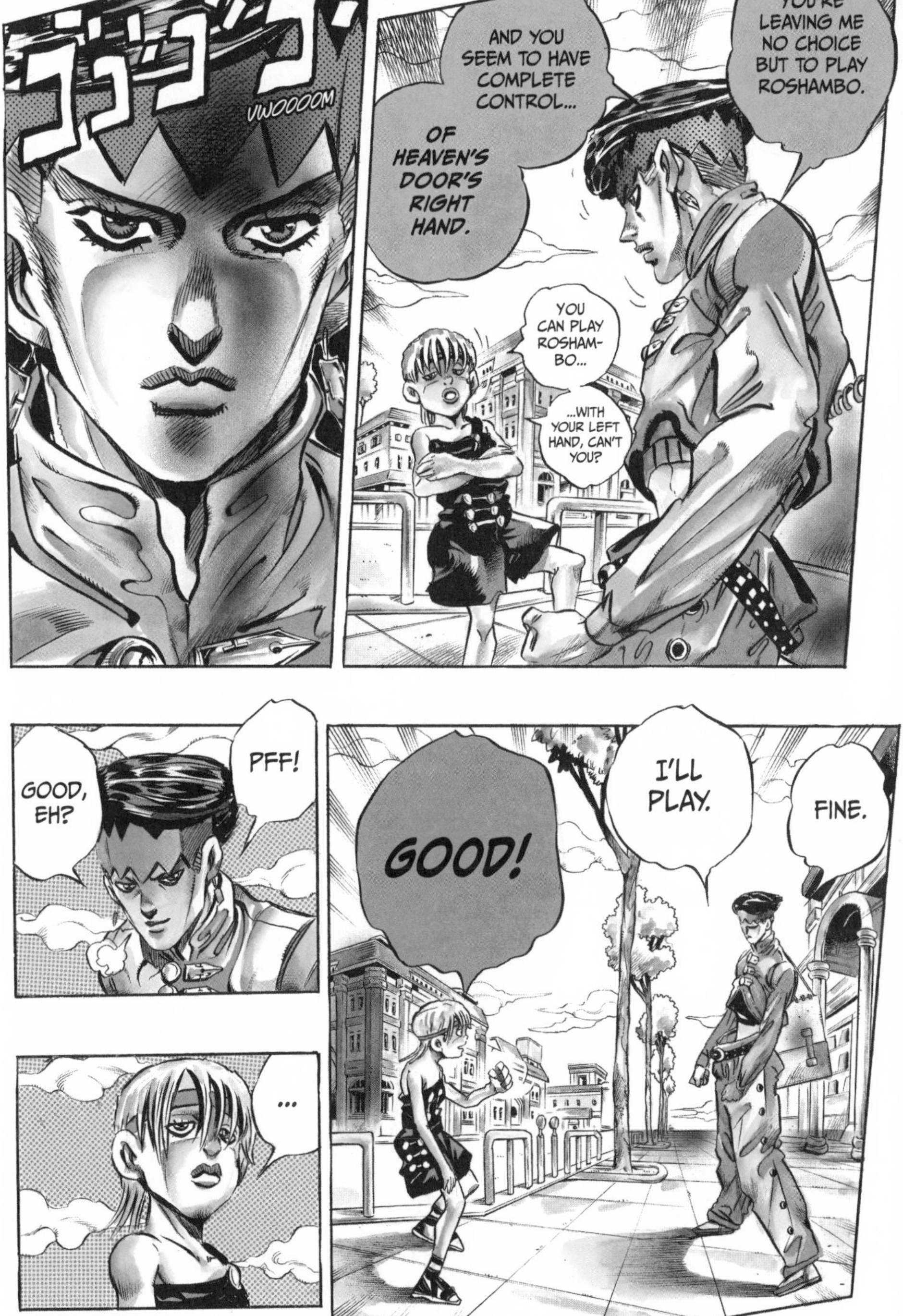
YOU'RE LEAVING ME NO CHOICE BUT TO PLAY ROSHAMBO.
AND YOU SEEM TO HAVE COMPLETE CONTROL...
OF HEAVEN'S DOOR'S RIGHT HAND.
YOU CAN PLAY ROSHAMBO...
...WITH YOUR LEFT HAND, CAN'T YOU?
VWOOOOM
FINE.
I'LL PLAY.
GOOD!
PFF!
GOOD, EH?
...

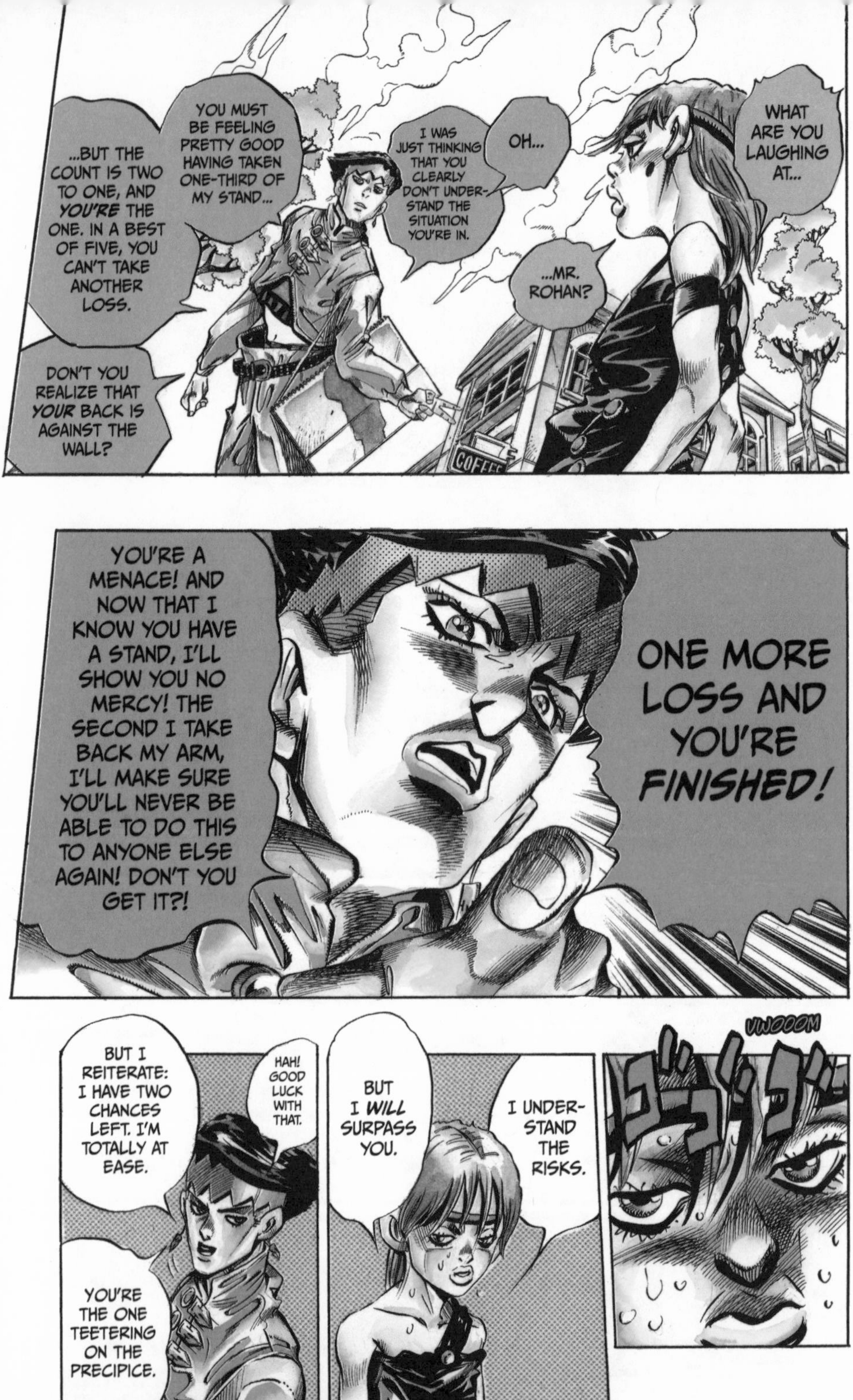
WHAT ARE YOU LAUGHING AT...
...MR. ROHAN?
OH...
I WAS JUST THINKING THAT YOU CLEARLY DON'T UNDER-STAND THE SITUATION YOU'RE IN.
YOU MUST BE FEELING PRETTY GOOD HAVING TAKEN ONE-THIRD OF MY STAND...
...BUT THE COUNT IS TWO TO ONE, AND *YOU'RE* THE ONE. IN A BEST OF FIVE, YOU CAN'T TAKE ANOTHER LOSS.
DON'T YOU REALIZE THAT *YOUR* BACK IS AGAINST THE WALL?
COFFEE
ONE MORE LOSS AND YOU'RE *FINISHED!*
YOU'RE A MENACE! AND NOW THAT I KNOW YOU HAVE A STAND, I'LL SHOW YOU NO MERCY! THE SECOND I TAKE BACK MY ARM, I'LL MAKE SURE YOU'LL NEVER BE ABLE TO DO THIS TO ANYONE ELSE AGAIN! DON'T YOU GET IT?!
VWOOOM
I UNDER-STAND THE RISKS.
BUT I *WILL* SURPASS YOU.
HAH! GOOD LUCK WITH THAT.
BUT I REITERATE: I HAVE TWO CHANCES LEFT. I'M TOTALLY AT EASE.
YOU'RE THE ONE TEETERING ON THE PRECIPICE.

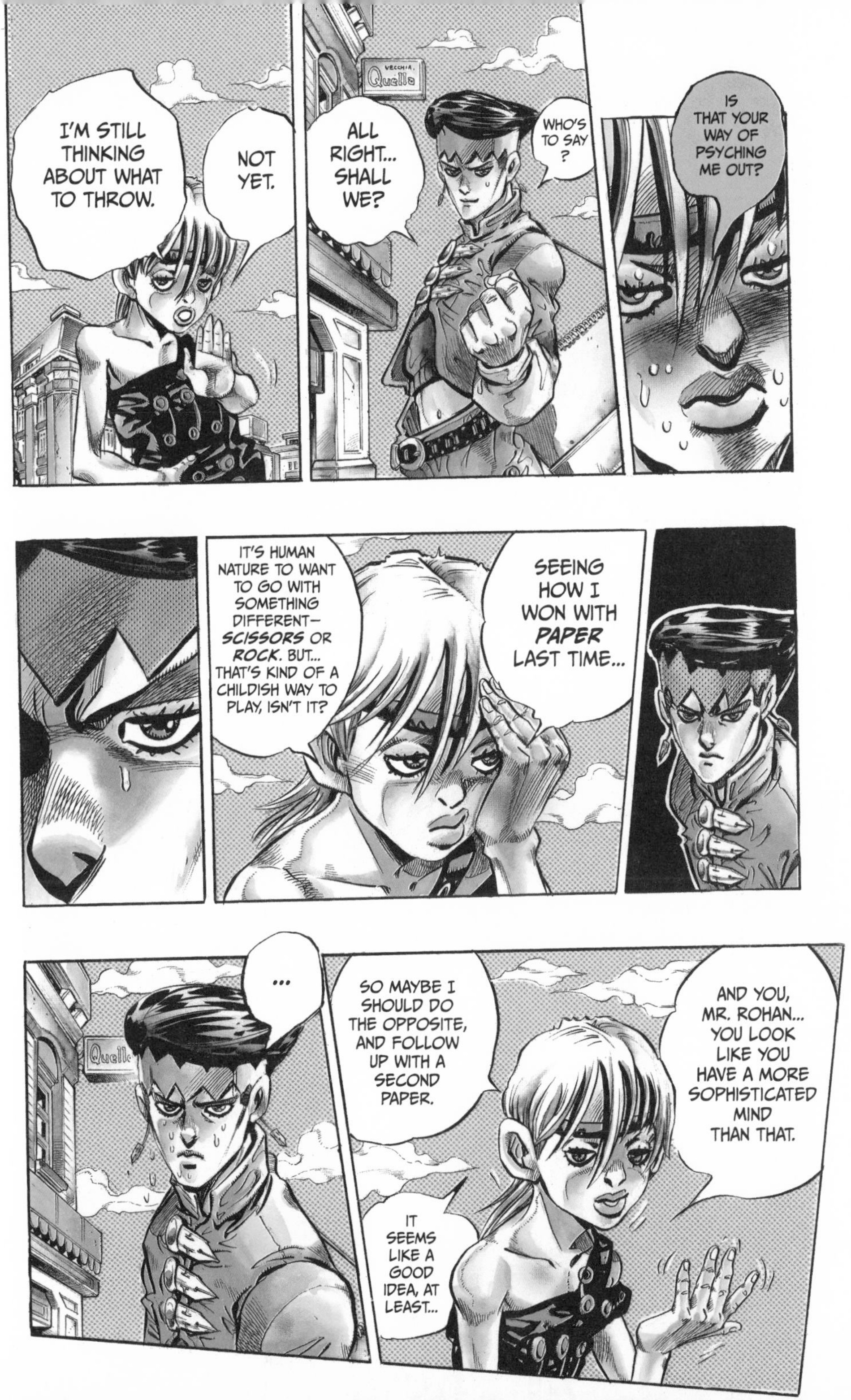
IS THAT YOUR WAY OF PSYCHING ME OUT?
WHO'S TO SAY?
ALL RIGHT... SHALL WE?
VECCHIA Quella
NOT YET.
I'M STILL THINKING ABOUT WHAT TO THROW.
SEEING HOW I WON WITH PAPER LAST TIME...
IT'S HUMAN NATURE TO WANT TO GO WITH SOMETHING DIFFERENT— SCISSORS OR ROCK. BUT... THAT'S KIND OF A CHILDISH WAY TO PLAY, ISN'T IT?
SO MAYBE I SHOULD DO THE OPPOSITE, AND FOLLOW UP WITH A SECOND PAPER.
IT SEEMS LIKE A GOOD IDEA, AT LEAST...
AND YOU, MR. ROHAN... YOU LOOK LIKE YOU HAVE A MORE SOPHISTICATED MIND THAN THAT.
...

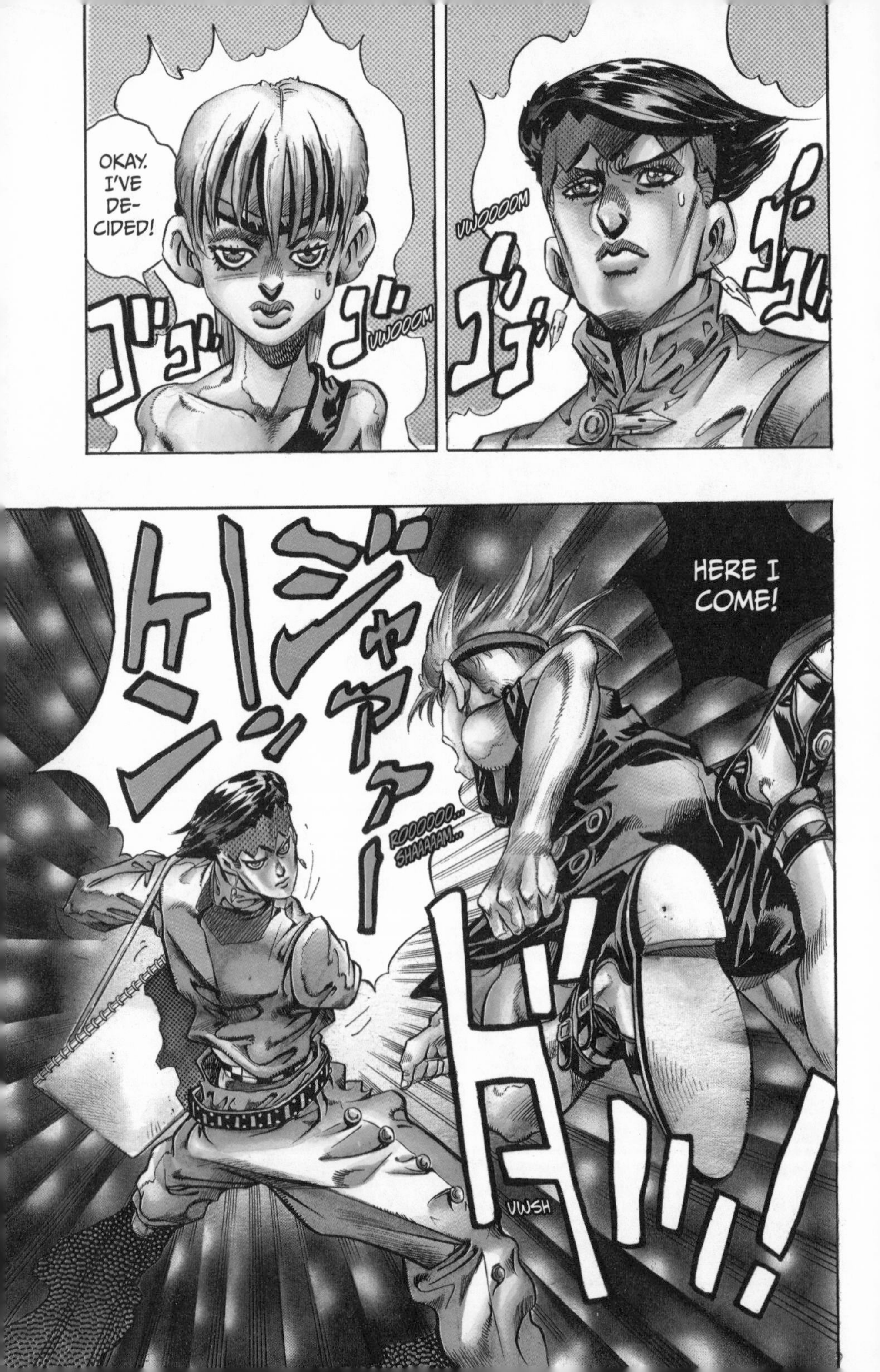
VWOOOOM
OKAY. I'VE DE-CIDED!
VWOOOM
HERE I COME!
ROOOOOO... SHAAAAAM...
VWSH

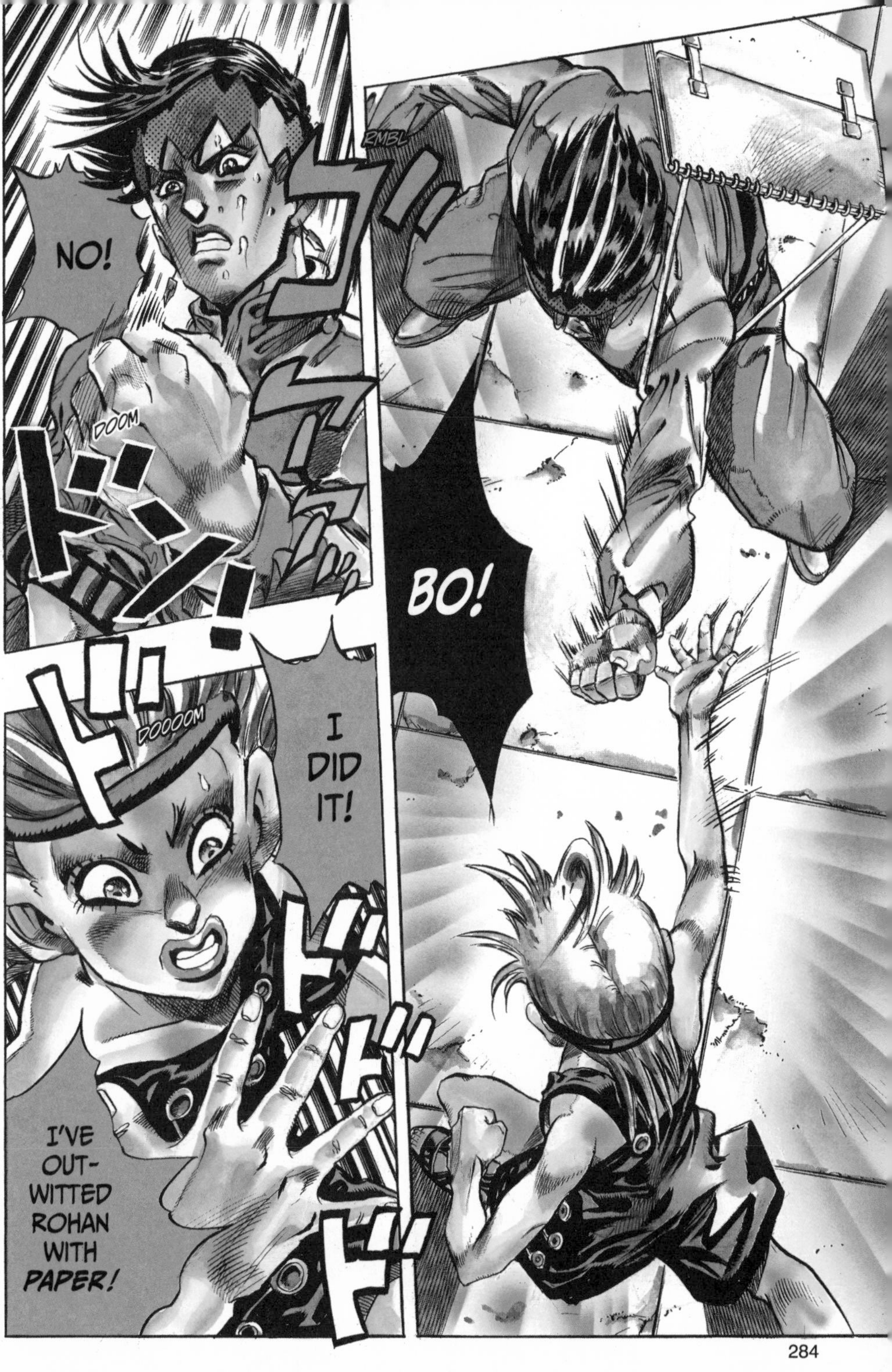
RMBL
BO!
NO!
DOOM
DOOOOM
I DID IT!
I'VE OUT-WITTED ROHAN WITH *PAPER!*

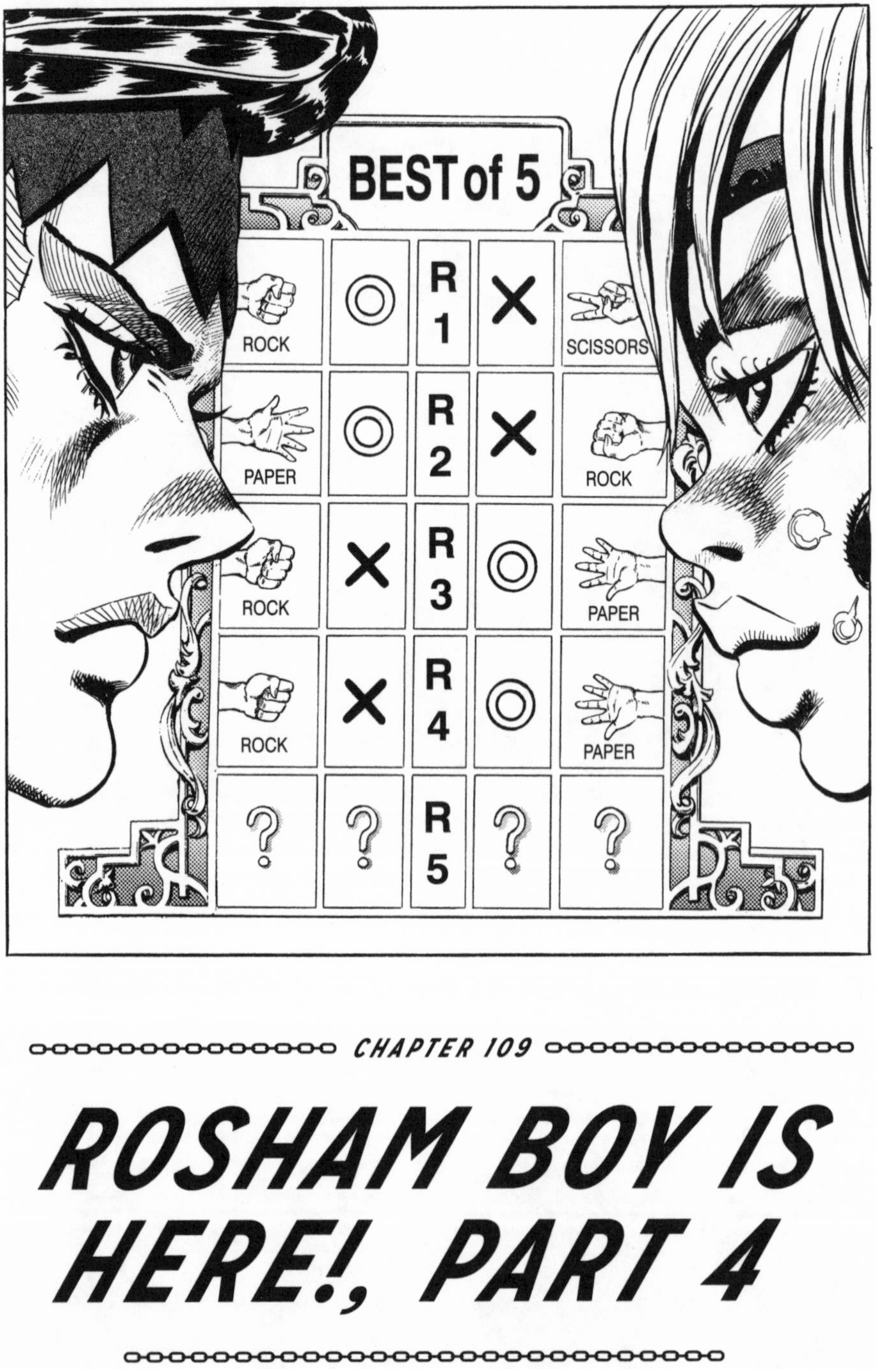
BEST of 5
ROCK
R 1
SCISSORS
PAPER
R 2
ROCK
ROCK
R 3
PAPER
ROCK
R 4
PAPER
?
?
R 5
?
?

CHAPTER 109

ROSHAM BOY IS HERE!, PART 4

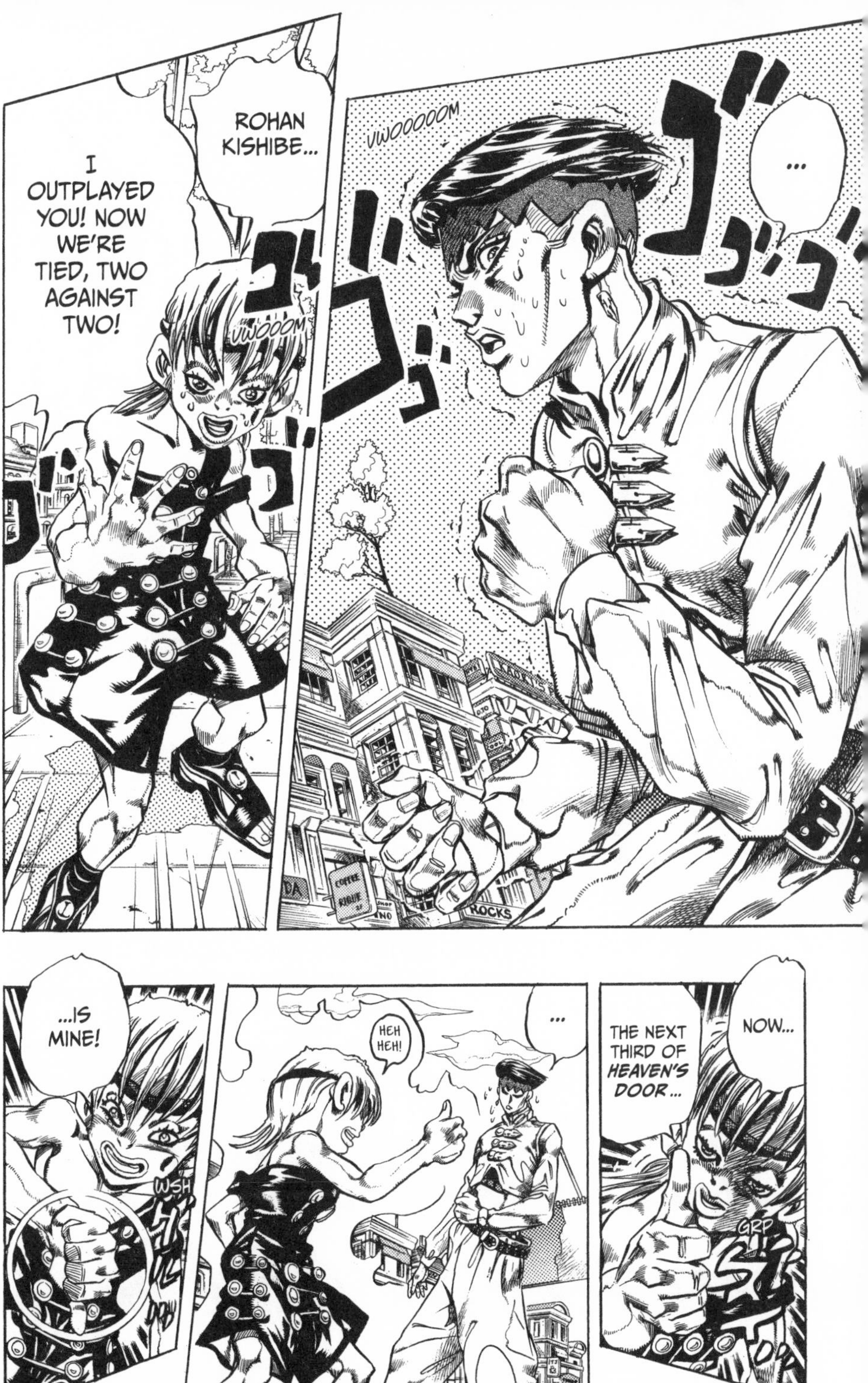
...
VWOOOOOM
ROCKS
ROHAN KISHIBE...
I OUTPLAYED YOU! NOW WE'RE TIED, TWO AGAINST TWO!
VWOOOM
NOW...
THE NEXT THIRD OF *HEAVEN'S DOOR*...
GRP
...
HEH HEH!
...IS MINE!
WSH

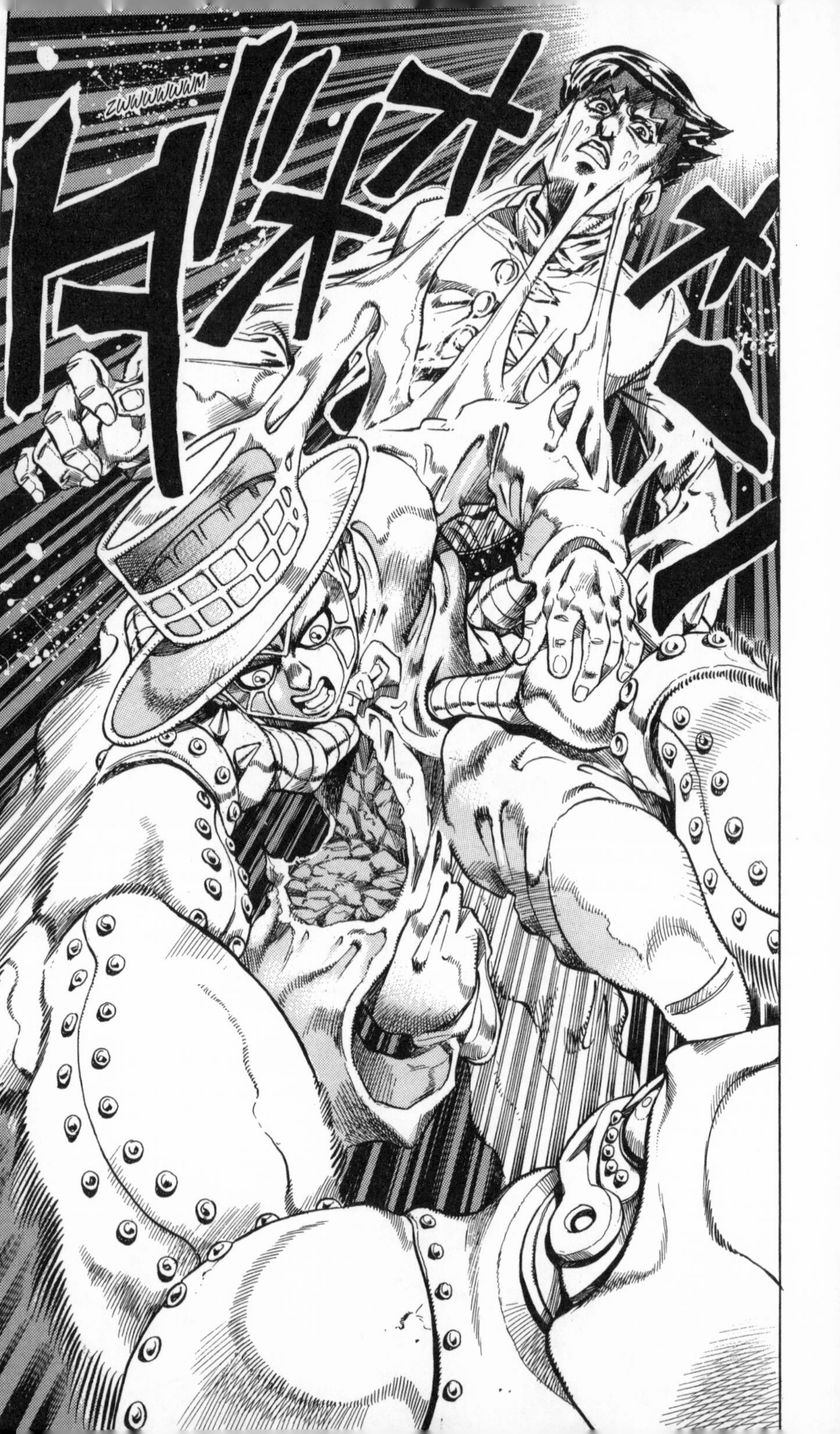
ZWWWWWWM

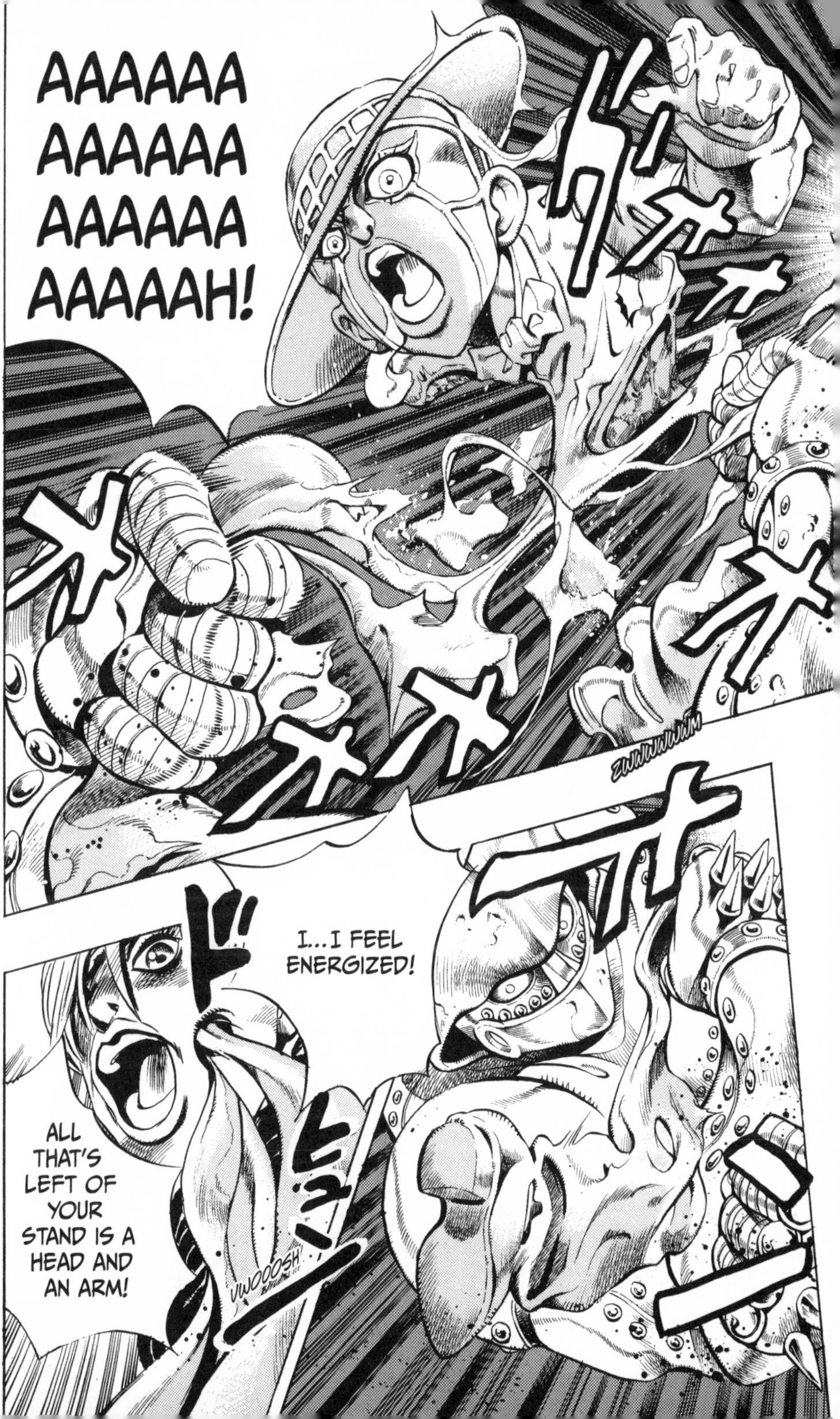
AAAAAA
AAAAAA
AAAAAA
AAAAAH!
ZWWWWWWM
I...I FEEL ENERGIZED!
ALL THAT'S LEFT OF YOUR STAND IS A HEAD AND AN ARM!
VWOOOSH

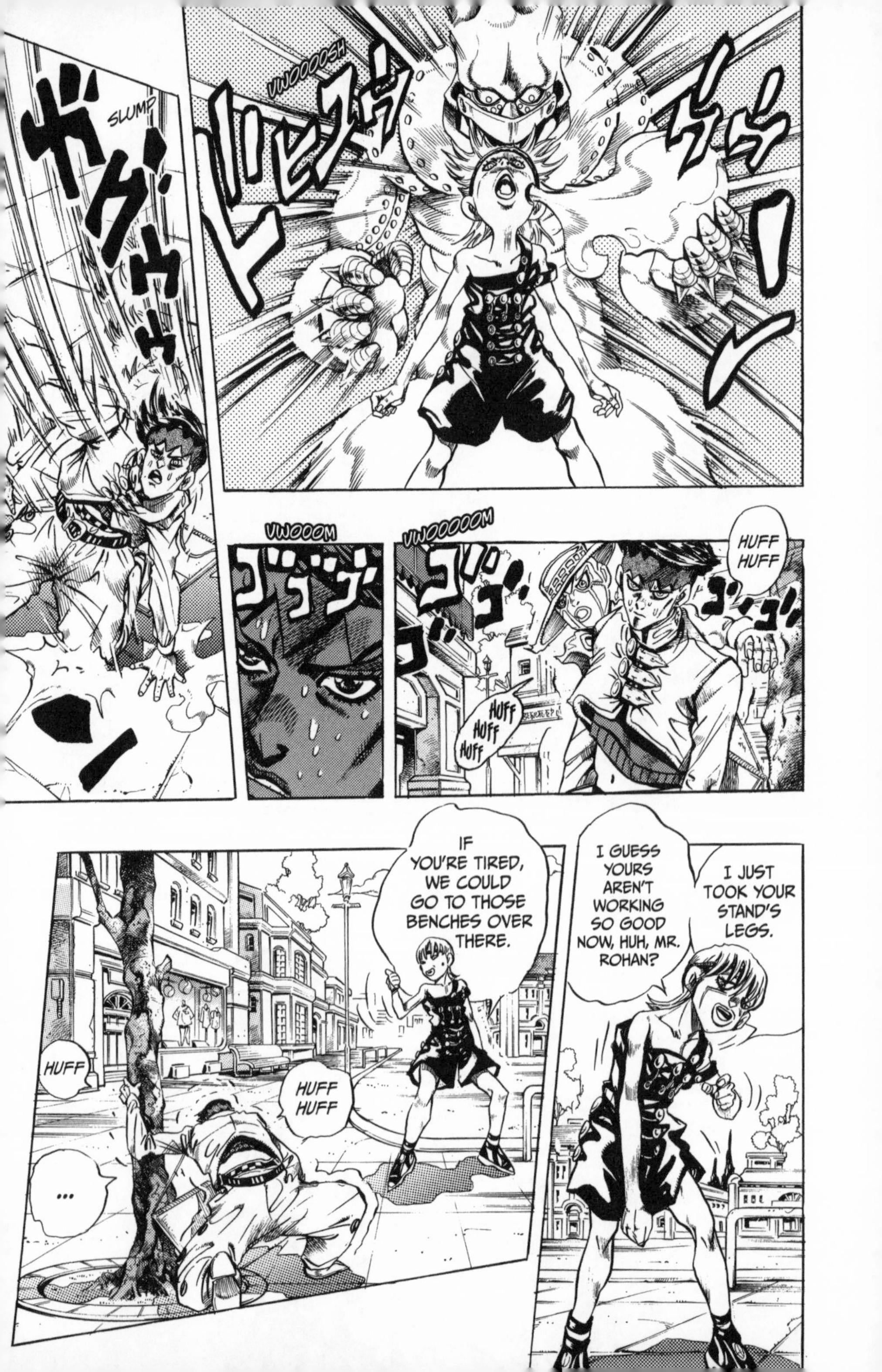
VWOOOOSH
HUFF
HUFF
VWOOOOOM
HUFF
HUFF
HUFF
VWOOOM
SLUMP
I JUST TOOK YOUR STAND'S LEGS.
I GUESS YOURS AREN'T WORKING SO GOOD NOW, HUH, MR. ROHAN?
IF YOU'RE TIRED, WE COULD GO TO THOSE BENCHES OVER THERE.
HUFF HUFF
HUFF
...

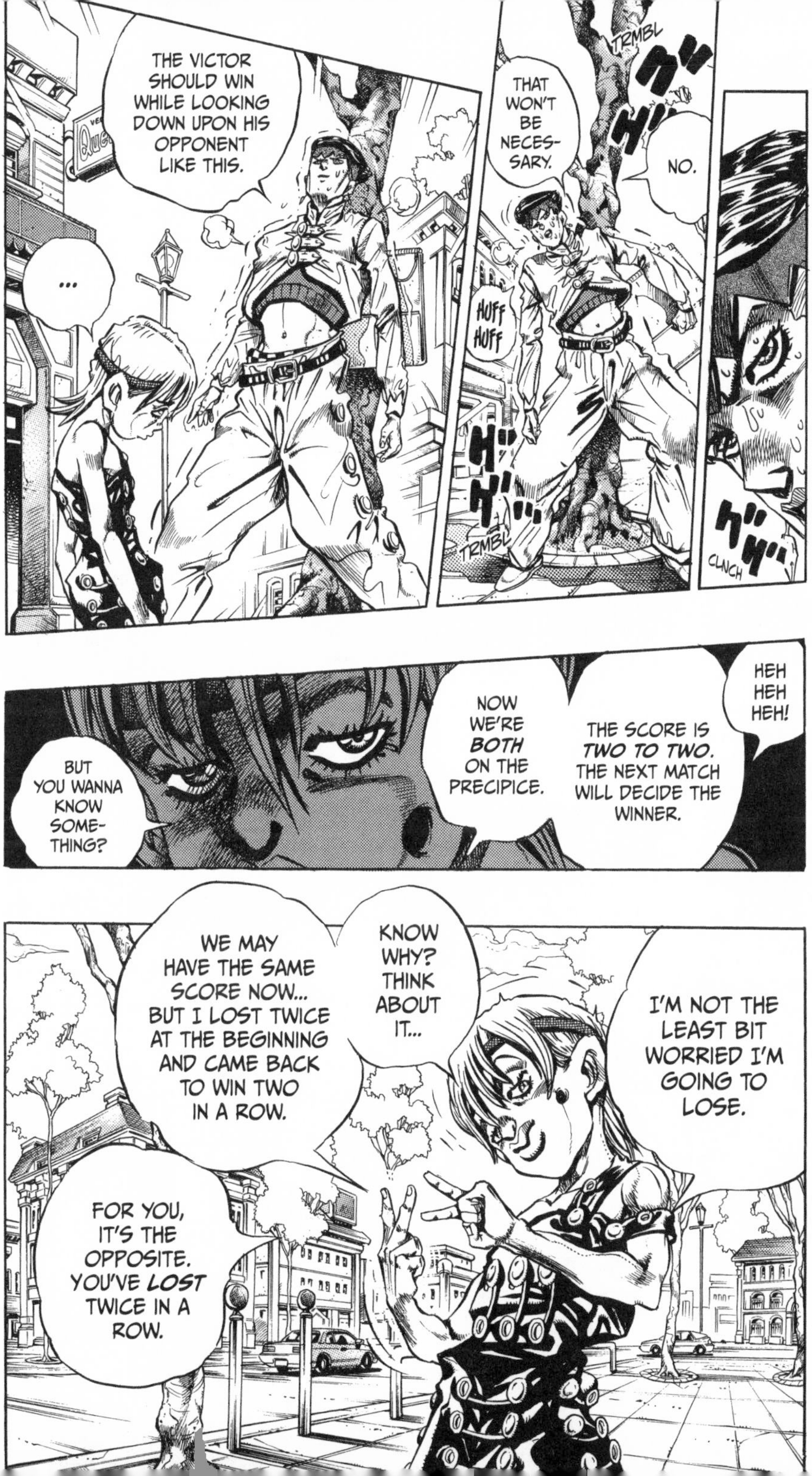
CLNCH
NO.
TRMBL
THAT WON'T BE NECES-SARY.
HUFF HUFF
TRMBL
THE VICTOR SHOULD WIN WHILE LOOKING DOWN UPON HIS OPPONENT LIKE THIS.
...
HEH HEH HEH!
THE SCORE IS *TWO TO TWO.* THE NEXT MATCH WILL DECIDE THE WINNER.
NOW WE'RE *BOTH* ON THE PRECIPICE.
BUT YOU WANNA KNOW SOME-THING?
I'M NOT THE LEAST BIT WORRIED I'M GOING TO LOSE.
KNOW WHY? THINK ABOUT IT...
WE MAY HAVE THE SAME SCORE NOW... BUT I LOST TWICE AT THE BEGINNING AND CAME BACK TO WIN TWO IN A ROW.
FOR YOU, IT'S THE OPPOSITE. YOU'VE *LOST* TWICE IN A ROW.

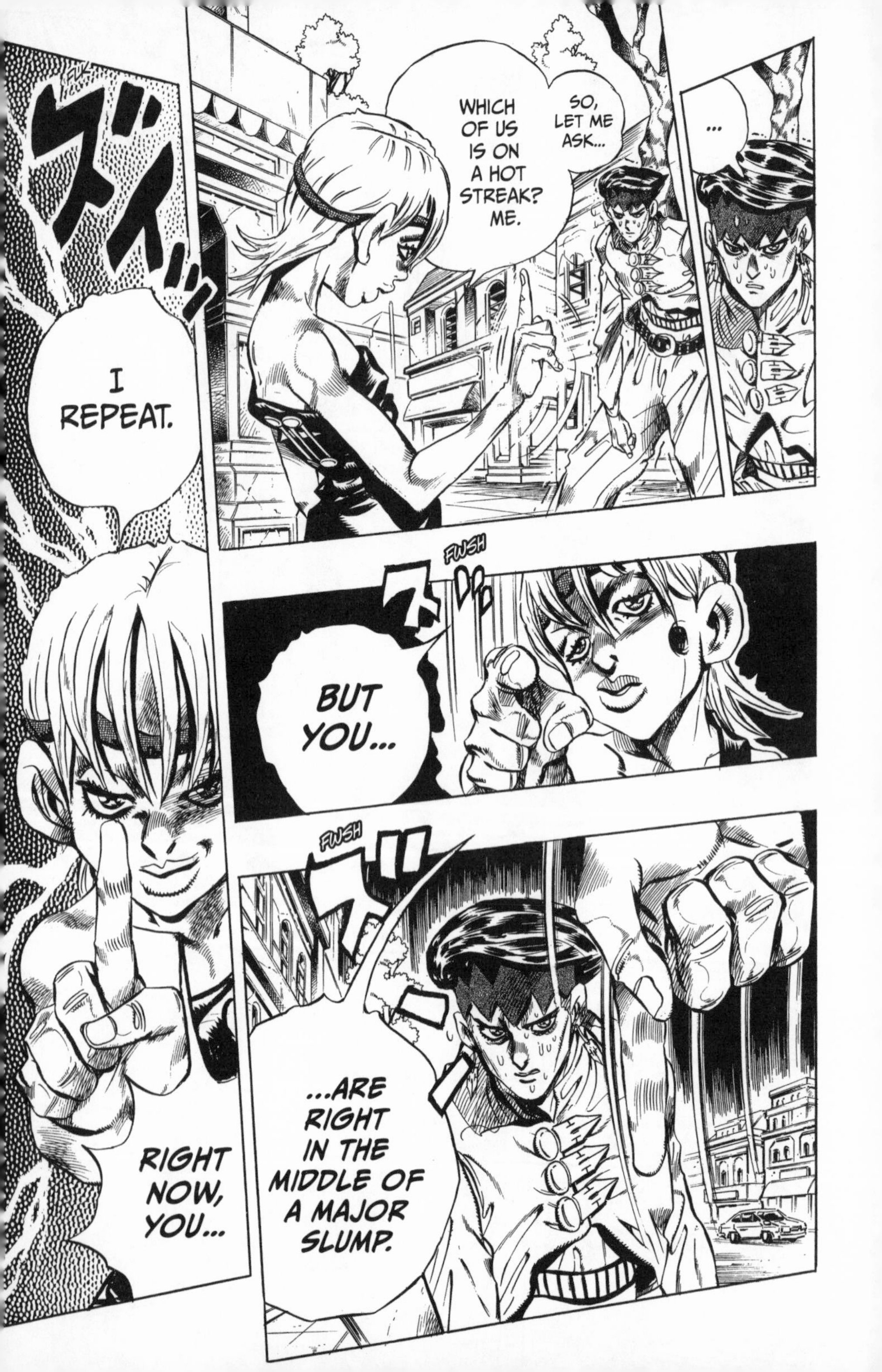
...
SO, LET ME ASK...
WHICH OF US IS ON A HOT STREAK? ME.
FWSH
BUT YOU...
FWSH
...ARE RIGHT IN THE MIDDLE OF A MAJOR SLUMP.
I REPEAT.
RIGHT NOW, YOU...

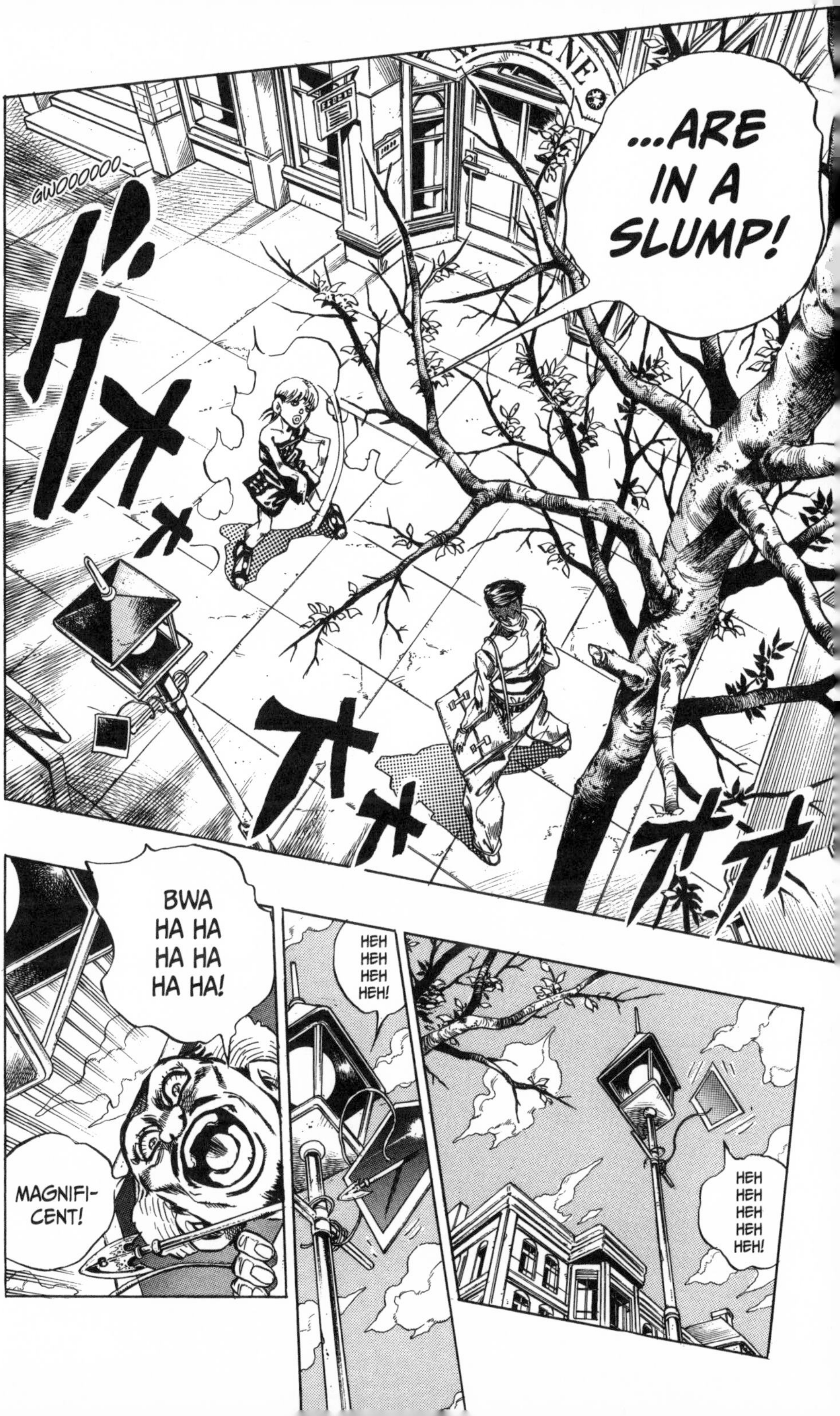
...ARE IN A SLUMP!
GWOOOOOO
HEH HEH HEH HEH HEH!
HEH HEH HEH HEH!
BWA HA HA HA HA HA HA!
MAGNIFI-CENT!

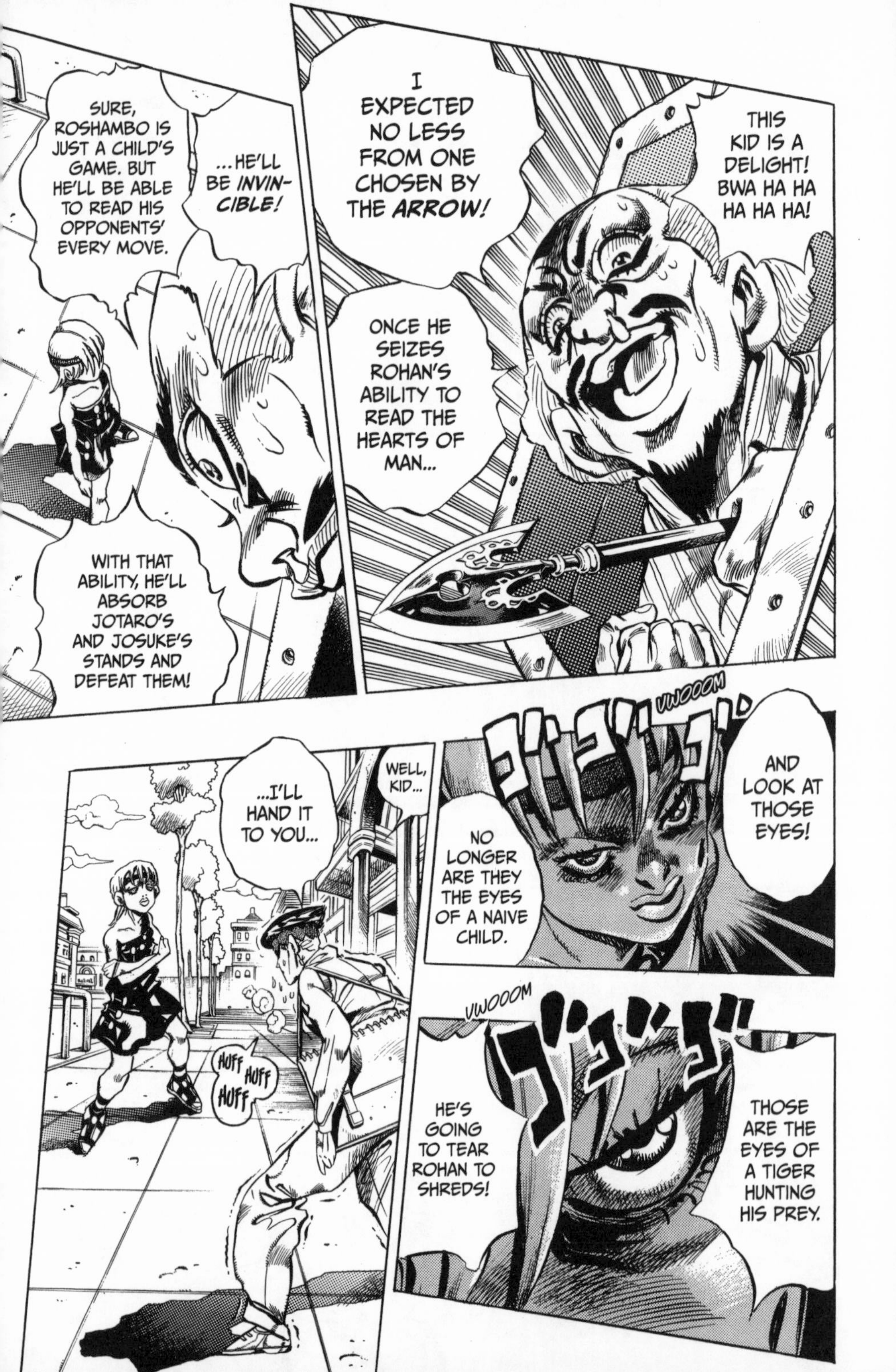
THIS KID IS A DELIGHT! BWA HA HA HA HA HA!
I EXPECTED NO LESS FROM ONE CHOSEN BY THE *ARROW!*
ONCE HE SEIZES ROHAN'S ABILITY TO READ THE HEARTS OF MAN...
SURE, ROSHAMBO IS JUST A CHILD'S GAME. BUT HE'LL BE ABLE TO READ HIS OPPONENTS' EVERY MOVE.
...HE'LL BE *INVINCIBLE!*
WITH THAT ABILITY, HE'LL ABSORB JOTARO'S AND JOSUKE'S STANDS AND DEFEAT THEM!
VWOOOM
AND LOOK AT THOSE EYES!
NO LONGER ARE THEY THE EYES OF A NAIVE CHILD.
VWOOOM
THOSE ARE THE EYES OF A TIGER HUNTING HIS PREY.
HE'S GOING TO TEAR ROHAN TO SHREDS!
WELL, KID...
...I'LL HAND IT TO YOU...
HUFF HUFF HUFF

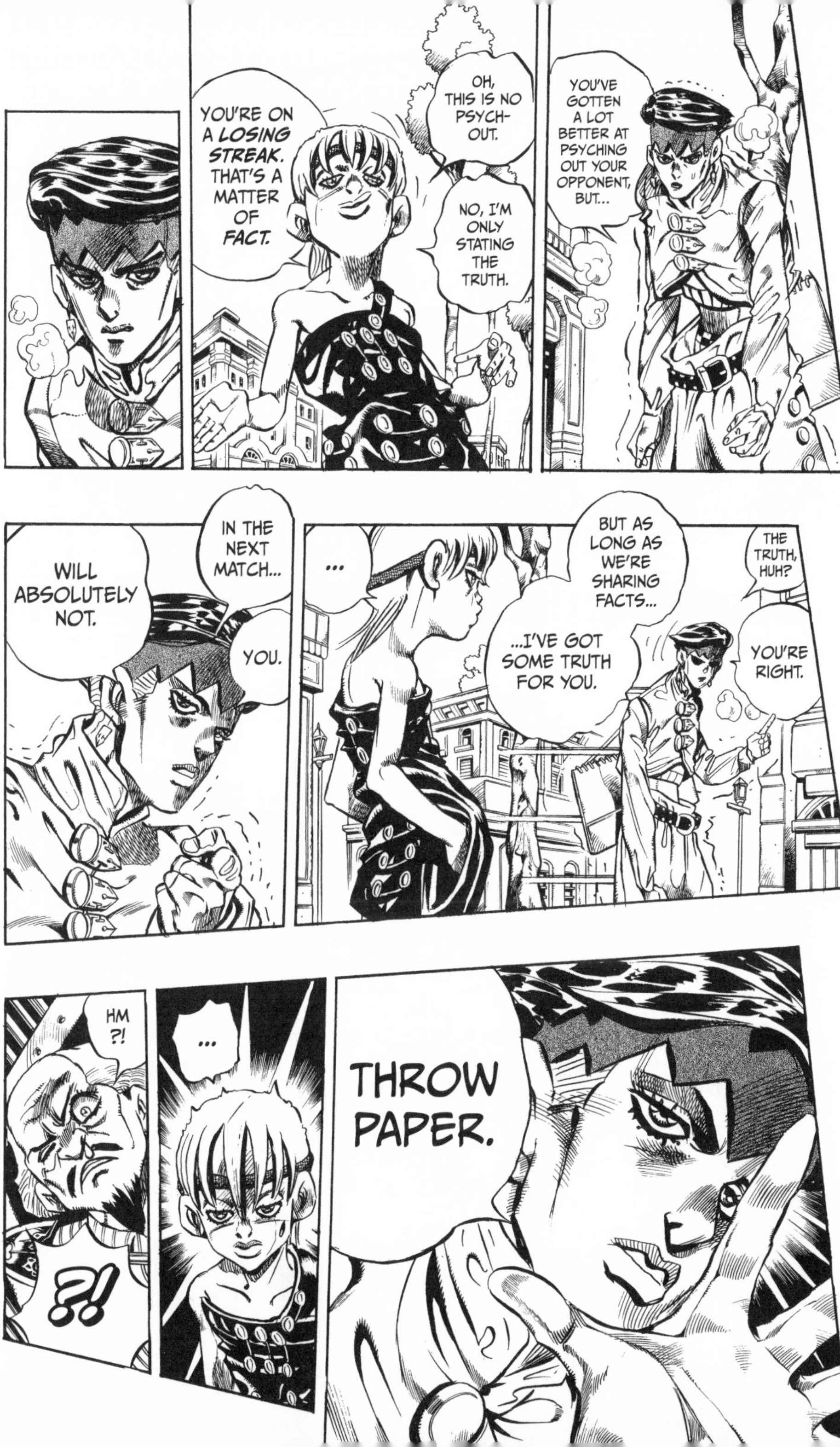
YOU'VE GOTTEN A LOT BETTER AT PSYCHING OUT YOUR OPPONENT, BUT...
OH, THIS IS NO PSYCH-OUT.
NO, I'M ONLY STATING THE TRUTH.
YOU'RE ON A LOSING STREAK. THAT'S A MATTER OF FACT.
THE TRUTH, HUH?
YOU'RE RIGHT.
BUT AS LONG AS WE'RE SHARING FACTS...
...I'VE GOT SOME TRUTH FOR YOU.
...
IN THE NEXT MATCH...
YOU.
WILL ABSOLUTELY NOT.
THROW PAPER.
...
HM ?!
?!

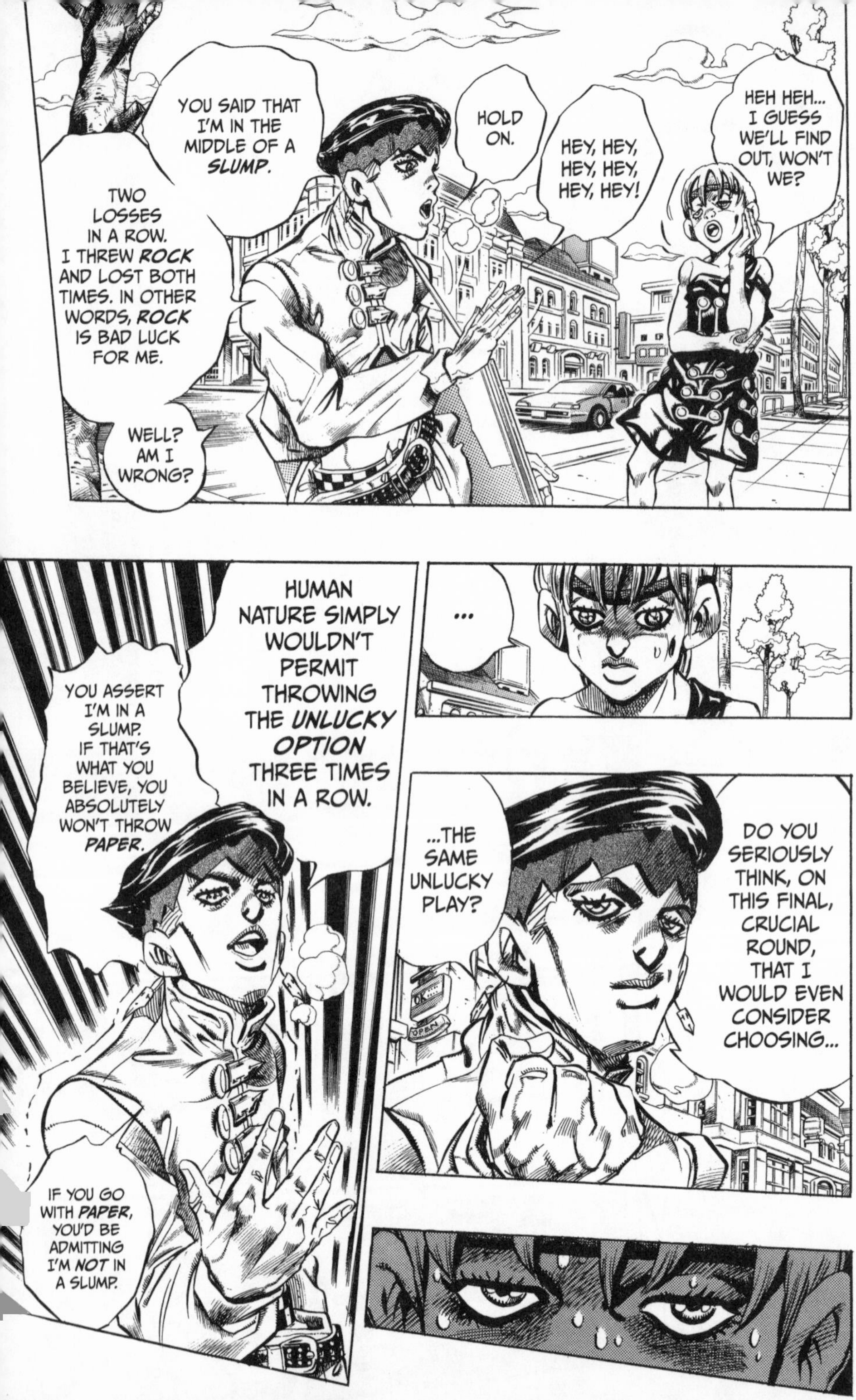
HEH HEH... I GUESS WE'LL FIND OUT, WON'T WE?
HEY, HEY, HEY, HEY, HEY, HEY!
HOLD ON.
YOU SAID THAT I'M IN THE MIDDLE OF A *SLUMP*.
TWO LOSSES IN A ROW. I THREW *ROCK* AND LOST BOTH TIMES. IN OTHER WORDS, *ROCK* IS BAD LUCK FOR ME.
WELL? AM I WRONG?
...
DO YOU SERIOUSLY THINK, ON THIS FINAL, CRUCIAL ROUND, THAT I WOULD EVEN CONSIDER CHOOSING...
...THE SAME UNLUCKY PLAY?
HUMAN NATURE SIMPLY WOULDN'T PERMIT THROWING THE *UNLUCKY OPTION* THREE TIMES IN A ROW.
YOU ASSERT I'M IN A SLUMP. IF THAT'S WHAT YOU BELIEVE, YOU ABSOLUTELY WON'T THROW *PAPER*.
IF YOU GO WITH *PAPER*, YOU'D BE ADMITTING I'M *NOT* IN A SLUMP.

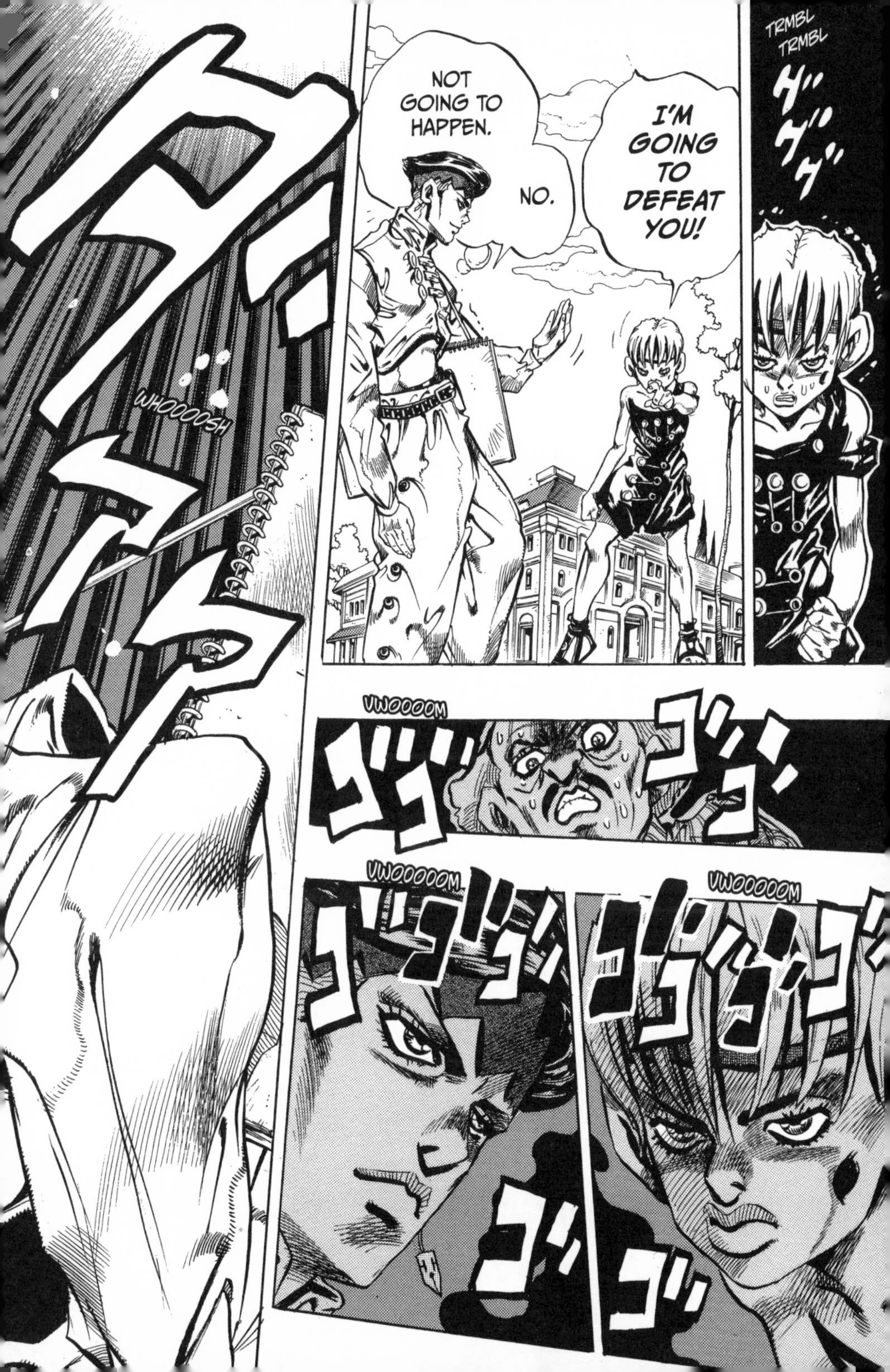
TRMBL TRMBL
I'M GOING TO DEFEAT YOU!
NO.
NOT GOING TO HAPPEN.
VWOOOOM
VWOOOOOM
VWOOOOOM
WHOOOOSH

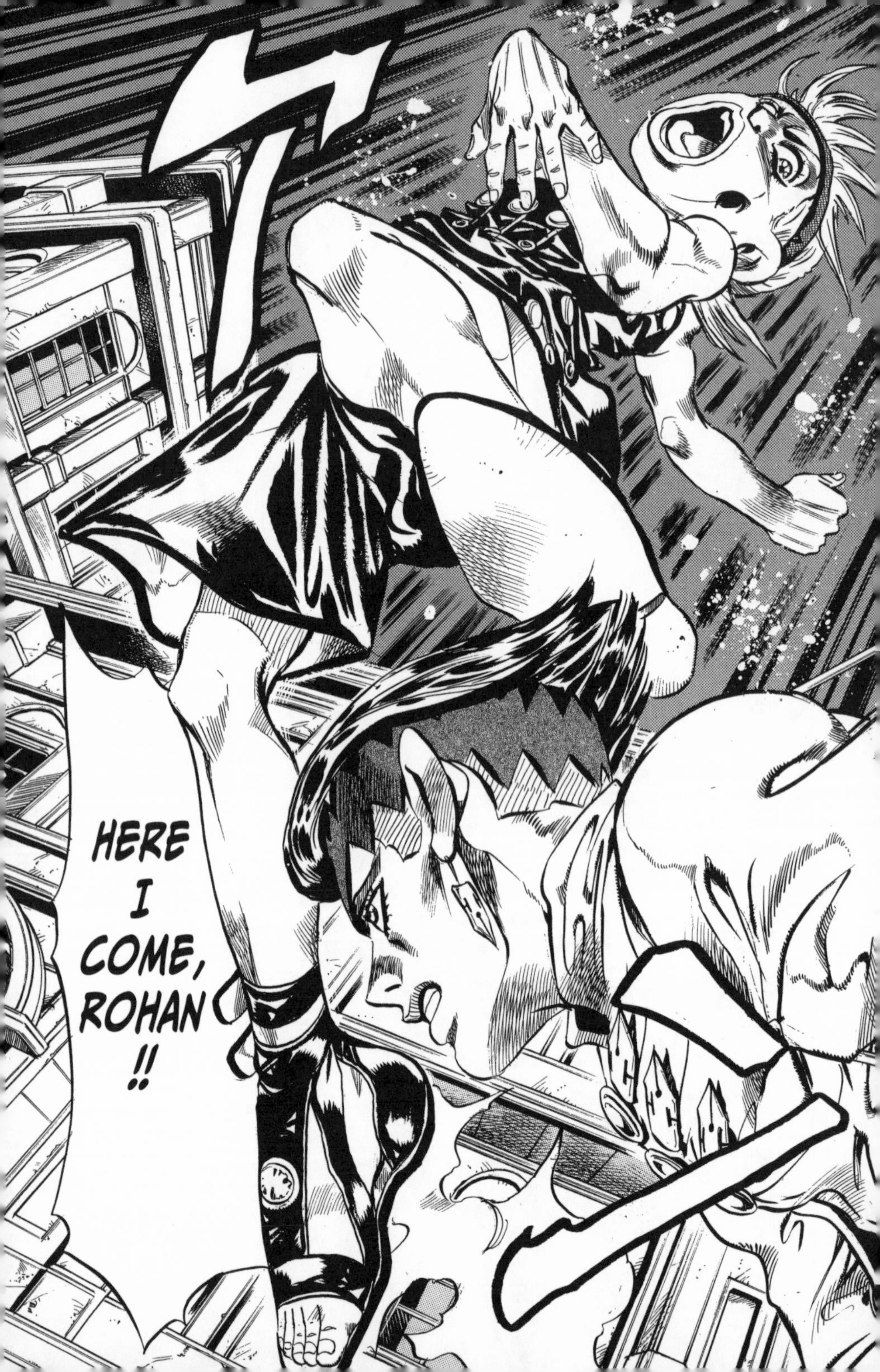
HERE I COME, ROHAN!!

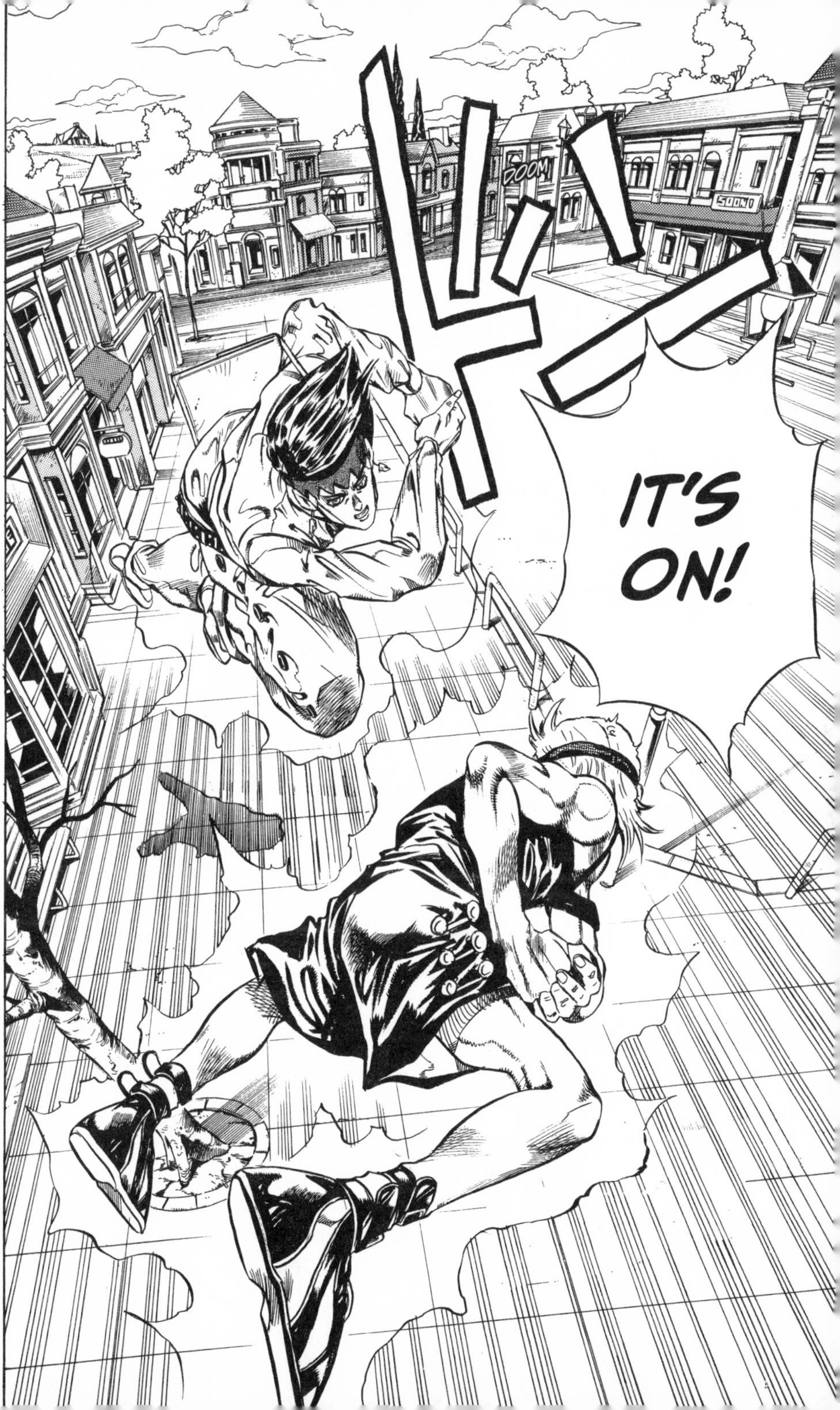
IT'S ON!
DOOM
SOON!

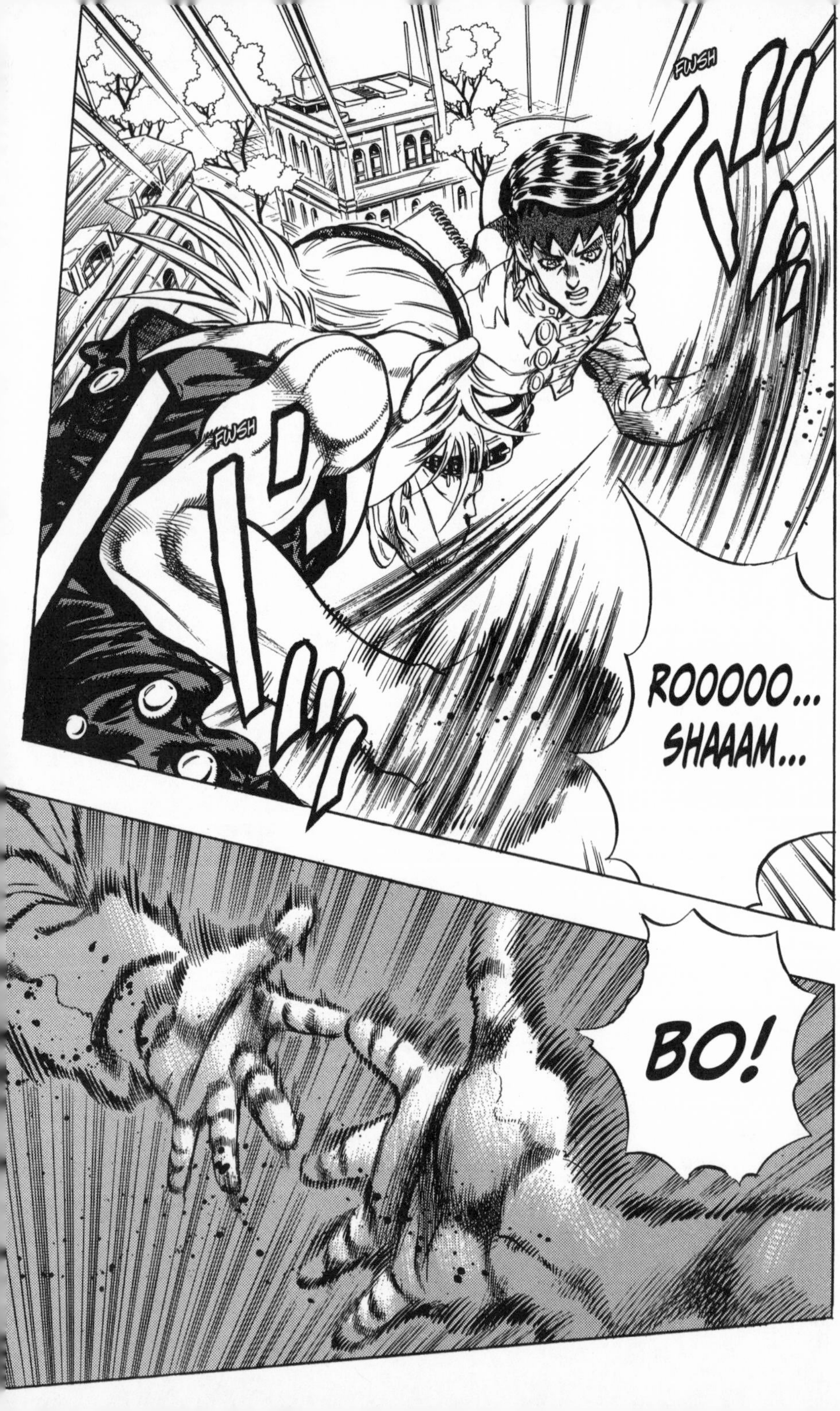
FWSH
FWSH
ROOOOO... SHAAAM...
BO!

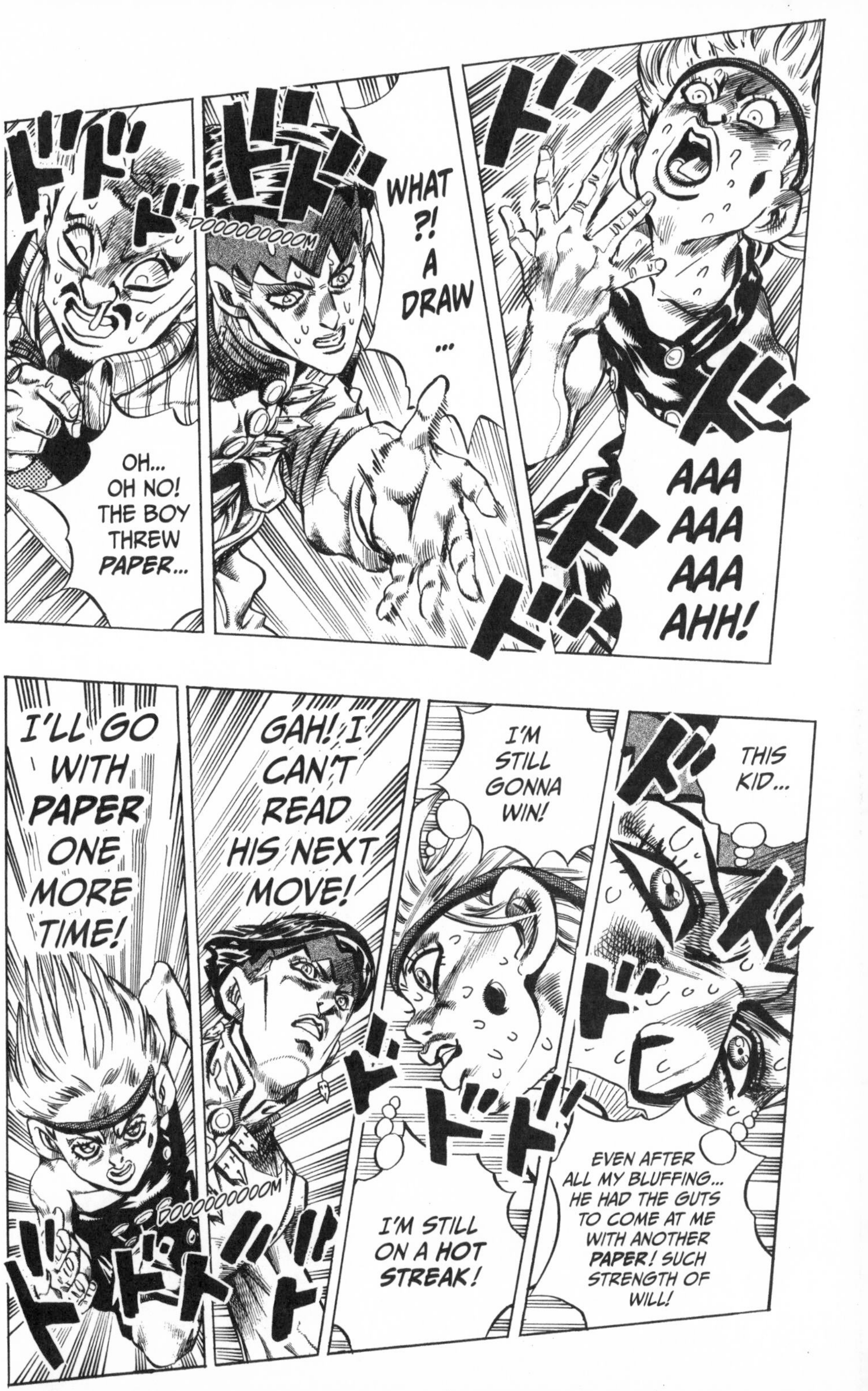
AAA AAA AAA AHH!
WHAT ?! A DRAW ...
DOOOOOOOOOOM
OH... OH NO! THE BOY THREW PAPER...
THIS KID...
EVEN AFTER ALL MY BLUFFING... HE HAD THE GUTS TO COME AT ME WITH ANOTHER PAPER! SUCH STRENGTH OF WILL!
I'M STILL GONNA WIN!
I'M STILL ON A HOT STREAK!
GAH! I CAN'T READ HIS NEXT MOVE!
DOOOOOOOOOOM
I'LL GO WITH PAPER ONE MORE TIME!

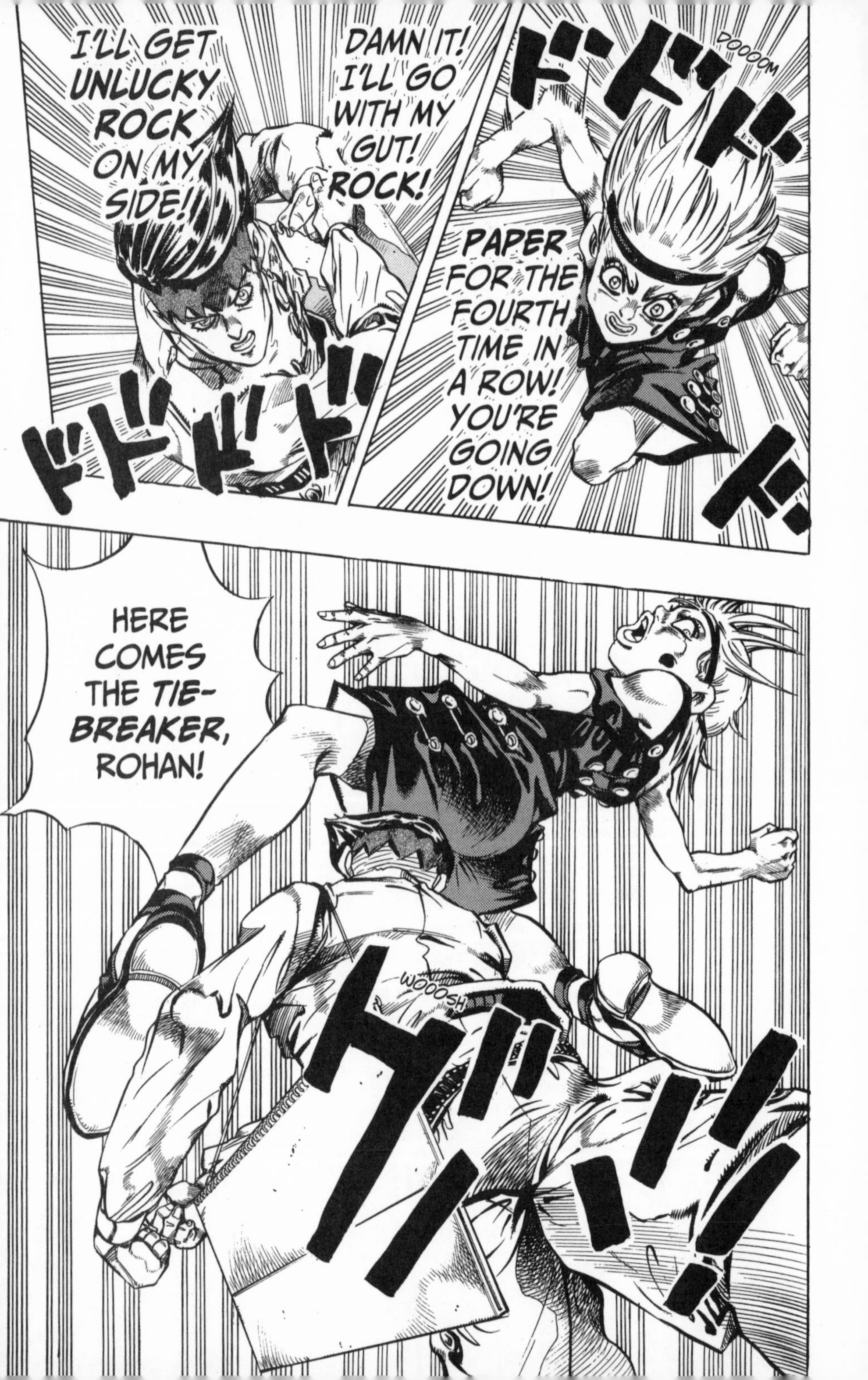
DOOOOM
PAPER FOR THE FOURTH TIME IN A ROW! YOU'RE GOING DOWN!
DAMN IT! I'LL GO WITH MY GUT! ROCK!
I'LL GET UNLUCKY ROCK ON MY SIDE!
HERE COMES THE TIE-BREAKER, ROHAN!
WOOOSH

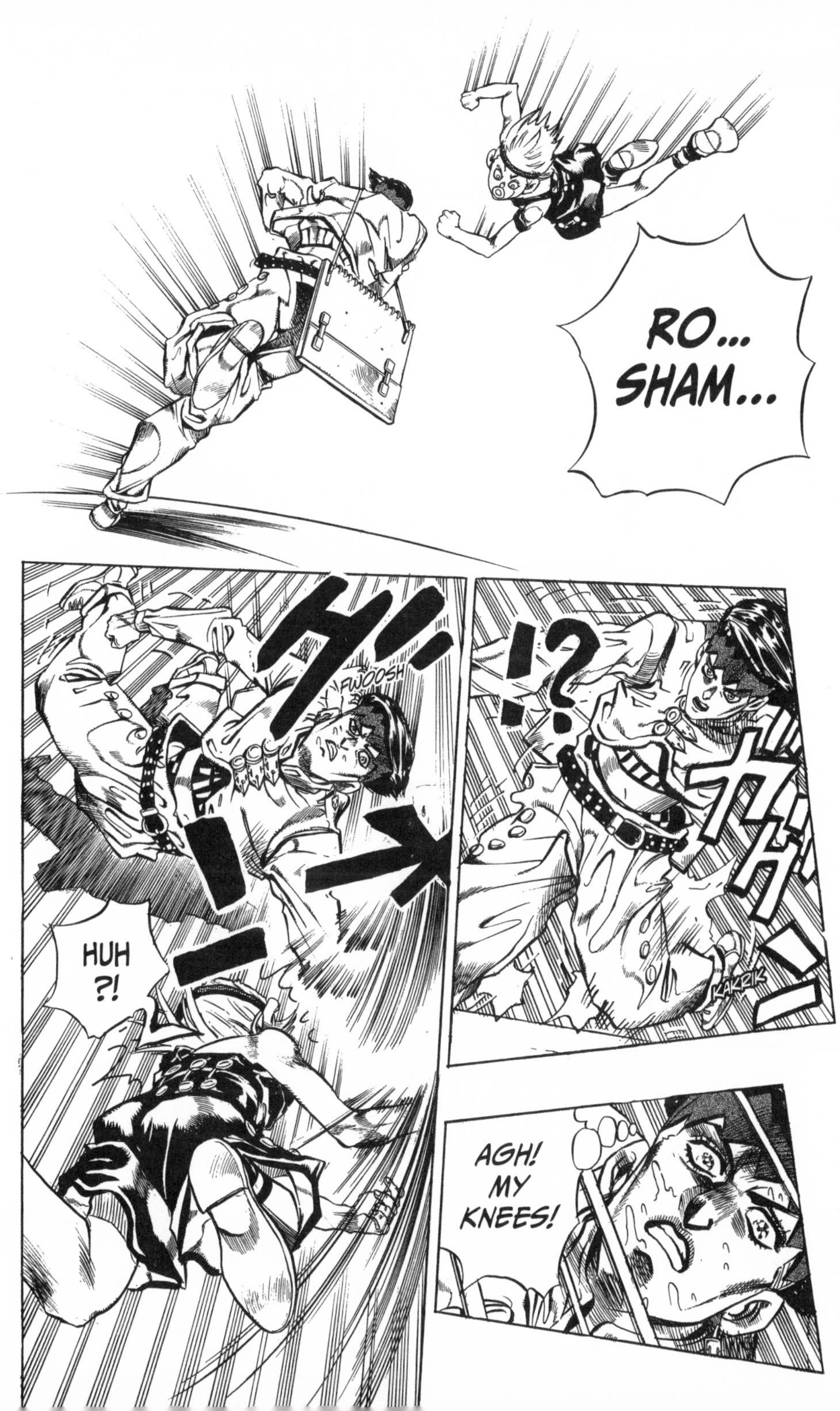
RO... SHAM...
!?
KAKRIK
AGH! MY KNEES!
FWOOSH
HUH ?!

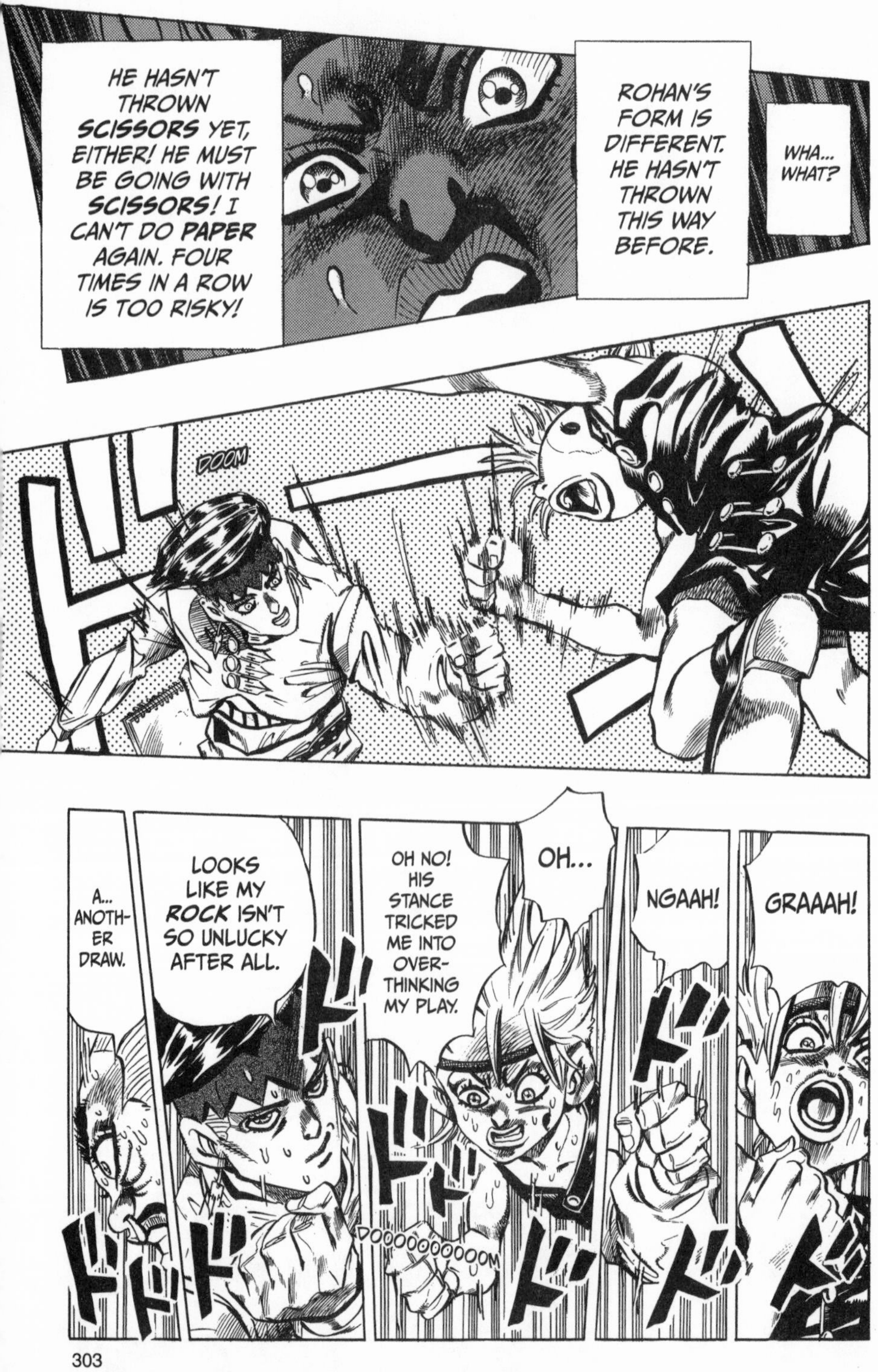

WHA... WHAT?
ROHAN'S FORM IS DIFFERENT. HE HASN'T THROWN THIS WAY BEFORE.
HE HASN'T THROWN SCISSORS YET, EITHER! HE MUST BE GOING WITH SCISSORS! I CAN'T DO PAPER AGAIN. FOUR TIMES IN A ROW IS TOO RISKY!
DOOM
GRAAAH!
NGAAH!
OH...
OH NO! HIS STANCE TRICKED ME INTO OVER-THINKING MY PLAY.
LOOKS LIKE MY ROCK ISN'T SO UNLUCKY AFTER ALL.
A... ANOTH-ER DRAW.
DOOOOOOOOOOOM

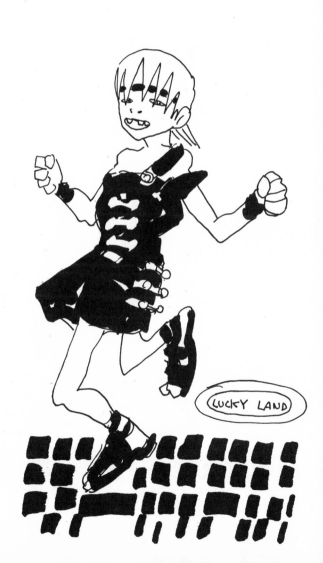
LUCKY LAND

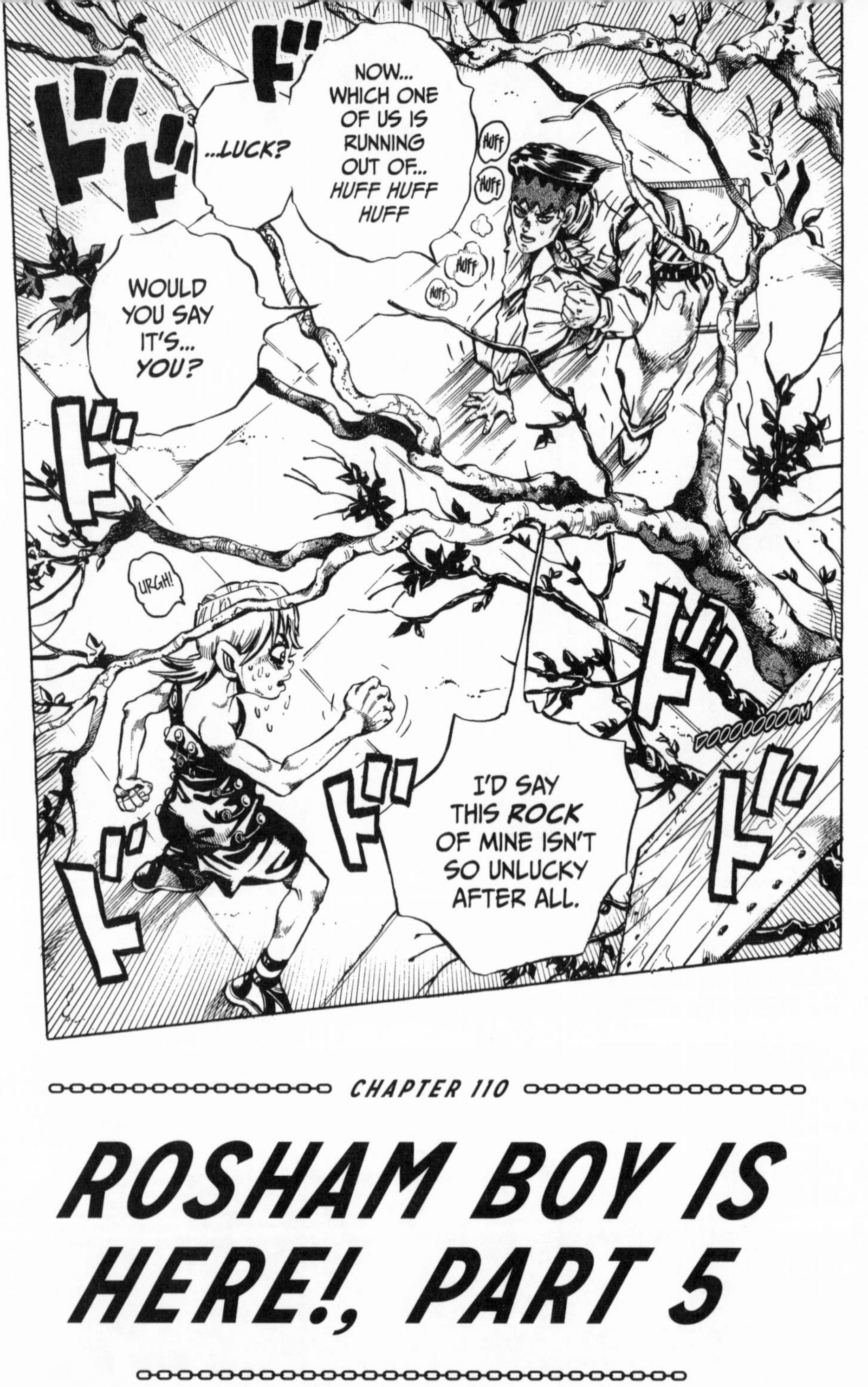
ドド
NOW... WHICH ONE OF US IS RUNNING OUT OF... HUFF HUFF HUFF
HUFF
HUFF
...LUCK?
ドドド
HUFF
HUFF
WOULD YOU SAY IT'S... YOU?
ドド
URGH!
ドド
DOOOOOOOOOM
ドド
I'D SAY THIS ROCK OF MINE ISN'T SO UNLUCKY AFTER ALL.
ドド
ドド

CHAPTER 110

ROSHAM BOY IS HERE!, PART 5

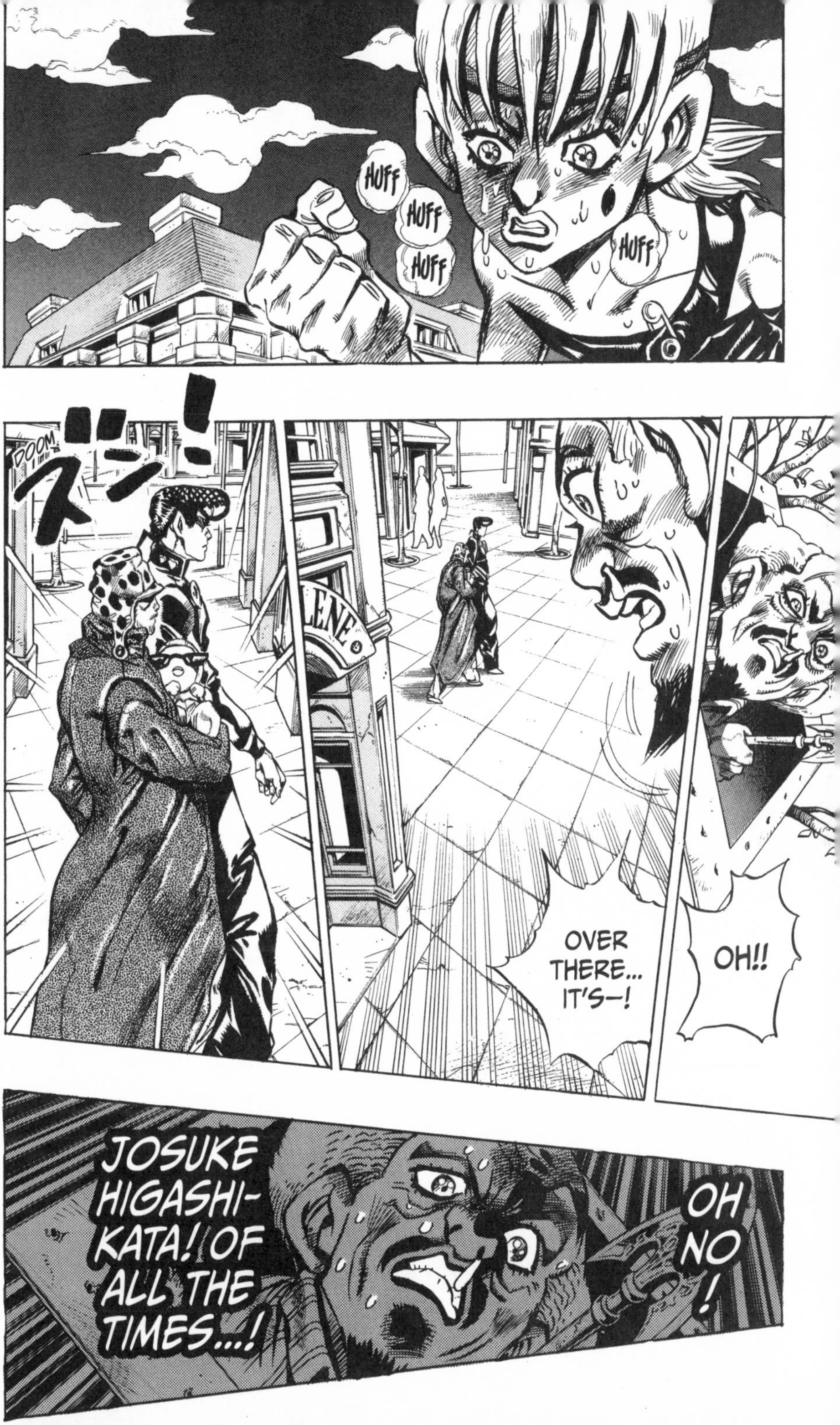
HUFF
HUFF
HUFF
HUFF
OH!!
OVER THERE... IT'S—!
DOOM
ズン!
OH NO!
JOSUKE HIGASHI-KATA! OF ALL THE TIMES...!

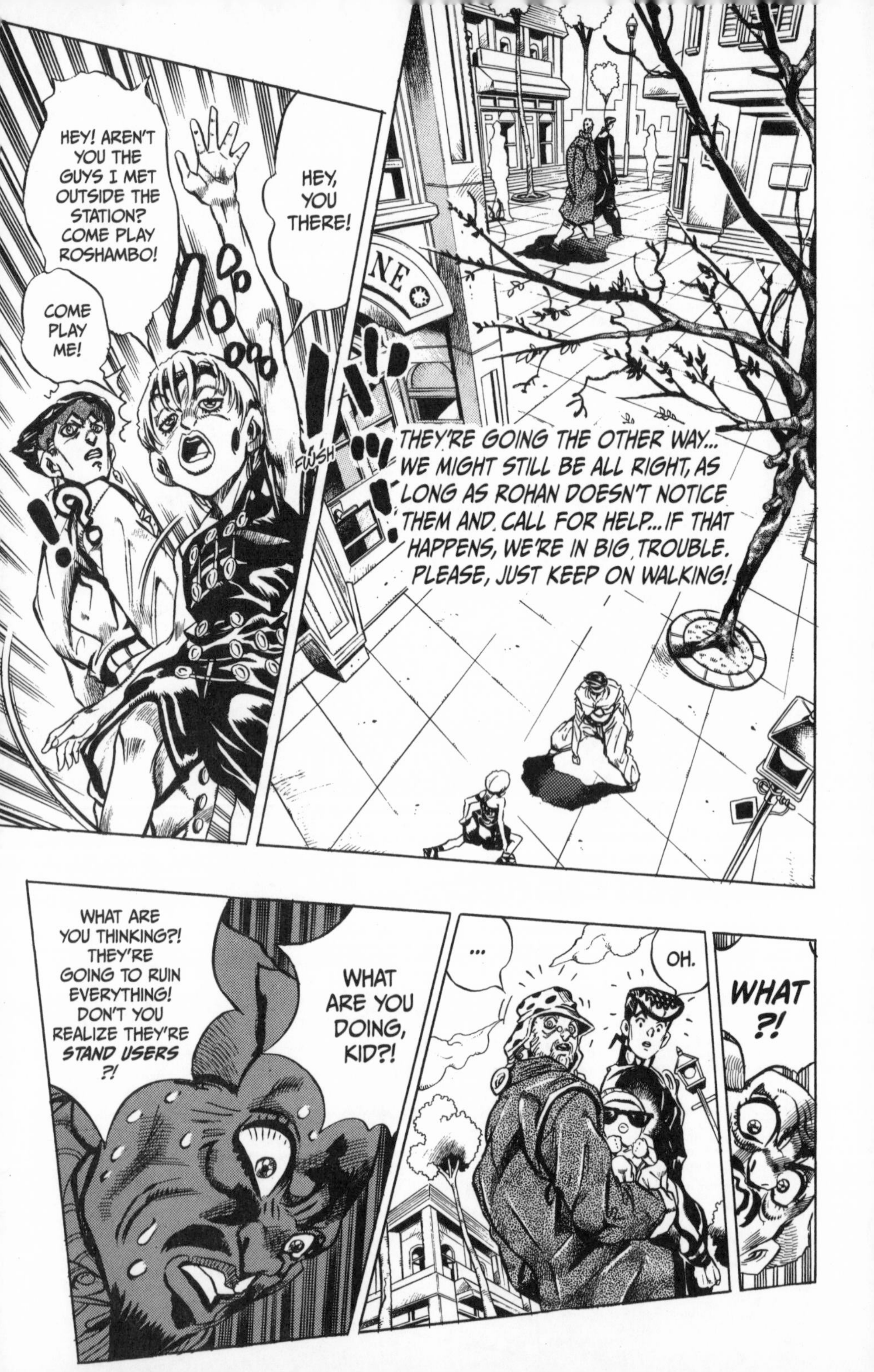
THEY'RE GOING THE OTHER WAY... WE MIGHT STILL BE ALL RIGHT, AS LONG AS ROHAN DOESN'T NOTICE THEM AND CALL FOR HELP... IF THAT HAPPENS, WE'RE IN BIG TROUBLE. PLEASE, JUST KEEP ON WALKING!
HEY, YOU THERE!
HEY! AREN'T YOU THE GUYS I MET OUTSIDE THE STATION? COME PLAY ROSHAMBO!
COME PLAY ME!
FWISH
WHAT ?!
OH.
...
WHAT ARE YOU DOING, KID?!
WHAT ARE YOU THINKING?! THEY'RE GOING TO RUIN EVERYTHING! DON'T YOU REALIZE THEY'RE STAND USERS ?!

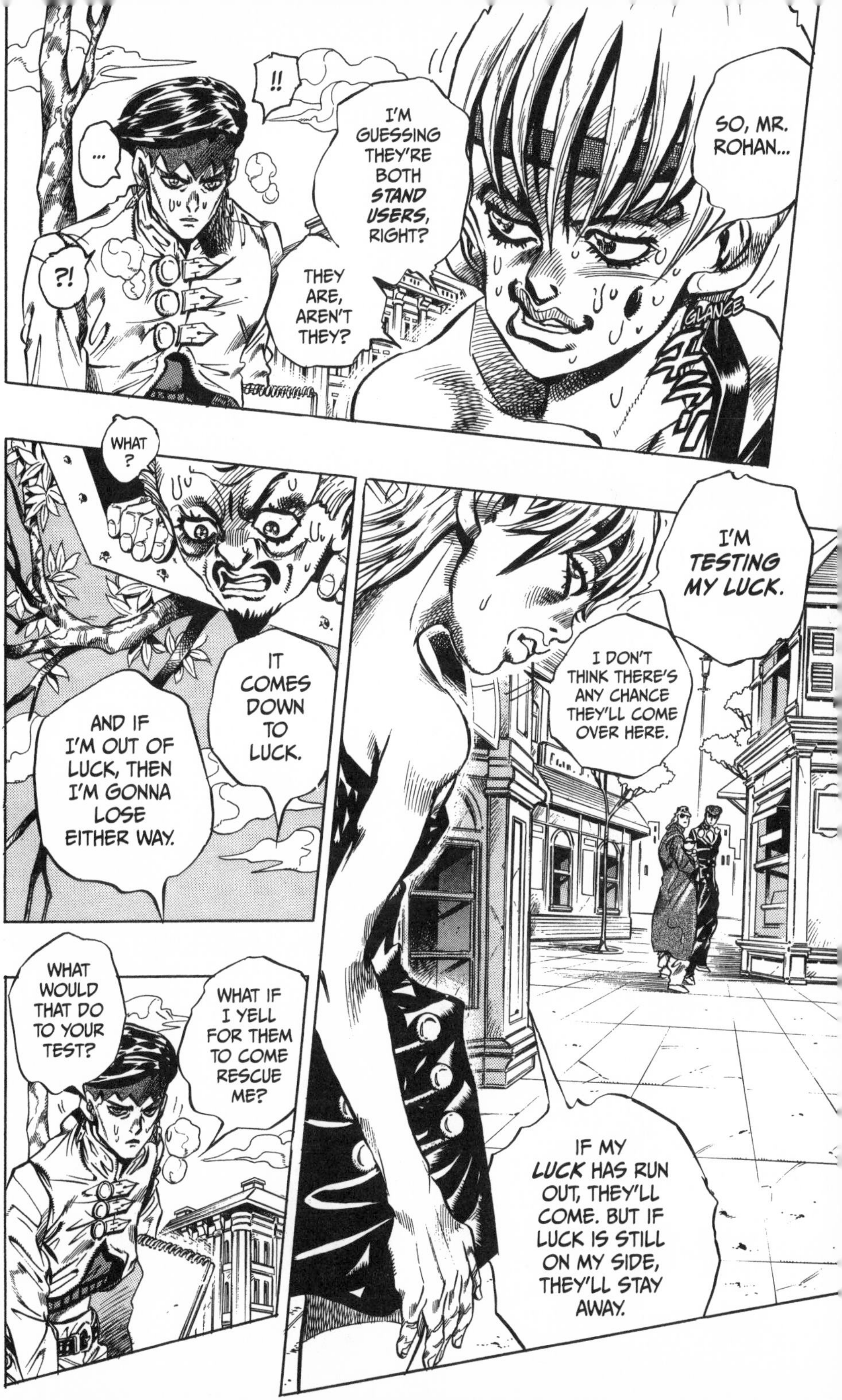
SO, MR. ROHAN...
GLANCE
I'M GUESSING THEY'RE BOTH STAND USERS, RIGHT?
THEY ARE, AREN'T THEY?
!!
...
?!
I'M TESTING MY LUCK.
I DON'T THINK THERE'S ANY CHANCE THEY'LL COME OVER HERE.
IF MY LUCK HAS RUN OUT, THEY'LL COME. BUT IF LUCK IS STILL ON MY SIDE, THEY'LL STAY AWAY.
WHAT?
IT COMES DOWN TO LUCK.
AND IF I'M OUT OF LUCK, THEN I'M GONNA LOSE EITHER WAY.
WHAT IF I YELL FOR THEM TO COME RESCUE ME?
WHAT WOULD THAT DO TO YOUR TEST?

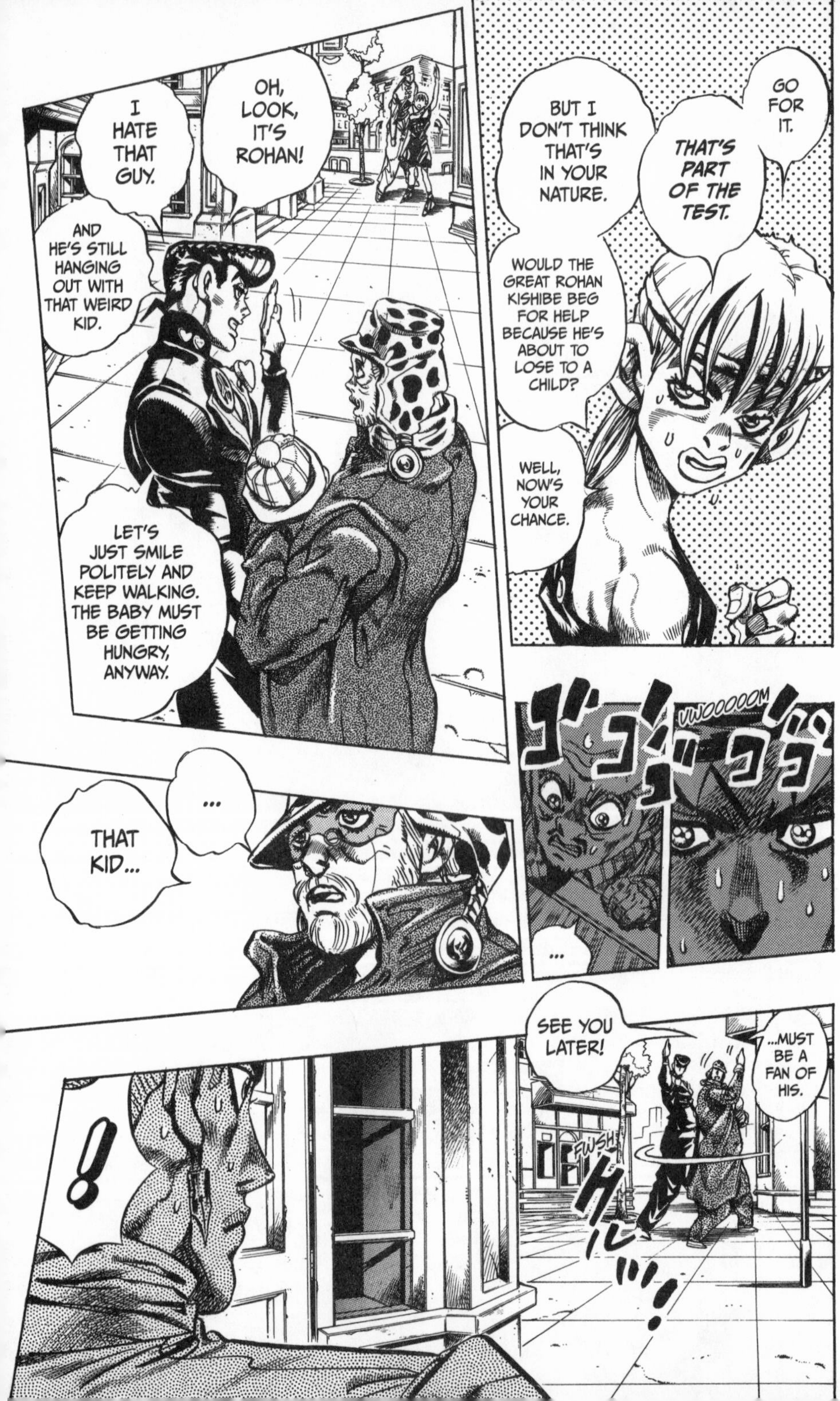
GO FOR IT.
THAT'S PART OF THE TEST.
BUT I DON'T THINK THAT'S IN YOUR NATURE.
WOULD THE GREAT ROHAN KISHIBE BEG FOR HELP BECAUSE HE'S ABOUT TO LOSE TO A CHILD?
WELL, NOW'S YOUR CHANCE.
OH, LOOK, IT'S ROHAN!
I HATE THAT GUY.
AND HE'S STILL HANGING OUT WITH THAT WEIRD KID.
LET'S JUST SMILE POLITELY AND KEEP WALKING. THE BABY MUST BE GETTING HUNGRY, ANYWAY.
UWOOOOOM
...
...
THAT KID...
SEE YOU LATER!
...MUST BE A FAN OF HIS.
FWSH
!

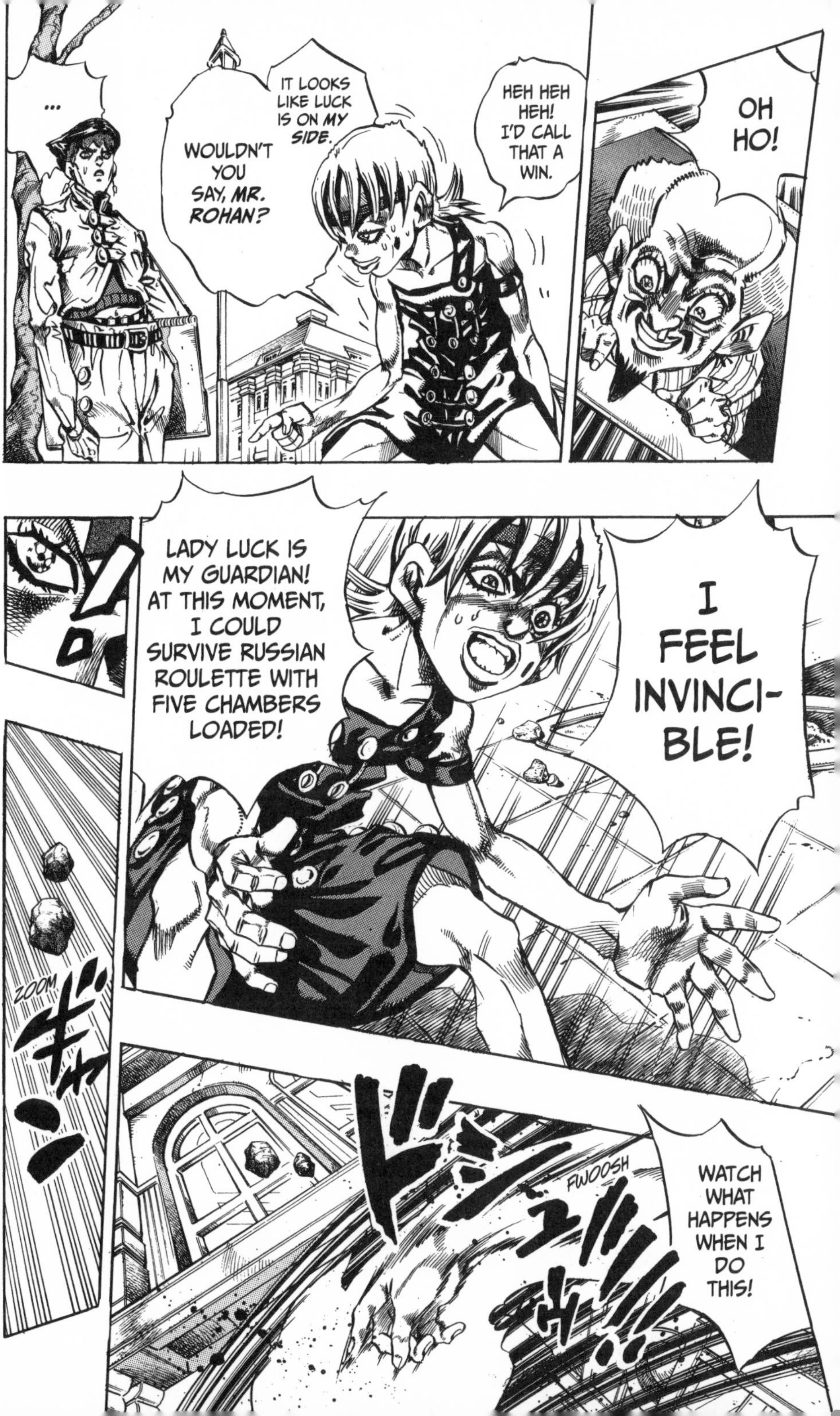
OH HO!
HEH HEH HEH! I'D CALL THAT A WIN.
IT LOOKS LIKE LUCK IS ON MY SIDE.
WOULDN'T YOU SAY, MR. ROHAN?
...
I FEEL INVINCIBLE!
LADY LUCK IS MY GUARDIAN! AT THIS MOMENT, I COULD SURVIVE RUSSIAN ROULETTE WITH FIVE CHAMBERS LOADED!
ZOOM
WATCH WHAT HAPPENS WHEN I DO THIS!
FWOOSH

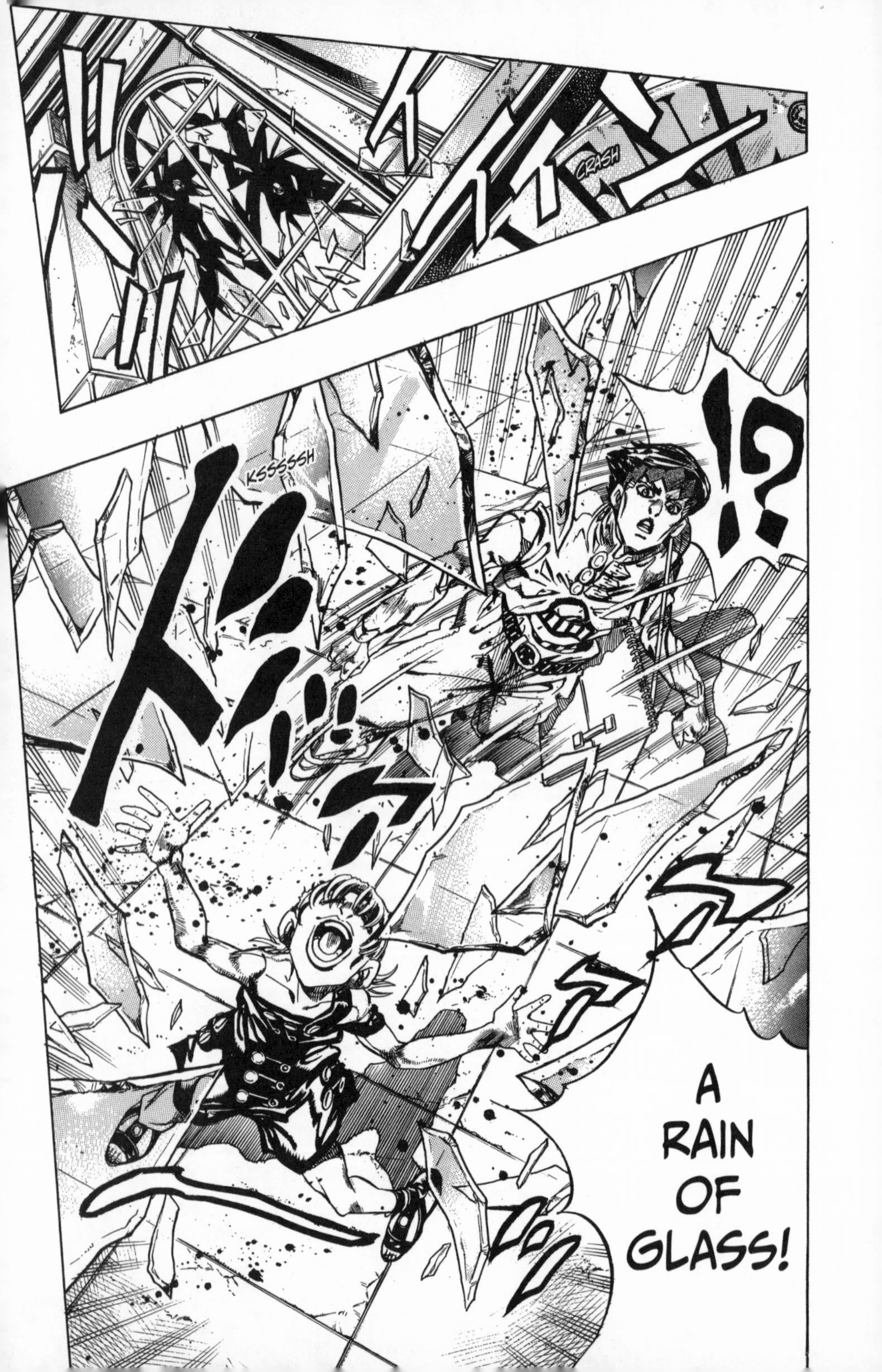
CRASH
!?
KSSSSSH
A RAIN OF GLASS!

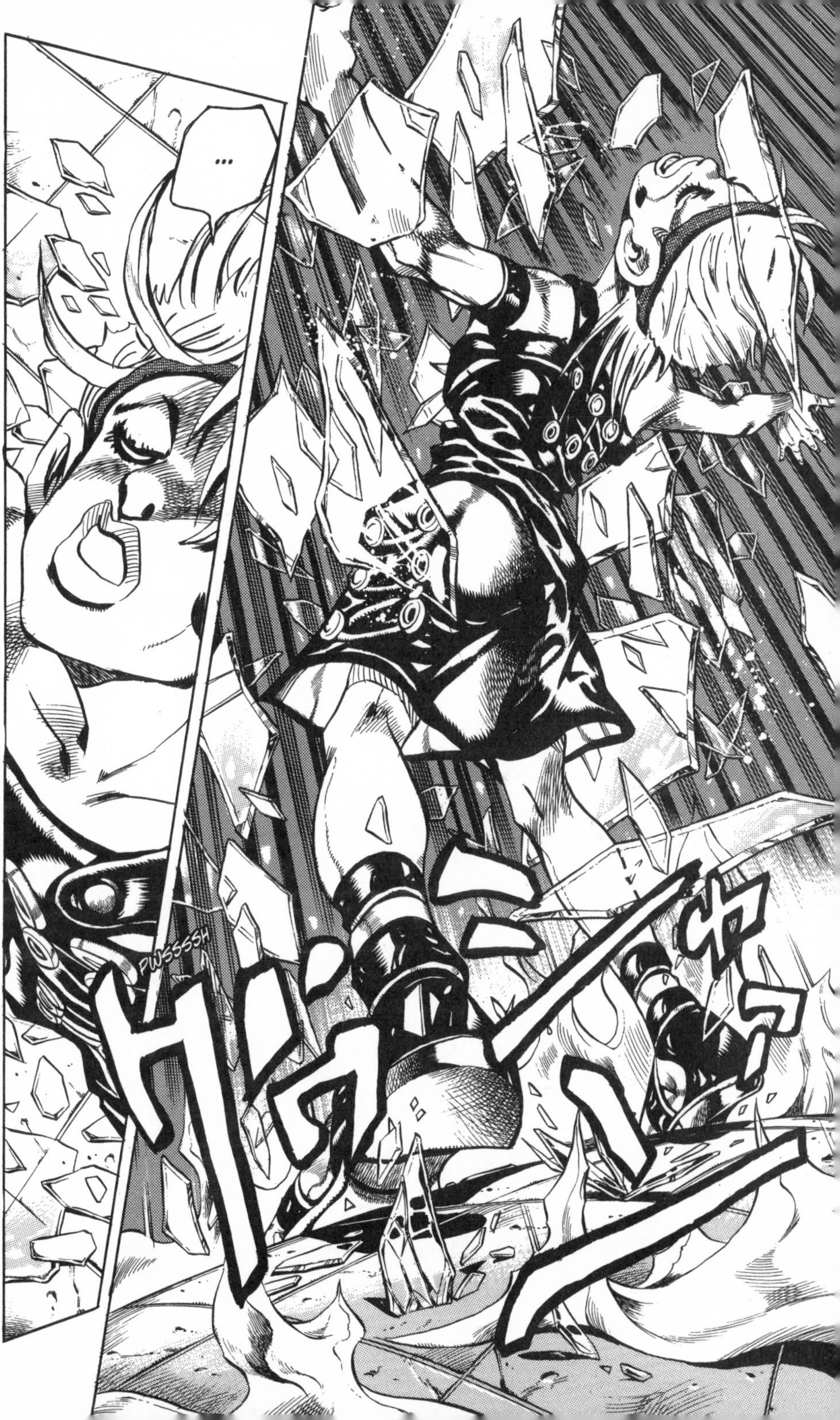
PWSSSSH
...

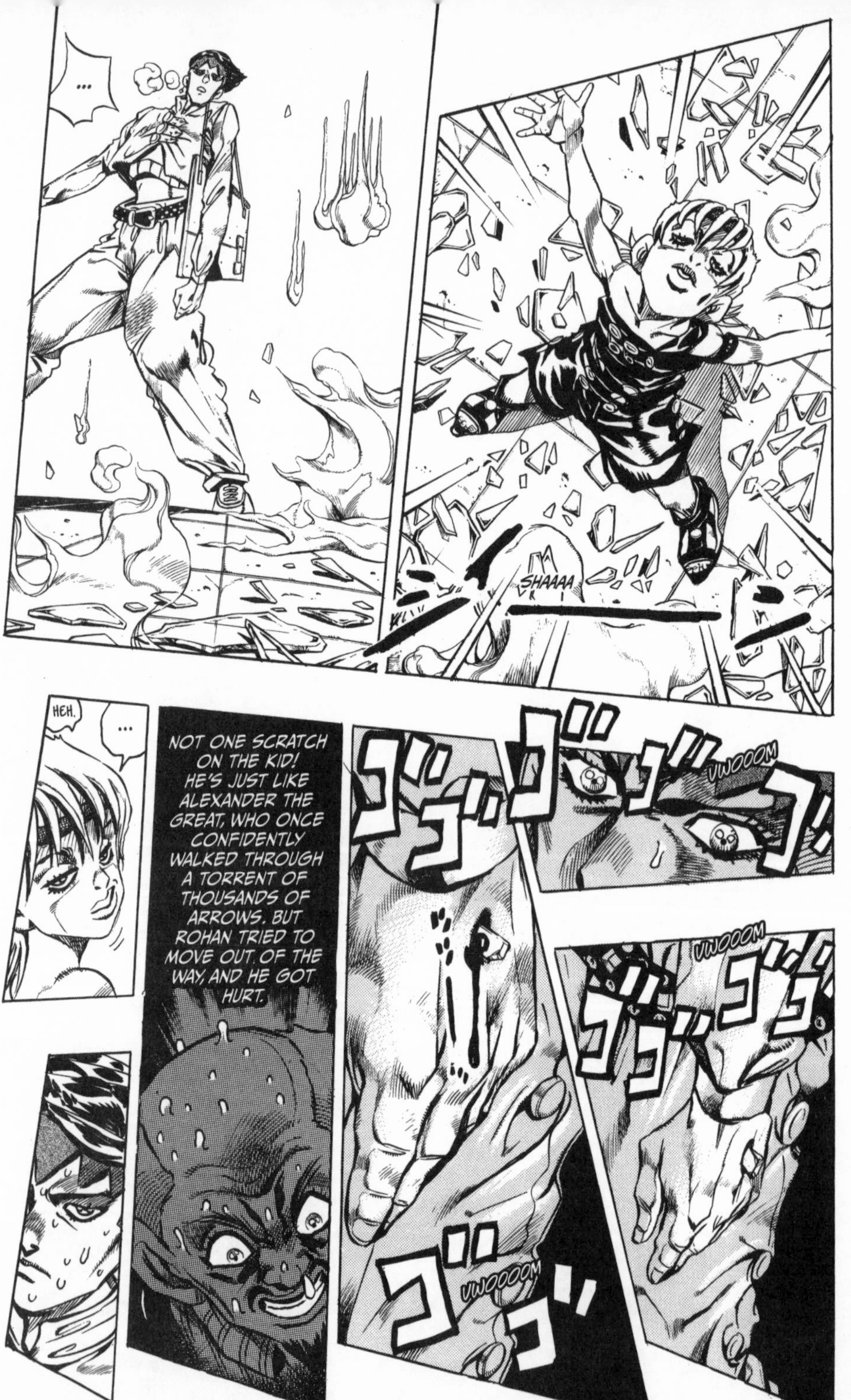
SHAAAA
...
UWOOOM
UWOOOM
UWOOOOM
NOT ONE SCRATCH ON THE KID! HE'S JUST LIKE ALEXANDER THE GREAT, WHO ONCE CONFIDENTLY WALKED THROUGH A TORRENT OF THOUSANDS OF ARROWS. BUT ROHAN TRIED TO MOVE OUT OF THE WAY, AND HE GOT HURT.
HEH.
...

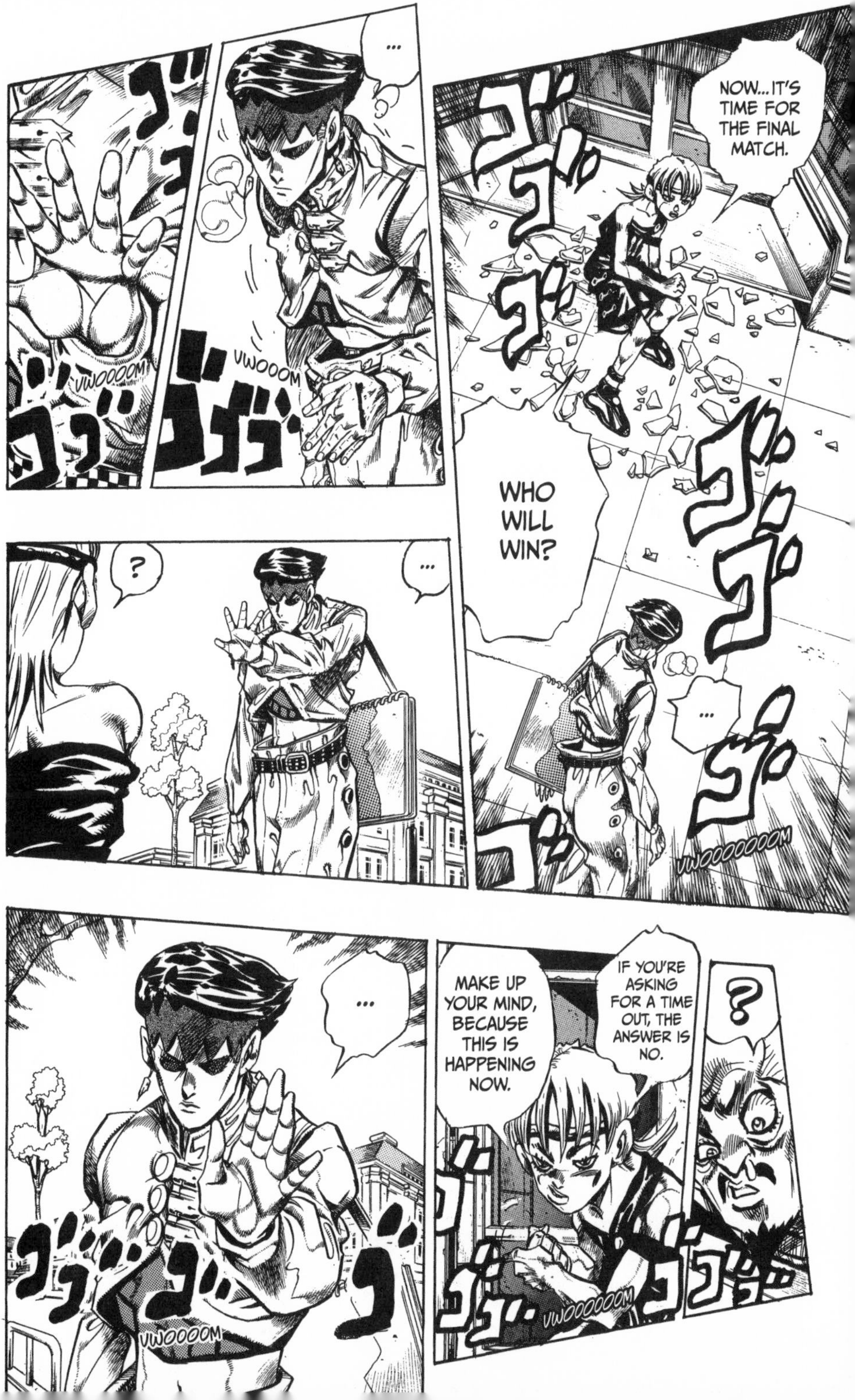
NOW...IT'S TIME FOR THE FINAL MATCH.
WHO WILL WIN?
...
VWOOOOOOOM
...
VWOOOM
VWOOOOM
...
?
?
IF YOU'RE ASKING FOR A TIME OUT, THE ANSWER IS NO.
MAKE UP YOUR MIND, BECAUSE THIS IS HAPPENING NOW.
VWOOOOOOM
...
VWOOOOM

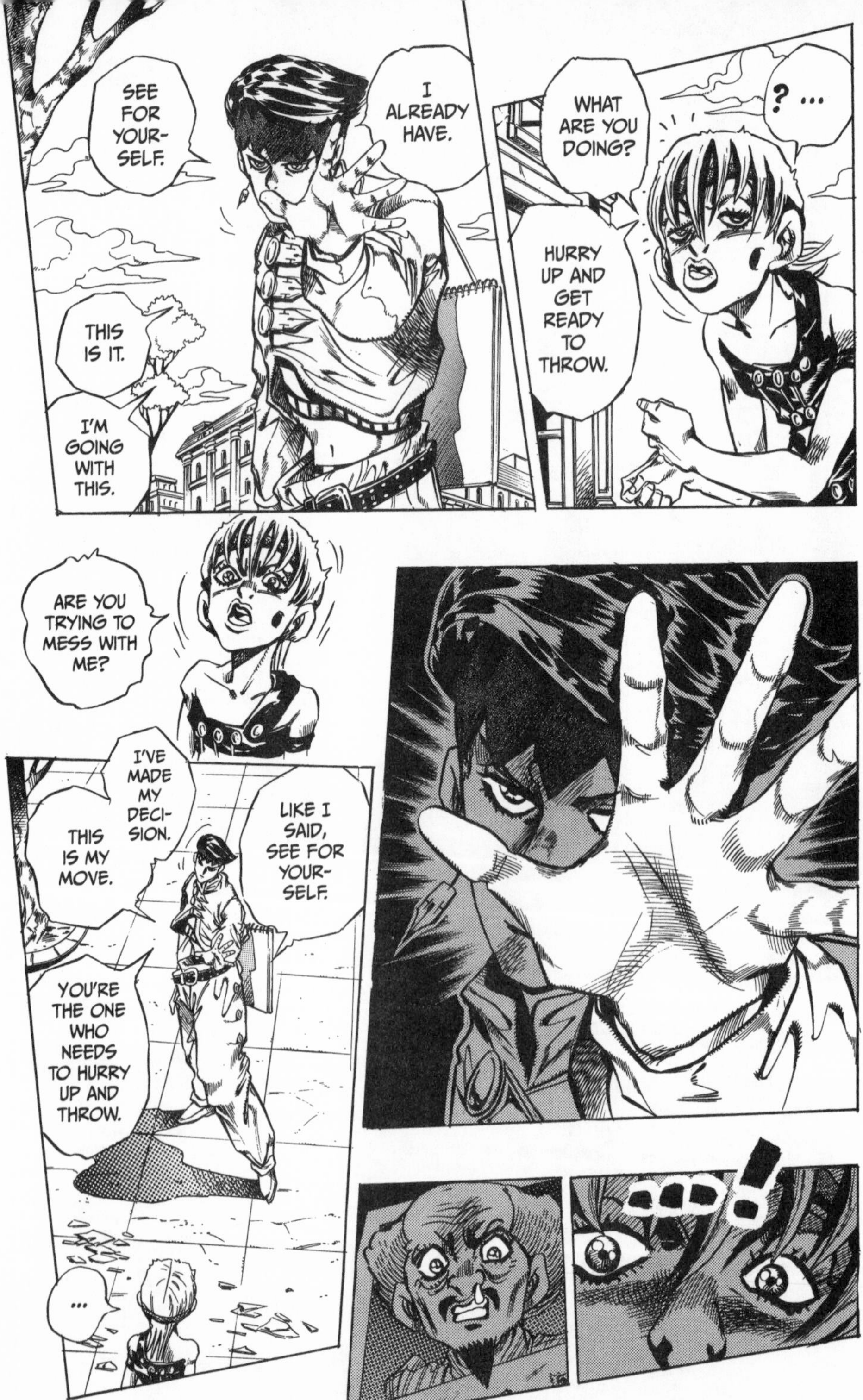
?...
WHAT ARE YOU DOING?
HURRY UP AND GET READY TO THROW.
I ALREADY HAVE.
SEE FOR YOURSELF.
THIS IS IT.
I'M GOING WITH THIS.
ARE YOU TRYING TO MESS WITH ME?
LIKE I SAID, SEE FOR YOURSELF.
I'VE MADE MY DECISION.
THIS IS MY MOVE.
YOU'RE THE ONE WHO NEEDS TO HURRY UP AND THROW.
...
...!

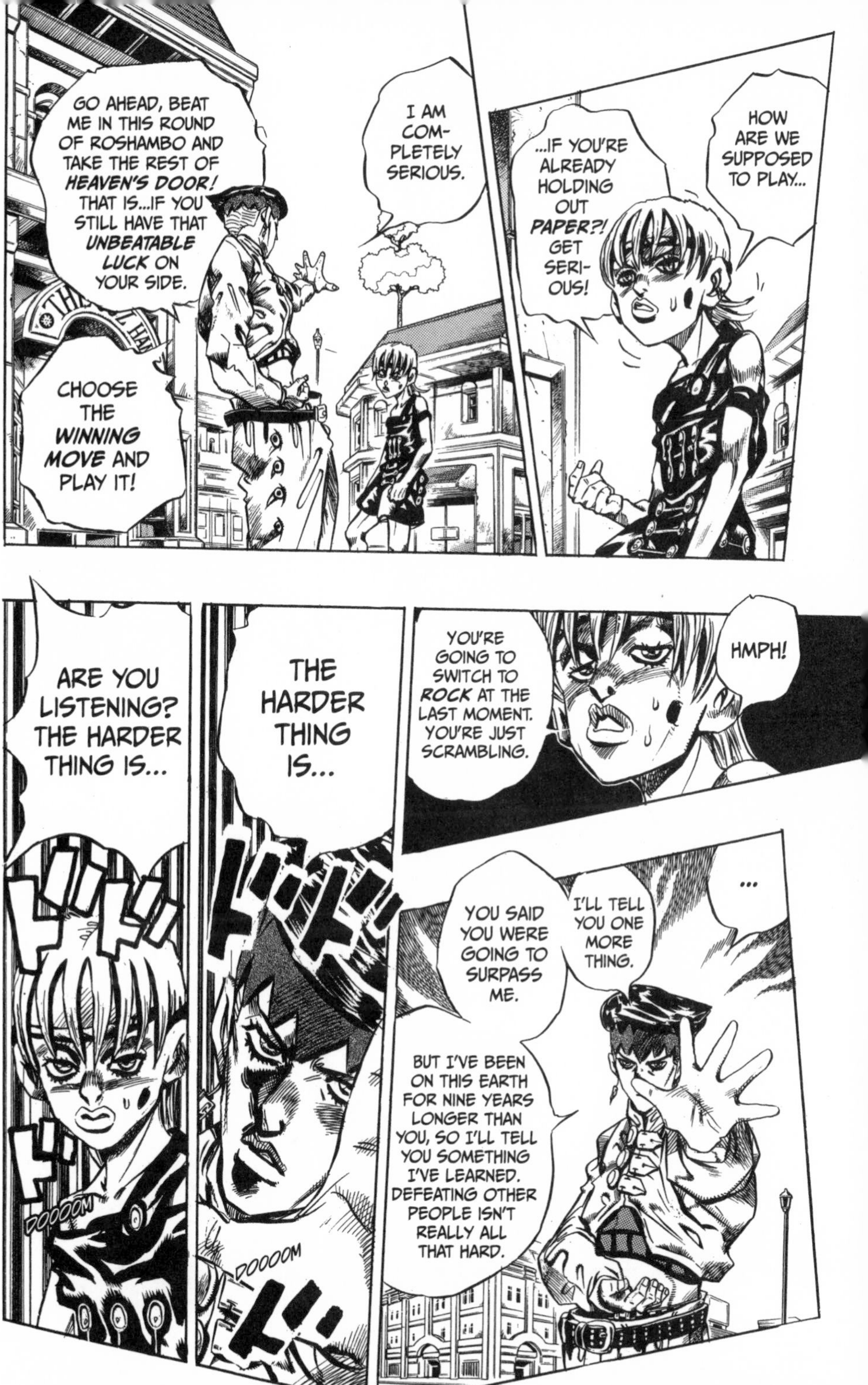
HOW ARE WE SUPPOSED TO PLAY...
...IF YOU'RE ALREADY HOLDING OUT *PAPER?!* GET SERIOUS!
I AM COMPLETELY SERIOUS.
GO AHEAD, BEAT ME IN THIS ROUND OF ROSHAMBO AND TAKE THE REST OF *HEAVEN'S DOOR!* THAT IS...IF YOU STILL HAVE THAT *UNBEATABLE LUCK* ON YOUR SIDE.
CHOOSE THE *WINNING MOVE* AND PLAY IT!
HMPH!
YOU'RE GOING TO SWITCH TO *ROCK* AT THE LAST MOMENT. YOU'RE JUST SCRAMBLING.
...
I'LL TELL YOU ONE MORE THING.
YOU SAID YOU WERE GOING TO SURPASS ME.
BUT I'VE BEEN ON THIS EARTH FOR NINE YEARS LONGER THAN YOU, SO I'LL TELL YOU SOMETHING I'VE LEARNED. DEFEATING OTHER PEOPLE ISN'T REALLY ALL THAT HARD.
THE HARDER THING IS...
DOOOOM
ARE YOU LISTENING? THE HARDER THING IS...
DOOOOM

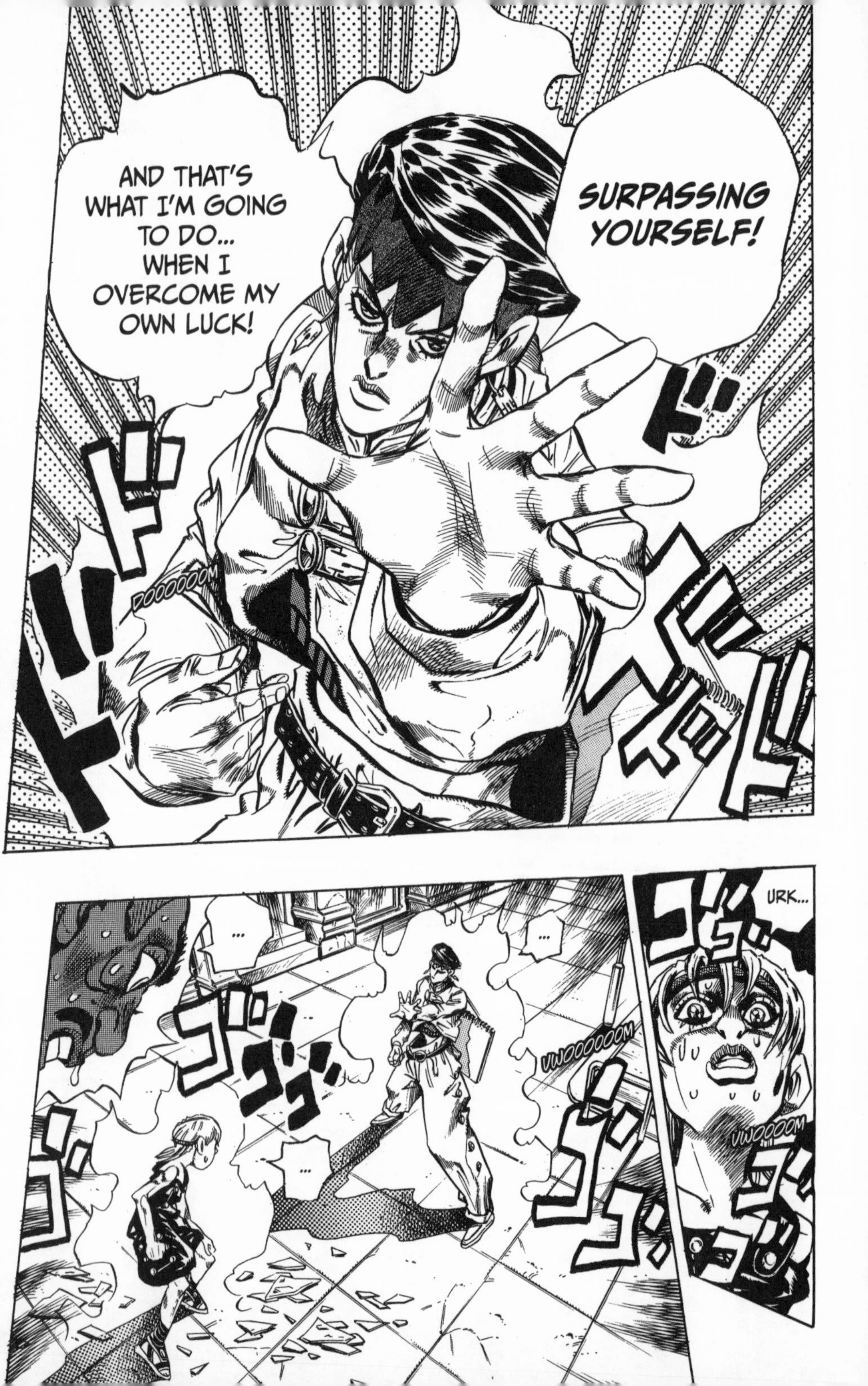
SURPASSING YOURSELF!
AND THAT'S WHAT I'M GOING TO DO... WHEN I OVERCOME MY OWN LUCK!
DOOOOOOOM
URK...
VWOOOOM
...
...
VWOOOOOOOM
...

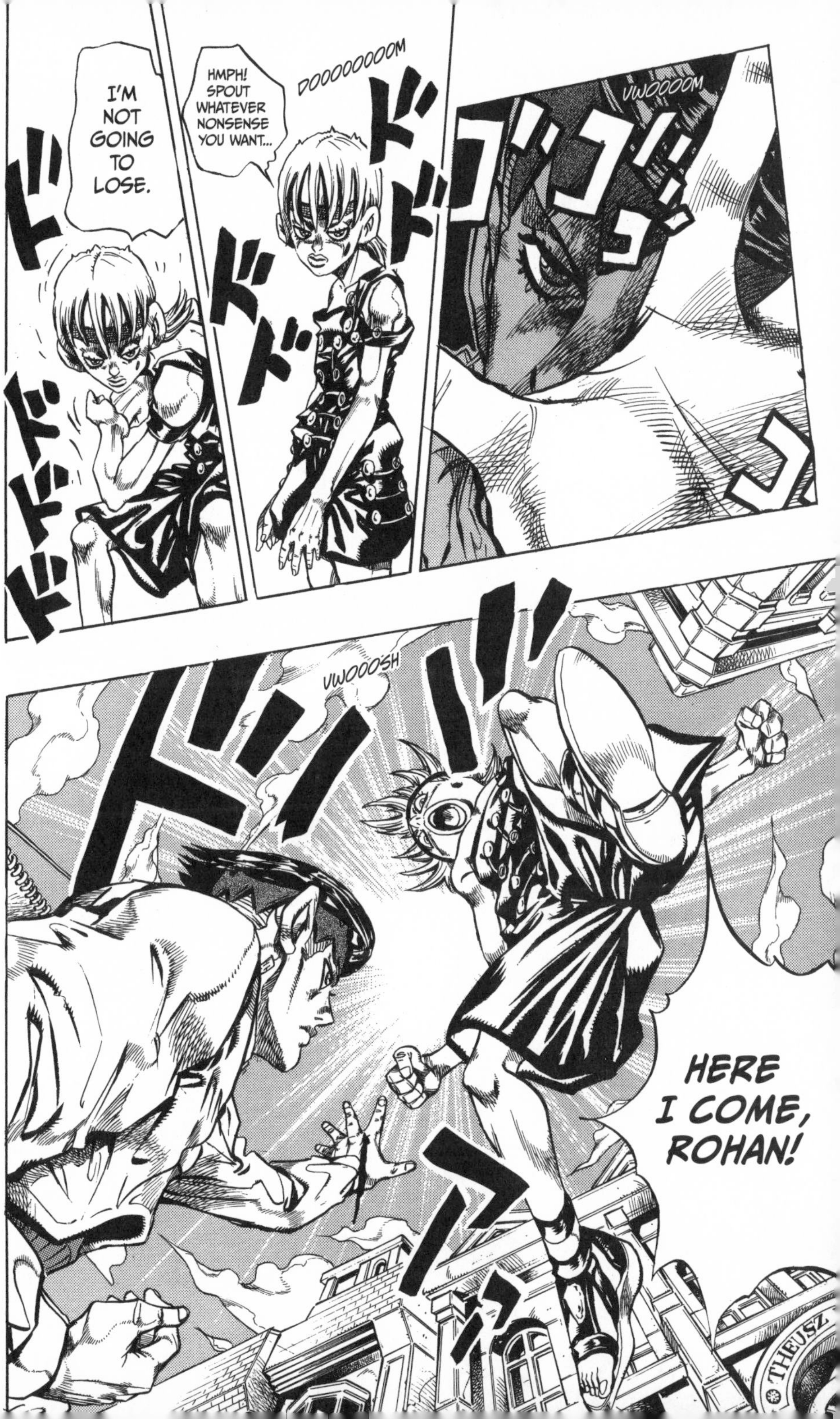
VWOOOOM
DOOOOOOOOM
HMPH! SPOUT WHATEVER NONSENSE YOU WANT...
I'M NOT GOING TO LOSE.
VWOOO'SH
HERE I COME, ROHAN!

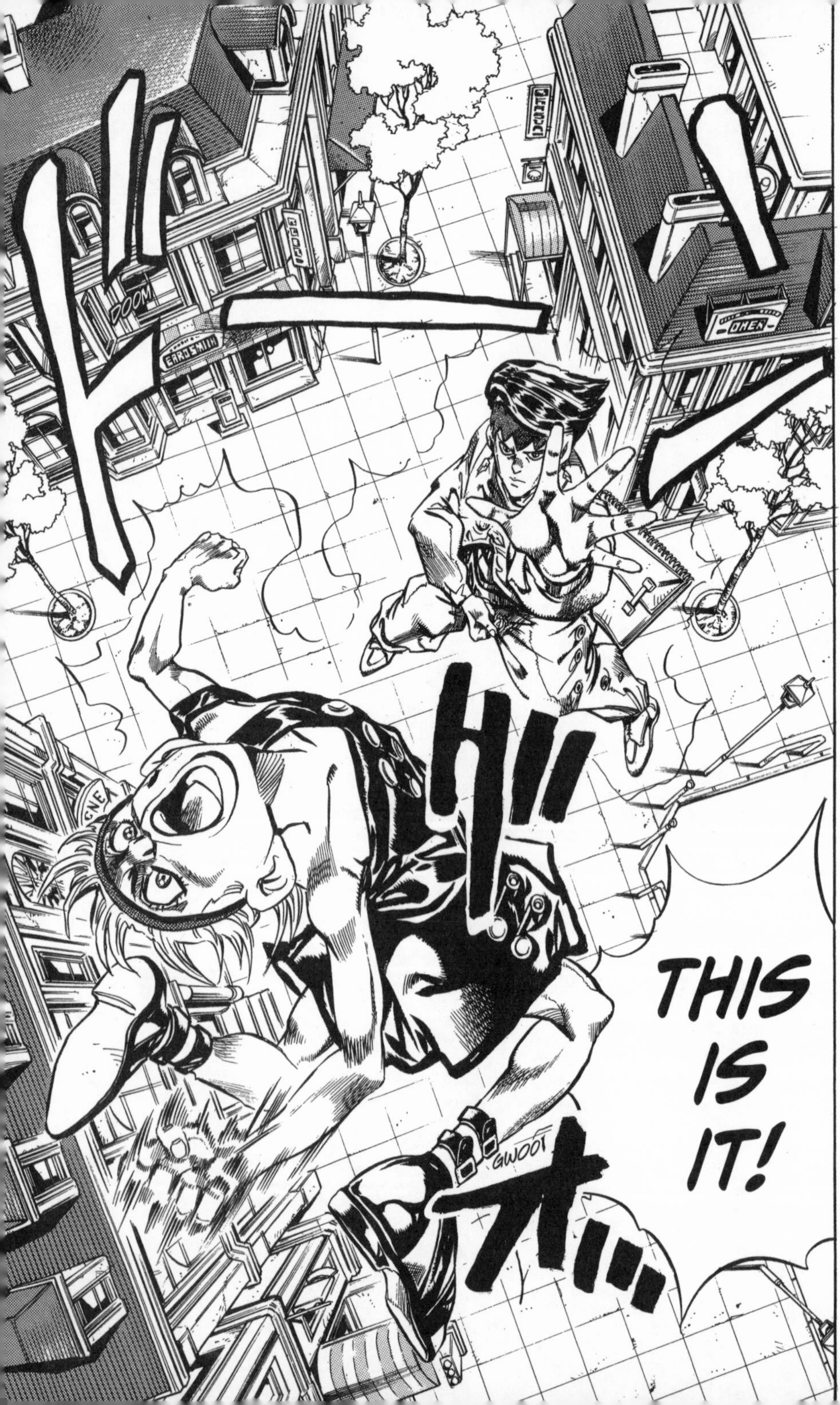
DOOM
THIS IS IT!
GWOOT

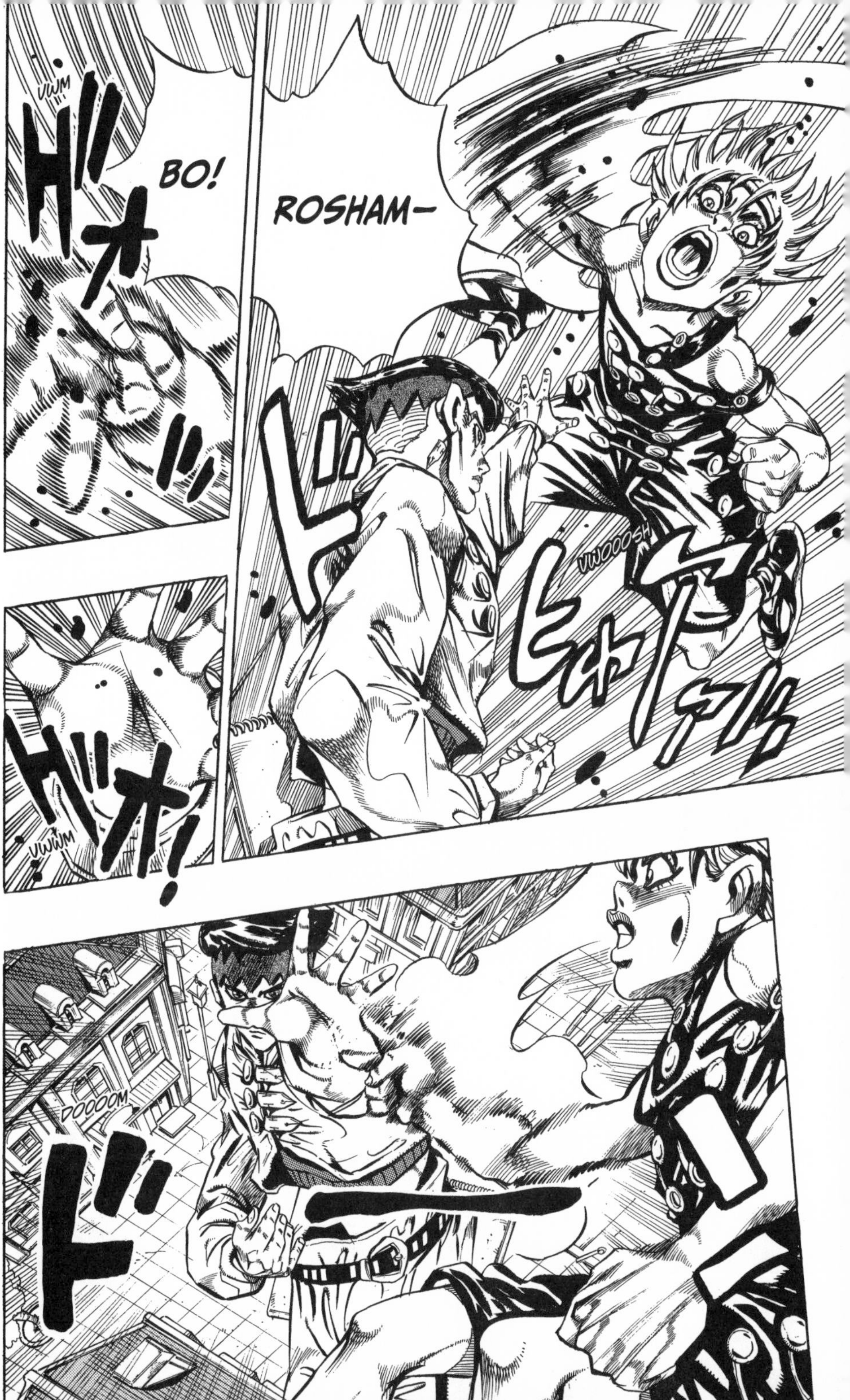
ROSHAM-
VWOOOSH
VWM
BO!
VWWM
DOOOOM

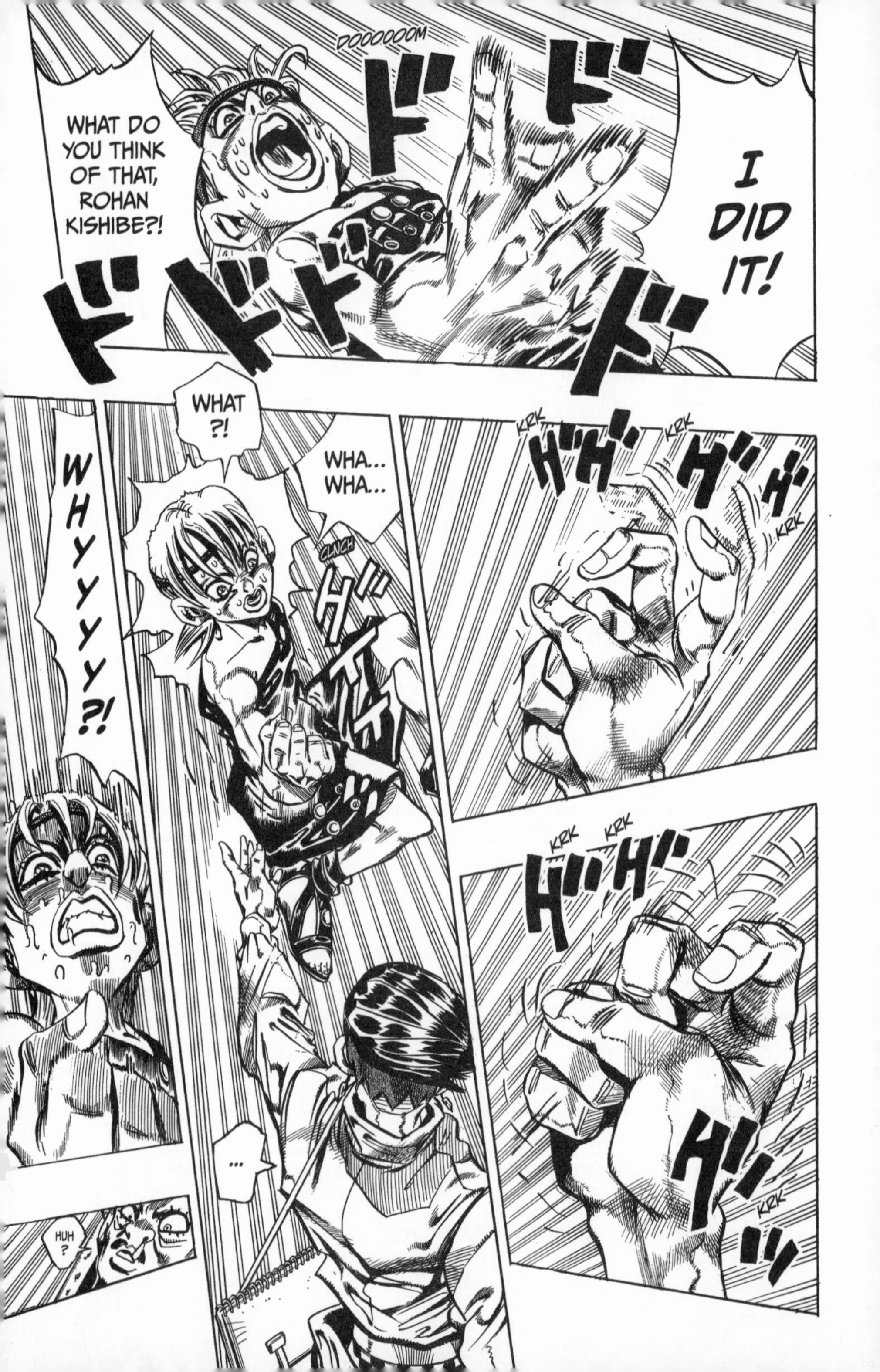
DOOOOOOM
I DID IT!
WHAT DO YOU THINK OF THAT, ROHAN KISHIBE?!
KRK
KRK
KRK
KRK
KRK
KRK
WHAT ?!
WHA... WHA...
CLNCH
...
WHYYYYYY?!
HUH ?

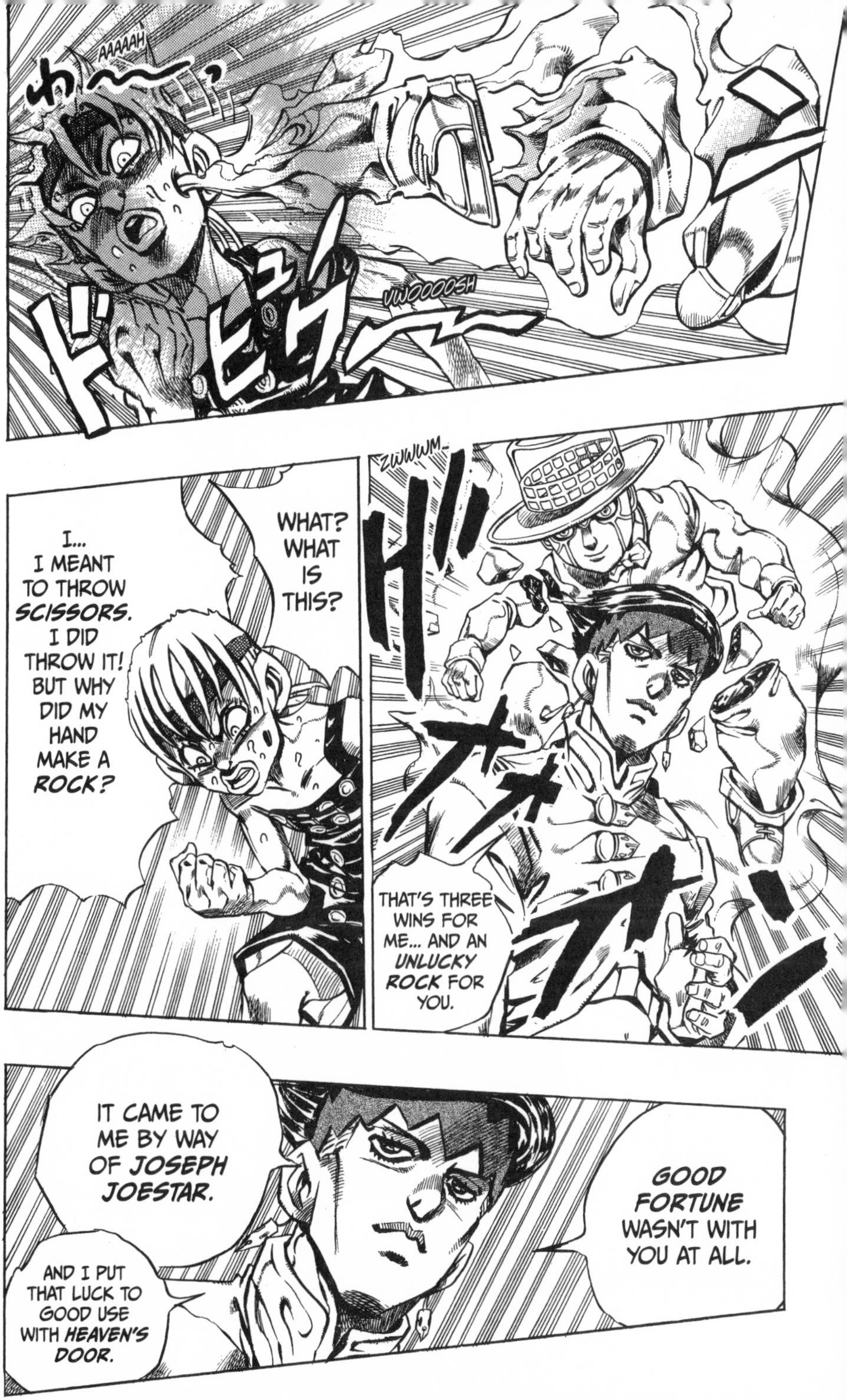

AAAAAH
わ〜〜
VWOOOOSH
ZWWWM
THAT'S THREE WINS FOR ME... AND AN *UNLUCKY ROCK* FOR YOU.
WHAT? WHAT IS THIS?
I... I MEANT TO THROW *SCISSORS*. I DID THROW IT! BUT WHY DID MY HAND MAKE A *ROCK*?
GOOD FORTUNE WASN'T WITH YOU AT ALL.
IT CAME TO ME BY WAY OF *JOSEPH JOESTAR*.
AND I PUT THAT LUCK TO GOOD USE WITH *HEAVEN'S DOOR*.

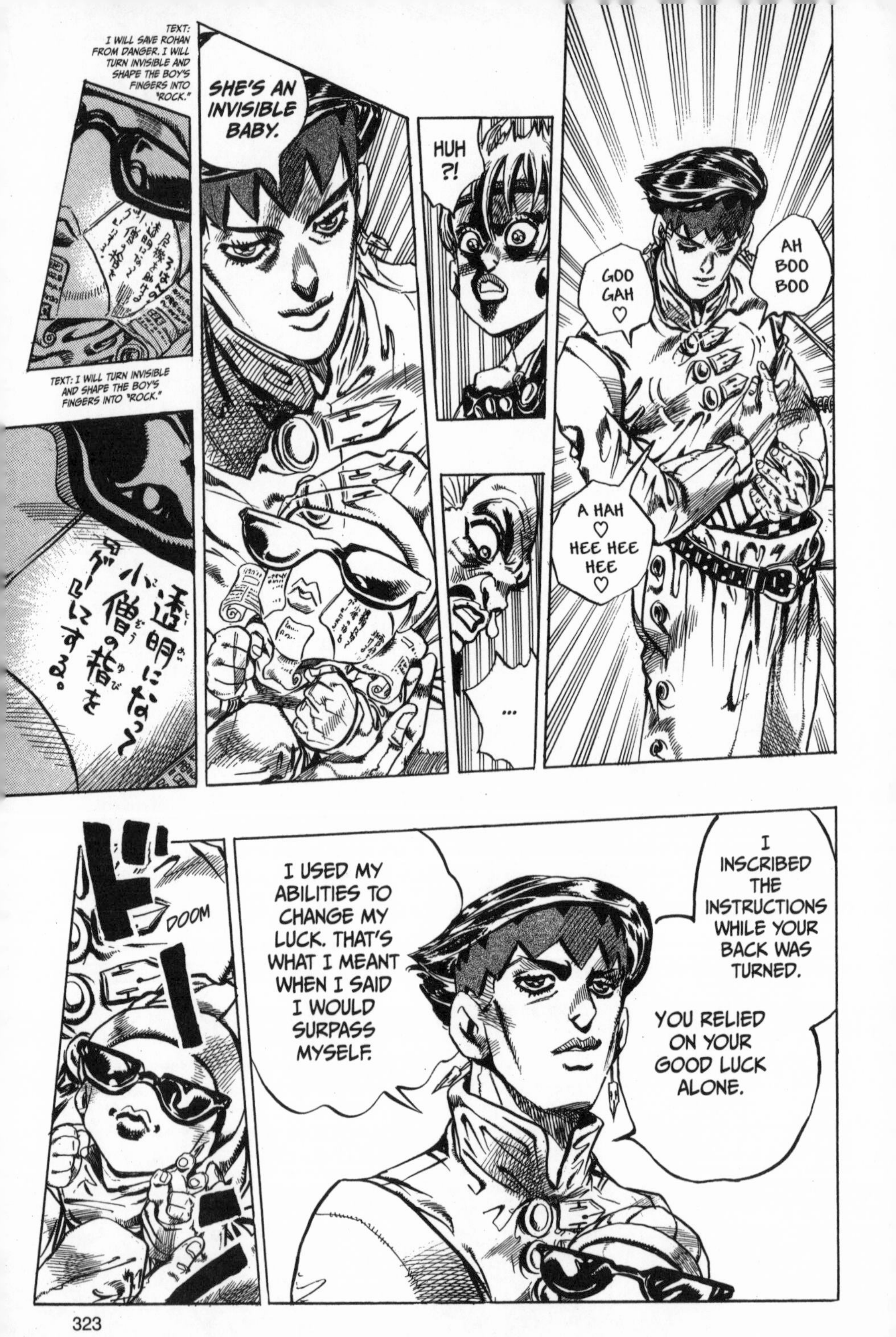
AH BOO BOO
GOO GAH ♡
A HAH ♡ HEE HEE HEE ♡
HUH ?!
...
SHE'S AN INVISIBLE BABY.
TEXT: I WILL SAVE ROHAN FROM DANGER. I WILL TURN INVISIBLE AND SHAPE THE BOY'S FINGERS INTO "ROCK."
TEXT: I WILL TURN INVISIBLE AND SHAPE THE BOY'S FINGERS INTO "ROCK."
透明になって小僧の指を『グー』にする。
I INSCRIBED THE INSTRUCTIONS WHILE YOUR BACK WAS TURNED.
YOU RELIED ON YOUR GOOD LUCK ALONE.
I USED MY ABILITIES TO CHANGE MY LUCK. THAT'S WHAT I MEANT WHEN I SAID I WOULD SURPASS MYSELF.
DOOM

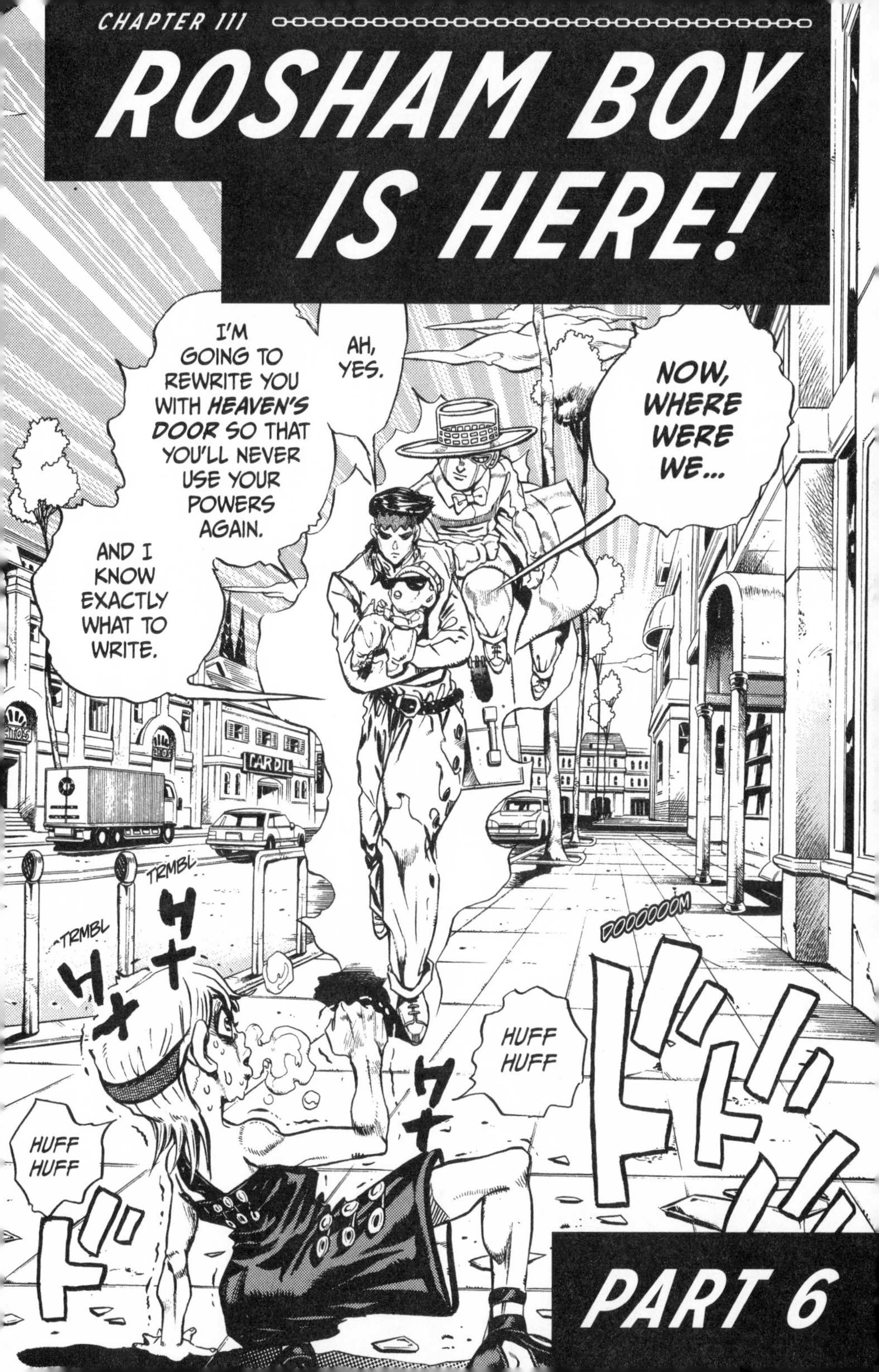
CHAPTER 111
ROSHAM BOY IS HERE!
NOW, WHERE WERE WE...
AH, YES.
I'M GOING TO REWRITE YOU WITH HEAVEN'S DOOR SO THAT YOU'LL NEVER USE YOUR POWERS AGAIN.
AND I KNOW EXACTLY WHAT TO WRITE.
DOOOOOOM
HUFF HUFF
TRMBL
TRMBL
HUFF HUFF
PART 6

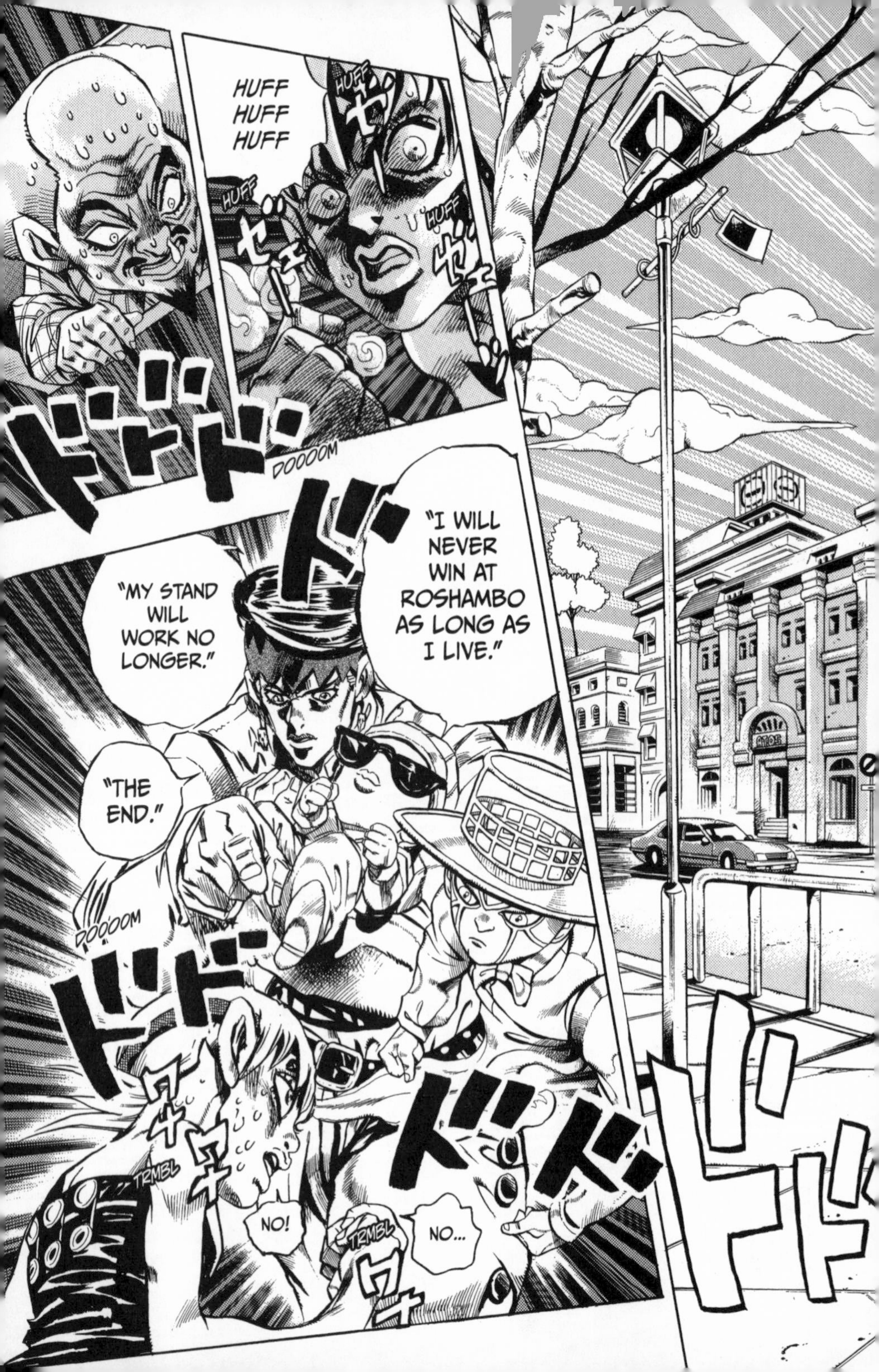
HUFF
HUFF
HUFF
HUFF
HUFF
HUFF
DOOOOM
"I WILL NEVER WIN AT ROSHAMBO AS LONG AS I LIVE."
"MY STAND WILL WORK NO LONGER."
"THE END."
DOOOOM
NO...
TRMBL
NO!
TRMBL

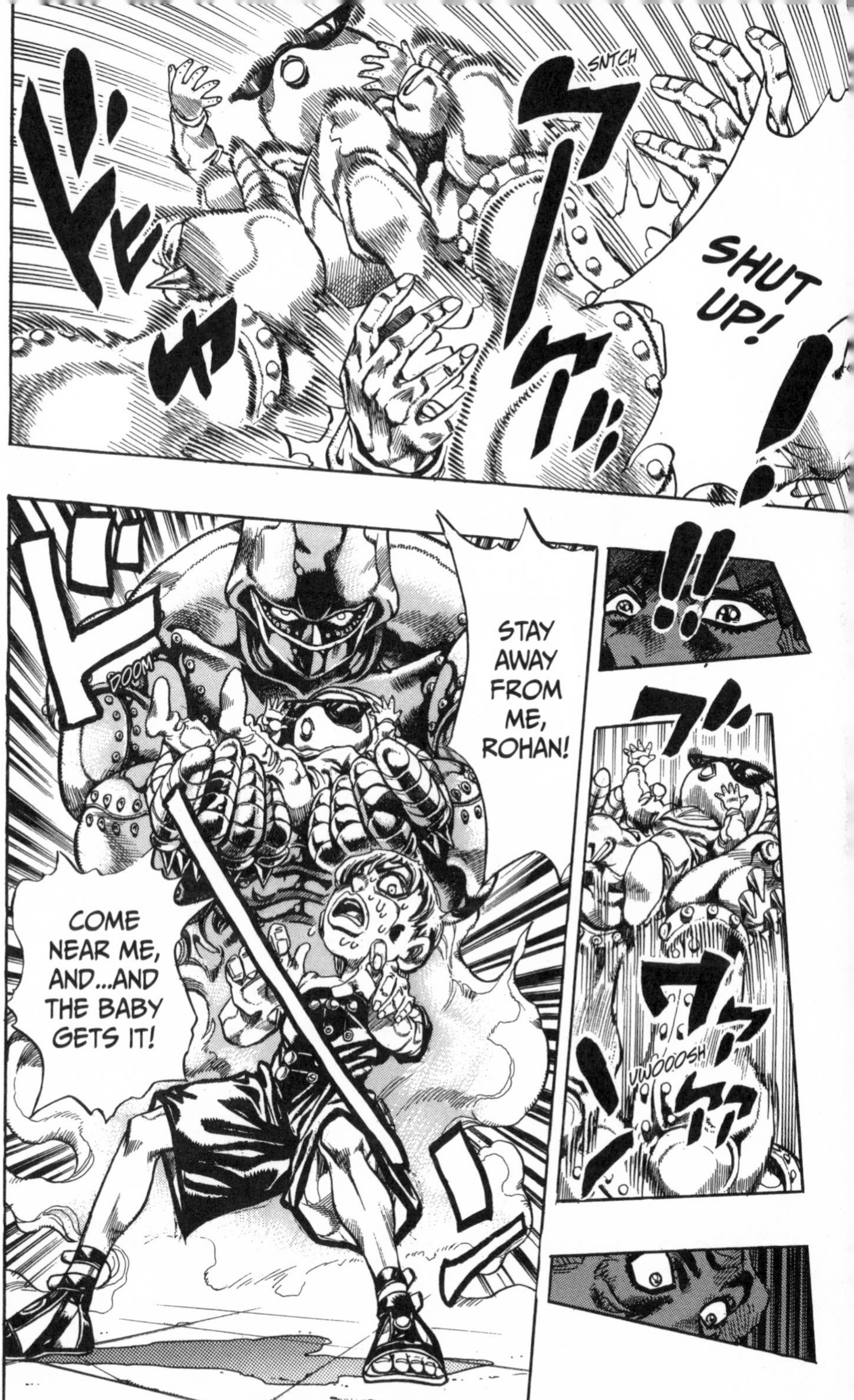
SNTCH
SHUT UP!
VWOOOSH
STAY AWAY FROM ME, ROHAN!
DOOM
COME NEAR ME, AND...AND THE BABY GETS IT!

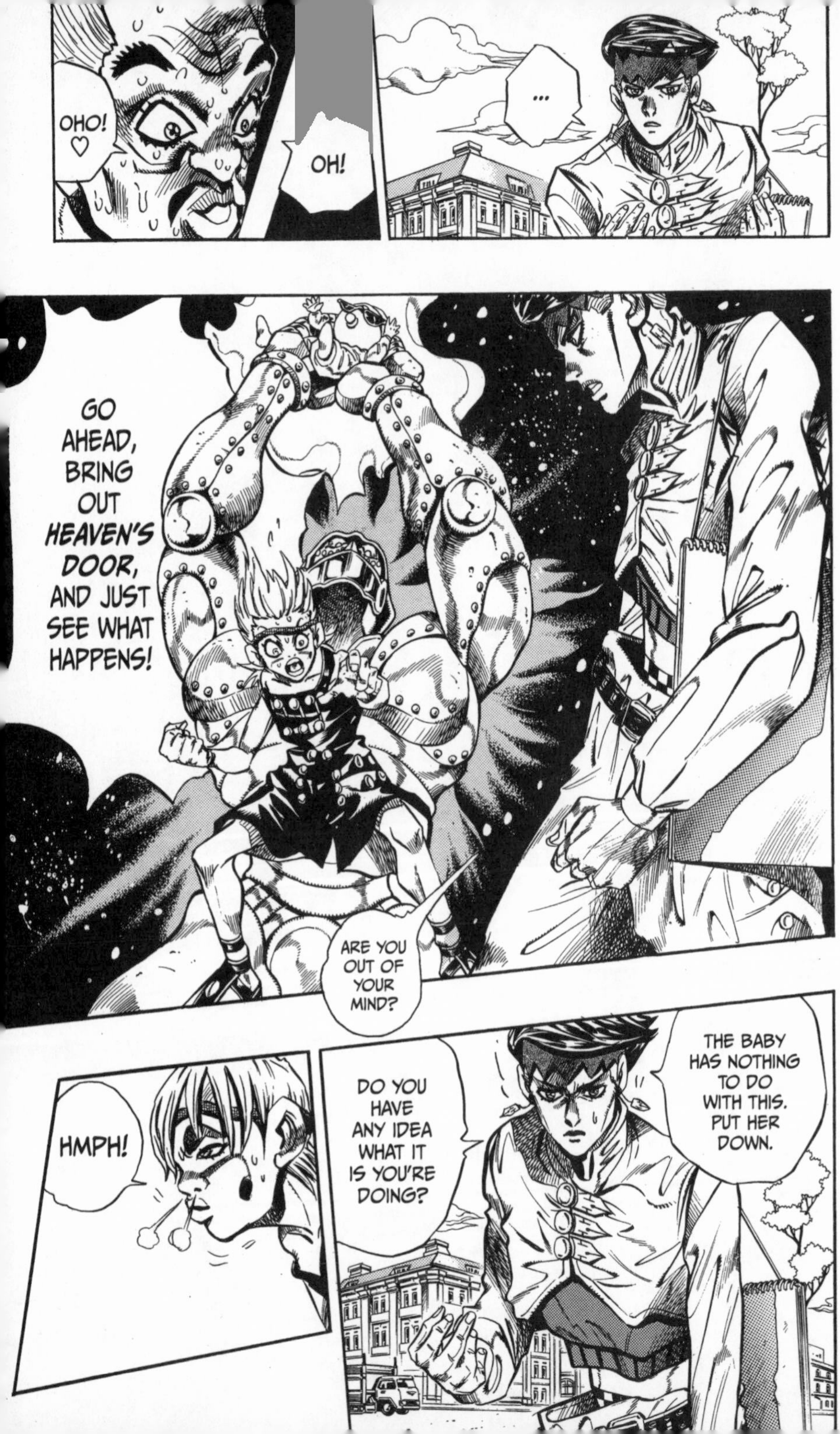
...
OH!
OHO! ♡
GO AHEAD, BRING OUT *HEAVEN'S DOOR,* AND JUST SEE WHAT HAPPENS!
ARE YOU OUT OF YOUR MIND?
THE BABY HAS NOTHING TO DO WITH THIS. PUT HER DOWN.
DO YOU HAVE ANY IDEA WHAT IT IS YOU'RE DOING?
HMPH!

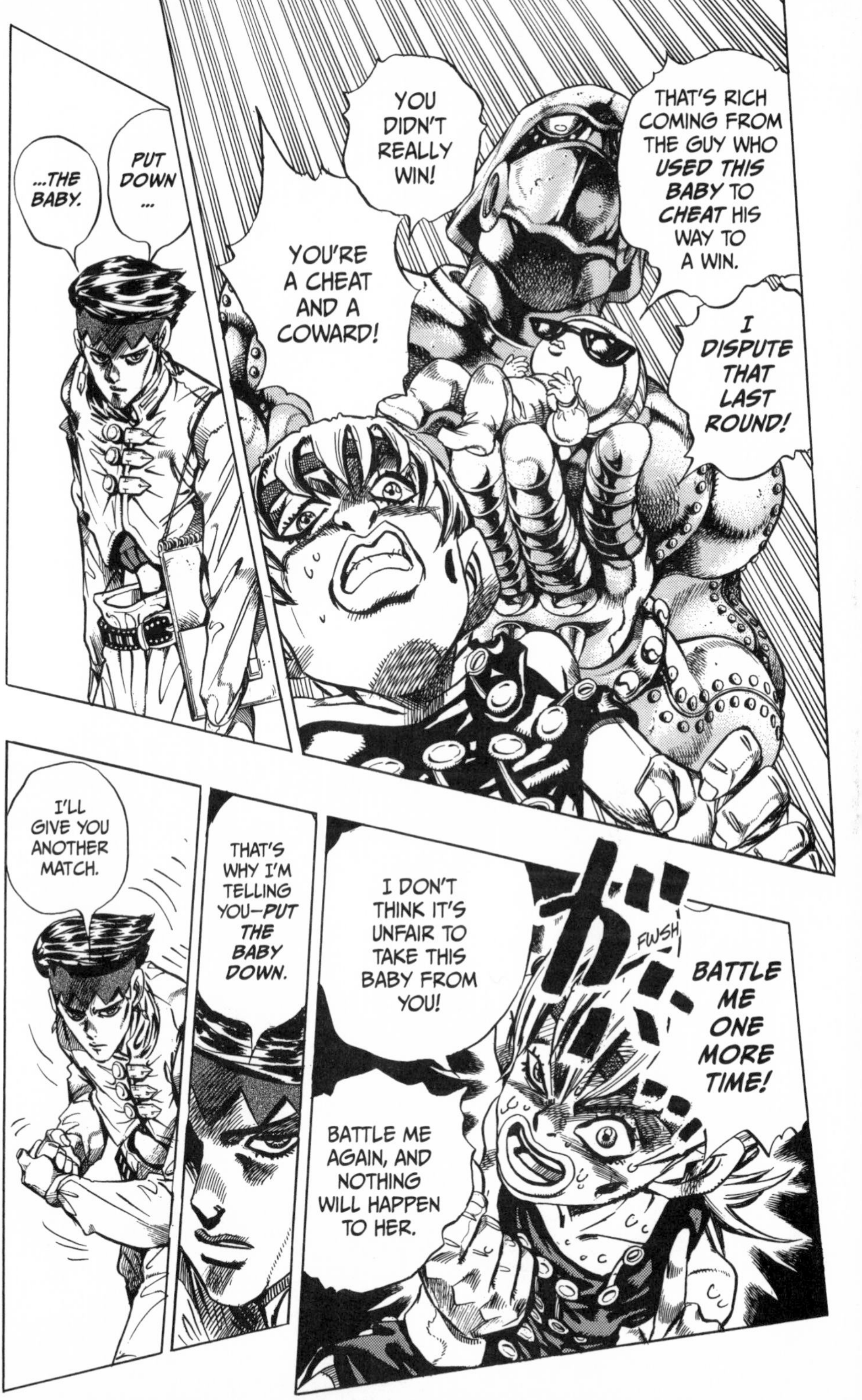
THAT'S RICH COMING FROM THE GUY WHO *USED THIS BABY* TO *CHEAT* HIS WAY TO A WIN.
YOU DIDN'T REALLY WIN!
I DISPUTE THAT LAST ROUND!
YOU'RE A CHEAT AND A COWARD!
PUT DOWN ...
...THE BABY.
BATTLE ME ONE MORE TIME!
FWSH
I DON'T THINK IT'S UNFAIR TO TAKE THIS BABY FROM YOU!
BATTLE ME AGAIN, AND NOTHING WILL HAPPEN TO HER.
THAT'S WHY I'M TELLING YOU—*PUT THE BABY DOWN.*
I'LL GIVE YOU ANOTHER MATCH.

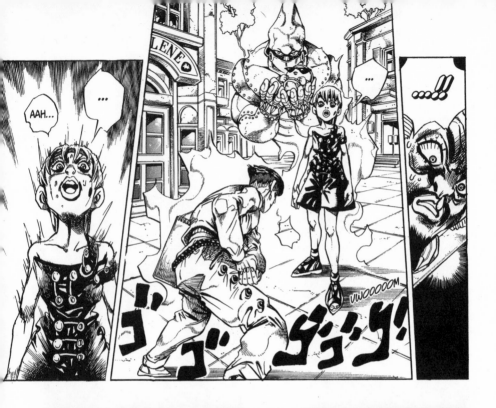

AAH...

...

...

...!!

UWOOOOOM

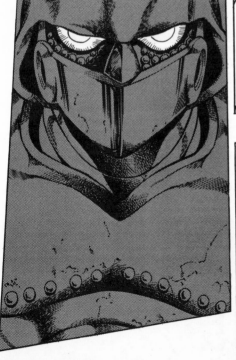

AAA
AAA
AAA
AAA
AAH!

AAAA
AAAA
AAAA
AAAA
AAAA
AAAA
AAA
AH!

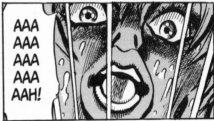

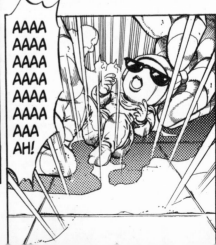

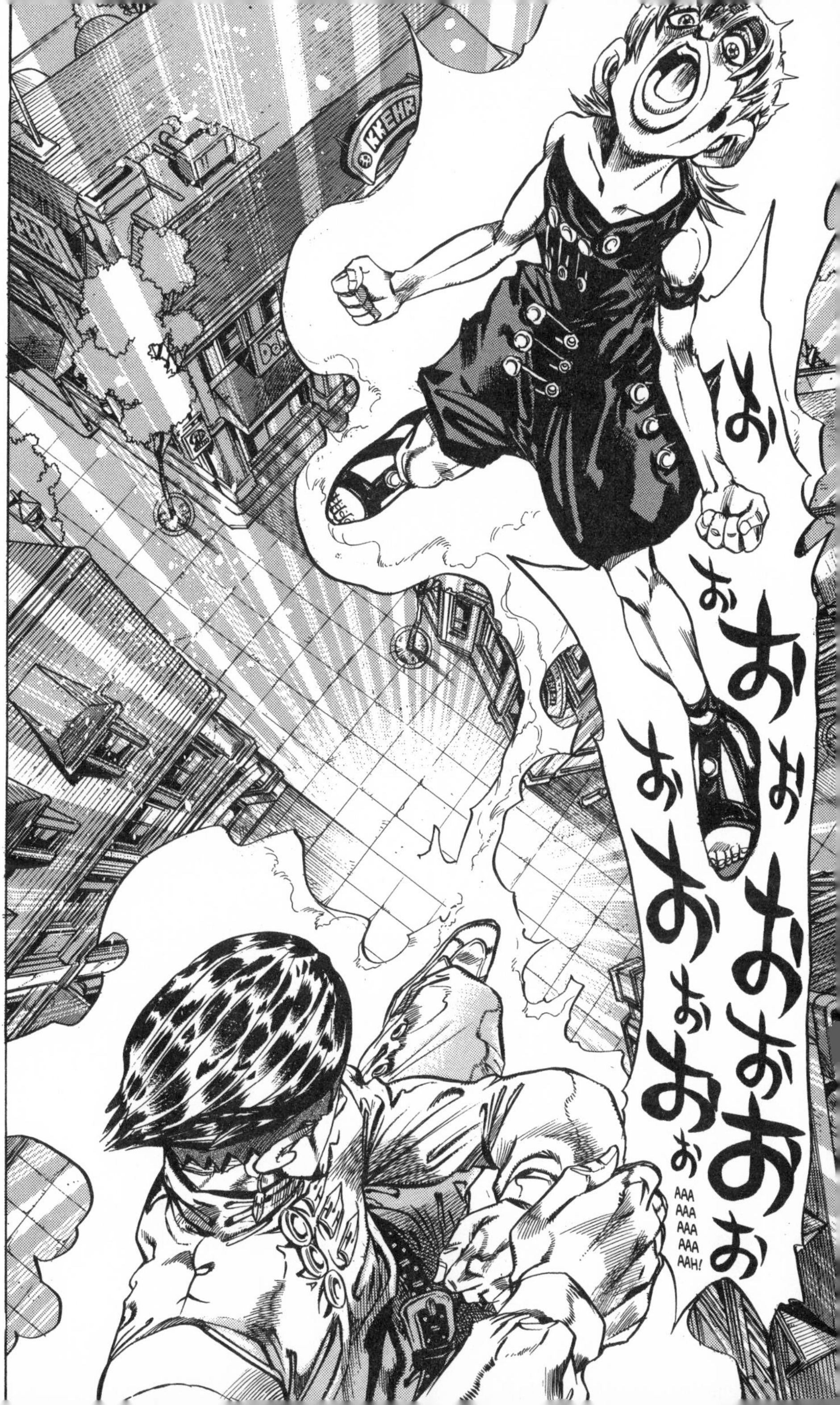
AAA
AAA
AAA
AAA
AAH!

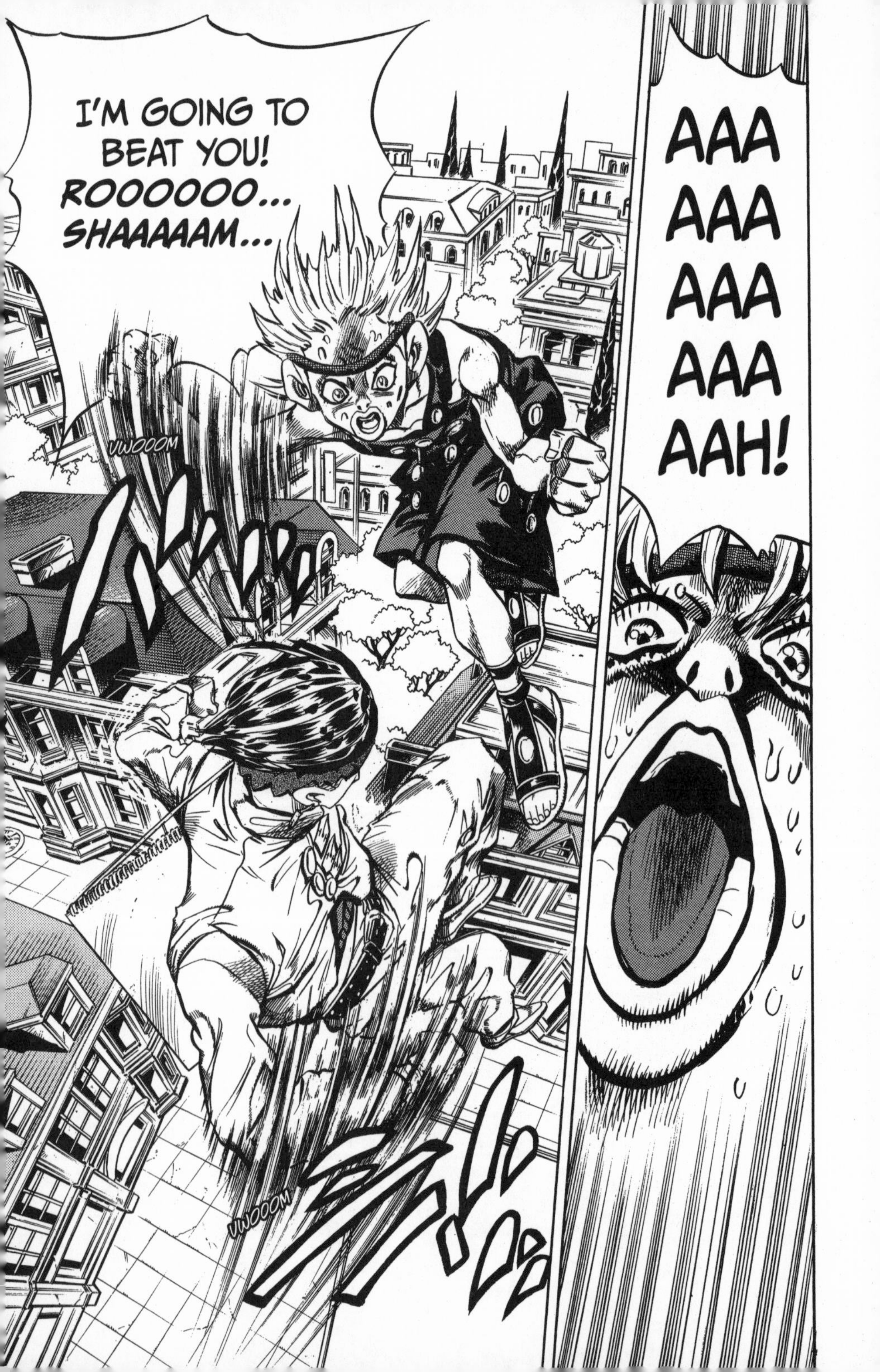
AAA AAA AAA AAA AAH!
I'M GOING TO BEAT YOU! ROOOOOO... SHAAAAAM...
UWOOOM
UWOOOM

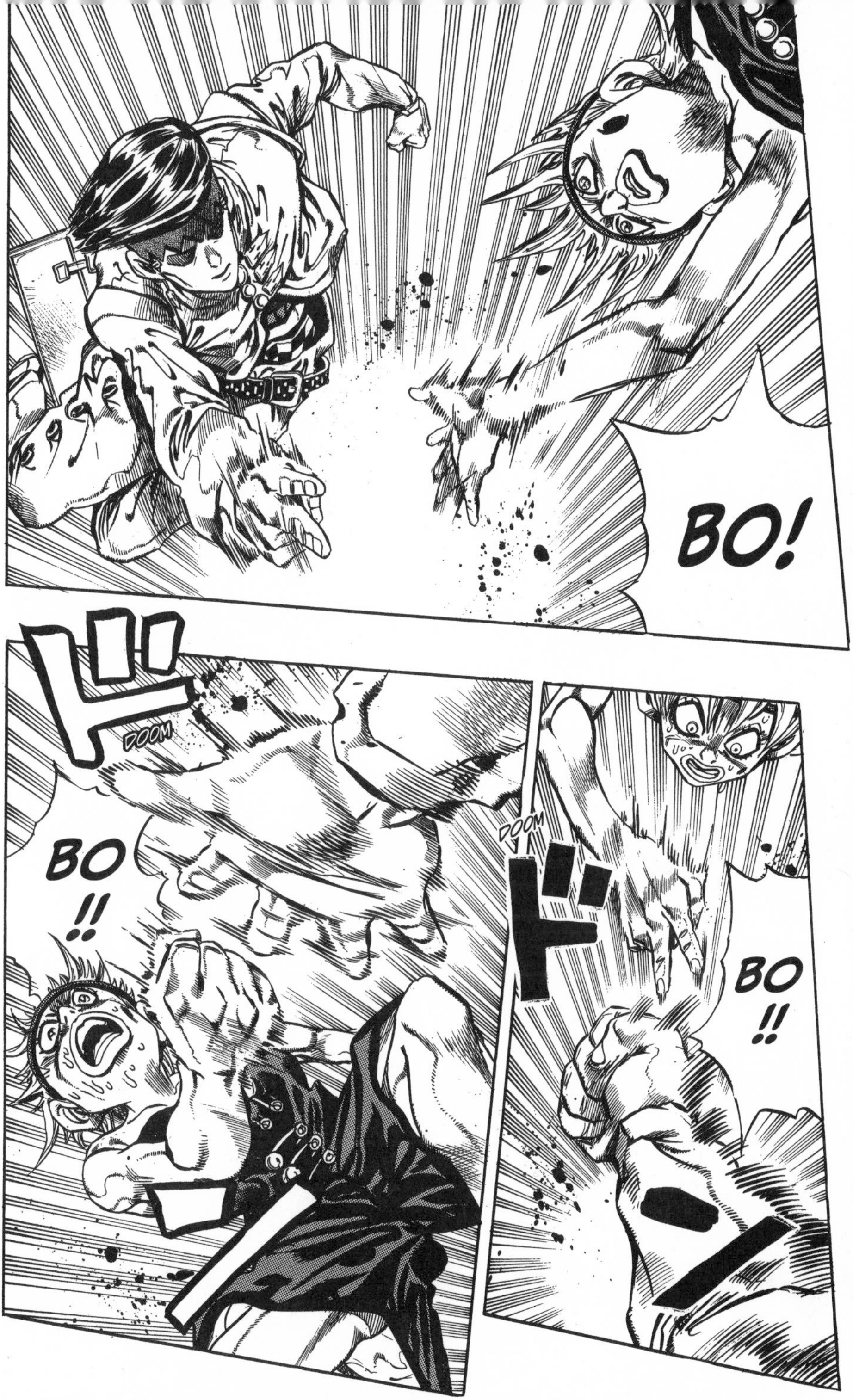
BO!
DOOM
ド
BO !!
ド
DOOM
BO !!

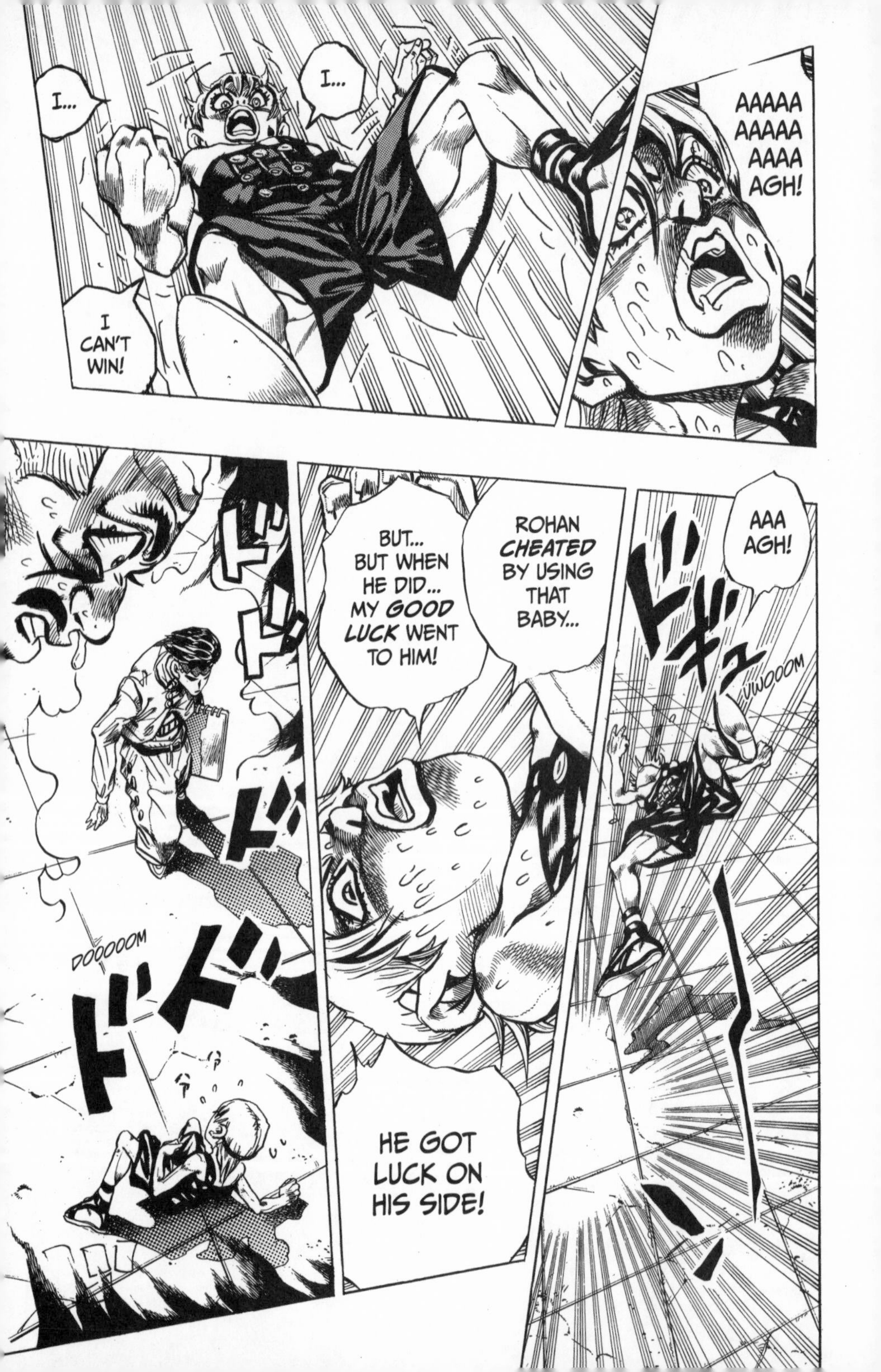
AAAAA AAAAA AAAA AGH!
I...
I...
I CAN'T WIN!
AAA AGH!
UWOOOM
ROHAN CHEATED BY USING THAT BABY...
BUT... BUT WHEN HE DID... MY GOOD LUCK WENT TO HIM!
HE GOT LUCK ON HIS SIDE!
DOOOOOM

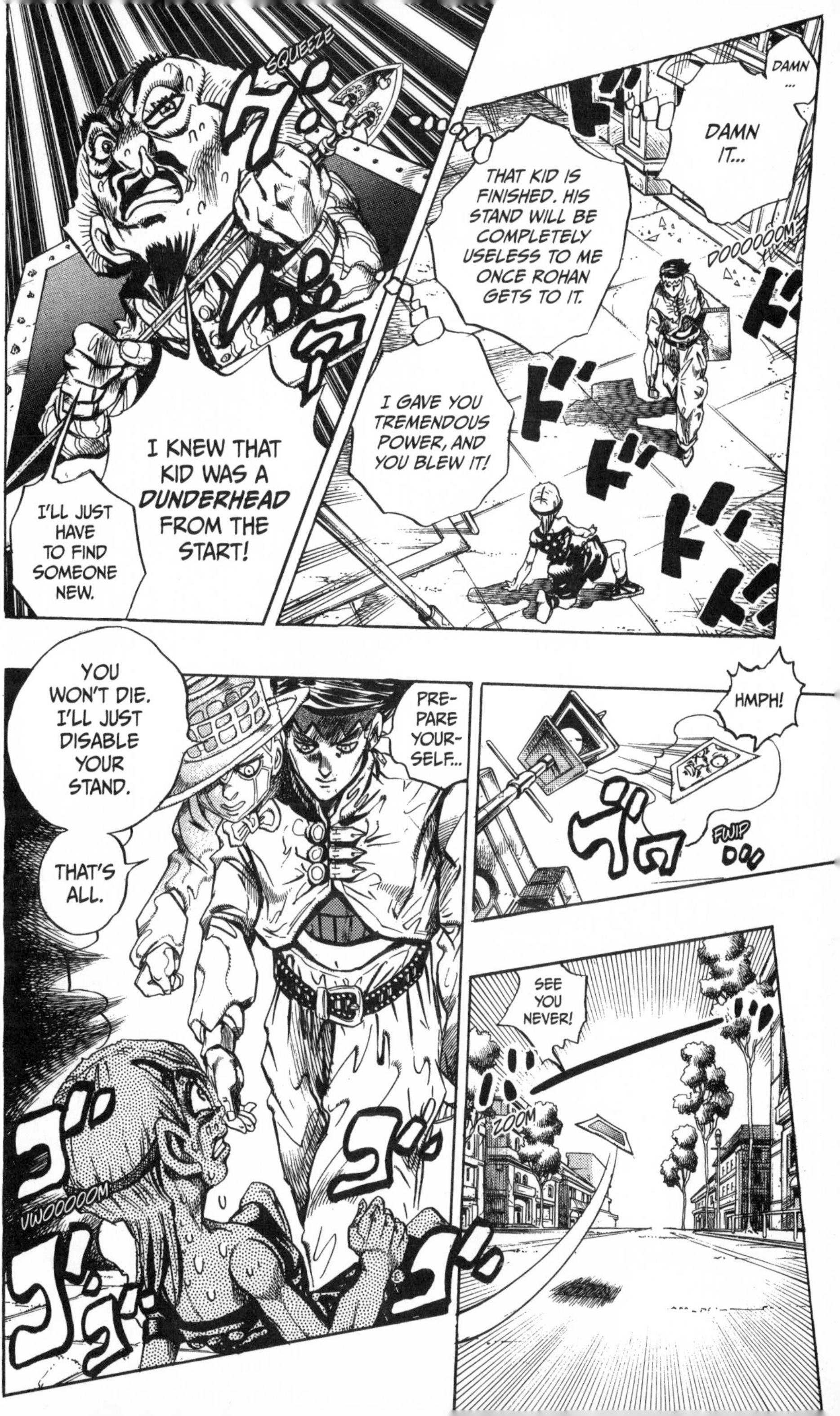
DAMN ...
DAMN IT...
THAT KID IS FINISHED. HIS STAND WILL BE COMPLETELY USELESS TO ME ONCE ROHAN GETS TO IT.
DOOOOOOOM
I GAVE YOU TREMENDOUS POWER, AND YOU BLEW IT!
SQUEEZE
I KNEW THAT KID WAS A *DUNDERHEAD* FROM THE START!
I'LL JUST HAVE TO FIND SOMEONE NEW.
HMPH!
FWIP
SEE YOU NEVER!
ZOOM
PRE-PARE YOUR-SELF...
YOU WON'T DIE. I'LL JUST DISABLE YOUR STAND.
THAT'S ALL.
VWOOOOOM

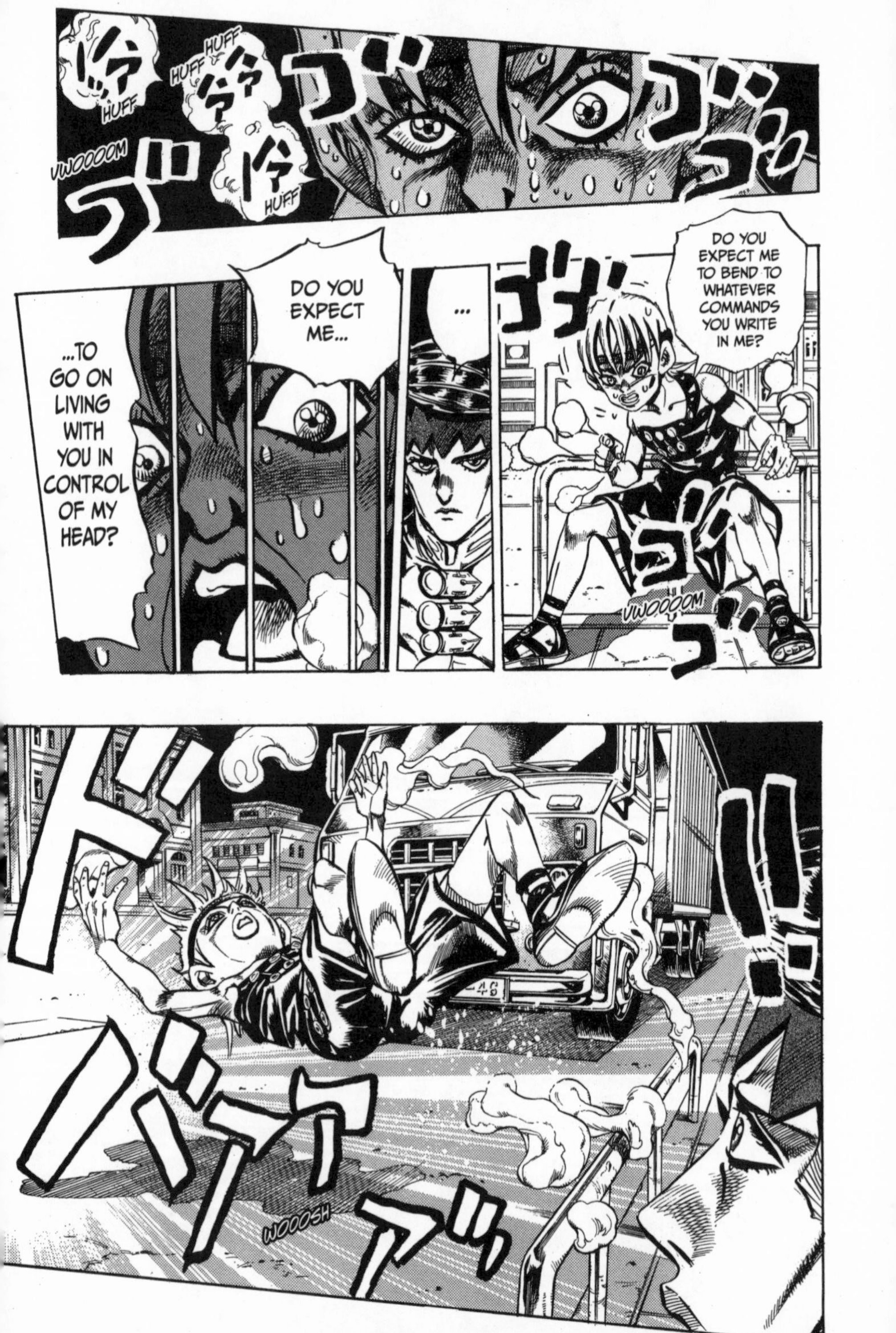
HUFF
HUFF
HUFF
VWOOOOM
HUFF
DO YOU EXPECT ME TO BEND TO WHATEVER COMMANDS YOU WRITE IN ME?
VWOOOOM
...
DO YOU EXPECT ME...
...TO GO ON LIVING WITH YOU IN CONTROL OF MY HEAD?
WOOOSH

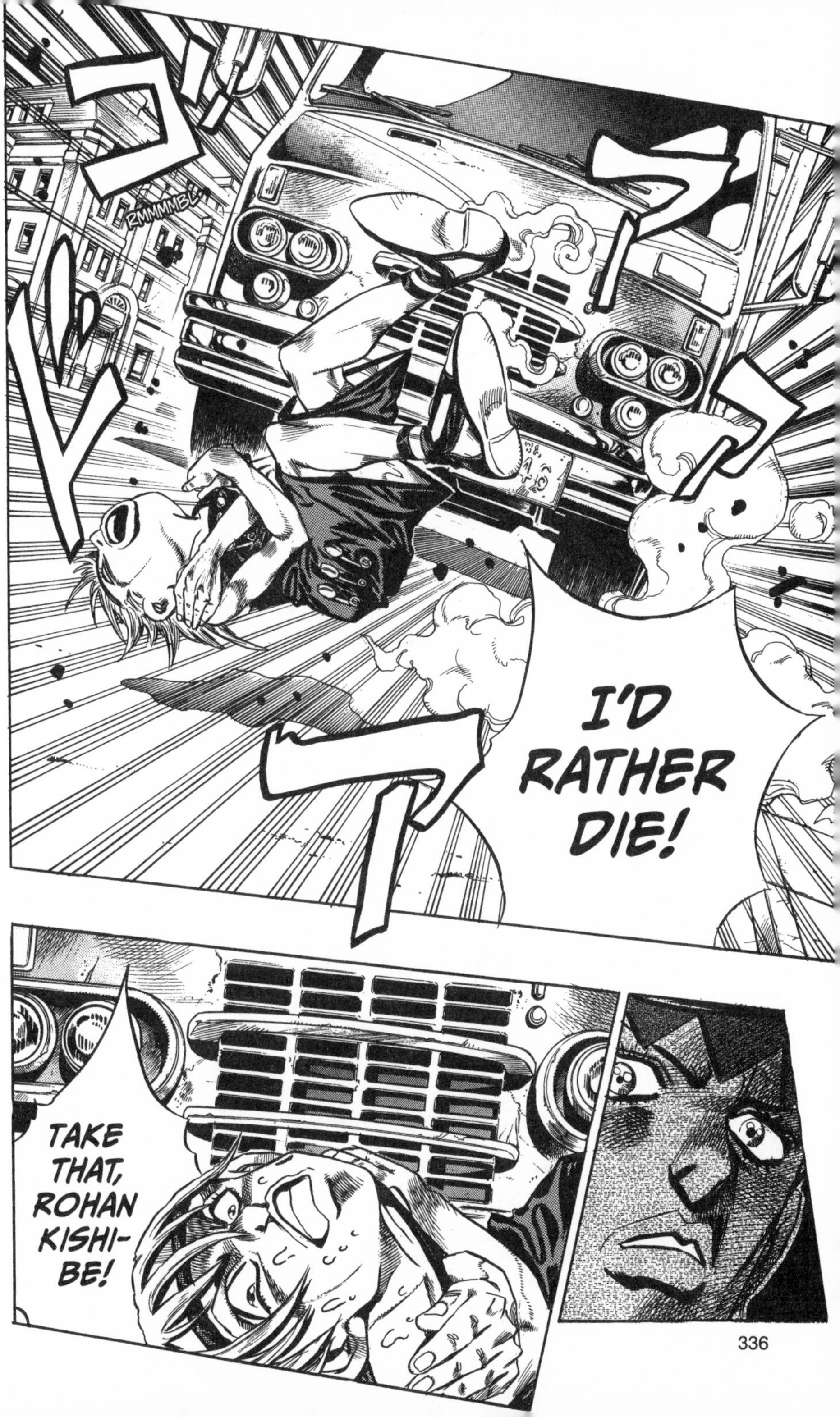
RMMMMBL
I'D RATHER DIE!
TAKE THAT, ROHAN KISHI-BE!

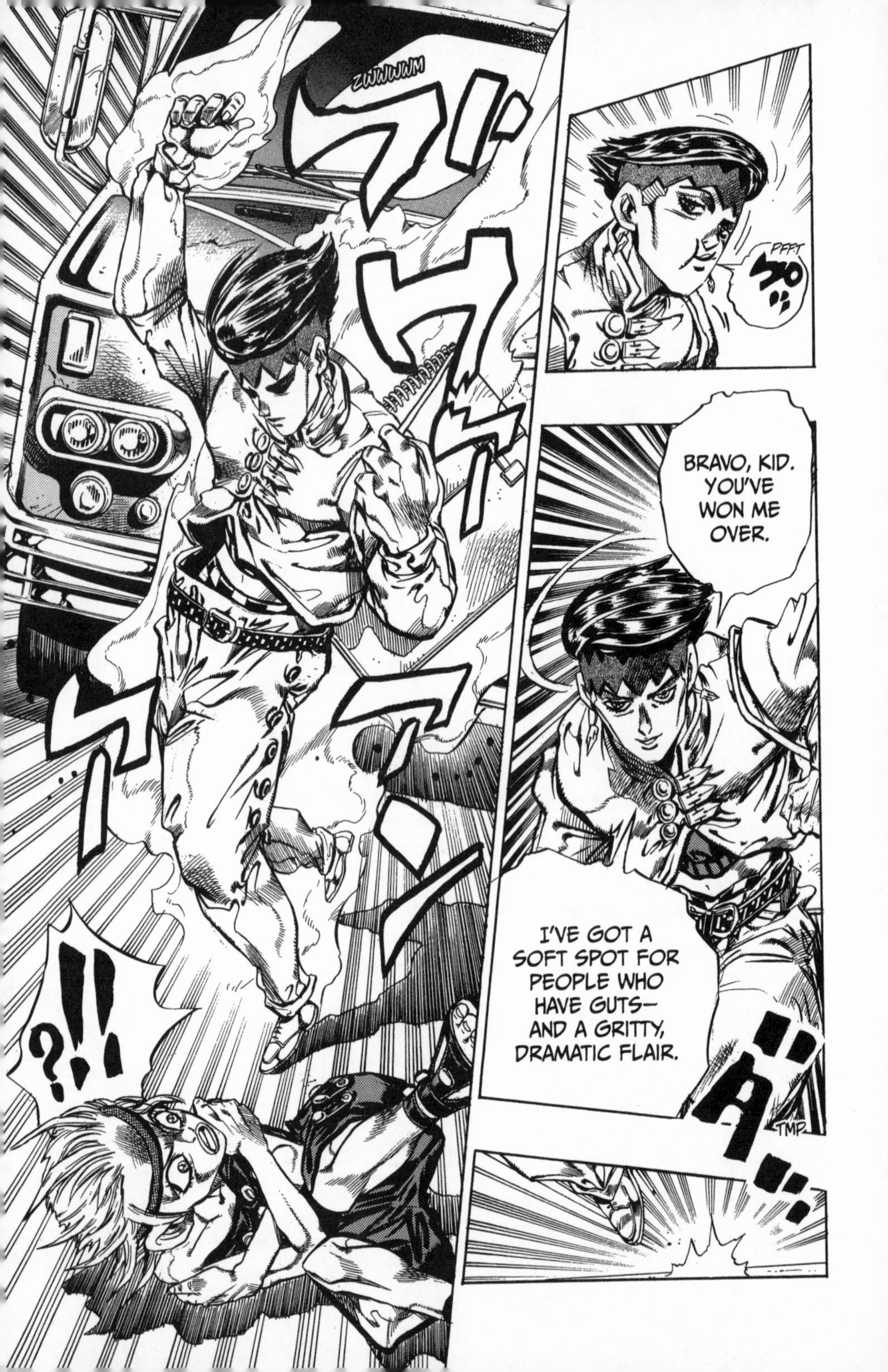
PFFT
BRAVO, KID. YOU'VE WON ME OVER.
I'VE GOT A SOFT SPOT FOR PEOPLE WHO HAVE GUTS— AND A GRITTY, DRAMATIC FLAIR.
TMP
ZWWWWM
?!!

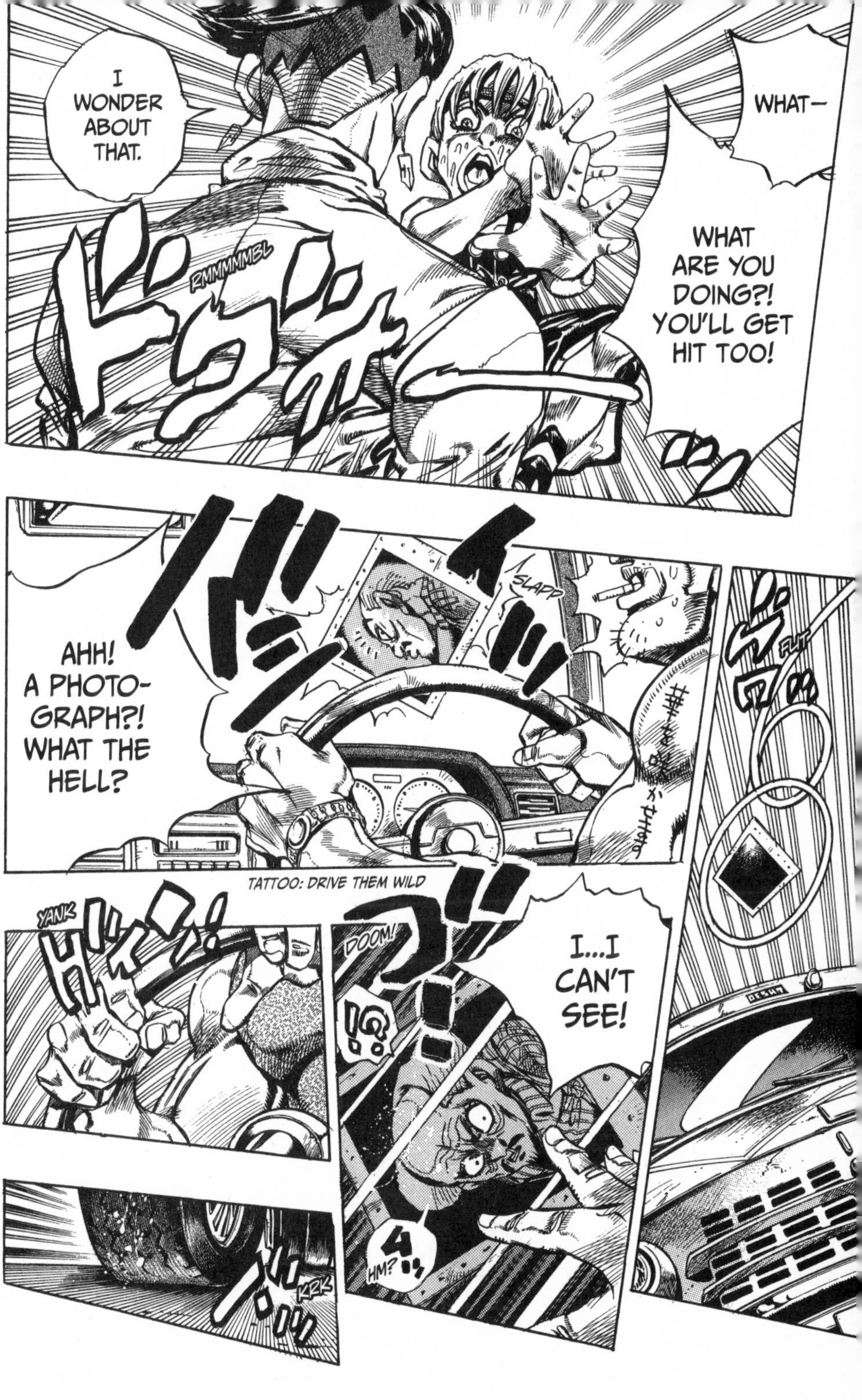
WHAT—
WHAT ARE YOU DOING?! YOU'LL GET HIT TOO!
I WONDER ABOUT THAT.
RMMMMMBL
FUT
SLAPP
AHH! A PHOTO-GRAPH?! WHAT THE HELL?
TATTOO: DRIVE THEM WILD
I...I CAN'T SEE!
DOOM!
HM?
YANK
KRK

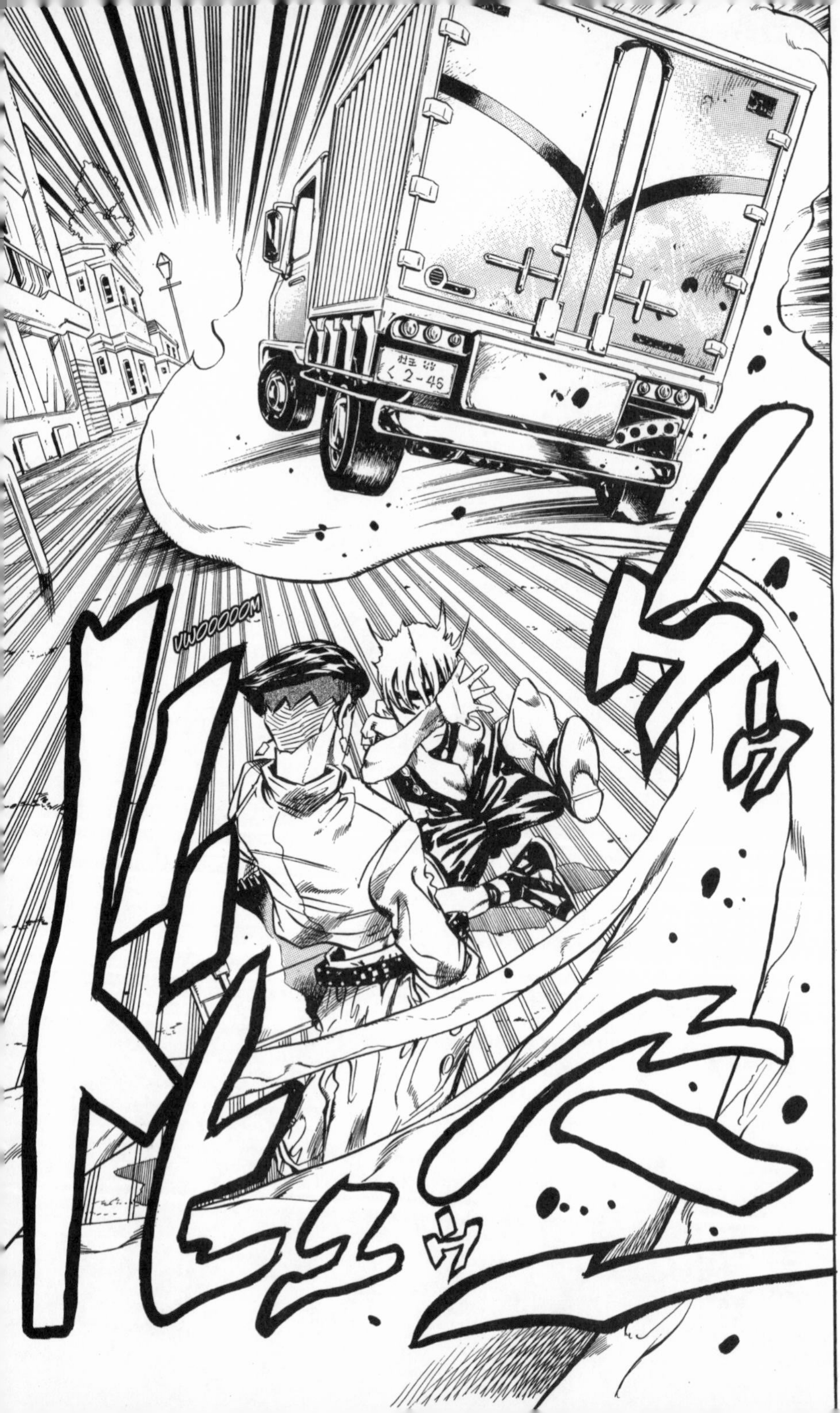
VWOOOOOM

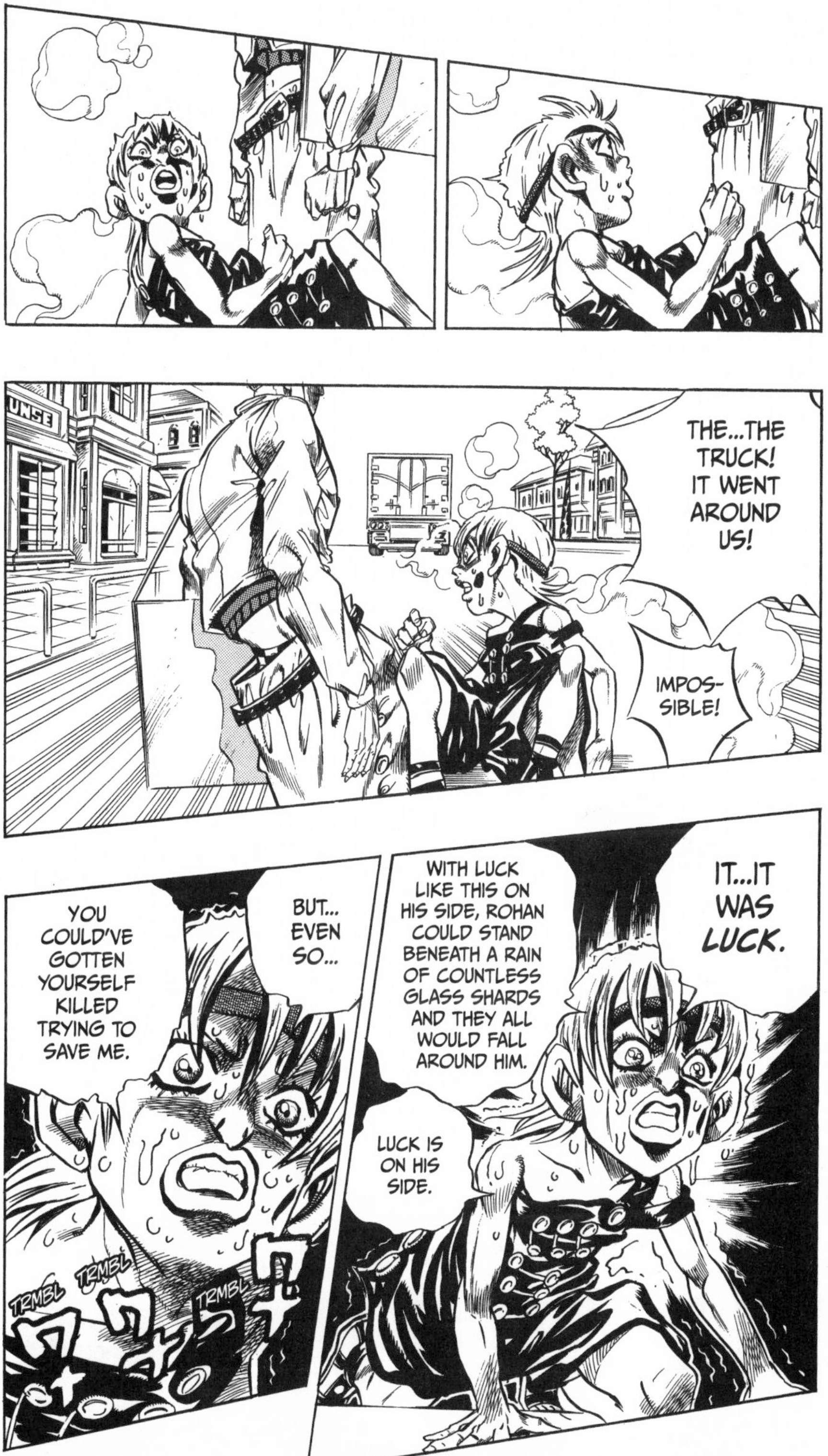
UNSE
THE...THE TRUCK! IT WENT AROUND US!
IMPOSSIBLE!
IT...IT WAS LUCK.
WITH LUCK LIKE THIS ON HIS SIDE, ROHAN COULD STAND BENEATH A RAIN OF COUNTLESS GLASS SHARDS AND THEY ALL WOULD FALL AROUND HIM.
LUCK IS ON HIS SIDE.
BUT... EVEN SO...
YOU COULD'VE GOTTEN YOURSELF KILLED TRYING TO SAVE ME.
TRMBL
TRMBL
TRMBL

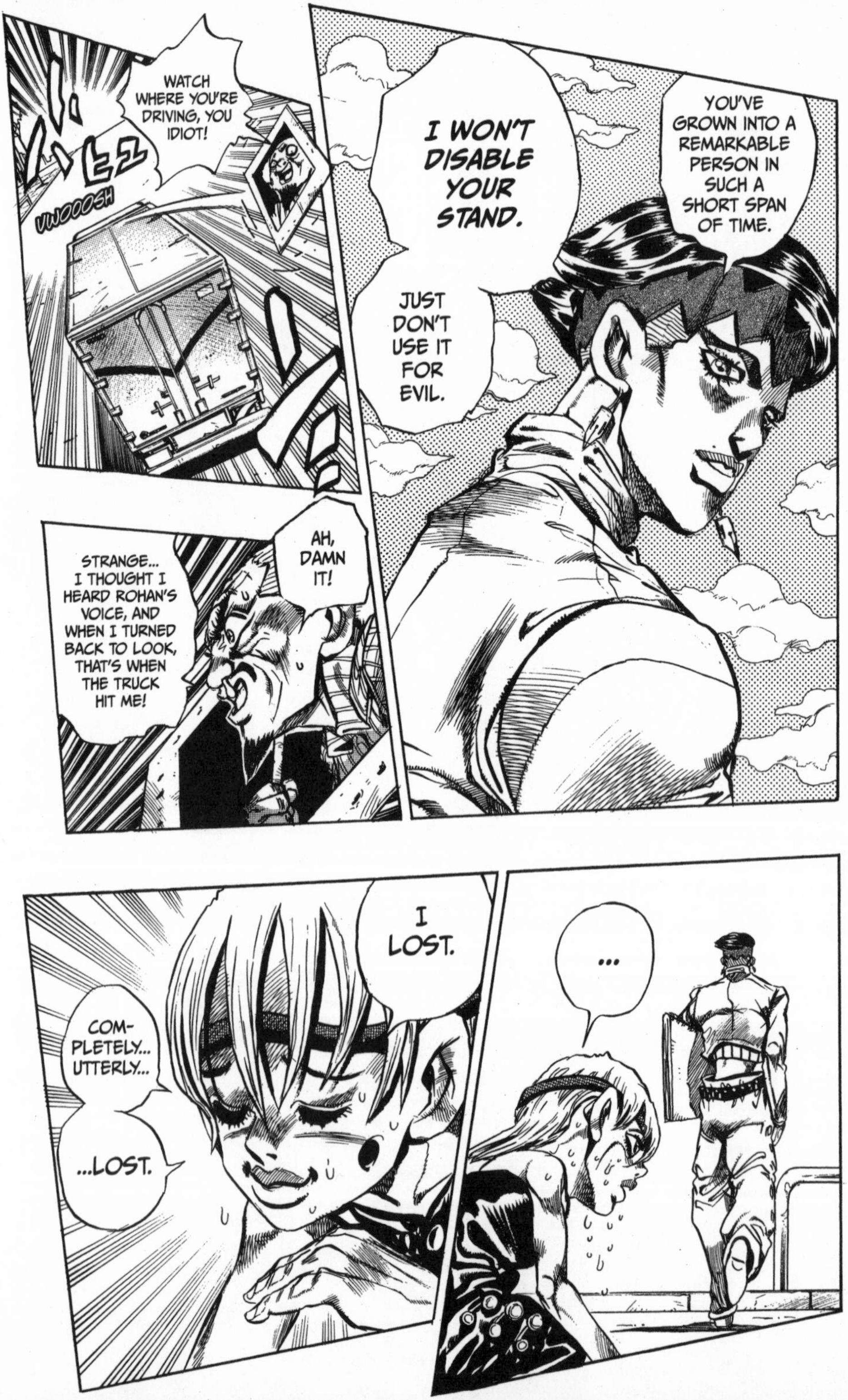
YOU'VE GROWN INTO A REMARKABLE PERSON IN SUCH A SHORT SPAN OF TIME.
I WON'T DISABLE YOUR STAND.
JUST DON'T USE IT FOR EVIL.
WATCH WHERE YOU'RE DRIVING, YOU IDIOT!
UWOOOSH
AH, DAMN IT!
STRANGE... I THOUGHT I HEARD ROHAN'S VOICE, AND WHEN I TURNED BACK TO LOOK, THAT'S WHEN THE TRUCK HIT ME!
...
I LOST.
COM-PLETELY... UTTERLY...
...LOST.

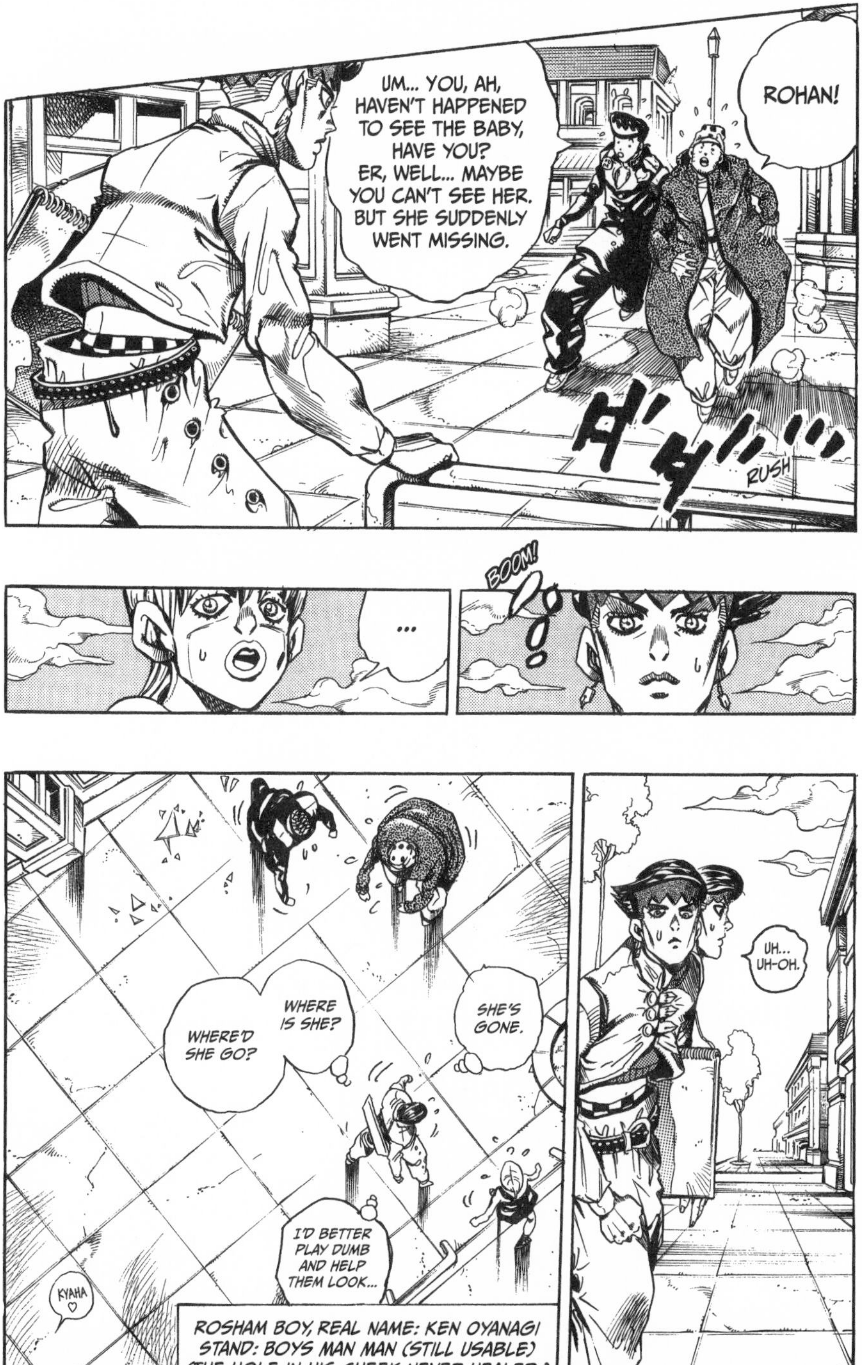
ROHAN!
UM... YOU, AH, HAVEN'T HAPPENED TO SEE THE BABY, HAVE YOU? ER, WELL... MAYBE YOU CAN'T SEE HER. BUT SHE SUDDENLY WENT MISSING.
RUSH
BOOM!
...
UH... UH-OH.
SHE'S GONE.
WHERE IS SHE?
WHERE'D SHE GO?
I'D BETTER PLAY DUMB AND HELP THEM LOOK...
KYAHA ♡
ROSHAM BOY, REAL NAME: KEN OYANAGI
STAND: BOYS MAN MAN (STILL USABLE)
(THE HOLE IN HIS CHEEK NEVER HEALED.)
TO BE CONTINUED....

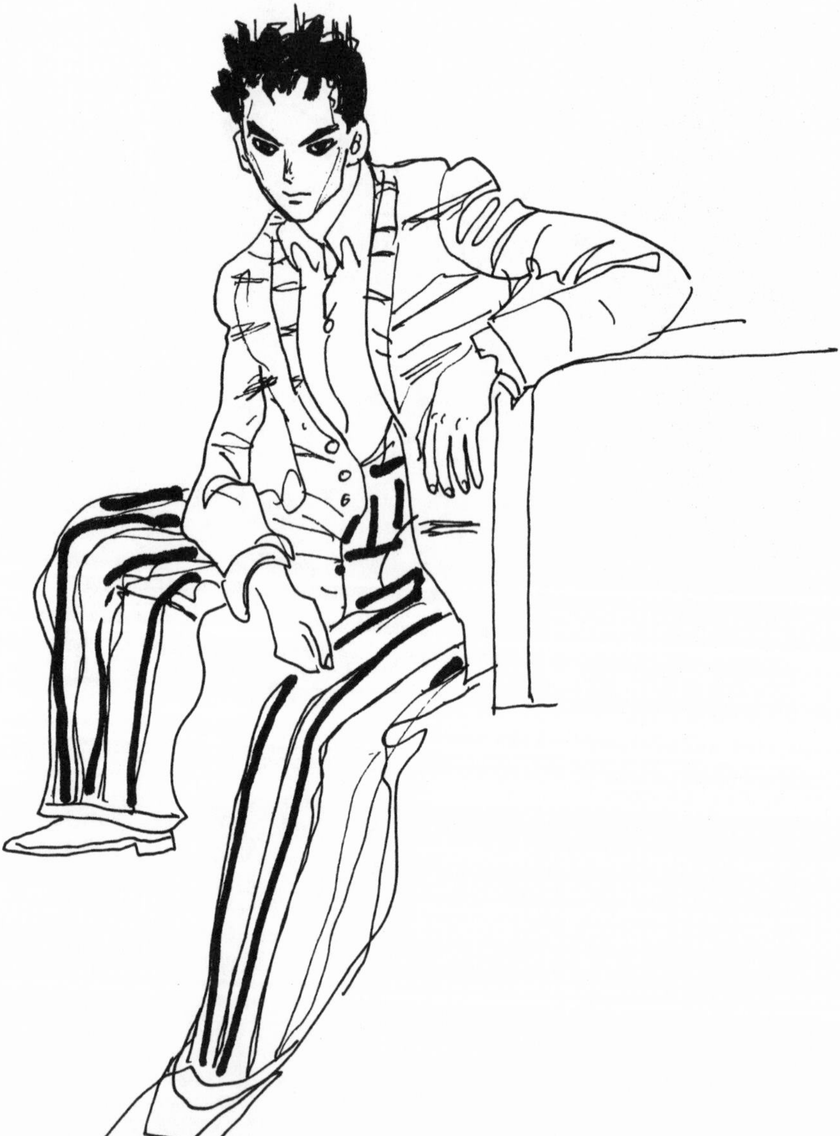

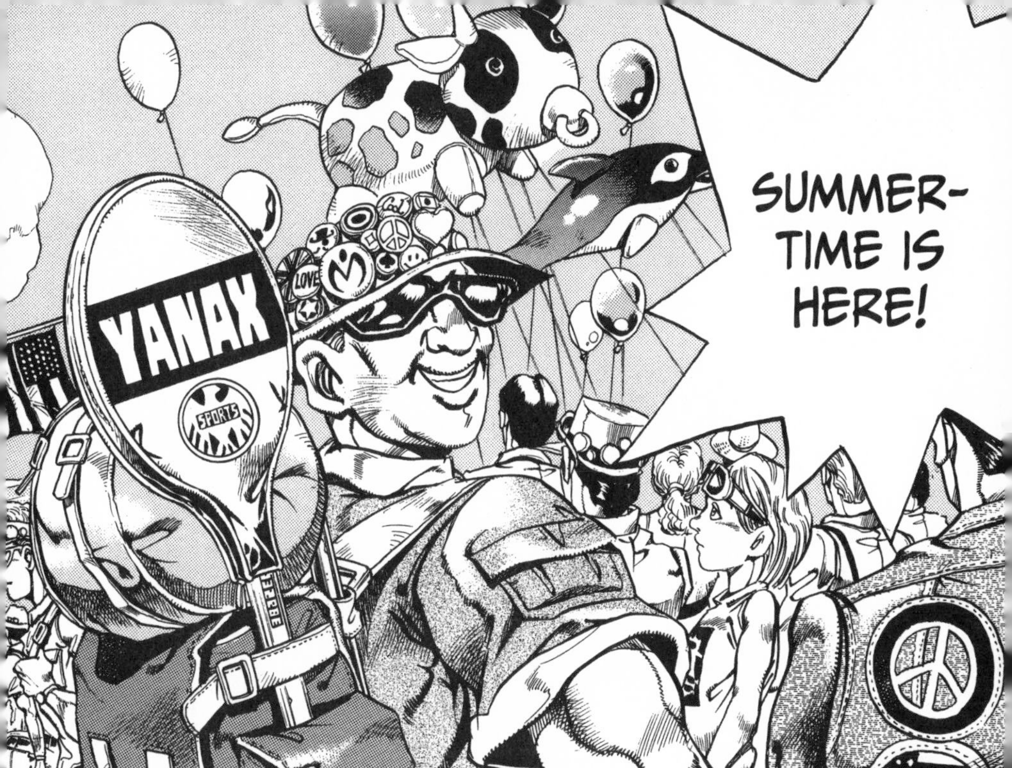
SUMMER-TIME IS HERE!
YANAX
SPORTS
LOVE
CAMP

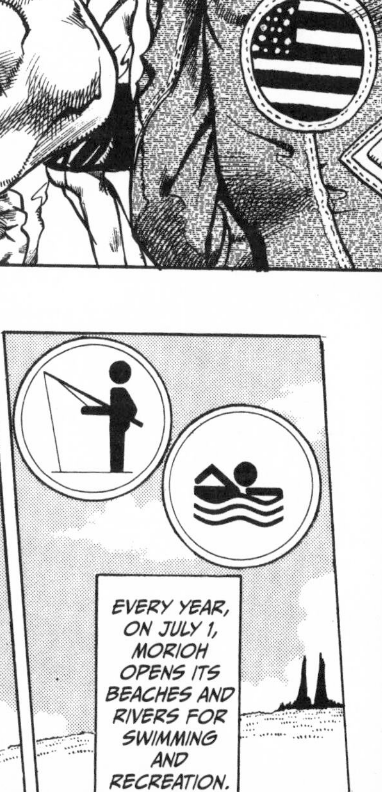
EVERY YEAR, ON JULY 1, MORIOH OPENS ITS BEACHES AND RIVERS FOR SWIMMING AND RECREATION.

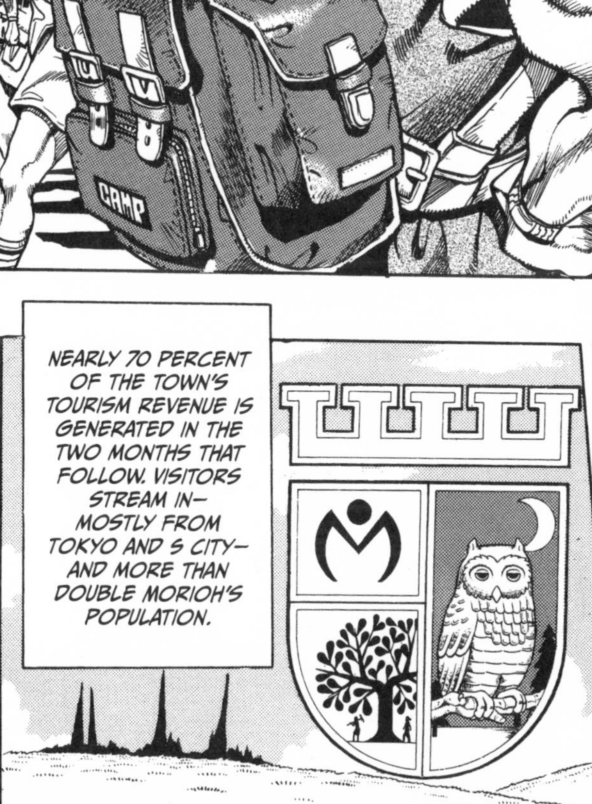
NEARLY 70 PERCENT OF THE TOWN'S TOURISM REVENUE IS GENERATED IN THE TWO MONTHS THAT FOLLOW. VISITORS STREAM IN—MOSTLY FROM TOKYO AND S CITY—AND MORE THAN DOUBLE MORIOH'S POPULATION.

CHAPTER 112

YOSHIKAGE KIRA'S NEW LIFE, PART 2

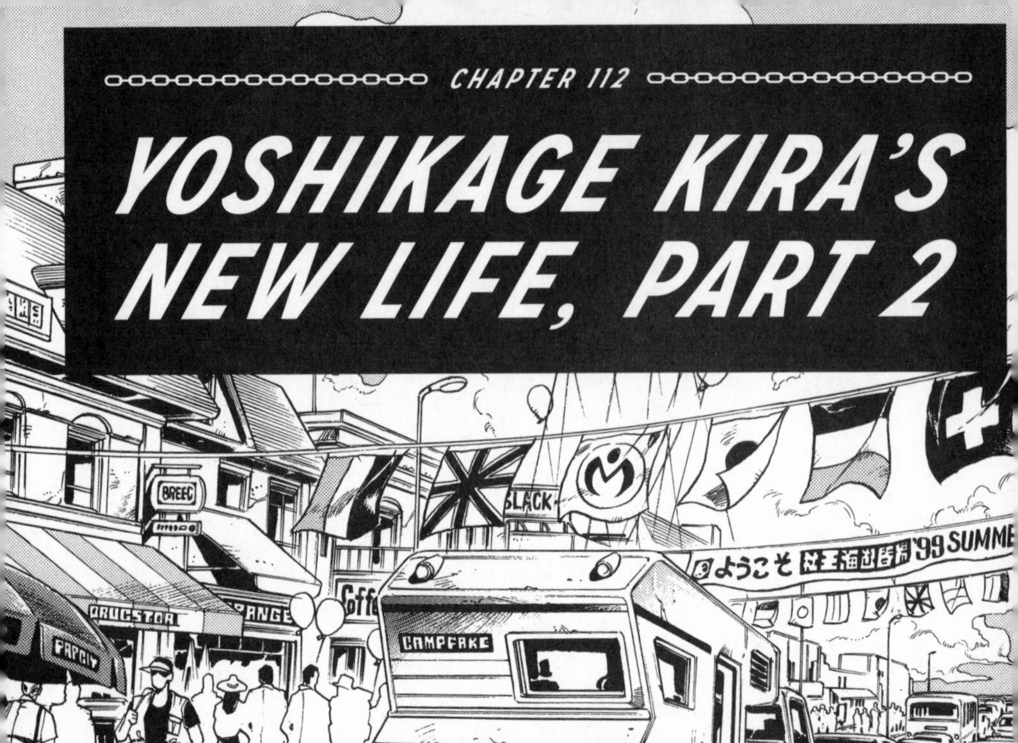
BANNER: WELCOME TO MORIOH BEACH FEST SUMMER '99

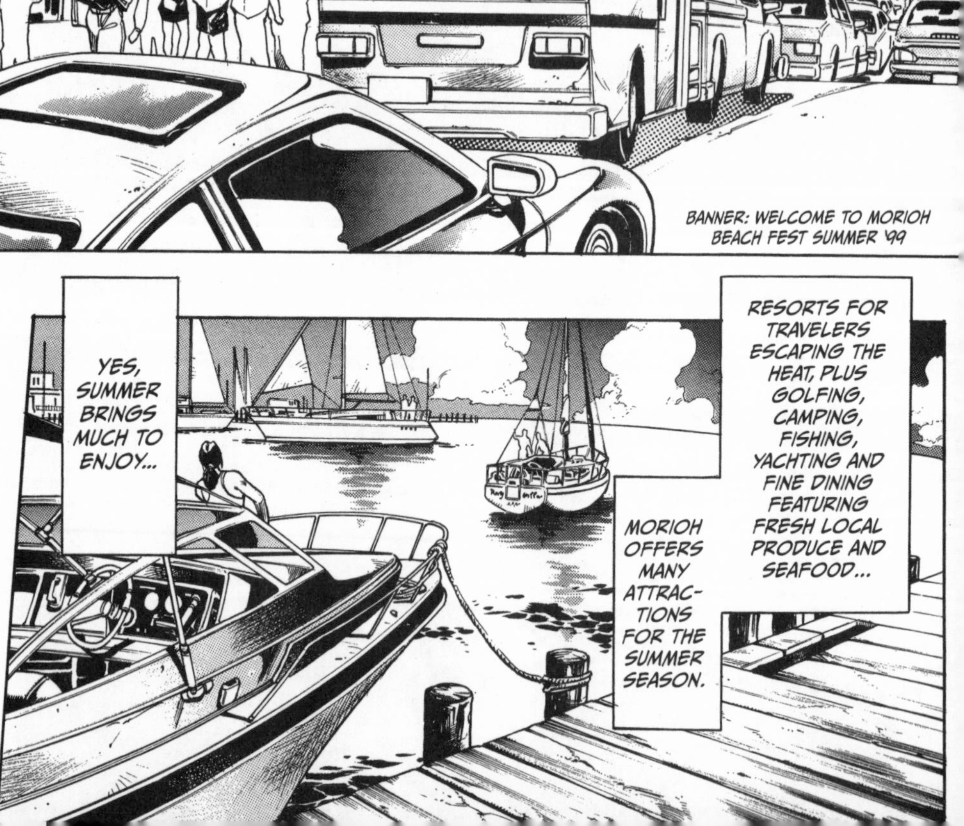
RESORTS FOR TRAVELERS ESCAPING THE HEAT, PLUS GOLFING, CAMPING, FISHING, YACHTING AND FINE DINING FEATURING FRESH LOCAL PRODUCE AND SEAFOOD...
MORIOH OFFERS MANY ATTRACTIONS FOR THE SUMMER SEASON.
YES, SUMMER BRINGS MUCH TO ENJOY...

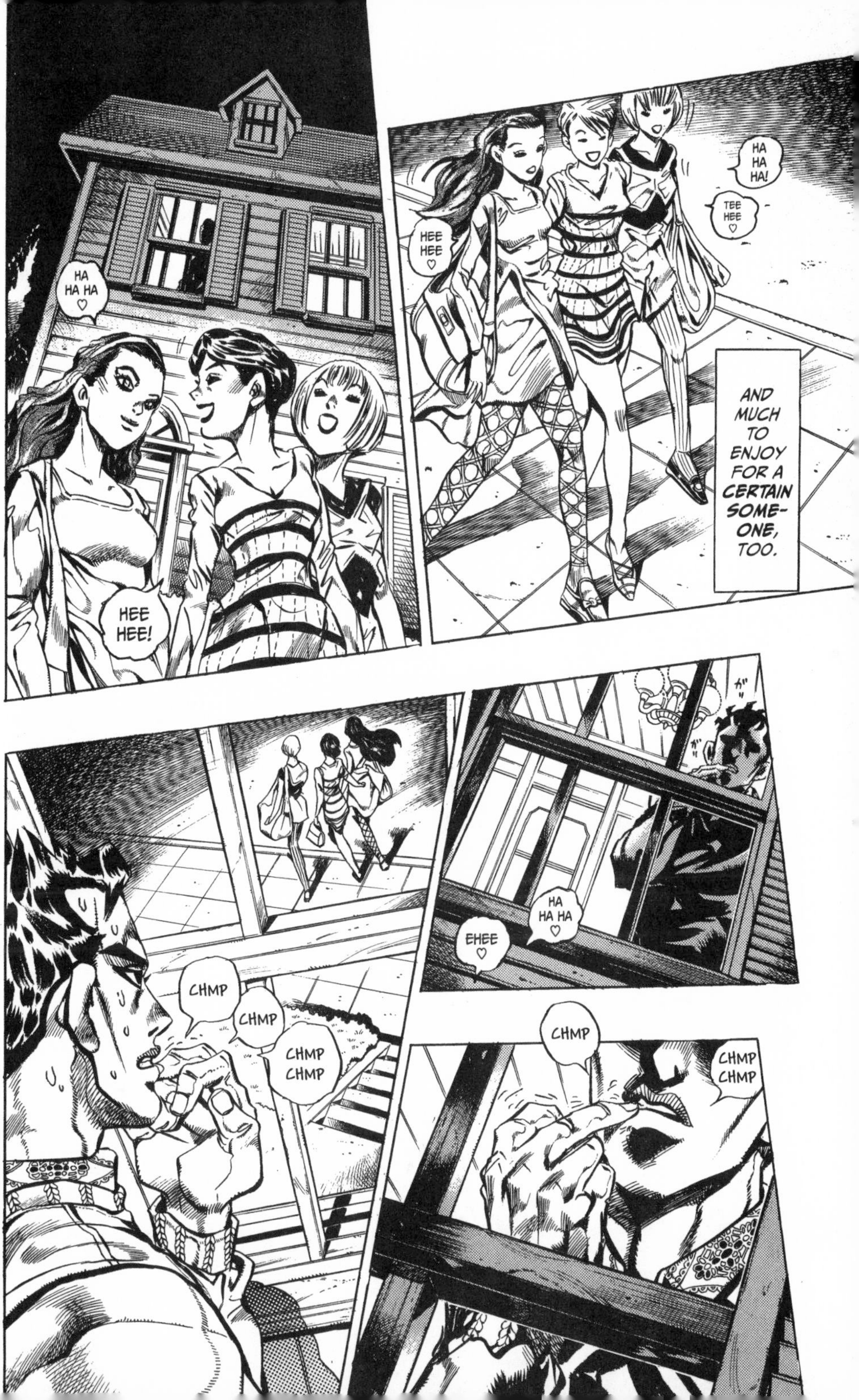
HA HA HA!
TEE HEE ♡
HEE HEE ♡
AND MUCH TO ENJOY FOR A CERTAIN SOMEONE, TOO.
HA HA HA ♡
HEE HEE!
HA HA HA ♡
EHEE ♡
CHMP
CHMP CHMP
CHMP
CHMP
CHMP CHMP

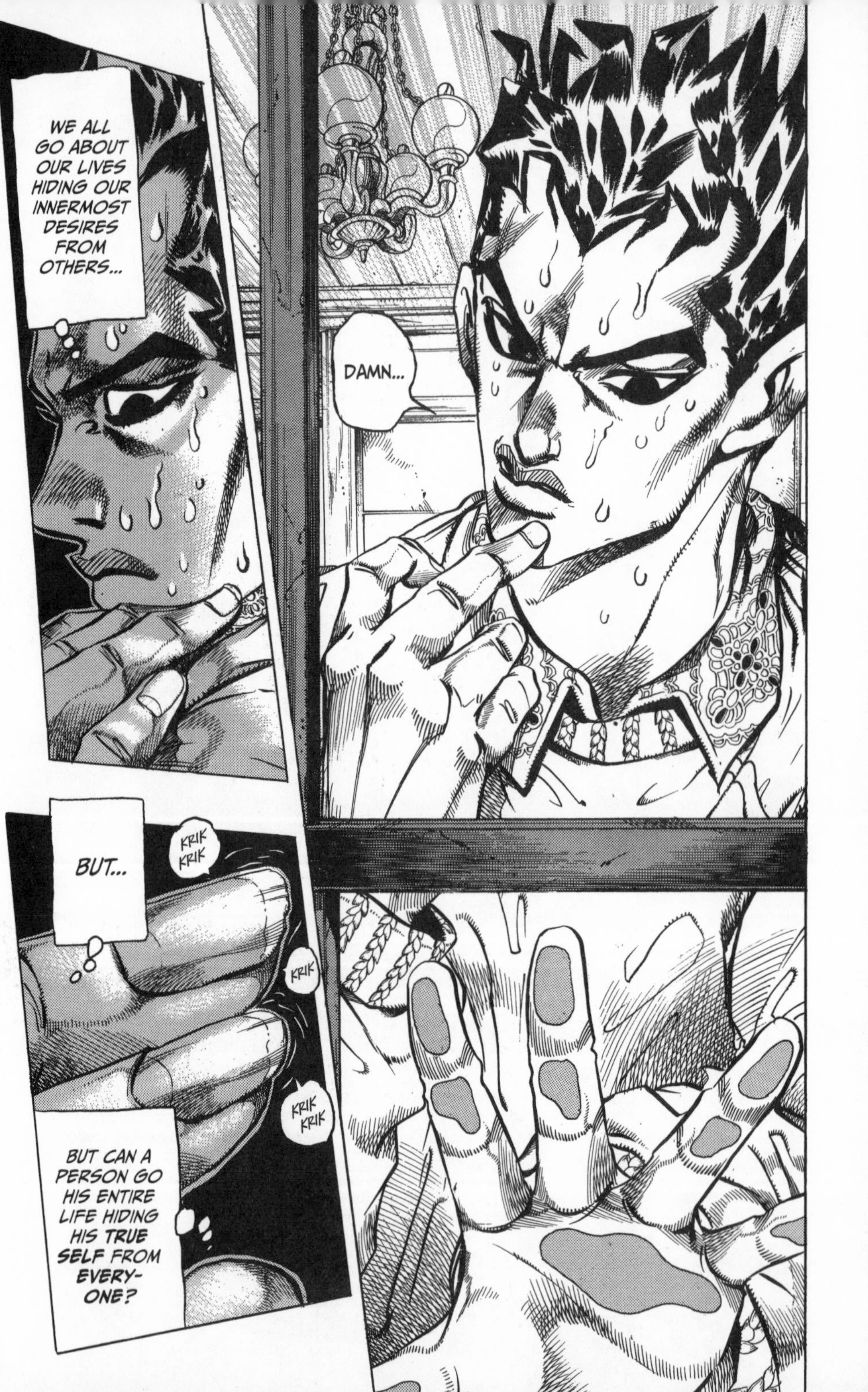
DAMN...
WE ALL GO ABOUT OUR LIVES HIDING OUR INNERMOST DESIRES FROM OTHERS...
BUT...
KRIK KRIK
KRIK
KRIK KRIK
BUT CAN A PERSON GO HIS ENTIRE LIFE HIDING HIS TRUE SELF FROM EVERY-ONE?

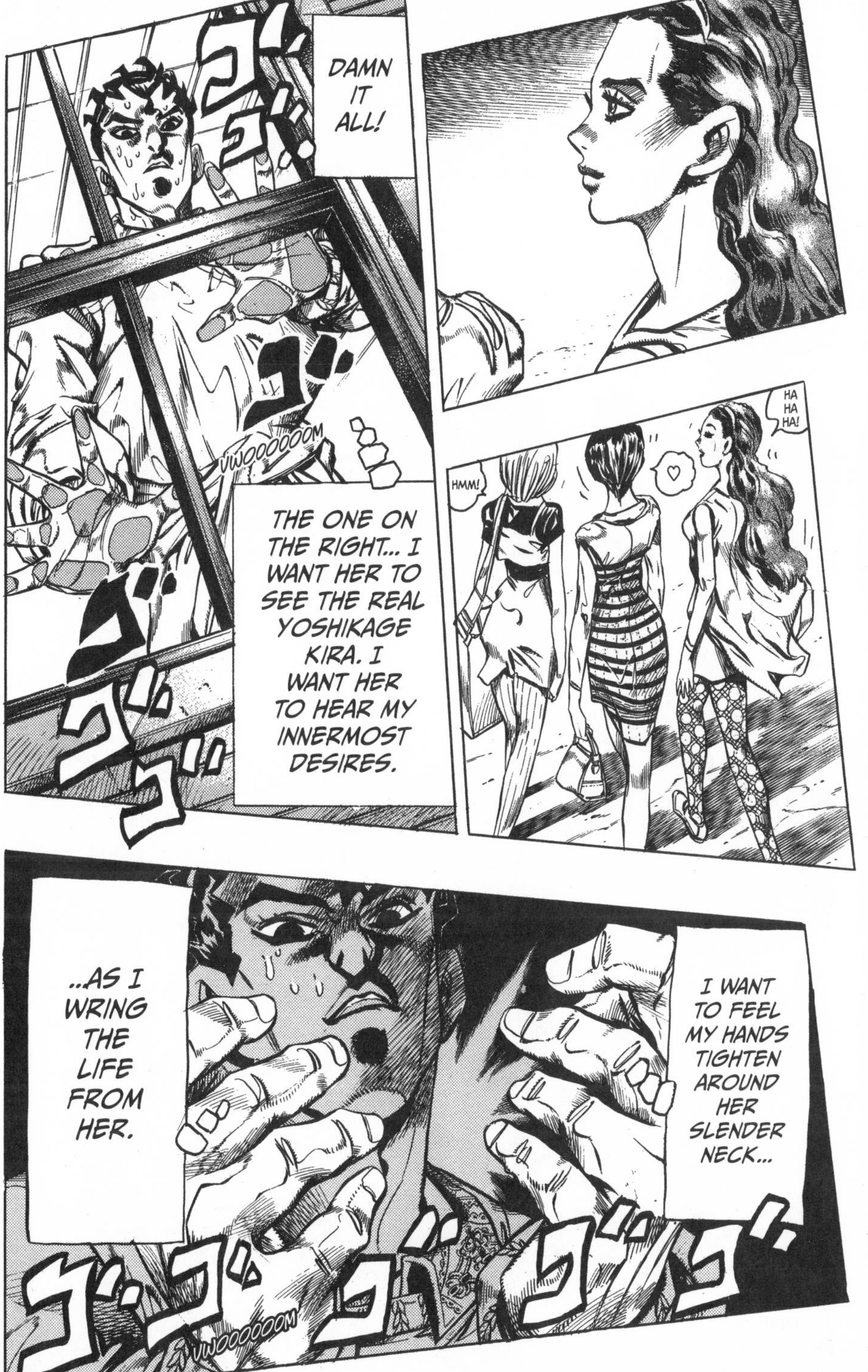
HA HA HA!
HMM!
DAMN IT ALL!
VWOOOOOOOM
THE ONE ON THE RIGHT... I WANT HER TO SEE THE REAL YOSHIKAGE KIRA. I WANT HER TO HEAR MY INNERMOST DESIRES.
I WANT TO FEEL MY HANDS TIGHTEN AROUND HER SLENDER NECK...
...AS I WRING THE LIFE FROM HER.
VWOOOOOOOM

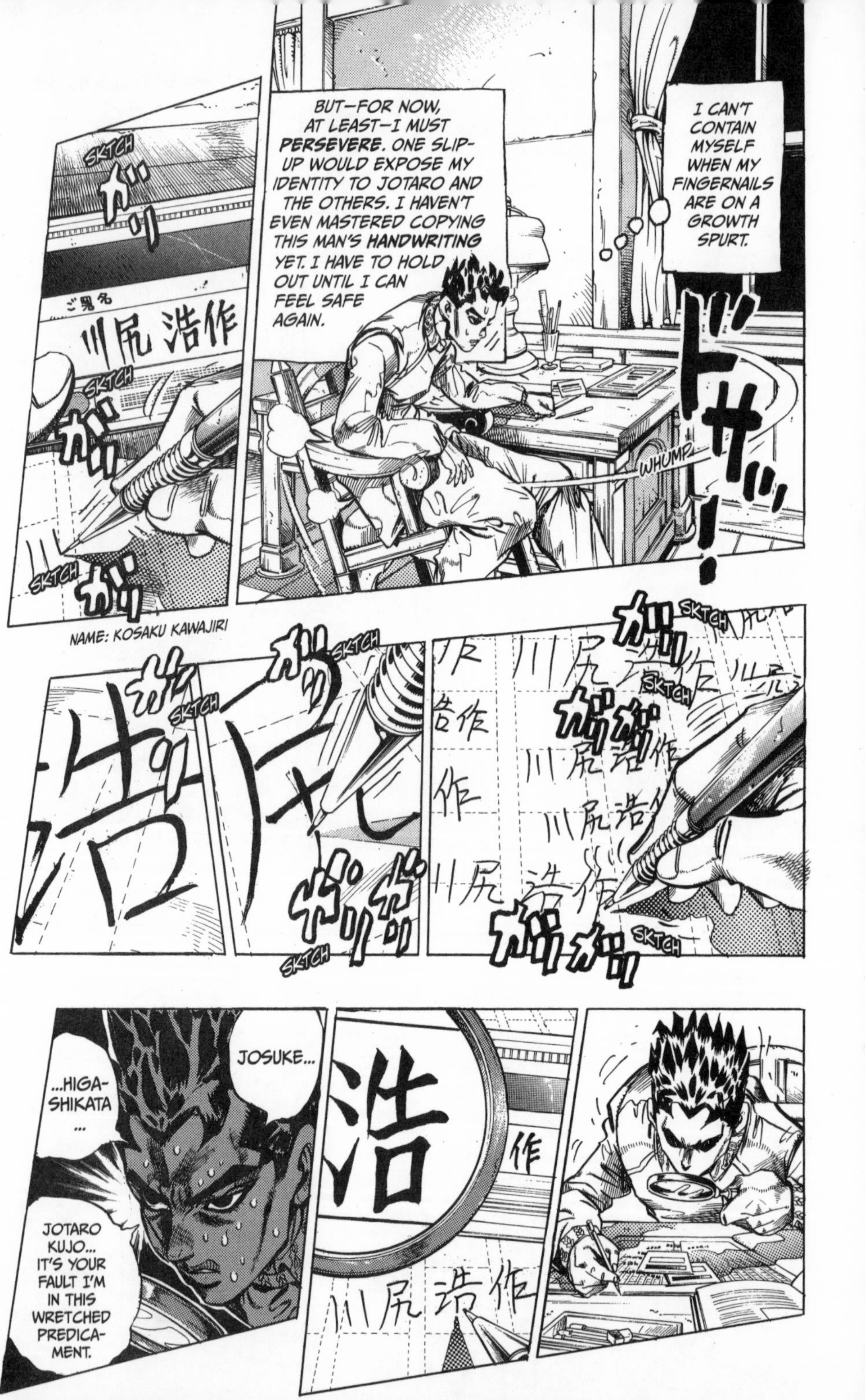
I CAN'T CONTAIN MYSELF WHEN MY FINGERNAILS ARE ON A GROWTH SPURT.
BUT—FOR NOW, AT LEAST—I MUST PERSEVERE. ONE SLIP-UP WOULD EXPOSE MY IDENTITY TO JOTARO AND THE OTHERS. I HAVEN'T EVEN MASTERED COPYING THIS MAN'S HANDWRITING YET. I HAVE TO HOLD OUT UNTIL I CAN FEEL SAFE AGAIN.
WHUMP
SKTCH
川尻浩作
SKTCH
SKTCH
NAME: KOSAKU KAWAJIRI
SKTCH
SKTCH
川尻浩作
SKTCH
SKTCH
SKTCH
SKTCH
浩
作
川尻浩作
JOSUKE...
...HIGA-SHIKATA...
JOTARO KUJO... IT'S YOUR FAULT I'M IN THIS WRETCHED PREDICA-MENT.

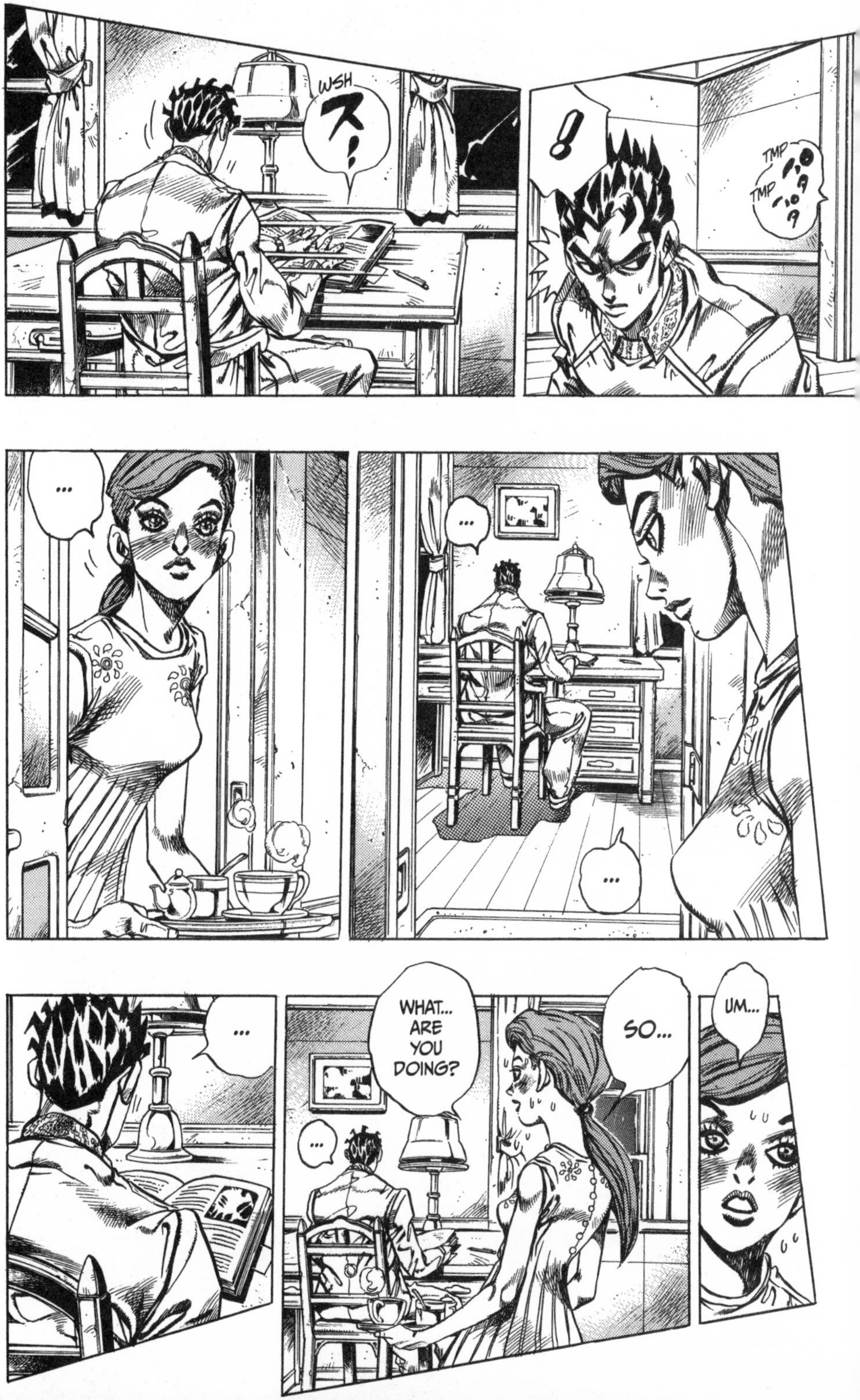
!
TMP TMP
パタ パタ
WSH
ス！
...
...
...
UM...
SO...
WHAT... ARE YOU DOING?
...
...

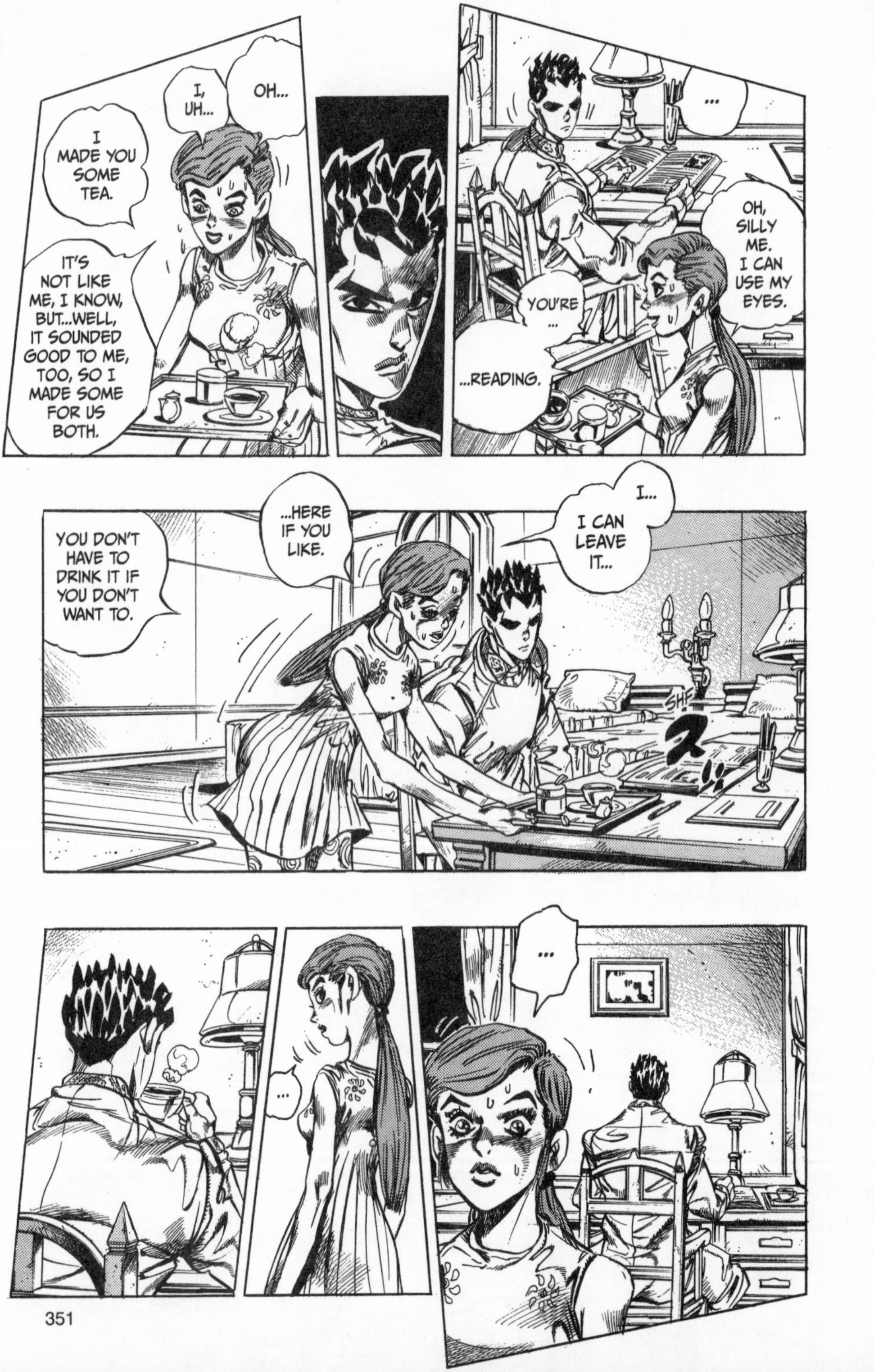
...
OH, SILLY ME. I CAN USE MY EYES.
YOU'RE ...
...READING.
OH...
I, UH...
I MADE YOU SOME TEA.
IT'S NOT LIKE ME, I KNOW, BUT...WELL, IT SOUNDED GOOD TO ME, TOO, SO I MADE SOME FOR US BOTH.
I...
I CAN LEAVE IT...
...HERE IF YOU LIKE.
YOU DON'T HAVE TO DRINK IT IF YOU DON'T WANT TO.
SHF
...
...

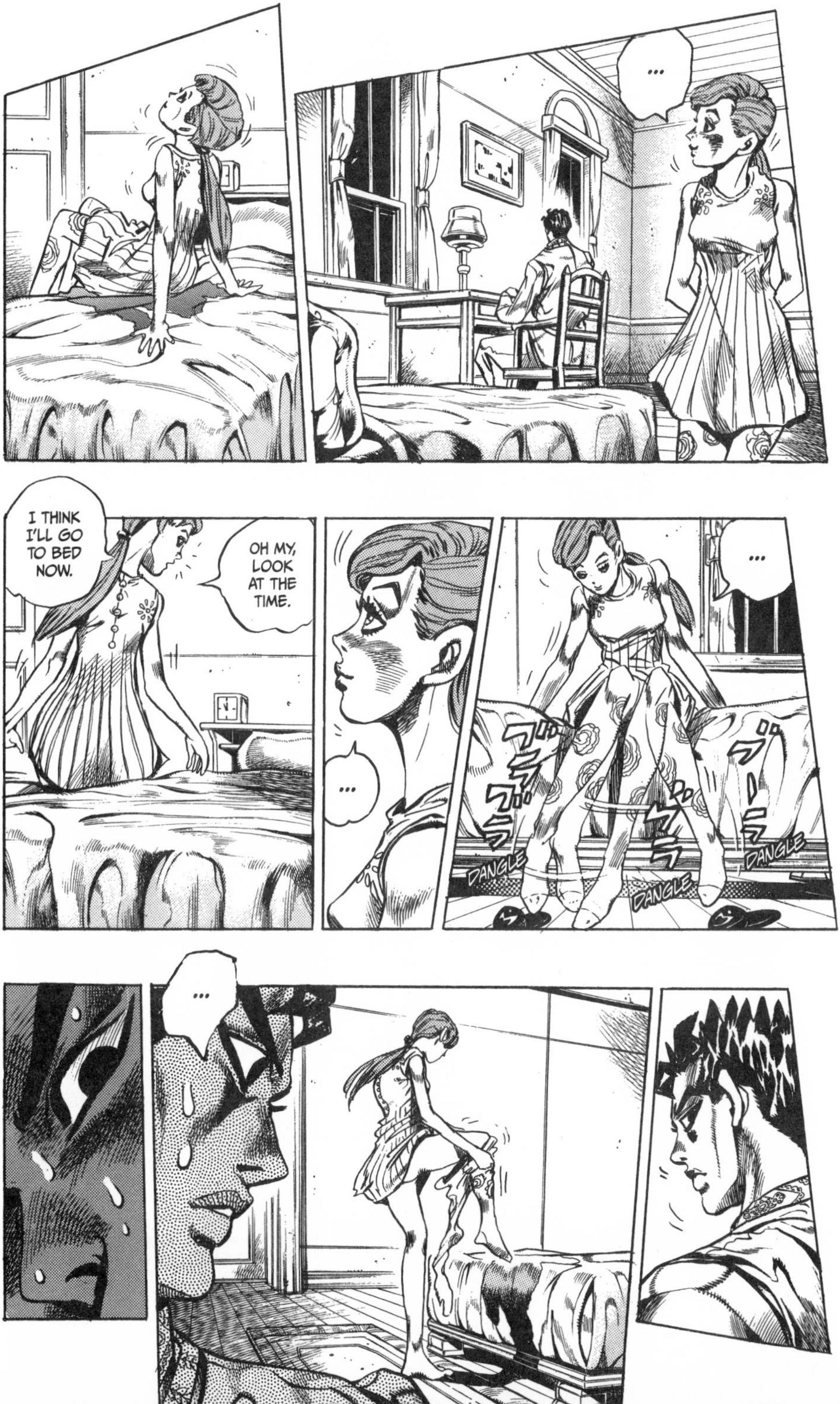
...
...
DANGLE
DANGLE
DANGLE
...
OH MY, LOOK AT THE TIME.
I THINK I'LL GO TO BED NOW.
...

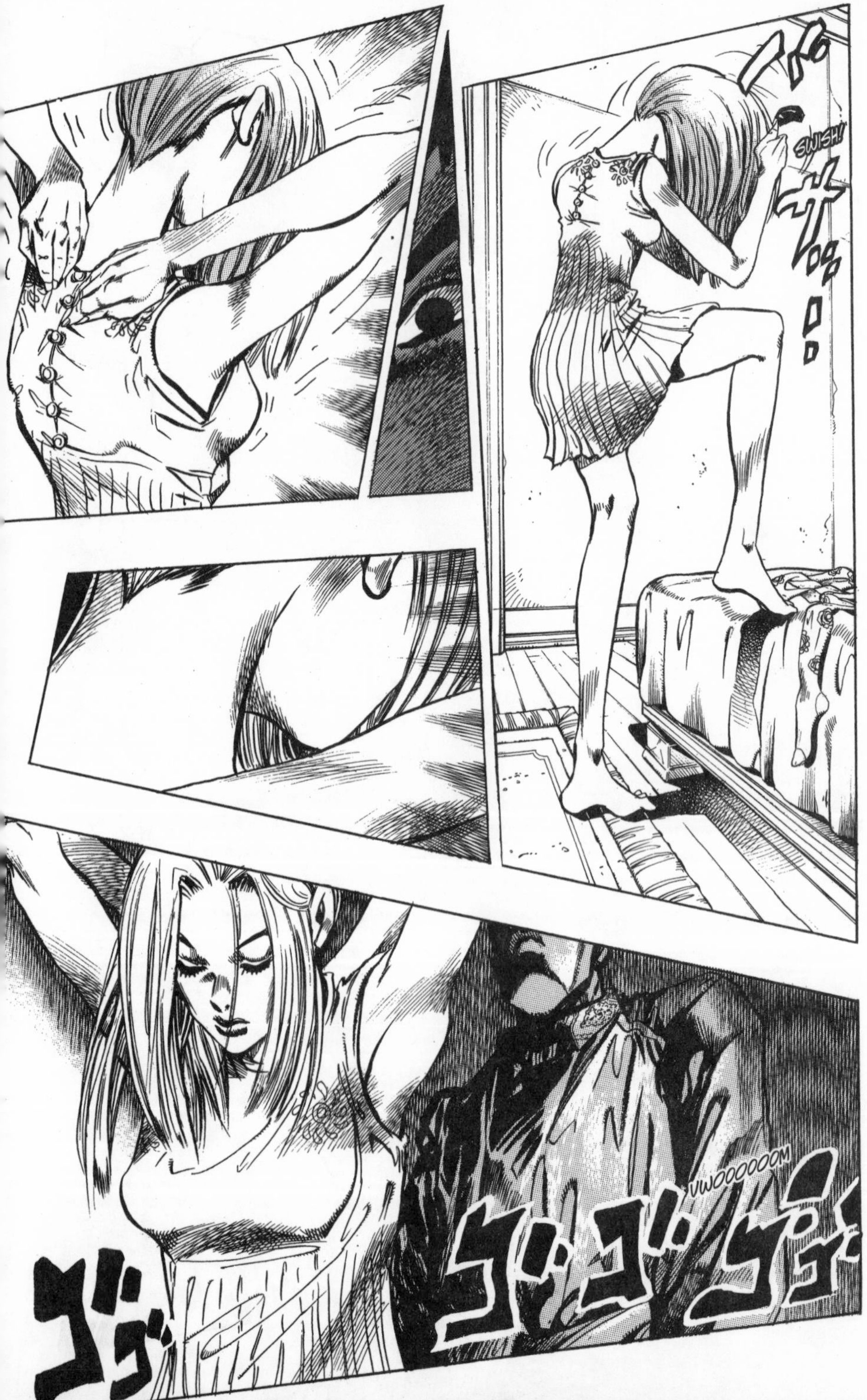
SWISH!
VWOOOOOOOM

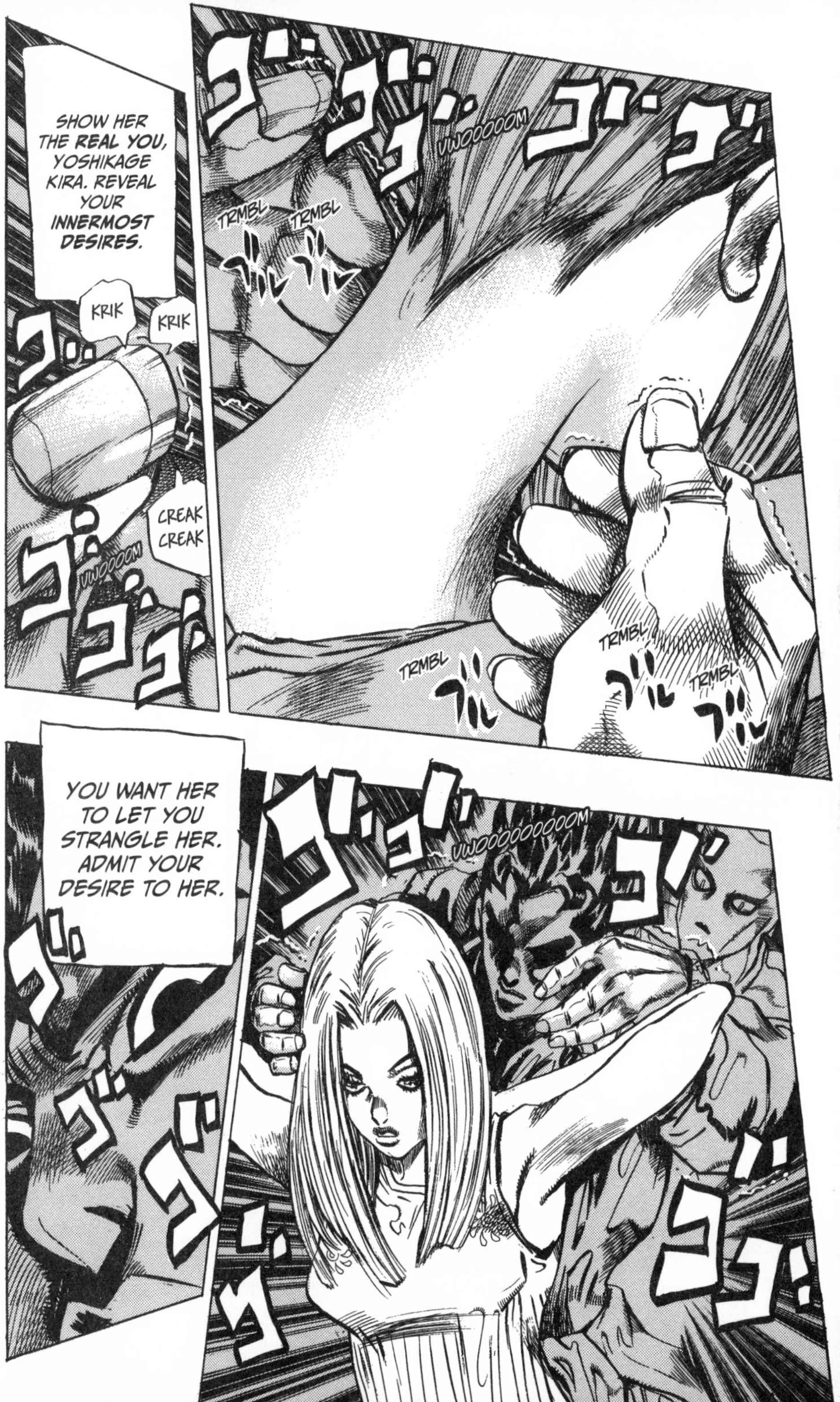

UWOOOOOM
TRMBL
TRMBL
TRMBL
TRMBL
TRMBL
SHOW HER THE **REAL YOU**, YOSHIKAGE KIRA. REVEAL YOUR INNERMOST DESIRES.
KRIK
KRIK
CREAK CREAK
UWOOOOM
UWOOOOOOOOOOM
YOU WANT HER TO LET YOU STRANGLE HER. ADMIT YOUR DESIRE TO HER.

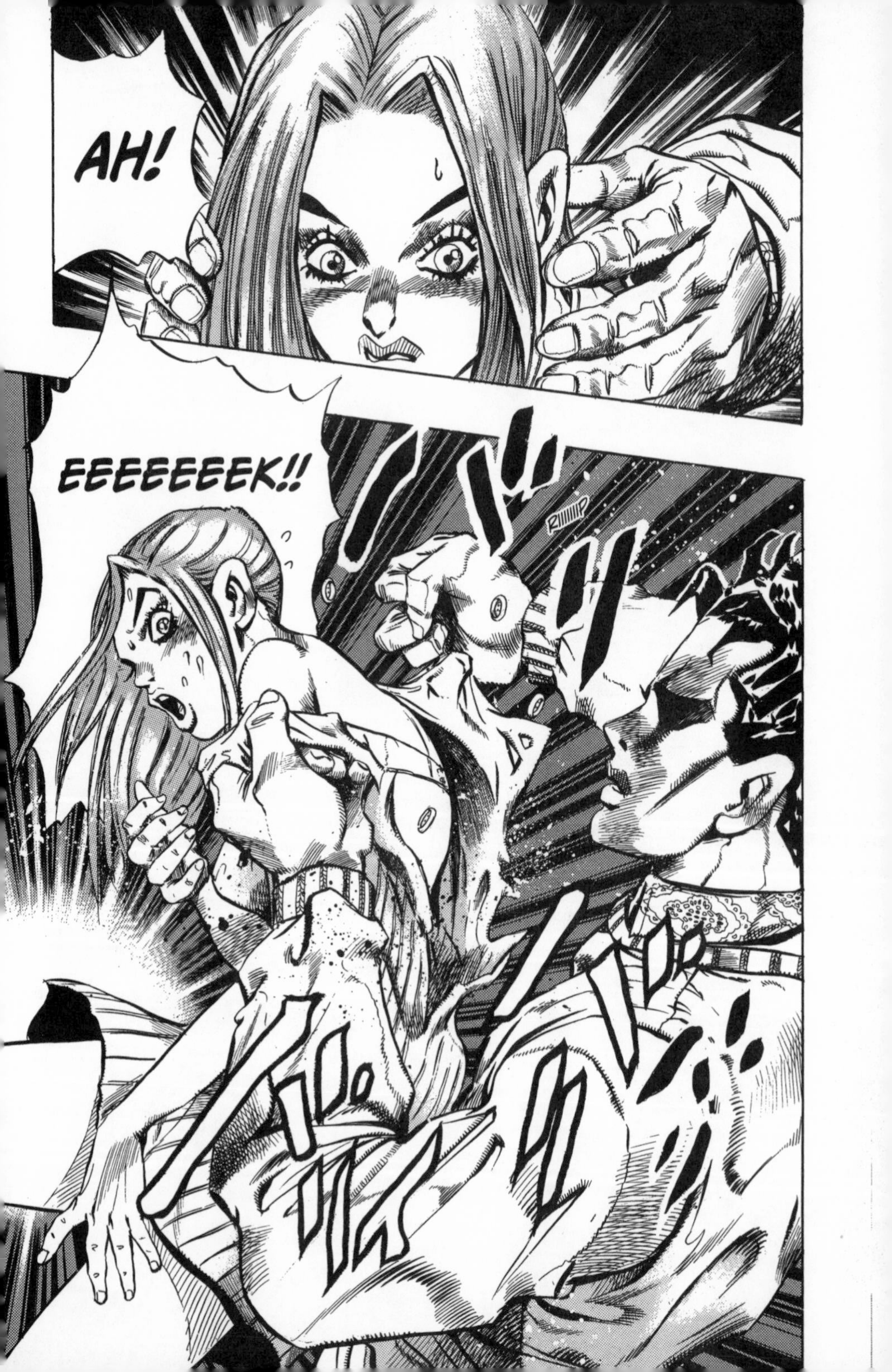
AH!
EEEEEEEEK!!
RIIIIIP

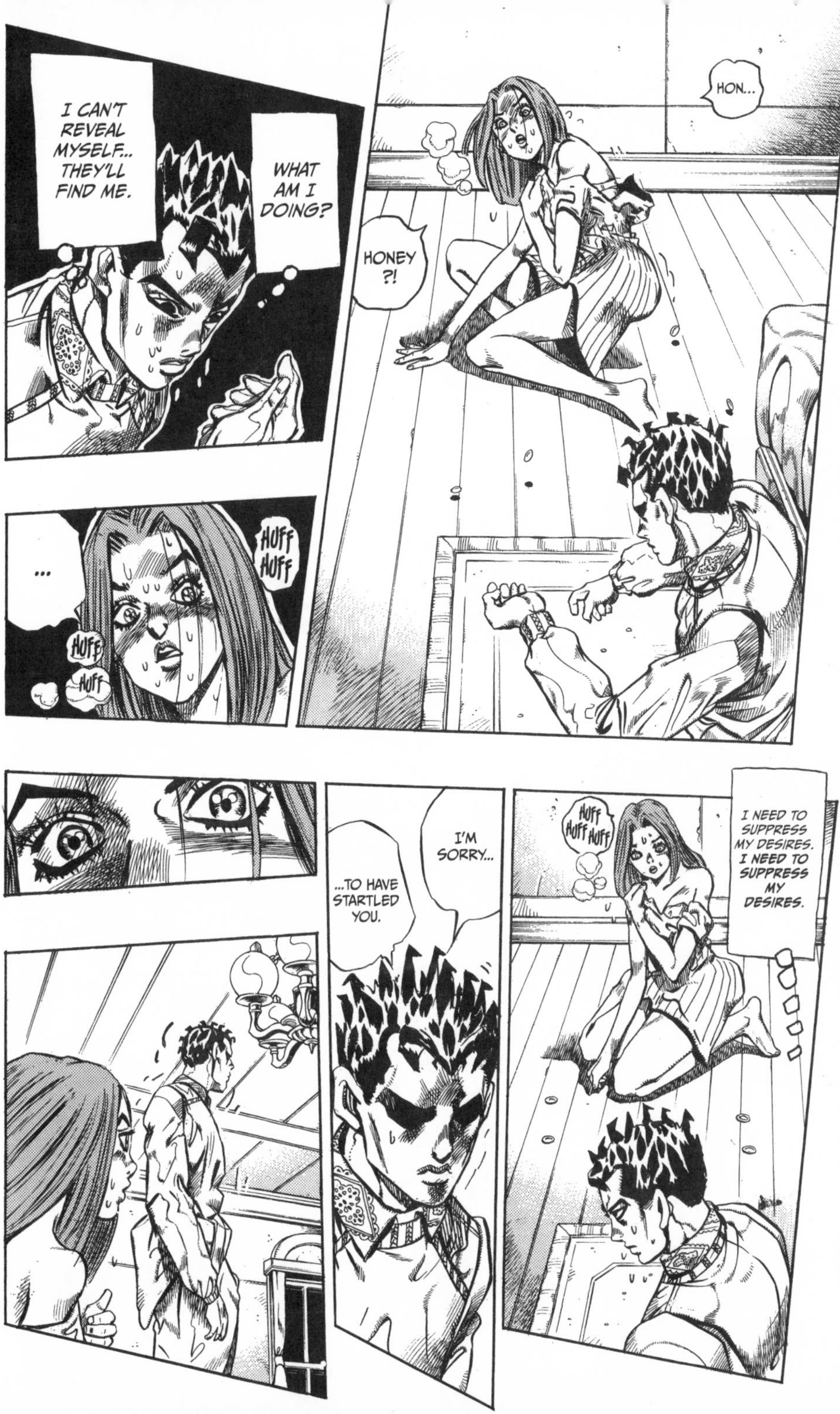
HON...
HONEY ?!
WHAT AM I DOING?
I CAN'T REVEAL MYSELF... THEY'LL FIND ME.
HUFF HUFF
...
HUFF
HUFF
I NEED TO SUPPRESS MY DESIRES. I NEED TO SUPPRESS MY DESIRES.
HUFF HUFF HUFF
I'M SORRY...
...TO HAVE STARTLED YOU.

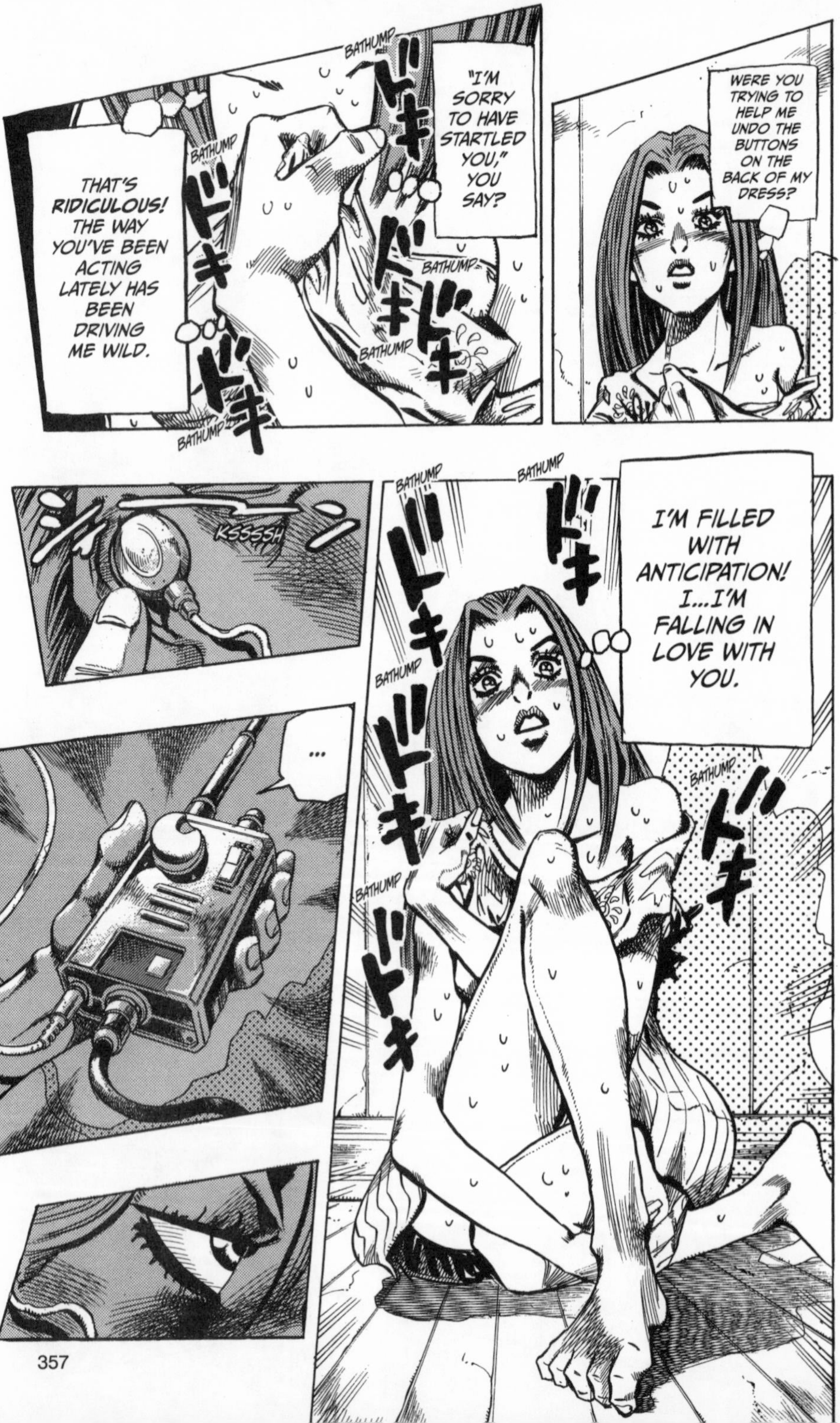

WERE YOU TRYING TO HELP ME UNDO THE BUTTONS ON THE BACK OF MY DRESS?
BATHUMP
"I'M SORRY TO HAVE STARTLED YOU," YOU SAY?
BATHUMP
THAT'S RIDICULOUS! THE WAY YOU'VE BEEN ACTING LATELY HAS BEEN DRIVING ME WILD.
BATHUMP
BATHUMP
BATHUMP
BATHUMP
BATHUMP
I'M FILLED WITH ANTICIPATION! I...I'M FALLING IN LOVE WITH YOU.
BATHUMP
BATHUMP
BATHUMP
BATHUMP
KSSSSH
...

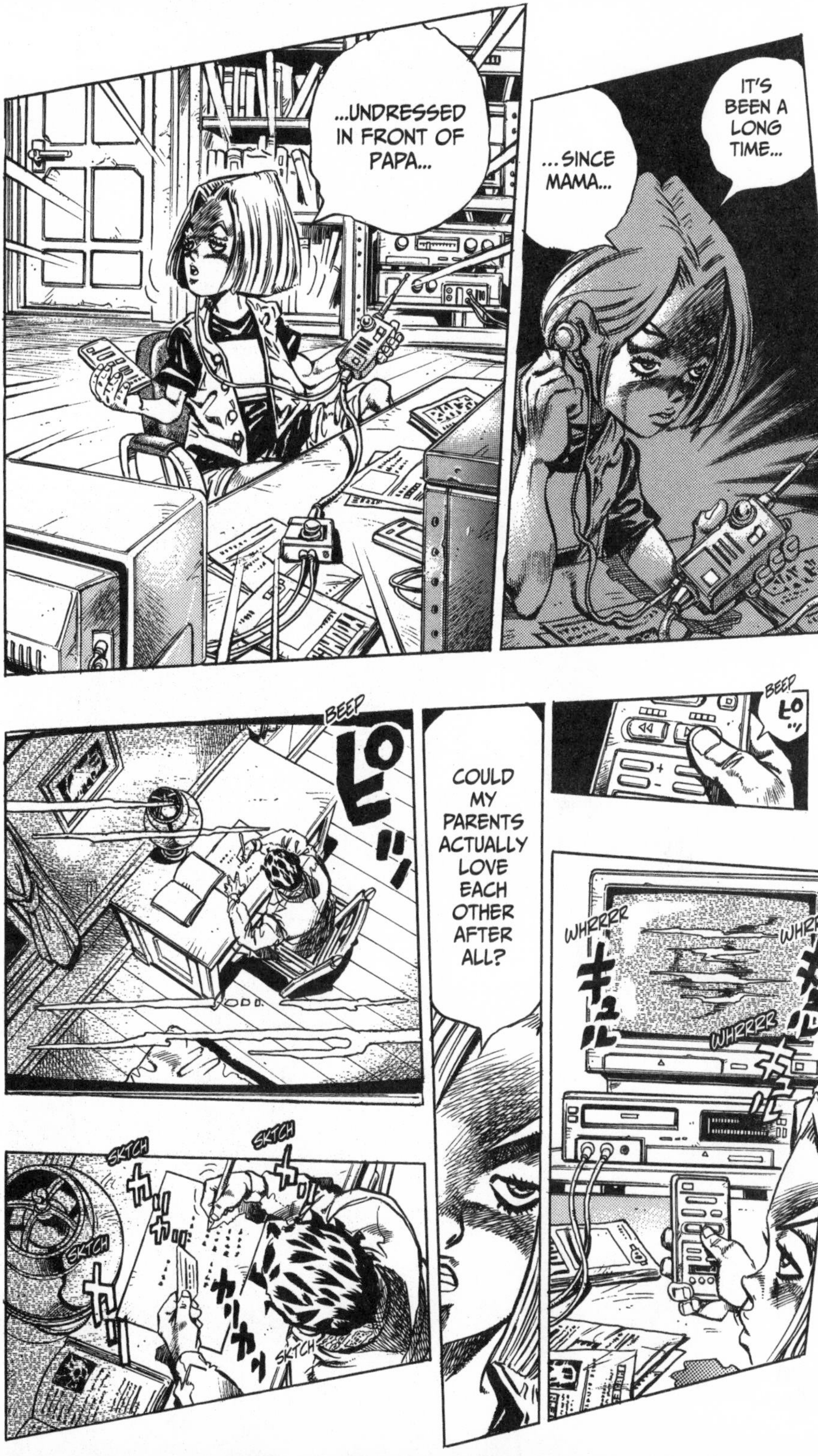
IT'S BEEN A LONG TIME...
...SINCE MAMA...
...UNDRESSED IN FRONT OF PAPA...
BEEP
WHRRRR
WHRRRR
WHRRRR
COULD MY PARENTS ACTUALLY LOVE EACH OTHER AFTER ALL?
BEEP
SKTCH
SKTCH
SKTCH
SKTCH

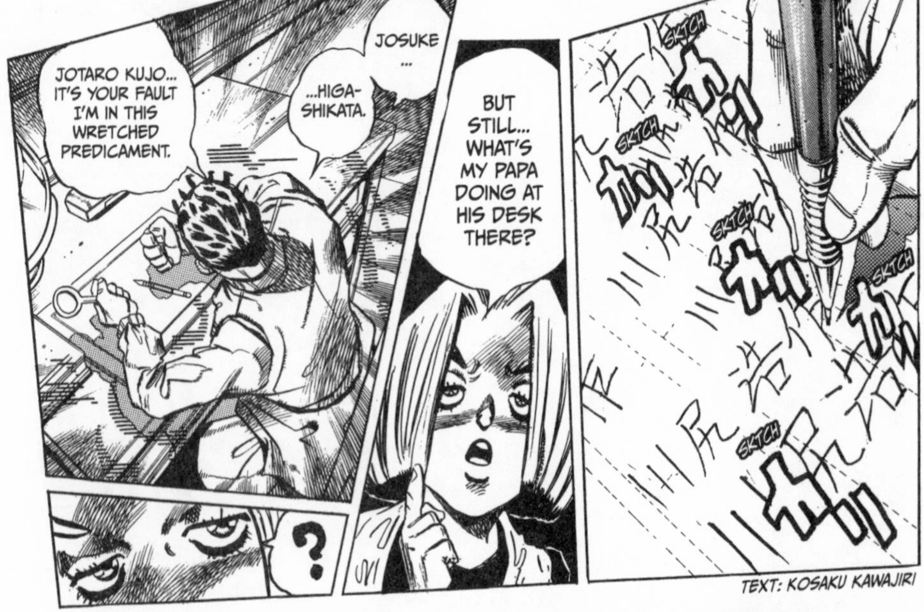
SKTCH
SKTCH
SKTCH
SKTCH
SKTCH
BUT STILL... WHAT'S MY PAPA DOING AT HIS DESK THERE?
JOSUKE ...
...HIGA-SHIKATA.
JOTARO KUJO... IT'S YOUR FAULT I'M IN THIS WRETCHED PREDICAMENT.
?

TEXT: KOSAKU KAWAJIRI

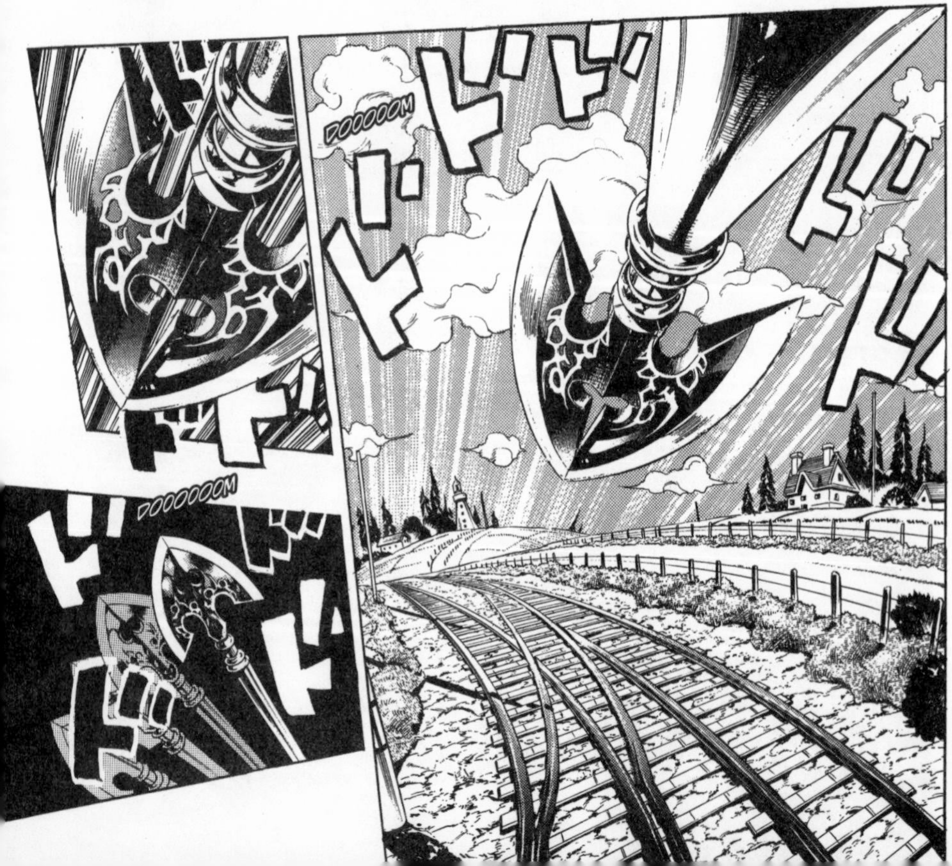
DOOOOOM
DOOOOOOM

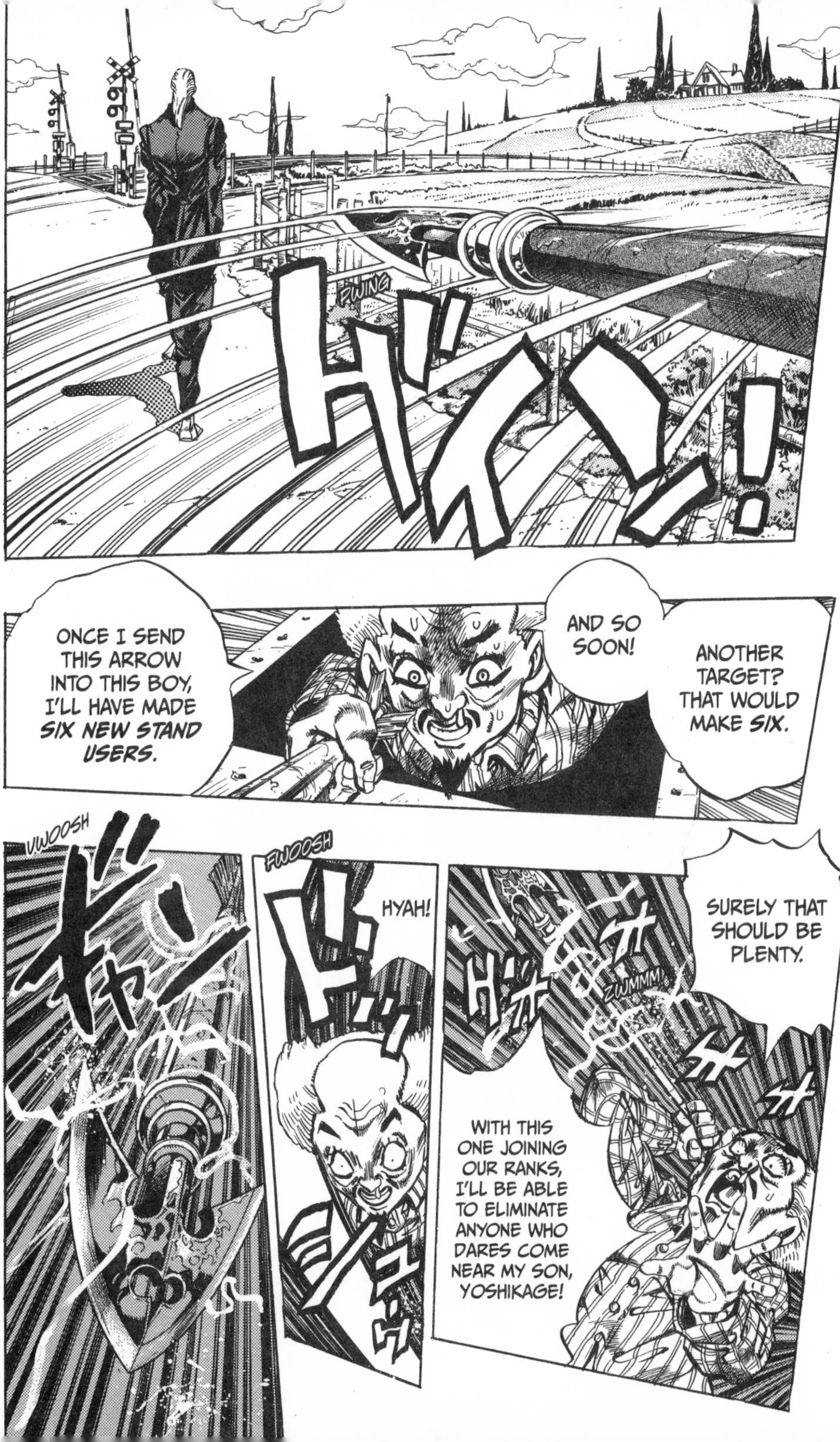
PWING
ANOTHER TARGET? THAT WOULD MAKE SIX.
AND SO SOON!
ONCE I SEND THIS ARROW INTO THIS BOY, I'LL HAVE MADE SIX NEW STAND USERS.
SURELY THAT SHOULD BE PLENTY.
ZWUMMM
WITH THIS ONE JOINING OUR RANKS, I'LL BE ABLE TO ELIMINATE ANYONE WHO DARES COME NEAR MY SON, YOSHIKAGE!
FWOOSH
HYAH!
UWOOSH

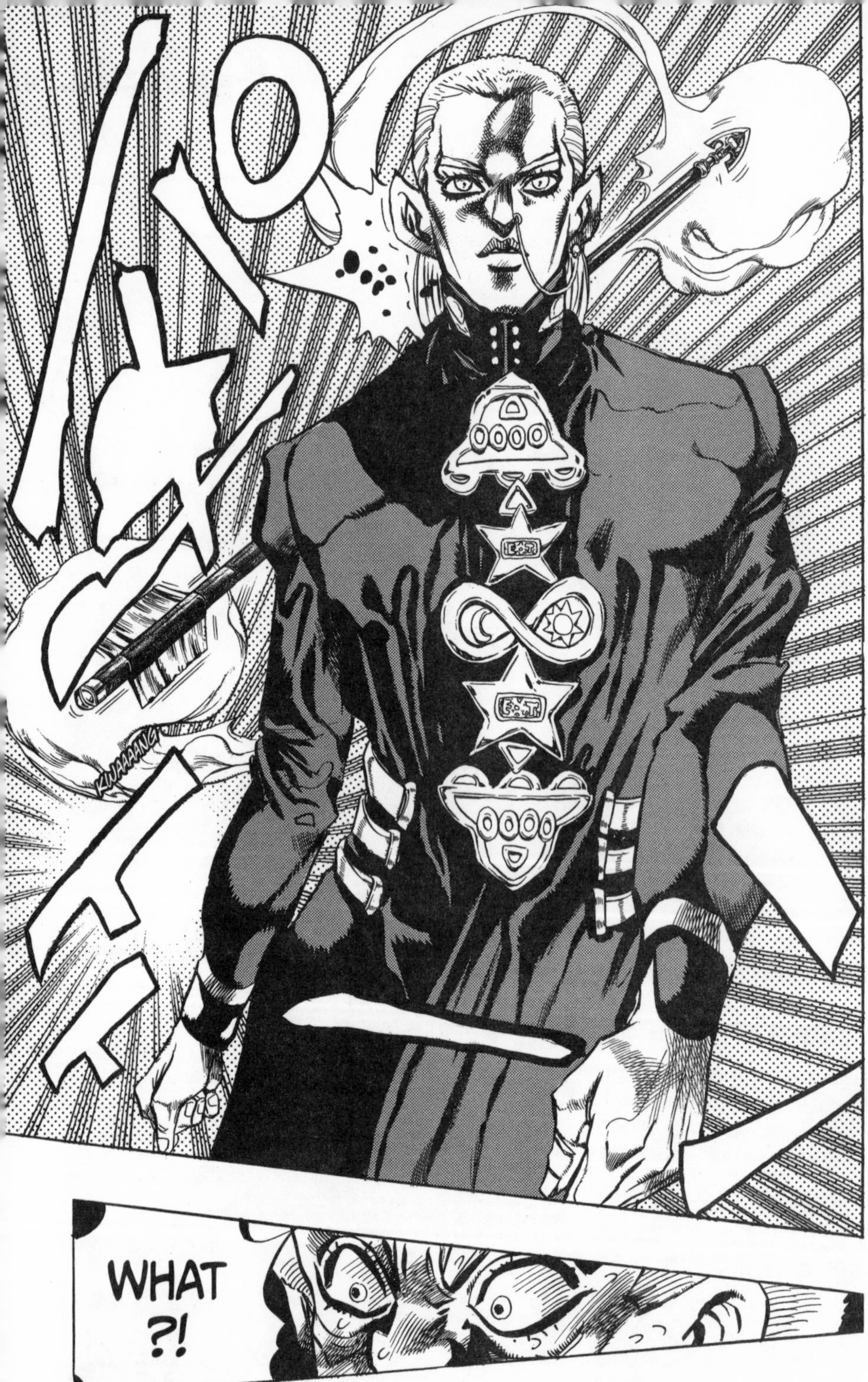
KWAAAANG
WHAT ?!

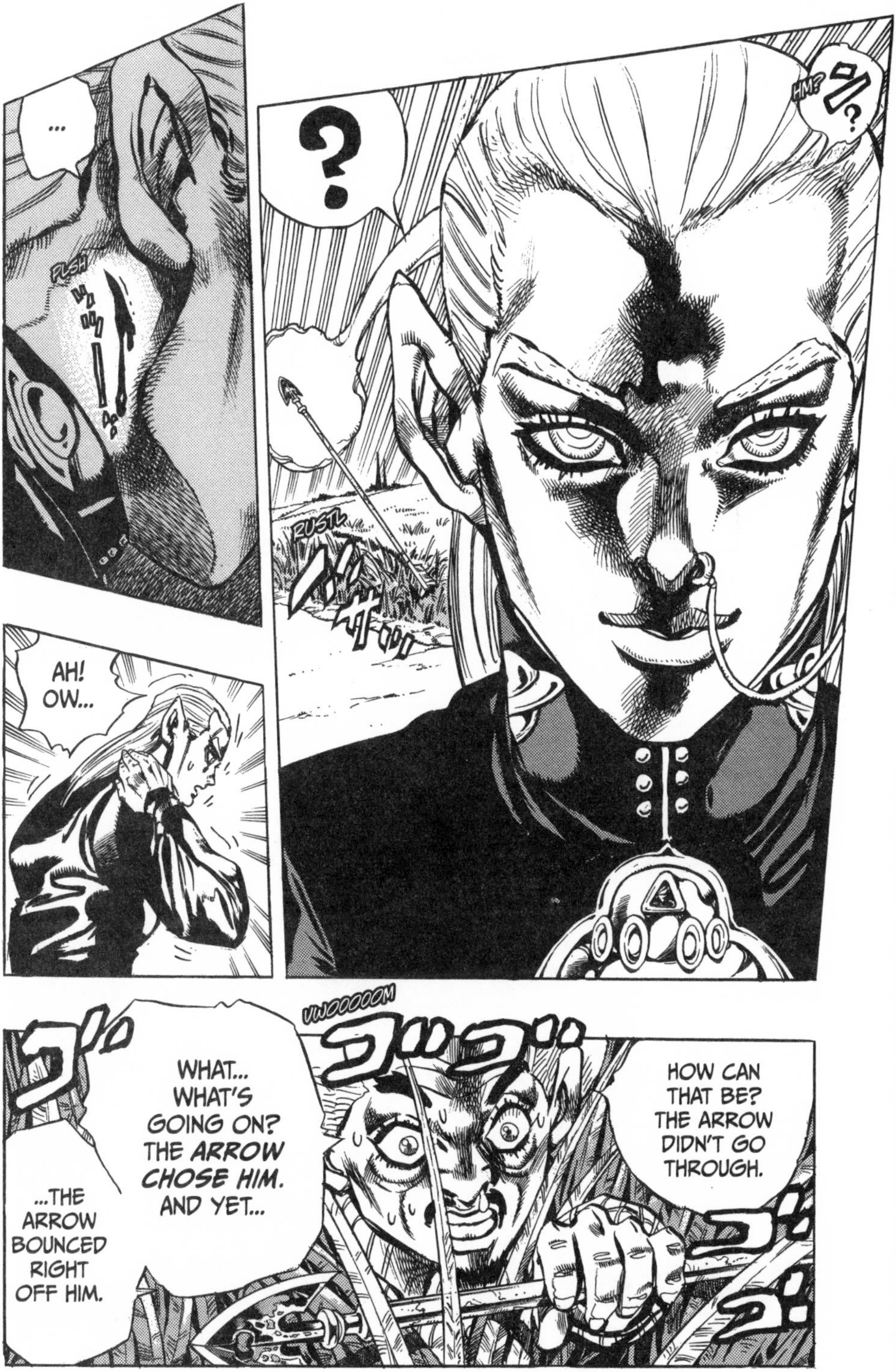
HM?
?
RUSTL
...
PLSH
AH! OW...
VWOOOOOM
HOW CAN THAT BE? THE ARROW DIDN'T GO THROUGH.
WHAT... WHAT'S GOING ON? THE *ARROW CHOSE HIM*. AND YET...
...THE ARROW BOUNCED RIGHT OFF HIM.

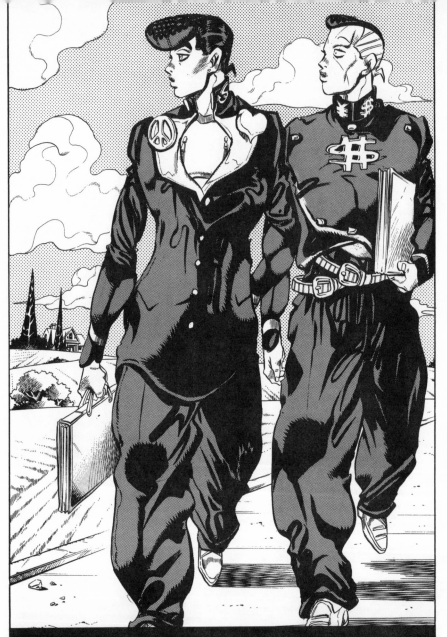

CHAPTER 113

I AM AN ALIEN, PART 1

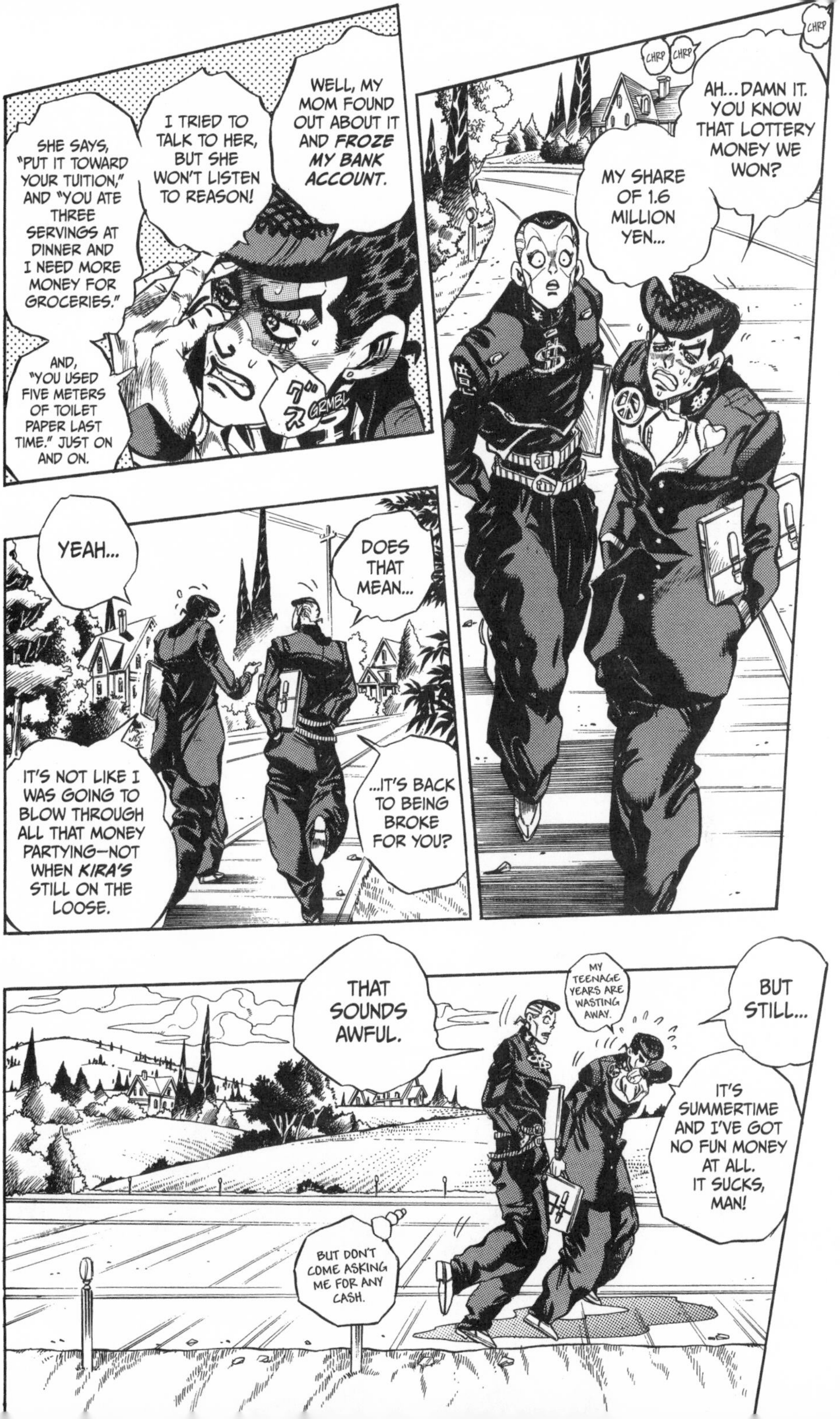
CHRP
CHRP
CHRP
AH...DAMN IT. YOU KNOW THAT LOTTERY MONEY WE WON?
MY SHARE OF 1.6 MILLION YEN...
WELL, MY MOM FOUND OUT ABOUT IT AND *FROZE MY BANK ACCOUNT*.
I TRIED TO TALK TO HER, BUT SHE WON'T LISTEN TO REASON!
SHE SAYS, "PUT IT TOWARD YOUR TUITION," AND "YOU ATE THREE SERVINGS AT DINNER AND I NEED MORE MONEY FOR GROCERIES."
AND, "YOU USED FIVE METERS OF TOILET PAPER LAST TIME." JUST ON AND ON.
GRMBL
DOES THAT MEAN...
YEAH...
...IT'S BACK TO BEING BROKE FOR YOU?
IT'S NOT LIKE I WAS GOING TO BLOW THROUGH ALL THAT MONEY PARTYING—NOT WHEN *KIRA'S* STILL ON THE LOOSE.
BUT STILL...
IT'S SUMMERTIME AND I'VE GOT NO FUN MONEY AT ALL. IT SUCKS, MAN!
MY TEENAGE YEARS ARE WASTING AWAY.
THAT SOUNDS AWFUL.
BUT DON'T COME ASKING ME FOR ANY CASH.

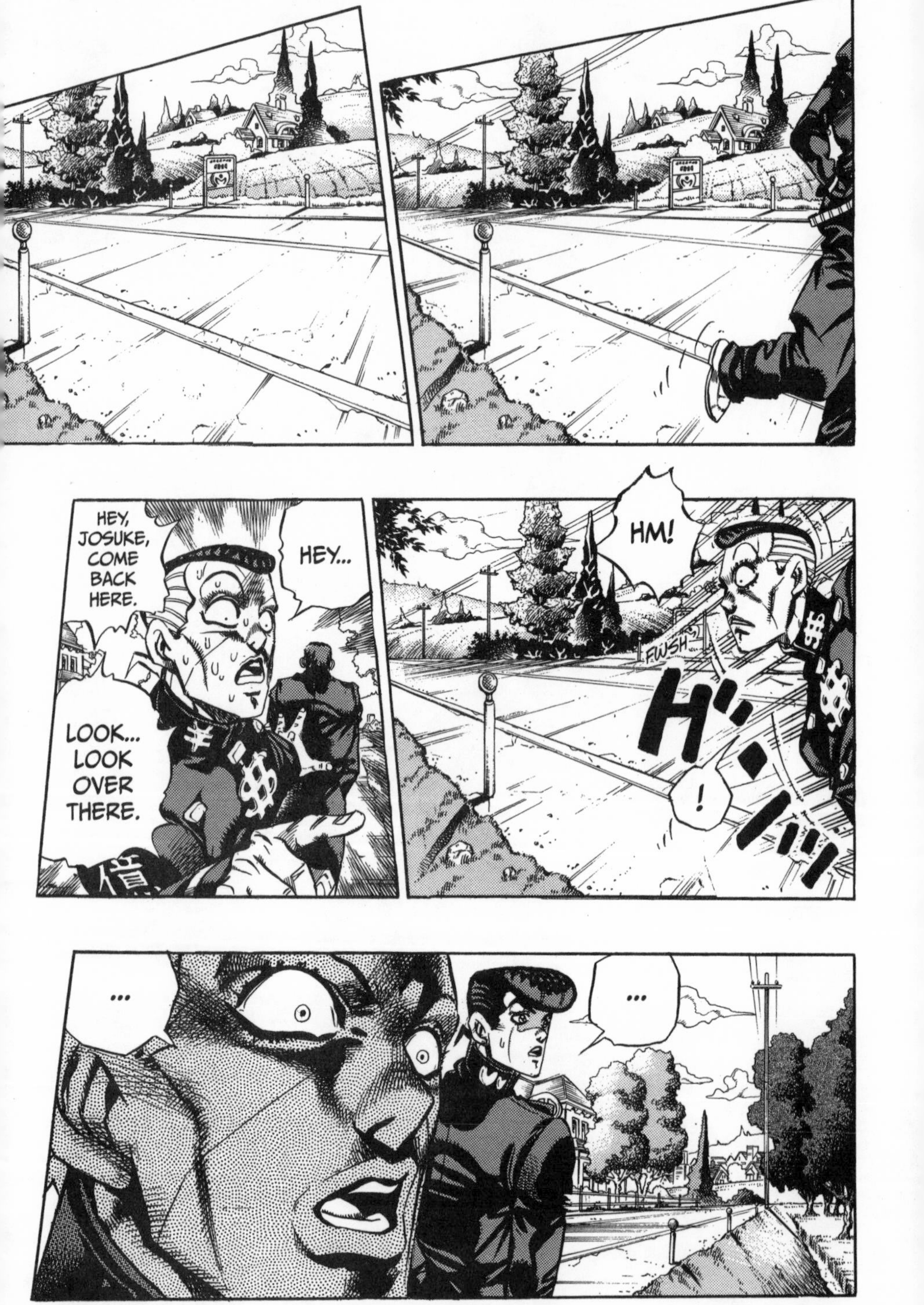
HM!
FWSH
!
HEY...
HEY, JOSUKE, COME BACK HERE.
LOOK... LOOK OVER THERE.
...
...

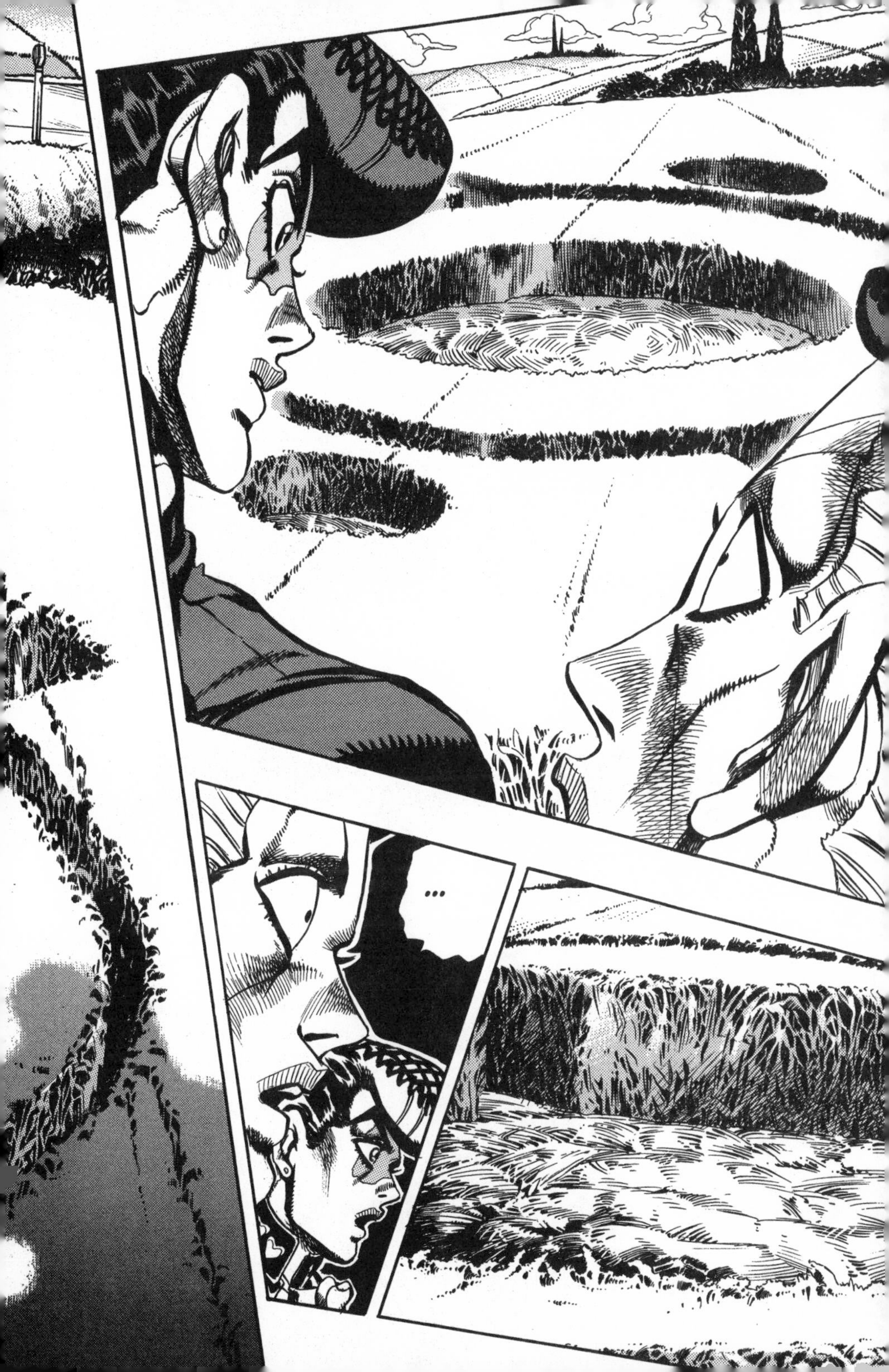
...

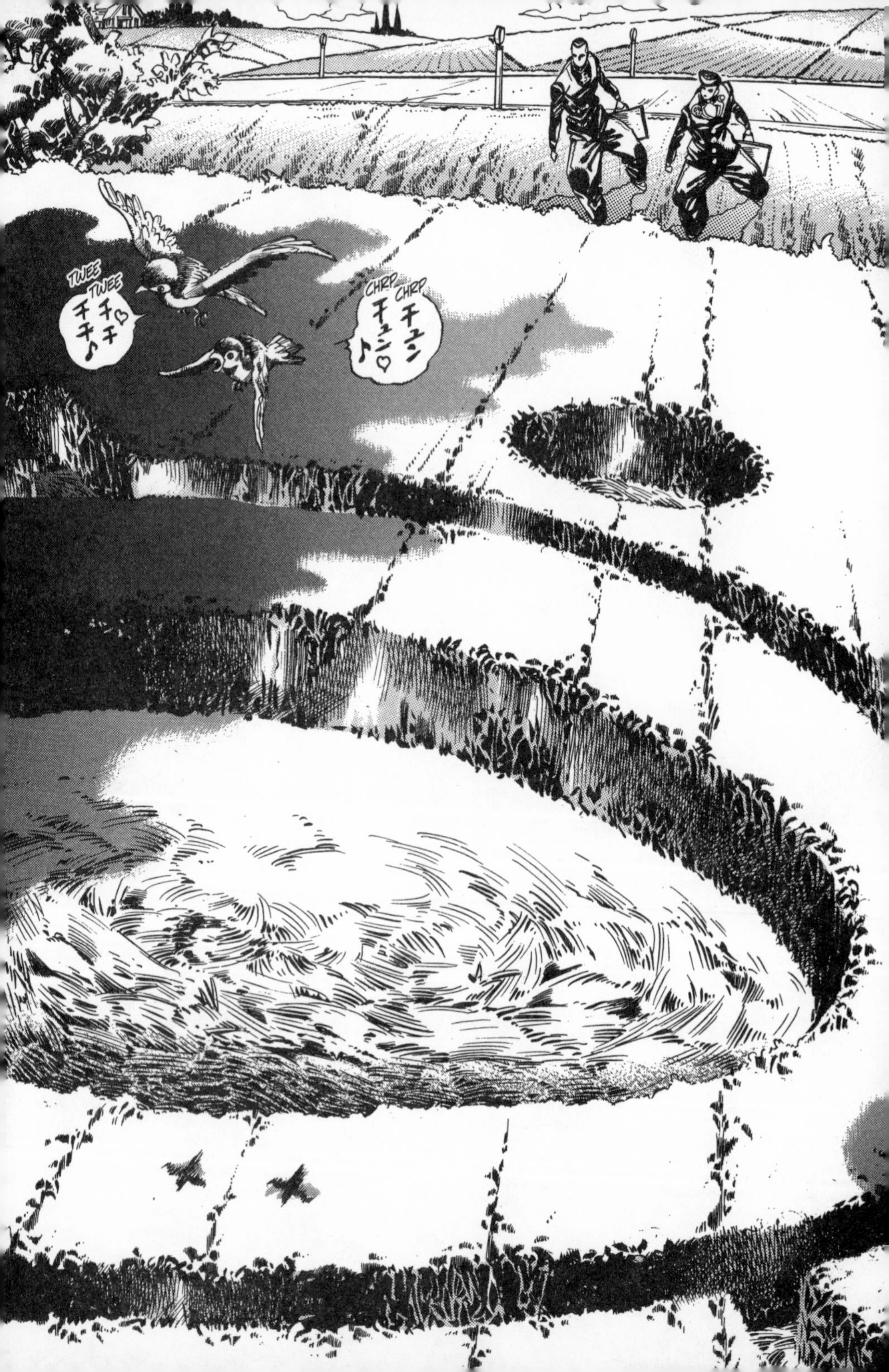

CHRP CHRP
チュン チュン♪♡
TWEE TWEE
チチ チチ♡♪

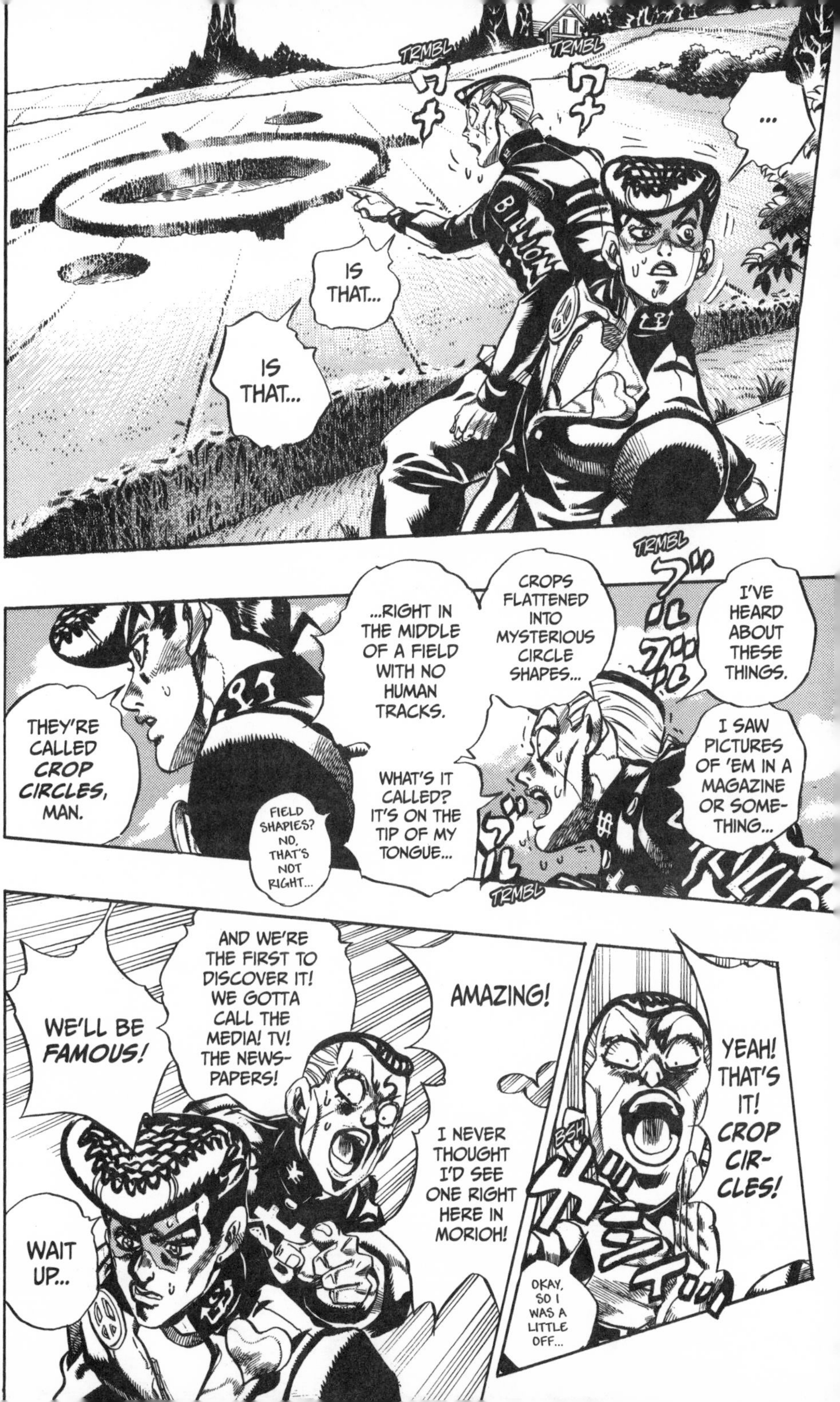

TRMBL
TRMBL
...
IS THAT...
IS THAT...
TRMBL
I'VE HEARD ABOUT THESE THINGS.
I SAW PICTURES OF 'EM IN A MAGAZINE OR SOMETHING...
CROPS FLATTENED INTO MYSTERIOUS CIRCLE SHAPES...
...RIGHT IN THE MIDDLE OF A FIELD WITH NO HUMAN TRACKS.
WHAT'S IT CALLED? IT'S ON THE TIP OF MY TONGUE...
FIELD SHAPIES? NO, THAT'S NOT RIGHT...
TRMBL
THEY'RE CALLED *CROP CIRCLES*, MAN.
YEAH! THAT'S IT! *CROP CIRCLES!*
BSH
OKAY, SO I WAS A LITTLE OFF...
AMAZING!
AND WE'RE THE FIRST TO DISCOVER IT! WE GOTTA CALL THE MEDIA! TV! THE NEWSPAPERS!
WE'LL BE *FAMOUS!*
I NEVER THOUGHT I'D SEE ONE RIGHT HERE IN MORIOH!
WAIT UP...

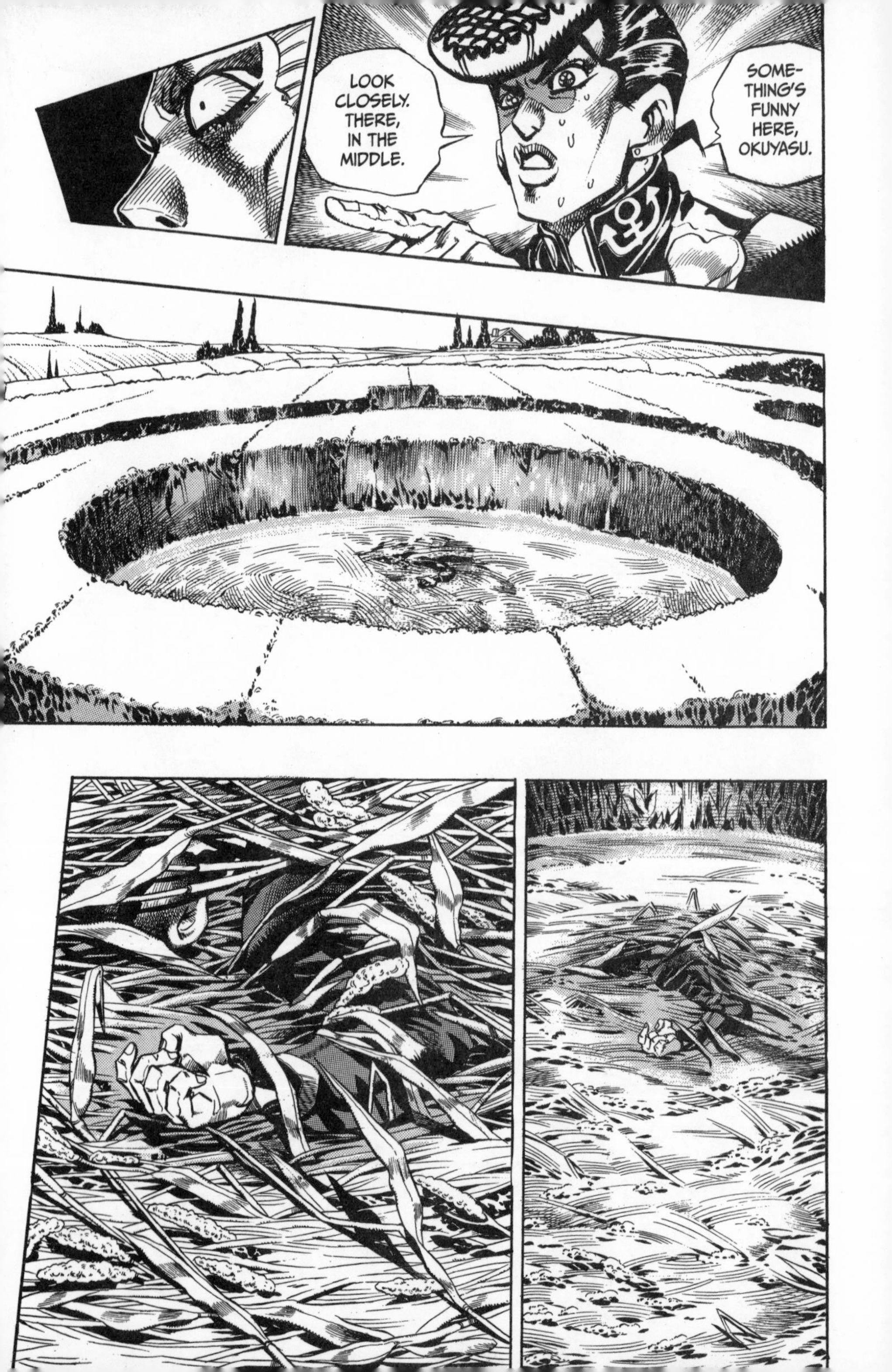
SOME-THING'S FUNNY HERE, OKUYASU.
LOOK CLOSELY. THERE, IN THE MIDDLE.

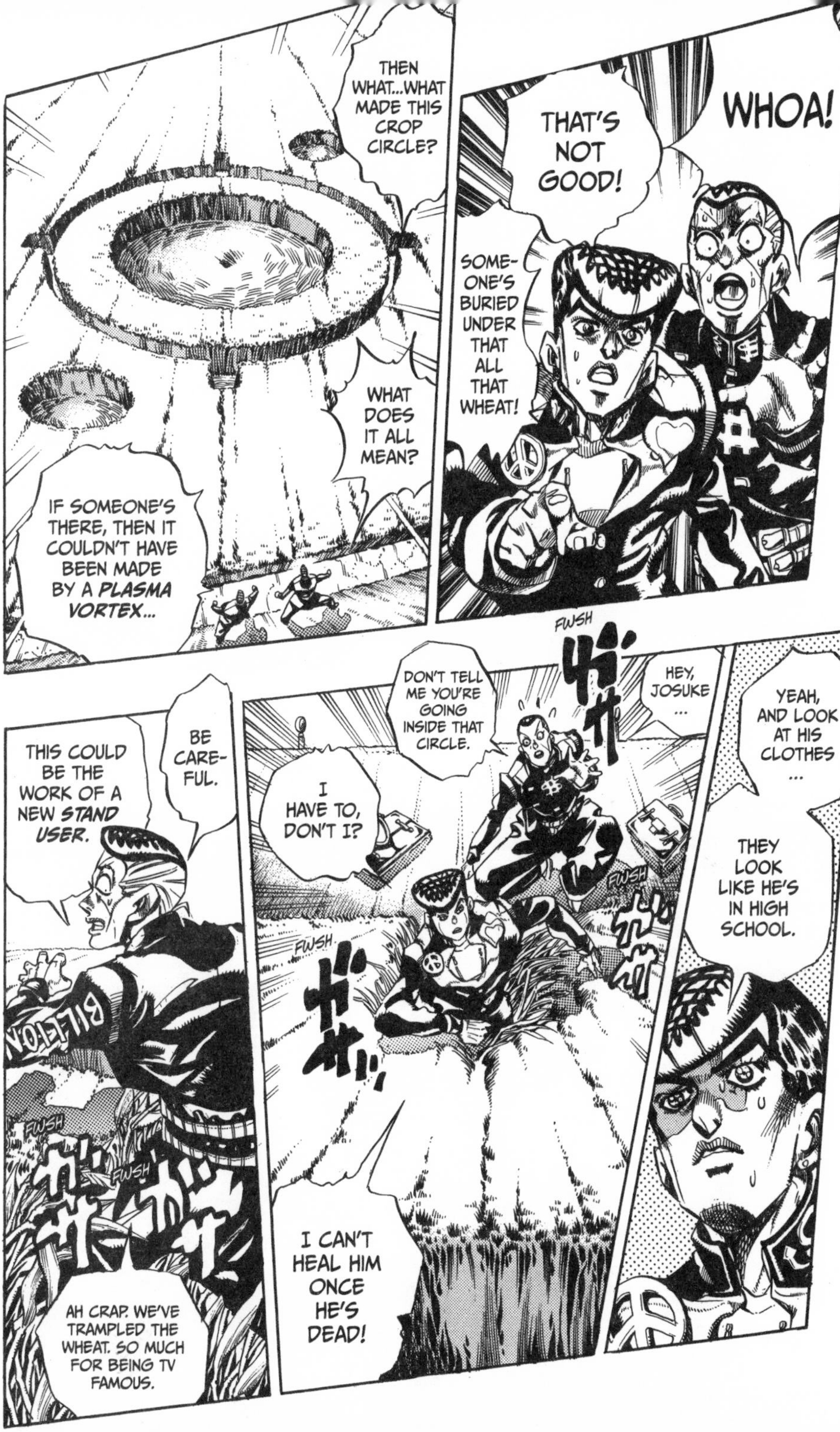
WHOA!
THAT'S NOT GOOD!
SOME-ONE'S BURIED UNDER THAT ALL THAT WHEAT!
THEN WHAT...WHAT MADE THIS CROP CIRCLE?
WHAT DOES IT ALL MEAN?
IF SOMEONE'S THERE, THEN IT COULDN'T HAVE BEEN MADE BY A *PLASMA VORTEX*...
YEAH, AND LOOK AT HIS CLOTHES...
THEY LOOK LIKE HE'S IN HIGH SCHOOL.
FWSH
HEY, JOSUKE...
DON'T TELL ME YOU'RE GOING INSIDE THAT CIRCLE.
I HAVE TO, DON'T I?
FWSH
FWSH
I CAN'T HEAL HIM ONCE HE'S DEAD!
BE CARE-FUL.
THIS COULD BE THE WORK OF A NEW *STAND USER*.
FWSH
FWSH
AH CRAP. WE'VE TRAMPLED THE WHEAT. SO MUCH FOR BEING TV FAMOUS.

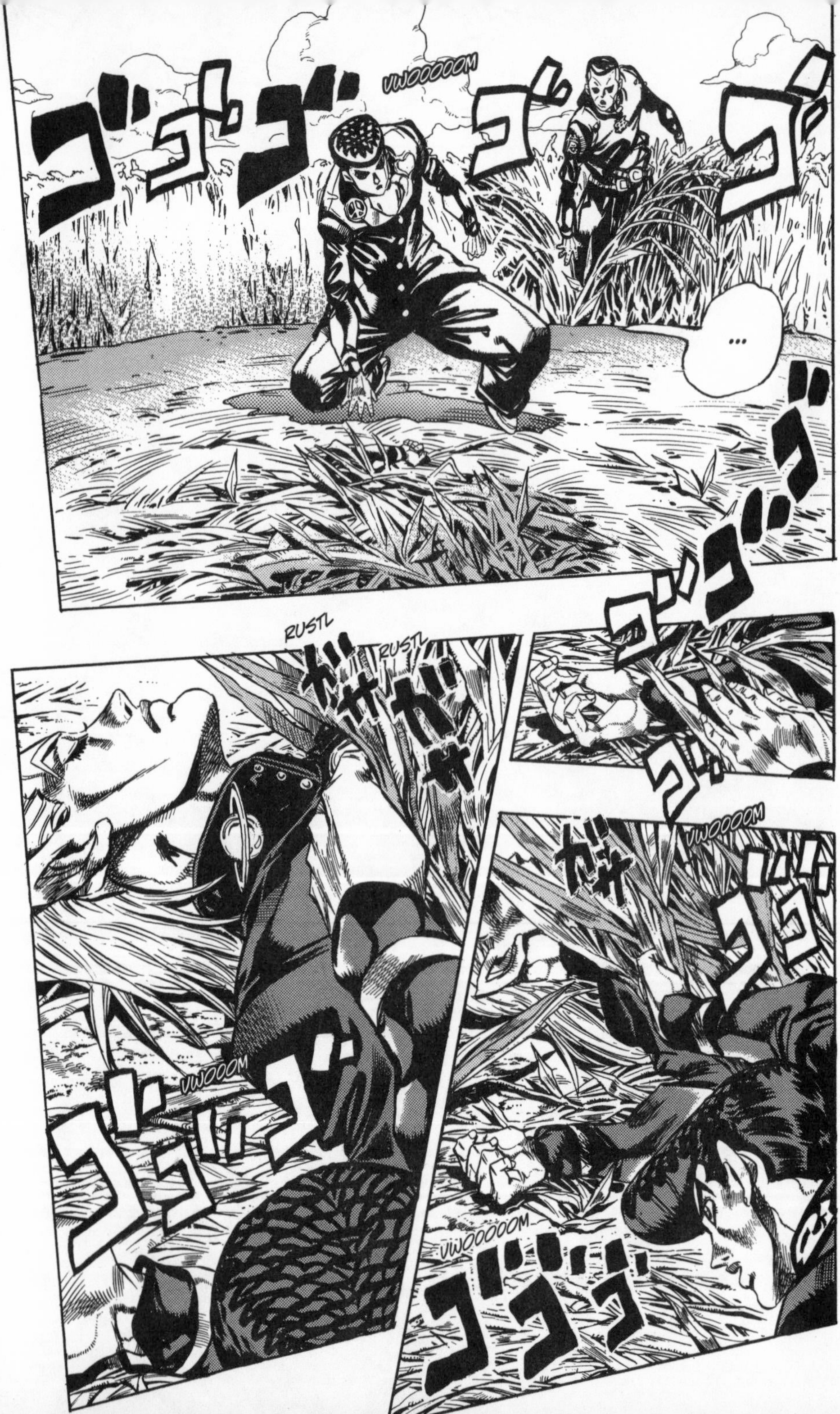
VWOOOOOM
...
VWOOOOM
VWOOOOOM
RUSTL
RUSTL
VWOOOM

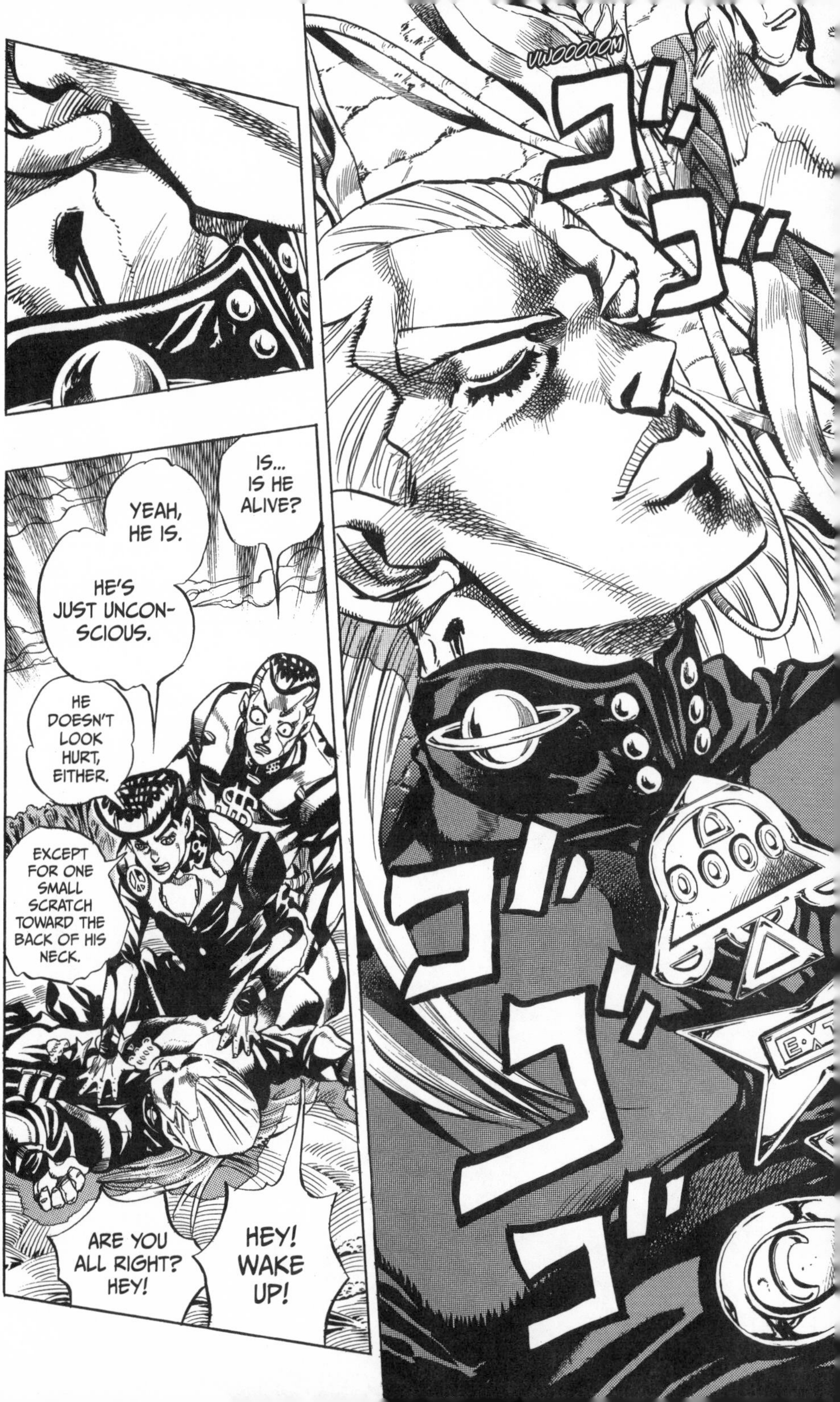
VWOOOOOM
IS... IS HE ALIVE?
YEAH, HE IS.
HE'S JUST UNCONSCIOUS.
HE DOESN'T LOOK HURT, EITHER.
EXCEPT FOR ONE SMALL SCRATCH TOWARD THE BACK OF HIS NECK.
HEY! WAKE UP!
ARE YOU ALL RIGHT? HEY!

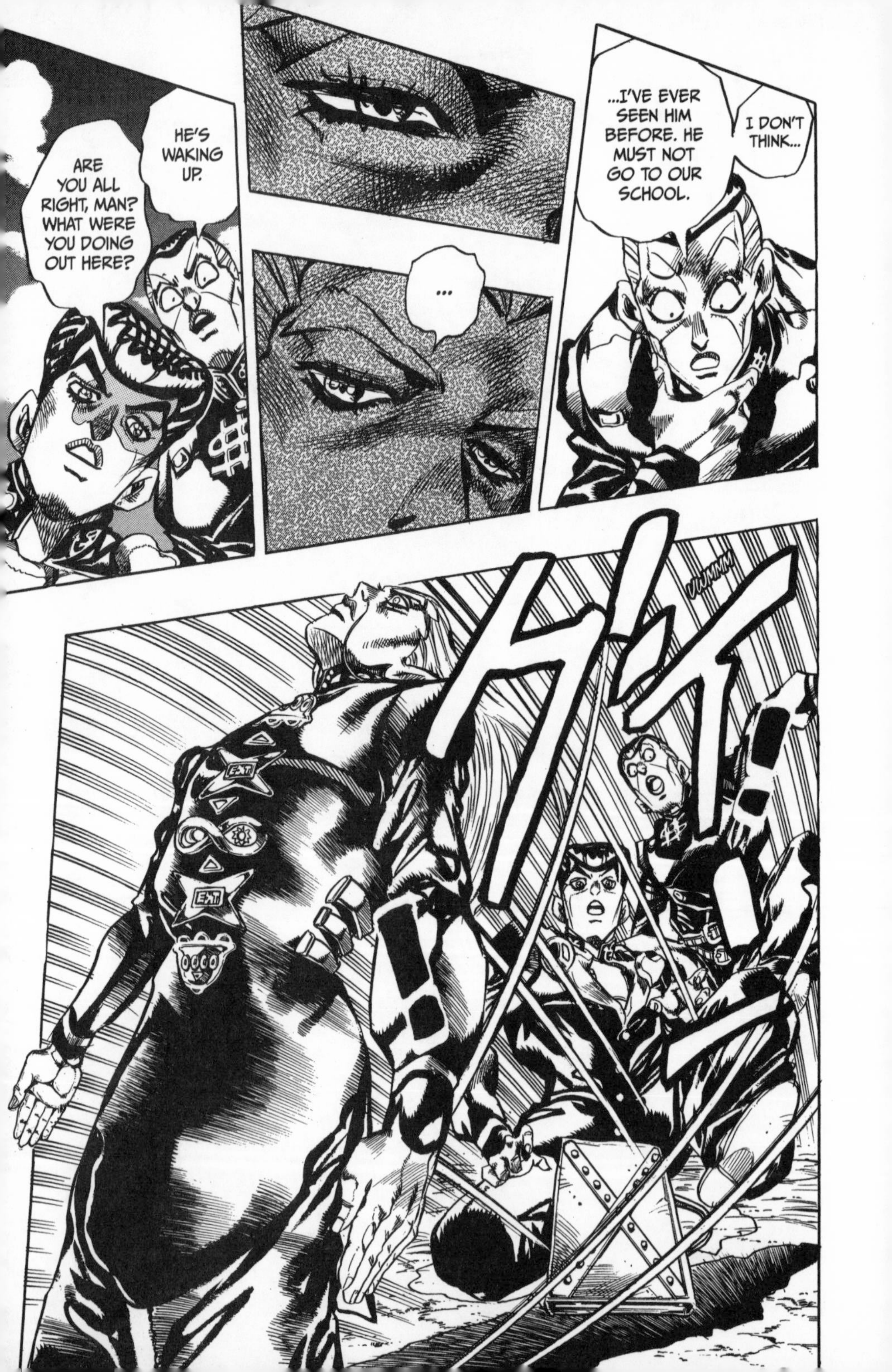
I DON'T THINK...
...I'VE EVER SEEN HIM BEFORE. HE MUST NOT GO TO OUR SCHOOL.
...
HE'S WAKING UP.
ARE YOU ALL RIGHT, MAN? WHAT WERE YOU DOING OUT HERE?
VUUMMM

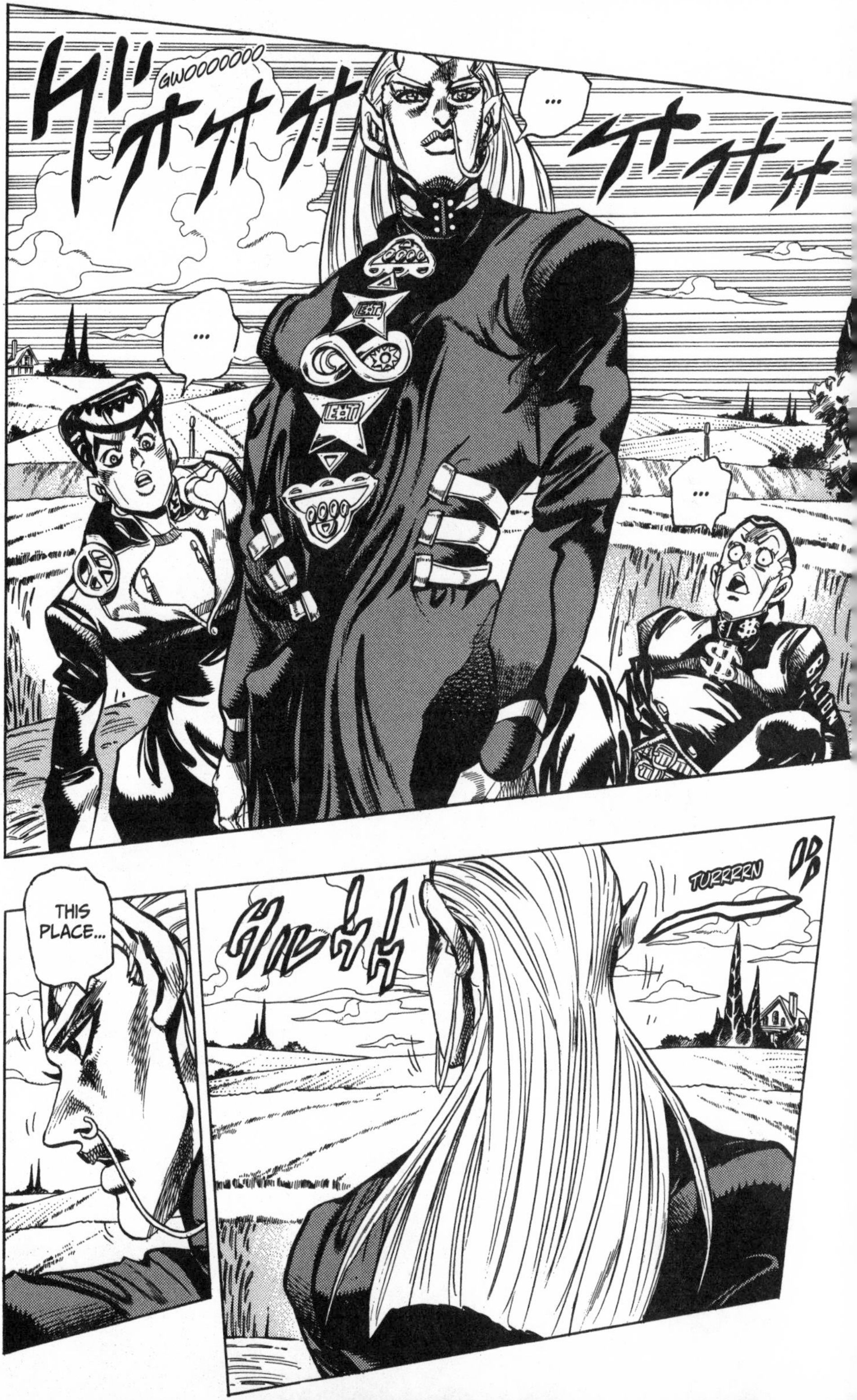
...
GWOOOOOOO
...
...
TURRRRN
THIS PLACE...

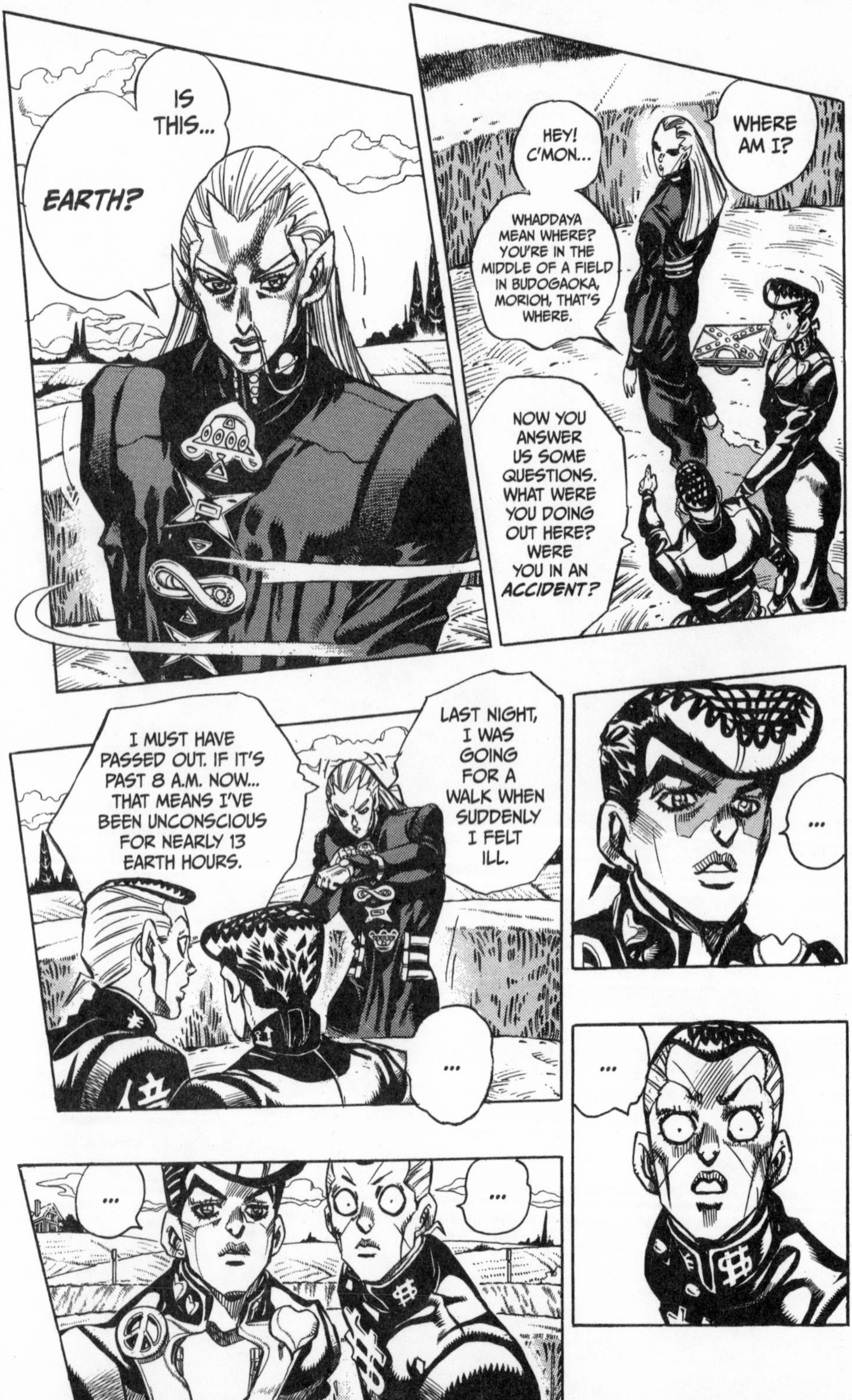
WHERE AM I?
HEY! C'MON...
WHADDAYA MEAN WHERE? YOU'RE IN THE MIDDLE OF A FIELD IN BUDOGAOKA, MORIOH, THAT'S WHERE.
NOW YOU ANSWER US SOME QUESTIONS. WHAT WERE YOU DOING OUT HERE? WERE YOU IN AN *ACCIDENT?*
IS THIS...
EARTH?
...
LAST NIGHT, I WAS GOING FOR A WALK WHEN SUDDENLY I FELT ILL.
I MUST HAVE PASSED OUT. IF IT'S PAST 8 A.M. NOW... THAT MEANS I'VE BEEN UNCONSCIOUS FOR NEARLY 13 EARTH HOURS.
...
...
...
...

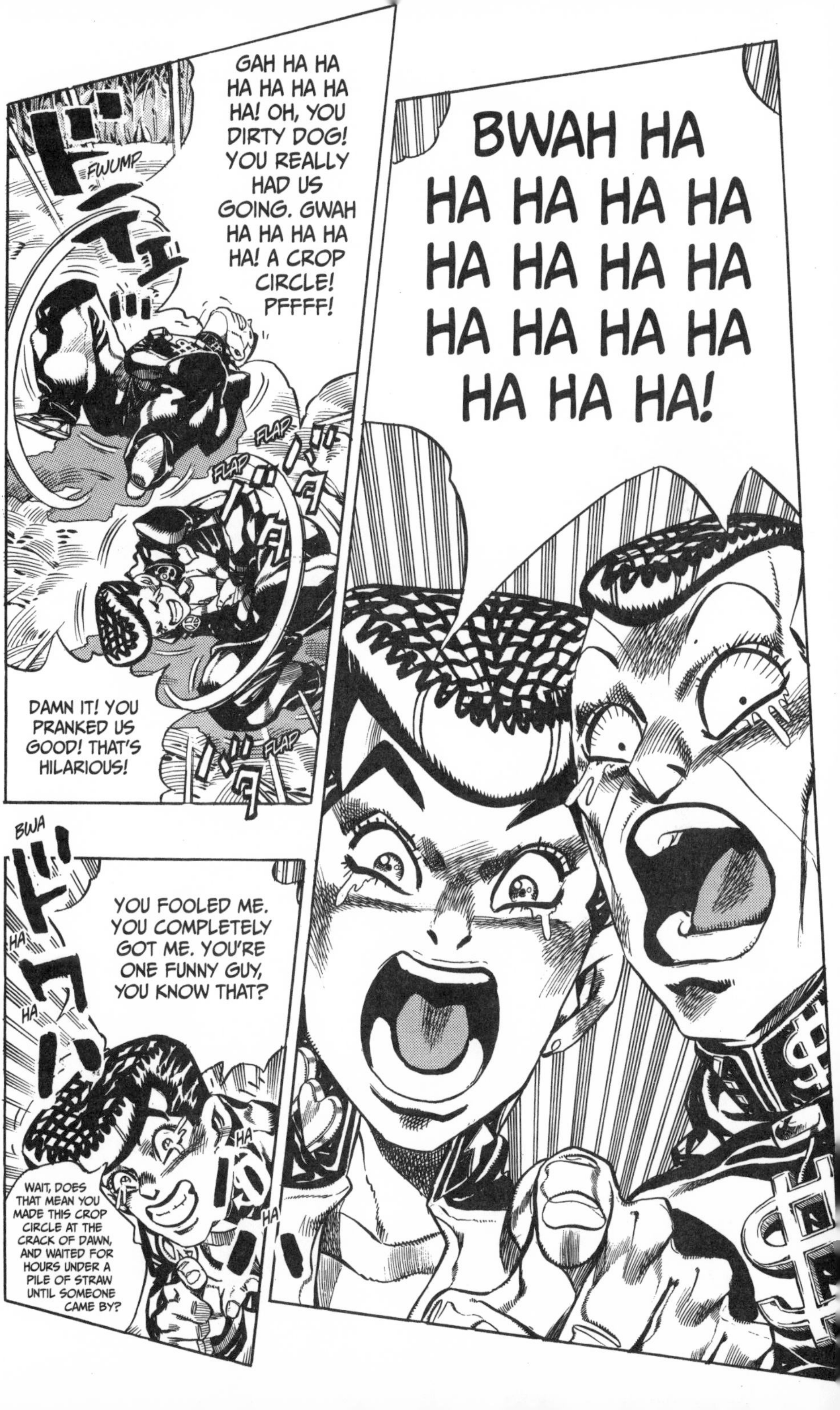
BWAH HA HA HA HA HA HA HA HA HA HA HA HA HA HA HA HA HA!
GAH HA HA HA HA HA HA HA! OH, YOU DIRTY DOG! YOU REALLY HAD US GOING. GWAH HA HA HA HA HA! A CROP CIRCLE! PFFFF!
FWUMP
FLAP
FLAP
FLAP
DAMN IT! YOU PRANKED US GOOD! THAT'S HILARIOUS!
BWA
HA
HA
YOU FOOLED ME. YOU COMPLETELY GOT ME. YOU'RE ONE FUNNY GUY, YOU KNOW THAT?
HA
HA
WAIT, DOES THAT MEAN YOU MADE THIS CROP CIRCLE AT THE CRACK OF DAWN, AND WAITED FOR HOURS UNDER A PILE OF STRAW UNTIL SOMEONE CAME BY?

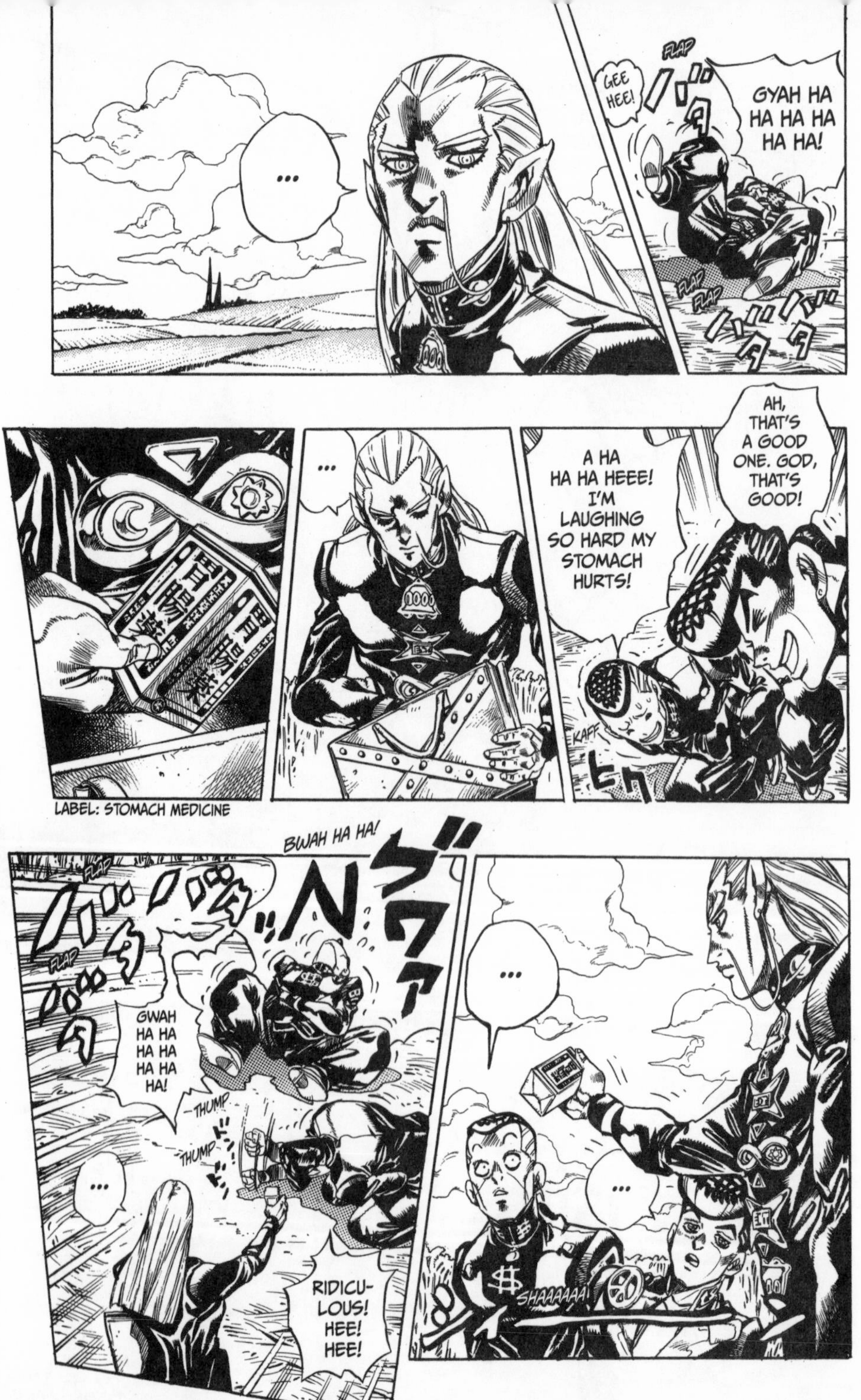
FLAP
GEE HEE!
GYAH HA HA HA HA HA HA!
FLAP FLAP
...
AH, THAT'S A GOOD ONE. GOD, THAT'S GOOD!
A HA HA HA HEEE! I'M LAUGHING SO HARD MY STOMACH HURTS!
KAFF
...
LABEL: STOMACH MEDICINE
...
...
SHAAAAAAA
BWAH HA HA!
FLAP
FLAP
GWAH HA HA HA HA HA HA HA!
THUMP
THUMP
...
RIDICU-LOUS! HEE! HEE!

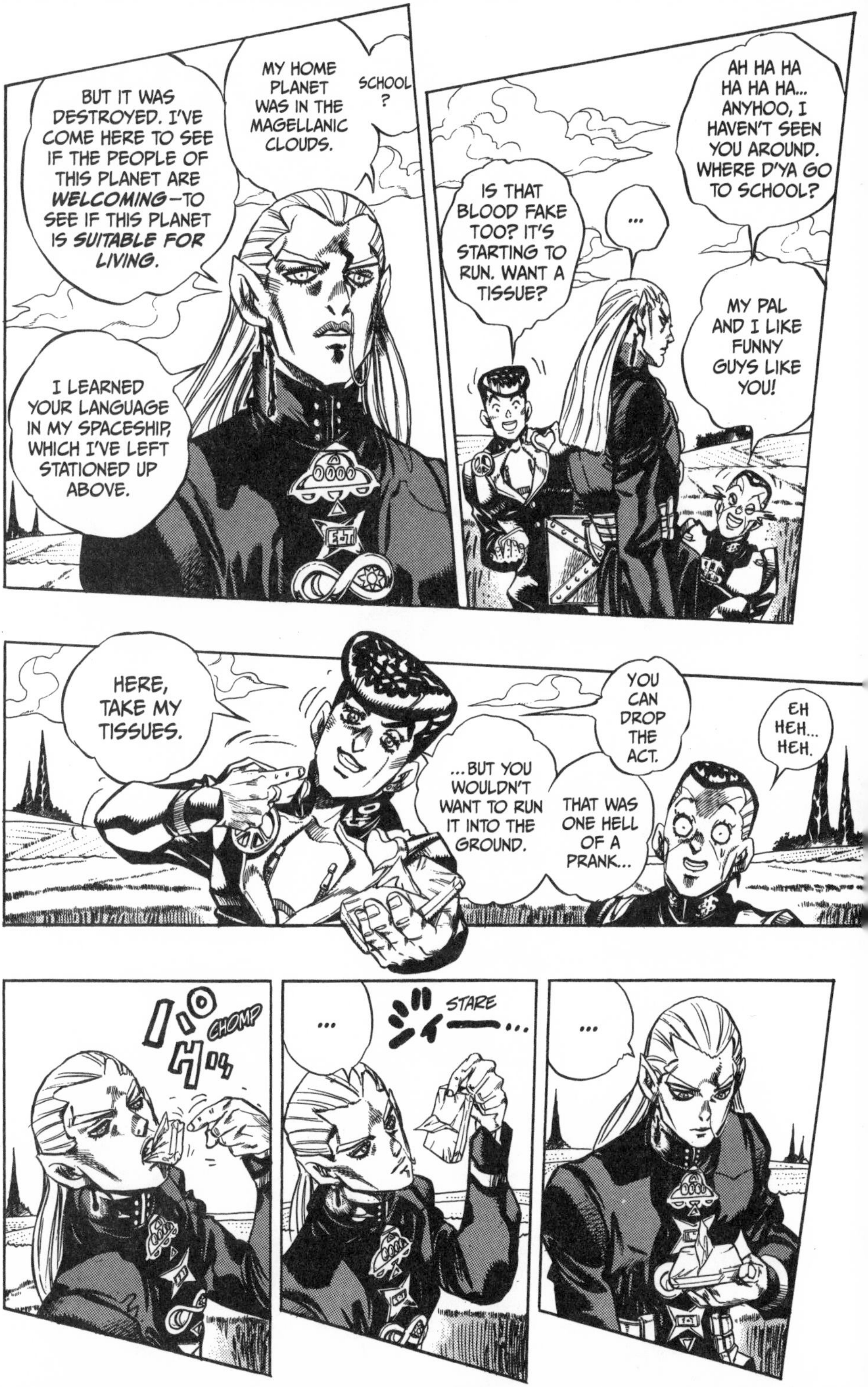
AH HA HA HA HA HA... ANYHOO, I HAVEN'T SEEN YOU AROUND. WHERE D'YA GO TO SCHOOL?
MY PAL AND I LIKE FUNNY GUYS LIKE YOU!
...
IS THAT BLOOD FAKE TOO? IT'S STARTING TO RUN. WANT A TISSUE?
SCHOOL?
MY HOME PLANET WAS IN THE MAGELLANIC CLOUDS.
BUT IT WAS DESTROYED. I'VE COME HERE TO SEE IF THE PEOPLE OF THIS PLANET ARE *WELCOMING*—TO SEE IF THIS PLANET IS *SUITABLE FOR LIVING*.
I LEARNED YOUR LANGUAGE IN MY SPACESHIP, WHICH I'VE LEFT STATIONED UP ABOVE.
EH HEH... HEH.
YOU CAN DROP THE ACT.
THAT WAS ONE HELL OF A PRANK...
...BUT YOU WOULDN'T WANT TO RUN IT INTO THE GROUND.
HERE, TAKE MY TISSUES.
...
STARE
...
CHOMP

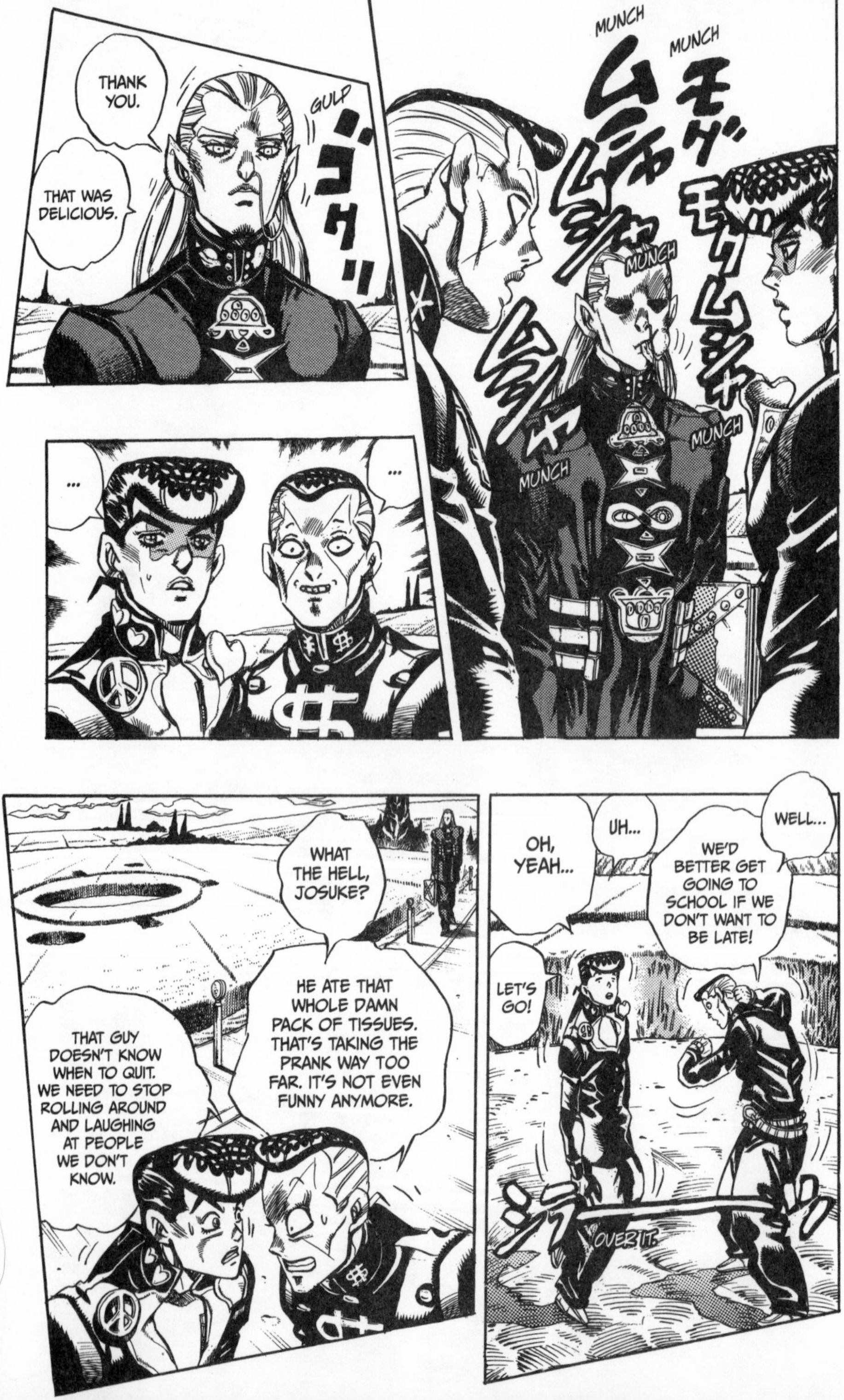
MUNCH
MUNCH
MUNCH
MUNCH
MUNCH
THANK YOU.
THAT WAS DELICIOUS.
GULP
...
...
WELL...
UH...
OH, YEAH...
WE'D BETTER GET GOING TO SCHOOL IF WE DON'T WANT TO BE LATE!
LET'S GO!
OVER IT.
WHAT THE HELL, JOSUKE?
HE ATE THAT WHOLE DAMN PACK OF TISSUES. THAT'S TAKING THE PRANK WAY TOO FAR. IT'S NOT EVEN FUNNY ANYMORE.
THAT GUY DOESN'T KNOW WHEN TO QUIT. WE NEED TO STOP ROLLING AROUND AND LAUGHING AT PEOPLE WE DON'T KNOW.

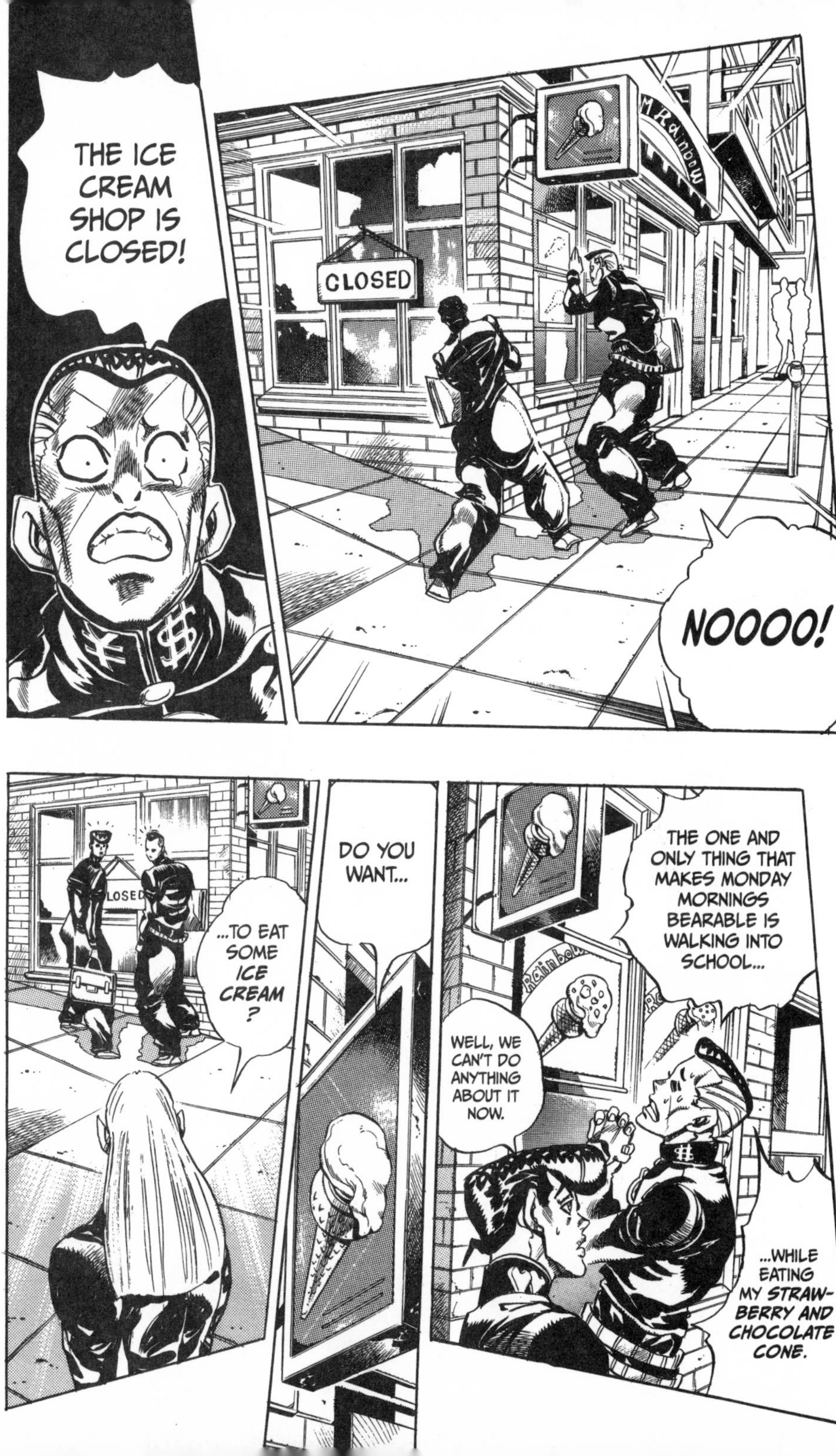
CLOSED
NOOOO!
THE ICE CREAM SHOP IS CLOSED!
THE ONE AND ONLY THING THAT MAKES MONDAY MORNINGS BEARABLE IS WALKING INTO SCHOOL...
WELL, WE CAN'T DO ANYTHING ABOUT IT NOW.
...WHILE EATING MY STRAWBERRY AND CHOCOLATE CONE.
DO YOU WANT...
...TO EAT SOME ICE CREAM?

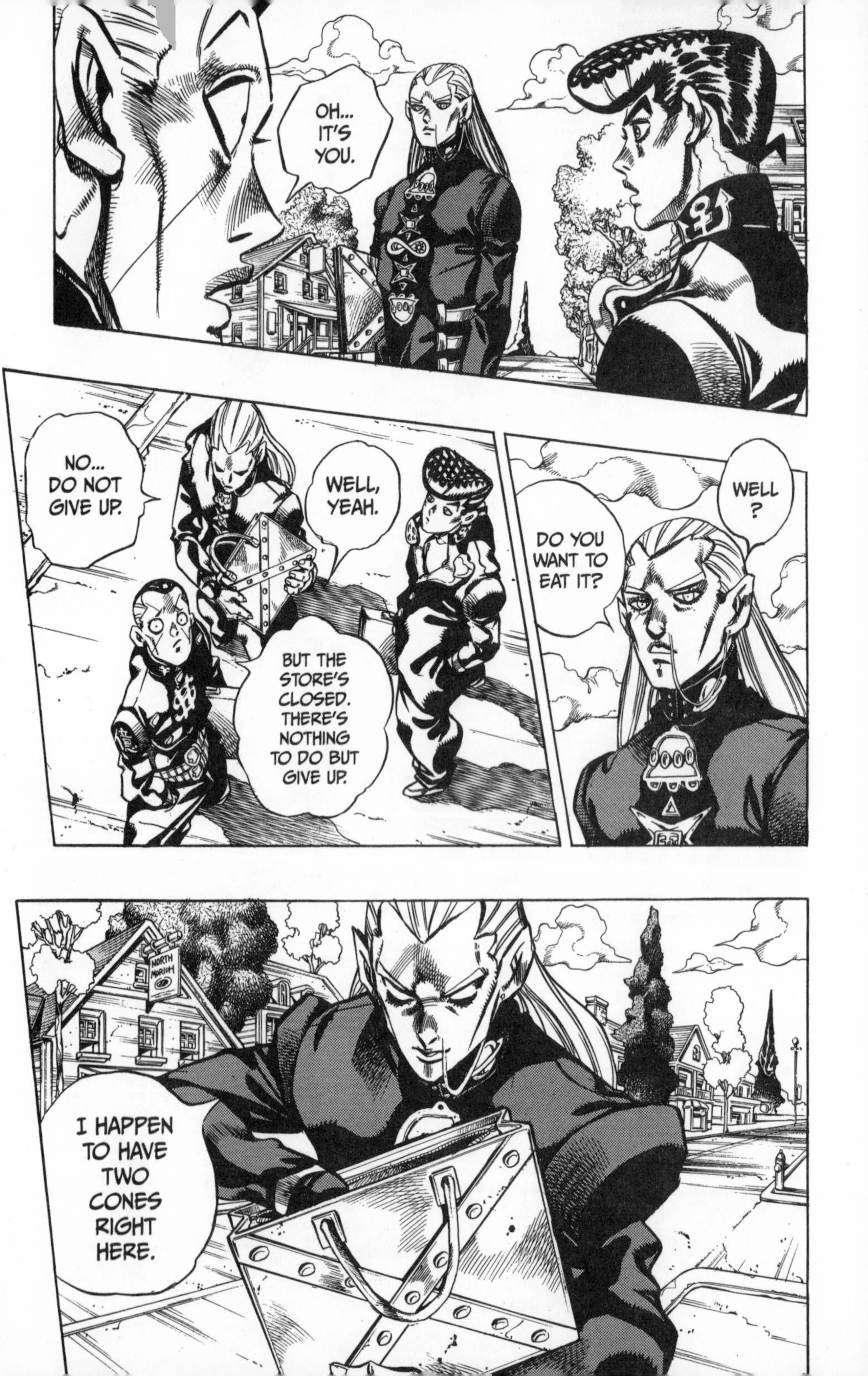
OH... IT'S YOU.
WELL ?
DO YOU WANT TO EAT IT?
WELL, YEAH.
BUT THE STORE'S CLOSED. THERE'S NOTHING TO DO BUT GIVE UP.
NO... DO NOT GIVE UP.
NORTH MORIOH
I HAPPEN TO HAVE TWO CONES RIGHT HERE.

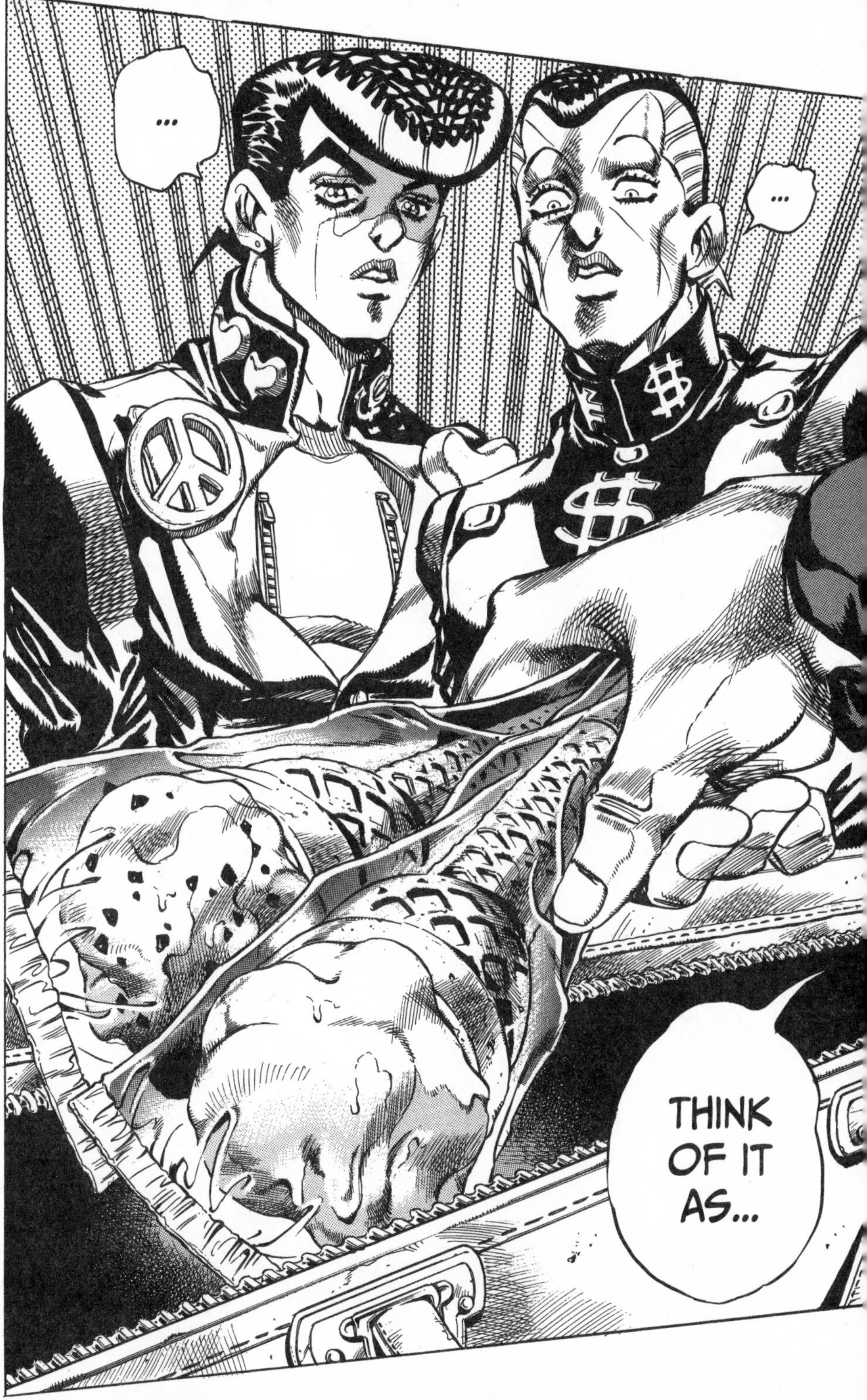
...
...
THINK OF IT AS...

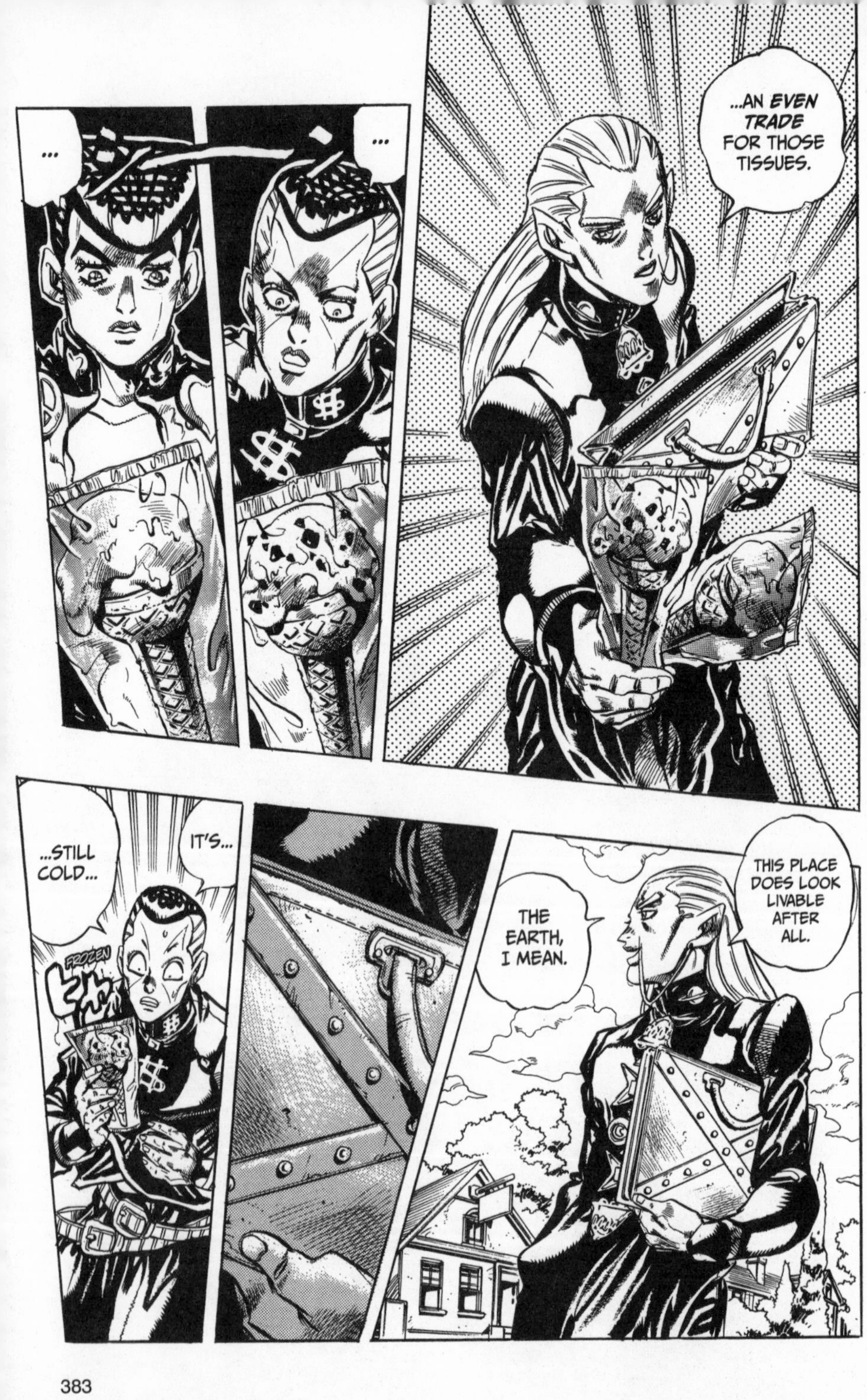
...AN EVEN TRADE FOR THOSE TISSUES.
...
...
THIS PLACE DOES LOOK LIVABLE AFTER ALL.
THE EARTH, I MEAN.
IT'S...
...STILL COLD...
FROZEN

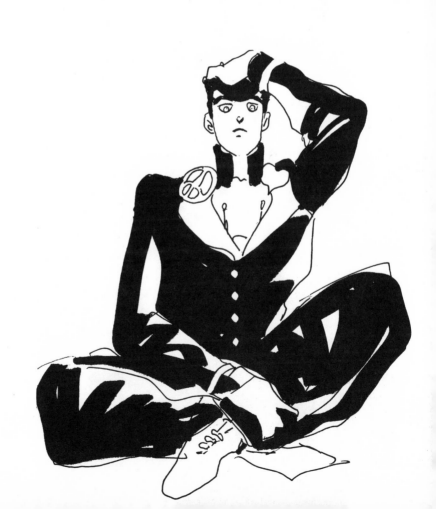

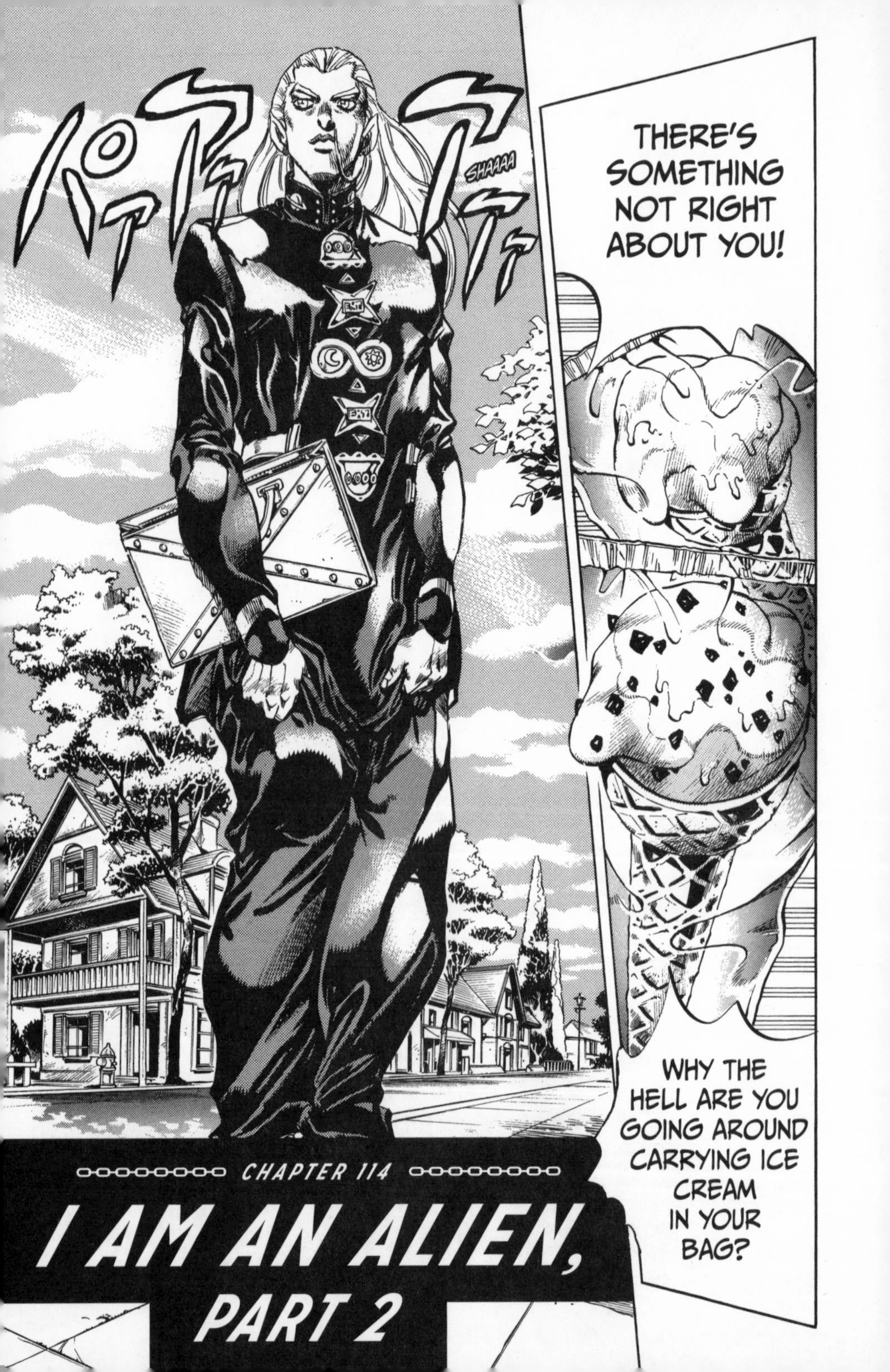
THERE'S SOMETHING NOT RIGHT ABOUT YOU!
WHY THE HELL ARE YOU GOING AROUND CARRYING ICE CREAM IN YOUR BAG?
SHAAAA
CHAPTER 114
I AM AN ALIEN, PART 2

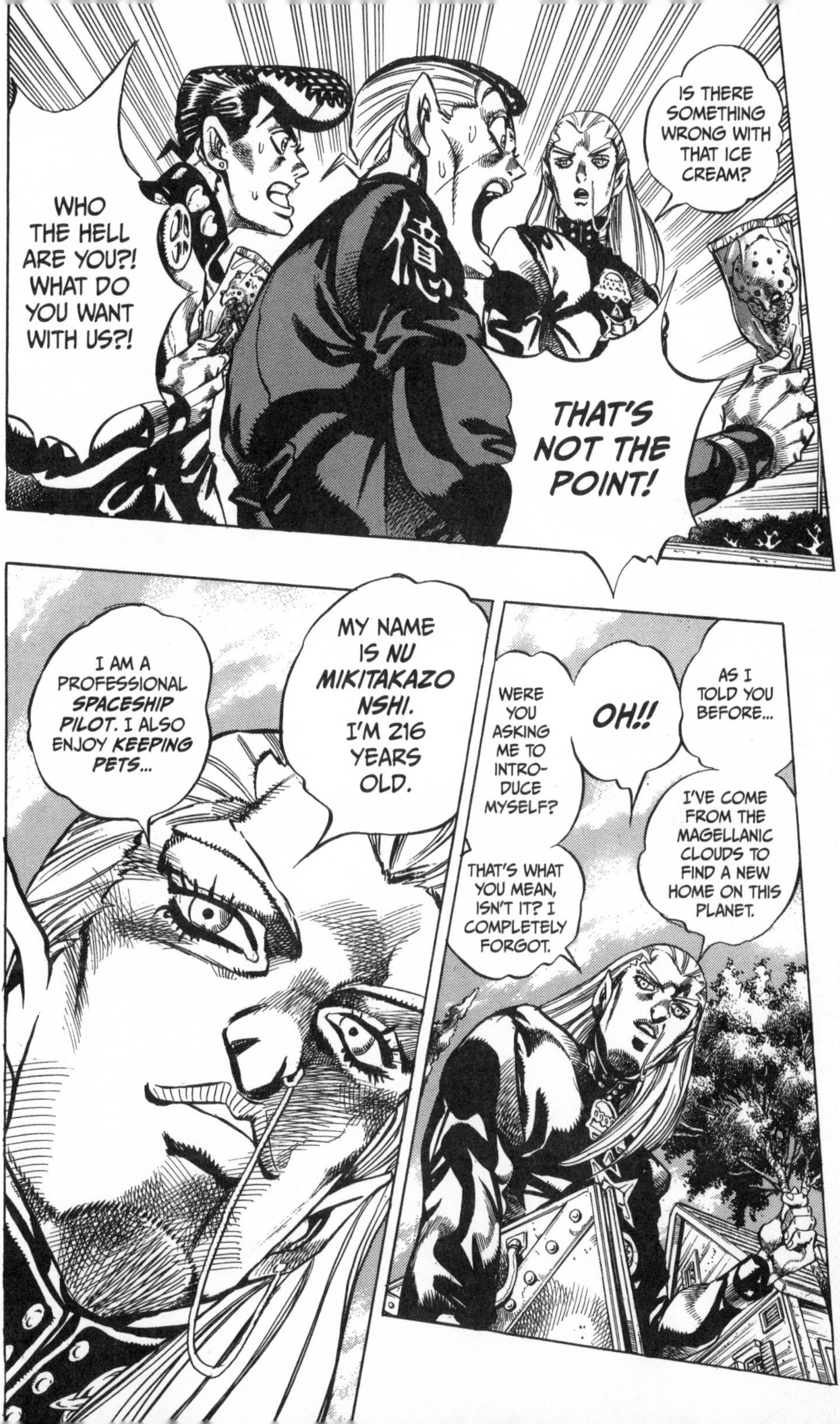
IS THERE SOMETHING WRONG WITH THAT ICE CREAM?
WHO THE HELL ARE YOU?! WHAT DO YOU WANT WITH US?!
THAT'S NOT THE POINT!
AS I TOLD YOU BEFORE...
I'VE COME FROM THE MAGELLANIC CLOUDS TO FIND A NEW HOME ON THIS PLANET.
OH!!
WERE YOU ASKING ME TO INTRO-DUCE MYSELF?
THAT'S WHAT YOU MEAN, ISN'T IT? I COMPLETELY FORGOT.
MY NAME IS *NU MIKITAKAZO NSHI*. I'M 216 YEARS OLD.
I AM A PROFESSIONAL *SPACESHIP PILOT*. I ALSO ENJOY *KEEPING PETS*...

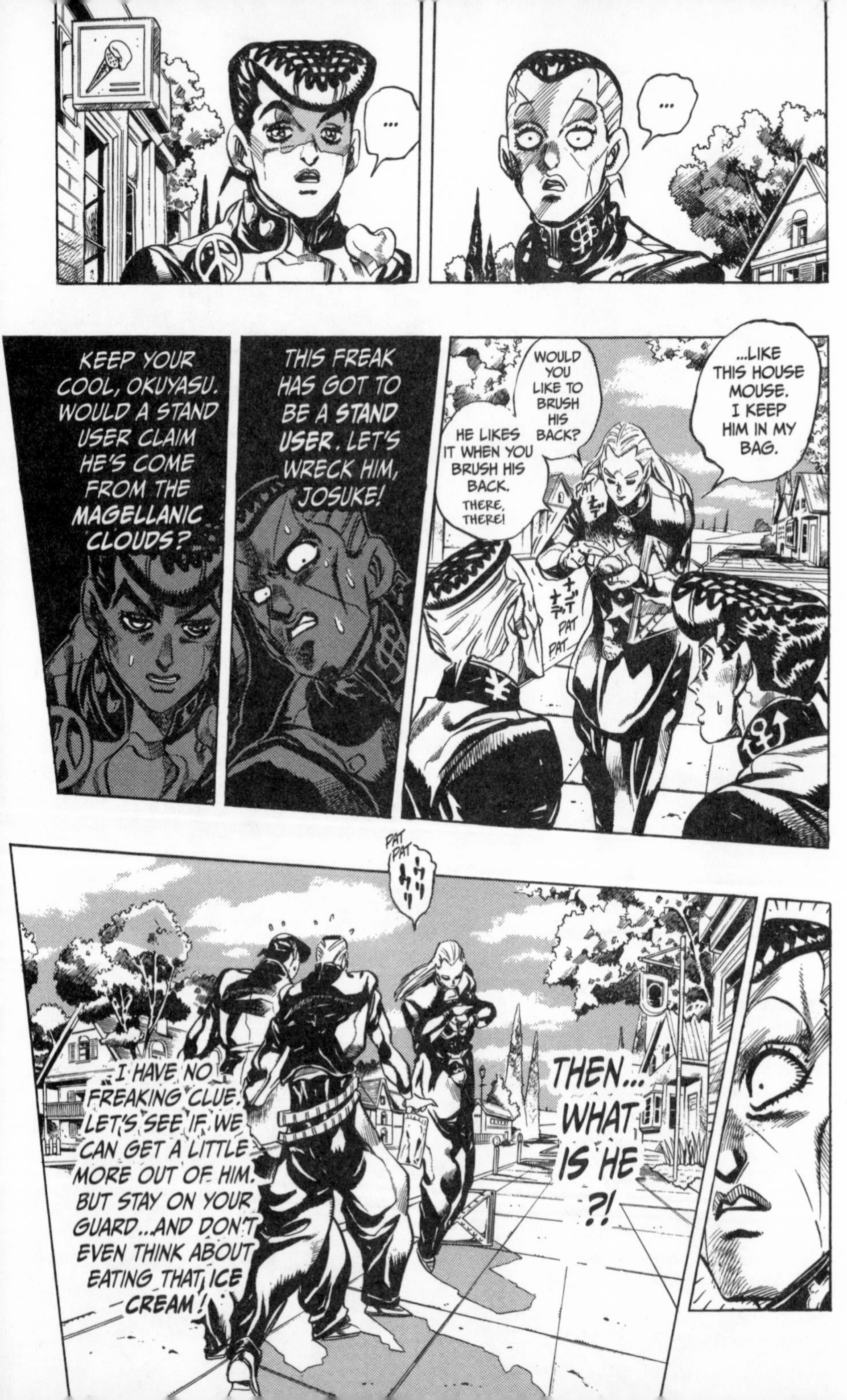
...
...
...LIKE THIS HOUSE MOUSE. I KEEP HIM IN MY BAG.
WOULD YOU LIKE TO BRUSH HIS BACK?
HE LIKES IT WHEN YOU BRUSH HIS BACK. THERE, THERE!
PAT
PAT PAT
THIS FREAK HAS GOT TO BE A STAND USER. LET'S WRECK HIM, JOSUKE!
KEEP YOUR COOL, OKUYASU. WOULD A STAND USER CLAIM HE'S COME FROM THE MAGELLANIC CLOUDS?
PAT PAT
THEN... WHAT IS HE ?!
I HAVE NO FREAKING CLUE. LET'S SEE IF WE CAN GET A LITTLE MORE OUT OF HIM. BUT STAY ON YOUR GUARD...AND DON'T EVEN THINK ABOUT EATING THAT ICE CREAM!

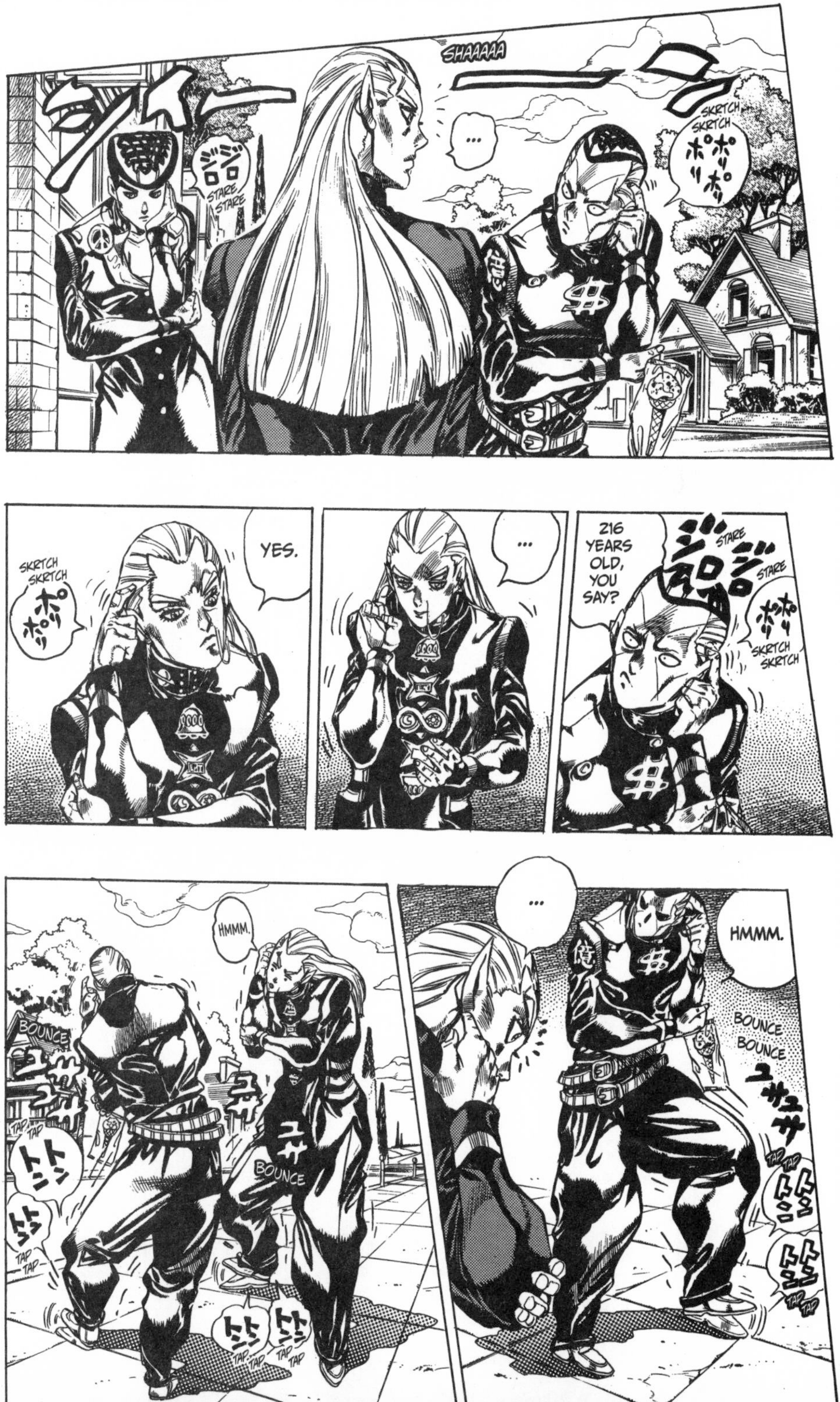
SKRTCH SKRTCH
ポリポリ
SHAAAAA
...
ジロジロ
STARE STARE
216 YEARS OLD, YOU SAY?
ジロジロ
STARE STARE
ポリポリ
SKRTCH SKRTCH
...
YES.
SKRTCH SKRTCH
ポリポリ
...
HMMM.
BOUNCE BOUNCE
ユサユサ
TAP TAP
TAP TAP
HMMM.
ユサユサ
BOUNCE
BOUNCE
ユサユサ
TAP TAP
トントン
TAP TAP
TAP TAP
TAP TAP

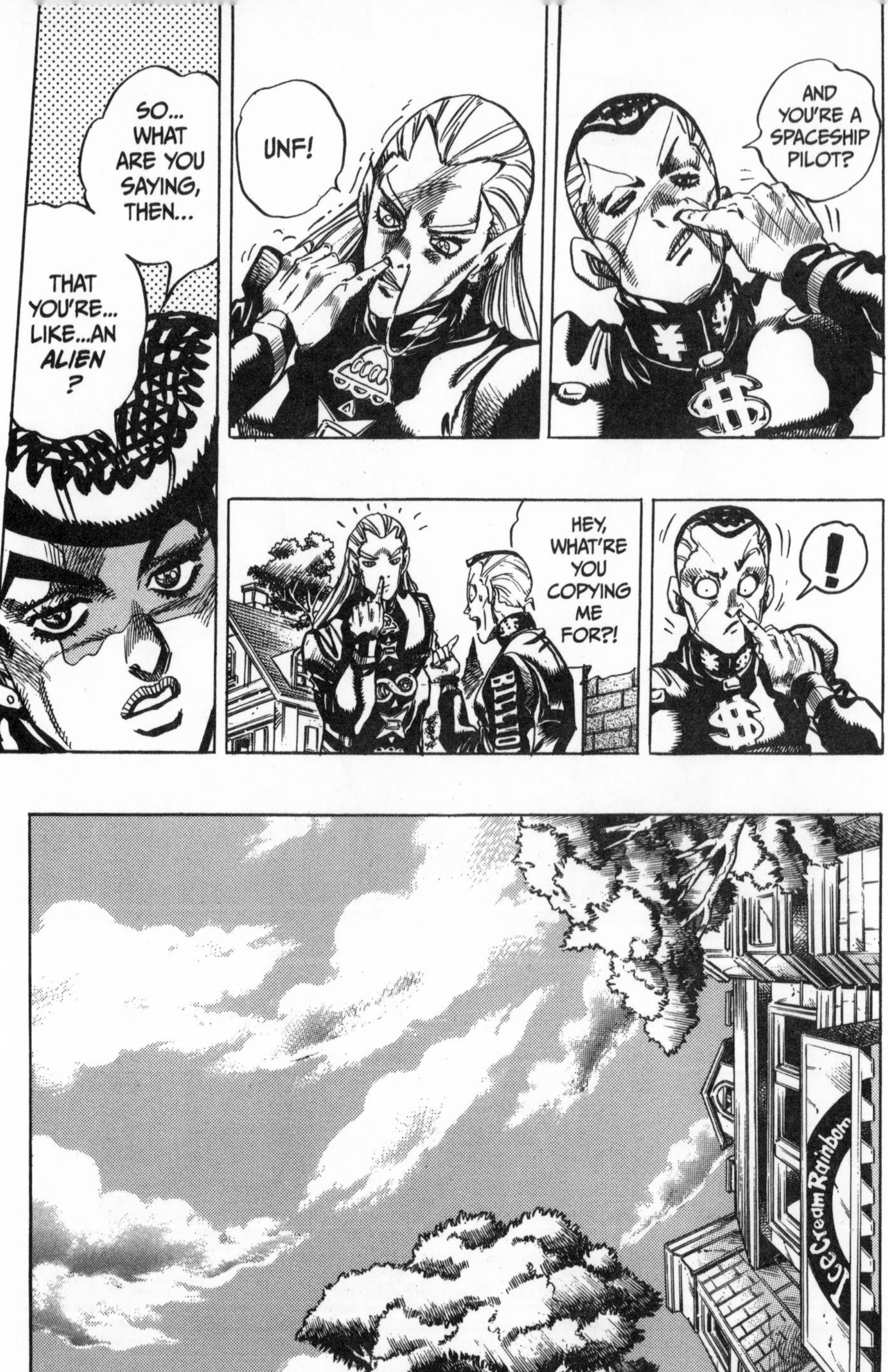
AND YOU'RE A SPACESHIP PILOT?
UNF!
!
HEY, WHAT'RE YOU COPYING ME FOR?!
SO... WHAT ARE YOU SAYING, THEN...
THAT YOU'RE... LIKE...AN *ALIEN* ?
Ice Cream Rainbow

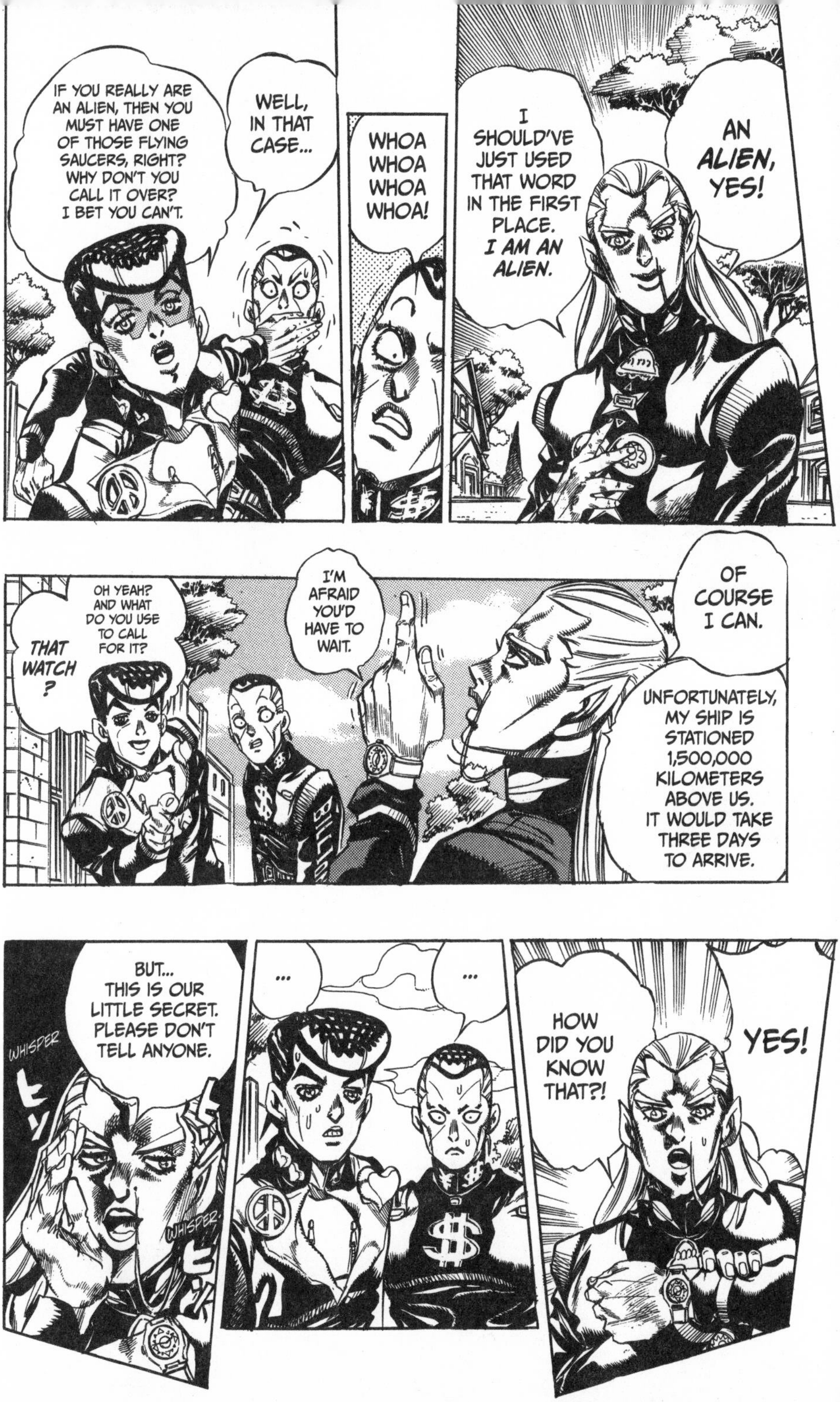
AN *ALIEN*, YES!
I SHOULD'VE JUST USED THAT WORD IN THE FIRST PLACE. *I AM AN ALIEN.*
WHOA WHOA WHOA WHOA!
WELL, IN THAT CASE...
IF YOU REALLY ARE AN ALIEN, THEN YOU MUST HAVE ONE OF THOSE FLYING SAUCERS, RIGHT? WHY DON'T YOU CALL IT OVER? I BET YOU CAN'T.
OF COURSE I CAN.
UNFORTUNATELY, MY SHIP IS STATIONED 1,500,000 KILOMETERS ABOVE US. IT WOULD TAKE THREE DAYS TO ARRIVE.
I'M AFRAID YOU'D HAVE TO WAIT.
OH YEAH? AND WHAT DO YOU USE TO CALL FOR IT?
THAT WATCH ?
YES!
HOW DID YOU KNOW THAT?!
...
...
BUT... THIS IS OUR LITTLE SECRET. PLEASE DON'T TELL ANYONE.
WHISPER
ヒソ
WHISPER
ヒソ

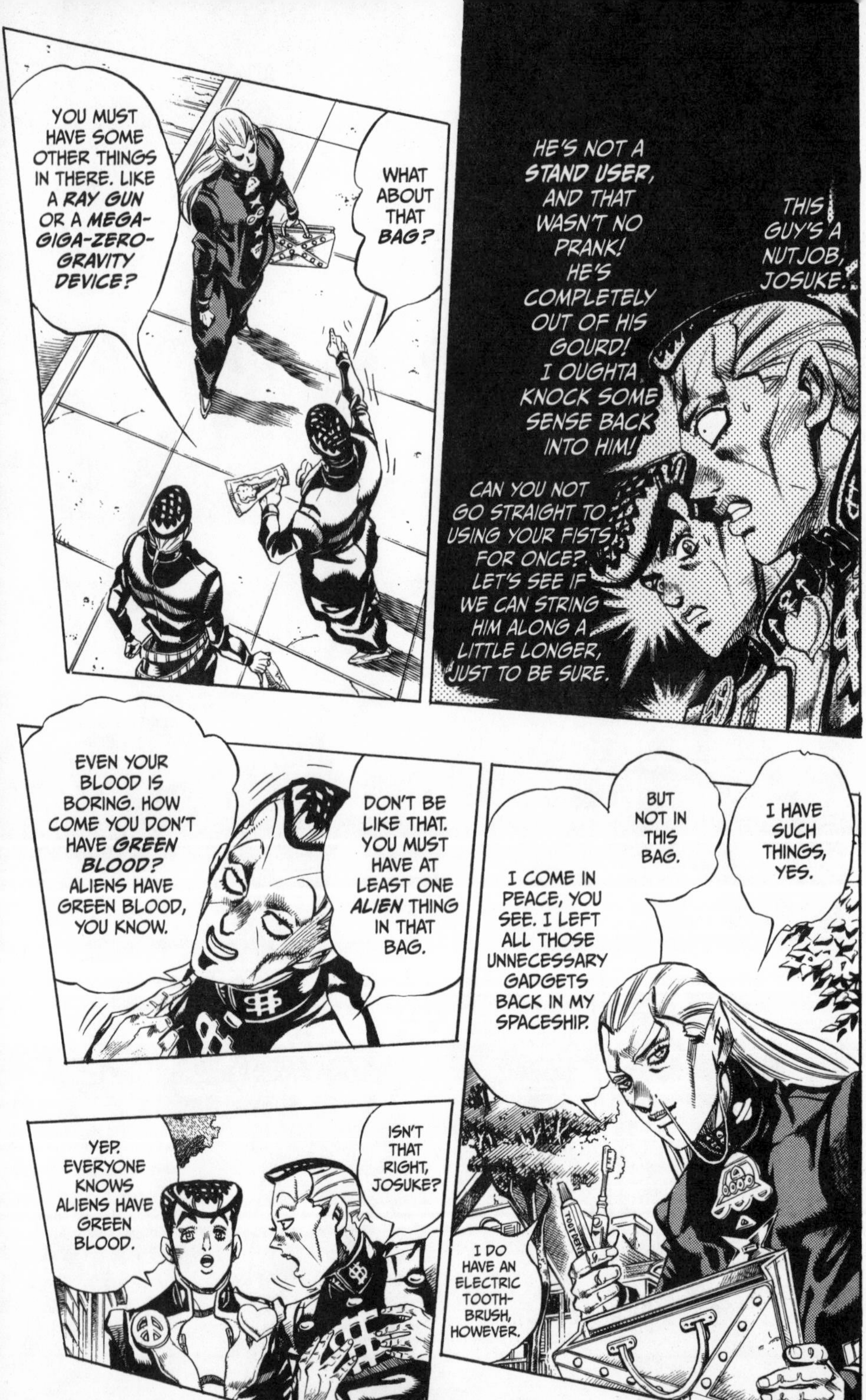
THIS GUY'S A NUTJOB, JOSUKE.
HE'S NOT A STAND USER, AND THAT WASN'T NO PRANK! HE'S COMPLETELY OUT OF HIS GOURD! I OUGHTA KNOCK SOME SENSE BACK INTO HIM!
CAN YOU NOT GO STRAIGHT TO USING YOUR FISTS FOR ONCE? LET'S SEE IF WE CAN STRING HIM ALONG A LITTLE LONGER, JUST TO BE SURE.
WHAT ABOUT THAT BAG?
YOU MUST HAVE SOME OTHER THINGS IN THERE. LIKE A RAY GUN OR A MEGA-GIGA-ZERO-GRAVITY DEVICE?
I HAVE SUCH THINGS, YES.
BUT NOT IN THIS BAG.
I COME IN PEACE, YOU SEE. I LEFT ALL THOSE UNNECESSARY GADGETS BACK IN MY SPACESHIP.
I DO HAVE AN ELECTRIC TOOTHBRUSH, HOWEVER.
DON'T BE LIKE THAT. YOU MUST HAVE AT LEAST ONE ALIEN THING IN THAT BAG.
EVEN YOUR BLOOD IS BORING. HOW COME YOU DON'T HAVE GREEN BLOOD? ALIENS HAVE GREEN BLOOD, YOU KNOW.
ISN'T THAT RIGHT, JOSUKE?
YEP. EVERYONE KNOWS ALIENS HAVE GREEN BLOOD.

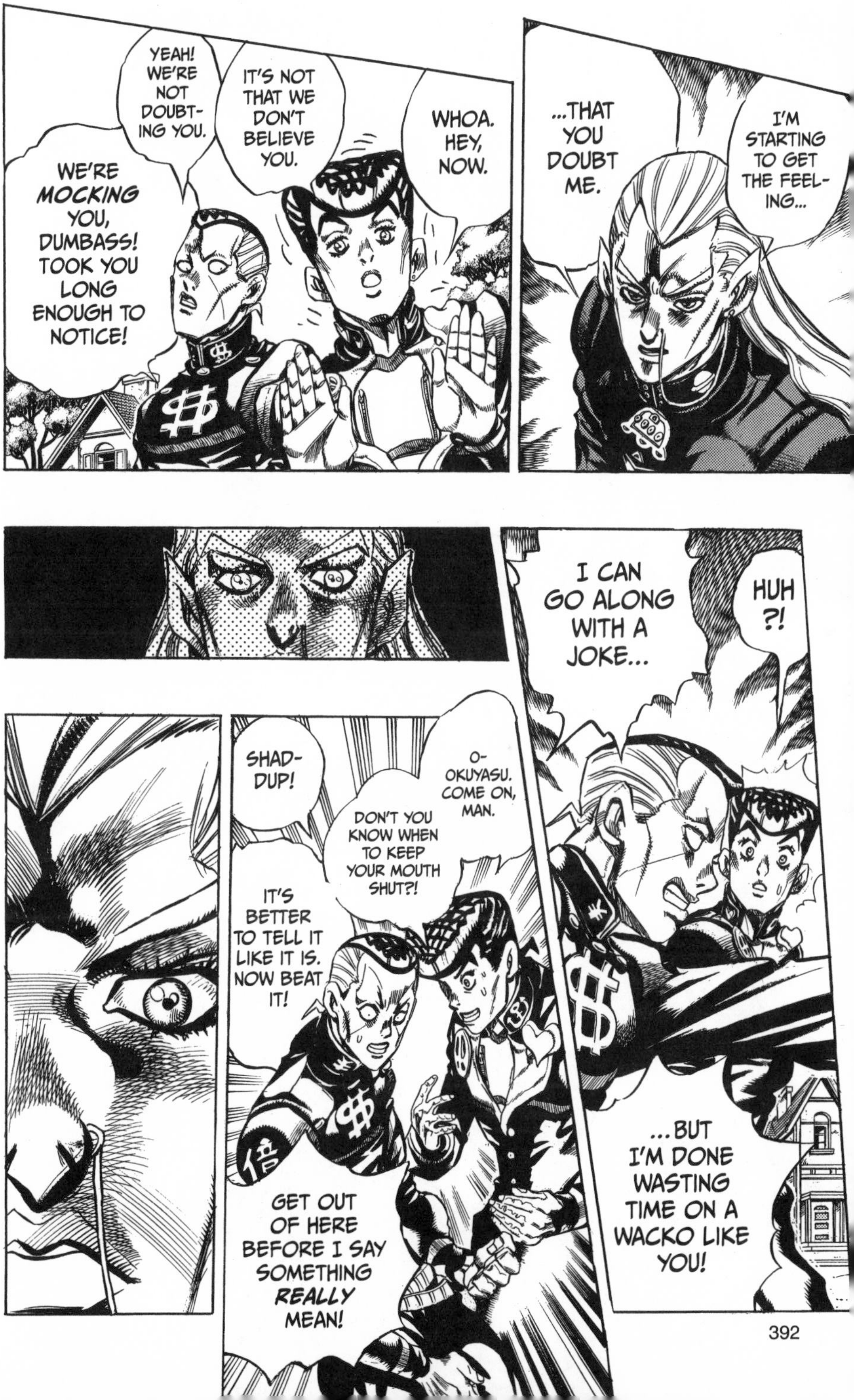
I'M STARTING TO GET THE FEELING...
...THAT YOU DOUBT ME.
WHOA. HEY, NOW.
IT'S NOT THAT WE DON'T BELIEVE YOU.
YEAH! WE'RE NOT DOUBTING YOU.
WE'RE *MOCKING* YOU, DUMBASS! TOOK YOU LONG ENOUGH TO NOTICE!
HUH?!
I CAN GO ALONG WITH A JOKE...
...BUT I'M DONE WASTING TIME ON A WACKO LIKE YOU!
O-OKUYASU. COME ON, MAN.
SHAD-DUP!
DON'T YOU KNOW WHEN TO KEEP YOUR MOUTH SHUT?!
IT'S BETTER TO TELL IT LIKE IT IS. NOW BEAT IT!
GET OUT OF HERE BEFORE I SAY SOMETHING *REALLY* MEAN!

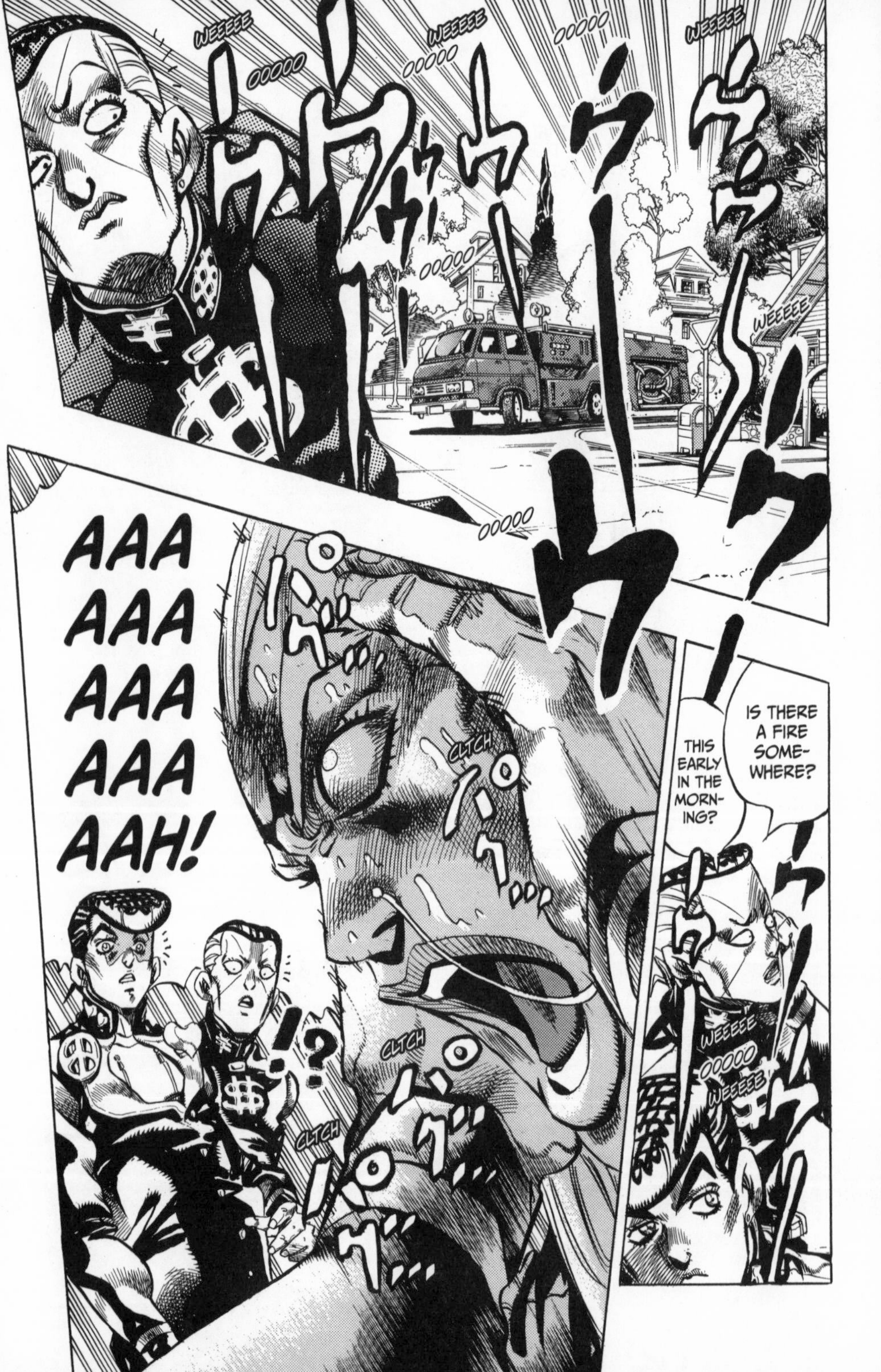
WEEEEE
OOOOO
WEEEEE
OOOOO
OOOOO
WEEEEE
OOOOO
WEEEEE
OOOOO
IS THERE A FIRE SOME-WHERE?
THIS EARLY IN THE MORNING?
WEEEEE
OOOOO
WEEEEE
AAA AAA AAA AAA AAH!
CLTCH
CLTCH
CLTCH
!?

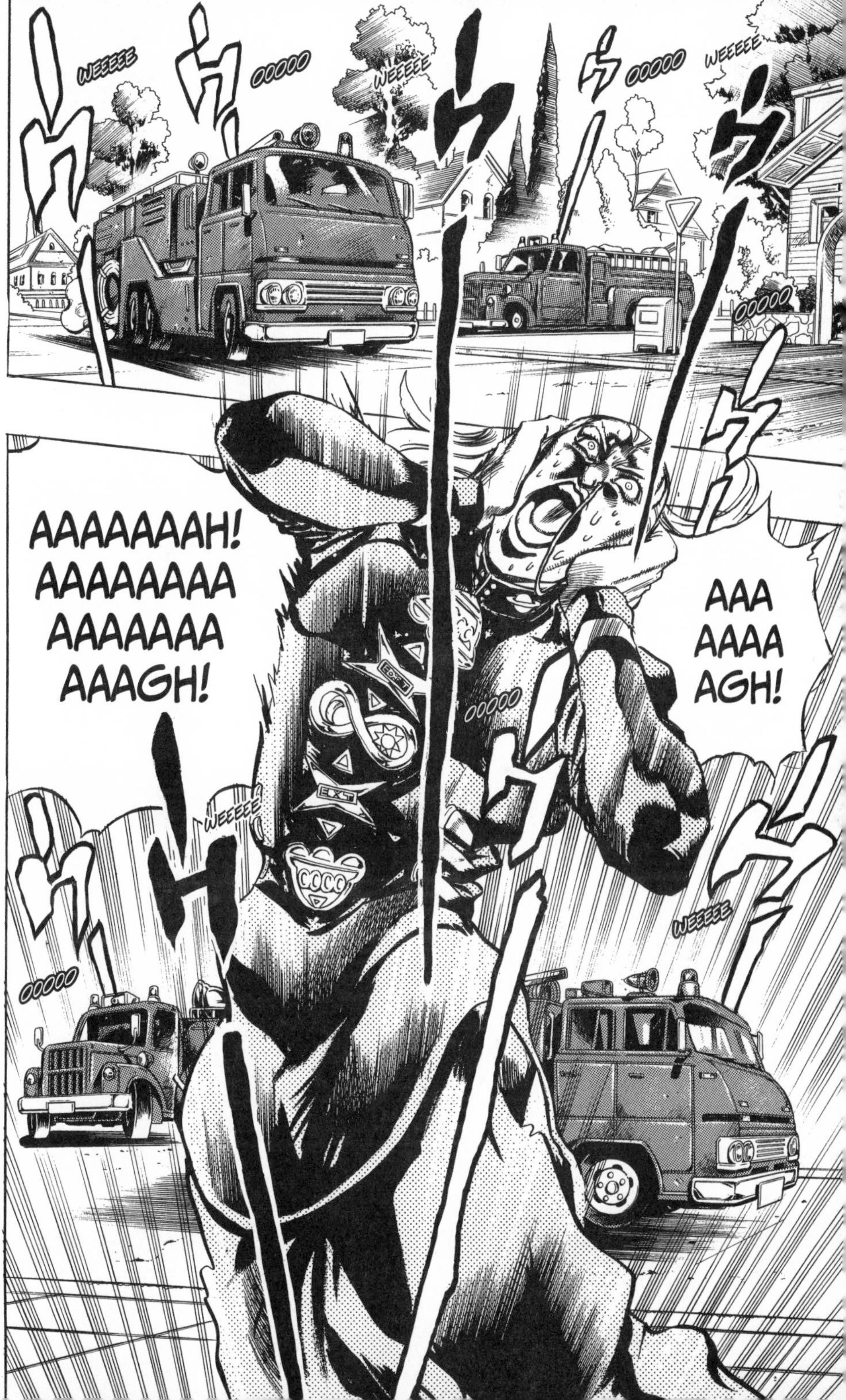
WEEEEE
OOOOO
OOOOO
WEEEEE
OOOOO
WEEEEE
AAA AAAA AGH!
AAAAAAAH! AAAAAAAA AAAAAAA AAAGH!
OOOOO
WEEEEE
WEEEEE
OOOOO

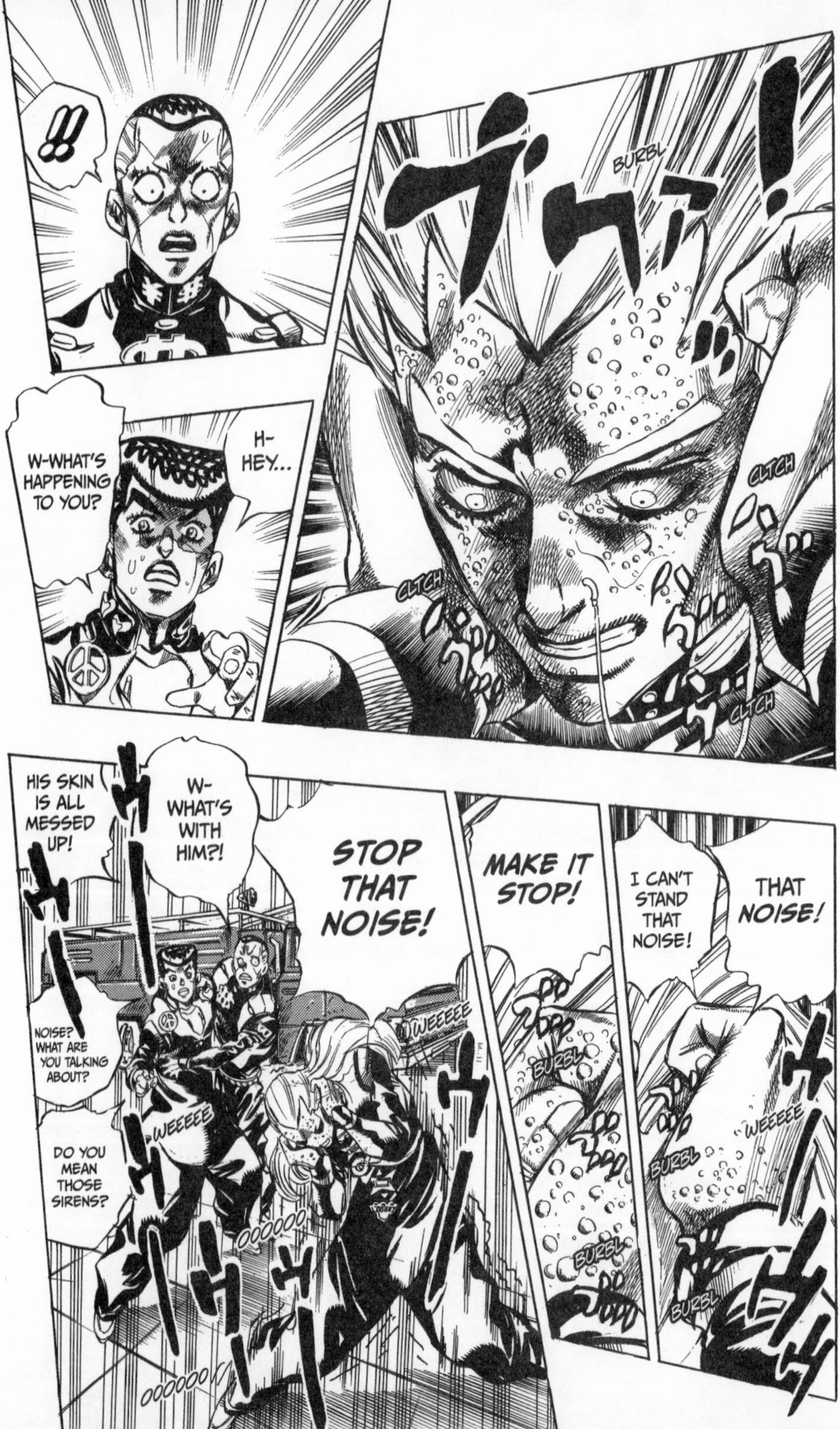

BURBL
CLTCH
CLTCH
CLTCH
!!
H-HEY...
W-WHAT'S HAPPENING TO YOU?
THAT NOISE!
I CAN'T STAND THAT NOISE!
WEEEEE
BURBL
BURBL
MAKE IT STOP!
BURBL
BURBL
STOP THAT NOISE!
W-WHAT'S WITH HIM?!
HIS SKIN IS ALL MESSED UP!
WEEEEE
NOISE? WHAT ARE YOU TALKING ABOUT?
WEEEEE
DO YOU MEAN THOSE SIRENS?
OOOOOO
OOOOOO

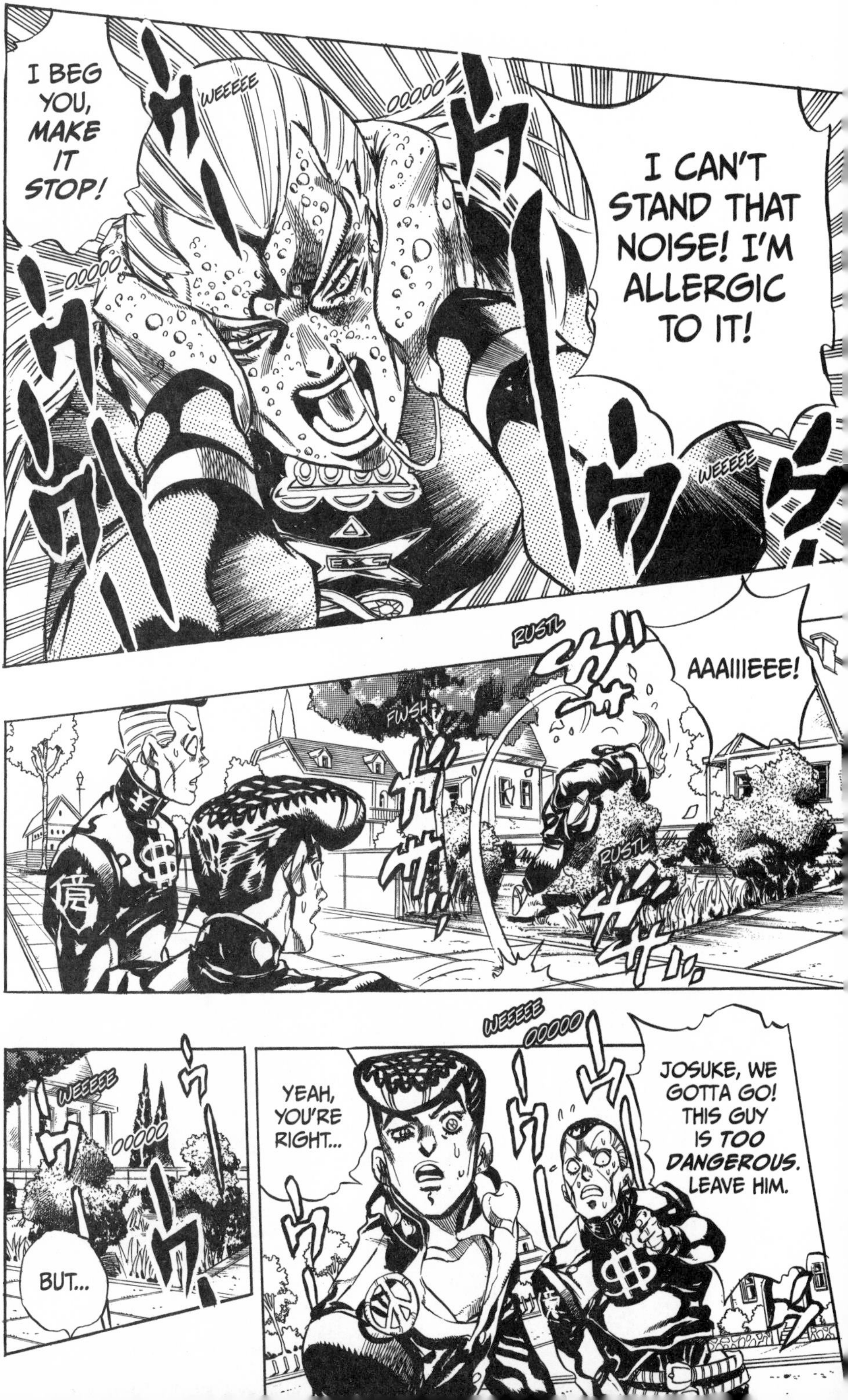
OOOOO
I CAN'T STAND THAT NOISE! I'M ALLERGIC TO IT!
WEEEEE
I BEG YOU, MAKE IT STOP!
OOOOO
WEEEEE
AAAIIIEEE!
RUSTL
FWSH
RUSTL
WEEEEE
OOOOO
JOSUKE, WE GOTTA GO! THIS GUY IS TOO DANGEROUS. LEAVE HIM.
YEAH, YOU'RE RIGHT...
WEEEEE
OOOOO
BUT...

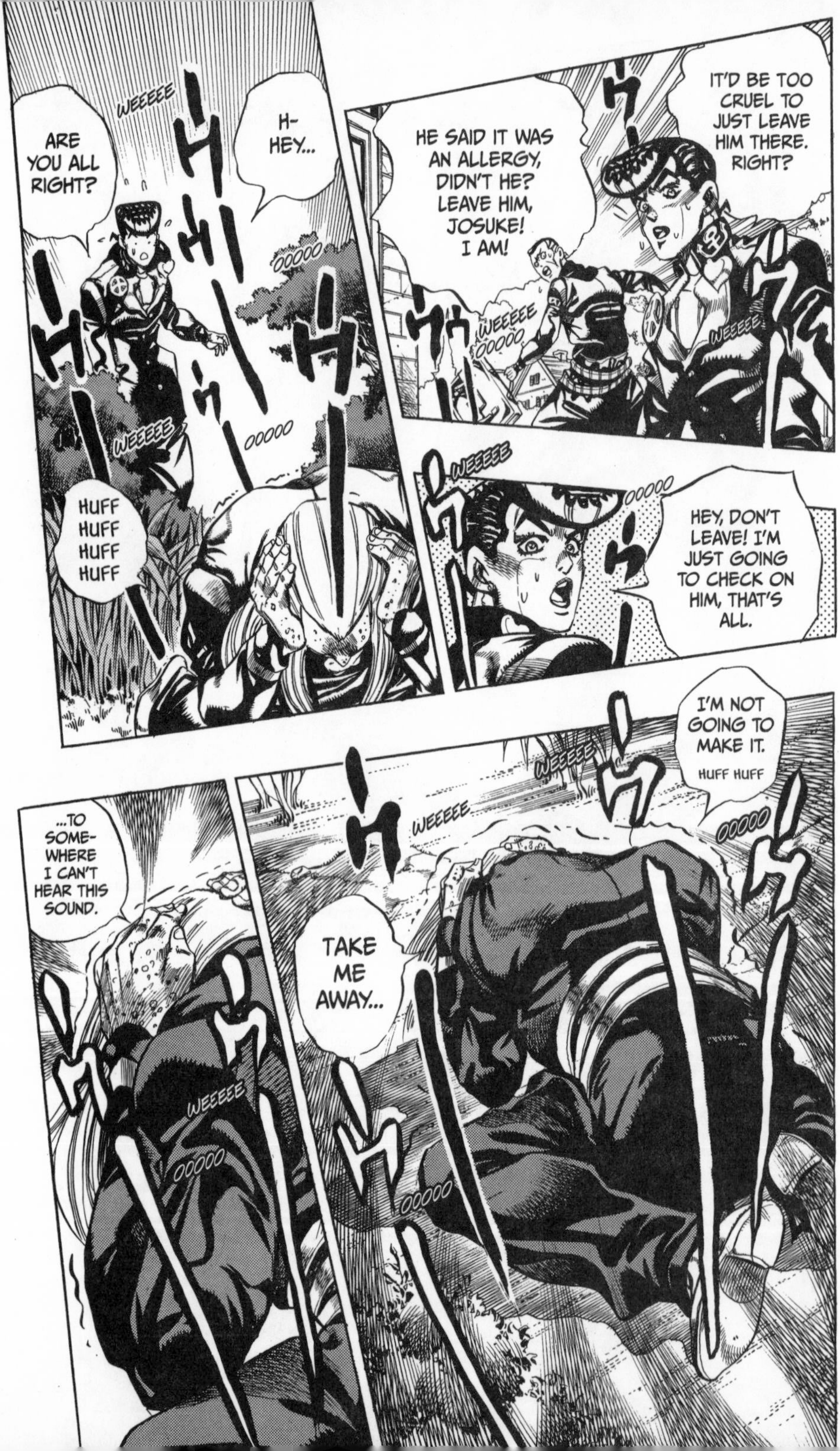

IT'D BE TOO CRUEL TO JUST LEAVE HIM THERE. RIGHT?
HE SAID IT WAS AN ALLERGY, DIDN'T HE? LEAVE HIM, JOSUKE! I AM!
WEEEEE
OOOOO
WEEEEE
WEEEEE
OOOOO
HEY, DON'T LEAVE! I'M JUST GOING TO CHECK ON HIM, THAT'S ALL.
WEEEEE
H-HEY...
OOOOO
ARE YOU ALL RIGHT?
WEEEEE
OOOOO
WEEEEE
HUFF HUFF HUFF HUFF
I'M NOT GOING TO MAKE IT.
HUFF HUFF
WEEEEE
OOOOO
WEEEEE
TAKE ME AWAY...
OOOOO
...TO SOME-WHERE I CAN'T HEAR THIS SOUND.
WEEEEE
OOOOO

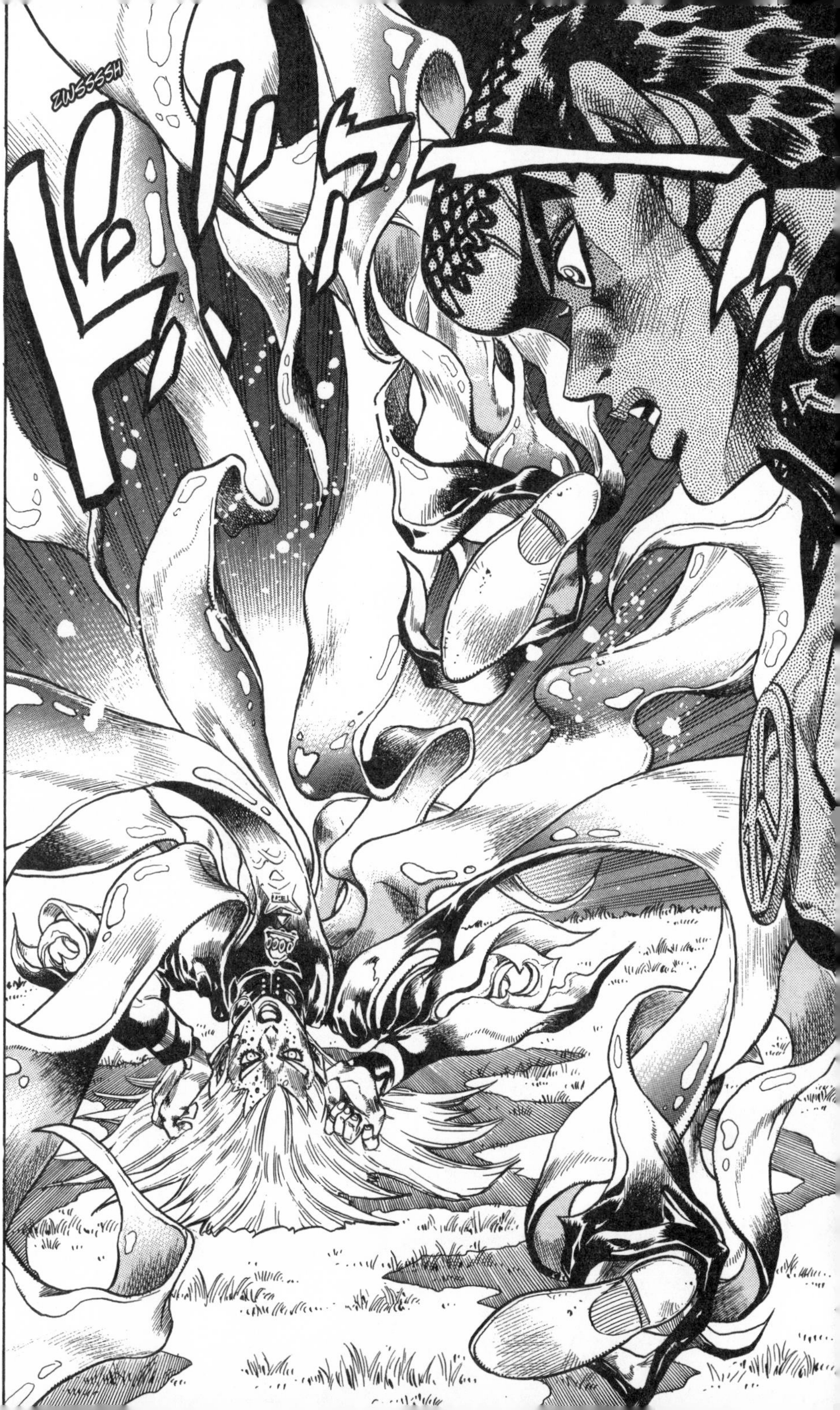
ZWSSSSH

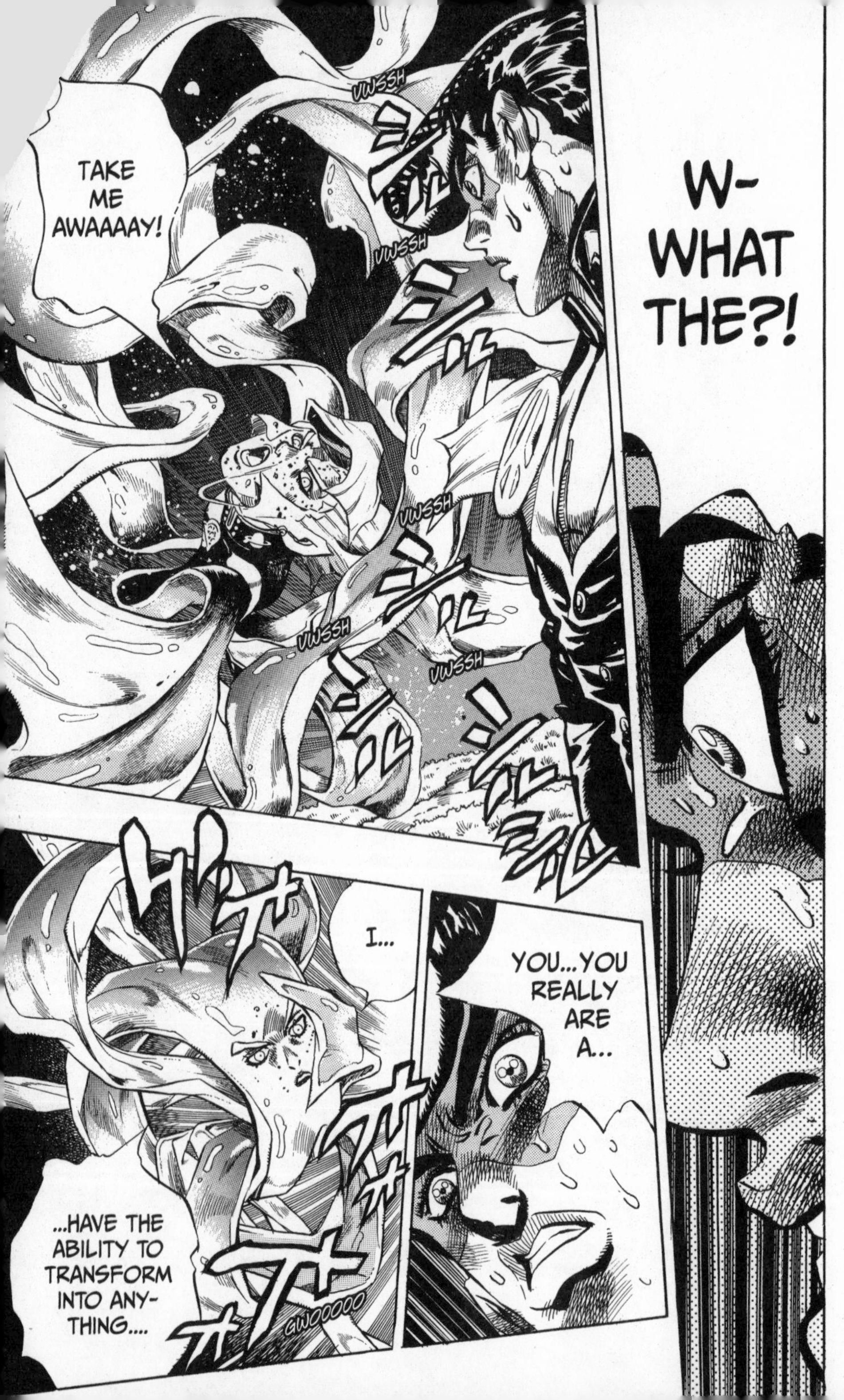
W-
WHAT
THE?!
TAKE ME AWAAAAY!
VWSSH
VWSSH
VWSSH
VWSSH
VWSSH
YOU...YOU REALLY ARE A...
GWOOOOO
I...
...HAVE THE ABILITY TO TRANSFORM INTO ANY-THING....

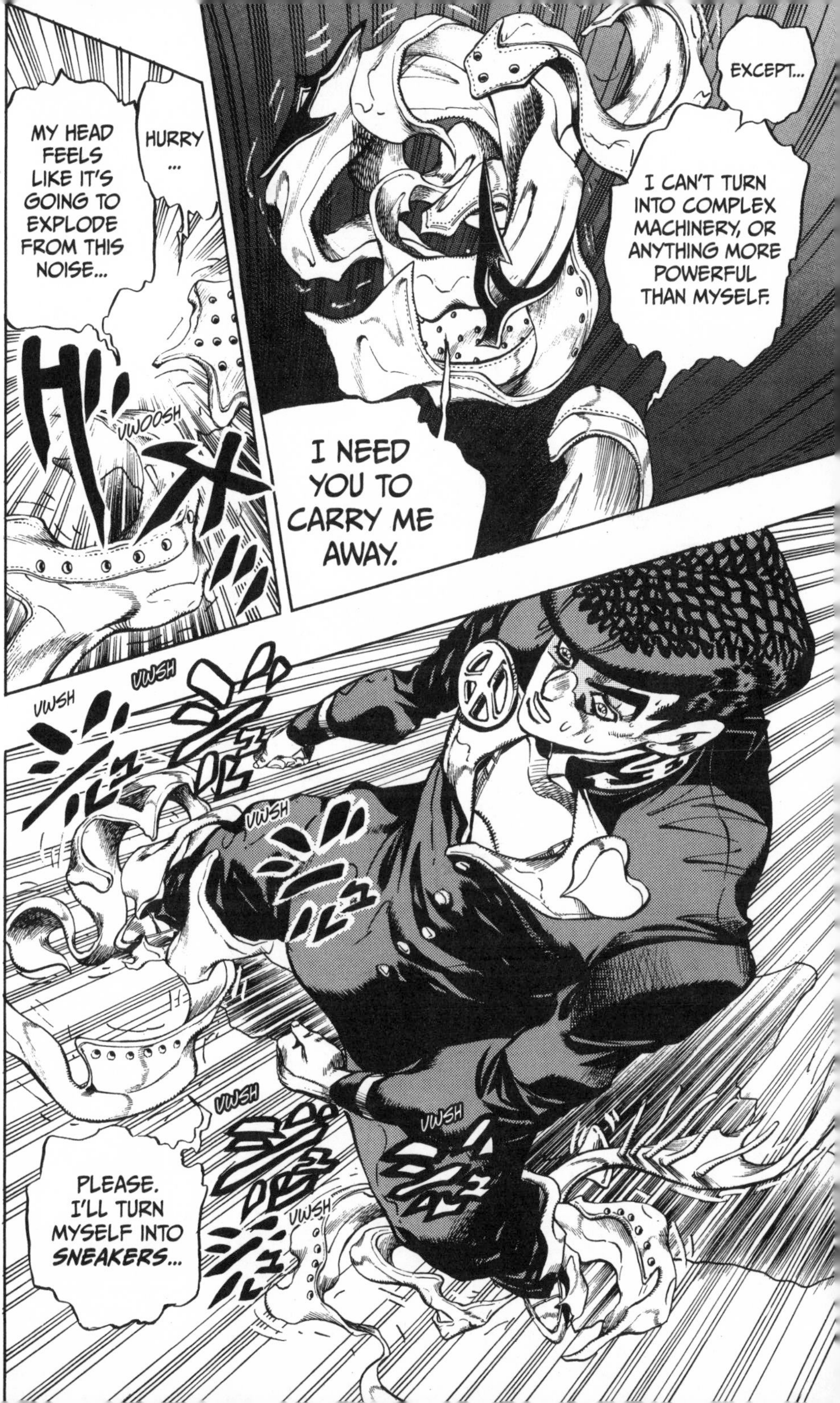
EXCEPT...
I CAN'T TURN INTO COMPLEX MACHINERY, OR ANYTHING MORE POWERFUL THAN MYSELF.
I NEED YOU TO CARRY ME AWAY.
HURRY ...
MY HEAD FEELS LIKE IT'S GOING TO EXPLODE FROM THIS NOISE...
VWOOSH
VWSH
VWSH
VWSH
VWSH
VWSH
VWSH
PLEASE. I'LL TURN MYSELF INTO SNEAKERS...

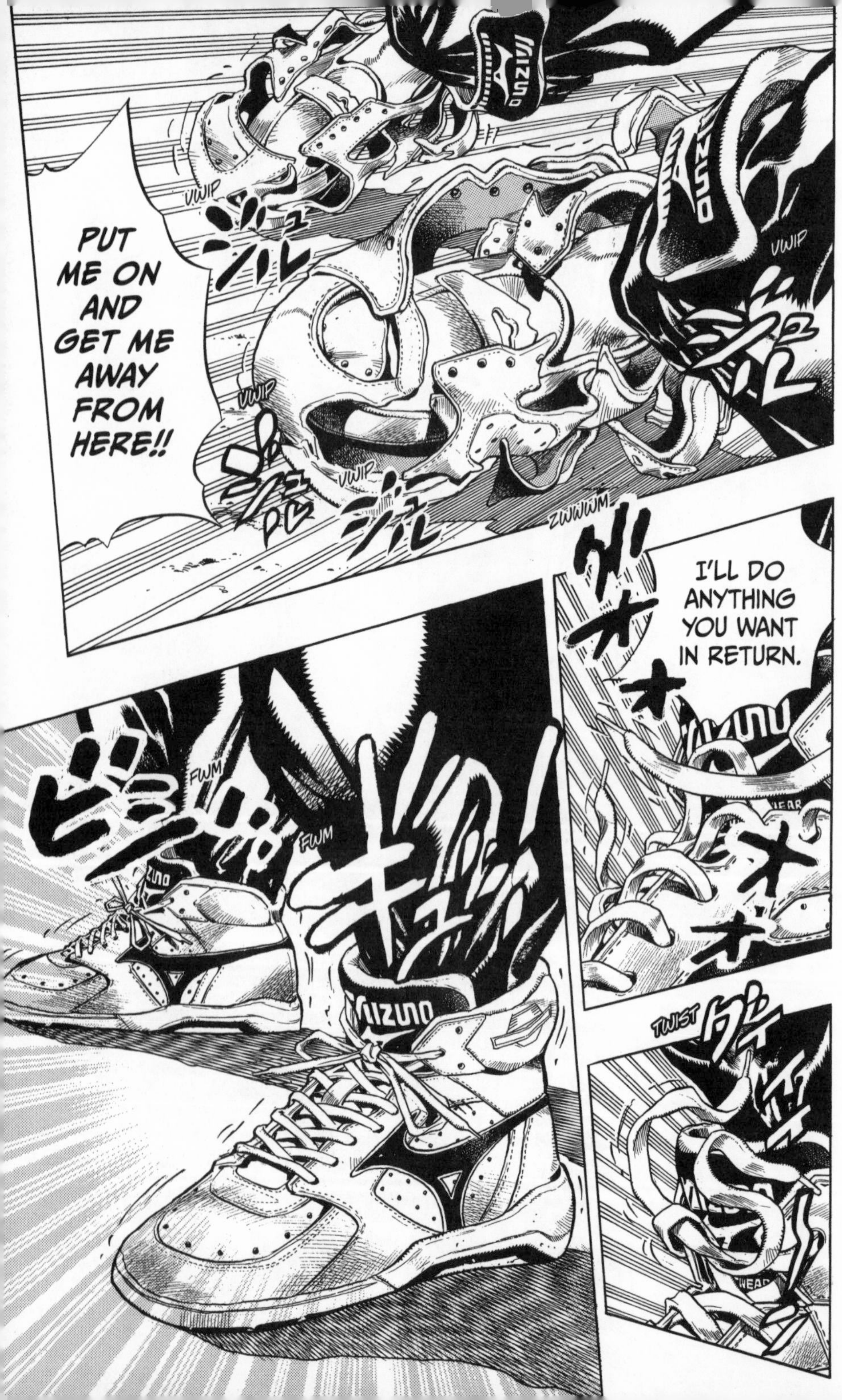
VWIP
PUT ME ON AND GET ME AWAY FROM HERE!!
VWIP
VWIP
VWIP
ZWWWM
I'LL DO ANYTHING YOU WANT IN RETURN.
TWIST
FWM
FWM

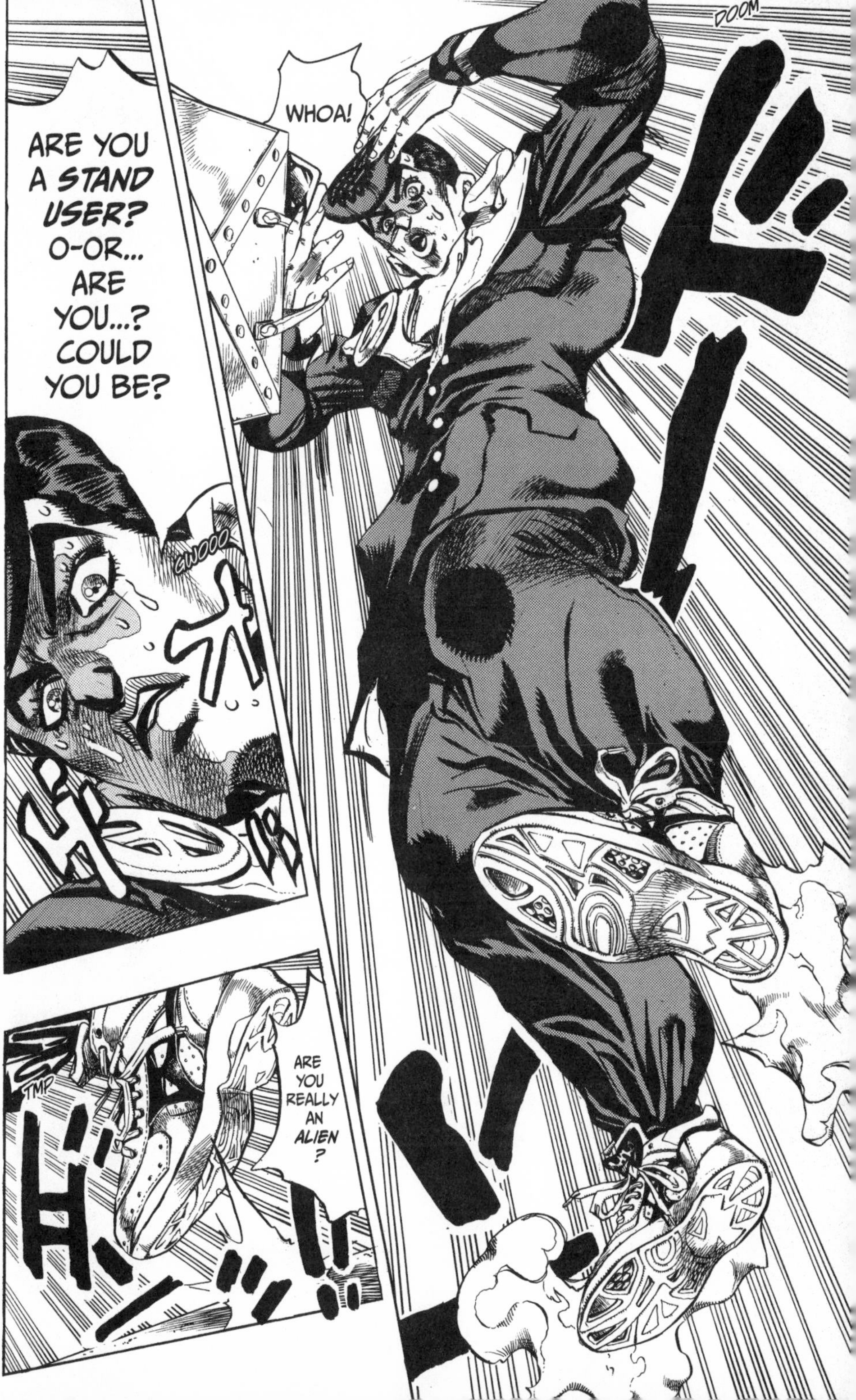
DOOM
WHOA!
ARE YOU A STAND USER? O-OR... ARE YOU...? COULD YOU BE?
GWOOO
TMP
ARE YOU REALLY AN ALIEN?

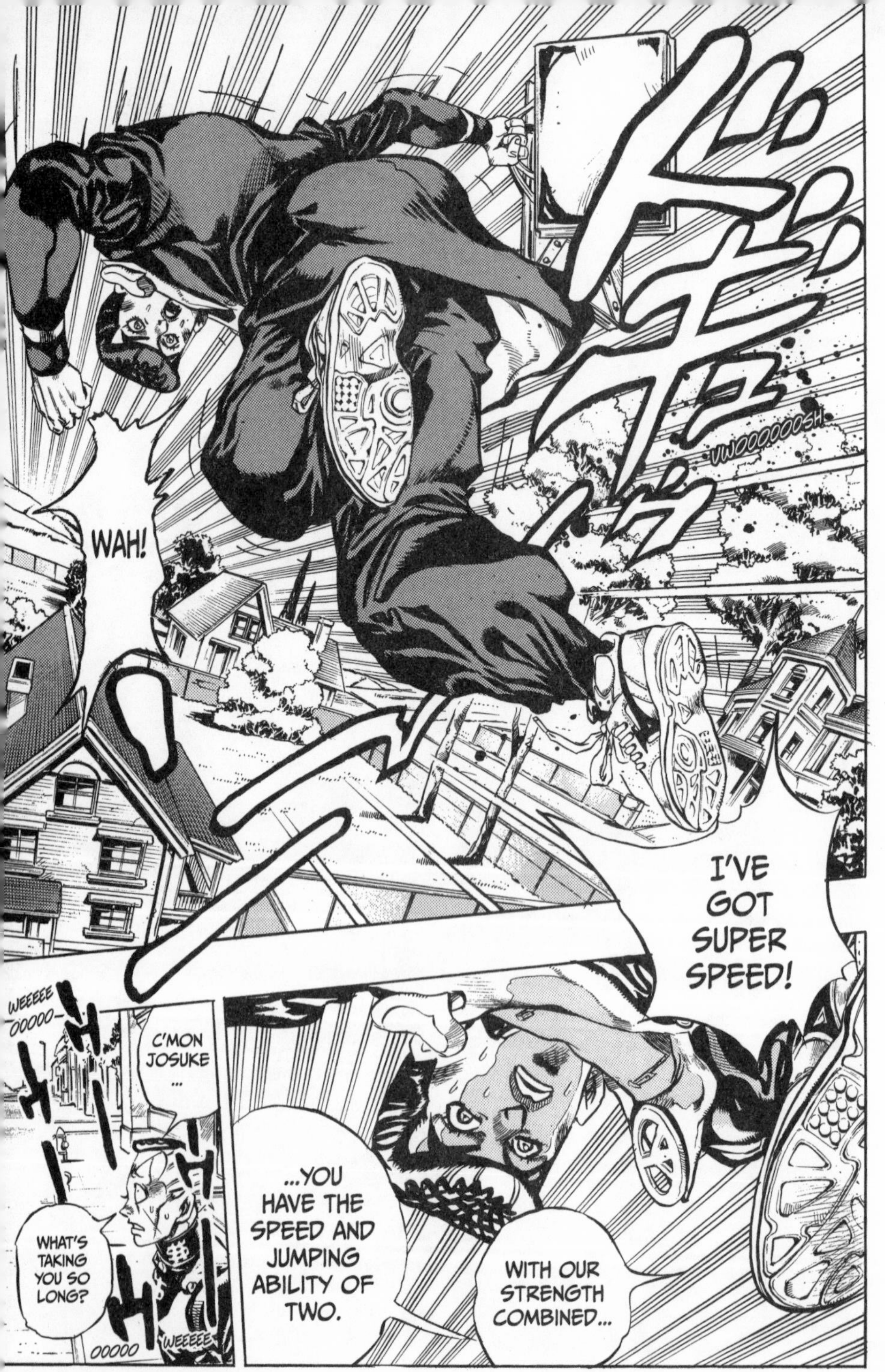
UWOOOOOOOSH
WAH!
I'VE GOT SUPER SPEED!
WITH OUR STRENGTH COMBINED...
...YOU HAVE THE SPEED AND JUMPING ABILITY OF TWO.
WEEEEE OOOOO—
C'MON JOSUKE ...
WHAT'S TAKING YOU SO LONG?
WEEEEE
OOOO

PART 4, VOLUME 6 / END

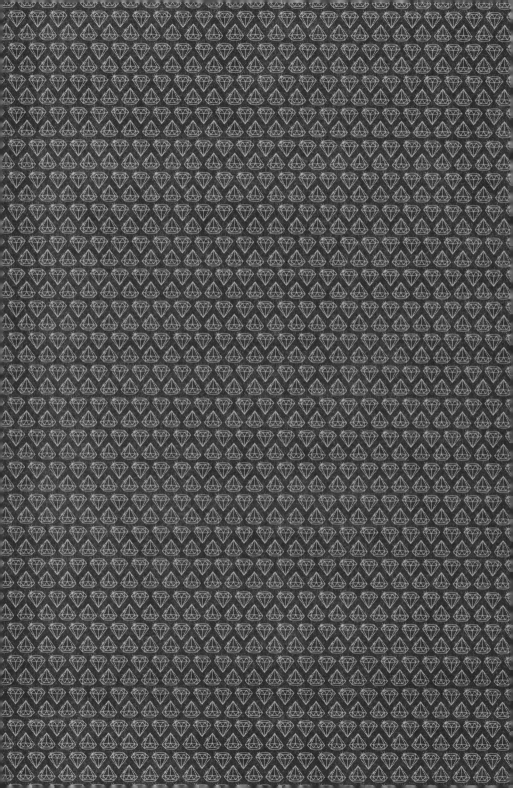

AUTHOR'S COMMENTS

There is a mystery in my life. Once, when I emerged from the swimming pool, a friend of mine looked at my soaking wet hair and said, "Whoa! Your hair looks just like Gokuraku-kun's," and fell over laughing.

"Gokuraku-kun" [Kid Paradise]? Who the heck is that? The protagonist of some famous manga or something?

I know Shinigami-kun [Kid Grim Reaper], Enma-kun [Kid Judge-of-the-Dead], Akuma-kun [Kid Demon], and Jigoku-kun [Kid Hell], but who is Gokuraku-kun? What kind of hair does he have? Later, I asked my friend about it, and this was the reply:

"Oh, did I say that?"

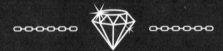

I love to read visual encyclopedias and guides. Whenever I see one for sale—from books on dinosaurs to movie stars—I can't help but buy it. The more details, the better. I want to read about when and where they were born, what they like to eat, and so on. I'll wind up reading the same entries over and over.

Recently, the two books I've been enjoying the most are *Supermodel Catalog* and *Cats of the World*. Both subjects just look so elegant.

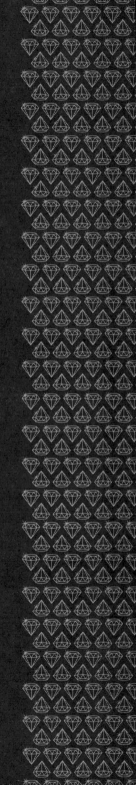

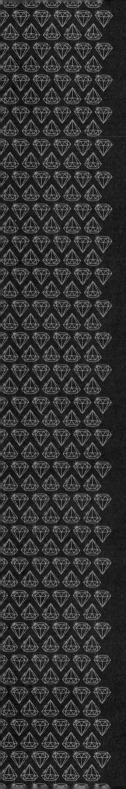

JoJo's
BIZARRE ADVENTURE

PART 4: DIAMOND IS UNBREAKABLE
VOLUME 6
BY HIROHIKO ARAKI

DELUXE HARDCOVER EDITION
Translation: Nathan A Collins
Touch-Up Art & Lettering: Mark McMurray
Design: Adam Grano
Editor: David Brothers

Printed in the U.S.A.

Published by VIZ Media, LLC
P.O. Box 77010
San Francisco, CA 94107

10 9 8 7 6 5 4 3 2 1
First printing, August 2020

viz.com

SHONEN
JUMP

shonenjump.com

THIS IS THE LAST PAGE

JoJo's
BIZARRE ADVENTURE

has been printed in the original
Japanese format in order to preserve
the orientation of the original artwork.